W9-BFF-226

TURKEY

MICHELIN

Travel Publications

Note to the reader

The chapter entitled "Practical Information" contains general information designed to help you prepare your trip. In the "Exploring Turkey" section, after each description of a city, site or itinerary, there is a practical section (eg "Making the most of Antalya", p 430) providing information pertaining to an area: how to get there, useful addresses, restaurants, entertainment, shopping etc. The tour itineraries described and shown on the maps give ideas for excursions off the beaten track. The symbol ■ indicates possible overnight stops.

While trying to keep in mind the skyrocketing inflation of the Turkish lira, hotel and restaurant prices are given by category (double occupancy basis) and in US dollars.

In Turkey, hotels, *pansiyons,* restaurants and shops spring up and disappear at a moment's notice. Therefore, the addresses shown may have changed since the guide was published. Furthermore, the opening hours of shops, museums or sites are also subject to numerous changes.

Lastly, as a result of the Kurdish conflict and the unstable conditions created in the eastern portion of the country, we have chosen not to include this part of the territory, in spite of its appeal.

Michelin Travel Publications
Published in 2000

◀ NE⊙S ▶

N ew – In the NEOS guides emphasis is placed on the discovery and enjoyment of a new destination through meeting the people, tasting the food and absorbing the exotic atmosphere. In addition to recommendations on which sights to see, we give details on the most suitable places to stay and eat, on what to look out for in traditional markets and where to go in search of the hidden character of the region, its crafts and its dancing rhythms. For those keen to explore places on foot, we provide guidelines and useful addresses in order to help organise walks to suit all tastes.

E xpert – The NEOS guides are written by people who have travelled in the country and researched the sites before recommending them by the allocation of stars. Accommodation and restaurants are similarly recommended by a 🏠 on the grounds of quality and value for money. Cartographers have drawn easy-to-use maps with clearly marked itineraries, as well as detailed plans of towns, archeological sites and large museums.

⊙ pen to all cultures, the NEOS guides provide an insight into the daily lives of the local people. In a world that is becoming ever more accessible, it is vital that religious practices, regional etiquette, traditional customs and languages be understood and respected by all travellers. Equipped with this knowledge, visitors can seek to share and enjoy with confidence the best of the local cuisine, musical harmonies and the skills involved in the production of arts and crafts.

S ensitive to the atmosphere and heritage of a foreign land, the NEOS guides encourage travellers to see, hear, smell and feel a country, through words and images. Take inspiration from the enthusiasm of our experienced travel writers and make this a journey full of discovery and enchantment.

G. Degeorge

Setting the scene   12

A KALEIDOSCOPE OF LANDSCAPES 14
  SCENERY 14
  A LAND OF TWO CLIMATES 16
  FLORA AND FAUNA 17
A LAND OF EMPIRES 18
  EARLY DAYS 18
  THE HITTITES AND THE FIRST ANATOLIAN EMPIRE 19
  FIVE HUNDRED YEARS OF FRAGMENTATION 19
  ROMAN DOMINATION 21
  BYZANTIUM 22
  THE OTTOMAN EMPIRE 25
  THE TURKISH REPUBLIC 29
  CHRONOLOGICAL TABLE 34
TURKEY TODAY 36
  ONGOING ECONOMIC DEVELOPMENT 37
  THE POPULATION 40
ART AND ARCHITECTURE 41
  GREEK ART OR THE AGE OF MARBLE 41
  ROMAN ARCHITECTS 42
  BYZANTINE ART 43
  THE SELJUKS AND THE INFLUENCE OF THE ORIENT 47
  OTTOMAN ART 48
  ART TODAY 51
  LEXICON OF ARCHITECTURAL TERMS 58

Meeting the people   60

A PEOPLE OF ASIAN ORIGIN 62
  THE TURKS TODAY 63
RELIGIOUS FAITHS 64
  ISLAM 64
  SUFISM 67
  RELIGIOUS MINORITIES 68
  POPULAR BELIEF 69
LITERATURE 70
CINEMA 72

DAILY LIFE **74**
    FAMILY PORTRAITS 74
    SLICES OF LIFE 76
    FAMILY CEREMONIES 78
    THE STATUS OF WOMEN 79
    FASHION TRENDS 80
TURKISH HOME **81**
    URBAN LIFE 81
    ANATOLIAN HOMES 83
HANDICRAFTS **84**
    CARPETS 84
MUSIC AND DANCE **87**
    RONDO À LA TURK 87
    FOLK DANCING 89
TRADITIONAL FESTIVALS **90**
HUMOUR AND SUPERSTITION **92**
TURKISH CUISINE **94**
SOCIAL ETIQUETTE **97**
    HOW TO MIX WITH THE LOCALS 98
LANGUAGE **100**

Practical Information   **102**

BEFORE GOING 104
GETTING THERE 108
UPON ARRIVAL 110
GETTING AROUND 113
BED AND BOARD 115
SPORTS AND PASTIMES 117
SHOPPING 120
HEALTH AND SAFETY 123
A TO Z 124
LOOK AND LEARN 126
USEFUL WORDS AND EXPRESSIONS 127

Exploring Turkey 132

THE MARMARA REGION 135
  İSTANBUL 138
    SULTANAHMET 144
    TOPKAPI PALACE 152
    BEYAZIT 157
    FROM ST SAVIOUR-IN-CHORA TO THE FATIH DISTRICT .. 162
    BEYOĞLU 165
    EYÜP 172
    ÜSKÜDAR 172
    MAKING THE MOST OF İSTANBUL 174
  AROUND İSTANBUL – THE BOSPHORUS 184
    THE PRINCES' ISLES 188
    ON THE BLACK SEA 188
  EDİRNE 190
  İZNİK 198
  BURSA 204
  THE DARDANELLES STRAITS (ÇANAKKALE BOĞAZI) 216
  TROY (TRUVA) 220

THE AEGEAN COAST 225
  ASSOS (BEHRAMKALE) 230
  AYVALIK 234
  PERGAMUM (BERGAMA) 238
  FOÇA 248
  İZMİR 252
  SARDİS – EAST OF İZMİR 262
  ÇEŞME 266
    THE BEACHES OF THE PENINSULA 266
  SELÇUK 270
  EPHESUS 276
  AROUND EPHESUS 286
    MERYEMANA 286
    ŞİRİNCE 287
    TIRE 287
    MAGNESIA AD MAEANDRUM 288

CLAROS 289
NOTIUM 290
NYSSA 292
PAMUKKALE-HIERAPOLIS.. 294
APHRODISIAS 302
KUŞADASI – DİLEK NATIONAL PARK 308
PRIENE 314
MILETUS 320
DİDYMA 326
HERAKLEIA AND LAKE BAFA 330
THE ROAD TO MİLAS 336
    IASOS 337
    STRATONICIA 339
BODRUM... 342

THE MEDITERRANEAN COAST..................................... 353
    KNİDOS AND THE DATÇA PENINSULA 360
    MARMARİS AND THE BOZBURUN PENINSULA 366
        THE CEDAR ISLANDS 368
    THE GULF OF KÖYCEĞİZ – KAUNOS 372
        KAUNOS 373
    FETHİYE 378
        KAYA KÖY 379
        THE BAY OF ÖLÜDENİZ 380
        THE ISLAND OF ST NICHOLAS 380
        TLOS 381
    FROM FETHİYE TO KAŞ – PINARA, XANTHOS, LETOÔN 386
        PINARA 386
        XANTHOS 388
        LETOÔN 391
        PATARA 392
        KALKAN 393
    KAŞ AND THE BAY OF KEKOVA 398
    MYRA (KALE, DEMRE) 408
        THE CHURCH OF ST NICHOLAS 408
    THE HEIGHTS OF FİNİKE 412
        LIMYRA 412

ARYCANDA 413
OLYMPOS 416
   CHIMAERA 418
PHASELIS 420
ANTALYA 424
TERMESSUS 434
PERGA 438
ASPENDOS 444
   THE SELGE ROAD 446
SİDE (SELİMİYE) 448
   ALARAHAN 451
ALANYA 454
THE CAPE OF ANAMUR – THE GATES OF CILICIA ... 460
   ANAMURIUM 460
   THE ANAMUR FORTRESS 462
CILICIA TRACHEIA –
  AN EXCURSION IN THE TAURUS REGION 464
   THE MONASTERY OF ALAHAN 465
CILICIA CAMPESTRIS –
  FROM SİLİFKE TO KANLIDİVANE 467
   OLBA-DIOCAESAREA 467
   KIZKALESİ 469
   KANLIDİVANE 470
THE PLAIN OF ÇUKUROVA – TARSUS AND ADANA ... 474
THE ROAD OF THE FORTRESSES –
  NORTHEAST OF ADANA 480
   YILANLI KALE 480
   ANAZARBUS 482
   KARATEPE 484
ANTAKYA (HATAY) 486
   SELEUCIA PIERIA 491

CENTRAL ANATOLIA 495

KONYA 498
LAKE EĞİRDİR – ISPARTA 506
   SAGALASSUS 508
ANKARA 512
GORDİON 526

THE LAND OF THE HITTITES 528
    ALACAHÖYÜK 529
    BOĞAZKALE (HATTUŞAŞ) 530
    YAZILIKAYA 532
SİVAS 536
NEMRUT DAĞI 540

CAPPADOCIA 547

THE HEART OF CAPPADOCIA 552
    ÜÇHİSAR 554
    PAŞABAĞ 556
    ZELVE 556
ÜRGÜP 558
THE GÖREME VALLEY 564
AVANOS 570
    SARI HAN 570
THE SOĞANLI VALLEY
AND THE UNDERGROUND CITIES 574
THE IHLARA VALLEY 580
AKSARAY 586
    AĞZIKARAHAN 586
    SULTAN HANI 587
NİĞDE 588
    THE MONASTERY OF ESKİ GÜMÜŞ 590
NEVŞEHİR 592
    THE HACIBEKTAŞ MONASTERY 593
KAYSERİ 596
    SULTAN HANI 600
    ERCIYES DAĞI 601

THE BLACK SEA 604

SAFRANBOLU 606
AMASYA 610
TOKAT 614
TRABZON 618
INDEX 632
MAPS AND PLANS 638

TURKEY

Official name: Turkish Republic *(Türkiye Cumhuriyeti)*
Area: 780 576sqkm
Population: 62 865 600
Capital: Ankara
Currency: Turkish lira

Setting the scene

J.S.R. / PIX

Sultan Hanı.
A caravanserai
in the middle of
the Anatolian plain

A KALEIDOSCOPE OF LANDSCAPES

If your idea of Turkey is just golden Mediterranean beaches and the vast arid expanses of Anatolia, then the country has plenty of surprises in store for you. From the mountains and forests of the Black Sea coast to the remote icy peaks of the east, you will be struck by the beauty and variety of Turkey's landscapes, source of a thousand legends.

Scenery

The country is vast! It has a surface area of 780 000sqkm, *(see map on inside cover)*, extending over 1 500km from east to west, and 500-600km from north to south. Almost 97% of its territory is in Asia **(Anatolia)**, but a small portion is in Europe (23 800sqkm), a left-over from previous Ottoman possessions in the Balkans.

This European part corresponds to **Thrace**, formed mainly by the Ergene basin which stretches north-eastwards to the wooded mountain range of Istranca (1 000m); its southern edge, meanwhile, is formed by the irregularly-shaped coastline of the Sea of Marmara. The area between the two consists of broad plains: a monotonous landscape that can be traversed without stopping.

The scenery finally changes southeast of the Taurus mountains, when the rugged peaks gradually give way to hills and then plains that continue to the horizon into Syria and Iraq.

Anatolian Plateau

Between the two lies Anatolia – the Asia Minor of Antiquity – whose Turkish name *Anadolu* comes from a Byzantine expression meaning "Levant". Wedged between the Black Sea (in the north) and the Mediterranean (in the south), the Anatolian plateau forms a vast peninsula, reaching out into the sea like the hand of Asia reaching out towards Europe. The average altitude here is 1 132m, and the land gently falls away from east to west to slip into the Aegean Sea.

Western Anatolia – The southwestern part of the plateau, previously the territory of ancient **Pisidia**, is a rugged landscape of limestone and volcanic massifs, cut by deep depressions that now harbour the Great Lakes (**Beyşehir**, 650sqkm, **Eğirdir**, 517sqkm). It is also the land of roses which have brought great fame to Isparta through time.

At the foot of a range of mountains that culminate with peaks of 2 000m, Konya marks the gateway to immense steppes. This region is the grainstore of Turkey, despite the northern part succumbing to regular flooding when the great salt lake of Tuz (**Tuz Gölü**, 1 642sqkm) bursts its banks.

Out towards the east, the landscape suddenly becomes outlandishly alien: the area between Nevşehir and Kayseri marks the start of **Cappadocia**, one of the most astounding Turkish provinces. Here, erosion has sculpted the lava from the Erciyes Dağı and the Melendiz Dağı, carving it into thousands of cones and "fairy chimneys" which the Byzantines hollowed out to form churches, monasteries and cave-dwellings. The very ground is riddled with troglodyte villages, some still waiting to be rediscovered.

Eastern Anatolia – Beyond Kayseri extend the Central Asian steppes, populated by great regiments of poplar trees. The average altitude never falls below 2 000m: the east of Turkey is mountainous and filled with high plateaux, crossed by the Euphrates (Fırat Nehri) which winds its tortuous route cross-country. The region of Commagene extends from Malatya to Diyarbakır, dominated by the legendary **Nemrut Dağı** (2 150m) where the Seleucid King Antiochus had a tomb built which was as immoderate as the man himself. Finally, further east, the land rises up to the edges of Armenia and Iran, where numerous summits exceed 3 000m, even reaching up above 4 000m, to form impressive rocky massifs dominating a few strangulated valleys. Then come the banks of the gigantic **Lake Van** (3 740sqkm) – like a Lilliputian sea suspended at 1 700m above sea-level, contained in a basin of seismic origin.

Mountainous country

The Anatolian plateau is flanked by two large mountain massifs stretching from east to west and finally joining up near Armenia. To the north, the chain of **Pontic mountains (Doğu Karadeniz Dağları)** borders the Black Sea and culminates to the east of Samsun (Kaçkar Dağı, 3 932m), to fall steeply away and down into the sea. An insuperable barrier between Armenia and the Black Sea, this volcanic massif has long played a historical role.

The same applies to the **Taurus mountains (Toros Dağları)**, a vast rocky range extending towards the south, facing out over the Mediterranean. But their relief is far more complex and broken: to the west, the massif of Bey Dağları rising to 3 086m, towers over the huge **Plain of Pamphylia** (Antalya). Further east, above the vast **Plain of Çukurova** (Adana), the mountain chain divides into two heading south-east to form the **Eastern Taurus** (Toroslar), that culminate in Cilo Dağı (4 135m) and border Kurdistan territory.

Towards the northeast, within the **Anti Taurus** (Aladağlar), the uplands increase in height as they reach up towards the Iranian and Armenian borders. Here stands the legendary **Mount Ararat** (Ağrı Dağı, 5 137m), the highest point in all Turkey. This mighty volcano, which has lain dormant since 1840, is the famous Urartu of the Bible, where Noah's Ark came to rest after the Flood subsided.

Underlying restlessness – More than 90% of Anatolia is subject to major tremors and occasional devastating **earthquakes** (like the ones which struck Erzurum in 1983, causing 1 330 deaths, Elazığ in 1997 and İzmit in 1999). This seismic activity is the result of pressure being brought to bear by the Afro-Arabian continental plate colliding with the European terrestrial plate. This tectonic fold resulted in the Taurus mountains and the many volcanoes strung across Cappadocia and Eastern Anatolia – Erciyes, Süphan, Ararat – all slumbering at present, but for how long?

Washed by four seas

No less than four seas bathe Turkey's shores: the Black Sea (1 695km of coastline), the Sea of Marmara (927km), the Aegean (2 805km) and the Mediterranean (1 577km).

The narrow coastal strip along the **Black Sea** (Karadeniz) is dominated by the Pontic Mountains, which are made up of a succession of folds and valleys that range from 600m to over 3 500m.

Between the Black Sea and the Aegean, the **Sea of Marmara** (Marmara Denizi) draws cool, brackish water from the north through the **Bosphorus Straits**, and conveys it to the Aegean, which in summer is subject to considerable evaporation and in need of replenishment. The Marmorean coastline is less rugged than in the west: the highest peak (2 543m) is Uludağ, near Bursa, and the region is mostly made up of large lake-filled basins (İznik, İzmit). The Sea of Marmara is itself a shallow subsidence basin.

The western coast, which also rises to lofty heights of over 1 000m is indented with islands, bays and peninsulas, along the shores of the **Aegean Sea** (Ege Denizi) like the teeth of a giant comb. Of the countless islands dotted along the coast, sometimes only a short way offshore, only two are Turkish – Gökçeada and Bozcaada – all the others having reverted to Greece as a result of the Treaty of Lausanne (1923) after the War of Independence (1922).

The same scenery continues along the shores of the **Mediterranean** (Akdeniz) – the **Turquoise Coast** – which should, ideally, be explored by boat. Untamed, often impassable, at times arid and in places covered with dense forests, the landscape is broken by mountains: protecting, to the west, the **beaches of Lycia**, amongst the most beautiful in Turkey, and further on, retreating from the coast to give way to the verdant pastures of Pamphylia. Thereafter, the cliffs of harsh **Cilicia** plunge straight down into the sea, and the land flattens out into the immense plain of Adana. Once infested with mosquitoes, this is now covered with endless fields of cotton.

The importance of water

The longest river in Turkey is the **Kızılırmak** (the "red river"), which finally flows out into the Black Sea after a journey of 1 182km through the heart of Anatolia. To the west and to the south, the rivers (the Büyük Menderes and the Gediz running into the Aegean; the Seyhan and the Ceyhan into the Mediterranean) are few and far between, and their flow is irregular. The deltas and plains which were formed over time as the rivers shed their loads of alluvium (the countless bends of the Büyük Menderes have given us the word "meander") tend to eclipse the actual importance of the many coastal cities that prospered in Antiquity – like Troy, Ephesus, Priene and Miletus – that were abandoned after their harbours silted up.

The eastern part of the country is watered by the **Tigris** (Dicle Nehri) and the **Euphrates** (Fırat Nehri) which rise in the Taurus mountains, traverse Mesopotamia, and join together just before flowing out into the Persian Gulf. Both rivers have witnessed the flowering of the most brilliant civilisations in Antiquity along their banks. The Turks have already built two enormous dams on the Euphrates (**Keban** and **Atatürk barajı**), and plans are afoot for another to be constructed on the Tigris, much to the displeasure of the countries situated downstream (Syria, Iraq), who fear the implications of the weakened flow of the river.

A land of two climates

With its sunny beaches on the Aegean Sea, the rainy slopes of the Pontic mountains and the arid expanses of Central Anatolia Turkey is like Greece, Switzerland and Syria rolled into one.

The **Mediterranean and Aegean coasts** are blessed with mild winters and very hot, dry summers (Antalya enjoys 300 days of sunshine per annum), with temperatures averaging 27.6°C and peaking at 40°C. Such a clement climate enables farmers to grow a selection of crops ranging from sugarcane to bananas (in Anamur) on the southern plains.

500km to the north, the **Black Sea coast** has a much wetter climate and regular rainfall throughout the year (879mm on average); winters are mild and temperate. In Sinop, for example, temperatures stabilise at 7.1°C in January and 21.2°C in August. The Pontic mountains act as a barrier, depriving Inner Anatolia of the benefits of the mild air currents blowing in from the Black Sea where the ambient temperature is 10°C to 24°C.

The **Anatolian plateau**, which lies between the two seas, is subject to more extreme conditions: summers are hot and dry, winters are harsh. In the course of a day, temperatures can range considerably and drop to below freezing at night even in summer. The effects of the continental climate are felt as far as Istanbul, where, in winter, it is not unusual to see Ayasofya covered in snow.

Annual average rainfall is 400mm, 200mm in the heart of Inner Anatolia where the rivers run dry, while further east, this increases progressively with regular summer and spring showers.

Few people inhabit the mountain areas of **Eastern Turkey** where the climate tends to be affected by altitude: with very high summer temperatures and winter temperatures dropping to between 0°C and -10°C. The annual rainfall, meanwhile, averages out at 500mm-1 000mm.

Further south, the **Taurus mountains** – rising to over 3 500m – are subject to heavy rains that allow the vegetation to grow profusely. In stark contrast, and with much harsher conditions, the eastern massif is altogether more arid, certainly less wooded. Finally, some dozen kilometres away, along the border with Syria, the southern slopes of the Taurus enjoy a Mediterranean climate with very dry summers, compensated for by heavy winter rain, creating ideal conditions for cultivating cereals and olives.

Flora and fauna

This mosaic of landscapes and climates gives rise to corresponding variations and diversity in species of plants and wildlife. In the west and the south, short narrow bands of coastal plain provide a habitat for **Mediterranean vegetation** (olives, figs and bay trees) flanked by fields of tobacco, maize and cotton. This is in stark contrast with the dense **forest** regions by the Black Sea, where great orchards (pears, apples, cherries, hazel) have thrived for generations. In the sunnier climes between Sinop and Samsun olives are grown and, further east, tea plantations cover some hills. In the Pontic Mountains – as in the Taurus ranges – the landscape covered with great expanses of forest (mainly pine, oak, fir, cedar, beech or spruce) is kept green and lush by abundant rains.

The conditions in Anatolia are quite different and the **steppe vegetation** (grasses, bulbous plants, poplars) is a reflection of this. In prehistoric times the Anatolian plateau was covered with forests that have now almost completely disappeared as a result of human intervention. Following the radical deforestation of large areas in the 19C, the present government is attempting to make amends by subsidising tree-planting programmes. Meanwhile large-scale building developments continue to mushroom along the coast.

Right across the Turkish countryside, domestic animals are reared, the most common being cattle, horses, donkeys, goats and sheep. Camels are also bred for use in competitions now that the age of the caravan is long dead. There are a few endemic species like the Kangal sheepdog and the great cat found around Lake Van, to name but two under protection and subjected to rigorous export controls.

The wildlife is comparable to that found in the Balkans: bears, stags, jackals, lynx, wild boars, wolves and even the occasional leopard (in the Dilek reserve).

Twice a year, **migratory birds** fly over Anatolia on their way to winter quarters in Africa. These include the grey crane, black kite, Egyptian vulture, lesser-spotted eagle, Levant sparrow hawk, red-backed shrike, various birds of prey and large gliders. In İstanbul, it is not unusual to see **white storks**: the Bosphorus is one of the routes they follow on their 12 000km journey to Africa.

Turkey maintains several national ornithological reserves: the one in **Kuş Cenneti** (the "Bird Paradise"), on the edge of the lake of Manyas (Kuş Gölü), between Bursa and Çanakkale, is a transit point for cormorants, herons, pelicans, spoonbills, glossy ibis, ducks and grey herons.

There are also many species of **reptile** to be found, most especially of land salamanders (in damp places), harduns (in rocky and mountain regions) and wall lizards. Watch out for snoozing snakes during the heat of the day!

Flora and fauna

A LAND OF EMPIRES

To go back into the history of Turkey involves following in the footsteps of the Hittites, the Persians, the Greeks, the Romans, the Turks and the Mongols, who in turn have flooded across the country in great waves, annihilating or assimilating the legacy of their predecessors. What do the eminently Christian and urbanised Byzantine civilisation, or the nomadic traditions of Islam have in common with the secular republic so dear to Atatürk? At first sight, nothing; but modern Turkey, founded in the aftermath of World War I, is a fusion of all three at the same time and thus an extraordinary cultural melting-pot. *(See chronological table at the end of the chapter.)*

Early days

The remains of the most ancient Anatolian, aged 150 000 years, were discovered in the **Karain Cave**, north of Antalya. The relief of prehistoric Anatolia allowed men to migrate freely across the steppes, and the first indications of their forming settlements are to be found in the southwestern part of the plateau. In the early part of the Quaternary Period, they were attracted there by the mild climate and the abundant resources provided by the forest.

After the age of unpolished, chipped stone came that of polished stone: the **Neolithic Age** (7000-6500 BC) marked the birth of agriculture and animal husbandry that was to lead to the settling of the population. It was from these beginnings that the first villages appeared, such as **Çatal Höyük**, as well as Söğüt, Canyönü and **Hacılar** where pottery was soon to make an appearance (between 6500 and 5000 BC).

Çatal Höyük, the original city

One of the first cities in the world had no streets! In Çatal Höyük, all the houses were joined together, and residents moved from one to another across the flat roofs. This highly original concept probably stemmed from a preoccupation with defending and safeguarding property. The walls, constructed of wood and covered in a mixture of cob and clay, had no windows or doors as such, only one or two hatches in the ceiling accessible by ladder. Each dwelling consisted of a vast central room (about 30sqm) lined with a bench and ornamented with bulls' horns or paintings. Furthermore, it seems that the bones of the deceased were buried beneath the floor of the house, after being left outside the city and picked clean by vultures. And so the living and the dead shared the same world.

A major technical revolution, the **discovery of bronze** at the dawn of the Third Millennium, propelled humanity into a new age. It was then that the first city-states were born. These were real urban complexes complete with a palace (and therefore a governor or a king), domestic housing and distinctive workshops, surrounded by walls and defended by armed men. One such example is **Alacahöyük**, the capital of the small **Hattian** kingdom, and founded by a people of unknown origin, who occupied the central part of the Anatolian plateau from 3500 BC. The Hattis were amongst the first peoples to develop the beginnings of an original civilisation in Anatolia, more or less at the same time as the foundations of **Troy I** were laid (3000 BC-2600 BC). Excavations of both cities have produced some remarkable bronze objects – weapons, tools, cult objects – and a magnificent collection of gold jewellery (Troy 2, 2600-2300 BC). The metalwork in question, which testifies to the considerable artistry and sophistication inherent in these young kingdoms, is the oldest in Anatolia. But it is only with the advent of the **written word**, introduced by **Assyrian merchants** between 1950-1800 BC, that Asia Minor really begins to make its impact on history.

The Hittites and the first Anatolian Empire
(19C BC-12C BC)

In around 1850 BC, the Hittites, an Indo-European people from the north, first appeared in Anatolia, settling first in **Kültepe** (Kanesh, near Kayseri) among a community of Hattis, before founding their own capital **Kussar** (the probable site of ancient Alaca Höyük), which was subsequently transferred to **Hattuşaş** (Boğazkale). It was the conquest of this second city, recorded on an inscribed tablet, in the 18C BC that marked the advent of the Hittite Empire.

During the **Ancient Empire** (17C BC-15C BC), **Labarnus II** waged war on Babylon – which he destroyed – and annexed the Mesopotamian realm of the **Hurrians** in the process. On his return, he had himself renamed Hattusilis I and transformed Hattuşaş into his capital – a city which was to remain the most powerful in Anatolia for several centuries thereafter.

Early transcriptions
Cuneiform writing ("wedge-shaped" writing) is deemed to have been invented by the Sumerians in the Fourth Millennium BC, but it was thanks to their neighbours the Akkadians, the Semitic ancestors of the Arabs and the Hebrews, that it was popularised. Within two thousand years, the Akkadian language was being spoken throughout the whole of Mesopotamia, diffused orally and, more importantly, in cuneiform writing on thousands of clay tablets. Even better, the same written language was used to transcribe other languages like Babylonian and Assyrian. Including receipts for goods, codes of law and legal treaties, scientific tracts, religious texts and even works of literature, these tablets constituted a fabulous means of correspondence and communication between the peoples of Mesopotamia and, thanks to the Assyrians, those of Anatolia.

The Hittites were able to consolidate their might and extend the boundaries of their kingdom largely as a result of using **horses**, which gave an edge and speed to their army over others. At the dawn of the 15C BC – and the rise of the **New Empire** – the Hittites ruled over the whole of Central Anatolia, extending their hegemony from the banks of the Euphrates to the Aegean coast. In time the realm absorbed the eastern part of the Mediterranean and stretched north to Damascus. In 1285 BC, **Hattusilis III** showed himself confident enough to take on the all-powerful **Ramses II** at the famous **Battle of Kadesh**. Neither emerged victorious. Instead they settled on the idea of securing a pact of non-aggression: Hattusilis III gave his daughter's hand in marriage to Ramses II, and together they signed the first peace treaty in history (1278 BC) each securing their share in the partition of Syria. Henceforth, the Hittites turned their swords into ploughshares, and the Empire embarked on a long period of peace and prosperity.

But this was also to be their swan-song, for around 1200 BC, the "Peoples of the Sea" swept through Anatolia, leaving a handful of small states intact in the southeast, like **Karatepe** (*see page 484*), which in turn were to crumble around 700 BC. And so the Hittite Era was brought to an abrupt end.

Five hundred years of fragmentation
(1000 BC-500 BC)

It is difficult to describe exactly what happened over the ensuing five centuries when no single body or power assumed control over the entire region of Asia Minor. But such political decadence did not prevent the emergence of great civilisations.

The west of Anatolia, in particular, faced the consequences of a Greek invasion from the 9C onwards as waves of **Achaeans**, **Aeolians**, **Dorians** and, most notably, **Ionians**, established colonies all along the Aegean coast (Smyrna, Ephesus, Miletus), the Sea of Marmara (Cyzique) and the Black Sea (Sinope), which before long developed into autonomous city-states. The Ionians implemented the use of an alphabet adapted from the Phoenician for a written language: this allowed literacy to be reinstated across Anatolia, having long been forgotten since the collapse of the Hittites. The hinterland meanwhile was colonised by the **Phrygians** (from 1200 BC), Indo-Europeans from Thrace who were to establish a vast central state that extended as far as Gordion. This empire reached its apotheosis during the reign of **Midas** (8C), largely as a result of the exploitation of fabulous gold and iron deposits (manna which earned the king his legendary reputation for turning everything he touched into gold).

In 696 BC the Phrygian empire fell into the hands of the **Cimmerians**, a people from Ukraine, highly skilled in the art of working metal, who established markets for their goods as far as Greece and Syria. These people also played a part in the downfall of the **Urartu kingdom** (near Lake Van) which eventually floundered and was overrun by the Scythians in around 650 BC.

Thirty years later the Cimmerians were forced to cede power to the **Lydians**, more Indo-Europeans this time from Persia, who also subdued the Greeks. The prosperity of this new empire, founded by King **Gyges**, was to reach considerable heights, boosted in particular by the mining and trading of Pactolus gold. It is on the banks of this providential river that the Lydians established their capital – Sardis – and invented money (minted in gold, of course). The whole of western Anatolia was thus Lydian until the Persian Cyrus the Great arrived (546 BC) and forced the legendary **Croesus** to abandon his empire and his fortune.

Median wars (490 BC-334 BC)

With the advent of **Cyrus the Great**, Asia Minor entered into a new era. This conqueror was the first of the **Achaeminid dynasty** and founder of the Persian Empire that included all of Anatolia, from central Asia to the Aegean Sea. To ensure unity, a sophisticated administration was meticulously structured and underpinned by an efficient network of communication.

When the Ionian cities realised how they had been weakened and impoverished by heavy taxes under Persian domination, they tried to rebel (499-493 BC), but **Darius I** (521-486 BC) was to prove merciless with his reprisals: Miletus, which had fomented the uprising, was simply obliterated and its population deported. When news of this terrible incursion reached Athens, the authorities took action and managed to topple Xerxes, Darius' successor. Following a succession of famous battles fought at **Marathon** (490), **Salamis** (480), Plataea and Mycale (479) Athens was eventually able to impose her sovereignty on Asia Minor.

At this point, the Achaeminids began their retreat, especially when it became increasingly obvious that the huge and unwieldy Persian empire was on the point of collapsing, weakened by disputing internal factions. For over time, some of the more remote satrapies (provinces) had become more or less independent – like **Caria**, for example, which was governed by the famous **Mausolus** – and the Persian rulers were finding it increasingly difficult to put down rebellions. So when Darius III came to the throne in 336 BC, his position was seriously weakened.

Greek revenge

With the coming of the King of Macedonia **Alexander the Great**, the tide of invasion now flowed from the west (334-327). In charge of the Hellenic confederation, the handsome young man overcame the Achaemenids and set out to conquer Asia Minor and extend his immense empire to the banks of the Indus.

Following the death of Alexander in 323, the land was divided among his generals (the Diadochi), with some considerable difficulty. **Lysimachus** retrieved Thrace and Ionia, while **Seleucus Nicator** ("the victor") seized the lion's share by taking command of Syria. Once installed there, he founded the **Seleucid dynasty** which remained in power until 64 BC, and helped sponsor a taste for Hellenistic art throughout Asia Minor (founding of Antiochus, Seleucia, Laodicea, Apamea).

During the 3C however, various assaults on the empire were mounted by the **Galatians**, a Celtic tribe from the Balkans, who ended up settling in central northern Anatolia and founding Galatia. More importantly, the Seleucids were gradually forced to cede to the dazzling **Kingdom of Pergamum**, founded by **Attalus I**. For having profited from the victory of their Roman ally against the Seleucid Antiochus III at **Magnesia of Sipylus** (189 BC), the Attalids were able to subjugate the whole Aegean coast, as well as the area from Hellespont (the Dardanelles) to Cappadocia.

Roman domination

A century of conquest

After the death of Attalus III in 133 BC, the Kingdom of Pergamum became the Roman bridgehead in Asia Minor, and was given the name "Roman province of Asia" in 129. But heavy taxes imposed by the Roman authorities soon caused the population to resent their masters and they needed little convincing when the King of Pontus **Mithridates VI** (88-63 BC), who had just invaded neighbouring Bythinia, asked them for help in expelling the Romans from Asia (resulting in the massacre of 80 000 Romans at Ephesus).

Before long, the brilliant **General Sylla** took charge of the situation and exacted a high price for the rebellion. After him, Lucullus and Pompey had little difficulty in reorganising the territories and extending Roman rule to the whole of Asia Minor, absorbing Lycia, Bythinia, Galatia, Cappadocia and Armenia. After his victory over Anthony (and Cleopatra) at the **battle of Actium** (31 BC), Octavius assumed the title of Augustus and became the first Roman emperor, thus marking the end of the republic.

The "pax romana"

From this point on, the Roman Empire was ruled as a genuine entity, and her provinces were either administered directly by the emperor or by the senate. The boundaries of the Empire were stable and peace reigned in the provinces. This was especially so after 150 AD as the Anatolian cities began to enjoy a period of prosperity. **Ephesus**, the sumptuous residence of the Roman governor with a population of 250 000 inhabitants, was embellished with prestigious monuments to celebrate the absolute power of Rome over her provinces, and the countryside was networked with roads, bridges and aqueducts, so that resources could be shifted easily between the different regions of the Empire.

Roman decline and rise of Christianity

Such prosperity was bound to arouse jealousy elsewhere. Finally, in the 3C AD, the Alans invaded and devastated Anatolia, while the Goths pillaged Ephesus (263). To facilitate the defence of his territories, **Diocletian** (284-305) decided to split the province of Asia into three dioceses that would be easier to manage: Asia henceforth included the Hellespont and Galatia, Pontus comprised the Black Sea coast, Cappadocia and Armenia, whilst Cilicia was attached to Syria.

At the same time, Christianity was spreading through Asia Minor. Ephesus had already been marked by the visit of **St John** and more especially by **St Paul**, who had founded one of the first Christian communities there. So this time, change was sweeping in from the east, and Rome was to succumb to Byzantium. In 312, the **Emperor Constantine** converted to Christianity and transferred the capital of the Empire to Byzantium, which he renamed **Constantinople** (330). Pagan cults were prohibited, temples abandoned and basilicas transformed into churches. A new civilisation, which was to last for 11 centuries, was dawning.

Byzantium
(395-1453)

After the death of Theodosius I (395), the Empire was divided between his two sons. Honorius inherited the Western territories (Rome) and **Arcadius** assumed control of the Eastern Empire (Constantinople) and became the first Byzantine emperor. This in turn precipitated the decline of Rome: for after being checked by the Byzantine forces, the Visigoths changed direction and marched south towards Rome causing the Western Roman Empire to collapse definitively in 476. Constantinople was henceforth the only heir to the Roman world: but, the "New Rome" was an oriental capital that was to be far more concerned with Hellenistic and Christian Asia Minor than with the Western world. This is further reflected in the fact that Ancient Greek soon replaced Latin across the Empire from the 7C onwards.

Justinian (527-565)

The 6C was marked by the brilliant reign of **Justinian**, who returned to the concept of universalism (a Christian doctrine stating that all mankind will eventually be saved) favoured by Roman emperors. He conquered almost all of the Mediterranean coastal regions (Italy, North Africa, Andalucia), making peace with the Persians and managing to contain the Barbarian threat in the Balkans. But Justinian is probably best remembered for his *Corpus Juris Civilis* on which modern civil law is formulated, and for the construction of the **Basilica of Ayasofya** (537) which symbolised the triumph of Christianity and embodied the artistic exuberance of the young Byzantine Empire. Alas, his achievements were short-lived: in the Balkans, the **Slavs** had already crossed the Danube, and in Italy, the Lombards were repelling the Byzantines southwards (565). Trouble broke out in the east as well; the Persians became a threat in the 7C and in 626, the Avars even camped for a while at the gates to Constantinople.

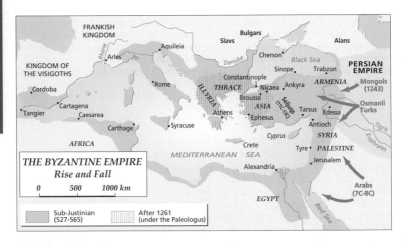

THE BYZANTINE EMPIRE
Rise and Fall

0   500   1000 km

Sub-Justinian (527-565)
After 1261 (under the Paleologus)

Arabs, Slavs and Bulgars

In 632, the **Arabs** launched their devastating conquest. In 636, the armies of Heraclius I were defeated near the River Jordan and the Arabs seized control of Syria, Palestine and Egypt before invading North Africa. After vain attempts to besiege Constantinople in 678, they tried once more in 717 and the city began to weaken. Leo III, the Isaurian (717-40), recovered his authority by winning a victory at

Akroïnon (740), but Antioch and Alexandria remained in enemy hands. Despite this, his successors continued to recover territory and at the end of the 8C the Slavs were finally evicted from the Peloponnese, mainland Greece, Thrace and Macedonia.

Under Nicephorus I (802-11), renewed infighting so undermined the central authority that the Emperor was forced to surrender Italy to Charlemagne (803) and pay tribute to the Caliph Harun ar-Rashid. Then more importantly, in 811, Constantinople was besieged and Nicephorus was vanquished by the **Bulgar Czar** Krum (who made his skull into a drinking-cup).

Conflict of iconography

Right from the start, the unity of the Byzantine Empire was undermined by religious controversy, that in turn stemmed from conflicting political and economic interests. To make matters worse, the Arabs were spreading the word of Muhammad. Weakened by these controversies, the Byzantine state needed to recover its vigour and change direction. First it tried to counteract Islam with Christianity; after all, this had been a unifying force from the outset. But to achieve this, the canons of Christianity needed to be reviewed, for these had been drawn up in the Eastern Church by hermits and monks working in the remotest corners of the countryside, and interspersed with rituals associated with images and holy relics. So, by the advent of the 8C, this cult was bordering on superstitious idolatry to the detriment of the religion itself as well as the image of the Emperor and his authority. Backed by the army, the Byzantine Episcopate decided to take decisive action and issue the edict of persecution in 730: Emperor Leo III thereby deposed the Patriarch and had the idolaters exiled or executed. Instead of figurative representations, church walls were decorated with more abstract symbols – like the cross – that better convey the idea of a powerful authority and were more closely allied to the refined sobriety of Muslim religious art.

The religious communities, which had a considerable following, reacted almost immediately by consolidating their influence in the rural areas. And so the Empire embarked upon a long period of crisis, which was to shake it to its very roots. Eventually, things came to a head during the reign of Constantine V, but the situation was calmed by the **Council of Nicaea** (787) when it was proclaimed that **iconoclasts** ("image-breakers") were heretics. This was to be but a brief interlude, for before long the quarrel erupted once more in 815 during the Council of Haghia Sophia, and was resolved eventually in 843.

A golden, but bloodstained, age (867-1057)

During the rule of the **Macedonian dynasty**, the empire recovered vast territories and re-established universalism once more. The taking of Crete (961) provided the Byzantines with control over the eastern Mediterranean; the Lombards were forced to surrender Italy and the German Empire was checked. Finally, several significant cities were won back from the Arabs (Melitene, Antioch and Edessa), although Jerusalem eluded them despite the attempts of John Tzimisces in 975. On the back of this age of expansion came a great artistic and intellectual renaissance that generated the encyclopaedia of Photius and the mosaics of St Mark's in Venice. This golden age lasted throughout the whole Comnenus dynasty. Throughout the 9C and 10C, Bulgaria continued to pose a threat as Czar Symeon (893-927), who longed to become *basileus* (official title given to Byzantine emperors, inherited from that bestowed upon Greek

Blind revenge

After Basil II carried off a victory at Stoumitsa (1014), he was given the unenviable nickname of Bulgaroctonus ("Bulgar Slayer") having ordered the eyes to be put out of some 15 000 of his prisoners. One in every hundred was spared so that he might lead them back to Czar Samuel, who died of grief on seeing his men reduced to such a state...

kings), narrowly failed to take Constantinople. There followed 16 years of bloody fighting, which concluded with **Basil II** (963-1025) annexing the Bulgar Empire and extending his kingdom to the banks of the Danube.

A little later, an alliance with Vladimir of Kiev enabled Basil II to extend his influence in Russia, whilst in the Caucasus, he annexed Georgia (Armenia was to fall in 1045). His reign, although bloodstained, marked the zenith of the Byzantine Empire: at his death, the treasury cof-

Byzantium and the West

The Roman Church had always considered Byzantium as a rival. Furthermore, the Byzantine Emperor, who claimed universality, did not show much respect for the Pope, especially when the Pope placed himself under the protection of the Franks and accepted large estates included in the Donation of Pepin (756), that in time were to become Church States. The rift was made worse when Charlemagne was crowned Emperor in 800, an act of treachery in the eyes of the "basileus". Finally in 1024, the Great Schism established a definitive break with Rome.

fers were full, the *nomisma* (Byzantine currency) was in circulation from the Baltic to the Red Sea, and Constantinople had the reputation of being the largest market place in the world.

But such commercial prosperity could not be maintained without risk to the authority of the *basileus* and the foundations of the Byzantine state: enterprising Italian merchants – Venetians, Pisans, Amalfitans and Genoese – trading from the capital managed to form an autonomous corporation. More importantly, the Byzantine aristocracy was becoming increasingly powerful as it progressively acquired the smaller available land-holdings, where the state had previously levied heavy taxes and recruited soldiers. All this was to provide the seed of decadence that was yet to come.

Constantinople in the 16C: the hill of Galata (Matrakçı miniature)

ROGER-VIOLLET

Turks and crusaders

In 1071, the Normans took the Italian city of Bari and threatened the borders of the Byzantine Empire. Fortunately, **Alexis Comnenus** (1081-1118), the head of the new dynasty in control of the Empire, managed to hold them back.

Meanwhile further troubles were festering in the east: in the mid 11C, the Seljuk Turks were launching increasing numbers of incursions *(see below)*. In 1071, in particular, a resounding victory over the Byzantines in **Manzikert** (today's Malazgirt) secured them open access to Asia Minor. All that Alexis Comnenus could do to repel them was to call on the **Crusaders** for help. Equipped with these reinforcements, the Turkish advance was checked in 1097, and almost all of Anatolia – save for Antioch – was recaptured. This was to be but a short-lived victory, alas, for the Byzantine army was defeated by the Turks in 1176.

On the domestic front unrest was brewing. The continued prosperity of the **Venetian merchants** and other Latin traders exempt from paying duty was no longer benefiting the Empire, and such privileges eventually aroused violent reactions from the Byzantine citizens (massacre of the Latins at Constantinople in 1182). In reprisal, the Crusaders took advantage of the anarchy following the fall of the Comnenes to ransack the town (1204), drive out the *basileus* and install their own Latin emperor. But Byzantine resistance was rallying: starting out from Nicaea, **Michael VIII Paleologus** soon retook control of Constantinople and reinvested the Empire (1261), lending his name to a tremendous artistic and cultural renaissance (mosaics in St Saviour-in-Chora). Byzantium, however, would never recover its economic position, for in the meantime the Ottomans were continuing their advance and, in 1368, gained a foothold in Europe after encircling the last remaining territories of the Empire.

Preoccupied by civil unrest, the Byzantines could only offer feeble resistance. But the Ottomans had other invaders at their heels, namely the Turko-Mongol troops of **Tamerlane** (Tamburlaine), who routed them at Ankara in 1402. It was a short respite for Constantinople, after which Mehmet II rallied his army, and took the town in 1453 with a flourish that signalled the fall of the Byzantine Empire.

The Ottoman Empire
(15C-20C)

The emergence of the Osmanlı

Back in the beginning of the 13C, the **Seljuks** – Turkomans from Central Asia – had succeeded in settling in eastern Anatolia and establishing other Turkoman tribes on the western marches of their properties so as to exert pressure on the Byzantines. In the following century, these tribes were to become formidable adversaries, not least for the Seljuks themselves: whilst the Karamanlı proceeded across Anatolia over Seljuk territory, the **Osmanlı** (soon to be known as the "**Ottomans**") attacked the rest of the Byzantine Empire in the west, crossing the Dardanelles so as to occupy Thrace (1345).The Osmanlı Emirate emerged as a force to contend with under **Murat I** (1362-89) who seized control

The Janissaries
Murat I made no particular effort to devise a specific term for his elite corps: the word "janissary" in fact comes from the Turkish "yeni çeri", which simply means "new troop". Originally the corps were made up with prisoners of war; later recruits came to be selected among the Christian communities across the Empire. Converted to Islam and trained in the martial arts, the young soldiers swelled the ranks of the infantry (later the artillery and the cavalry) and proved themselves to be formidable warriors and vital players in a number of the Empire's military victories. The most brilliant members were promoted to the "Acemioğlan", whose task was to assist the Sultan. Extremely close to the seat of power, these Janissaries eventually came to be a threat to the Sultan, and so the entire corps was disbanded in 1826.

after defeating the Karamanlı and the Serbs (Kosovo). It was he who established his capital at Adrianople, instituted a centralised administration (known as the *divan*) run by a grand vizier, and founded the corps of **Janissaries**: only then did he proclaim himself **Sultan**. Murat I, in turn was succeeded by his son **Beyazıt I Yıldırım** ("the streak of lightning", 1389-1403), under whom the kingdom was extended across Anatolia, to the gates of Hungary. He then went on to defeat the crusaders at Nicopolis (1396).

In 1402, **Tamerlane's** Mongols defeated the Ottomans at Ankara, slowing their advances but not actually stopping them: **Mehmet I** (1413-21) reclaimed the territory in Anatolia and quashed the rebellions, handing over to his successor **Mehmet II** (1421-51) a real Empire complete with an efficient administration and a powerful army. He had even instigated an agreement with the Genoese and the Venetians, who agreed to share their monopoly of maritime trade. During the reigns of Mehmed II and Beyazıt II, Constantinople and the Balkans gradually became peopled with Turks, while

The capture of Constantinople

On 18 April 1453 Mehmet II ordered 80 000 soldiers to attack the city. The basileus (Byzantine Emperor) had only 20 000 men with which to mount a counter-offensive, but his defences were reputed to be impregnable. In order to gain access to the Golden Horn, which was barred with a mighty chain, Mehmet laid a timber track from Dolmabahçe to Kasımpaşa (8km). During the night of 23 April, 70 galleys were thus conveyed across land so as to bombard the walled defences surrounding the Golden Horn, cut off Constantinople from Galata and destroy the Byzantine fleet. When the Emperor turned down the renewed offer of surrender, the Sultan issued orders for a general assault on the evening of 28 May: at the Edirne Gate, the Ottoman soldiers opened up a breach, incurring heavy losses to themselves, and overcame the defending troops. Fighting continued for several hours thereafter, while the inhabitants found refuge in the churches. That evening, Mehmet II (known as Fatih Mehmet, the conqueror) rode into town on horseback.

Süleyman the Magnificent on his divan (16C Ottoman miniature).

Correr Museum, Venice/GIRAUDON

Selim I pursued plans to expand the Empire by defeating the Persians at Chaldiran (1514), and then subjugating Azerbaijan and Kurdistan. Furthermore, he assumed control of the entire eastern Mediterranean basin and proclaimed himself protector of the Holy cities (essentially Mecca and Medina). In this way, the Ottomans established their rule over the whole Arab world (excluding Algeria and Morocco) until the 20C.

The Ottoman Empire at its peak

The capture of Constantinople was deemed to be a major victory of Islam over Christianity. It also enabled the Empire to endow itself with a capital worthy of the name: in the wake of the Byzantines, the Ottomans were keen to respect the local traditions practised across the various states and to transform their capital – renamed **İstanbul** – into a major centre for the arts and culture. This was the beginning of a golden age that was to culminate with the reign of **Süleyman the Magnificent** (1521-26).

Süleyman the Magnificent – nicknamed the "Legislator" (*Kanuni*) – is considered the most brilliant sultan in Ottoman history. In the space of 13 military campaigns, he managed to extend the limits of his empire to include the coasts of Arabia, Iraq and North Africa (Maghreb), and seize Belgrade, Rhodes, Hungary and Transylvania in Europe before making Western governments quake in their boots as he marched on to besiege Vienna (1529). Contesting Emperor Charles V's hegemony over the continent, he formed an alliance with the French king Francis I in exchange for important trade concessions (the "capitulations"). By this time, the Genoese and Venetian monopoly was crumbling, and so the Ottomans were quick to take control of the very profitable maritime trade routes in the Indian Ocean, subsidising their indomitable corsairs (including the infamous **Barbarossa**) to spread terror across the Mediterranean. Having installed himself at the helm of the Empire and consolidated his power-base in the Topkapı Palace, Süleyman set about asserting his authority as absolute sovereign and spiritual leader using the army when required (particularly the elite **Janissary** corps). The Sultan was also a great patron of the arts, endowing İstanbul with its most beautiful mosques designed by the great architect Mimar Sinan, as well as commissioning many great works of literature and poetry.

Early signs of decline (17C-18C)

Alas, no successor could match the brilliance and personality of Süleyman, and none showed any ability in dealing with the rising European nations. True, the Empire acquired control of Cyprus, Tunis, Georgia and Azerbaijan, but there was no longer any driving ambition, and before long the Ottomans suffered a series of defeats in Europe, notably the famous naval **Battle of Lepanto** (1571) against the Holy League, and in Hungary against the Habsburgs.

By the end of the 16C, corruption and rebelliousness were rife in the army as each successive sovereign neglected to modernise what used to be a formidable artillery. In the early 17C, the Sultan was so ineffectual that the Janissaries were able to assassinate Osman II (1622) without fear of reprisals. While the Sultans vied for power, the economy floundered and the administration collapsed.

Fortunately, a spectacular turnaround took place in the latter half of the century through the dynamic reforms implemented by the **Köprülü**, an Albanian family who produced five great viziers for the Empire. But even their collective measures proved to be insufficient; the **Peace of Carlowitz** (1699) reassigned Hungary and Transylvania (surrendered to Austria) as well as a number of other territories. Further losses were incurred later in the 18C when the Caucasus was surrendered to the Persians (1736), and Crimea to the Russians (1783). Despite this, it should be noted that the Ottomans allowed Russia free access to the Black Sea and the right of transit through the Straits.

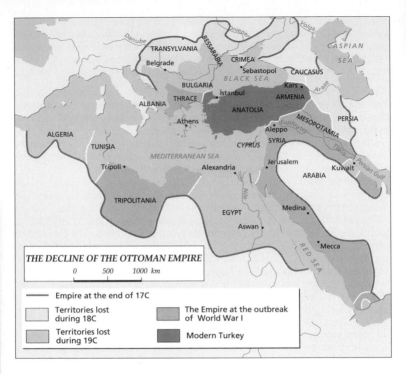

THE DECLINE OF THE OTTOMAN EMPIRE

0   500   1000 km

— Empire at the end of 17C

Territories lost during 18C

Territories lost during 19C

The Empire at the outbreak of World War I

Modern Turkey

The "Eastern Question"

By the close of the 18C, the rival governments of Britain, Russia, France and Austria saw the Ottoman Empire as the key controlling the maritime trade routes to India and the Far East. Conscious of the need to consolidate power, **Selim III** (1789-1807) reformed his navy; but when he attempted to do the same with the corps of Janissaries, they assassinated him. In retrospect, his reign was catastrophic; he was powerless to stop the Russians from making new conquests and from checking Napoleon's invasion of Egypt (1798). Meanwhile, a spirit of nationalism stirred in the Balkans and the Middle East, and eventually resulted in the loss of Mecca. In 1826, Mahmud II (1808-39) restructured his army and had the Janissaries executed for contradicting his authority. In spite of this, the Empire continued to shrink inexorably; Bessarabia passed to Russia, Serbia became autonomous (1812), and Greece won its independence (1829) as did Egypt.

Eventually, Russia's gradual advances came to preoccupy France, Britain and Piedmont; an alliance was formed to help Turkey and this precipitated the gruesome **Crimean War** (1854-55). The after-shock of this terrible interlude gave the Ottoman Empire some respite to address pressing internal issues. **Abdülmecid I** (1839-61) initiated a series of vital reforms that later became known as **Tanzimat**: all citizens became equal before the law (whatever their religion), a system of proportional taxation was implemented, sections of the judiciary were secularised and public life was modernised.

But nothing could prevent further decline. France and Britain withdrew their support for Turkey in favour of Egypt (opening of the Suez Canal by the French in 1869); the Russians encouraged nationalism in the Balkans, and the **Treaty of San Stefano**

(1878) approved their triumphal hegemony in the region. That same year the **Congress of Berlin** sparked off more troubles. Serbia and Romania were granted independence, Bulgaria became autonomous and the Ottoman Empire was forced to sign away Bosnia, Herzegovina, Thessalia, Cyprus and North Africa.

"The sick man of Europe"

Collapse now seemed inevitable. **Abdülhamit II** (1876-1909), backed by the reformers, was quick to take action. Having promulgated a Constitution, he promptly suspended it in 1878 so as to take a more reactionary line. Then, after inciting a pan-Islamic movement, he set about attacking minorities (which led to the dreadful massacre of Armenians in 1894 and 1896). Although hostile to the West, financial crisis forced him to delegate the management of the national debt and the collection of revenue to the Ottoman Bank (Anglo-French capital). This promptly gave foreign companies the right to come and exploit valuable resources like oil, and take charge of building a railway to Baghdad (conceded to Germany). But not everyone approved of the Western powers taking such liberties; in 1908, a group of officers and progressive intellectuals sparked the **Young Turks** to rally and provoke a nationalist uprising in Salonica that was to force the sovereign to reinstate the 1876 Constitution. Beyond the borders, other problems were brewing: the first **Balkan War** (1912) forced Turkey to cede almost all of Thrace to Russia – a situation that was reversed the following year by the second Balkan War.

In 1914 even greater troubles erupted, prompted in part by the Ottoman Empire's loss of integrity, and the Young Turk government of **Enver Paşa** deciding to side with Germany. After the Russians systematically crushed the Turkish troops on the eastern front, the Turks took revenge on the Armenian population, massacring and deporting them on a massive scale for having supported the enemy (1915-16). Meanwhile, in the Dardanelles, the Turks managed to repel the Allies and check their plans to occupy the Straits so as to supply arms to Russia.

After the **Armistice of Mudros** (30 October 1918), the country spent two years struggling against disintegration; the Allies occupied İstanbul and divided Anatolia among themselves, while the long-standing enemy – the Greeks – seized control of Smyrna and Thrace.

At last the country awoke from its torpor when Captain **Mustafa Kemal** challenged the powerlessness of the Sultan and repudiated the disastrous Treaty of Sèvres (1920). Two years of fighting ensued before he was able to expel the Greeks from Anatolia; with the **Treaty of Lausanne** (1923) full sovereignty was restored to Turkey along with Thrace, Smyrna, Trebizond, Erzurum and control of the Straits. This in turn prompted a massive **exodus** of Greeks (amounting to a million or more) leaving Turkey. Totally discredited, the Sultanate was abolished in 1924 after the proclamation of the Turkish Republic by the Grand National Assembly of Ankara (the GNA) held on 29 October 1923. Its leader was Mustafa Kemal, thereafter known as Atatürk: "Father of the Turks".

The Turkish Republic

Ne mutlu Türküm diyene (Happy he who may call himself a Turk) cried Atatürk to the crowd in 1927. With the same words, Mustafa Kemal planted the idea of an independent nation with what he considered to be a fundamentally Turkish identity liberated from the Islamic heritage of the Ottoman era.

Atatürk's achievements (1923-38)

The state envisaged by Atatürk was to have three fundamental attributes. Firstly, it should be modern and forward-looking like the Western nations; secondly, it ought to have a secular and democratic political regime (modelled on the French

Republic); thirdly, its cultural identity should be built on the foundations inherited from one of the most ancient civilisations in Anatolia. Henceforth, to be Turkish was to correspond to a political, social, cultural and economic reality.

To this end the Constitution of 1924 installed a parliamentary system consisting of a single assembly and a president of the Republic with a four-year term, elected by universal suffrage (women were granted the right to vote in 1934). But Kemal was realistic: all the members of the assembly belonged to the one and only Republican People's Party (RPP) and as the all-powerful president, he was able to crush any opposition, muzzle religious resistance and put down Kurdish separatism.

The Kurdish question

The Kurds, an Indo-European people from Central Asia, settled in the marches of Anatolia in the 6C. Like all other Muslims, the Kurds are followers of Muhammad; unlike their neighbours however, they have their own language and preserve a culture that is marginally different. Indeed, it was not without resistance that Kurdistan was eventually subjugated to Ottoman domination in the 16C. Then in the early 20C, with encouragement from the Russians, the Kurds revolted. Eventually, the Treaty of Sèvres (1920) attempted to restore peace by proposing the creation of an autonomous territory, but Atatürk's new Republic was quick to ensure the project came to nothing and the Kurds refused to be assimilated with the Turkish people. It must be said that Kurdistan is not confined to southeastern Turkey but extends across the northern part of Iraq to include a section of Iran, and only 10 million Kurds out of an estimated population of 60 million live in Turkish Kurdistan. The creation of a Kurd State therefore involves three separate countries. A complex problem, to say the least. It has been exacerbated since their persecution by Iraq's Saddam Hussein.

The omnipresent father figure Atatürk

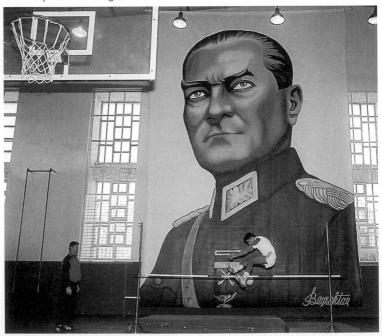

Manaud/HOA QUI

30

Furthermore, judging Islam to be the root cause of the Ottoman decline, he secularised the State and the justice system, abolished Koranic schools, religious tribunals and the brotherhood of the dervishes. In 1923 he moved his capital to Ankara in Anatolia, abandoning the Ottoman capital İstanbul, and in 1935 turned his back on Ayasofya, the most awe-inspiring religious monument imaginable, leaving it to its fate as a hollow museum.

Inspired by the same spirit of reform, Kemal abolished the caliphate, adopted the Latin alphabet and imposed Western ethics on Turkish society; in town, the Ottoman *fez* was gradually replaced by the felt hat, and polygamy was outlawed in 1927.

On the economic front, Atatürk nationalised the foreign companies and poured money into equipping the country with a modern infrastructure (mines, dams, roads). The aims of his foreign policy, meanwhile, were to sustain peaceful relations with neighbouring states, and to pilot Turkey towards joining the League of Nations.

When he died prematurely in 1938, Turkey was still in its infancy. Before long the man who had been the great visionary and grand architect of the new country became the personification of the modern power.

Atatürk, father of the Turkish nation
Mustafa Kemal, known as Atatürk, died on 10 November 1938 at the Palace of Dolmabahçe (İstanbul) at 9.05am, which is the time still shown on all 156 clocks in the palace, in honour of the man who had founded the Turkish Republic. His body was transported by train to Ankara, and transferred to the National Assembly where, on 21 November, the whole country came to pay him homage. Since then, Atatürk has been revered like a god with countless statues and portraits installed everywhere, conveying the image of an ambitious and reassuring "father" figure: eyes looking into the distance, his strong jaw set in an expression of nobility and authority.

Even today, every village has a monument of Atatürk, standing tall on a plinth, astride a horse or in the form of a portrait bust; his photograph hangs everywhere, in post offices as well as in the back room of the smallest grocery shop.

After Atatürk

Atatürk's successor was his close friend and long-standing colleague **İsmet İnönü** who adopted an authoritarian approach in keeping with the original single party system. Throughout the Second World War, Turkey managed to remain neutral while the conflict consistently undermined the economy. Before long, the regime was forced to become more hard-line and Muslim extremists began exerting their influence in politics (clamouring for the right to broadcast on radio, seeking approval of the pilgrimage to Mecca, expecting tolerance of religious brotherhoods and the reopening of religious schools).

Eventually, in 1950, the Turkish people were allowed to exercise their right to choose and voted the opposition Democrat Party, led by **Adnan Menderes**, to power. Fearing the country might have to cede certain territories to the Soviets, Turkey renounced her neutrality and sided with the western allies. In 1951, Turkey agreed to the Marshall Plan and joined NATO; in 1955, she signed the Baghdad Pact with Iraq aimed at keeping the USSR out of the Middle East. But the tension with Greece over Cyprus remained high, provoking violent demonstrations in İstanbul and the expulsion from the city of the last remaining Greeks in 1955.

More importantly, as the country faced increasing economic problems, opposition to Adnan Menderes' government grew, especially when it was revealed that the party was becoming more and more authoritarian, curbing political freedom and gradually arresting numerous intellectuals for insubordination.

From one military coup to another

On **27 May 1960**, the military as guardians of the Kemalist regime, decided to take action and seize control. New parliamentary elections were organised (a tactic employed following each successive intervention), various members of the Assembly were arrested, Menderes was executed and a new Constitution was drawn up. Conservatism was restored with General Gürsel elected as President, and Inönü nominated as Prime Minister. In the elections of 1965, the Justice Party (JP) of **Süleyman Demirel**, the successor to the Democrat Party, was swept to victory, but this was not enough to quash the ongoing speculation and raging economic crisis. Eventually, the continued suppression of left-wing factions provoked violent demonstrations.

The dark years – In **March 1971** the army intervened again, seizing control of the Parliament and forcing Demirel to step down in favour of **Nihat Erim**. The following decade was to be troubled and violent, as the government teetered on the brink of collapse, and terrorism wrought havoc across the country (Kurdish extremists were responsible for 1 000 deaths in 1978).

In 1974, Ecevit's Social Democrat RPP formed a coalition with the National Salvation Party – with pro-Islamic and nationalist tendencies. It was this government that decided on military intervention in **Cyprus** to protect the Turkish minority there from possible Greek reprisals; the result was the partition of the island.

Turkey's future

E. Valentin/HOA QUI

The 1975 parliamentary elections restored Demirel (JP) to office, supported by the extreme right. The government increased the national debt, causing the home economy to flounder (inflation rose over 100%) and the country to succumb to depression. On 12 September 1980, General Evren ordered **another military coup** in the hope that this would assuage public opinion and reassure the business sector which had been unnerved by the wave of violence. Instead, the action precipitated the abolition of the Constitution and the suspension of public liberties. The political parties, trade unions, the press and university all suffered from this, and Ecevit's arrest followed. Although condemned by the international community, particularly Europe, the *putsch* eventually managed to win over the Americans who, since the Iranian revolution, had been keen to find a friendly regime in the area.

A long haul back to democracy – Finally, in 1983 the Turkish people elected to power **Turgut Özal**, the head of the Motherland Party (ANAP, *Ana Vatan Partisi*), and a civil government was reconstituted. The compromise now was between the democratic powers and the military authorities. In this way, the army was able to intervene directly in economic matters and assume control in the Kurdistan war that from 1984 was devastating southeastern Anatolia.

In 1993, Süleyman Demirel replaced Turgut Özal as President, and appointed the first female Prime Minister **Tansu Çiller**, leader of the True Path Party (DYP, *Doğru Yol Partisi*), to head his government. During her term, fighting broke out once more in Kurdistan, and, the Refah Islamists (Welfare Party, *Refah Partisi*) succeeded in rallying support that was to win them success in the parliamentary elections of 1995. In July 1997, after only a year in power, the army toppled the coalition government (RP and DYP) led by the Islamist **Erbakan**, and instituted an unusual alliance run by **Mesut Yılmaz** (ANAP). Could it be a chance for a genuine return to democracy? In 1998, **Bülent Ecevit**, the leader of the leftist DSP (*Demokratik Sol Partisi*) was nominated Prime Minister. Since 1999, his government has been in a coalition with the MHP, an extreme right nationalist party (*Milliyetçi Hareket Partisi*, also known as the Grey Wolves), the ANAP and the Muslims of the Virtue Party (*Fazilet Partisi*). The latter replaced the former RP, banned in 1997.

A highly strategic position
"We feel ourselves to be both European and Asian. We consider this duality to be an advantage," İsmail Cem, minister of foreign affairs, declared in December 1997. A close look at Turkey's neighbours – Bulgaria and Greece on the Balkan side; Syria, Iraq and Iran in the Middle East; Georgia, Armenia, Azerbaijan (Nakhichevan) in the Caucasus – reveal her position as an eminently strategic one that is not without danger. This was especially evident in 1991, at the height of the Gulf War when Iraq made a number of incursions into Kurdistan, while American forces took up defences in various military bases in the eastern part of the country that at one time provided a front-line position on the edges of the Soviet empire.

After the break up of the USSR, Ankara turned to the young turkophone republics in the **Caucasus** and **Central Asia** (Azerbaijan, Turkmenistan, Uzbekistan, Kyrgyzstan, Kazakhstan) in the hope of tapping into the natural oil reserves there. But this initiative was to be fruitless in all but reawakening mistrust among Russians and Iranians. As for relations with Europe, the customs union came into force in 1996, but the real issue at stake remains Turkey's full membership in the **European Union**. Since 1987, Turkey has repeatedly applied for candidacy, but each time the government has been reprimanded for its abuses of human rights and reproached for its backward economic policies. Or, as İsmail Cem has suggested, is the unspoken reason that Turkey is a Muslim country? For the present, there is considerable opposition from both Germany and **Greece** especially, with whom Turkey remains at loggerheads over a number of outstanding conflicts (Aegean Sea, Cyprus).

Five thousand years of history

Dates	Events	Places
15000-7000 BC	Paleolithic period	*Karain caves*
7000-5500 BC	Neolithic period: first villages	*Çatal Höyük*
5500-3000 BC	Chalcolithic period (age of copper)	*Hacılar, Mersin*

Bronze age (3000 BC-800 BC)

Dates	Events	Places
3000-2600	Foundation of Troy	*Troy 1*
	Hatti civilisation	*Alaca Höyük*
1950-1800	Apparition of writing in Anatolia	*Kültepe*
	Assyrian trading colonies	
1800-1200	Hittite civilisation	*Hattusas,*
		Yazılıkay
1300-1250	Trojan war	*Troy 7*
900	Rise of the Carians, the Lydians	*Halicarnassus*
	and the Phrygians	*Sardis, Gordion*
800	Foundation of the Ionian League	*Ephesus, Priene...*
800-600	Greek colonisation of the Aegean coast	*Smyrna, Ephesus*
		Miletus

Antiquity (7C BC-4C AD)

Dates	Events	Places
Around 700	Birth of Homer	*Smyrna*
700-300	Carian and Lycian civilisations	*Halicarnassus,*
		Xanthos
667	Foundation of Byzantium	
561-546	Reign of Lydian King Croesus	*Sardis*
546	End of the Lydian Empire: the Persian King	
	Cyrus Invades western Anatolia	
490	First Median War	
	Defeat of Darius at Marathon	
480	Second Median War, led by Xerxes	
	Second Persian defeat	
386-334	Third Median War	
334-327	Alexander the Great drives out the Persians	*Gordion, Tarsus*
	and conquers Asia Minor	*Miletus*
305-64	Seleucid dynasty	*Antiochus, Edessa*
261-241	Eumenus I founds the Kingdom of Pergamum	*Pergamum*
230	The Galatians invade Anatolia	
197-159	Zenith of the Kingdom of Pergamum	
129	Rome founds the province of Asia	*Ephesus*
64 BC	The Romans colonise almost all Asia Minor	
47-54 AD	Journeys of Saint Paul	*Antiochus, Ephesus*
313	Christianity becomes state religion	

The Byzantine Era (330-1453 AD)

Dates	Events	Places
330	Foundation of Constantinople by Constantine	
395	Start of the Byzantine Empire	
476	End of the Western Roman Empire	
527-565	Reign of Justinian. First zenith	
	of Byzantine Empire	
678-717	Sieges of Constantinople by the Arabs	
726-787	First Iconoclastic crisis	

811	Siege of Constantinople by the Bulgars	
815-843	Second Iconoclastic crisis	
867-1057	Advent of the Macedonian Dynasty: Second Byzantine Golden Age	
1054	Eastern schism	
1071	Victory of the Seljuks at Manzikert	
1071-1243	Seljuk Sultanate in Anatolia (Rum)	*Konya*
1204-1261	Capture of Constantinople by the Crusaders Latin Empire	
1240	Turks invade western Anatolia	
1261	Michael VIII Paleologus restores Byzantine Empire	
1402	The Mongol Tamerlane pushes back the Turks	*Ankara*
1453	Capture of Constantinople by Mehmet II	

The Ottoman Era (1453-1922)

1520-1566	Reign of Süleyman the Magnificent Golden Age of the Ottomans	
1571	Conquest of Cyprus by the Turks	
1683	Failure of second siege of Vienna	
1789-1839	Decline of the Ottoman Empire	
1826	Massacre of the Janissaries	*İstanbul*
1829	Greek Independence	
1854-1876	Crimean War	
1876-1909	Reign of the last Sultan, Abdülhamit II	*İstanbul*
1912-1913	Balkan Wars: loss of territories	
1915	Battle of the Dardanelles: Turkish victory over the Allies	*Gallipoli*
1919	Division of Anatolia (Antalya to the Italians, Adana to the French, and Smyrna to the Greeks)	
1919-1922	Turkish War of Independence Defeat of Greeks, who leave Anatolia	*Smyrna*

Modern times

1923	Treaty of Lausanne (Turkish sovereignty) Proclamation of the Republic	*Ankara*
1938	Death of Atatürk	
1946	Turkey becomes a member of the UN	
1951	Turkey joins NATO	
1960	Military coup. Condemnation of Adnan Menderes	
1971	Army forces Süleyman Demirel to resign	
1974	Invasion of Cyprus	
1980	Military coup by Kenan Evren, who becomes President	
1984	Start of the war with Kurdistan	
1989-1993	Turgut Özal is President	
1991	Gulf War	
1996	Customs Union with European Union	

TURKEY TODAY

A secular republic

Atatürk envisaged a secular, parliamentary-based republic, and in order to see his dream fulfilled, he put all his energies into selling his idea to the Turks, among whom he had a great following. Several decades later, despite many a political setback, Turkey has remained faithful to the original system, although details have been revised three times since the Republic's inception – the latest **Constitution** was devised in 1982 shortly after the last military coup.

Guardian of the Constitution and of national unity, the **president** is elected to serve a seven-year term of office (non-renewable) by the Turkish Grand National Assembly **(TGNA)**. This legislative body consists of a 450-member assembly, elected for a five-year period by universal suffrage. The **prime minister**, who is accountable to the assembly, is the head of the Executive: he is chosen by the president from within the party or from the coalition with the largest majority.

What is unique about this democracy is the political role of the **army**, which wields considerable power as the guardian of the secular republic so dear to Atatürk's heart. Within the framework of the National Security Council, the military is actually mandated to preserve the integrity of the State (article 118).

For administrative purposes, Turkey is divided into 76 **provinces** (il) comprising 700 districts (ilçe), headed by prefects and sub-prefects appointed by the Minister for the Interior, with the help of elected councils. At the bottom of the scale, each **locality** made up of more than 2 000 inhabitants has its own elected mayor and local council.

Lively political activity

Since the demise of Atatürk at the close of the 19C, electoral battles have been fought by two principal political dynasties. The one embodying Kemalism is authoritarian, secular and in favour of State control; its delegates are to be found in the Republican People's Party **(CHP)** led by Deniz Baykal, and the Democratic Left Party **(DSP)** run by Bülent Ecevit, a long-standing political figure.

Voice of the press

It is quite impossible to ignore the proliferation of newspapers in Turkey, with kiosks everywhere swamped with four-colour newsprint and periodicals. But circulation is relatively small for all but the tabloid press. Most of the major newspapers run serious editorials tinged with militant tendencies, which regularly upset the authorities. The one with the largest circulation is probably "Milliyet" (Nationality) which sets the standards for the population at large (circulation 600 000). In 1979, the editor-in-chief was assassinated by Mehmet Ali Ağca, the man who shot Pope. The highly secular and serious "Sabah" and "Cumhuriyet", meanwhile, are two other major dailies, while mention should be made of the political weekly "Nokta" (circulation 15 000), which is also fairly politically committed.

The other faction, conservative and favouring an open economy, corresponds to the Democrat Party which at present is represented by the True Path Party **(DYP)** run by Mrs Tansu Çiller (Prime Minister 1993-95), and the Motherland Party **(ANAP)** led by Mesut Yılmaz (Prime Minister in 1995 and 1997). Personal hostility has led the two leaders to fall out, but the two parties are nevertheless ideologically very close and play a key part in almost all coalitions. Although it represents something of a bugbear for those in favour of a secular State, mention must be made of the Islamic Welfare Party **(RP)** headed by the practised politician Necmettin Erbakan, who brought his party to power in 1996-97. Suppressed by the military authorities in 1997, the RP was succeeded a year later by the *Fazilet Partisi* (FP).

Since the Democratic Party disbanded in 1993, the **moderate Kurds** have formed their own people's democratic party **(HADEP)**. However it is still not represented in parliament since it lacks the necessary votes and faces many obstacles and police pressure. This group suffers from the violent image created by the **separatist Kurds** who group themselves under the single banner of the **PKK**, an ideological organisation with Marxist-Leninist leanings.

At the other end of the spectrum is the ultra-nationalist party **(MHP)** founded by Alparslan Türkeş, the leader of the Grey Wolves. This party is known for its violent behaviour towards Kurds and leftist personalities. After his death in April 1997, Türkeş left his seat to Devlet Bahçeli. The Grey Wolves thus obtained the necessary votes during the last elections (April 1999) to enter the governmental coalition with the CHP.

In recent years the country has been wracked by instability, partly as a result of the piecemeal political arrangement, but also because of successive financial scandals. It is not unusual for coalition majorities to shift mid-term as opportunist alliances are set up almost on a whim to fight a particular issue.

Ongoing economic development

Turkey appears to be suffering all the symptoms of a major economic depression, with three-figure inflation, political instability, excessive interest rates, trade deficit and over-valued currency. Despite this, the country achieved an impressive growth-rate of 7.2 % in 1996. Such a state of affairs can be explained by the fact that the country is undergoing a process of development, and is categorised by the World Bank as a middle-income economy. The average purchasing power (US$4 750 in 1994) is higher than that of the Middle East, but lower than that of Greece and only about 25 % of that of the UK.

The paradox with respect to the Turkish economy is the discrepancy between the rapidly developing social and political structures (if only in fits and starts), and economic factors which often fail to keep pace. During the 1980s, the country underwent a complete revolution, moving away from a Kemalist planned economy to a more liberal one. Industry, previously protected by customs barriers, was abruptly exposed to foreign competition, and external trade doubled in 10 years. In order to facilitate international business, the authorities passed a decree in 1989 allowing the Turkish lira to be freely traded on world markets.

On the one hand this was a good thing, but the effect on the economy was devastating. The currency was devalued and salaries were reduced to a pittance; although Turkey increased her share of the market in certain sectors, these proved to be the less competitive ones.

Whatever the case, it cannot be denied that in the last decade the economy and social structure of the country have gained in flexibility and appear to be better equipped to cope with the shock of foreign competition. Furthermore, the trade deficit has been reduced thanks largely to a massive growth in tourism (9 million visitors in 1997), but also due to funds being transferred by people working abroad (especially in Germany). More recently, the "suitcase trade" has provided additional income, as nationals from the former eastern block countries and the Commonwealth of Independent States have flooded in.

As cross-border regulations were relaxed and traffic increased, the European Union decided to approve the **Customs Union** (1 January 1996) allowing Turkey to sell half of its export output to Europe in return for financial assistance. But the promised investments remain blocked by Greece, whose animosity towards Turkey continues.

Under-exploited potential

In spite of all these changes, Turkey remains a profoundly rural country in which 43% of the working population is employed in some form of **agriculture** (14% of GDP in 1993), thereby ensuring the country is self-sufficient in food. Since the time of Atatürk, huge areas of land have been turned over to farming and this has resulted in striking increases in production. However, the country has yet to undergo its "green revolution". Progress is already evident in terms of mechanisation, improving the selection of seed and the choice of varieties. Things have still some way to go, for nomadic tradition weighs heavily on farming practices (seasonal migration); terraced installations are few and far between, and the average size of holdings remains small. Twenty-one dams have now been completed along the Euphrates and the Tigris in southeast Anatolia thereby controlling a supply of irrigation water sufficient for 1.7 million hectares of land.

Crops vary considerably from one region to the next. While much of Inner Anatolia concentrates on growing **cereals** (wheat and barley), **sugar-beet** and **stockbreeding** (sheep, goats and cattle), various smallholders have diversified into such lucrative crops as **tobacco** (on the Aegean coast and the Black Sea), **hazelnuts** and **tea** (eastern shore of the Black Sea), and **vineyards** (Thrace, Cappadocia and southeast Anatolia). The Aegean and Mediterranean coasts are veritable oases. **Cotton**, **olives**, figs and grapes (raisins) are grown in the west; **citrus fruits** and other **fruit and vegetables** on the southern coast. Mention must also be made of the famous **roses** from Isparta which are used to perfume soaps, *eau de toilette* and **Turkish Delight**, as well as the opium poppy (grown for its pharmaceutical properties under State control), pulses (chickpeas, lentils, beans), pistachio nuts and aromatic herbs and plants (bay, mint, sage, lavender etc).

Little can be said for Turkey's efforts at exploiting the **sea**. Despite being surrounded by water, the Turks are not great **fishermen**, preferring to make do with mackerel and anchovy *(hamsi)* from the Black Sea and the Sea of Marmara, without contemplating any industrial exploitation of the resources.

The country has few **natural mineral resources** save for a handful of coal mines in Zonguldak-Eregli, some lignite and a little crude oil. Until the outbreak of the Gulf War, Turkey piped Iraqi crude oil from the field directly to its refineries in İzmit, İskenderun, Batman and Mersin. In recent years, alternative supplies have been imported.

Hydro-electric power stations generate sufficient amounts of electricity to supply 60% of national need (Keban dam on the Euphrates). As the installations in southeast Anatolia *(mentioned above)* come on line, the grid should receive an additional 27 billion KW.

Turkish **industry**, especially concentrated (25%) in and around İstanbul remains somewhat underdeveloped despite the efforts of Atatürk and his successors. Manufacturing concerns do, however, provide for most of the country's economic growth with **textiles** (wool, silk, clothing, hand made carpets) topping the list of exports over and above **cultivated foodstuffs**.

The **steel industry**, which helps sustain the engineering industry, is undergoing considerable expansion at present (Karabük, İskenderun and Ereğli) as it strives to satisfy demands from the domestic market. Principal players include the construction and chemical industries, as well as the car assembly plants near Bursa (Renault and Fiat), whose growth testifies to the emergence of a considerable domestic market – Turkey's real trump card as far as industry is concerned.

Harvesting cotton is women's business

38

Finally, thanks to **tourism**, which has just boomed over the last 20 years, the **services sector** now represents more than half of the Turkish GDP. This is not without cause, for Turkey has made large-scale investments in this area in the past and continues to market the country's natural heritage and history. Unfortunately the proliferation of hotel construction, together with neglect of the necessary infrastructure, tends to mar rather than enhance areas of particular interest.

The population

The population has almost doubled in the space of 30 years, which is bringing Turkey into line with other European and Middle Eastern heavyweights. This is a considerable problem for the country needs to modernise its infrastructure, narrow the divide between East and West, town and country, and between the aspiring, ever-affluent classes and an ever-increasing underclass.

Developments beyond control

The population of Turkey – 31 million inhabitants in 1965 – reached **62 million** in 1999: that is an increase of one million per year (annual growth is 3%). Currently, that rate is declining somewhat and, although it has some way to go before any similarities can be made to Western countries, Turkey is no longer compared to the Third World. According to forecasts, there should be 70 to 80 million inhabitants by 2005.

The lure of the town

The average population **density** is 77.3 inhabitants per square kilometre. But this conceals the enormous discrepancies between regions. İstanbul remains the largest city in the country with a population of 10 million (suburbs included), way ahead of Ankara (3 million) – which only had a population of some 20 000 at the beginning of the 1920s – and İzmir (2.1 million). Right across the country, people are choosing to leave the countryside in favour of towns. Over the past 30 years, the country has witnessed a massive **rural exodus** that has considerably altered the size and appearance of many towns. In the space of a single decade (1985-95), the urban population has risen from 52% to 67% and forecasts state this should reach 82% in 2005! For country people, the towns represent a tangible means of enjoying a Western way of life complete with all its supposed advantages. İstanbul, whose streets might be considered to be paved in gold, appears to be the prime attraction, luring hapless people from Anatolia to the overcrowded outskirts of the city. There they pile into *gecekondu*, insalubrious small houses put up overnight without planning permission *(see page 81)*.

Another preoccupation among the Turkish population is its youth. Life expectancy is 57 years and, in 1995, the censor counted 27.6 million individuals – two-thirds of the total population – under the age of 30. As each year passes, the number of people **eligible for work** increases. This inevitably will lead to serious problems of unemployment. At present, 62.5% of Turks are of working age (15-65), whereas the rate of employment (45% in 1995) is not supposed to reach a figure higher than 47% in 2005!

Irrespective of whether these statistics are interpreted positively or negatively, the growth of the population coupled with renewed interest in the Turkish peoples of Central Asia will play a considerable role in greatly influencing governments of the future.

ART AND ARCHITECTURE

Rather than embarking on a fastidious history of Turkish art, this chapter is designed to describe the main developments, especially where Classical Antiquity is concerned. A more detailed picture is given in the regional sections, and, of course, in the site descriptions. For quick reference, readers may like to turn to the plates and glossary at the end of this chapter.

Since the first historians and archeologists set off on their expeditions to Turkey in the 19C, countless treasures have been brought to light and have rekindled some of the spellbinding history of Anatolia. This land of empires possesses an extraordinary heritage with Hittite palaces built of dark basalt, Greek and Roman cities clad in polished marble, luminous mosaics glistening with gold from Byzantium, fabulous Ottoman mosques covered in iridescent glazed earthenware tiles. No wonder the country's monuments are considered a glorious reflection of some of the most brilliant civilisations in the world.

Even the Neolithic Age contributed to the country's heritage, notwithstanding the fact that the concept of "art" had yet to be devised. After all, the flamboyant mural paintings decorating the houses in **Çatal Höyük** (7th millennium BC) and the generous clay goddesses in **Hacılar** (6th millennium BC) must surely rank as works of art. The same applies to the heavy swords and fabulous gold jewellery, almost 4 000 years old, which the archeologist Schliemann discovered beneath the ruins of **Troy**, or the figurines and amazing bronze solar discs of **Alaca Höyük.**

The first great impact on Anatolia was made by the **Hittites** (2nd millennium BC). The excavation of their capital **Hattuşaş** (Boğazkale), has revealed powerfully evocative remains of enclosure walls, temples and palaces, while the striking bas-reliefs and statues of **Yazılıkaya** and **Karatepe** suggest the art of sculpture was already well established. Several peoples were to flourish in Anatolia after the passing of the Hittite Empire. The **Phrygians** (1200-700 BC), for example, emerge as great architects and adept structural engineers from excavations at the **tumulus of Midas** (near Gordion).

The **Lydians,** meanwhile, were annihilated by the Persians so little remains of their Kingdom and famous capital at Sardis (Aegean coast). Only the engraved gold plaques and the precious stone necklaces found in the tombs of Alyatte, the gigantic **necropolis of Sardis**, provide an inkling of the fabulous wealth enjoyed by King Croesus.

The **Lycians** (6C-3C BC) manifested their particular talent in building burial chambers, excavating the mountains of **Xanthos** and **Fethiye** (western Mediterranean) so as to accommodate hundreds of temple- or house-fronted tombs.

Greek art or the age of marble

Turkey possibly has more precious Ancient Greek treasures than Greece itself. Furthermore, these monuments provide a very clear idea of the munificence of that civilisation with innumerable fragments of cities serving as a reminder that, long before the Turkish invasions, Asia Minor was a great showcase for Hellenistic culture. In the 8C-7C BC, it was in Anatolia and not Greece that **Ionian** art flourished as the Greeks laid the foundations of successive prestigious cities like Ephesus, Priene and Miletus. In due course, signs would appear of monuments being planned, with each building being conceived as an individual work of art. Theatres, temples (Temple of Athena at **Assos**), *agoras* surrounded by covered galleries supported on elegant marble columns, are but a few illustrations of the refinement of Greek taste. Then as if beauty alone did not suffice, a second element is introduced into urban planning: in the 6C BC, the eminent philosopher **Hippodamus of Miletus** conceived the ideal city *(see page 316)* as being laid out on a grid-system articulated by broad avenues lined with covered galleries.

During the Persian occupation (5C BC), work progressed and Greek architecture produced two of the Seven Wonders of the World (unfortunately destroyed): the **Artemesion of Ephesus** (450 BC) and the **Mausoleum of Halicarnassus** (Bodrum), built a hundred years later by the Carian King Mausolus.

At the end of the 4C BC the successors to Alexander in Asia Minor, the **Seleucids**, and the **Attalids**, brilliant kings of Pergamum, heralded the golden age of Hellenistic culture which extended well beyond the marches of Asia Minor, from Italy to the Caspian Sea, and from the Nile to the Hindu Kush. The Hippodamian model of the *polis* (city) was being imposed everywhere, and with it spread a taste for monumental architecture, executed with the help of talented sculptors. Ephesus, Miletus, Priene, Sardis, Pergamum **(great altar of Zeus)** and Antiochus were all embellished with monuments and statuary reflecting the Greek ideal of beauty.

This liking for monumentality and prestige was to culminate in the extraordinary Commagene sanctuary of **Nemrut Dağı**, built at the start of the period of Roman domination (1C BC) by King Antiochus I. This immense conical tumulus, guarded by colossi, illustrates just how deeply Hellenistic art penetrated into eastern Anatolia, and how local and Mesopotamian design could be integrated into it.

Roman architects

The other undisputed lovers of monumentalism, the Romans, were also to use their architects and urban planners to establish imperial power in offshore territories. In all four corners of the Empire, builders were active in every town: temples, baths and theatres were erected, while ever bigger, more complicated and ambitious **projects** involving roads, bridges and aqueducts were being implemented. These highly sophisticated developments were no longer limited to religious monuments. Water

Nemrut Dağı or the tomb of the Gods

was used to symbolise the might and power of the Roman Empire and therefore it could be seen everywhere and in abundance; sumptuous **nymphaea** were built to ornament town squares. However the Romans demonstrated a profound respect for the Hellenistic heritage: many edifices were restored or modernised, and new architectural projects were carefully designed in harmony with the prevailing local styles. Two major structural innovations – the arch and **vaulting** – became widespread, and the Corinthian order, a decorative variant of the Ionic order, was also introduced.

Meanwhile the Romans refined the concept of a rectilinear street system, in keeping with the Hippodamian original, after considerable experimentation in laying out their military camps.

Roman **statuary**, however, was to adhere to Hellenistic prototypes, for better or for worse. Enormous quantities were reproduced, of varying quality, with the inevitable result that the style became increasingly conventional.

N. F. Carteret/HOA QUI

Byzantine art

By the 4C AD, Rome was in decline, the Empire was fading, and the new Emperor transferred his capital to Constantinople. Before long, the Roman ideal was giving way to a new aesthetic combining Hellenistic influences with Christian iconography. In time the Byzantine Empire had a hold on all the former Roman colonies, and was imposing its new culture on Greece (Athos), Serbia, Italy (Ravenna, Venice), Armenia and across the Middle East (the monastery of St Catherine in the Sinai). Meanwhile, the Byzantine civilisation assimilated Sassanian and above all Arab elements, like the **arabesque**, notably for use in the decorative and applied arts (and ceramics) at which it excelled.

Constantinople occupied a central position in a vast and disparate State. Not only did the city attract ideas and wealth from the furthest provinces, it also set the standards of taste and moulded artistic creativity. Gradually the city-dwelling nobility lost out to a class of rich landowners who settled in Anatolia (9C-10C). One such migrant was **Phocas**, the creator of one of the jewels of Cappadocia, namely the second **Church of Tokalı** (Göreme), covered in frescoes that recall the beauty of distant Constantinople. As countless other monasteries prospered in the region, each diffused its own extraordinary repertoire of holy images, modelled on the mosaics in the churches of the capital.

The consequences of the eminently political **Iconoclastic crisis** *(see page 23)* were disastrous for the arts, especially for the religious institutions in Constantinople which were powerless to prevent great masterpieces from being destroyed.

But after the dark days came the brilliant **Macedonian renaissance** (9C) which marked the start of a new golden era that was to last until 1204. Artists abandoned Classical Antiquity – which they associated with paganism and regarded as suspect – and turned instead to traditional religious representation and elements peculiar to the Paleochristian Age. Furthermore, they made no attempt to master realism, preferring to search for profound truth and depict a more spiritual world. The slow decline, which began at the end of the 11C, did not prevent the arts from flourishing, especially during the rule of the **Comnene** dynasty when several sumptuous **monasteries** were built. Frescoes and mosaics showed a gradual return to realism with figurative representations becoming increasingly expressive and emotionally demonstrative. This was entirely in keeping with developments in Byzantine society as individuals learned to assert their personality and give voice to inner consciousness.

Indeed, it is interesting to note that this was when the concept of the artist first emerged, but the Empire had to wait until the disastrous Latin occupation was over (13C) before succumbing to a veritable **Humanist renaissance**. Byzantine architecture and the art of the **icon** attained hitherto unknown levels of refinement, but the State was no longer in a position to pay for their ambitious policies – the restoration of the **monastery of St Saviour-in-Chora** being very much an exception. Henceforth, the best Byzantine art was no longer to be found in Constantinople, but in Mistra and in Salonica in Greece.

Byzantine architecture

The brilliance of Byzantine architecture is best appreciated in **religious buildings**. The fact that so many survive intact must surely bear witness to the importance of Christianity's role in contemporary society, providing the foundations for legitimising power and acting as a cement to hold the Empire together. The survival of the buildings is surely due in part to the solid way in which they were constructed, but above all to their design, prompting the Ottomans to alter, rather than destroy them.

It was Constantine, at the beginning of the 4C, who provided the real impetus for Christian art, encouraging new sanctuaries to be constructed on the lines of the **timber basilica**, which was significantly different from the ancient temple. Modelled on the Roman basilica – a purely functional building for assembling people – the Byzantine sanctuary is fronted by an atrium and a narthex, reserved for the catechumen. Churches were generally orientated to face the East, for that was where the light announcing the Second Coming of Christ was to come from. In some instances, a transept was added. Among the Paleochristian sanctuaries to be built in Anatolia in the 4C-6C, one should mention the basilicas at **Alahan** (to the north of Silifke) and **Hierapolis**.

The rise of the dome – Throughout the 6C, **Justinian** peppered Constantinople with monuments, and provided an incentive for a tremendous surge in artistic creativity right across the Empire. The **dome**, long since perfected by the Romans, was adopted as the prime feature of all future major Byzantine edifices. Indeed, eastern practices required the faithful and officiants to be present in the same unified space. This

Cappadocia, the hidden treasures of the churches of Göreme

eventually gave rise to the idea of capping the basilica with a dome, transforming it into a centralised space. But the spirit of the age is best embodied in the monumental dimensions of great complexes, like the masterly **Basilica of Ayasofya** *(see page 145)*.

After the iconoclastic crisis during Macedonian rule (9C), churches proliferated, although they were built to reduced dimensions. The most effective format, the **Greek cross plan**, being perfectly suited to the scale of office celebrated by small private chapels or monastic communities, quickly became widespread. This comprises a central dome rising from a drum, studded with a ring of windows, endowing the building with an elegant profile. The dome is suspended over the intersection of two barrel vaults, to produce four arms of equal lengths – similar to a Greek cross – sometimes contained within a square (hence the term **inscribed cross**).

In the 9C, the first **rock churches of Cappadocia** began to appear, consisting of a single sanctuary hewn out of the extraordinary cones of volcanic tufa. Then, in the 11C, builders began experimenting with other forms like the **tetraconic plan**, which had been popular in the Paleochristian Era, and was possibly reintroduced by Armenians. In this instance, the four arms of the cross terminate in simple apses; the eastern one is often larger so that it can serve as the sanctuary.

After the Latin occupation, the demand for new churches dwindled, although projects continued to be conceived on an ambitious scale. The sanctuary area remained fashioned like a Greek cross, but the interior space became increasingly open and the load-bearing piers deliberately masked (**Church of St Saviour-in-Chora** in İstanbul).

Byzantine civil architecture is relatively little known, with the exception of village dwellings in **Pergamum** (12C-13C) and the town dignitaries' houses in **Ephesus**. In İstanbul, nothing remains of the sumptuous Imperial Grand Palace, the hippodrome, nor of the ancient forums with covered galleries built by Constantine and his successors. However, some elements of the **Palace of Constantine Porphyrogenitus**

(Tekfur Sarayı) survive, as do sections of the famous **Valens aqueduct** (4C) and various underground cisterns (**Yerebatan Sarayı, Binbirdirek**), with their mass of columns reflected in the water.

From a planning point of view, Constantinople preserves formidable ramparts and a street system from late Antiquity, arranged around the *Mese*, a broad transversal thoroughfare. The only real improvements were made in the 5C, when Theodosius II erected new ramparts and installed a vast water supply system, complete with cisterns. No subsequent ruler was ever to attempt to implement such radical town planning policies again, preferring to make their mark with religious buildings.

Military architecture is much better known largely in terms of the impressive city walls of **İstanbul** and **İznik** which reflect the use of Roman techniques of alternate courses of stone and brick.

Mosaic, painting and miniatures

Mosaic was to become the most expressive medium in Byzantine art, a technique artists imported from Ancient Greek and Rome. The mosaic pavement was extremely popular in homes and churches in towns throughout the Empire up until the 7C. The floors of the Imperial Grand Palace (5C-7C) in Constantinople reflect antique traditions notably in the choice of subject matter (mythology, pastoral scenes, sporting events), a taste for the picturesque, expressive sensitivity and feeling for movement. Some remarkable examples are displayed in the Archeological Museum in Antakya, ancient Antioch.

But it is in mural mosaics that the Byzantine style really comes into its own. The mosaic is a perfect vehicle for simple narratives, and artists imbued these with a particular spirituality that completely transformed the Holy Scriptures. All the buildings were covered with figurative, albeit highly stylised, images, boldly offset against a gold background and so devoid of perspective. In time every vault and wall became crowded with wide-eyed ghost-like figures. The Byzantine style in fact was largely forged in Constantinople (churches dedicated to St John the Baptist of Studius, St Polyeuktus, the Holy Apostles); although many of the mosaic cycles were badly damaged by the iconoclasts so one should look to **Ravenna** (Italy) and Salonica (Greece) for worthy comparisons.

After the restoration of images, all forms of pictorial representation were reviewed, most especially the treatment of sacred figures (*Virgin and Child* in the apse of Ayasofya). The Greek cross church provides the perfect context for evangelical scenes, arranged hierarchically and radiating from the central space so as to allow the uninitiated to follow the story as if reading a comic strip.

In the 11C, as a new class of wealthy citizens evolved, taste shifted towards the use of a more dramatic expressionism and strong vibrant colour which inevitably affected the style of church mosaics. Immediately after the Latin occupation, under the **Paleologus**, the art form underwent a complete transformation as is apparent in the *Deisis* in the southern tribune of Ayasofya (13C) and the whole of the Kariye Camii (14C) in İstanbul. For the first time, the figures seem to have individual personality, they are animated with profound realism, and their gestures are remarkably graceful.

Fresco painting meanwhile adhered to the same stylistic forms as mosaic, and followed much the same historical evolution. The only real distinction between them was one of cost, so frescoes tended to be used in many of the lesser churches and, in particular, in the monasteries of **Cappadocia**, as decoration in tombs.

The other important Byzantine art form is the icon. These were small paintings on wooden panels, and being transportable, provided a popular way of interceding with God and obtaining protection from evil. In time, icons grew to be so revered that in the 6C, legends were emerging of *acheiropoeietic* icons (that is icons "not made by man"). Inevitably, most of the Palaeobyzantine icons were destroyed by iconoclasts save for the odd one preserved in St Catherine's monastery in the Sinai.

In the meantime, religious **miniatures** – meticulously copied by monks and laymen – were being produced for distribution across the Empire (most Christians being illiterate). The art of illustration was particularly perfected in Armenia, and of course, Russia. Of the few examples to survive today, one of the most remarkable is surely the very well-known profane manuscript the *Dioscoride*, in Vienna, which consists of a 1C thesis on pharmocopoeia, copied in 512. The drawing conforms to Greco-Roman prototypes, and being highlighted in gold betrays Byzantine influence.

Sculpture and applied arts

Sculpture was never to enjoy the same success as painting in Byzantium, although in the early days "New Rome" was keen to preserve the Imperial art of portrait busts and figurative sarcophagi. It would appear that remarkably little statuary adorned buildings and civic centres save for the countless effigies pillaged from pagan temples; for Byzantine artists seemed to rate highly-stylised forms over Roman realism. Up until the 5C, Egyptian porphyry was especially fashionable because its purple colour was associated with dignity; a throwback, perhaps, to Imperial times. It was only in the 6C that a genuine Byzantine style became apparent in incised ornament-on-column capitals and carved sarcophagi (Silifke, Archeological Museum of İstanbul), with figures portrayed in very simple terms among highly stylised elements.

Sculpture modelled in the round and on a monumental scale suffered a marked decline in the 6C. Furthermore, most of the works that were completed were destroyed by the Crusaders in the early 13C with the exception of some **statues of Constantine**, a marble portrait of Heraclius, a bronze colossus from Barletta, not forgetting, of course, the superb **horses of St Mark's** in Venice which originally graced the hippodrome in Constantinople.

It is perhaps in the applied arts, however, that Byzantine craftsmen showed particular brilliance, notably working in **ivory** brought from India and Africa by caravan. The consular diptychs produced between the 4C-6C are especially exquisite, populated by the stylised figures so typical of Byzantine art. Similarly, the larger, imperial diptychs show the Emperor as a hieratic figure be it in military scenes or with his wife.

The goldsmiths, while perpetuating an ancient tradition, proved to be equally remarkable, with gold and silver jewellery, plate and furniture playing an important role in ornamenting both palaces and churches. But it is in **cloisonné enamel** that the Byzantine artists excel, skilfully wedding the brightness of the precious metal with the colours of precious stones. Stylised figures, floral motifs and birds combined in iridescent scenes provide a vivid insight into contemporary tastes. The same iconography is translated into luxurious **textiles** (linen, silk, wool), dyed purple and embroidered with gold thread to be made up into garments fit for the Emperor, or fashioned into heavy **tapestries** that insulated palace and church interiors against draughts (imagine the Ayasofya decked with sumptuous drapes). The main workshops were situated in Egypt, where Coptic weavers excelled at their trade, but also in Syria, Thrace and in Constantinople itself.

The Seljuks and the influence of the Orient

The arrival of the Seljuks in Asia Minor in the 11C, motivated by a new and different faith, instituted a radical change of direction. Their contribution was to be both prolific and highly original, especially in the field of architecture where they managed to blend Byzantine elements with oriental ones, often derived from Iranian sources. The best examples of Seljuk art and design are to be found in southeast Turkey, as well as in **Konya**, the capital of the Sultanate of Rum and in the north of central Anatolia **(Sivas)**.

Religious architecture

The standard at that time for a religious complex was the great Umayyad mosque in Damascus (715). This comprised a vast prayer hall, supported on columns, and an open courtyard surrounded by a portico. The Seljuk **mosque**, meanwhile, could be arranged in a variety of ways. In accordance with oriental prototypes, this complex comprised a central courtyard, flanked by three or four separate rooms *(iwan)*, and a fountain for ablutions. In Anatolia, this format was adapted to suit the rigorous climate: the courtyard was made progressively smaller and covered by a dome, thereby providing an extension to the hall of prayer, which was also domed. This is the case with the **Alaaddin Mosque** in Konya, the **Great Mosque of Hunat** (Kayseri) and of that of **Sivas**. Other mosques are adaptations of the Byzantine basilica, such as those at **Amasya** and **Niğde.**

In keeping with the mosques, the Seljuks injected a wholly original spirit into the building of **medrese** (Koranic schools) and *imaret* (public kitchens) in all the towns of the sultanate. Mention should also be made of the elegant **türbe** (mausoleums), built of stone or brick, roofed with playful variants of a rounded dome, cone or pyramid (Konya, Niğde, Kayseri and Erzurum).

As in Iranian art, Seljuk **sculptural ornaments** decorated walls with floral and geometric designs, and Koranic verses written out in highly stylised and fluid calligraphy. The doorways of mosques, medreses and caravanserais are often adorned with human and animal forms, represented as slender and lithe, almost dancing figures, suggesting an Indian influence transmitted through Eastern and Iranian shamanism **(Gök Medrese of Sivas)**. This 13C Seljuk style, luxurious, dense, highly decorative, and representing the middle way between the living and the spiritual worlds, has often been described as "baroque".

The other important component of the style is the colourful arrays of blue, white and black **tin-glazed earthenware** with which many buildings are tiled. This form of decoration, which originated in Tabriz (Iran), was to find complete expression at **Konya**.

Secular buildings

Of the mighty **palaces** of the Sultans of Rum, embellished with enamelled earthenware tiles, there is, alas, not a single trace. Indeed, our knowledge of Seljuk secular architecture derives almost entirely from the **caravanserais**, or fortified hostels, which provided shelter for the large caravans. In stark contrast with the austerely plain walls, the gateway is topped with a concave tympanum elaborately carved with a profusion of *muqarnas* (stalactites), stars and intertwined loops. The portals of Seljuk caravanserais are expressions of exquisite artistry as those of the two **Sultan Hanı**, between Konya and Sivas, will testify.

Furthermore, the Seljuks demonstrated considerable know-how in their upkeep of the **fortifications** of the towns in their possession, sometimes adding a **citadel**, as in Diyarbakır, Van, Konya, Amasya, Niğde and Ankara.

Ottoman art

The Seljuks were toppled by an invasion of Mongols; the Ottomans seized control of Asia Minor and installed the Osmanlı dynasty on the throne. And under their auspices, a genuinely "Turkish" style evolved in three distinct phases. At Bursa (13C-15C), the architecture of the mosque was perfected and tiled decoration superseded all forms of sculpture. The so-called Classical Period (15C-17C), saw a culmination in the art of dome-building – and a golden age for architecture with the advent of Mimar Sinan. Finally, the Baroque and Rococo phase (17C-20C) saw the influence of European tastes, especially in surface decoration.

Bursa architects

The achievements of Ottoman architects are all the more admirable when one stops to think how, before the conquest of Bursa (1326), the Turkish people were leading nomadic lives and sleeping in tents. The new capital Bursa challenged mosque architects, vying with one another, to increase the internal space of the new buildings. The two possible solutions being a **hypostyle interior** or an inverted T.

The first consists of a single space, articulated with rows of columns into several bays and covered with domes (**Ulu Cami**, 1399). In this case, the courtyard is covered, providing an even larger space interspersed with columns.

The second option – the **inverted T mosque** – adapted from the Seljuk mosque and better adapted to harsh winters, became the more popular. The single dome symbolised the sky (as in Byzantine churches). The square prayer-hall represented the earth and its four cardinal points while the internal domed courtyard was capped with a lantern. On either side of the courtyard were arranged a series of studies (*iwan*), giving the plan its T-shape. The whole complex was preceded by a gateway which was often two storeys. Early prototypes include the Nilüfer Hatun mosque in İznik, but it is in Bursa that the format was refined and established with the **Mosque of Orhan** (1340) and the famous **Green Mosque** (1424).

A change occurred with the **Mosque of Beyazıt I** where the gateway was reduced to a simple archway, and far more soberly decorated than the exuberant Seljuk portals. The main concern was for the architect to conceal the basic structural elements; to this end, they devised the pendentive which ensures the weight of the circular dome is distributed down through a succession of arches to the square fabric of the building. These were then encrusted with a flourish of *muqarnas*, blurring the separations between dome, drum and pillar. From below, the dome appears to hover above the vast internal space.

The age of Imperial mosques

After the capture of Constantinople (1453), mosques continued to be built to centralised plans. The Ottomans remained in awe of the boldness in design of the Ayasofya, and dreamed of surpassing it: but it was to take them another 50 years before any sign of this appeared in the mosque of **Beyazıt II** (İstanbul).

The art of the Ottoman Empire reached new heights in the 16C with the work of **Mimar Sinan**, chief architect to Süleyman the Magnificent. His colossal output included some 334 projects: city walls, aqueducts, bridges, *türbe*, caravanserais, Turkish baths and mosques – notably the

Şehzade and **Süleymaniye mosques** in İstanbul, and that of **Selim II**, in Edirne. At Edirne, Sinan managed to match the prowess of the dome of Ayasofya, even surpassing it in elegance. The subtle interaction of elements border on perfection here: for beneath the central dome, the internal space tapers up to a pyramidal form; while on the outside, the tall silhouette is counterbalanced by spear-like minarets.

Sinan, the architect of Islam

Mimar Sinan (1489-1588) is unquestionably the most famous Ottoman architect. Born in Kayseri, he was enrolled as a young man in the Janissary corps, where he turned out to be an excellent military engineer. In 1539 the Sultan Süleyman appointed him his personal architect, and Sinan set about producing the finest mosques in the Empire, all based on the concept of the basilica of Ayasofya. Like the Roman Vitruvius who wrote his books on Imperial architecture, Sinan wrote a history of Ottoman architecture.

Many of Sinan's followers were also to produce brilliant adaptations of classical models: Davut Ağa (1597-1663) built the **Yeni Cami** in İstanbul, while Mehmet Ağa was the architect of the famous **Blue Mosque** (1609-16). But there was no further innovation and the age of the great Imperial mosques soon came to an end.

The rise and fall of Ottoman palaces

Far more examples of religious buildings survive than secular ones. For according to Muslim ideology (and many other ancient civilisations), secular buildings and dwelling places should be provisional in character, like life on earth. To this end, stone tended to be used only for religious and funereal buildings like the medrese, mosque and mausoleum. Exception is made for **Turkish baths (hamams)**, where all true Muslims go for purification, as well as for the defence of cities and for **caravanserais**.

In addition, according to ancient beliefs, all dwellings should remain incomplete in some way or another. In the case of the **Topkapı Palace**, it was assumed that each sultan would in some way change or extend the structure, and being an Imperial palace, the buildings should be constructed of stone, and stand as a symbol of the Empire, steadfast and eternal.

The last palace to be built was the **Dolmabahçe Palace**. It is a harmonious entity, and was completed in two years (1843-54). It also shows the influence of the West when the Ottoman Empire was in decline, both with regard to the layout and to the decoration borrowed directly from the French Baroque and Rococo. This is also when wealthy İstanbul families were building their yalı, elegant tall wooden town houses painted in pastel colours, overlooking the Bosphorus.

Tin-glazed earthenware (faience)

One of the most striking qualities of the Ottoman fine and decorative arts is the uniformity of style permeating the medium of fresco, miniatures, ceramics, silks and velvet. This may partially be explained by the eminent role played by the painters of the *nakkaşhane,* one of the various bodies or corporations of artisans employed by the court.

The importance attached to ceramics was a Seljuk legacy (albeit borrowed from Iran and China), but it was only then that the craft was refined into an art of such beauty as to become the preferred form of ornament for palaces and mosques. Besides the tiles, however, mention should be made of the potters producing countless dishes, cups and bowls.

The most famous pottery was produced in the **İznik workshops** from the late 15C, although in the 18C their production was superseded by workshops in **Kütahya** and **Tekfur Sarayı** (even if they never reached quite the same level of quality).

In the early days, the main colour that could be applied to the white background was cobalt blue (as in Dutch Delft). But in time, turquoise, then black and pastel shades of linden green, pale lilac, grey, and manganese violet became available. Eventually, in the mid 16C, red was added, while the rage was for "blue and white" motifs inspired by Chinese Ming porcelain, interspersed with swirling **arabesques**, ribbons of cloud, angular lettering and elegant foliated scrolls.

In the 16C there were two dominant polychrome styles of composition: the **"four-flower"** comprising bouquets of peonies, tulips, hyacinths or carnations, sometimes roses, and **saz** ("reed and forest") – a design devised by a painter from Tabriz. Echoing motifs found in Chinese and Iranian art, these patterns symbolise the rebirth of nature in spring, often involving dense foliage, sprigs of flowers, mythical animals and fairy creatures (*peri*) executed in a highly skilled stroke of the brush. The *saz* style also became highly fashionable in 16C **painting**, with its underlying decorative and abstract qualities. But painting took on a wholly different aspect at this time with strong narrative and realist elements, notably evident in portraiture and the illustrations accompanying biographies of eminent personalities (like Süleyman the Magnificent).

Calligraphy

Calligraphy, an ornament in itself (Ottoman funerary stele)

D. Ball/DIAF

The art of writing Arabic was considered sacred, as it was an instrument of divine revelation, and so calligraphy was held in high esteem and calligraphers applied their talents to books, walls, ceramics and talismans. There were six predominant forms of written Arabic, the most common being the *Kufic* (early angular form with static characters and elongated stems). However a combination of *Nâskhi* (more fluid with continuous lines) and *Thuluth* tended to be used on a large scale on the walls of mosques and medrese.

To produce an Ottoman manuscript, in particular the Koran, the calligrapher collaborated with a *warraq* (preparer of paper), painters, guilders, binders and illuminators, who used great quantities of gold and lapis-lazuli to set off their sumptuous floral motifs. History records two artists: Sheikh Hamdullah (1429-1520) and Ahmed Karahisari (16C). But countless inspired geniuses – Seljuk and Ottoman – have fashioned clay and plaster on walls and doorways to mosques with extraordinary interlaced lettering, as an expression of Muslim fervour.

Art today

Today various ancient traditional Anatolian art forms are undergoing a revival: at İznik for example, various tile workshops have been recreated. However, Turkish artists are finding it very difficult to free themselves from their Ottoman heritage and from Western influence. Turkish 20C **architecture**, in particular, is having difficulty in formulating a style of its own. After a preoccupation with monumental architecture (imposing and clinical **Atatürk Mausoleum** in Ankara) that lasted until the 1950s, the modern buildings cluttering the city centres are rather souless affairs constructed of concrete and glass; but these should not be seen as the expressions of a burgeoning "Turkish school". Instead, a regional style is emerging from the designs of Sedat Eldem who uses modern techniques to build traditional forms (**Atatürk Library** in İstanbul).

When the republic was founded, **sculpture** was considered a dead art form. Since then, it is slowly learning to shed its pompous style exalting the regime (future archeologists will no doubt wonder at the immense powers of this god Atatürk, whose statue is everywhere!). The first generation of sculptors and **painters** of the young Turkish Republic formed the "Group D" movement, with Elif Naci, Nurullah Berk, Abidin Dino and Zeki Faik İzer amongst its ranks. Open to Western trends, the group became involved in cubism and constructivism. However, **Ali Hadi Bara** and **Zühtü Müritoğlu**, who are reputed to have introduced abstraction into Turkish statuary, were making their mark back in the 1950s.

In the course of the 1940s, **Turgut Zaïm** and his daughter Oya Katoğlu went off in a different direction, keen to return to the genuine roots of Turkish culture. For them, inspiration was derived from provincial painting, rural life and popular artistic expression, calligraphy and miniature painting. This continues to be the most productive area of contemporary work.

At the same time, tourism has stimulated an interest in traditional Turkish crafts, notably in pottery and onyx (Cappadocia), as well as kilim-weaving and carpet-making. As is often the case though with these particular crafts, the quality of production does vary.

Art today

ARCHITECTURE OF ANTIQUITY

THE TEMPLE

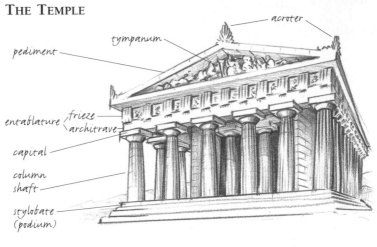

acroter

tympanum

pediment

frieze

entablature

architrave

capital

column

shaft

stylobate
(podium)

statue of the god

naos (cella, inner cell or sanctuary)

peristyle

pronaos
(narthex or
vestibule)

opisthodomos
(treasure chamber, reserved for priests)

THREE CLASSICAL ORDERS

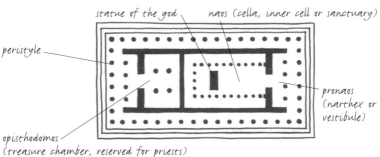

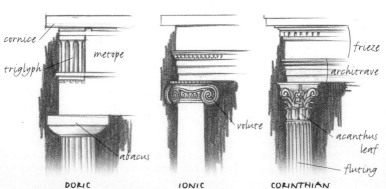

cornice

metope

triglyph

frieze

architrave

volute

abacus

acanthus
leaf

fluting

DORIC

IONIC

CORINTHIAN

H. Choimet

THE ROMAN AMPHITHEATRE

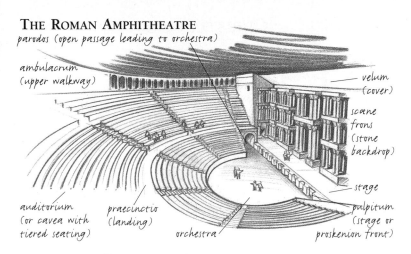

parodos (open passage leading to orchestra)

ambulacrum (upper walkway)

velum (cover)

scæne frons (stone backdrop)

stage

pulpitum (stage or proskenion front)

orchestra

praecinctio (landing)

auditorium (or cavea with tiered seating)

THERMAE OR BATHS

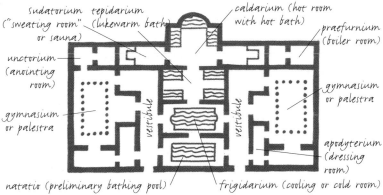

sudatorium ("sweating room" or sauna)

tepidarium (lukewarm bath)

caldarium (hot room with hot bath)

praefurnium (boiler room)

unctorium (anointing room)

gymnasium or palestra

gymnasium or palestra

vestibule

vestibule

apodyterium (dressing room)

natatio (preliminary bathing pool)

frigidarium (cooling or cold room)

tubuli (wall heating ducts)

swimming pool or bath

brick piles

hearth

HYPOCAUST HEATING SYSTEM

H. Choimet

CHRISTIAN ERA

ROMAN BASILICA

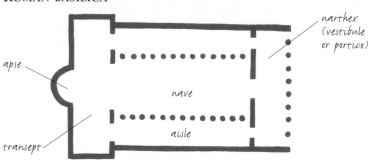

narthex (vestibule or portico)

apse

nave

transept

aisle

BYZANTINE CHURCH

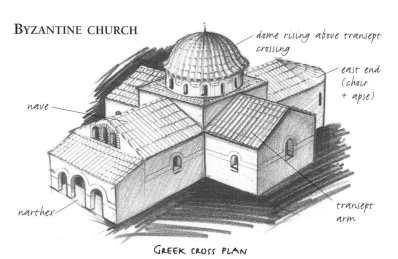

dome rising above transept crossing

east end (choir + apse)

nave

transept arm

narthex

GREEK CROSS PLAN

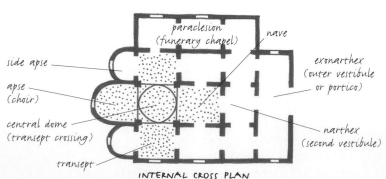

paraclesion (funerary chapel)

nave

side apse

exonarthex (outer vestibule or portico)

apse (choir)

central dome (transept crossing)

narthex (second vestibule)

transept

INTERNAL CROSS PLAN

H. Choimet

DOMES

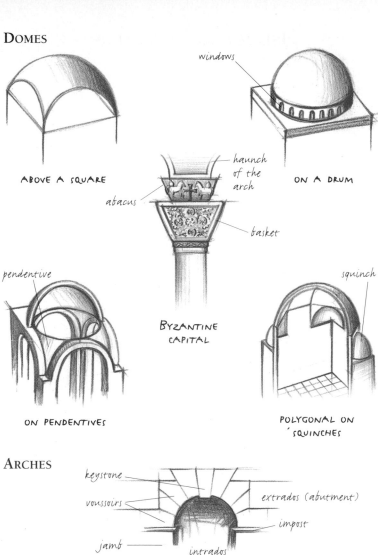

ABOVE A SQUARE

windows

ON A DRUM

haunch of the arch

abacus

basket

BYZANTINE CAPITAL

pendentive

ON PENDENTIVES

squinch

POLYGONAL ON SQUINCHES

ARCHES

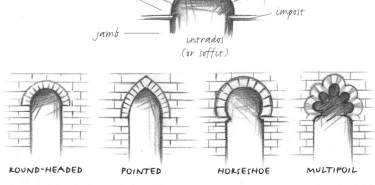

keystone

voussoirs

jamb

extrados (abutment)

impost

intrados (or soffit)

ROUND-HEADED

POINTED

HORSESHOE

MULTIPOIL

H. Choimet

ISLAMIC ARCHITECTURE

OTTOMAN MOSQUE

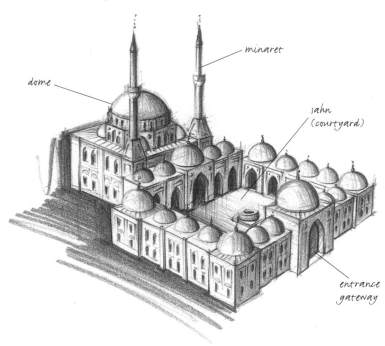

minaret

dome

sahn
(courtyard)

entrance
gateway

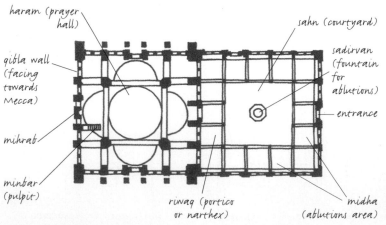

haram (prayer
hall)

sahn (courtyard)

qibla wall
(facing
towards
Mecca)

sadirvan
(fountain
for
ablutions)

entrance

mihrab

minbar
(pulpit)

riwaq (portico
or narthex)

midha
(ablutions area)

H. Choimet

MINARETS

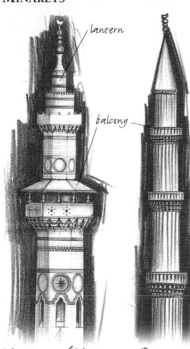

lantern

balcony

MAMELUKE (MIDDLE
EAST)

OTTOMAN
(TURKEY)

MUQARNAS
("STALACTITES")

FURNISHINGS

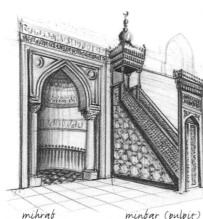

mihrab

minbar (pulpit)

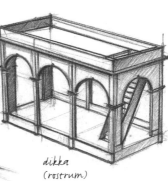

dikka
(rostrum)

kursi (lectern)

H. Choimet

Lexicon of architectural terms

Antiquity and general terms

Acanthus   Artichoke-like plant with scalloped leaves carved to decorate the Corinthian capital.

Acropolis   Citadel built on the highest point above Greek cities – enclosing main temples and public buildings.

Adobe   Sun-dried mud brick.

Adytum   Inner sanctuary of a Greek temple reserved for priests.

Agora   Open space in Greek cities used for public meetings and market; often surrounded by a portico as in a Roman forum.

Anastylose   Reconstruction of a ruined building using the original materials.

Andron   Meeting place for men in the Greek, Roman and Byzantine periods.

Anta   Corner (in antis) pilaster of a different order from the rest of the building.

Bond   Arrangement of stones (or bricks) in a wall.

Bouleuterion   Covered council (boule in Ancient Greek) chamber fitted with tiered seating like a theatre, built in the agora. Also used as an odeon.

Cardo   Street running on a north-south axis across a Roman city, parallel to the main thoroughfare known as the cardo maximus and perpendicular to the decumanus.

Decumanus   Street running east-west across a Roman city.

Exedra   Semicircular or rectangular recess with raised seats. Also used to denote the stone bench of the same shape, a niche for statuary or an apse.

Forum   See "agora".

Gymnasium   Sports complex in Antiquity, including various buildings (changing-rooms, exercise rooms, anointing rooms etc) and open-air areas (running tracks).

Hypostyle   Classical temple or palace with a roof supported by columns (the Greek *stylos* meaning column).

Iconostasis   Screen inset with icons, separating the nave from the choir of Orthodox churches.

Insula   A residential quarter or block delimited by the streets, in ancient cities.

Megaron   Large oblong hall in palace complex, considered to be the antecedent of the Doric temple. Also used to allude to Neolithic and Bronze Age rectangular living-room with a central hearth (Troy, Gordion), preceded by porch and vestibule.

Mosaic   Assembly of coloured tesserae for decorative effect, applied to floors and walls in early buildings (see also sidebar on page 488).

Nymphaeum   Natural spring or artificial fountain dedicated to the nymphs. In Roman cities, the monumental fountain might honour an emperor and symbolise the power of the Empire.

Odeon   Small theatre, usually covered, for concerts and public readings.

Opus   See "bond".

Order   Classical style of architecture defined by a system of proportion, and distinguished by the ornament applied to the capital of a column and the treatment of the entablature.

Orthostate   From the Greek meaning "standing stone": carved and cut upright block of stone used to form the base of a wall and support a bas-relief panel.

Peristyle   Gallery (stoa in Greek), or colonnaded portico surrounding a temple or courtyard.

Pilaster   A shallow pier or rectangular column, protruding from the wall.

Portico   Covered gallery supported by a colonnade.

Praetorium   Residence of a Roman governor, or barracks.

Propylaeum   Monumental gateway to an important public building, sanctuary, sacred precinct, or a citadel.

Prytaneum	Official headquarters of the administrative organisation of a Greek city. Seat of the Prytaneis or magistrates in charge of the bouleuterion.
Stucco	Plaster (gypsum), used for surface mouldings and carved wall and ceiling decoration.
Temenos	A sacred precinct around a sanctuary, bounded by the peribole, where the faithful assemble. Sacred esplanade of an acropolis.
Tessera	Small cube of stone or coloured glass used in the making of mosaics.
Tetrapylon	From the Greek "tetra" meaning "four". Monument comprising four piers marking the intersection of two Roman thoroughfares.
Tholos	Circular temple with a conical roof or dome.

Byzantine buildings

Ambo	Stand raised on a few steps from which the Gospels and Epistles are read: replaced in the 14C by the pulpit.
Apse	Vaulted semicircular or polygonal extension often added to a chancel or choir.
Archivolt	Continuous architrave moulding on the extrados of an arch.
Basilica	Rectangular civil building divided into three parallel aisles, used by the Romans for public meetings and tribunals. Name given to the first Christian churches built on this plan.
Bema	The raised area in an Orthodox church, often before an apse, where the altar and the bishop's throne were placed.
Chancel	Low balustrade dividing the choir from the nave in a church.
Diaconicon	The sacristy in Byzantine churches, where the clergy kept their vessels and vestments.
Fresco	From the Italian "fresh": used to refer to wall paintings applied in Byzantine times to the bare stone, later to fresh plaster, providing a finer ground for the pigment.
Narthex	Vestibule or covered porch before the main body of a church where penitents and catechumens assembled before baptism.
Prothesis	Sacristy located to the left of the main apse, opposite the diaconicon (see above) where the bread and wine of the sacrament were prepared before consecration.
Synthronon	Bench or benches reserved for the clergy arranged around the apse or in rows on either side of the bema (see above) in Early Christian and Byzantine churches.

Islamic buildings

Caravanserai	Fortified hostelry built along the principle trade routes across the Middle and Far East where caravan travellers could stop and rest, unload their cargo into secure warehouses and stable their animals; usually located at 25km intervals or a day's ride.
Hamam	Turkish steam baths found across the Muslim world, adapted from Roman prototypes although with no actual pool; as in accordance with Muslim ideology, water should run freely and liberally (through a fountain or "sebil").
Iwan	Small room opening out onto a courtyard, enclosed on three sides, found in secular and religious Muslim complexes.
Mashrabiya	Known as moucharaby in English. Window or balcony of a traditional Muslim house, screened off with wooden or stone lattice-work allowing the women to see out without being seen.
Mihrab	Niche in a mosque indicating the direction of Mecca.
Minbar	Raised pulpit in a mosque with a flight of steps, from which Friday prayers are addressed.
Serail	Ottoman palace, a seat of administration.
Tekke	Sufi monastery, dervishes convent.
Türbe	Muslim funerary monument, tomb or mausoleum.

Meeting the people

E. Valentin / HOA QUI

The fish market
at Kadıköy

A PEOPLE OF ASIAN ORIGIN

Oriental stereotype

At one time, it would have been normal to expect Turkish men, clad in baggy trousers, to be strong, moustachioed, swashbuckling and belligerent fellows with an aptitude for fighting like tigers. Their women, meanwhile, might be seen as lascivious creatures living in harems. Such clichés – propagated by the likes of the Romantic Orientalists Flaubert, Lamartine and Delacroix in France – were suggestively exotic and erotic (if highly misleading) depictions of Turkish life and society. The real Turkey is as far removed from such 19C stereotypes as it is from the compelling film *Midnight Express*! If you ask travellers who have been to Turkey what their overriding impression was, you will find that it is probably the people's tremendous sense of hospitality.

From the steppes of Central Asia to the Anatolian plateau

It is as well to clarify that the Turks, although Muslim, are not Arabs; their languages, for a start, are quite different. Whereas Arabic originates from a group of southern Semitic languages, the roots of Turkish are to be sought much further east in the **Altay Mountains**, on the border between Russia and China. So the Huns, Genghis Khan, Tamerlane, the Mongols and the Turks all share the same origins. A vast family of Asian nomads, the Altay peoples originally lived in the Siberian forest. They then migrated southwards, towards the steppes of central Asia, where they regrouped to form a huge confederation (6C-8C). This "Tujue" Empire (perhaps the origin of the word *Turk*) incorporated the whole of upper Asia and extended as far as the marches of Sassanid Persia. In the 9C, various Turkish tribes were impelled by the Uygurs – a dissident people allied to the Chinese – to flee towards the southern reaches of eastern Europe where they later became known as Bulgars, Khazars, Pechenegs and Cumans.

As these nomadic shepherds and horsemen came to mix with Iranians, they converted to Islam and henceforth became known as the **Turkomans**. Over the ensuing centuries, they migrated westwards and formed disparate communities and small states across the region, clashing periodically with each other but gradually being assimilated by the local Greeks, Kurds and Armenians.

In the 11C, the **Seljuks** – a powerful dynasty of Oğuz Turks founded by **Selçuk** – emerged on the scene. It was not long before the Seljuks had permeated all the territories held by the Arabs, spreading across Iran, Mesopotamia, Syria, right up to the Byzantine lands of Anatolia, where they established their capital (Konya).

A century later, a wave of **Turko-Mongol** people arrived and settled in the area, adding their personality to the Turkish identity. Under their leader Timur-Lang **(Tamerlane)**, this tribe managed to found a veritable Turkish Empire that incorporated Siberia, Asia Minor and the Crimea, stretching as far as eastern Turkestan.

This Empire was to be short-lived, having been quickly overrun by advancing **Osmanlıs** or **Ottomans**, who were a different Turkish people descended from the same stock as the Seljuks, through the Oğuz line. The Ottoman (*osmanlı* in Turkish) dynasty, established by **Sultan Osman** in 1290, extended their rule across a vast region reaching the gates of Vienna and including the Berber countries of North Africa (16C), before retreating into Anatolia at the end of the 19C. And it is in this land, turned into a nation state in 1923 by Atatürk, that the majority of the Turkish population is now concentrated. But ethnic Turks are also to be found beyond the borders of modern Turkey, spread over a large area in central and southern Asia: of the 80 million Turkish people in all, almost half are distributed across Azerbaijan, Turkmenistan, Uzbekistan and Kyrgyzstan. Small Turkish minorities also live in Iran, the Balkans, and even in China (in Xinjiang).

The Turks today

At the crossroads of East and West, Turkey can claim to have a rich cultural heritage that is evidently apparent in the diversity of its people: Greeks, Celts, Armenians, European Jews, Circassians. It is still quite disarming to find just how diverse looking the Turks on the street are: green- or blue-eyed blondes jostle with high cheek-boned individuals with almond-shaped eyes, jet-black hair, and aquiline noses.

Superficial unity

Generally speaking, the boundaries of the Republic correspond to the same as those of the ancient Ottoman Empire, populated in the main by Turks save for Armenia (northeast) and Kurdistan (southeast). Until the 19C, the various populations lived peaceably side by side in Anatolia under the watchful and tolerant eye of the Ottomans: the Greeks remained on the coasts and in the west, while the Armenians and the Kurds occupied the eastern territories. It was not until the First World War that the co-existence of these populations was abruptly questioned. In the turmoil of war, countless **Armenians** were massacred by the Turks (1915). Then after the War of Independence (1922) many **Greeks** were exchanged with the Turks in Greece. Nowadays, these two communities are only really to be found in any numbers in İstanbul (50 000 Armenians, 6 000 Greeks, with a good proportion in İzmir). Much the same applies to the **Jews**. The **Kurds**, on the other hand, still represent a considerable minority, indeed it is the main one, accounting for some 15 % of the national population. But their complete integration remains a delicate issue as the Kurds wish to safeguard both their language (so different from Turkish) and their customs (as Alawite Muslims). They are concentrated in and around İstanbul and, above all, in the southeastern part of the country (Turkish Kurdistan).

Turkey boasts several other minorities, notably in the region of Hatay, near the Syrian border, where numerous Syriac Christian (rather than Muslim) **Turks of Arab origin** reside.

Mention should also be made of two Caucasian peoples: the **Lazes** (some 100 000) who have lived in the area near the present border of Georgia (the Black Sea region) since the 1C, and the **Cherkessians** who sought to escape from the Russian invasion in the 19C. Their communities are so dispersed as to make the numbers difficult to quantify, rather like the **Muslim gypsies** who tend to live in urban areas.

Another often overlooked statistic is that a quarter of the Turkish population is descended from the great waves of **refugees** (*muhacir*) flooding in from lost Ottoman territories from the 18C onwards: in this way, almost 10 million Turks originate from the Balkans alone (Bosnia, Macedonia, Greece, Bulgaria).

The last category of people are the **nomadic populations**, who are essentially concentrated in Kurdistan. The **Yörüks** (*see page 428*), a semi-nomadic people, are increasingly opting for a more settled way of life mainly among the southwest Anatolian mountains, although in the last few decades many have been streaming down from the Taurus mountains attracted by the agricultural plains.

RELIGIOUS FAITHS

Throughout its history, the Ottoman Empire was a multi-denominational state and a cosmopolitan land where Christians, Jews and Muslims of different creed could cohabit in peace while enjoying a considerable level of autonomy in religious, administrative and cultural practices. Organised into **millets** (nations), each community managed its own affairs and appointed its own representative at the "Ottoman Porte". But the advent of the Turkish nation at the beginning of the 20C was to upset this balance. In his desire to eliminate ethnic diversity, Atatürk crushed the religious minorities, in particular the Jews, Orthodox Christians (Armenian and Greek Churches), and certain marginal Muslim groups.

In spite of the State being secularised, Islam remains the predominant religion across the country today with 90% of the population being Muslim. Other minority factions have sought refuge in the larger towns and their numbers are dwindling. To be Turkish means to be Muslim, which implies that non-Muslims are not entirely Turkish.

Islam

In the beginning, the early nomads from the Altay Mountains adhered to Shamanism. But in time, depending on where they chose to settle, they converted either to Buddhism or to Eastern Christianity. Then, in the 8C, as the Arabs progressively conquered the entire region, Islam was spread across the whole of central Asia, bringing with it new social and cultural values.

The story of Muhammad

Born in Mecca around 570, Muhammad began life as a modest shepherd. He gradually he made a name for himself as a caravan guide, journeying as far as Syria. It was only in 610, at the age of 40, that he had his first revelations while living out in the desert. For the following 10 years, the Prophet preached the word of God, declaring that Allah was all-powerful and the one and only god. But his proselytising displeased the dignitaries in Mecca and, in 622, Muhammad and his disciples were forced to flee to Medina: a period of exile that was to mark the beginning of the **Hegira** (*Hidjra*), the Islamic Era. Following in the wake of Abraham, Moses and Jesus (whom he revered for having brought the first glimpses of the true light), Muhammad continued to preach until his death (632), converting countless followers to his faith.

The word of Allah to Muhammad has been transcribed into the **Koran** by his disciples, verse by verse into 114 chapters **(suras)** and it is this complete body of scriptures that the students in the **medrese** (Koranic schools) have to learn by heart: a formidable task by all accounts. Besides the Koran, there is also the **Sunna** (or tradition): a collection of more or less legendary tales (*hadith*) about the life of Muhammad and his followers. This work also clarifies certain obscure parts of the Koran, completing its precepts and dealing with various aspects of daily life as affected by the teachings of Islam.

The "five pillars" of Islam

"There is no God other than Allah and Muhammad is his Prophet." Such is the Muslim **profession of faith** resounding from the muezzins at each call to prayer. In Sunnite Islam there is neither clergy nor sacrament. Prayer alone brings the faithful together, guided by an eminent scholar, the Imam.

Zefa/HOA QUI

Inside the Mosque

On the other hand, the Koran does lay down **five obligations**: the profession of faith – act of conversion to Islam; prayer (five times a day); fasting for Ramadan; charity *(sadakat)* and the pilgrimage to Mecca *(hadjadj)* which every good Muslim should perform at least once in his life.

In addition to these fundamental principles, the Muslim religion prescribes certain rules by which the faithful should abide: alcoholic (fermented) drinks are prohibited, as are pork and non-*halal* meat (derived from animals – like game – from which the blood has not been drawn). Gambling and usury are disapproved of, charity is encouraged as is a disdain for certain worldly goods.

During your stay in Turkey, you will not fail to hear the **call to prayer** *(ezan)* intoned over the loudspeakers of the minarets. This always starts with the incantation "*Allah Akbar*" ("God is great") repeated four or five times in different registers. The muezzin (or rather the tape-recording!) carries on with the profession of faith, inviting the faithful to pray in the mosque or elsewhere, provided they turn to face Mecca.

Cleanliness of the body reflects that of the soul: so every adherent must perform his ablutions, according to a strict ritual. Then, after removing their shoes, the faithful may enter the mosque, take their place facing towards the *mihrab* (a recess hollowed out in the wall facing Mecca) and start their **prayer**. This consists of repeated prostration in three movements (standing – kneeling – bent to the ground), to the chant of verses from the Koran.

Friday *(cuma)* is the day of **solemn prayer**, accompanied by a sermon. Over recent years, Turkey has witnessed such a considerable increase in the number of practising Muslims that in some places, the people are forced to pray out in the street. Crouched on their heels, the long lines of prostrated figures bow down in silence, intent on the murmur of orisons and readings from the Koran.

Feast days and holy days

The Hegiran year is a lunar year, composed of 12 months of 29 or 30 days each. It is therefore shorter than the solar year and gains about 10 days advance on it each year. This means that the main religious festivals and the month of Ramadan are not at a fixed date on the Gregorian calendar.

The official religious festivals in Turkey are as follows:

New year's day in the Muslim calendar;

The 6th day of the Hegira **(birth of the Prophet)**;

The **Şeker Bayramı**, or feast of sugar, which celebrates the end of Ramadan. After the fasting, everyone feasts on confectionery, sweets and cakes, which families offer each other;

The **Kurban Bayramı**, or feast of the sacrifice (of Abraham), which takes place 40 days later. On this occasion, nearly three million sheep or cattle are sacrificed and eaten in the space of a few days, a third of the meat being kept by the family, a third going to friends and relations, and the final third going to the poor and needy.

Calendar of Muslim Holy Days				
Anno Hegirae	1421	1422	1423	1424
New Year	05/04/2000	25/03/2001	14/03/2002	03/03/2003
Prophet's Birthday	14/06/2000	03/06/2001	23/05/2002	12/05/2003
Beginning of Ramadan	27/11/2000	16/11/2001	05/11/2002	25/10/2003
Şeker Bayramı (end of Ramadan)	27/12/2000	16/12/2001	05/12/2002	24/11/2003
Kurban Bayramı	05/03/2001	22/02/2002	11/02/2003	31/01/2004

N.B.: the dates shown above may vary by one or two days due to the difficulty in calculating the precise start of a lunar month.

The most striking demonstration of Muslim life is **Ramadan** (ramazan), which corresponds to the ninth month of the lunar year. Ramadan affects all adults physically capable of respecting the requirements (expectant mothers, the sick, the elderly or travellers in transit are exempt). For its duration, the faithful should respect a period of fasting (oruç) and abstinence, refraining from eating during daylight hours from sunrise to sunset (announced by the muezzin), "when a white thread can no longer be distinguished from a black thread".

Even in the secular country that Turkey is now, certain aspects of daily life still revolve around the constraints of Ramadan: employees cease their work to respect iftar (breaking of the fast) at the office, taxi-drivers stop taking clients in order to return home more quickly, some shops close earlier and night-life is considerably reduced.

Alawites

Islam comprises two factions: the (orthodox) **Sunnite** (by far the majority in Turkey) and the (heretical) **Shia**, which includes the **Alawites**. The difference between them hinges on the legitimacy of Muhammad's successor: the Sunnis recognise the first four caliphs as worthy representatives of the Muslim community, while the Shiites are followers of the Prophet's son-in-law **Ali**, and they await the "hidden Imam" who will restore the Prophet's true lineage.

It is impossible to ascertain the exact number of Shiites because the adherents are sworn to secrecy, but estimates put the figure at 10 million in Turkey, mainly **Kurds**. Turkish Shiism, as distinct from Iranian Shiism, has had a history of uneasy cohabitation with the Sunnites, punctuated by many a bloody incident. Even today, the term "alawite" if used by a Sunni is intended as an insult, for considerable prejudice is weighted against the followers of Ali. Regarded as heretics, they were quick to side with Kemalism, which expounded the segregation of religion from politics. It must be said that the Alawites have their own peculiar interpretation of Islam: promoting greater tolerance, but abiding by unwritten rules of silence and secrecy. Their religious rituals remain shrouded in mystery and their commitment is a private affair free from dogma.

However, there are no converts to this faction: followers are Alawites by birth and to be a true believer, they must undergo a special initiation ceremony beginning with the *Cem* (the union), accompanied by music and ritual dances. Under the auspices of the master *(Pir)*, each new member has first to choose a "godfather"; only then can he dedicate himself completely to his induction and the beginning of his life's journey towards perfection. There are four stages in this "apprenticeship": the first is knowledge of the **Shariah** (Islamic law) as specified in the Koran and defined by tradition. The second step in personal fulfilment is the *tarikat* (the path), followed by the *marifet* or mystical knowledge of God providing access to *hakikat*, or knowledge of divine reality.

Sufism

By leading exemplary lives, ascetics and wandering poets have exercised profound influence on tradition. They are the fundamental embodiment of oriental **mysticism**, or Sufism, charged with spawning new ideas to this day.

Sufism first appeared in the 1C of the Hegira, but it was only in the 3C that the practice was specified and approved, giving rise to a variety of different confraternities *(tarikat)*. The word Sufism *(tassavuf* in Turkish) is thought to derive from the Arabic word *souf* meaning "wool", probably a reference to the woollen robes that members of these communities wore.

In keeping with the way Islam was disseminated in the beginning, the precepts of Sufism were passed from master to novice, with the help of teachings from the founders and their successors, and also with **music** and a specific series of rites pertaining to each brotherhood. Common to all meanwhile, is the quest for divine knowledge through the collective repetition of the name of God *(zikr)*: a new form of prayer accompanied by certain gestures, music and quotations from the Koran. In 1925 Atatürk prohibited the convening of these mystic brotherhoods and confiscated their assets. Over the past 20 years, these clandestine organisations have begun to resurface and reaffirm their claim for a more tolerant Islam.

Sufi confraternities

The best known Sufi brotherhood in Turkey is that of the Mevlevi **Whirling Dervishes**. This was founded by **Mevlana Celaleddin-i Rumi** (1207-73), a preacher from Konya who bequeathed an immense body of work including the Masvani, a sort of philosophical and religious poem peppered with tales written in Persian *(see Literature page 70)*.

Probably the most distinctive ritual of the Whirling Dervishes is the **sema**, a dance enacted to the mellifluous sounds of a flute. The main branch of the Order is situated in Konya, in a vast convent **(tekke)** overshadowed by the mausoleum of Mevlana which today is an important place of pilgrimage *(see p 498 and 505 for the festival which takes place)*.

The other famous brotherhood is the **Bektaşis** or followers of Hacı Bektaş, a mystic from Khorassan, who is said to have arrived in Anatolia in the 13C at the same time as the dervishes. Hacı Bektaş is commemorated by the *tekke* he founded in Cappadocia and a village *(see page 593)* bearing his name.

Religious minorities

Christians

At the close of the 19C, Anatolia claimed to have more Christians than any other province in the Ottoman Empire. In theory, all Turkish citizens have had the same rights since the creation of the secular republic, be they Christian or Muslim. In practice, however, things are very different with non-Muslims finding themselves excluded from almost all walks of public life and notably discriminated from high office in administrative roles, the State and the army. As a result, the minorities that were so much part of the cosmopolitan nation of Turkey are fast disappearing. Indeed, the Christian community here is smaller than in any other Middle Eastern country. Of the 90 000 members today (as compared to 340 000 in 1937), the majority are Greek, Armenian or Syrian Orthodox – complemented by a few thousand Catholics and Protestants.

The **Armenians** form the main Orthodox Christian community in the country (40 000-50 000 adherents). The largest numbers are concentrated in İstanbul, İzmir and Ankara, although small enclaves continue to subsist in their ancient eastern homelands of İskenderun, Malatya and Sivas. This faction has its own patriarchy based in İstanbul (in the Kumkapı district), as well as 30 places of worship, some 20 associations, two newspapers, several schools and a hospital. There is also a small community of **Catholic Armenians** as distinct from the Orthodox Christians, divided between İstanbul, Ankara, İzmir and Kayseri, who worship in the Latin churches. Since the dawn of the 20C, the **Greek community** has considerably shrunk from 1 500 000 to some 6 000 individuals today. This is explained by the massive exodus of Greeks after the signing of the Lausanne Treaty (1923) and the repatriation of yet more in 1955 when the Conference of London (relating to Cyprus) was agreed upon, provoking considerable anti-Greek feeling and rioting in İstanbul, İzmir and Ankara. Today, the only substantial pocket of Greek Orthodox Christians is congregated in the Fener district of İstanbul, around their Patriarch who represents the interests of all Orthodox Greeks in Turkey and northern Greece.

Unlike the Greek and the Armenian Patriarchies, the **Orthodox Syrians** (or **Syriacs**) are not officially recognised: in Ottoman times, their community never obtained the status of "millet" and, nowadays, they still have no legal status. Their institutions (schools, churches) are merely tolerated, and the Syriac language cannot be taught as such and its use is restricted to the liturgy. Since the early 20C therefore, many have migrated to the southeastern region of Tur Abdin whence they originally came or, more especially, to Damascus, the seat of the Syriac Church. Of the 100 000 or so believers living in Turkey at the turn of the century, only 20 000 remain and they tend to live in Midyat (east of Mardin) or in İstanbul.

Jews

When the Sephardim were subjected to persecution in Spain and Portugal in the 15C, they were offered asylum in the Ottoman Empire by Sultan Beyazıt I. Large numbers settled in İstanbul along the Golden Horn, among the *Romaniotes* or Byzantine Jews. The community gradually grew until the early 20C, when a sudden influx of 60 000 refugees – victims of late 19C pogroms – arrived from Salonica, Romania and Russia. By the 1920s the Jewish population accounted for some 100 000 individuals, divided between İstanbul, İzmir and Edirne.

In 1948, shortly after the Turkish authorities had imposed a hefty wealth tax on Jewish people, punishable by forced labour (1942), a substantial number left Turkey to settle in the newly formed State of Israel.

Today, about 15 000 Jews live in İstanbul and 2 000 in İzmir. They preserve all their institutions intact including the Great Rabbinate (in İstanbul), a rabbinic seminary, 18 synagogues, schools, cultural and charitable associations, a weekly newspaper, and a foundation created in 1992 to commemorate the 500th anniversary of the arrival of the Sephardim in the Ottoman Empire. The older members of the community still speak *Ladino*, the liturgical Judeo-Spanish dialect derived from Castilian in the 15C and written phonetically, into which Turkish, Greek and Hebrew terms have been assimilated.

Popular belief

Turkish Islam is permeated with pre-Islamic beliefs and rites, especially among religious **women**: practices such as the worship of saints and other prominent Christian figures, which are widespread both in town and country.

On St George's Day (23 April), for example, Muslims and Orthodox Greeks are likely to make the pilgrimage to the monastery on Büyükada, one of the Princes' Isles *(see page 188)* together. Furthermore, the knotted rags and scraps of paper tied to the trees along the steep route up to the monastery will have been placed there for luck by pilgrims of both religions. On arrival at the monastery, prayers and rituals are offered up to the saint, then each woman places a coin on the various icons: if the coin remains balanced there, their wish will come true.

Equally, every Tuesday, the Catholic Church of St Anthony of Padua in İstanbul is open to any woman irrespective of her faith, who wishes to offer up a prayer or seek help and consolation from the patron saint.

There are countless other places reputed to be holy: springs of water with healing powers, unusual landscapes, even mausoleums that the Turks have honoured since time immemorial by tying strips of coloured cloth and pieces of paper to the branches of a nearby tree. You will see them all over the country.

The most important centres of pilgrimage include the tomb of Mevlana in Konya and the house of the Virgin (Meryemana) in Ephesus which attracts large numbers of women in the region. In Sarıyer, on the banks of the Bosphorus, newly-weds come to the tomb of Telli Baba to pay homage and to offer up some gold or silver threads from the bride's veil *(ince gelin teli)* in the hope that they will be rewarded with fertility and a healthy family.

J.-F. Galmiche

In the shade of the mosque, booksellers dispense every type of culture

LITERATURE

Although contemporary Turkish literature might be regarded as conforming to Western literary forms, its subject matter is very obviously drawn from the Ottoman tradition, and is heir to a deeply poetic legacy from the Orient. True, modern times have prompted a radical change of outlook and stirred a move towards realism and a stark view of modern society, but the old themes and ancestral rhythms recur nonetheless, bearing a spirit of the East to the edges of Europe.

Poetry at court and poetry for the people

Right from the outset when the Turkish people first settled in Anatolia in the 11C, there were two vastly different types of literature: while the nomads maintained the **oral poetic tradition**, sung in Turkish by wandering troubadours (the **aşık**, *see page 88*), the educated poets sustained **Persian culture**. These two traditions echoed the split within Islam for the country folk were predominantly Shiite, and the literate townspeople tended to be Sunni. This dichotomy was also reflected geographically in the differences between the eastern and western Turks: the former saw themselves as poets of the Turkish language, and the latter adhered to more Arab and, more importantly Persian influence.

Yunus Emre (13C-14C) and **Mevlana Celaleddin-i Rumi** (13C), who are often considered to be the representatives of **oriental mystic poetry**, reinforce this ambivalence. Emre's verses were transmitted in Turkish and continue to impress contemporary poets; meanwhile Mevlana, who founded the order of whirling dervishes, wrote his masterpiece the *Masvani* in Persian.

Yunus Emre, the poet of the invisible
The Sufi poet Yunus Emre was the first known aşık. He lived in the region of Sivrihisar and travelled throughout eastern Anatolia, living off the hospitality offered him by village people. His mystic poetry sings of the essence of nature, be it visible or invisible, bearer of the love of God. His "Divan" remained unpublished until 1885, but the aşıks passed it on and imitated it over the centuries, to such an extent that many of his poems are deemed apochryphal. Yunus Emre has become an important and colourful figure in the Turkish popular psyche, and his works, on the periphery of Ottoman courtly poetry, continue to enjoy a considerable following.

The aşıks perceived the world in realistic terms, highly charged with emotion and rooted in daily life. The *Dede Korkut*, the first major epic transcribed in the 16C, relates the story of the Oğuz in 12 episodes. To this day, this **popular sung poetry** has been fundamental to the development of Turkish culture.

The 16C is considered as the classic age of **Divan literature** with **Mehmed Süleyman Fuzuli** and **Mahmud Abdül Baki**, the "sultan of poets", experimenting with the different styles – *zarifane* ("elegant"), *levendane* ("leisurely"), *şuh* ("sensual"), and *taz* ("fresh"). In the 17C this mannered literature evolved closely in association with Persian culture. This dependence eventually provoked a major counter-reaction with some writers becoming pro-Arab and some pro-Turk. At last, divan literature became exposed to Western influence in the 18C, but its rigorous observance to form prevented it from being adaptable enough to reflect the changes in the social climate of the time: as the Empire crumbled, this artistic form dwindled into oblivion.

The emergence of modern literature

Both erudite and popular literary forms continued to flourish in parallel until the mid 19C. Then, at the close of the century, the country was subjected to a series of radical reforms known as the **Tanzimat**. Translations of Western works, particularly French literature, flooded the cities challenging longstanding schools of thought, and introduced new forms of expression such as plays, literary criticism, novels, essays, and journalism. The first to rise to the challenge and publish a novel and stage a play in Turkish was **Namık Kemal** (1840-88) who thereafter became the figurehead of modernism and modern literature. The other prominent figure of the Tanzimat was the journalist and poet **İbrahim Şinasi** who founded the Turkish press and worked at simplifying the language.

Contemporary literature

After the Balkan war and the disintegration of the Empire, Turkish writers set about forging a new national identity, hesitating between the Panislamic, Ottoman and Turkish. Some simply wanted to restore ancient folk literature to its former glory and use spoken Turkish as a literary medium. After the First World War, the quest for an identity became all the more important; as İstanbul intellectuals discovered the true facts about Anatolia this search assumed social and political implications. Finally, when the Turkish language and alphabet were reformed in 1928, links with Arab and Persian influence were decisively broken.

From this point on, **poetry** oscillated between modernity and tradition. The poets of the young Republic opted for simple language and regular metres. **Nazım Hikmet** (1902-63) was the first to attempt free verse, while **Mehmet Emin Yurdakul** (1869-1944) revived and revised aşık poetry, and **Zeki Ömer Defne** and **Arif Nihat Asya** returned to ancient folklore.

When it came to the **novel**, Turkish authors showed a similar concern for writing in an accessible style and found their politics being translated into social realism. Novelists took to describing rural folk in sentimental and melodramatic terms, condemning the injustices of being born a peasant and fated to working the soil. **Yakup Kadri Karaosmanoğlu** (1889-1974) for example, blamed the intelligentsia for the dire poverty of a peasant's lot in his novel *Yaban (The Stranger)*. This same realism continues to pervade the genre today.

The next generation comprises writers of peasant or working-class origin, like **Fakir Baykurt** (b 1929) and **Mahmut Makal** (b 1930) who wrote *Turkish Village*. The tendency here is towards a munificent humanism, coloured by a love for the land and for rural traditions, and expressed in a style that is both epic and lyrical. The result is an extremely committed "village literature". Perhaps the best-known writer of this form is **Yaşar Kemal** (b 1922), although mention should be made of other highly committed political writers such as **Orhan Kemal** (1914-70) who was assassinated as he tried to leave the country, and **Kemal Tahir** (1910-73) who wrote *On Fertile Lands* and spent 15 years in prison.

Certain novelists born in the 1950s, like **Nedim Gürsel** and **Orhan Pamuk,** abandoned the countryside and set their stories in urban contexts, homing-in on the hopes and fears of the middle classes. The 20C was also marked by the emergence of women writers such as **Latif Tekin** (b 1957) who is considered the most prominent. She produces "social" novels and shows a keen interest in linguistics.

Yaşar Kemal, the voice of the Taurus Mountains
Yaşar Kemal was born in a village up in the hills shielding Çukurova. His air of good-natured roughness, crossed with a rebellious soul, came from his peasant father as well as his mother, who was descended from a band of *eşkiya* – bandits who took refuge from the oppression of the "ağa" in the Taurus Mountains. This self-taught man learned the art of story-telling from the aşık, turning his hand to all sorts of jobs before offering to write for the *Cumhuriyet* in İstanbul. Very rapidly, his poems, short stories and "papers" on rural life in his country earned him a national reputation. But it was his first novel, *İnce Memed (Mehmet the Thin)*(1955), a work of powerful realism and poetry that runs ice-cold and burning hot from the mountain bedrock, that secured him the title of best Turkish writer and brought him recognition from abroad.

CINEMA

Few Turkish films have made much of an impact on Western audiences to date, with only a handful of directors like Yılmaz Güney being known outside Turkey. The industry has been going through a severe crisis over recent years, and there are probably more films being screened in independent cinemas in Paris and Brussels than in cinemas in İstanbul or İzmir, which prefer to show less contentious but nonetheless popular second-rate movies.

A slow start

The first Turkish film was made in the Balkans (Ottoman at the time) in 1911 and the first cinema opened its doors in İstanbul in 1914. But Turkish cinema took years to assert itself, as it struggled to shed the influence of theatre and the tradition of popular literature. So until the 1950s, the productions remained rather timorous, and were dominated by the director **Muhsin Ertuğrul** (1892-1979).

The **"film-director era"** began in 1950, resulting in many new films. Following in the wake of the pioneer **Lüfti Ömer Akad** (*In the Name of the Law*, 1952) came such prolific film-makers as **Atıf Yılmaz**, the director of some 100 or so films, and **Metin Erksan** who made *Dry Summer*, which won him the Golden Bear award at the Berlin Film Festival in 1964. After this, the industry boomed with some 300 films being made in 1972 as compared with 113 in 1961. This was also when the **popular cinema** *arabesk* (*see this word, page 87*) took off, making catalogues of cheap musical comedies and sentimental melodramas, that ensured the future prosperity of the Yeşilçam studios.

The 1961 Constitution brought a breath of fresh air to the scene, allowing directors a new-found freedom in making films with greater political weight. The genre became the vehicle for intellectual debate, especially when seen through the lens of **Halit Refiğ** and Metin Erksan, who, at the head of the national movement (*Ulusal*), advocated a return to Turkish cultural values stripped of all Western influence. Aware of the impact of the silver screen, directors threw themselves into highlighting the social realities of their country, painting a harsh picture of life in rural Anatolia. **Yılmaz Güney** (1937-84) for one, exchanged his career as a popular actor for a more controversial role spent exposing the injustice and poverty in society, fully aware of the dangers and prepared to suffer the consequences with repeated stays in prison. It is to him that we owe such artistic and beautiful films as *Hope* (1970), his masterpiece. During the 1970s a broad range of other films were made – historical sagas, melodramas, partisan films and erotic comedies – with considerable success.

New Turkish cinema

In the 1980s, output was subjected to a series of highly repressive measures and the Turkish film industry was crippled by a prolonged period of crisis, despite efforts to de-politicise the genre and satisfy the demands for increased numbers of television channels. The number of cinemas fell from 3 000 in the 1970s to 363 in 1995. That year only 35 films were made, and only 10 found distributors. Meanwhile, 90% of the films on show were American: even **Tevfik Başer**, one of the most talented filmmakers of the new generation, failed to secure backing. But the crisis did not prevent the production of high-quality work. Ten directors grouped together under the auspices of the Cinema Foundation – the **Sinema Vakfı** – while others like **Zeki Ökten**, **Ömer Kavur** and **Şerif Gören** followed in the footsteps of Güney and set about producing highly original and artistic screenplays that were soon to gain recognition abroad. In this way, **Erden Kıral** was awarded the Silver Bear at the Berlin Film Festival for his *A Season in Hakkari* (1983).

In 1979, several of these directors cooperated in the making of **overtly political works**: Kiral filmed the novel by Orhan Kemal, *On Fertile Lands.* One year later, Zeki Ökten wrote *The Enemy* based on a screenplay by Yılmaz Güney. But the first successful Turkish film to enjoy a broader distribution was *Yol*, made by **Şerif Gören** under the direction of Yılmaz Güney while serving a prison sentence, and was awarded the Golden Palm at the Cannes Film Festival in 1982.

In the meantime, the young **"symbolic naturalism"** movement was producing some interesting films portraying a realistic view of everyday life, but imbued with poetic sensitivity. Examples of this style include **Ali Özgentürk's** *Hazal* (1980).

Urban cinema

The 1980s witnessed the birth of a new genre with rural settings being displaced by urban contexts. In 1989, Halit Refiğ scored a commercial hit with *The Lady,* which glorifies İstanbul. Meanwhile, Ömer Kavur turned his hand to "road movies" like *The Secret Face.*

These films are enacted by more realistic characters – occasionally by women – far removed from the insubstantial heroic persona animating epic literature. It should be said, however, that these achievements have been attained by a few leading women like **Cahide Sonku** and **Bilge Olgaç** (1940-94), with the support of many more female Turkish directors.

As the country remains burdened with a troubled economy, Turkish cinema is fighting for survival. Rather than historic films, the public prefer **literary adaptations** – a reflection of their torments – bringing (with a greater or lesser degree of success) Fuzuli, Nazim Hikmet, Yaşar Kemal and Aziz Nesin to the big screen. But the crisis is affecting even the most popular cinema, which the very stars themselves – **Kemal Sunal**, **İlyas Salman**, **Şener Şen**, **Zeki Alasya** and **Metin Akpınar** – can no longer keep afloat.

A scene from Yol – the masterpiece by Şerif Gören and Yılmaz Güney (1982)

CATS COLLECTION

Cinema

DAILY LIFE

Daily life in rural Turkey is markedly different from that in its cities. In the remote countryside, practises remain closely rooted to ancestral Anatolian customs despite the progress in mechanisation: still you will see the womenfolk working out in the fields, picking cotton or tobacco, dressed in their traditional flowered şalvar (baggy trousers) and coloured headscarves to keep out the sun; the men, meanwhile, will be loading up the donkey or the cart, before heading off to the café to join their friends. In town, it is quite a different story, with a resolute desire for modernity. Over the last few decades there has been a flourishing of the middle classes, who are attracted by Western patterns of consumerism and who cultivate European ideas and habits. One sign of the times is the considerable increase in the number of car-owners and you will be surprised by the number of petrol stations around the country!

But in fact, this apparent modernity conceals a very hierarchical society. The young respect their elders, the poor envy the rich, but accept their inferior status. All the odd jobs of bygone days – shoe-shine boy, street porter, street vendor – are still very much around the place, all the more so as unemployment is rife. One thing you will never see, however, is a beggar; even the most poverty-stricken offer a service of some sort, even if it is just an old weighing machine, for weight-conscious passers-by. For, however modest it may be, this "work" entitles them to respect.

Family portraits

In Bebek, a smart area of İstanbul

Mr Hakan Kahramanoğlu and his wife Ayşe have three children: Cengiz, Can and Melisa. They live in a luxurious villa on the banks of the Bosphorus; they have two cars, a chauffeur and two mobile phones. Hakan studied at the American University of İstanbul and is now manager of his own company, representing a major foreign brand of electronics. His office is in Levent, in one of the large, glass, air-conditioned multi-storey blocks.

Ayşe studied Italian at university. She does not work, but brings up the children (all three are at a foreign school in İstanbul), runs a bridge-club and spends some of her afternoons at the beauty-parlour or having tea with friends. She loves shopping in the smart boutiques in town, when she is not busy at home, helped by her two servants.

In Fatih, working-class İstanbul

The Cetin family are the owners of an apartment. Ali and Zeynep worked hard to acquire it and furnish it properly: a flashy bedroom with a gold bed, covered in blue satin, a veneered wardrobe with mirror and dressing-table. The bedroom is part of Zeynep's dowry. Ali was responsible for producing the green velvet three-piece suite, the sideboard with golden handles and the dining table, not to mention the television and all the kitchen equipment. When they are home, Zeynep and Ali use the everyday living-room, the other being kept for guests.

Ali is a tradesman, he rises very early in the morning to sell fruit and vegetables in the markets, until about 2pm-3pm. Zeynep does not work, but she knits jerseys and babywear for neighbours and their relations. They hope to have children, but not until they have finished paying for the apartment. Some evenings, Ali replaces his cousin Mehmet, who is a taxi-driver. Ali's only entertainment: a football match from time to time, and for Zeynep, a few hours relaxation at the Turkish baths.

The Berktay's house in Islamic Konya

Ömer is a copper craftsman. His day starts at seven in the morning in winter, and at five-thirty in summer. He never misses the first prayer of the day, and leaves for work with the frugal meal that Emine, his wife, has prepared for him. Ömer is a very religious man, who believes that respect for the teachings of the Koran will lead to a better life. Every day, he interrupts his work to pray, and never misses the preaching every Friday at the mosque. All day long, he supervises the work of his apprentices, drinks tea with his colleagues and discusses issues he feels strongly about. The main topic of conversation at present, is the government's closing of Koranic schools. Ömer is worried, for his two sons attend one of these same schools, and he feels that it would be a catastrophe to send them to a secular state school. He is very concerned that they should be good Muslims, even good imams.

Emine does not work. She brings up their four children. When she goes out to the market or to visit her parents, she puts on the traditional dark cloak and covers her head with a scarf. It is the local section of the Muslim Party that provides them with clothes and food during the *bayram* or Muslim New Year's Day.

The Galatasaray team

Just by looking at the delirious atmosphere in the football stadiums and the number of matches shown continually on television, which enliven most of the restaurants in the country, it does not take long to realise the degree of passion raised by this sport in Turkey. The Galatasaray team (İstanbul), especially, one of the best in the league, participate regularly in European competitions. A product of the Galatasaray college back in 1905 (whose colours they wear; red and yellow), they are considered to be more "intellectual" than the more popular, working-class Beşiktaş and Fenerbahçe teams. In 1996, after their victory over Paris-St-Germain (4-2) at the Ali Sami Yen stadium, in front of a crowd of 32 000, the streets around Taksim were overrun by exuberant fans.

At Ortaköy, an Anatolian village

Kemal is a peasant farmer. He works the fields, dressed in *şalvar* like his wife Azize, who is as busy as he is, in her white scarf. Their house is small and the furniture basic: three chests given by Kemal, when they were engaged, in which Azize keeps her dresses and her dowry; some rectangular cushions by way of seats, and a bench covered in cloth for guests. The little, round, low table (*meydan*) is used for meals. Kept in cupboards during the day, the mattresses are unfolded in the evening to sleep on. In the winter, the whole family snuggle up under heavy quilted blankets, as the wood-fired stove (*soba*) is not always sufficient to heat the communal room.

Very early in the morning, Azize gets her three children ready for school. Dressed in their blue overalls, they leave on foot for the village, 3km away. Like the children, Kemal and Azize start their day's labour with a hot bowl of lentil soup (*mercimek çorbası*), before heading for the fields or carding the wool.

After school, the children help their parents, either by tending the few goats they possess, or, for the girls, helping prepare the meal, bake the bread or clean the house. Once a week, Kemal and Azize go to the village: Kemal spends the day at the café, while Azize visits her women friends or buys one or two things at the grocer's.

Family portraits

Playing cards

Slices of life

At the café

The most important institution of all is the café (*kahve*), which is an entirely male haunt. Men meet here for hours of low-voiced discussion of the family, the harvest, the price of barley, the rain and the drought, the price of cotton or of tobacco. When not working, this is where they spend most of their time. They read the newspaper and comment on the news, watch television, play *tavla* (the equivalent of backgammon), watch for the arrival of the coach coming back from town. They drink tea or coffee, quenching their thirst in summer with *ayran*, a savoury glass of yoghurt. Some head off for the mosque when the call comes from the muezzin, but more of them attend at Friday noon, for the main prayer ceremony.

At school

In the school (*okul*) playground, under the bust of Atatürk, boys and girls play together in their regulatory blue overalls with white collars. The girls have a ribbon in their hair, the boys have almost all had their hair cropped short. Previously, the boys and girls were kept separated, boys attending in the mornings and girls in the afternoons. Every morning, the pupils sing the national anthem in chorus and attend the raising of the flag. Seated in rows, two by two in front of the teacher, they stay in class until 4pm and then go off to fly their kites.

At the grocer's

There is often a weekly market in rural areas, but this in no way detracts from the grocery store (*bakkal*), where local people like to go to buy a few items and keep up with the latest gossip (*dedikodu*). It is true that the grocer takes great care of his produce, watering his lettuce, giving the fruit and vegetables a quick shine and even going so far as to decorate his display with flowers, calling his clients with cries of *"Buyurun"* — literally "command", you will be served!

The bazaar, or Ali Baba's cave

The bazaar *(carşı or pazar)* is a covered market, a maze of dome-topped galleries, concealing any number of treasures. In spite of the competition from manufactured products, this remains the centre for traditional business and flourishing craft activities. The

The country of the moustache
Turks show a veritable devotion to the moustache and have a certain artistic talent for cultivating the unshaven look. Going by the number of hairdressers and barbers, popping up all over the place, hair-cutting appears to be a prosperous business. After a massage, the cheeks are shaven to smooth perfection. Some barbers even go so far as cutting protruding nasal hair and singeing excessive growth in the ears.

vast number of booths, no larger than cupboards, stacked up to the ceiling with produce, and the workshops with their feverish activity preserve an atmosphere of the past, imbued with smells, colours and sounds that conjure up the exoticism of the Orient.

Street vendors

Vendors of bread-rolls with sesame-seed *(simit)*, soft drinks, bird seed, people offering to weigh you, write your official correspondence for you, hawkers, beartamers, itinerant second-hand or antique dealers, fruit and vegetable salesmen with little chicks dyed in bright colours, *aryan* sellers, the streets are teeming with the activity of vendors and craftsmen, shouting out their wares. Markets and bazaars are above all the realm of the street porters *(hammal)*, bearing huge loads on their backs, while shoe-shiners are everywhere, seated in front of their magnificent copper chests, which are polished as diligently as their clients' shoes. Other activities appear and disappear throughout the seasons: autumn showers provide work for the umbrella menders; when the sun shines, out come the smartly-dressed water vendors, with their reservoirs slung across their backs, and also the sellers of *yoğurt*, ice-cream, fruit juice (the cherry juice, **vişne suyu** is delicious) or of **turşu suyu** (salted vegetable water), kept in large coloured jars. Autumn belongs to the chestnut and sweetcorn sellers, while the first chill of winter delights the vendors of fermented millet *(boza)*, of scorching-hot orchid powder, seasoned with cinnamon *(sahlep)* and sesame-seed oil *(tahin)*.

The samovar at tea-time

J.-F. Galmiche

The hammam or Turkish baths

A place traditionally associated with Islam, the Turkish baths *(hamam)* are often situated near the mosque. The baths provide hygiene, but more than that, they provide a congenial meeting-place. Once a week, the women meet there, sometimes staying all day. Here, they can pick out young girls of marriageable age and discuss the latest local gossip. They bring drinks and food, as well as all the necessary toiletries: a *pestemal* (a sort of striped bathrobe), a *kese* (horse-hair flannel), soap, shampoo, depilatory wax and razor. After washing, steam baths, cold water and massages comes the moment to relax: reclining on mattresses in the rest-room, they are served with tea. Sheer delight!

Family ceremonies

Circumcision (sünnet)

Carried out at the age of six or seven, circumcision marks the boy's entry into the world of men. Without this rite of passage, the child is considered to be impure. In the morning he goes in pilgrimage with his family and friends to the tomb of St Eyüp (İstanbul), to whom prayers are offered, so that all may go well, and to ask for "blessings" for the future man.

The actual circumcision may take place at home, at hospital or in a special room hired out by the town hall. Islamic town halls offer a "complete service" circumcision- circumcisor (sünnetçi) and ceremonial meal! In this case, the circumcisions take place in groups, several children undergoing surgical removal of the foreskin at the same time. Afterwards, all the guests pray once again with the sünnetçi. Then the child is decked out in ceremonial costume, usually white (a sign of purity), and rather like a parade outfit. Finally, the party starts with all the friends and neighbours invited, who give the boy all sorts of presents, or even banknotes, which are attached to the costume.

Weddings (nikah)

In towns, weddings are becoming more and more westernised, but in the countryside, where the festivities can last for three days, tradition holds good, and each region has its own customs.

On the eve of the wedding-day (düğün), the women go to the Turkish baths: mother, mother-in-law, sisters, cousins and close girlfriends accompany the future bride in order to prepare her. They depilate her, wash her hair, give her advice and good wishes; together they eat, drink and have a good-humoured chat. That same evening sees the start of the **night of henna** (kına gecesi); the women bring the preparation on a large tray covered in candles, which the bride must blow out. They then smear her hands, feet and hair with henna, after which there is dancing, singing and eating.

R. Valaucher/PIX

Young boys on the day of their circumcision

The next day, everyone leaves in a procession for the **town hall** in cars, decked with ribbons and flowers, hooting vigorously on the way. The bride and bridegroom, who were engaged one year previously, will henceforth wear their wedding-ring on the right hand rather than the left. After the ceremony, the only official one – this is a secular state, after all – it is time for the **party** to begin. In the countryside, it will take place in the garden beside the house. In towns, a municipal or private room (düğün salonu) will be hired as well as caterers, all paid for by the bridegroom, with wine and rakı if the budget will go that far.

Daily life

At the party, the newly-weds are given presents: gold *Cumhuriyet* (the equivalent of gold sovereigns), cash, gifts for the home. The young girl brings a **dowry** of a bedroom suite, crockery, carpets (handmade by her, if she is a country girl). As for the young man, he provides the apartment or the house, the furniture, electrical household goods and sometimes the car. In the village, the young girl will have been embroidering her trousseau since the age of six: sheets, tablecloths, towels and household linen.

At the end of the day, the **religious ceremony** takes place in the presence of the imam *(imam nikahı)*. This ceremony is widespread throughout all social circles, despite the fact that it has no official status. In rural areas, although polygamy is prohibited in Turkey, it is known for a man to marry two or three women, one in the presence of the Mayor and the other two in the presence of the imam.

In towns, it is no longer an essential prerequisite for the bride to be a virgin, and contraception is available. But most young women, however westernised, will not have sexual relations before marriage. In the countryside, the custom of exhibiting the blood-stained sheet to the family, the day after the wedding-night, as proof of deflowering is happily on the way out, although the tradition is still to be found in southeast Anatolia.

Funerals (cenaze)

Only the men go to the cemetery; the women just attend the religious service, while the deceased lie outside in a coffin placed on a table at the entrance to the mosque. They are buried on the day immediately following their demise, wrapped in a white shroud and placed directly into the earth of the grave. The body must be in direct contact with the earth, in order to return to dust, the original state of man. Muslim tombs are of great simplicity: a small rectangle of grass, watered by the rain and bordered by a white marble curb-stone.

The status of women

In Turkey, a vast and variegated land, the condition of women varies considerably from one region to another, from town to country and depending on the degree of education, on race and on religion. As a result, in southeastern regions, arranged marriages are still common, and the values of family honour are still very much alive. On the other hand, in İstanbul or Ankara, a number of women hold down jobs as executives in large firms, banks or the media. Many female intellectuals or artists – painters, film-makers or writers – have acquired a certain celebrity and live either alone or in relationships.

However, the majority of women are **housewives**, bringing up their children. A number of them have left the countryside for the town, where, no longer tied down by agricultural tasks, they adopt a pattern of western life as conveyed by a television culture: stylish furnishings, electrical household appliances, in short, everything symbolising town life. Curiously, these women do not abandon certain traditional customs as a result. They continue to wear the Islamic scarf, arrange marriages for their daughters, go to the hamam, etc, mixing the old ways quite naturally with the most modern of habits.

The eighties witnessed the arrival of an important **feminist movement**. Already in the 19C, women fought hard to combat polygamy, and to obtain the right to wear western clothing, the right to work and to education. With Atatürk, they obtained a number of reforms in their favour, such as the adoption of a Civil Code, based on the Swiss model, to replace the *Shariah* (Islamic law), and the right to vote and to eligibility (1934).

But in a patriarchal society like Turkey, women still have a lot on their plate. At present, they are mainly concerned with consolidating the rights they have already obtained and making progress in obtaining more personal support: the creation of refuges for battered women, feminist newspapers, fighting against sexual harassment at work and in public places. In 1990, they managed to obtain a revocation of the article in the 1926 Civil Code, which subjected a woman's right to work to authorisation from her husband.

Fashion trends

While the inhabitants of large towns – Ankara, İzmir, İstanbul, Antalya – have adopted western fashions, şalvar (baggy trousers) still predominate in the countryside. They are worn by both men and women, the latter often wearing a long, brightly-coloured skirt over the top. In the southeastern part of the country, the villagers tie wide belts around their waist and wear dark-coloured boleros under their jackets.

Islamic veil or simple headscarf?

Desirous of establishing a secular state, Atatürk prohibited all ostentatious signs of religion in Turkish dress: men were to abandon the *fez* and women the veil. But for ten years or so now, with the resurgence of Islamic tendencies, the veil has been reappearing in certain Turkish towns (or within certain neighbourhoods). You will therefore quite frequently come across women entirely covered in black; this is the traditional *çarşaf* in the countryside, and women wear it in town as a sign of their adherence to traditionalist circles. However, most countrywomen who have emigrated to the town prefer wearing a grey or navy-blue raincoat, very much an urban uniform (possibly even less flattering!), which characterises their modest social origins. The only sign of adornment, the headscarf, is always brightly flowered.

But let us not generalise: if the countrywomen cover their heads, it is above all to protect themselves from the sun and the dust, when working in the fields.

TURKISH HOME

Each province has its own type of house. Turkish dwellings vary according to region, climatic conditions and traditions: Anatolian houses, whitewashed or painted in pastel colours, along the Aegean and Mediterranean coasts; stone, pisé or cob houses further inland; wooden houses on the Black Sea and grey stone in the mountainous regions of the east; houses dug into the ground towards Doğubeyazıt and the southeast. All sorts of variations which, unfortunately, are gradually disappearing and being replaced by breeze-blocks and reinforced concrete. Apartment buildings are replacing individual houses and on the outskirts of large towns, *gecekondu* or shanty-towns are proliferating to pack in the countryfolk looking for work in town.

Urban life

Apart from the historic parts, which give most of the towns their charm, the makeshift modern housing (built any old how) is singularly lacking in interest.

The concrete invasion

In order to house the vast population that has been pouring into the towns over the last few decades, a number of soulless **housing estates** have been built, based on European models in the sixties: fifteen-storey tower-blocks perched on windy plains, where nothing grows, and there are not even any shops and services. As for the **business centres**, they are just pale imitations of American skyscrapers.

Concrete is rife in tourist regions too, particularly on the Aegean and Mediterranean coasts: like leprosy, gigantic hotel complexes or holiday villages are eating away at thousands of hectares of land around Kuşadası, Bodrum or Antalya; not to mention the villas, that the nouveaux riches have had built bordering on the Sea of Marmara or on the banks of the Bosphorus.

Today, only the older parts of town retain the character of the past. This is where you have to go to see some beautiful architecture: 19C mansions, neo-classical houses belonging to the old Levantines (Greeks and Armenians) in İzmir and İstanbul *(see sidebar page 253)*, citadels with closely built houses and cobbled alleyways (Ankara), stone dwellings in old Erzurum, Ottoman houses, *konak*, *yalı* and little villas from the thirties overlooking the Bosphorus or the beautiful wooden residences in Safranbolu.

The "gecekondu" or houses of the night

A law, promulgated in 1947, stipulates that once a house has been built, it cannot be destroyed. This is how, on the edges of towns, it was possible for a multitude of shacks to spring up overnight on municipally-owned land; by the next morning it was too late for the authorities to react. Today, the outskirts of İstanbul, İzmir or Ankara are invaded by these *gecekondu* ("placed in the night"), forming veritable urban conglomerations. They are huge in size and form a haphazard maze of huts, made of brick and breeze-block, without streets or sewers, with no water nor electricity. The population of these shanty-towns consists mainly of rural peasants, who have transferred their modest country lifestyle here. A vast reservoir of cheap labour, the inhabitants of the *gecekondu* are potential voters who give their support mainly to the Islamic parties: weary of their poverty-stricken conditions, disenchanted with broken promises, they frequently break out in protest, as in March 1993 in the Alawite district of Gazi Osman Paşa (İstanbul), when the rioting was cruelly repressed.

Anatolian homes

In the Taurus Mountains, the **Yörük nomads** still live in **tents**, veritable canvas homes with several "rooms", separated by drapes. The inside is organised in accordance with propriety, each member of the family having their own space, according to sex and generation, and an area is also reserved for the livestock.

Whatever its size – bourgeois *yalı*, fortified dwelling *(kasır)* or palace *(saray)* – the **Anatolian house** always follows the same layout: a **central room** with a sofa (or *baş oda*) giving access to the different parts of the house. The nerve centre of the whole system, the *baş oda* must be comfortable: apart from the sofa, it is decorated with carpets and surrounded with a bench *(divan)* covered with cushions.

The richer the house, the greater the number of rooms *(oda)*, which may be installed on several floors. In the houses of dignitaries (the *Ağa*) and

In the tent of a Yörük chief

Come in, you "Ağa", said a bearded Yörük. Bending their heads at the doorway, they entered the tent. Memet was amazed. He was struck by the beauty of the interior. It was the first time he had seen the inside of a tent. He did not even hear Yörük's welcome. He only had eyes for the decoration. The end of the tent was covered with embroidered canvases (…) Where did the light in the tent come from? The light and the intertwined colours swirled around (…). The central pole was decorated with flying stags. Stags, whose coat shone… as if in pure mother-of-pearl. Hey, dreamer, wake up! said Cabbar. Memet pulled himself together and smiled – I never saw the inside of a tent. It's paradise. It's so pretty! he said. (Yaşar Kemal, "Memet the Thin")

in the Imperial residences, the apartments are often divided into two quarters: that of the men *(selamlık)*, which is also used for receptions, and that of the women *(haremlik)*. It is even possible to find small Turkish baths, as well as *köşk* (kiosks), which are a kind of private belvedere, making a pleasant addition to the house.

The Anatolian house makes much of using the same space for different purposes. Thus, in the most modest dwellings, the central room can be used as a bedroom, a dining room or a workshop for sewing, embroidery etc, and in the evening the mattresses are taken out of their cupboards *(dolap*, nooks hollowed out of the walls and closed off by elaborate doors) and laid out here. In the wealthier houses – like the **konaks in Bursa**, İstanbul or Edirne, rich, 19C, wooden houses – the ceilings *(tavan)* are painted and the windows are fitted with moucharabies *(kafes)*, elegant wooden trellises preserving the privacy of the home.

The **entrance** to the Anatolian house is usually via a **courtyard** or a garden – a place for work, getting together or relaxation in the summer. In regions where the climate is harsh, the courtyard is covered. On the other hand, in regions where the summers are hot, the courtyard may be placed centrally, the traditional *baş oda* being replaced by an airy patio. This is the case in houses in **Diyarbakır**, but also in **Cappadocia**, thus resembling the Arab model much more, like those to be found in **Antalya**, **Konya** and **Malatya**, where the flat roof forms a terrace.

In the several-storey (wooden) houses on the **Black Sea**, the ground floor includes the kitchen *(mutfak)*, the storeroom (for wood and food supplies), the bath, the toilets and the stable, while the upper storey overhangs the façade to include the actual living quarters of the family *(see also page 606)*.

It should be noted that this type of dwelling is not to be found in Turkey alone: it is the **Ottoman house**, that can also be seen in the Balkans, northern Greece, Syria, Egypt and Arabia, with many a variation, depending on the region.

Finally, we must not omit the **Aegean home** (Bodrum), little turret-like, whitewashed houses, recalling those of the Greek Islands.

İzmir, from the old town to the modern metropolis

A. Thévenart / MICHELIN

Anatolian homes

HANDICRAFTS

Turkish handicrafts have regained their popularity in recent years, largely as a result of tourism. Pottery and onyx from Cappadocia, fine gold jewellery, copper-work from Diyarbakır: all these treasures are available from the bazaars across the country, waiting to be discovered and acquired after careful deliberation. *See also chapter "Shopping" page 120.*

Jewellery

Some idea of the Ottoman taste for exquisite finery may be gleaned from the fabulous collections on display in the Topkapı palace (İstanbul). **Gold** is used in jewellery, ornaments, weapons, tableware and caskets with such precious materials as mother-of-pearl, polished gem stones and ivory. For anyone unable to purchase these fabulous treasures, consolation may be sought in the bazaar.

Silver is used in combination with all kinds of other things: to plate copper, to inlay into wood, to be drawn into embroidery. Translucent brown agate, the aptly named turquoise, spangled yellow amber, jade, lapis-lazuli – blue as the night and studded with gold star – watered green malachite, are all contrived into modern settings or imitation ancient jewellery. In the bazaars, silver belts and anklets jostle with mother-of-pearl earrings. For the last few years, the distinctive chunky silver and agate jewellery of the Turkoman nomads has been especially popular, as has the famous **evil eye** *(göz)*, a glass-paste amulet that protects the wearer from harm *(see page 93)*.

Skins and hides

Be it jackets, bags or shoes, **leather** *(deri)* is made up into a variety of articles – especially footwear. Turkish markets are full of leather goods. Having said that, Turkish shoes are not exactly made to last. Turkey is definitely the place to buy a jacket or coat. Whether suede or sheepskin, the leather is generally well textured, supple and soft and on sale at a very reasonable price.

Stone, wood and pottery

The carved **onyx** from Cappadocia can be particularly fine. This is turned out in a multitude of forms: vases, dishes, ornamental eggs, ashtrays, boxes, lamp-bases, chess-pieces, each one variegated by a different grain and colour (the greener the onyx, the more highly prized).

The other great thing is **meerschaum** (magnesium silicate) which comes from the region of Eskişehir. This white or off-white porous stone is also reasonably soft and therefore easily worked, and fashioned to appear like ivory. Traditional objects include pipe bowls (carved heads of turbaned pashas) and chess sets.

Wood is used a great deal to make boxes often carved with floral motifs, and inlaid with mother-of-pearl, and marquetry furniture, not forgetting the sets of *tavla* (Turkish backgammon) forged out of various different coloured woods.

The **pottery** is also quite distinctive and tends to conform to designs associated with the town of Kütahya. Most of the stuff produced is practical: tiles, dishes, plates and bowls decorated with the traditional Ottoman mix of turquoise and dark blue, highlighted with the red used in İznik.

Carpets

It would be impossible to talk about Turkish handicrafts without mentioning carpets, an important part of Anatolian culture. Well before Marco Polo admired the beauty of Seljuk craftsmanship, carpets were ornamenting the walls of the Çatal Höyük houses, some 8 500 years ago.

E Valentin/HOA QUI

Carpet-makers at their loom

Although the carpet-making tradition continues to thrive, the patterns, techniques and materials have evolved. For the carpet has never been merely decorative, but a valuable commodity denoting family origins and status. It is as well to spend considerable time examining the different textures and learning the meaning of the designs: this will provide an insight into the very soul of Turkish culture.

In the beginning, the nomads wove carpets for insulating their tents and then as a currency with which to trade for salt and other vital commodities. But the use of carpets radically altered with the rise of Islam when they became an integral part of prayer. Anatolia has always been of prime importance in carpet manufacture, and continues to be so today: Ghiordes, Kars, Konya **(Ladik)**, Kayseri (**Sivas**, Cappadocia), Diyarbakır being some of the most famous centres for carpet weaving. The industry also thrives on the Aegean coast, at Pergamum and **Milas**. **Hereke** (near İstanbul) meanwhile is famous for its exquisite silk rugs with delicate floral patterns and glorious pastel tones (inspired by Persia), in demand since 1891 when they were first produced as furnishings for the salons of the Imperial palaces, such as Dolmabahçe.

Carpets

Knotted pile as opposed to woven carpets

The main distinction between different sorts of carpets is the technique by which they are made: the true carpet (*halı*) has a knotted pile, while the kilim, soumak and cicim (pronounced "jijim") are woven. The word *halı* may be derived from the Iranian *kali* ("that which does not age"), which would have been applied to the most valuable parts of a bride's trousseau, namely the carpets that she would have started weaving from a tender age.

There are two ways of making a **knotted carpet**: in Anatolia, the **Turkish knot** (or **Ghiordes knot**) is more common, and involves the knot being tied around two warp threads. In Kayseri and Isparta, however, the **Persian knot** (or **Sehna knot**) is more popular with the yarn being looped around a single warp thread. The Turkish knot produces a thicker and stronger pile, but the Persian knot allows more subtle and finer designs to be created. For this reason, the Persian knot is the preferred technique for making silk carpets, and is used to produce the small Hereke carpets – considered as luxury items – that may consist of anything up to a million tiny knots!

The knotted carpet comprises several sections: a central motif (*göbek*), four inside corner designs (*köşe*), an inner border (*iç dar*) and an outer border (*enli bordür*) which indicates the carpet's place of origin.

Woven carpets (non-*halı*) – **kilim**, soumak and cicim – at one time comprised the prime element of nomad furnishing. These were highly practical, reasonably lightweight and usable up or down side as drapes, for seating, to cover cushions or as saddle-rugs for camels or horses.

Cicims are composed of several bands, 30-40cm wide and 3-4m long, sewn together and are used as curtains or blankets.

What makes the **sumak rugs**, which traditionally come from the Caucasus, so distinctive, is the embroidered animals and loose yarn left hanging at the back.

Carpet iconography

Each design and colour is associated with a particular region, and is rooted in very ancient beliefs. **Red** (*kirmızı*), for example, is linked to the cult of fire and the homestead, and thereby allied to the traditions of the Altay peoples. **Blue** (*mavi*) alludes to the sky god, all-powerful benefactor and bringer of good fortune (like the protective glass amulets warding off the evil eye).

Many of the designs used in knotted carpets are stylised organic forms – flowers and interlaces for the most part. Kilims, on the other hand, draw on geometric patterns. Among the favourites is the **triangle** which represents the three divine gods of the heavens, sun and fire, and the ram's horn (*koç boynuzu*) which symbolises fertility. Other elements, like the camel's horn (*deve boynuzu*), nine navels (*dokuz göbek*), calf's eye (*dana gözü*), eight-pointed stars (*sekiz köşeli yıldızlar*) and the broken mirror (*kırık ayna*), have been used since time immemorial.

Another easily recognised type of carpet is the **prayer mat** (knotted) or *seccade* (pronounced "sejaday") or *namazlık*, which has one or more mihrabs. Where these individual panels are assembled over large areas like the floor of a mosque, they become known as a *saf*. Besides the mihrab, prayer mats often display stylised motifs representing candles (enlightenment), columns (strength), mosques (religious belief), trees (life) and houses (family).

Materials

In the main, carpets (knotted and woven) are made using **sheep's wool** – rather than goat or camel hair – because it tends to be softer and more pliable. Cotton is used for the warp and weft, especially for the larger pieces. The sheep are sheared twice a year, in May and autumn: spring wool is known as *"yapağı"* and the autumn one as *"yün"* (the general term for wool). The fleeces are then washed and carded with a comb. The wool is spun by the women with a *kırman* (spindle) and wound into skeins for dyeing. Having said this, a coarse **cotton yarn** is used for making rugs in Isparta and Kayseri, while the Kurds, Yörük and Turkmen opt for **goat's wool** and in Urfa, Gaziantep and Artvin, carpets are made from a mixture of **camel hair** and goat's wool. Neither of these two rougher materials will take any kind of dye, not even a vegetable one, and so remain in their natural colour.

The **silk** used to make the Hereke and Kayseri carpets is spun by the women who keep silkworms. But beware: in Kayseri, cotton is sometimes mixed with artificial (rayon) silk to produce a soft pile with a special sheen.

The traditional **dyes** used are vegetable-based and derived from plant roots, leaves, shrubs or bark. The colour red is imparted by pomegranate peelings or the roots of the madder plant; green from a concoction of vine-leaves and black from walnut leaves. The women, who usually have the task of making the dyes, anoint their fingers with henna to protect their nails and prevent the skin drying. Obviously, industrial dyes are also available but they tend to fade more quickly.

MUSIC AND DANCE

Music is to be heard everywhere in bars, minibuses, on the ferries heading up the Bosphorus, on the village greens, on the radio and television. Whether it is the sound of *saz* (distinctive oriental chanting), the syrupy voices of *arabesk* singers, traditional airs sung in chorus by a large group of people, each and every moment in life is an excuse for music-making, be it a festival, some official ceremony or a simple gathering of friends.

Rondo à la Turk

Turkish music tends to fall into three categories: Ottoman, classical and popular, which in turn conform to two trends: *şarkı* (urban) and *türkü* (rural).

"Arabesk"

This is a mixture of Arab sounds and Western melodies. It really came into its own in the 1970s at a time when a new urban middle class was emerging: 200 million *arabesk* tapes are bought each year by former Anatolian country people severely affected by the harsh reality of urban living. Such success hinges largely on the music's ability to express the dichotomy between tradition and modernity, the malaise and nostalgia felt by these displaced people who are unable to reconcile the two worlds, and consider themselves to be excluded from society. This insecurity has become a subject of mockery and disdain for the pro-Western and anti-Arab mainstream. However, this has not been sufficient to check the popularity of *arabesk* and its high ratings on radio and television. Furthermore the singers, caked in heavy make-up and attired in flashy sequinned outfits, are far from fashionable: yet still their syrupy voices echo through every town in the country, broadcast over the radio to the delight of street-vendors, taxi or dolmuş drivers, and shopkeepers everywhere. The best known performers include **İbrahim Tatlıses**, who shot to fame and became the archetypal self-made Turkish man; Orhan Gencebay and Bülent Ersoy – the notorious transvestite beloved by the public. **Zeki Müren** (who died in 1996) should also be mentioned as his voice appealed to people from all walks of life.

"Poptürk"

The first bars sound much like disco music. But then the percussion instruments are sounded and a vaguely oriental element is introduced. Trumpets, electric guitars and synthesiser complete the picture.

There are many different bands and groups propagating *poptürk* culture with its jerky rhythms, topical lyrics, nostalgic melodies and loud beat. Individual singers come and go. Those who make it – like **Sezen Aksu** – have acquired a style that falls somewhere between Western pop and traditional Turkish music.

Others, like **Tarkan**, are immensely successful within Turkey and when on tour, provoke collective hysteria among their teenage fans. Riots also accompany live gigs given by Rafet el Roman, Nilüfer, Burak, Candan Ercetin and Mahsum Kırmızıgül.

Turkish classical music

The roots of Turkish classical music are to be found in ancient Arab and Persian music-making. A modal, homophonic form, underpinned by the human voice, enjoyed particular success in Ottoman times (15C). But in those days, classical music was a **scholarly pursuit** enjoyed by a small elite. Eventually, as the works of Western composers like Donizzetti (1797-1848) permeated through to Turkey and successful musicians of Greek, Armenian or Jewish origin practised their art there, new sonorities and harmonies became integrated into the vernacular form.

Symphonic music only really emerged during the Republic with encouragement from Atatürk, who, in 1924, founded the National Conservatory of Music and the Orchestra of the Republic. Formative influences include the work of Bela Bartok, who spent some time in Turkey during the 1930s, together with a rich heritage of traditional music: both elements are apparent in modern compositions by **Adnan Saygun** (1907-91, *Yunus Emre*) and **Cemal Reşid Rey** *(Fatih)*. More recently a new generation, led by **İlhan Mimaroğlu**, is attempting to break away from this great heritage and preferring to turn to contemporary music from abroad for inspiration.

Turkish classical musical instruments are more or less the same as those of the Middle East, with one or two adaptations over the centuries. It is interesting to note that the violin, hitherto associated predominantly with gypsies, was only integrated into Ottoman music-making by European players.

Sephardic music and songs

There are two styles of Jewish music in Turkey: the ancient Hebraic orisons and the melodies popular among Jewish city-dwellers.

The religious chant settings show a number of similarities with Ottoman music. Partly because their composer Rabbi Selomo Ben Mazaltov, a contemporary of Süleyman the Magnificent, and the choir of David Sevi Maftirim (17C), were greatly influenced by Mevlevi music (the Whirling Dervishes).

As for popular Sephardic music, its roots are to be found in Judeo-Spanish romances: lullabies once sung by mothers to their children, and songs of exile that have been revived recently by the traditional group **Los Pasaros Sefarditas**.

Asıklık music

Aşıks are the troubadours of love (their name in Arabic means "lover"). These popular songsters have roamed Anatolia with their *saz* slung over a shoulder since the 11C, earning their living from wandering through the country villages and singing about their love of life, nature, God and of making love.

Although musicians and poets combined, the aşıks are often illiterate: for centuries their repertory has survived by being transmitted orally, in stark contrast with the scholarly culture of the Divan and far removed from the Ottoman language of the elite. This valuable element of the Turkish traditional heritage has only been preserved since the early 20C – with the support of Atatürk – when a handful of secular scholars set about transcribing the material before it disappeared. Fortunately, **aşıklık** remains extremely popular even though progress is sweeping through the countryside.

No country fete or celebration would be complete without an aşık to provide entertainment. For these veritable champions of improvisation are able to move from the epic to the satirical, from village tale to deep metaphysical reflection with incomparable dexterity, while adding their own personality and coloured interpretation to the popular repertory. Throughout the evening, the entertainer runs through his poetic jousts and animated dialogues, while respecting the required rules and regulations, accompanied by his *saz*, which has become such an integral part of aşıklık poetry as to be known as the "stringed Koran".

The **Alawites** and the **Bektaşis** have one or two famous aşıks of their own: these were so successful at perpetrating their anti-establishment ideas and humanist poetry in Anatolia that they caused several peasant and nomad uprisings. The most famous of these "troubadour poets" remains Yunus Emre (13-14C, *see p 70*), but the modern heirs of this faction include the *saz* player **Talip Özkan** and the singers **Ruhi Su** and **Zülfü Livaneli**.

Rebetika and mehter

Mention should also be made of two other forms of Turkish music. **Rebetika**, which originated in the slums of Athens, was imported from Greece and is highly popular in the Greek community of İzmir. Nowadays, the songs – which can be sung in Greek or Turkish – animate the taverns of İstanbul after nightfall.

Mehter, the **music of the Janissaries** (the ancient army corps of the Sultans), largely survives because it was played by soldiers on the battlefields. It can be heard in İstanbul, at the Military Museum and at the Topkapı palace.

Traditional musical instruments	
Bağlama	traditional stringed instrument
Bendir	tambourine without cymbals
Cenk	harp
Darbuka	drum comprising an earthenware (or metal) cylinder with a taut skin membrane
Davul	drum with small cymbals
Def	large tambourine without cymbals
Kanun	zither-like instrument
Kemence	small viol, widespread around the Black Sea, played like a cello
Küdüm	a double drum
Ney	long reed flute
Rebap	stringed instrument, with the belly sometimes made of a coconut / a gourd viol
Santhur	zither-like instrument with 72 strings
Saz	long-necked lute
Tambur	mandolin
Tef	cymbals
Ut/Ud	lute
Zurna	oboe-like instrument with a nasal sound

Folk dancing

There are as many and varied Turkish dances as there are regions in this vast country, and only the most famous ones can be described here. The **dance of the Horon**, from the **Black Sea** area, brings together a troupe of men dressed in black costumes embroidered with silver thread, who dance around in a tight circle, holding hands. The fast, jerky rhythm of the dance evokes the leaping of anchovies caught in the fishing nets: the dancers move their shoulders spasmodically and beat the ground with their feet to the twanging of the *kemence*.

In the **east** and the **southeast** (Erzurum, Urfa, Diyarbakır), there is a more or less similar dance – the **Halay** – where men and women dance slowly round in a circle, led by a dancer waving a handkerchief accompanied by the *zurna* and the *davul*. In **Bursa**, the **Kılıç Kalkan** is a dance that symbolically re-enacts the town's capture by the Ottomans: dressed in coats of mail and armed with shields, the dancers mark the beat by clashing their sabres together.

In **Konya** and **Silifke**, men and women come together to dance the **Kaşık Oyonu** ("game of spoons"), so called because the dancers clash the spoons in their hands with each musical beat.

One final mention for the famous **Zeybek** from along the **Aegean coast:** a slow, virile dance full of bravado, during which the dancers, their swords tucked into their belts, beat the ground with their knees.

Folk dancing

TRADITIONAL FESTIVALS

Turkey is still very much a rural country, so **agricultural festivals** play a significant role in the annual calendar. Each season brings its own task: grape-picking, seed-sowing, beating the olive-trees etc and each area celebrates the end of harvest with merrymaking and dancing be it cherries on the Aegean coast, watermelons in Diyarbakır, or apricots in Adıyaman.

Return of spring

Everyone has his own way of giving thanks at the advent of fine weather. The gypsies mark **Hidrellez** (5-6 May) by paying homage to water, the most beneficial of the elements and indispensable to life itself. To mark the occasion huge numbers of people gather together and immerse themselves collectively in the river or sea; then the women and young girls tie rings or little coin-filled pouches to the branches of trees, in the hope that they will be rewarded with good fortune or marriage. This is well portrayed in the splendid film *The Time of the Gypsies*.

The Alawites and Kurds celebrate spring earlier around **Nevruz**, which in fact com-memorates the birth of the Prophet's son-in-law Ali (equivalent to the Iranian *Nowruz*, which means "new day"). On this occasion, people prepare **Aşure**, a sweet mixture of boiled wheat, sugar, almonds, raisins and chickpeas. The women pay visits to sacred tombs before rejoining their families and partaking in two days of festivities, dancing and excursions.

Wrestling tournaments

Turks love any contest in which men and / or animals are pitched one against the other, and consider this sport to be a virile match for both strength and strategy. The expression "strong as a Turk" is well deserved; especially if a Turkish wrestling tournament or **yağli güreş** ("oiled combat") is anything to go by, when several pairs of fighters confront each other, covered from top to toe in olive oil (making it highly difficult to grip). The most popular championships are those hosted by **Kırkpınar**, near Edirne, which are watched by thousands of spectators from all over the country *(see also sidebar page 191)*.

Cirit – a variant of the Afghan *bushkhasi*, tests a **horseman's** skill and ability to their limit. The aim is for the participants to try, at a gallop, to retrieve a lance from the ground, armed with nothing but a short javelin with which to fight off their charging opponents. This equestrian sport from the region of Adıyaman (near the Nemrut Dağı), an ancestor of polo, requires a great deal of strength and precision. The Cirit festival usually takes place at the end of August (although this practice is dwindling).

Camel fighting (Deve Güreşi)

Camel fighting, which is unique to the Aegean region, enjoys as much of a following as *yağlı güreş*, if not more so. This sport was invented at the end of the 19C, when the great camel caravans gave way to road and rail transport. Various championships are held at Pergamum, Germençlik (near Aydın), Milas and Yatağan (near Muğla), as well as across the region of İzmir: Selçuk (Ephesus), Torbalı, Menemen, Turgutlu, Salihli and Manisa.

Events can only be organised during the rutting season, generally in January and February, when bulls stop eating and live off the reserves of fat in their humps. The fighting camels – the *türlü* – are the result of a camel (two humps) being crossed with a female dromedary (one hump), so as to produce a taller and heavier animal (800-1 200kg).

Before the fight, the combatants are decked out with blankets and ornamental strings of blue and white glass beads, bells, shells, multicoloured pom-poms and little mirrors contrived on the spot. A plate inscribed with the owner's name and the indispensable **Maşallah** warding off the evil eye provide the finishing touches. Thus prepared (and muzzled), the camels are led in procession to the sound of a playing *davul* and *zurna* and a colourful retinue of enthusiastic spectators follows, laden with ice-boxes, deck-chairs, demijohns of water and baskets of food. All these people head towards the fighting arena, where smoking braziers are ready to receive the *köfte* and the *kebab*.

The animals are classed into different categories according to weight, age or style of combat: left-footed, right-footed, those who trip up, those who butt with the head, those who knock their opponent over etc. Betting becomes frenzied and wagers reach extortionate heights. The commentator cracks a joke, broadcasts a glowing description of each animal and stirs up the crowd. A camel is beaten when he cries out in pain, leaves the arena or falls down. If neither animal has won when the fight-time prescribed by the umpires has elapsed, the *urgancı* (rope holders) intervene to separate them by pulling the ropes attached to the front legs, and the match is declared a draw. At the end of the season, the best camel receives the title of champion of the Aegean.

Fighting camels: mind the hump!

G Sioen/RAPHO

HUMOUR AND SUPERSTITION

Since time began, the Turks have had an innate sense of humour. They are especially fond of stories, jokes and flamboyant characters, as well as satire, which is in evidence everywhere in illustrations and literature. Two figures, in particular, embody the critical and good-natured side to their character: Karagöz, the hero of the Turkish shadow theatre, and Nasreddin Hoca (pronounced "Hodja"), the legendary protagonist of numerous tales.

Turkish humour also pervades a notable literary genre by the likes of the leading writer and novelist **Aziz Nesin** who has demonstrated great talent as a cartoonist. In the same vein, the best-known cartoonists illustrate a number of local and foreign daily papers, and the Turkish press counts a dozen or so satirical weeklies, the most famous of which, Gırgır, has a circulation of nearly 400 000.

Humour is so important in Turkey that there is even a museum of humour and caricature in İstanbul. In fact, Turkish satirists have always used both the pencil and the pen to criticise society, highlight the absurdity of certain situations and denounce injustice or bureaucratic red tape. To date, these have proved to be more formidable than direct confrontation.

Karagöz

Like the Indonesians, the Turks have evolved their own **shadow theatre**. Using silhouettes cut out of painted leather and mounted on a stick, the story is enacted before a lighted screen. The comparison is apt because Karagöz was probably modelled on the Javanese Wayang kulit, a form of entertainment imported into Egypt by the Arabs. From the 16C onwards, the shadow theatre enjoyed considerable success at the İstanbul court.

Others, however, maintain that Karagöz is wholly Turkish in origin and dates back to the 14C. According to them Karagöz and Hacivat – the two main heroes – were hired as workmen on a mosque building site in **Bursa**. But the two cronies were pretty half-hearted about doing any actual work, preferring instead to spend their time keeping their fellow workers amused. To punish such idleness, the Sultan Orhan decided to make an example of them and had them hanged. Over the ensuing days, the townspeople missed the clowns so much that a certain Şeyh Küsteri came up with the idea of making a pair of puppets in their effigy that could be used to perpetuate their stories. This, so it is said, is how the Turkish shadow theatre (zill-i hayal) was born.

Whatever the truth, Karagöz quickly became hugely popular, as it is today. In spite of competition from television, the antics of the redoubtable pair continue to raise laughs amongst the public, when performances are given at circumcision ceremonies, weddings and religious festivals.

Like a comedy of manners, Karagöz is an expression of social satire enlivened by a number of taklit or characters personifying the various professions (shopkeepers) and archetypes (town dignitary, country bumpkin), not forgetting representatives of the various nationalities (Arab, Jew, Armenian) and religions. The main hero Karagöz ("the black eye") is a kind of Turkish Punch, an inveterate talker always ready to mock

Karagöz

the awkwardness or naïvety of the Anatolian peasant. He represents the ordinary man in the street, illiterate and idle, noisy, impulsive, cheeky and garrulous. The show always starts with Hacivat dancing to the beat of the tambourine and singing a song (*semai*). He is looking for a friend and calls out for Karagöz, who makes his entrance. Now the story can begin, interrupted systematically by fights and by numerous interventions from the *taklit* or from the *djinns* (evil spirits), witches, dancers or monsters.

Mortal jar
One day, Nasreddin Hoca went to borrow a jar from his neighbour. A few days later, he brought it back, together with another, smaller jar. The neighbour expressed his surprise. Ah yes, said Nasreddin, your jar gave birth while it was with me. A month went by and Nasreddin came back to borrow the jar again. The neighbour lent it to him again eagerly, but the weeks went by and no jar came back. He went to see Nasreddin, who said to him: Oh! Your jar died. – My jar died? Said the neighbour. But a jar doesn't die! Is it not said, replied Nasreddin, that all that gives forth life will die?

Nasreddin Hoca

Between 6-10 July, Akşehir hosts the **caricature and cartoon festival**, which ends with the election of the best cartoonist of the year under the auspices of the legendary Nasreddin Hoca. The existence of the character has never been proved, but according to tradition he lived in Akşehir in the 13C. There is even a grave inscribed with his name, which attracts a number of pilgrims. Legend or reality, Hoca became famous for his countless stories and witty anecdotes, which have long since become proverbs, adapted through time by each successive generation. He embodies the common sense, good-heartedness, indulgent philosophy and disarming candour of the Anatolian peasant, which in no way prevents him from being an irreverent critic.

Superstition

The Turks are forever preoccupied with warding off the evil eye. Everyone wears a blue stone (*nazar boncuk*) or blue glass eye (*göz*) around their neck or wrist. This blue eye can be seen everywhere: in buses, dolmuşes, shops, houses, at the market or worn by children. It comes in all shapes and sizes: heart-shaped, round, tapered, magnetised, pierced. It is either attached to a horseshoe – also blue – or decorated with multicoloured beads. Similarly, people who have blue eyes are considered capable of keeping away the evil eye or, on the contrary, of attracting it!

Other gestures and everyday customs show how tenacious superstition can be. Compliments should never be made to a child or new-born baby, as this could bring them bad luck, unless the obligatory *Maşallah* is uttered and any risk of incurring bad luck is averted.

Additional "lucky incantations" – embroidered or printed on material – are to be seen inside the taxicab or minibus: *"Allah korusun"* (may God protect us), is one favourite in the hope that this might prevent an accident.

You, yourself could bring good fortune to a shopkeeper. If you are his first customer of the day, you may see him passing your money under his chin as a mark of his pleasure, and saying *Bereket versin* ("may this bring you luck") to you, because the first sale of the day, known as *siftah*, is a sign of good luck for the rest of the day.

D. R.

and his croney Hacivat

TURKISH CUISINE

Most people will already be familiar with *kebab* or *shish kebab*, the universally reputed cubes of meat grilled on a skewer, but to limit Turkish cooking to this alone would be like saying that the British eat nothing but fish and chips! In fact, there is a great panoply of dishes to be tasted and savoured – *meze*, *köfte*, *baklava* – devised over time from simple nomadic staples into refined and sophisticated concoctions perfected by the grand chefs of the Ottoman sultans. Hence such highly evocative names of certain dishes like *hünkar beğendi* ("the Sultan has appreciated"), *imam bayıldı* ("the Imam was in raptures"), *bülbül yuvası* ("nightingale's nest"), *kadın budu* ("thigh of woman"). The other fundamental influence to have fashioned the outcome of Turkish food is Mediterranean cooking, notably in the use of olive oil and the way in which fish is prepared.

Unlike Western traditional "meat and two veg", the main element of a Turkish meal is a dish contrived from an assortment of vegetables and cereals, with the meat as an accompaniment on the side. In the simpler restaurants, where the dishes are all displayed on a counter, a choice of lentil soup *(mercimek çorbasi)* or rice in yoghurt *(yayla çorbasi)* is followed by courgette *dolmas*, stuffed aubergines or peppers, vegetables in sauce *(türlü)*, *gombos* with tomato *(bamya)*, with a portion of meat stew on the side. In eastern Anatolia the menu is much more basic, the main staple being rice and *bulgur*, prepared *pilav*-style (cooked in mutton-tail fat). In town, the *pilav* is somewhat more sophisticated, flavoured with cinnamon and currants.

"Meze"

This is the Turkish equivalent to the mixed starter and consists of countless small dishes, served hot and cold, with savoury, sweet and spicy flavours all mixing happily in a delicious combination. Typical specialities include cucumber in yoghurt *(cacık)*, anchovies from the Black Sea in vinegar *(hamsi)*, spinach with garlic *(ıspanak)*, corn-salad in yoghurt *(semizotu)*, shrimps *(karides)*, stuffed mussels *(midye)*, baked beans in tomato sauce *(fasulye* or *pilaki)*, fried squid *(kalamar)*, liver Albanian style *(arnavut ciğeri)*, pastrami in flaky pastry *(pastırmalı börek)*, spicy tomato purée *(ezme)*.

The döner kebab, or the oriental-style roast

Local folklore has it that in the late 19C a man named Iskender (Alexander) had the novel idea of placing lamb's meat vertically on a spit to roast it. And so the famous "döner" (literally: "which constantly revolves") was born.

In the taverns *(meyhane)* or at friends' houses, a meal of meze can count anything up to 30 dishes, always accompanied by a bottle of the famous *rakı*.

Meat

The most widely eaten meat is mutton or lamb: boiled and then roasted in the oven *(kuzu fırın)*, or in *döner*, kebabs *(shish kebab)*, or spicy meatballs *(köfte)*. Veal *(dana)*, cut into small pieces is delicious served with a vegetable stew. Finally chicken, which was scarcely eaten in Turkey 40 years ago, is now very popular because of its price. It is available grilled *(tavuk ızgara)* or roasted, and can be bought in quarters or half-portions for picnics.

Fish

Surrounded by four seas, Turkey has a wide variety of fish *(balık)* to offer, but as the fishing trade has not been commercialised, fish remains fairly expensive. This, however, should not put you off trying it grilled or fried, served with lemon, dill or rings of spring onion. Depending on where you happen to be and the time of year,

Black, green, plain or stuffed olives, take your pick!

menus may include sea-bass, mullet, bonito, anchovies, sardines (delicious!), sea-bream or fresh-water fish like the highly-prized grilled trout. In winter, do not miss the opportunity of tasting **lakerda**, smoked fish or fish-roe, preserved in wax *(balık yumurtası)*.

The pick of the vegetables

Vegetable preserves – one of Turkey's typically Mediterranean specialities. Drizzled in olive oil *(zeytin yağlı)*, they make a refreshing salad. Almost all vegetables lend themselves to this treatment: cooked artichoke hearts, green beans, red peppers, best eaten with a squeeze of lemon juice.

Pickled vegetables *(turşu)*, meanwhile, are cooked in vinegar and are eaten as a side dish to meat or mezze: green tomatoes, white cabbage, radishes, beetroot, green almonds, garlic, carrots, haricot beans. In summer, the Turks often quench their thirst with a glass of juice from these vegetables, purchased at the *turşucu* (pickled-vegetable maker).

Pride of place is given to the delicious and versatile **aubergine** or egg-plant *(patlıcan)*. This is prepared in a hundred different ways: diced and cooked in tomato sauce *(domatesli patlıcan)*, as a hot purée served with veal *(hûnkar beğendi)*, as a cold purée meze *(patlıcan salata)*, fried and covered in yoghurt *(patlıcan tava)*, accompanying meat kebab *(patlıcan kebabi)*, or even stuffed *(kanıyarık)*.

Dairy products

Descended from nomadic forefathers, Turks have a passionate liking for milk products (from goat and sheep) including **yoghurt** *(yoğurt)* and **ayran**. The first is eaten plain and unsweetened with meat and with certain vegetables preserved in olive oil. *Ayran* is more liquid – made with yoghurt, water and salt – and deliciously thirst-quenching when the weather is hot and dry.

The Turkish tea-rooms or *muhallebici* provide the opportunity to taste all sorts of appetising **milk puddings** like *sütlaç* (rice pudding), *muhallebi* (milk with cornflower) or *tavuk göğsü* (chicken breast in sweetened milk).

Fast food

Wherever you may be in Turkey, you will have no trouble in finding something to eat. Long before the advent of hamburgers and fries in the West, the Turks had perfected the concept of the nourishing snack, with even the remotest village possessing countless little restaurants providing quick meals for next to nothing. Between two museums or monuments, appease your appetite with a **lahmacun** still hot from the oven – a sort of pizza with minced meat, a **pide** – a roll filled with egg, meat or salami *(sucuk)*, or a half-portion of grilled chicken. Alternatively, you could pop into a *büfe* for a selection of canapés, cheese or *döner* sandwiches, fruit or fresh vegetable juices (orange, banana, kiwi, grapefruit or carrot).

Drinks

Tea (çay) is the national drink. It has only been grown since the start of the century in the Black Sea region, but it now features prominently in every Turk's daily life, with some people drinking anything up to 10 cups a day! It is prepared samovar-fashion (with the water below steaming up through the tea leaves), and served in little narrow-necked glasses. In some places, tea is made with mint or with apples: either way, you will be offered *çay* everywhere, whether bargaining for a carpet or calling on friends. You should never turn it down, but if you find it too bitter or too strong, ask for it *açık* – clear.

Another very popular drink is **Turkish coffee** (türk kahvesi), which tends to be weaker than the tea and less strong than Arab coffee. According to taste, it is drunk *şekerli* (sweet), *orta* (medium) or *sade* (unsweetened), and always accompanied by a glass of water to wash down the taste of the coffee-grounds. Instant coffee is obviously also widespread in restaurants in the large towns.

Other popular drinks include **sahlep**, an infusion of orchid roots sold by the street vendors, or **boza** made with millet, especially when winter is in the air.

Although the majority of Turks are Muslims, many are happy to drink wine and spirits. The most popular spirit is **rakı**, which ranks with tea as the nation's favourite drink. Like the Greek *ouzo* and Syrio-Lebanese *arak*, the aniseed-flavoured rakı is reputed to have beneficial qualities and boost strength, hence its nickname "lion's milk" *(arslan sütü)*. When served as an aperitif, it is accompanied by salted roasted chick peas, pistachio nuts or meze. A single measure *(tek)* or a double *(duble)*, depending on one's drinking capacity, can be diluted with water or drunk neat.

Wine is consumed with food, with the choice of red (Selection, Doluca or Yakut) or white (**Kavaklıdere** or Doluca) being determined by the dishes on offer.

SOCIAL ETIQUETTE

In Turkey, visitors are not foreigners but *misafir* (guests), a term which clearly illustrates the importance the Turks give to being hospitable. Wherever you go, people are happy to drop everything to help out, provide information or just engage in conversation. Similarly, every problem has a solution: if your innkeeper does not have exactly what you want, he will buy it from the next-door grocer's, just for you. This attitude of nothing being impossible and there always being a solution if you look for it, is the *idare* which literally translates as the "arrangement".

Hardware, carpets, food: a general store Turkish-style

Social etiquette

Temperament
Turks are reputed to be irascible, violent even. They certainly are particularly sensitive to questions of honour touching on family, women or money: in rural areas it is not unusual to see knives drawn, and vendettas are not uncommon in Central Anatolia, particularly amongst Kurds and the Black Sea Lazes.

But visitors from abroad are not likely to be affected. When it comes to foreign travellers, the Turks are extremely friendly and hospitable. On asking the way, for example, you will be showered with all sorts of directions, rather than the slightest admission of ignorance. In their eyes, it is of great import not to disappoint; being of service is vital to life and goes without saying. Female travellers will also appreciate the gallantry of Turkish men giving up their seats on public transport. In the same way, women are never expected to queue in administrative buildings.

Hospitality
If you are invited into a Turkish family home, start by introducing yourself and pronouncing your name to your host. Then, remove your shoes and leave them on the doorstep alongside the many other pairs already scattered there. When you are

Turkish toilets

Although most tourist hotels and restaurants are now equipped with Western-style toilets (in all but the furthest flung eastern regions), Turkish toilets with neither seat nor bowl are still the norm in private houses. Although these may be deemed to be less comfortable, they are in fact more hygienic, as they avoid all body contact. A small tap is provided, but the Turks do also use toilet paper. Nevertheless, it is as well to have some with you, just in case.

welcomed with *Hoş geldiniz* (welcome) you should reply *Hoş bulduk* (which literally translates as "we have found pleasant"). These pleasantries having been exchanged, you will be ushered into the formal reception room reserved for guests (a second one is used for ordinary day-to-day living). This is crowded with sofas, carpets, cushions, glass cabinets displaying the family treasures; gilt-framed photographs, cut-glass and porcelain tea-sets, plates, brightly gilded vases, mother-of-pearl boxes, lace mats and such like.

There follows a great procession of dishes piled high with food, all prepared especially for you. Refusing a second helping is simply out of the question as it could offend your hostess. Instead, you should exclaim your delight at such delicacies with *Elinize sağlik* (pronounced *aylinizay sarlik*) which means "may your hand be full of health".

Finally, when you leave, your hostess may empty a glass of water behind you: a gesture symbolising the hope that your onward journey will flow smoothly like water. *Güle güle* will be her parting words, to which you will reply *Allahaıssmarladık* (may God be with you).

How to mix with the locals

In the street

You will have no difficulty in establishing a rapport with a stranger on the street, because the Turks are born with an innate curiosity for anything new or foreign, and their inquisitiveness knows no bounds. They are ever happy to offer help without expecting anything in return, and always keen for a glass of tea so as to enjoy the opportunity of a chat. So you do not have to be overcautious, although in tourist areas this attention may sometimes have money-making motives. If this is the case, just state clearly where you stand and your wishes will be respected.

Do's

There is a polite turn of phrase for each occasion: for the sick, you wish them *Geçmiş olsun* – "may it be over"; to someone working hard *Kolay gelsin* – "may that be easy for you"; you take your leave of the shopkeeper standing at the shop-door with a friendly *Hayırlı işler* – "may your work be profitable", and so on.

It is not worth even trying to learn all of these phrases, your stay will be too short. Settle for a few as a mark of respect for your hosts. Showing awareness of the local customs will flatter your host, so here are a handful of tips:

Typical bus journey
6pm. The coach doors open and the passengers have just got on, men and women settle themselves on different seats. A lone tourist, you end up sitting next to a teenage girl wrapped in a grey coat and a headscarf. As soon as you set off – punctually as usual – the "steward" comes to pour a little eau-de-cologne into each person's hands while strains of "arabesk" are broadcast over the radio. Then people start to converse with a mixture of gestures and words plucked from all different languages. The young girl attends a religious school, and in time she will marry the fiancé of her parents' choice. The coach has reached its destination by dawn and the passengers, exhausted by the restless night, take leave of each other with a brief but cordial *mersi!*

– remove shoes before entering a house or mosque
– women should cover their head before entering a mosque
– in restaurants, couples or groups of women should make their way to the family room (*Aile salonu*).

Don'ts

Certain behaviour can both shock and cause offence:
– avoid criticising Atatürk or the fact that his portrait is to be found all over the place in offices, shops, hotels, guest houses etc
– do not mock the national obsession with sport and the Turks' passion for football
– do not mention the Kurdish conflict
– do not confuse Turks with Arabs
– do not photograph local women without their consent (the men will be happy to pose)
– do not shake hands or embrace a woman unless she makes the first move
– avoid wearing revealing or suggestive clothes like shorts, mini-skirts, tight T-shirts (except in southern beach resorts). Even if nobody openly objects, it is not really to Turkish taste
– do not launch straight into English or German; it is as well at least to try a few words of Turkish
– avoid explicit and overt demonstrations of affection towards your partner in public
– do not stare at any of the female members of the family when invited into a Turkish home
– do not pass judgement on the Muslim religion or on local beliefs, and try not to confuse Muslims with fundamentalists.

The complete shoe-shining kit includes Oriental goddesses and gleaming brass pots

G Degeorge

LANGUAGE

It is estimated that a hundred million people speak Turkish between China and the Balkans, including the shores of the Mediterranean. This makes it the eleventh most spoken language (according to UNESCO listings).

Turkish, a language of the Ural-Altaic group, is described as agglutinative because suffixes are attached to words to qualify place, time, person and number, or to conjugate the verbs.

For example, the word *ev* which means "house" becomes *evde* to denote "at home"; *eve* for "towards the house"; *evim* for "my house"; *evimde* for "in my house"; *evime* for "towards my house"; *evimden* for "of my house"; *evler* for "the houses", and so on.

It is also a very concise language: a single word is often sufficient for what, in English, requires a whole phrase. *"Alısamıyorsun"* is translated by "you can't get used to it".

See also "Useful words and expressions", page 127.

Old Ottoman and modern Turkish

Up until the early 20C, Turkish was written like Arabic (Ottoman Turkish) and 80 % of its vocabulary consisted of **Arab and Persian** words. In 1928 all this was radically changed: Atatürk abruptly imposed the use of the Latin alphabet and reformed the language in a programme related to his policy of westernising the young Turkish nation. The first stage of the initiative involved replacing the Arabic script with phonetic equivalents written in the Latin alphabet, but adapted with various diacritical marks to help with the pronunciation of certain specific sounds. This resulted in a Turkish alphabet of 29 letters.

The second stage, implemented simultaneously, involved "purging" the language of all Arab and Persian-derived terms, and devising equivalents in *öztürk* or true Turkish, in accordance with the language spoken by the first Turks of Anatolia.

In spite of Atatürk's best efforts, old Ottoman survived in a number of areas, and even today, older people might still use an Ottoman word rather than the *öztürk* one: where young people use the new word *anıt* (monument), their grandparents will probably use the Arabic word *abide*. Nowadays, some 30 % of the vocabulary is of Arab or Persian origin, including such current terms as *portakal* (orange), *şarap* (wine), *sabah* (morning), *dakika* (minute), *saat* (hour), *meydan* (square), *cami* (mosque) and *dükkan* (shop).

There are also a few very common **Greek words** in the Turkish language, carried over from the Byzantines and the Greeks that once lived there: *pilaki* (haricot beans), *karides* (shrimps), *domates* (tomatoes), and such like.

Western corruptions

Modern Turkish has absorbed many **Italian words**, especially to allude to maritime subjects: *iskele* (ladder, landing stage), *ruta* (heading), *pusula* (compass), *vapur* (steamboat), but also *lamba* (lamp), *tabela* (roadsign), *borsa* (purse), *banyo* (bath), *manifatura* (small factory).

More recently, **English words** have become assimilated to refer to fashionable trends and modern imports: *filim* (film), *sov* (show), *hostess*, *gey* (gay).

But it is **French** which has had the biggest influence on the language, as French spelling adapts very easily to the Turkish alphabet. Thus, "tunnel" has become *tünel*, "garde-robes" (wardrobe) has become *gardırop*, "photocopie" is written *fotokopi*, "intéressant" (interesting) *enteresan*, "virage" (bend) *viraj*, "accessoire" (accessory) *aksesuar.* A certain number of culinary terms (obviously!) have also been adopted from the French, such as *pötifur* (petit-four) or *pötibör* (petit beurre biscuits). Others are borrowed to describe urban features: *garaj*, *bulvar* (boulevard), *tuvalet* (toilette), *banliyö* (banlieu – suburbs), *bilet* (billet – ticket), *kartpostal* (carte postale – postcard), *reklam* (réclame – advert), *şezlong* (chaise longue – deckchair), *bisiklet* (bicyclette – bicycle), *adres* (adresse) or *müze* (musée – museum). There is a lengthy list.

In return Turkish has imparted certain words to French and English: divan, sofa, kiosk *(köşk)*, tea *(çay)*, yoghurt (from *yurt* the nomadic tent) and horde (*ordu*, army). Mention should also be made of Romani and Russian linguistic imports notably since the disintegration of the Soviet Union and the flood of former USSR citizens into Turkey. The word *Nataşalar* (the Natashas), for example, has entered the vernacular to refer to Russian women of easy virtue.

Catching up with the football results between customers

E Valentin/HOA QUI

Language

Practical Information

Manaud/HOA QUI

The Bosphorus
Bridge, linking
Europe and Asia

BEFORE GOING

• Time difference

Turkey is 2hr ahead of Greenwich Mean Time, 7hr ahead of Eastern Standard Time, 8hr ahead of Central Mountain Time, 10hr ahead of Pacific Time, 8hr ahead of Sydney, Australia and 10hr ahead of Auckland, New Zealand.

• International dialling

To call Turkey from the UK and Australia, dial 00 90, from the USA / Canada dial 011 90 followed by the number you are calling. For local city codes, see p 112.

• When to go

If you have the choice, go in the **spring** (from April to mid-June) or at the beginning of **autumn** when temperatures are mild and tourism is still relatively slow. In October, the water temperature on the Gulf of Antalya fluctuates around 27°C (80°F). Cappadocia in April and May is a delight.

During the **summer** months, and July in particular, the country is flooded with both foreign and Turkish holiday-makers. Countless coaches travel through the country's roads, be it on the coast, İstanbul, or Cappadocia. Towards the end of August, hotels begin to empty again and it's easier to find a room without making a reservation in advance. It's also easier to meet the Turks and conversation is more convivial.

For those not interested in seaside holidays, **winter** is also a very nice time to visit. Exploring Cappadocia under a blanket of snow is particularly unforgettable, as is the light over the Bosphorus. The Taurus Mountains – another dreamlike setting – welcome many skiers. This is another way to discover Turkey.

• Packing list

Clothes

Here's a tip: whenever you visit, bring a cotton windbreaker that you can roll up and put in your bag. This is ideal for the gusty winds along the Bosphorus (which are glacial in the winter months), the windy mountain summits or on the coast (with the exception of the southern coast), and it's just as warm as a bulky jumper.

Plan to bring light clothing in the **summer** (particularly cotton and not synthetic fabrics). Don't forget a hat and sunglasses which are essential throughout the country. If you go in the spring, add a couple of light woollies as it can still get a bit chilly in the evening depending on the region, and a raincoat if you are in İstanbul. In **winter**, be sure to bring a coat, a heavier one for İstanbul and Cappadocia and a lighter jacket if you are on the Mediterranean coast.

If you plan to visit archeological sites, bring along a good pair of shoes. Most of the sites are in fact not cleared and you will wander amongst thistles and fallen rocks. To visit the **sacred sites**, remember that you are on Islamic ground and women, in particular, should consider covering their head, shoulders and legs. A skirt that is easy to wear over shorts and a scarf (or better yet, a large shawl) will be sufficient. In larger cities, trousers are tolerated, however in more rural settings, in less touristy towns and in Konya, pay more attention to your attire. If you inadvertently wish to visit a village mosque and you are somewhat scantily dressed, smile and humbly ask if you can enter all the same. In general, your reply will be a nod that implies you can enter and that nothing was seen. For men, trousers are of course more appropriate than shorts (which go unnoticed on the coast but are less common in cities).

Taking gifts

Turks are generally very hospitable. To thank them for their welcome, you may want to bring some small items from home. In general, many foreign goods are appreciated. On the other hand, avoid bringing alcohol or food. Turkish women will be happy to receive a small bottle of perfume or a coloured scarf. As for the men, since most are smokers, try offering them a cigar or a packet of cigarettes. Don't forget to bring along a box of pencils or some other small trinkets to give to the children in the villages.

• A trip for everyone

Travelling with children

Children are kings in Turkey. If you go as a family, you will be welcomed with open arms and your hosts will bend over backwards to make you comfortable.

Women travelling alone

A woman travelling on her own has nothing to fear in Turkey as long as she respects certain basic rules, of course. But avoid wearing provocative clothing and taking walks alone in the evening.

Disabled persons

Unfortunately, there is no infrastructure adapted for disabled persons. You can count more on the kindness of locals than on facilities for the handicapped.

• Address book

Tourist information

United Kingdom – 170-173 Piccadilly, London, WV1 9DD, ☎ (0171) 734 8681 / 355 4207, Fax (0171) 491 0773.

USA – 821 United Nations Plaza, New York, NY 10017, ☎ (212) 687 2194, Fax (212) 599 7568.

1717 Massachusetts Avenue, N.W., Suite 306, Washington, D.C. 20036, ☎ (202) 429 9844 / 833 8411, Fax (202) 429 5649.

Canada – 360 Albert Street, Suite 801, Ottawa, Ontario, K1R 7X7, ☎ (613) 230 8654, Fax (613) 230 3683.

Australia – Suite 101, 280 George Street, Sydney, NSW 2000, ☎ (2) 223 3055, Fax (2) 223 3204.

Internet sites

There are several interesting sites that provide a variety of information to help you prepare for your trip. The following is a selection:

Travel Cities – www.travelocity.com. This interactive site allows you to research whatever you are looking for in each destination or by theme (practical information, family travel, skiing etc). You will find various research sites on large tourist centres in Turkey.

www.turkey.org. This site provides a variety of practical information, bibliographical information, destination information etc.

Turkish Government – www.turkey.org/turkey

Ministry of Tourism – www.turizm.gov.tr

Ministry of Foreign Affairs – www.mfa.gov.tr

Turkish embassies and consulates abroad

United Kingdom – 43 Belgrave Square, London, SW1X 8PA, ☎ (0171) 655 421, Fax (0171) 235 80 93.

USA – 1714 Massachusetts Avenue, N.W., Washington, D.C., 20036, ☎ (202) 659-8200 / 659-0032, Fax (202) 659-0744.

Turkish Center – 821 United Nations Plaza, 5th Floor, New York, NY 10017,
☎ (212) 934-0188 / 934-0149.
Canada – 197 Wertemburg Street, Ottawa, Ontario,
☎ (613) 232-1577, Fax (613) 232-5498.
Australia – 60 Mugga Way, Red Hill, Canberra, A.C.T. 2603,
☎ (6) 295-0227 / 295-0228, Fax (6) 239-6592.

• Documents required
IDs, visas
If you are a British subject, you can obtain a sticker visa at the border for up to
3 months. Citizens of the United States can obtain a visa in advance from the Turkish
Consulate or upon entering Turkey for US$45. Canadian and Australian nationals
can enter Turkey for up to 3 months with a valid passport; a visa is not required.
Nationals of all other countries require a visa which can be obtained at the nearest
Turkish embassy or consulate.
If you enter Turkey from Bulgaria (via train, coach or car), you will need a transit
visa which you must obtain from the Bulgarian consulate in your own country.
Customs
There is no restriction on the amount of money you can bring into the country. On
the other hand, smokers are only allowed to import one carton of cigarettes and
50 cigars and wine lovers can only bring a maximum of 5 litres (but not to worry
– Kavaklıdere, wine produced in Ankara, is excellent!). If you wish to bring your
mobile phone, you must obtain a certificate with the phone's details beforehand.
Health regulations
There are no particular health regulations needed to enter the country.
Vaccinations
Although no vaccinations are required, it is still a good idea to check when you last
had your Tetanus and DTP vaccination. As a precaution, you might also get a vaccination against Hepatitis A and B (there is currently one vaccination that protects
you against both – **Twinrix** – which can be given in 3 injections).
Driver's licence
If you plan to drive in Turkey, you will need to show your passport, national or
international driver's licence and proof of international car insurance. If you enter
Turkey by car, you must absolutely leave with it, whether you're driving it or even
if it's a wreck (your licence plate will be written in your passport when you arrive).
If you cross through Turkey en route to Bulgaria, a transit visa is necessary (*see the
section on "IDs, visas" above*).

• Local currency
Cash
The Turkish monetary unit is the *lira (TRL)*. At the time of writing, the current
exchange rate is approximately 480 000 lire to one US$. Considering the soaring
level of inflation, make sure you check the going exchange rate ahead of time. If you
change money on site, pay attention to the state of the bills; because of inflation,
notes are found in wads and some of them are so worn they look as though they'll
fall apart as soon as you touch them.
Exchange
You can only exchange money upon arrival. Because of inflation, it is better to change
only enough for your immediate needs. In cities, there are many exchange offices
(*Döviz Bürosu*). You may also change your money at the airport or the post office, as

well as in banks and hotels (for the two latter, the exchange rate is less desirable, of course). Make sure you keep the receipts of your transactions; these could be useful if you plan to reconvert your remaining Turkish money at the end of your trip.

Travellers' Cheques
These can only be used in the more touristy centres and larger cities. They can, however, be exchanged in all post offices (in general before 4pm).

Credit Cards
You can find automatic cash dispensers for **Visa** or **Mastercard** in every city and in the main tourist sites (expect to pay approximately US$5 fee for the transaction). In some cases, banks even allow you to take out money using your credit card, with approximately 3% commission. Many hotels accept payment with bank cards, and more and more establishments are putting this in place. This is not as common in smaller hotels.

• Spending money
Accommodation, restaurants, shopping and living in general is very inexpensive in Turkey, with the exception of İstanbul. There are numerous guest houses (pansiyon) in the country where you can stay for approximately US$8, including breakfast on the terrace. You will even find deluxe hotels at reasonable rates which will allow you to splurge on one or two more luxurious nights during your trip.

The same goes for restaurants: for US$5 you can enjoy a delicious *pide* or *meze* in any small establishment. If you go when the weather is at its best, you may want to plan for picnics. This is still the cheapest way to eat and there is no shortage of beautiful spots to stop and relax.

Entering sites and museums is also inexpensive. The same goes for travelling around – coaches, buses, and shared taxis (dolmuş), which are ubiquitous. And finally, when shopping, take the time to barter while drinking the çay (tea) that is offered.

In İstanbul however, the hotels and restaurants are much more costly. You should expect to pay approximately US$42 for a nice room, and US$8-17 for a good meal. This amounts to roughly US$75-85 a day, without taking into consideration your transport (which is less costly).

In conclusion, with a budget of approximately US$45 a day per person, you can count on enjoying your vacation without depriving yourself. For those on a smaller budget, US$25 should be sufficient if you plan to travel by bus, eat *meze* and *pide* (US$8 for 2 meals), and stay in modest hotels.

• Booking in advance
Although the hotel infrastructure is very developed (it's even proliferating!), it is better to make advance reservations if you go during the high season, especially along the Aegean and Mediterranean coasts, in Cappadocia and in İstanbul. After mid-August, there are fewer problems and you can usually show up without warning. For travelling on domestic airlines, it is better to book your ticket several days in advance through a local Turkish Airlines agency (*see the section "Getting around"*).

• Repatriation insurance
Plan to take out travellers' insurance before leaving (if you go through a tour operator, repatriation insurance is generally included in the price of your trip). Ask your local insurance company for details.

• Turkish lessons
The best way to communicate with the Turks is to learn their language. Ask your local consulate for details on language schools teaching Turkish near you.

GETTING THERE

• By air

If you plan to go during the summer, reserve your flights at least 2 months in advance. Like everywhere, you can carry up to 20kg of luggage on scheduled flights and 15kg on charter flights.

Scheduled flights

Turkish Airlines Offices

United Kingdom – 125 Pall Mall, London SW1Y 5EA, ☎ (0171) 766 9300 / 33, Fax (0171) 976 1733 / 38.

United States – 437 Madison Avenue 17-B, New York, NY 10022, ☎ (212) 339 9650, Fax (212) 339 9661.

Canada – RepWorld, Inc., 372 Bay Street, Suite 405, Toronto, Ontario, ☎ (416) 955 8591, Fax (416) 955 9157.

Australia – 603/16 Barrack St., Sydney, N.S.W. 2000, ☎ (02) 9299 8400, Fax (2) 9299 8443.

Delta Airlines also offers regularly scheduled non-stop flights from the U.S. All major European airlines, such as **British Airways**, **Lufthansa**, **Air France**, **Alitalia**, **Sabena**, and **Swissair**, operate services to İstanbul via major European cities. **Malaysian Air** offers direct flights from Australia.

Charter flights

There are numerous charter companies with weekly departures for Turkey from several European cities. Ask your local travel agency for information and for departure days. Remember that some larger airline companies also have charter prices on some of their regular flights.

Confirmation

To be on the safe side, always remember to confirm your return flight at least 48hr prior to departure.

Airport taxes

Airport tax varies between US$20 to US$30 depending on the airline company or the travel agency you go through. In general, tax is included in the price of your ticket but make sure you confirm this to avoid any unpleasant surprises when you arrive.

• By train

For those who have romantic memories of the Orient Express, there are daily departures from Paris (Gare de l'Est) at 5.49pm. The journey is long (at least 3 days) and complicated: you will bypass former Yugoslavia and go via Vienna, then Budapest where you must make a connection (at 11.58am). Your train will then leave at 11.55pm and will arrive in İstanbul the next morning at 8.30am. Since the rate of inflation of the Turkish lira is soaring, it is impossible to guarantee rates for Paris-İstanbul. On the other hand, the price of a ticket from Paris to Budapest is stable: approximately US$200. Contact your local travel agency for details.

• By bus

There is a bus that departs from Paris for İstanbul (nearly 3 600km)! This is a very long trip, however it is an experience for those who have the time.

Eurolines, international bus terminal, 28 avenue du Général du Gaulle, 93177 Bagnolet (metro Gallieni), France. ☎ (33 1) 49 72 51 51. The bus operates only during the months of July to September. There is one departure a week on Saturdays at 3pm. Arrival in İstanbul is Tuesday at 5am. Price: approximately US$175.

• By car

Your journey will be much shorter if you go through Italy and take your car on the ferry (*see below*). You can drive your car in Turkey for up to 6 months. If you plan to stay longer, you must contact the **Touring Automobile Club** of Turkey or the customs main office.

TAC in İstanbul: Birinci Oto Sanayi Sitesi, Yanı, Dördüncü, Levent, ☎ (212) 280 44 49 / 282 78 74, or Soğukçeşme Sok, Sultanahmet, ☎ (212) 513 36 60.

TAC in Ankara: Maresal Fevzi Cakmak Cad 31/8, Beseler. ☎ (312) 222 87 23.

(Also see the sections "Address book", "Consulates" and "Driver's licence".)

• By boat

There are boats to Turkey from both Italy and Greece.

From Italy

Bari-Çeşme. Boats operate from February to June and October to December. Departures every Tuesday (8pm and midnight). From July to September, departures on Tuesdays and Saturdays. Crossing time: 36hr.

Turkish maritime lines

Venice-İzmir. Departures throughout the year on Saturdays at 9pm. Crossing time: 2 1/2 days.

Venice-Marmaris or Antalya. From 14 June to 15 October. Departures every 2 weeks on Saturdays at 5pm. Crossing time: 3 1/2 days.

Brindisi-Çeşme. From 18 June to 25 September. Departures on Tuesdays (1am) and Saturdays (7pm). Crossing time: 35hr.

From Greece

Be aware that ferries between the Greek islands and the Turkish coast only operate during the summer. Main connections: Rhodes-Marmaris, Kos-Bodrum, Samos-Kuşadası, Chios-Çeşme, Lesbos-Ayvalık.

• Travel agencies

(See the section on "The sea")

Turkish tourist offices abroad can provide lengthy lists of travel agencies that promote Turkey. Here are some examples:

United Kingdom

Westminster Classic Tours – Colquhoun House, 5 Richbell Place, London WC1N 3LA, ☎ (0171) 404 37 38, Fax (0171) 404 36 38.

United States

Blue Voyage – 323 Geary Street, Suite 401, San Francisco, CA 94102, ☎ (415) 392 0146 / (800) 81-TURKEY, Fax (415) 392 9125.

Far Horizons – P.O. Box 91900, Albuquerque, NM 87199-1900, ☎ (800) 552 4575 / (505) 343 9400, Fax (505) 343 8076.

Canada

Turcan Tours, Inc. – 1575 West Georgia Street, 3rd Floor, Vancouver, B.C., ☎ (604) 682 9566, Fax (604) 687 7787.

Australia

Skylink Travel – Suite 35, Level 7, 84 Pitt Street, Sydney, NSW 2000, ☎ (02) 9223 4277, Fax (02) 9221 4281.

Getting there

UPON ARRIVAL

• Address book

Tourist information

Every tourist area, whether large or small, has its own tourist information centre, which is often well-stocked with information and managed by competent staff. The centres are well worth a visit.

Ankara (regional office): Gazi Mustafa Kemal Bul 121, Tandoğan, ☎ (312) 231 5572, Fax (312) 231 55 72.

İstanbul (regional office): Meşrutiyet Cad 57, Tepebaşı-Beyoğlu, ☎ (212) 243 37 31, Fax (212) 252 43 46.

There is another office in Sultanahmet (the historical quarter), Yerebatan Cad 2, ☎ (212) 528 53 69.

Also located at the Hilton Hotel: Hilton Oteli Girişi Elmadağ, ☎ (212) 233 05 92.

Consulates in İstanbul

British Consulate General – Meşrutiyet Cad 34, Tepebaşı, Beyoğlu, ☎ (212) 293 75 40, Fax (212) 245 49 89.

American Consulate – Meşrutiyet Cad 104-108, Tepebaşı, ☎ (212) 251 36 02, Fax (212) 251 25 54.

Canadian Consulate – Büyükdere Cad 107 K3, Begün Han, Gayrettepe, ☎ (212) 272 51 74, Fax (212) 272 34 27.

Australian Consulate – Tepecik Yolu 58, Etiler, ☎ (212) 257 70 50, Fax (212) 257 76 01.

Embassies in Ankara

British Embassy – Sehit Ersan Cad 46/A, Çankaya, ☎ (312) 468 62 30 / 42, Fax (312) 466 29 89.

United States Embassy – Atatürk Bul 110, Kavaklıdere, ☎ (312) 468 61 10, Fax (312) 467 00 19.

Canadian Embassy – Nenehatun Cad 75, Gaziosmanpaşa, ☎ (312) 436 12 75 / 76 / 77, Fax (312) 446 44 37.

Australian Embassy – Nenehatun Cad 83, Gaziosmanpaşa, ☎ (312) 446 11 80 / 87, Fax (312) 446 11 88.

• Opening times

Administrative offices and some public establishments close during the summer on the Aegean and the Mediterranean. Hours are decided upon by the prefecture and change yearly. The following are for information only.

Banks

Open Mondays to Fridays, 8.30am-12noon and 1.30pm-5pm. In tourist areas, branch offices of the larger banks are open weekends.

Post offices

Central post offices are open Monday to Saturday, 8am-midnight and Sundays, 9am-7pm. All other post offices are open Monday to Friday, 8.30am-12.30pm and 1.30pm-5pm.

Shops

Open daily (except Sundays), 9.30am-7pm. Many shops actually open earlier and in tourist areas they often stay open late into the evening. The Grand Bazaar in İstanbul is open Monday to Saturday (closed Sundays), 8am-7pm in summer, and 8am-6pm in winter.

Restaurants

You'll get the impression that these never close! Hours vary according to the establishment but you'll always be able to find restaurants serving *meze* at any time.

Offices

The working day begins at 9am and finishes at about 5pm, except during Ramadan when it's shorter.

J.-F. Galmiche

• Museums, monuments and archeological sites

Times

Monuments and archeological sites are open 7 days a week, usually 8am-6 or 7pm. Museums are closed on Mondays, with the exception of Topkapı Palace (in İstanbul) which closes on Tuesdays and Kariye Camii (the church of St Saviour-in-Chora), also in İstanbul, which closes on Wednesdays. Most museums are open 9am-5pm, but may sometimes close between 12 and 1pm.

Rates

Except in some rare cases (ie recently restored monuments), entrance to museums and archeological sites is very inexpensive. Students receive a discount in most places if they show an international student ID.

• Post offices

Turkish post offices are easily recognisable by their yellow signs indicating "PTT". The Turkish postal service functions well and you shouldn't hesitate to use it to send postcards (*kartpostal*), letters (*mektup*) or packages (*koli*). Post boxes are yellow and if you wish to send mail abroad, be sure to look for those that are marked *Yurtdışı*. Stamps (*pul*) and telephone cards can only be purchased at the post office. On the other hand, telephone tokens can be bought at any newspaper stand (*see below*). Most of the post offices have phone booths outside and have a money exchange service (be aware that the currency exchange office often closes one hour before the post office). Also, you can receive all types of correspondence through poste restante (*Post restant*) for a fee and upon showing your passport.

• Telephone

The telephone network is well developed and efficient. Blue phone booths are ubiquitous, at a bend in the road, in the bazaars or across from the post offices. The phones operate with either a phone card or with a token.
Three types of **tokens** (*jeton*) are used: the largest (*büyük jeton*) are for international calls, mid-sized tokens (*orta*) are for long distance calls within Turkey, and the smallest (*küçük*) for local calls. You may also call from your hotel but the cost will be much higher. For long distance calls, it is advisable to call from the post office.

International calls

To make an international call from Turkey, you must dial 00 followed by the country code, area code and number you are trying to call.

USA/Canada	1
United Kingdom	44
Australia	61
New Zealand	64

Local calls

Each region has its own 3 digit area code in parentheses. İstanbul and its suburbs are considered a region of their own and have 2 area codes – one for the European side and one for the Asian side of the city. This area code comes before the 7 digit phone numbers (ie (212) 257 11 11).

– For local calls within the same district, dial only the 7 digit number you are trying to call (ie 257 11 11).

– For calls to a different district, dial 0, then the area code for that region, followed by the 7 digit number you are trying to call (ie 0 (212) 257 11 11).

Domestic information

Dial 118.

Main area codes

Adana	322	European İstanbul	212
Afyon	272	Asian İstanbul	216
Aksaray	382	İzmir	232
Amasya	358	İznit	262
Ankara	312	Kars	474
Antalya	242	Kayseri	352
Aydın	256	Konya	332
Bursa	224	Malatya	422
Çanakkale	286	Manisa	236
Cyprus	392	Mersin (İçel)	324
Denizli	258	Muğla	252
Diyarbakır	412	Nevşehir	384
Edirne	284	Niğde	388
Erzurum	442	Samsun	362
Eskişehir	222	Sinop	368
Gazientep	342	Tekirdağ	282
Hatay (Antakya)	326	Trabzon	462
İsparta	246	Van	432

Upon arrival

• Public holidays

1 January	New Year's Day
23 April	International Children's Day (school parades)
19 May	Youth and Sports Day (in commemoration of the Independence War of 1919)
29 May	Celebration to Commemorate the Conquest of Constantinople by the Turks in 1453
30 August	Victory Day (over the Greeks in 1922)
29 October	Republic Day (military parades)

10 November is not a holiday but is commemorated by cannon fire and sirens going off throughout the city at 9.05am on the dot, the exact time of Atatürk's death (1938). At this very moment, Turks stop whatever they are doing to have a moment of silence.

There are a number of religious holidays to add to the above list of non-religious holidays. The dates of these vary from year to year according to the Muslim calendar.

GETTING AROUND

• By car

Rental

Unlike in the United States, car hire is relatively expensive depending on the model and its state. Count on spending at least US$250 a week. There are, of course, several national rental agencies: **Sun**, **Ekan** etc. While their rates may be more attractive than their foreign competitors, the quality of the cars and their service may be lacking. It's better to stick with the well-known international agencies: **Avis**, **Budget**, **Europcar**, and **Hertz**, which have offices all over the country. For several pounds more, you will be sure to have a car that's in good shape (the model may be a bit old but well maintained).

Rental conditions, which are specified in each agency, generally adhere to the minimum age of 21 years, with initial payment via cash or credit card when you hire the vehicle. In summer, you may have to wait for several hours before getting your car. Be patient – it will arrive eventually!

Road network

The quality of the roads is not bad but the main routes are not wide enough to support the heavy traffic. You will often find yourself stuck behind a large lorry that is coughing out black smoke without any chance of overtaking it. Since the railway system is underdeveloped, nearly everyone travels by road. The motorways are expanding but there is still a long way to go and in the meantime journeys remain long and tiring.

Moreover, the country has innumerable **tracks** that still need to be paved over. Of the 381 028km of road calculated in 1992, only 15% was paved. Today, this percentage is much higher but there are still many difficult roads. Even the best-known archeological sites, such as Cnide, are accessible only via stony routes, often impassable unless you have a 4-wheel drive. Nonetheless, this adds to the charm of your trip.

Highway code

In Turkey, you must drive on the right hand side of the road. In principle, the speed limit is 50kph in towns and 90kph on motorways. Of course, the reality is somewhat different. It's survival of the fittest here, and in cities you'll be able to force your way onto the road if you adopt the local habit of honking your horn.

On the road, Turks can be rather reckless (overtaking another car on a bend does not seem to faze them!). A piece of advice: respect the security distance between cars.

Fuel

There is no problem filling your car up (except perhaps if you need Super or Unleaded petrol which are less available). Service stations have increased in number and you will find them without any trouble throughout the country, except in mountains and very remote parts of the country. It pays to plan ahead and make sure you avoid some roads if you don't have a half-full tank.

Petrol is much less expensive than in many countries. Be aware that even if some stations have the sign for *Visa/Mastercard*, it doesn't necessarily mean that they are equipped to accept payment with credit cards.

Parking in town

There is no free parking in towns, even in distant areas. An attendant will exit a nearby café and ask you for several lira in exchange for a ticket (*makbuz*). Once your car is parked, don't touch it! Driving in the large cities with your own car is very trying – traffic jams, the racket of horns, one-way streets, ground signs that are often strange – you will quickly find that it's better to walk or take public transport.

In emergencies

In due form a report must be written by a police officer who will give you a copy. With this report, a mechanic will be able to repair your car. Mechanics are everywhere and are often ingenious – able to restore the worst wreck. If your car is truly irretrievable, it is mandatory to take it to a customs office before leaving the country.

• By taxi and "dolmuş"

There are a large number of long distance buses, taxis and *dolmuş* (shared taxis) in all of Turkey's cities – regardless of their size – and their rates are very inexpensive. **Taxis** *(taksi)* are all painted yellow which makes it impossible to miss them. Verify that the meter *(köntör)* is turned on so you don't have to pay more than the going rate. The most affordable (and the most picturesque) type of transport is by **dolmuş** (shared taxis), which are either large American cars or minibuses that the driver decorates with photos, hanging trinkets etc. Itineraries are pre-established and the rate varies according to the length of the trip. Dolmuşes (which means "stuffed" in Turkish) leave as soon as they are full (9-12 passengers). The wait is rarely long but this is what discourages most tourists. If you're not in a hurry, it's ideal. They serve both the cities and their outskirts, particularly surrounding archeological sites.

• By train

Mustafa Kemal's passion for trains was not sufficient enough to develop the Turkish railroads. The 8 452km of railway tracks are insufficient to cover the entire country. Trains are nonetheless the most practical means of travelling from İstanbul to Ankara (by night). There are 3 departures daily (from the Asian banks), some of which are in blue *Pullman* trains (7hr).
Besides that, the absence of coastal lines, the usual delays and the average speed of the **TCDD** trains (80kph) makes it preferable to take the buses which are more numerous.

• By bus

Most travellers (more than 90%) uses buses to explore the country. The network, covered by private companies, is dispersed throughout the country. Rates are reasonable and there is an *otogar* (bus terminal) in nearly every city (most often on the outskirts rather than the centre, unfortunately!). There is always a pleasant atmosphere. Families will not hesitate to share their picnic with you. There is a good level of comfort (the larger bus companies have air-conditioned coaches) and more recently smoking on board has been banned. The main companies are **Varan Turizm**, **Kamil Koç**, **Ulusoy** and **Pamukkale**.

• By boat

For longer distances, you can save time by taking a boat. There are a large number of ferries that depart from İstanbul for the Marmara Sea, the Bosphorus, the Dardanelles and the Aegean coast as far as İzmir. The crossing to the Dardanelles operates several times a day, between Çanakkale and Eceabat, or Gelibolu and Lapseki. From Monday to Saturday, a ferry departs from İstanbul for Bandırma and İzmir (embark at Eminönü at 9am, except Fridays: evening departure at 8pm). *(See "Making the most of İstanbul", p 174.)* Be aware that shuttles to the Greek islands only operate in the summer.

• Renting a bike, moped or motorcycle

Like cars, you can hire mopeds, motorcycles and bicycles in the main tourist sites, and in the Princes' Isles, bicycles are the most common form of transport. Here too, the state of the machine can vary.

At the jetty

• Hitch-hiking

Hitch-hiking is not very common. You may risk waiting a very long time before somebody stops. Don't forget, there are many buses and dolmuşes.

• Domestic flights

Planes belonging to **Turkish Airlines** *(THY: Türk Hava Yolları)* have daily services to all the large cities in the country: İzmir, İstanbul, Ankara, Trabzon, Adana, Antalya and Dalaman.

THY agencies in İstanbul – Cumhuriyet Cad 199-201, Taksim, ☎ (212) 225 05 56, reservations: ☎ (212) 663 63 63, Atatürk Bul 162, Aksaray, ☎ (212) 511 92 22.
THY agency in Ankara – Atatürk Bul 154, Kavaklıdere, ☎ (312) 428 02 00.

• Organised tours and excursions

Local travel agencies organise numerous excursions to neighbouring archeological sites or even to some further afield. Excursions include a guide and a meal at very reasonable prices. For those who don't have a car, it's often a very practical way to visit a site. Ask for information at your hotel.

BED AND BOARD

The hotel infrastructure has developed considerably from simple family-run guest houses to deluxe hotels. You will find places to stay all over the country without any problem. The welcome is generally friendly, particularly in the smaller hotels where there is often a warm atmosphere. Unfortunately, cleanliness leaves much to be desired and many transit towns don't have anything suitable to offer. While the beds are universally of good quality (firm mattresses) – even in the smaller hotels – the same cannot be said for the bathrooms: cleanliness and attractive amenities are rare. Since hotels are quite inexpensive, you may decide to select a 2- or 3-star hotel (determined by the Ministry of Tourism). If you wish to spend your holiday on the coast during the summer, make reservations as soon as possible (especially on the Mediterranean): all the vacation resorts and hotels are booked very early and you will have a lot of trouble finding a room in a decent hotel.

Bed and board

Prices

The range of prices mentioned in this guide is calculated on the basis of a double room with breakfast in high season. Single travellers will often pay less, particularly in the smaller hotels where beds rather than rooms are rented. In low season, room rates are generally one-third less or even half as expensive.

• Different types of accommodation

Hotels

Good hotels which combine charm and comfort are rather rare. Instead you will find innumerable mediocre establishments – cement blocks built hastily and equipped with second-rate bathrooms (we won't even count the number of new hotels that have bathtubs so deteriorated that the enamel is completely worn off!). Cleanliness is often dubious, even in hotels supposedly of good standing. For our selections, we have therefore focused much attention on the cleanliness and state of the bathrooms.

Guest houses

Guest houses (*pansiyon*) offer simple comfort, modest prices (US$5 to US$12) and a generally warm family atmosphere. A number of them are well-located and they therefore form the most practical, most pleasant, and typically Turkish type of accommodation. Rooms often have private baths (generally minuscule but that's always the case!), and undoubtedly this is why some are granted the title of hotel. And they sometimes deserve it! Moreover, the *pansiyon* is a good place to get advice: if you become friendly with the owner or his son, you will get all types of tips to organise a trek, visit a site by boat etc.

Camping

Camp sites are primarily concentrated in the coastal areas, between Çannakale and Marmaris, and in Cappadocia (in Nevşehir). Outside the controlled areas, camping is not authorised. Open from April / May to October, the grounds approved by the Ministry of Tourism are relatively well equipped and in pleasant surroundings.

Resorts

Resorts (*tatil köyü*) have multiplied during the last 10 years, particularly along the Mediterranean coast, like pimples on a pretty face. They have colonised everything, from beaches to rocky inlets and even to the edge of some ancient sites. They are very comfortable and equipped with swimming pools, restaurants, bars, nightclubs that blare music as soon as night falls, and many holidaymakers stay there the entire summer in near isolation. Although expensive, these resorts can nevertheless be an option for one night if the hotels in neighbouring cities do not appeal to you.

Youth hostels

Youth hostels are not widespread in Turkey. Guest houses, which are also inexpensive, take their place.

Bed & Breakfast

Bed and breakfasts are not very common but you'll often find a family atmosphere when you stay in a guest house.

• Eating out

Restaurants are as ubiquitous as guest houses, if not more so. Between the *kebab*, the *köfte*, the *pide* and the traditional *meze*, you will always find something to appease your hunger (and to have a delicious meal!), quickly and for a low price. Turkey abounds in cheap unpretentious restaurants with neon lights on the ceiling and TVs in the corner tuned into a current or past football game. The food is always good with a pleasant atmosphere.

In the larger cities and the tourist areas, there are also more upscale restaurants, of course, in more refined settings. The menu is a bit more varied but not necessarily better.

In the hotels and guest houses

You can often eat much better in the guest houses where tasty traditional dishes are prepared than in larger hotels where bland westernised cooking is served to please the tourists.

In the markets

In the streets you will find many food stands serving *simit* (round sesame bread),

Guest house above grocer's shop

çay (tea), orange juice (in the south) or ice-cream. You can also buy a sandwich with slices of *döner kebab* or other delicacies to satisfy your appetite for the remainder of the day!

Where to drink alcohol

Although Muslim, Turks don't balk at a glass of wine, a beer, or *rakı*, the traditional alcohol in the country which is flavoured with aniseed (40°). With the exception of the city of Konya, which is strictly Muslim, *rakı* is consumed everywhere.

SPORTS AND PASTIMES

• Cross country

Walking

If you love walking, this is the place for you. Turkey is covered with paths, trails, archeological sites, and nature parks where walking is a delight. Whether you're a sportsman or prefer easy walks, everyone will find a path to suit. For those who particularly enjoy both history and nature, **Cappadocia** should not be missed unless you decide to escape to the summits of the **Taurus Mountains** or along the **Lycian coast**. Experienced climbers may want to look for adventure on the Kaçkar massif, on the Black Sea, or on the slopes of the famous Mount Ararat, on the Iranian border.

You can organise your own trekking holiday prior to leaving if you go through one of the specialised agencies (*see the section "Getting there" above*). Of course, it is also possible to prepare for your hike once you arrive according to your itinerary. Travel agencies and the local tourist information offices also organise all sorts of day trips, or excursions that can last several days. In some areas, such as **Herakleia at Latmos** on the Aegean coast, you only need to inquire at the hotels which often organise excursions themselves.

Horse riding

Many hiking trails can also be done on horseback. Rates are inexpensive and, seen from a little higher up, the countryside can appear even more beautiful. Among the possibilities, **Cappadocia** is once again the leader, but the areas around Alanya, Çeşme and Daday (north of Ankara) are also very attractive. In the same way as for trekking, the most practical means is to inquire at the local tourist information office, in travel agencies or in local guest houses.

• The sea

Sailing

Sailing is without a doubt the most pleasant way to discover the Turkish coast, particularly along the superb Mediterranean coast. Each year, countless sailboats coast along the Gulf of Antalya and along the Lycian coast, to ancient ruins and white-sanded beaches searching for the last untouched inlets that are inaccessible by road. At each stop, dolmuşes are available to take you to the sites set back from the shore, and, aboard a ship, you are like a *paşa* in the sun!

With the success of sailing, **wooden ships** have made a comeback in all the shipyards. Local sailing agencies call them **"gulet"**, a term derived from the French word "goélette" (schooner) which actually describes any sailboat that sleeps 8 to 10 passengers, equipped with a raised and larger stern. This "pigeon's nest" has two benefits: it allows the cabins on the deck to be larger for greater comfort and it provides a very pleasant deck where you can find some shade under the sails. You can eat, take a nap, or chat with the captain.

The **turquoise cruise** from Ayvalık to Silifke is considered a classic today. Nothing is easier than hiring a *gulet* before leaving home or once you arrive, directly at the port. Whether you're travelling with family or friends, this is ideal. As for single travellers, they can sign up individually to form a group. In general, boats are rented with a captain and a cook and you will find all the necessary equipment aboard to go scuba diving or windsurfing. Rates are reasonable, especially during the off-season (in the summer, count on spending US$65-85 per day per person). It's even cheaper if you rent a boat on site; since they are moored to the quay, you can compare prices from one crew to the next.

Addresses

Huntley Yacht Vacations, 210 Preston Road, Wernersville, PA 19565 USA, ☎ (610) 678 2628, Fax (610) 670 1767, www.huntleyyacht.com

Ocean Voyages, 1709 Bridgeway, Sausalito, CA 94965, USA, ☎ (415) 332 4681, Fax (415) 332 7460, www.apparentwind.com

Prime Travel, 14 North Spruce Street, Suite 101, Ramsey, NJ 07446, ☎ (800) 887 5493 or (201) 825 1600, Fax (201) 825 4153, www.primetravel.com

Westminster Classic Tours Ltd, Suite 120, 266 Banbury Road, Summertown, Oxford, OX2 7DL, England, ☎ (01865) 728 565, Fax (01865) 728 575.

Scuba diving

Take advantage of your stay on the coast by learning how to scuba dive or to perfect your skills. The depths of the Aegean and Mediterranean coast are very beautiful, particularly along the Gulf of Gökova. The local agencies at the port provide tailor-made equipment and certified instructors (with PADI or CMAS licences, in Turkish: *Balık Adam Belgesi*). Be aware that it is strictly forbidden to scuba dive near **archeological sites** (identified by signs erected by the Ministry of Culture). Don't take the risk of fishing out a piece of stone or even a small fragment of pottery: this too is forbidden and the crackdown is very severe *(see the section below "A to Z")*.

Addresses
Huntley Yacht Vacations, 210 Preston Road, Wernersville, PA 19565 USA, ☎ (610) 678 2628, Fax (610) 670 1767, www.huntleyyacht.com
Prime Travel, 14 North Spruce Street, Suite 101, Ramsey, NJ 07446, ☎ (800) 887 5493 or (201) 825 1600, Fax (201) 825 4153, www.primetravel.com

Riding the waves
Those who enjoy marine adventures have the choice between rafting, water skiing or jet-skiing on the Dalaman (in Anatolia) or the rivers near the Black Sea and the Mediterranean.
The best surfing areas are in Bodrum (Gümbet Beach), in Antalya and on the coast along the Sığacık peninsula. It's useless to load yourself down with equipment; the clubs in the area can rent it all out.

• A healthy mind and a healthy body
Spas
Why not tie your trip in with a visit to a spa? This country of mountains and volcanoes is swarming with hot springs – from sulphur to clay – full of all sorts of benefits. Most of them are concentrated along the Aegean coast. You can get information in local tourist information offices.

Turkish baths
Your trip to Turkey wouldn't be complete without a visit to a *hamam*. They are ideal to relax or to wipe away the fatigue after an excursion in the heat. The establishments are open alternate days for women and for men or else provide separate rooms for each gender. Only those that are visited by tourists have become mixed. The atmosphere is obviously much less authentic in these, but they are sometimes cleaner and, in general, are the nicest Turkish baths.

• Night life
Cinema
You will not often see the works of the great Turkish directors in Turkey. The films showing are usually mediocre with mostly action films and low-grade comedies. Moreover, if you don't speak Turkish, there will be limited interest. There are however two international festivals to keep in mind: one in İstanbul and the other in İzmir (both in April).

Bars and nightclubs
For those who enjoy nightlife, there is plenty to do in all the larger cities and the tourist centres, particularly along the coast. If you like techno and pop songs, not to mention the Turkish hits of the summer, you will be happy. You'll have a much harder time if you prefer to listen to jazz, rhythm & blues or traditional Turkish music (except in İstanbul, which hosts an annual jazz festival).

• Cultural life
Many cities and tourist centres have their own music and traditional dance festivals (*see p 89*). Whether it's folklore, military, or religious, music and dance can be found everywhere in Turkey and liven up festivals and commemorative ceremonies.

Some holidays
January
Camel Wrestling Festival in Selçuk.
April – May
Tulip Festival – Emirgan (İstanbul).
İstanbul International Film Festival.
International İzmir Film Festival.

May
International Yachting Festival – Marmaris.
International Music and Folklore Festival – Silifke.
June
Kırkpınar Wrestling Festival (Edirne).
Bergama Festival.
Rize Tea Festival (east of Trabzon).
Foça Music, Folklore & Watersports Festival.
International Wine Festival – Ürgüp.
June – July
International Music Festival – İstanbul.
International Music Festival – İzmir.
July
Nasreddin Hoca Festival – Akşehir (northwest of Konya).
Carpet Festival – Isparta.
Ihlara Art and Culture Festival – Aksaray.
Konya Rose Festival.
August
Music and Folklore Festival – Ephesus (in the ancient theatre).
Troy Folklore Festival – Çanakkale.
September
Bodrum Art and Culture Festival.
İstanbul International Jazz Festival.
International Meerschaum (White Gold) Festival – Eskişehir.
İzmir International Trade Fair.
October
Antalya Film Festival (Golden Orange).
International Akdeniz Song Contest – Antalya.
International Regatta – Marmaris.
November
Karagöz Festival – Bursa.
December
St Nicholas Theatre Festival – Antalya.
Mevlana Commemoration Ceremony – Konya.

SHOPPING

• What's on offer

Also see the section on "Handicrafts", p 84.

Carpets and kilims

Turkey is the kingdom of carpets. Every effort is made to tempt you to buy one: Turkish merchants have been practising bragging about the quality of their products for centuries, strengthening their arguments with tea. Moreover, nothing is easier than shipping a carpet home. If you leave a deposit, your vendor will take care of everything (the cost of shipping is generally quite low, but count on it taking 2-3 months for your carpet to arrive).

You can purchase a carpet anywhere in Turkey. However, you may wish to avoid the Grand Bazaar in İstanbul as the merchants there pay higher taxes than elsewhere, which obviously affects prices. In general, carpets carry the name of the place they were woven.

The quality (and, in principle, the price) depends on the number of knots (starting with 30 per sqcm for a good carpet). You'll therefore need to spend around US$650 for a 2m by 1.5m carpet and the same price for a silk carpet half that size. Kilims (carpets that have been woven but not knotted) are much cheaper.

Pay careful attention to carpets that are said to be antique. What is supposed to be silk can turn out to be mercerised cotton. Take the time to look around and don't hesitate to go through entire stacks of carpets to find one.

Copperware

Veritable Ali Baba's caves, the bazaars overflow with polished and embossed copperware – from ewers to flowerpots to beaten copper plates, tea services etc, hanging in clusters on the walls of the stalls. The quality of the work varies – look closely. The finer articles come from the **East**, in Urfa and Diyarbakır.

Onyx

Onyx articles are relatively expensive. The greener the onyx, the more precious the stone. If you have a penchant for white onyx, be careful about imitations in **alabaster** which is more fragile and therefore less expensive. While onyx is veiny, alabaster, when you look at it against the light, has all sorts of scales similar to cracked earth (also pretty). If you buy a vase, pay attention to the veins on the stone: if they are too pronounced, that one should be avoided!

Leather goods

A trip to Turkey might be a good occasion to replace your old leather jacket. The price of leather is very good for its quality and, although cuts remain somewhat standard, you can always find nice things. Look carefully to be sure the leather is well-tanned and well-finished (cut, stitching etc). Don't hesitate to barter as prices are always a bit inflated.

Gold and silver

Gold and silver, sold by the weight, are also very inexpensive (but be aware that in Turkey, gold tends to be 14 carat). You can buy it in most bazaars. For a low price, you'll find a vast number of rings, bracelets, and oriental-style necklaces that seem to have come out of Sheherazade's jewellery box. You can even have copies of jewellery made if you provide the model. Silverwork is not always well made but the jewellery is nonetheless attractive. Be careful about false turquoise that will lose its colour when you put it under the tap.

Pipes

Sculpted designs are so numerous that you'll have trouble making a selection. Let the finesse of the artist's work guide you, but be aware that pipes that are more finely-worked may mask a defect in the stone. The most simple patterns are therefore often the best.

Hookahs

Be it a simply-decorated article or used to smoke tobacco (and only tobacco!), the hookah is without a doubt one of the most symbolic items of the exotic East. If you buy one to smoke from, you may consider purchasing the rolls of tobacco sold with it. Try the pure Turkish tobacco (very strong) or Egyptian tobacco that is scented with fruit. In any case, ask for the *Tömbeki Tütünü* brand.

Antiques

Exporting antiques is forbidden. The antique articles you will find in antique shops are no more than 100 years old or else they are fakes. If you want to tell if a stone article is really an antique, lick it. If it sticks to your tongue slightly, it is new. The sheen over time will make the surface of the stone completely smooth.

Spices and sweets

Colours and perfumes... don't leave without buying some small packets of spice or pistachios (the best are from Gaziantep), for their flavour, colour, and for a souvenir of the country when they are on your table at home. In any case, it's impossible to resist the appeal of the enormous canvas bags that line up in all the markets, filled with red, ochre, yellow, and brown powder – a blaze of colours as hot as fire (their taste will also remind you!).

If you like **lokum** (Turkish delight) you will be in heaven: there are multitudes of flavours, with hazelnuts, pistachios, orange, or even rose (very sweet).

Miscellaneous

In the large bazaars, don't pass by the small shops that contain antiques, jewellery, fabrics and leather bags stacked on top of each other under a heavy coat of dust. These are curiosity shops where you must take the time to look through everything in order to find the rare treasure. You may also find stunning small boxes made in **camel bone**, painted with hunting scenes in Persian-style with a delicate black stroke.

• Where to shop

What to buy where

Other than the bazaars in İstanbul, villages in Cappadocia are especially good places to go shopping. Here you will find all imaginable Turkish handicrafts, and this region is one where the traditions are the best preserved (particularly carpets, pottery, and onyx articles).

With the exception of İstanbul, everything is cheaper in the country than in cities and you will have more pleasant contact with the people. Avoid buying anything in tourist centres that you can find elsewhere: the prices are generally much higher there and the quality is not as good. In the country, the proprietor of the hotel will try to sell you his carpets. It's worthwhile to discuss this with him over a glass of çay.

The bazaar

Each city has its own bazaar. In general, the larger ones are divided into districts according to each craft (carpet district, jewellery district etc).

The entrance to the bazaar

J.-F. Galmiche

The advantage of shopping in the bazaars is that everything is gathered together. These are therefore the most practical places to go shopping, compare the products etc. But the bazaar in İstanbul, particularly, has become so touristy that good deals are better found outside its walls, in the innumerable **shops** that are squeezed together in the surrounding alleys, or in the Egyptian bazaar nearby.

• Bartering

Aside from the shops where prices are indicated – this is therefore not the place to do your shopping – bartering is de rigueur. In the East, everyone haggles. No matter what the time, you must chat or tell your life story with a sense of humour. Don't offend the person you're speaking to by asking what his best price is immediately. Look at the item that interests you, show him the defects in it, weigh it, then let him give you a price and tell him yours, taking into account the observations you have just made. Don't hesitate to offer half of the merchant's asking price, even if his reaction will be to burst out laughing. And if language is creating a barrier, communicate with gestures, and always with a smile. If nothing can be done, leave the shop slowly and continue on your way. If the merchant doesn't chase after you, your asking price was truly too low. In this case, go back and start again!

• Duty

KDV, Turkish VAT, is always included in marked prices (between 12 % and 15 % depending on the product).

• Mailing things home

You can send your purchases by mail without any risk, or leave them in the hands of the salesman if he offers (particularly for carpets which is common). For information only, the shipping rates are indicated in the post offices.

HEALTH AND SAFETY

• Precautions

There are no particular illnesses you will need to fear more than in other parts of Europe. The most common worry travellers are likely to encounter is intestinal problems provoked by the change in food. In Turkey, you will eat lots of salads that have not always been washed or preserved as well as they should be. Also, dishes tend to be rather spicy, which doesn't always agree with everyone. To be on the safe side, wash fruit and vegetables you buy. Only drink mineral water (*maden suyu*), never tap water (use this only to wash your hands and brush your teeth). When you're in a restaurant, be sure that the bottle is opened in front of you (generally this is done).

Medical kit

Bring a small emergency medical kit, containing aspirin, anti-diarrhoea medicine, suntan lotion (this is indispensable in the summer), adhesive plasters, cotton balls, and antiseptic lotion for small cuts. In case of emergency, Turkish pharmacies will have whatever you need. Remember that AIDS is raging in Turkey, as it is everywhere. Remember to protect yourself.

• Health

First aid

Small Turkish hospitals are hardly ever recommended – the supplies and cleanliness leave much to be desired. It's also better to purchase good repatriation insurance before leaving home.

Hospitals
There is an international hospital and foreign hospitals in İstanbul that are able to treat you; however, in more serious cases, repatriation is preferable.
International Hospital – Çınar Oteli Yanı 82, Yeşilyurt, ☎ (212) 663 30 00.
American Hospital – Güzelbahçe Sok, Nişantaşı, ☎ (212) 231 40 50.
Chemists / Pharmacies
The pharmacies (*eczane*) issue many types of medication without a prescription, including certain antibiotics.
Doctors
Some doctors speak English, German, and French. But, if possible, wait to go home if you need to see a practitioner.

• Emergencies
Dial 112.

A TO Z

• Antiques
Exporting antiques is strictly forbidden: anything that is more than 100 years old cannot leave Turkish soil, without risking a heavy fine or even several days in prison. Don't ever pick up anything on the archeological sites – fragments of stone or pottery, even if they seem insignificant. The laws are very strict for this type of robbery.

• Drinking water
Only drink bottled water without ice. In urban settings, water (*su*) is generally drinkable but has a strong taste of chlorine. In short, it's not advisable to drink it. Bottled mineral water (*maden suyu or şişe suyu*) is not expensive and is sold everywhere, from shops to street vendors. A little language tip: in Turkey *mineral water* or *soda* means "carbonated water".

• Electricity
220 volts, as in the rest of mainland Europe. On the other hand, electricity failures are quite common throughout the country.

• Laundry
Besides the public laundrettes, most of the larger hotels provide a laundry service that is inexpensive and efficient. Some smaller hotels also have washing machines.

• Newspapers
Most of the larger foreign daily newspapers are available a day after they are printed. If, during your trip, you don't want to lose track of local and international news, read the *Turkish Daily News*, that also publishes a weekly selection of quality articles in the *Turkish Probe*.

• Radio and television
Since the State's monopoly disappeared in 1989, innumerable private channels have flourished. Most revolve around political debates, and the quality of the programmes leaves much to be desired.
You can find news in English and German on the second national channel, every day in the summer after 10pm.

• Smoking
Since November 1996, it has been forbidden to smoke in public places and on public transport. This said, until the Turks respect this new dictate, it's not certain that the cafés will be any less smoky.

• Taking photographs
Unless you have a favourite brand, you will not have any difficulty buying film in Turkey (however you'll find print film easier to find than slide film). Prices are usually better than elsewhere. Make sure you check the expiration date, however, and avoid buying film that has been exposed to the sun in the shop window. With the exception of the countryside, people are not opposed to being photographed. However, while men like to pose, women tend to be more shy. Make it a habit to ask before you snap a picture, with a smile and a friendly *"lütfen"* (please).

• Thefts
In Turkey, it is not done to steal from one's guests, so theft is more common with tourists than locals. In tourist centres, watch your luggage carefully. Elsewhere, there is almost no risk.

• Tipping
You will never be asked to tip but there is no reason not to leave one. As in Europe, it is customary to leave something (add approximately 10% of your bill) in cafés, restaurants, and even for the taxi driver. This will always please the young student who serves you *çay*, or the shoe cleaner camped out in the street.

• Units of Measurement
Distances in this guide are given in kilometres. As a rule of thumb, one kilometre is five-eighths of a mile: 5 miles is therefore about 8 kilometres, 10 miles is about 16 kilometres and 20 miles is about 32 kilometres.

Consult the table below for other useful metric equivalents:

Degrees Celsius	35°	30°	25°	20°	15°	10°	5°	0°	-5°	-10°
Degrees Fahrenheit	95°	86°	77°	68°	59°	50°	41°	32°	23°	15°

1 centimetre (cm) = 0.4 inch
1 metre (m) = 3.3 feet
1 metre (m) = 1.09 yards
1 litre = 1.06 quart
1 litre = 0.22 gallon
1 kilogram (kg) = 2.2 pounds

• Weather forecasts
Weather reports are broadcast daily on TV and in newspapers. There is no need to understand Turkish; you only need to look at the small suns and clouds that cover the country's map!

A to Z

LOOK AND LEARN

• History and archeology

Brown, Dale M., *Anatolia: Cauldron of Cultures*, Time Life, Inc., 1995.

Bryce, Trevor, *The Kingdom of the Hittites*, Clarendon Press, 1998.

Davison, Roderic, *Turkey: from Empire to Republic*, Prentice Hall, 1968.

Freely, John, *Classical Turkey*, Chronicle Books, 1990. An architectural guide for travellers.

Freely, John, *Istanbul: The Imperial City*, Penguin, 1998.

Kinross, Lord, *The Ottoman Centuries: The Rise and Fall of the Turkish Empire*, William Morrow, 1977.

Koester, Helmut, *Pergamon Citadel of the Gods*, Trinity Press International, 1998. A comprehensive study of this ancient city from Hellenistic to Byzantine times.

Lewis, Bernard, *Istanbul and the Civilization of the Ottoman Empire*, University of Oklahoma Press, 1963.

Lloyd, Seton, *Ancient Turkey: A Traveler's History*, University of California Press, 1989.

MacFie, A.L., *Ataturk*, Addison-Wesley Publishing Co., 1994.

MacQueen, J.G., *The Hittites*, Thames & Hudson, 1996. An introduction to the people whose culture and power represent early Anatolian civilization.

Shaw, Stanford Jay, *History of the Ottoman Empire and Modern Turkey*, Cambridge University Press, 1977.

Stoneman, Richard, *A Traveller's History of Turkey*, Interlink Books, 1993.

Wood, Michael, *In Search of the Trojan War*, University of California Press, 1998.

Zurcher, Erik J., *Turkey: A Modern History*, St. Martins Press, 1998.

• Society

Arat, Zehra, F., (editor), *Deconstructing Images of the "Turkish Woman"*, St. Martins Press, 1998. Collection of essays on the images of Turkish women from late 19th century to the present.

Coco, Carla, *Secrets of the Harem*, Vendome Press, 1997. Focuses on the harems of the Sultans of Turkey.

Croutier, Alev Lytle, *Harem: The World Behind the Veil*, Abbeville Press, 1998. From first-hand accounts and memoirs, explores life in the world's harems focusing on Topkapı Palace.

Kelly, Robert et al., *Country Review, Turkey 1998/1999*, Commercial Data International, Inc., 1998.

Martin, Ramela, *Out of Darkness: An Armenian Woman's Story*, Lost Coast Press, 1997.

Settle, Mary Lee, *Turkish Reflection: A Biography of a Place*, Touchstone Books, 1992. A cross-country journey in search of the country's soul.

• Religion

Garnett, Lucy M., *The Dervishes of Turkey*, Octagon Press, 1991.

Itzkowitz, Norman, *Ottoman Empire and Islamic Traditions*, University of Chicago Press, 1980.

• Literature

Kemal, Yasar, *Memed My Hawk*, Harvill Press, 1998.

Pamuk, Orhan, *The New Life*, Farrar Straus & Giroux, 1997.

Pamuk, Orhan, *The White Castle*, Vintage Books, 1998.

Look and learn

Phillips, Michael, **A Rift in Time**, Tyndale House Publishing, 1997.
Unsworth, Barry, **The Rage of the Vulture**, WW Norton, 1995. A story of one man's revenge against the Ottomans amid the breakdown of the Turkish empire.
Poetry
Hikmet, Nazım, **Rubaiyat**, Copper Beech Press, 1986.
Hikmet, Nazım, **Poems of Nazım Hikmet**, Persea Books, 1994.

• Films
Hammam: A Turkish Bath, 1998. A young Italian inherits a dilapidated hammam and more as he enters into the exotic culture of İstanbul.
Midnight Express, by Alan Parker, 1978. The chilling true story of an American imprisoned in Turkey for drug smuggling.
Topkapi, by Jules Dassin, 1964. A comic thriller about jewel thieves planning to steal a priceless dagger from Topkapı Palace in İstanbul.
Yol, by Şerif Gören, 1982. Portrait of modern Turkey as seen through the eyes of 5 prisoners on temporary leave. Winner of the Golden Palm at the Cannes Film Festival.

• Music
Art of the Turkish Ud, Munir Nurettin Beken, Rounder Records, 1997.
Ashiklar – Turkish Folk Music, Golden Horn, 1999.
Masters of Turkish Music, Rounder Records, 1995.
Turkish Belly Dance: Desert Night Dance, Hüseyin Turkmenler, Arc, 1999.
Turkish Sufi Music – Folk Lute of Anatolia, Ali Ekber Çiçek, Lyrichord, 1992.

• Maps
Turkey, general map (for East and West) by Langenscheidt's American Map series, 1/800 000.
Turkey, general map by Bartholemew, 1/800 000.

USEFUL WORDS AND EXPRESSIONS

Since Atatürk loved France, he integrated many French words into the Turkish language during its reformation. Many Turkish words are phonetically identical to the French word. For example, "douche" (shower) is *duş* in Turkish, "telephone" becomes *telefon*, "chauffeur" (driver) is *şoför*, "coiffeur" (hairdresser) is *kuaför*, and "charcuterie" (delicatessen meats) becomes *şarküteri* (veal-based products – not pork of course). If dialogue is difficult, you may want to try your school French. In any case, words are not needed if you know how to smile!

Pronunciation
The letters *q*, *w*, and *x* don't exist in the Turkish alphabet. Conversely, the letters ğ, ı, ş, ö, and ü are specific to Turkish. Finally, some letters are pronounced differently. To sum up:

e	*e*	ğ	silent (a bit like *h*). Lengthen the vowel that precedes it.
c	*dj*	ö	*eu*
ç	*tch*	ü	*u*
ş	*sh*	u	*ou*
g	*gue*	ı	between *i* and *e*, with a guttural sound.

Common expressions

hello	iyi günler
good morning	günaydın
hi	merhaba
good evening	iyi akşamlar
goodbye	allahaısmarladık
(when you're leaving)	
goodbye	güle güle
(when you're staying)	
please	lütfen
thank you	teşekkür ederim / teşekkürler / mersi
yes	evet

no	hayır, yok
OK	tamam
Excuse me.	Affedersiniz.
I don't understand.	Anlamıyorum.
I don't speak Turkish.	Türkçe Bilmiyorum.
Do you speak English?	Ingilizce biliyormusunuz?
I want	istiyorum
there are	var
there are not	yok
I / you / he / she	ben / sen / o / o
we / you / they	biz / siz / onlar

Basic conversation

How are you?	Nasılsınız?
Where are you from?	Nerelisiniz?
You are my friend.	Arkadaşım.

I am British.	Ingilizim.
I am American.	Amerikalıyım.
I am Canadian.	Kanadalıyım.
I am Australian.	Avustralyalıyım.

Time

What time is it?	Saat Kaç?
It is 7 o'clock.	Saat yedi.
today	bugün
yesterday	dün
tomorrow	yarın
morning	sabah
evening	akşam
early	erken
late	geç
night	gece

hour	saat
day	gün
week	hafta
Monday	pazartesi
Tuesday	salı
Wednesday	çarşamba
Thursday	perşembe
Friday	cuma
Saturday	cumartesi
Sunday	pazar

Common adjectives

handsome	güzel
expensive	pahalı
inexpensive	ucuz
new	yeni
old	eski
big	büyük
small	küçük / ufak
closed	kapalı

open	açık
hot	sıcak
cold	soğuk
good	iyi, nefis (delicious)
bad	kötü
fast	hızlı, çabuk
slow	yavaş

Colours

white	ak / beyaz
blue	mavi
yellow	sarı

black	kara / siyah
red	kızıl (or kırmızı)
green	yeşil

Directions and visiting

here	burada
there	orada
north	kuzey (K)
south	güney (G)
east	doğu (D)

village	köy
What's the name of this village?	Bu köyün isimi nedir?
square	meydan
town centre	şehir merkezi

west	batı (B)	street	sokak
to the right	sağa	avenue	caddesi
to the left	sola	boulevard	bulvar
straight ahead	doğru	road	yol
where is...?	nerede...?	tourist office	turizm bürosu
museum	müze	post office	postane
church	kilise	entrance	giriş
mosque	cami	exit	çıkış
caravanserai	han	lake	göl
hotel	hotel	beach	plaj
guest house	pansiyon	tea room	çay bahçesi
restaurant	lokanta	holiday village	tatil köyü

Public transport

bus	otobüs	railway station	istasyon
ferry	feribot	ticket	bilet
airplane	uçak	return ticket	gidiş-dönüş bileti
train	tren	service station	benzin istasyonu
bus station	otogar	garage	garaj
port	liman	super	süperbenzin
airport	hava alanı	petrol (gas)	motorin
	(or hava limani)	full tank	ful / tam depo

Hotel

passport	pasaport	ladies	bayanlar
luggage	bagaj	gentlemen	baylar
half-board	yarım pansyon	sheets	çarşaf
(bed)room	oda	soap	sabun
single bed	tek yataklı	towel	havlu
double bed	çift yataklı	blanket	battaniye
room with	banyolu bir oda	key	anahtar
private bath		breakfast	kahvaltı
shower	duş	room rate	oda fiyatı
toilet	tuvalet	laundry	çamaşır temizleme
toilet paper	tuvalet kağıdı	dry cleaning	kuru temizleme

Restaurant

eat	yemek	coffee	kahve
drink	içmek	knife	bıçak
table	masa	spoon	kaşık
menu	yemek listesi	fork	çatal
salad	salata	salt	tuz
grilled	ızgara	pepper	kara biber
meat	et	rice	pilav
chicken	piliç, tavuk	sugar	şeker
fish	balık	yoghurt	yoğurt
dessert	tatlı	milk	süt
drink	içki	egg	yumurta
water	su	olive	zeytin
mineral water	maden suyu	soup	çorba
fruit juice	meyva suyu	bread	ekmek
wine	şarap	The bill, please.	Hesap lütfen.
tea	çay	tip	bahşiş

Post office

stamp	pul	air mail	uçakla
Do you have stamps?	Posta pulu var mı?	telegram	telgraf
envelope, letter	mektup	token	jeton
package	koli	normal token, large	normal jeton,
send	göndermek		büyük jeton

Purchasing

How much does this cost?	Ne kadar? Kaç para?	silver	gümüş
		gold	altın
This is too expensive	Çok pahalı.	cigarettes	sigara
It's beautiful.	Çok güzel.	credit card	kredi kartı
money	para	travellers' cheques	seyahat çeki

Emergencies

breakdown	arıza	doctor	doktor
Warn the police.	Polise haber verin.	hospital	hastane
There was an accident.	Bir kaza oldu.		

Numbers

0	sıfır	30	otuz
1	bir	40	kırk
2	iki	50	elli
3	üç	60	altmış
4	dört	70	yetmiş
5	beş	80	seksen
6	altı	90	doksan
7	yedi	100	yüz
8	sekiz	200	ikiyüz
9	dokuz	1 000	bin
10	on	1 000 000	bir milyon
20	yirmi		

Gesticulating

Whether or not you have trouble speaking Turkish, the language of gesticulation proves to be very useful and often more efficient than words. It's therefore better to understand their meaning when the words are foreign to us. For example, to say "no", Turks customarily lift their head and raise their eyes to the sky while lightly clicking their tongue.

To say "yes", on the contrary, they lower their head and eyes slightly. These signs, which are hardly noticeable by those who are not used to them, can be sufficient to push away an aggressive salesperson or a cruising taxi.

At the same time, other gestures express emotions or social manners. For example, clicking your tongue several times indicates disagreement or reprobation, and touching wood wards against bad luck, as in our cultures.

Then and now

Alexandretta	İskenderun
Andrianople	Edirne
Angora	Ankara
Antioch	Antakya (Hatay)
Brusa	Bursa

Byzantium, Constantinople	İstanbul
Caesarea Cappadociae	Kayseri
Ephesus	Efes, Selçuk
Halicarnassus	Bodrum
Hellespont	Dardanelles (Çanakkale Boğazı)
Iconium	Konya
Myra	Kale (Demre)
Nicaea	İznik
Nicomedia	İzmit
Pergamum	Bergama
Phocaea	Foça
Sardes, Sardis	Sart
Sebastea, Sebasteia	Sivas
Smyrna	İzmir
Tarsus	Tarsus
Trapezus, Trebizond	Trabzon
Troia	Truva (Troy)

Useful words and expressions

Exploring Turkey

N. F. Carterer/HOA QUI

The old port
at Antalya

The Ortaköy Mosque, İstanbul

G. Simeone/DIAF

THE MARMARA REGION

Marmara... an enchanting word for the sea named after the marble shipped from the islands to build the ancient world's most beautiful cities. It is a sea wedged between two bodies of water and gripped between two worlds, the Orient and Europe, and linked to the outside world via two narrow corridors. Towards Asia the **Bosphorus**, the straits running northward for 32km towards the Black Sea, the Caucasus mountains and the eastern steppes. Towards Europe the **Dardanelles**, a 68km-long channel spilling into the Aegean Sea and stretching to the coastlines of Greece and the Balkans. The windswept banks of the Dardanelles, the ancient Hellespont, gave rise to a legendary Homeric city, **Troy**. However, Constantine chose Byzantium, on the Bosphorus, to build the Roman empire of the East.

A maritime waterway, bridge or barrier to mankind, both straits have seen a hundred conquerors and countless ships filled with wheat, silk, spices and black gold. Each strait has also been the scene of bloody battles which reddened its waters and changed the course of history. Troy may have sunk into oblivion, but Constantinople's star rose, and the city went on to become the capital of several empires.

As a result, **İstanbul** holds the greatest concentration of the region's history, from Byzantine Anatolia to Mustafa Kemal's Turkey. Even though the latter ended İstanbul's political role, the city has not lost any of its aura or power. It is one of the country's most industrialised regions, housing an enormous population, which in turn creates the unavoidable problems of pollution and urbanisation.

A strategic point of entry, İstanbul is the gateway to Turkey for most visitors. They become swept away in its hubbub, array of colours, perfumes and marvels before escaping to open spaces and tranquil shores.

To the north, **Edirne** lies withdrawn and isolated in the small European portion of Turkey. To affirm its Ottoman culture, the city has endowed itself with one of the most beautiful mosques in the world, designed by the indefatigable Sinan for Süleyman the Magnificent. On the other side of the Sea of Marmara lies Anatolia, another land to discover, following in the footsteps of Alexander the Great or the explorers of the 19C.

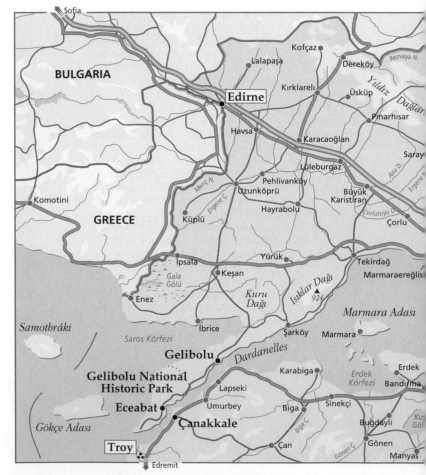

To the south is **İznik**, the city of blue and red tiles which decorate the mosques of the region and far beyond. The tiles are as blue as the waters of the lake where the reflections of the old Byzantine ramparts can be seen.

Toward the west, **Bursa**, the "green" city, was the final destination of the Silk Road and the gathering point of caravans arriving from Persia filled with the silken treasures of the Orient. Located at Europe's doorstep, it is undoubtedly the most Ottoman of the great cities of the north.

Further west are the Dardanelles, then Troy on its sombre hilltop overlooking the plain, its eroded walls mute testimony to the exploits of Ulysses and Agamemnon.

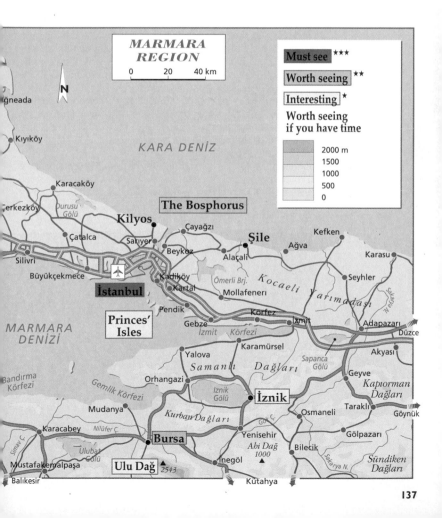

İSTANBUL ★★★
Provincal capital – 450km from Ankara
pop 7 million (10 million in the metropolitan area)
Mediterranean climate subject to cool winters

Not to be missed
The historical district of Sultanahmet
The Süleymaniye Mosque and the mosaics in the Church of St Saviour-in-Chora (Kariye)
A walk through the Grand Bazaar and on to İstiklal Caddesi
A boat trip on the Bosphorus (see p 184) and a visit to the Dolmabahçe Palace

And remember...
Visit Ayasofya early in the day when the light is at its best
The Beyoğlu district becomes lively at nightfall
Spend a day in the Princes' Isles, far from the city's hustle and bustle (see p 188)

Byzantium, Constantinople, İstanbul – each name, past and present, attributed to the great city on the Bosphorus, invokes powerful images of splendour and eastern promise. Travellers arrive in İstanbul to follow in the footsteps of writers such as the French author Pierre Loti, inspired by myths rooted in ancient Byzantium and stories of the eminent city ruled by Süleyman the Magnificent. The sands of time that have run their course have seen the city successively dominated by Roman, Byzantine, Christian, Muslim, and then secular conquerors. Each imparted his own mark on the city by building magnificent monuments celebrating the prosperity and brilliance of his realm, presiding over a hundred different peoples from the Balkans to the Persian Gulf, the Caucasus to Egypt.

Today, İstanbul is no longer the capital city but it retains the role of Turkey's window overlooking Europe. Following the rural exodus of the peasants from Anatolia, Russians, Ukrainians, Bulgarians and Uzbeks are reviving ancient trade ties and re-establishing

The Golden Horn's Seraglio Point or the Fires of the Orient

old cosmopolitan traditions. The excitement that one experiences in İstanbul, a megalopolis with a frenetic pace, is due to this mixture of people: countless street vendors, throngs of rushing workers, traffic congestion, perfume-laced markets.

The city gives the impression of being an urban monster, enlivened by the comings and goings of the boats on the Bosphorus and the sound of their sirens. Architecture buffs will discover some of the finest accomplishments of that art. But beyond the beautiful monuments, there are thousands of other ways to appreciate İstanbul: strolling in its alleys, enjoying grilled fish on its quaysides, sailing up the Bosphorus, smoking a hookah or tasting meze (starters) with rakı (aniseed flavoured liqueur) and of course, meeting İstanbul's residents.

A Great Destiny

The foundation of the first colony at the mouth of the Golden Horn is owed to the legendary King **Byzas** (c 660 BC). Very quickly, *Byzantion* became an extremely rich trade centre. This in turn made the neighbouring states envious of its wealth: the Persians, Greeks (5C BC) and Macedonians succeeded each other in possessing it. The city regained its independence and its prosperity under Alexander the Great who allowed it self-rule and ushered it into the Hellenic (Greek) world (333 BC). The invasion by the **Galata Celts** (279 BC) marked the beginning of a darker period: Byzantium bought back its freedom from the barbarians by paying a substantial tribute. The Galatas agreed to pull back only to settle on the eastern bank of the Golden Horn, facing the city's ramparts (today's Galata district). Their presence was a constant threat and was further exacerbated by the endless conflicts among the neighbouring principalities.

Fearing renewed attacks, the city asked for the protection of the Kingdom of **Pergamum**, Roman allies (202 BC). This was a fatal mistake which, little by little, diminished its independence until the city became a subject of Rome (146 BC). Emperor Septimius Severus covered the city with prestigious monuments, and surrounded it with city walls following the model of all the great cities of the Empire.

İstanbul

J.-F. Galmiche

The New Rome – When **Constantine I (Constantine the Great)** came to the throne in 306 AD, Rome was already a declining capital. Because of the expansion of Christianity, an Eastern religion, the ancient world's centre of gravity was moving eastwards. This was surely what motivated Constantine to move the capital of the Empire further East, to the Bosphorus. Byzantium with its Seven Hills (as in Rome) was the ideal site to create the "New Rome" (324). Within a few months, huge construction projects were undertaken so that *Constantinopolis* "the city of Constantine" would have the facilities worthy of its status as capital. New ramparts rose which Theodosius II reinforced in 447 to defend the city against **Attila the Hun.**

The Byzantine Era – Following the sacking of Rome by the Ostrogoths (476), Constantinople became the only heir to the Roman Empire and subsequently spread its influence to all the cities of Greece and Asia Minor. In the Greek language and the Christian religion, the Byzantine Empire possessed a powerful uniting force. Nevertheless, peace remained fragile: the city witnessed many social and religious conflicts, the most important being the **Nika Riot** (532) which nearly led to the downfall of **Justinian**. His reign (527-565) nevertheless marked the first Golden Age of Byzantium, of which the greatest achievement was Ayasofya, a symbol to all of a unique ideological and artistic renewal. The prosperous city reached a population of 1 million. Upon his death, the Empire, now at peace, stretched along most of the Mediterranean shores as it had during the Roman period.

Turmoil and Renewal – Peace was precarious and did not last long. In the 7C and 8C, Constantinople once again entered a dark period of history with renewed attacks by the Avars, the Persians and the Arabs. The city survived but lost numerous territories, especially in Africa. In addition, there was the **Iconoclastic Crisis** (726-843) during which fires and bloodshed destroyed numerous religious works of art.

The advent of the **Macedonian Dynasty**, from the 9C to the 11C, ushered in Constantinople's second renaissance with the arrival of numerous merchants on the shores of the Bosphorus. Latins, Venetians (Byzantine subjects) and Genoese settled in the cosmopolitan district of Galata, which acquired the status of an independent city in the 14C.

The Treachery of the Crusaders – To halt the advance of the **Seljuks**, who had won the Battle of Malazgirt (1071), the Emperor requested the aid of the Crusaders by promising them considerable commercial favours. Unfortunately the solution was worse than the problem. In 1204, the barons of the fourth crusade pillaged Constantinople and placed a **Latin emperor** on the throne. Basing himself at **Nicea**, refuge of the last Byzantines, Michael VIII took over the city in 1261 and founded the **Paleologus Dynasty**.

Byzantium, however, would never recover its past splendour. The age of decline was near: Ottomans, successors to the Seljuks, continued to take over the lands of the Empire, putting Anatolia under submission, followed by Thrace, before reaching the north shores of the Bosphorus in 1393. In 1402, the long siege of Constantinople began, only to be interrupted by the victory of the Turco-Mongol **Tamerlane**, who managed to crush Sultan Beyazıt I in Ankara.

The Ottoman Era – After a short interval, on May 29 1453, **Mehmet II's** capture of the city marked the **Fall of Constantinople** and the end of the Byzantine Empire, now confined to the city and its surroundings. After four years of construction and transformation of most of the churches into mosques, Constantinople became İstanbul, the Ottoman capital. The Sultan made it a priority to repopulate the city (which had shrunk to 35 000 inhabitants!) by encouraging trade and being tolerant towards other religions. Slowly under the reign of Beyazıt II, Selim I, and especially **Süleyman the Magnificent** (1520-1566), numerous foreign colonies established themselves in İstanbul which by now was once again very prosperous, economically as well as culturally. With the palace of Topkapı and the masterpieces of the architect **Sinan**, the city renewed its status as an artistic centre worthy of Constantine's vision.

The End of an Era – After Süleyman, the Empire, now governed by inept sultans, began experiencing endless internal disruptions and lost control of its economy to European powers. In the 19C, the Germans, French and British began sharing trade on the Bosphorus and brought it into the modern era with electricity and railways. In spite of the efforts of the last sultans, the Empire was in decline. The construction of the luxurious Dolmabahçe Palace on the banks of the Bosphorus was a futile attempt to mask the precarious situation.

The Faded Glory of a Capital – After the defeat of 1918, İstanbul had to bear the humiliating occupation by the Anglo-French forces. However, **Mustafa Kemal,** the future Atatürk, drew the Turks into a battle of independence against the Greeks and Western powers. In 1922, the last Sultan was overthrown and the following year the Allies left İstanbul which lost its role as the country's capital, ceding to Ankara. After the departure of the Greek and Armenian communities, İstanbul abruptly lost its cosmopolitan flavour and replaced it with a distinctive Turkish identity.

Greater İstanbul – Even though it lost its political might, İstanbul has remained the cultural and economic capital of Turkey, possessing over one-third of the industry and one quarter of the country's wealth. On the flip side of the coin, however, it receives the bulk of the **rural immigrants**. Since 1950, the population has grown from 1 to 9 million creating urban havoc on the shores of the Bosphorus. Frenetic and uncontrolled growth has led to numerous problems: housing, traffic, pollution and unhealthy living conditions in the *gecekondu*, shacks built overnight on the outskirts of the city. This situation explains the election, in 1994, of an Islamic mayor in a city which is normally European in outlook.

Since the early 1990s, the authorities have been trying to improve roads and many neighbourhoods have benefited from facelifts. The local authorities are trying hard to preserve the historical sights, making them more attractive. Population growth has slowed somewhat and a wide-reaching campaign to improve city life has begun. This long and arduous task is still in its infancy.

Bridging Two Continents

At the crossroads between Europe and Asia, İstanbul's location is exceptional. The city stretches over the shores of the Boğaziçi (the Bosphorus, *see p 184*), the 32km long straits linking the waters of the Black Sea and the Sea of Marmara. The European shore, where nearly two-thirds of the population lives is cut in half by the Golden Horn **(Haliç)**, a 7km-long natural harbour which is sheltered from the Bosphorus' strong currents. From one shore to the other, one continent to the other, every district of Greater İstanbul is a village with a unique atmosphere.

A City of Seven Hills – The never-changing landscape of domes and minarets on the west bank of the Golden Horn is the site of the ancient *Byzantion*. The first hill, **Sultanahmet** (Map 1 C4-5), includes İstanbul's most prestigious Byzantine and Ottoman monuments. To the west, one enters the heart of **Beyazıt** (Map 1 B3, C3), home of the Grand Bazaar and the magnificent Süleymaniye Mosque (third hill). Heading slightly north, the district of **Fatih** (Map 1 B4), the fourth hill, and a network of alleys, draws you into the religious atmosphere of deepest Anatolia.

İstanbul

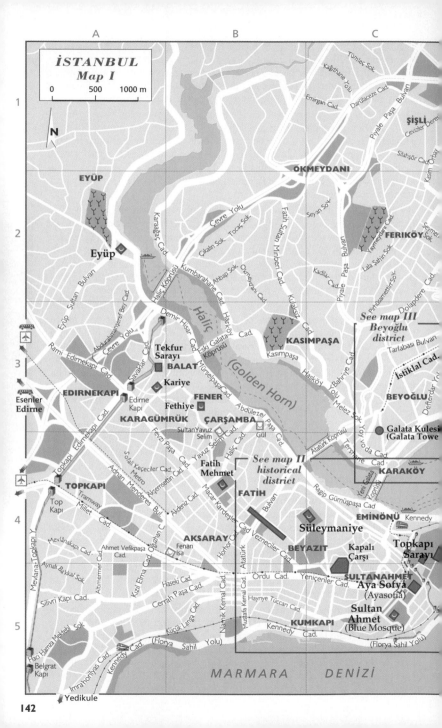

İSTANBUL Map I

0   500   1000 m

N

A   B   C

1

2

EYÜP

Eyüp

ŞİŞLİ

OKMEYDANI

Kağıthane Yolu

Emirgan Cad.

Piyale Paşa Bulvarı

Cevizler Sok.

Silahşör Cad.

Karaağaç Cad.

Çıkalın Sok.   Tocar Sok.

Fatih Sultan Minden Cad.

Seyran Sok.

FERİKÖY

Taynıpaşa Cad.

Laia Şahin Sok.

Seymen Sok.

Dolapdere Cad.

Eyüp Sultan Bulvarı

Abdurrahmangezi Bey Cad.

Çevre Yolu

Kumbarahane Cad.

Ahbap Sok.

Okmeydanı Cad.

Kadılar Cad.

Piyale Paşa Cad.

Kuralsız Cad.

Pirhüsamettin Sok.

3

Rami Edirnekapı Cad.

Demir Hisar Cad.

Tekfur Sarayı

BALAT

Eski Galata Köprüsü

Mürselpaşa Cad.

Haliç

(Golden Horn)

KASIMPAŞA

Kasımpaşa Cad.

Hasköy Cad.

Bahriye Yolu

Melez Sok.

Yolu Cad.

See map III
Beyoğlu district

Tarlabaşı Bulvarı

İstiklal Cad.

BEYOĞLU

Defterdar Cad.

Esenler
Edirne

EDİRNEKAPI

Edirne Kapı

Kariye

Fethiye

FENER

Abdülezel Paşa Cad.

KARAGÜMRÜK

ÇARŞAMBA

Galata Kulesi
(Galata Tower)

KARAGÜMRÜK

Fevzi Paşa Cad.

SultanYavuz Selim

Yavuz Selim Cad.

Haliç Cad.

Gül

Atatürk Köprüsü

Tersane Cad.

Yeni Galata Köprüsü

KARAKÖY

4

Topkapı Edirnekapı Cad.

Fatih Mehmet

FATİH

See map II
historical district

Macar Kardeşler Cad.

Ragıp Gümüşpaşa Cad.

Sofalı Keçeciler Cad.   Metro

Adnan Menderes Bul.   Akşemsettin Cad.

Akdeniz Cad.

Atatürk Bulvarı

Süleymaniye

EMİNÖNÜ   Kennedy

TOPKAPI

Top Kapı

Tramway   Millet Cad.

Mevlânâkapı Cad.

Ahmet Vefikpaşa Cad.

Fenari İsa

AKSARAY

Horhor

Veznecaler Cad.

BEYAZIT

Kapalı Çarşı

Topkapı Sarayı

SULTANAHMET
Aya Sofya
(Ayasofia)

Altınmermer Cad.

Kızıl Elma Cad.

Özhan C.

Haseki Cad.

Cerrah Paşa Cad.

Ordu Cad.

Namık Kemal Cad.

Mustafa Kemal Cad.

Yeniçeriler Cad.

Hayriye Tüccarı Cad.

KUMKAPI

Sultan Ahmet
(Blue Mosque)

5

Mevlana Topkapı Y.

Aynalı Bakkal Sok.

Silivri Kapı Cad.

Küçük Langa Cad.

İmrahoniliyas Cad.

Kennedy Cad.

(Florya Sahil Yolu)

Kennedy Cad.

(Florya Sahil Yolu)

Hacı Hamza Mektebi Sok.

Belgrat Kapı

Yedikule

MARMARA   DENİZİ

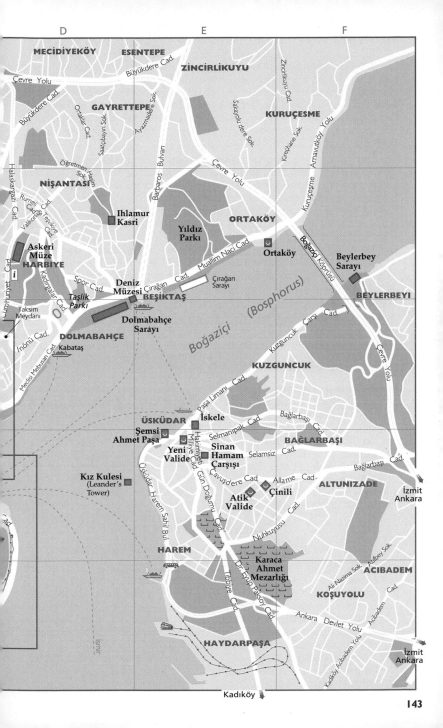

D   E   F

MECİDİYEKÖY   ESENTEPE

Çevre Yolu

Büyükdere Cad.

ZİNCİRLİKUYU

Zincirlikuyu Cad.

Büyükdere Cad.

GAYRETTEPE

Ortaklar Cad.

Saatçıbayırı Sok.

Öğretmen Haşim Sok.

Ayazmadere Sok.

KURUÇEŞME

Sakayolu dere Sok.

Kireçhane Sok.

Arnavutköy Yolu

Kuruçeşme

Çevre Yolu

NİŞANTAŞI

Halaskargazi Cad.

Rumeli Cad.

Teşvikiye Cad.

Valikonağı Cad.

Kadırgalar Cad.

Barbaros Bulvarı

İhlamur Kasri

Yıldız Parkı

ORTAKÖY

Ortaköy

Boğaziçi Köprüsü

Beylerbey Sarayı

Askeri Müze

HARBİYE

Cumhuriyet Cad.

i

Spor Cad.

Taşlık Parkı

Deniz Müzesi

Çırağan Cad.

Muallim Naci Cad.

Çırağan Sarayı

Boğaziçi (Bosphorus)

BEYLERBEYİ

Taksim Meydanı

İnönü Cad.

DOLMABAHÇE

Dolmabahçe Sarayı

Kabataş

Meclisi Mebusan Cad.

Boğaziçi (Bosphorus)

KUZGUNCUK

Kuzguncuk Çarşı Cad.

Çevre Yolu

Paşa Limanı Cad.

ÜSKÜDAR

İskele

Bağlarbaşı Cad.

BAĞLARBAŞI

Şemsi Ahmet Paşa

Hakimiyeti Milliye Cad.

Selmanipak Cad.

Yeni Valide

Sinan Hamam Çarşışı

Selamsiz Cad.

Gün Doğumu Cad.

Çavuşdere Cad.

Allame Cad.

Bağlarbaşı Cad.

Kız Kulesi (Leander's Tower)

Üsküdar Harem Sahil Bul.

Çinili

ALTUNIZADE

İzmit Ankara

Atik Valide

Çavuşdere Cad.

Nuhkuyusu Cad.

HAREM

Karaca Ahmet Mezarlığı

Dr. Eyüp Aksoy Cad.

Tıbbiye Cad.

Ali Nazıma Sok.

Atıfbey Sok.

ACIBADEM

KOŞUYOLU

Acıbadem Cad.

Ankara Devlet Yolu

Kadıköy Acıbadem Yolu

İzmit Ankara

HAYDARPAŞA

İzmir

Kadıköy

143

Next you reach **Fener** (Map 1 B3), the ancient Greek quarter built on the slopes of the fifth hill which spreads along the Golden Horn. The western side of the city's boundaries is defined by the **Theodosian Walls**, a snake-like stone structure which runs along the sixth and seventh hills between the Edirne (Edirne Kapı) and Cannon (Topkapı) Gates. At the northern edge, beyond the fortification, the quiet district of **Eyüp** (Map 1 A2) overlooks the river valley. Seen from the Pierre Loti café located on the hilltop, the sunset turns the waters below to gold. The **Kumkapı** fishermen's district on the Sea of Marmara (Map 1 B5) is an evening rendezvous for those who are fond of fresh grilled fish.

The European City – On the other side of the Golden Horn, **Beyoğlu** (Map 1 C3) is the European showroom of İstanbul. Topped by a majestic Genoese tower, the Galata Hill is lively with shops and craftsmen, while İstiklal Caddesi, the ancient **Pera** (Map 1 C3) and the former embassy district, is a concentration of the city's cultural and night-life. To the north, the pedestrian avenue spills into Taksim Square where most of the large hotels are located. Beyond, the **Şişli** (Map 1 C1) district contains modern office buildings and elegant boutiques.

Back on the shores of the Bosphorus, Dolmabahçe is the last palace of the Ottoman sultans, and the jewel of the **Beşiktaş** (Map 1 D2,E2) district. Further along, on the far eastern side, picturesque **Ortaköy** (Map I E2), with its pleasant restaurants, spreads out near the Bosphorus bridge, a gigantic structure linking two continents.

Oriental İstanbul – On the other side of the bridge you are in Asia. To the south, is the busy district of **Üsküdar** (Map 1 E3–4). This is a residential and business area. It overlooks the shores of the Bosphorus and reveals the soul of 19C Ottoman İstanbul: the elegant *yalı*, princely homes surrounded by distinctive hanging gardens, flank the humbler, pastel-coloured wooden homes of fishermen, gathered around the fish markets along the shore.

Four Days in İstanbul

1st day: Ayasofya; Yerebatan Sarayı; the Blue Mosque; the Hippodrome; the Museum of Turkish and Islamic Arts; the Grand Bazaar; the Süleymaniye Mosque. Dinner in Kumkapı.

2nd day: The Topkapı Palace and the Archeological Museum complex. Dinner in Sultanahmet.

3rd day: St Saviour-in-Chora (Kariye Camii), the Beyoğlu district; the Dolmabahçe Palace. Dinner in the Çiçek pasajı.

4th day: a boat trip on the Bosphorus *(see next chapter)*; the Egyptian Bazaar; a walk around Üsküdar. Dinner in Ortaköy.

Sultanahmet★★★

Allow 2 days to visit. All sights are within walking distance (see Map II, p 148-149).

Overlooking Seraglio Point **(Sarayburnu)**, at the mouth of the Golden Horn, the Sultanahmet district covers the first hill, fief of the ancient *Byzantion* and the political and cultural heart of the Byzantine and Ottoman city. Few places in the world host such a concentration of architectural jewels, examples of brilliant civilisations, in such a small perimeter. Sultanahmet, easily explored on foot, is perfectly accustomed to welcoming foreign guests: there are hotels, restaurants, cafés, newsagents, not forgetting the countless carpet sellers, and shoeshine boys who will accost you even if you are wearing trainers! The district has the atmosphere of a living museum proudly looking back on its past, far away from the bustle of the modern businesses and oriental bazaars of İstanbul.

Ayasofya★★★ (Aya Sofya Camii) (Map II E4)

9am-4pm, galleries closed 11.30am-1pm; closed Mondays. Entrance fee. Allow 2hr. If you arrive near closing time, it is best to begin with the galleries.

Even though the basilica has lost a large portion of the gold which illuminated its walls, the majesty of the place is stunning, especially when you know that such an architectural feat has been unmatched in the last one thousand years! Built for Christianity's glory, it became the Ottomans' symbol of triumphant Islam, and served as a model to the Empire's builders. From the exterior, it is difficult to appreciate the elegance of the work which is masked by the thick supporting pillars designed to protect the walls against earthquakes. The building's proportions are nevertheless striking.

For the glory of Christianity – Destroyed in 532 during the Nika Riot, the old Church of the Divine Wisdom (*Haghia Sophia*, in Greek) was rebuilt by Emperor **Justinian** who decided to construct on its foundation a sanctuary which would be worthy of the New Rome and capable of surpassing the temple of Solomon. To reach his objective, he called upon **Anthemius of Tralles** and **Isidore of Miletus**, two of the Empire's most eminent architects. Construction took less than six years to complete and involved 10 000 workers. Justinian had the most precious materials brought in, and didn't hesitate to pillage Delphi, Athens and Ephesus. The inauguration, held with great pomp, took place on December 26, 537. A gigantic dome henceforth dominated Seraglio Point; exceedingly large, it collapsed in 558 during a violent earthquake. To avoid a recurrence, the dome's diameter was reduced, but the dome was raised by 6m (to 56m in all).

After the conquest of the city in 1453, the basilica was converted into a mosque. Later, the Byzantine mosaics disappeared under a layer of plaster decorated with mediocre paintings, and enormous green medallions carrying the names of Allah, Muhammad and the four caliphs were placed at the top of the large columns. It was only in the 19C that the Fossati family undertook to renovate the building and to uncover the mosaics prior to Atatürk's decision to convert the site into a museum, in 1935. Not all of the plaster has been cleared, but the beauty of the space and the visible mosaics leave onlookers astonished.

A garden precedes the basilica, where some of the vestiges of the ancient church of Theodosius II lie. The narrow **exonarthex** which stands in half-darkness leads to the **narthex**, a grand 60m-long vestibule which opens through three doors into the nave, the

The Architects of Wisdom

Breaking away from the Roman rectangular pattern, Justinian's basilica was the first church to opt for a central plan by combining the basilica layout and the dome, symbol of the celestial sphere and the Kingdom of God. This concept agreed perfectly with the demands of the Eastern Orthodox creed which required that the priests and congregation be assembled together. In order to cover this enormous space without partitioning it, the architects of Ayasofya had a stroke of genius: a lightweight cupola built of bricks from Rhodes rests on a square plan, its weight distributed to four corner piers by pendentives in the form of quarter-spheres. The idea was a such a success that all Islamic architecture is derived from it.

main area of the basilica. The **Imperial door**, in the centre, is topped by one of the most beautiful mosaics, showing Emperor Leo VI kneeling in front of a **Christ in Majesty★★**. Mary and the archangel Gabriel are visible in the medallions on each side. The impression is awe-inspiring as you enter into the **nave★★★**, an immense space, almost square with sides 70m long, and surprisingly austere. Rays of light pierce the windows of the dome and the side galleries, plunging to the ground like arrows. Multicoloured marbles and mosaics adorn the surroundings. A feast for the eyes! Justinian spared no expense: white marble from Marmara, green from Euboea, pink from Synnada and yellow from Africa. The sumptuous **opus sectile**★ in green and red marble, in the southeast corner of the nave, gives the visitor an idea of the original floor's appearance. As far as the 107 columns of the basilica are concerned, some are ancient, removed from the most beautiful Greek temples, while the remainder were carved especially for the construction and are decorated with magnificent **capitals**★ with the monograms of Justinian and his wife Theodora.

During the Byzantine period, almost all of the walls were covered with **mosaics**★ laid onto a golden background – crosses, geometrical motifs and floral patterns, with human representations making an appearance at a later post-iconoclastic period. Three of them in particular, representing the **patriarchs** of Constantinople and Antioch (9C), are preserved in the niches located at the bottom of the northern tympanum. The **cherubs** with six wings which decorate the pendentives of the dome (14C) as well as the charming **Virgin Mary with Infant**★★ hidden at the back of the **apse** (9C) are also noteworthy.

During the conversion from church to mosque, several modifications occurred. Besides the large green **medallions** with golden calligraphy, a **mihrab** decorated with blue İznik tiles, as well an **Imperial tribune** (19C) were installed in the apse. Murat III added his touch with two enormous **alabaster urns** impressively flanking both sides of the entrance. Designed for ablutions, each can contain no less than 1 250 litres! Ahmet III had the **minbar** added, on the right of the apse, as well as the gigantic **chandelier**★ which hangs down from the dome. Last but not least, a **library** was created in the lower southern side in 1739. Behind its metal grilles, several niches hold thousands of Ottoman books and manuscripts.

Back towards the entrance, on the right side, the **sweating pillar** of St Gregory the Thaumaturge had a reputation for curing the blind and making women fertile. A hole was pierced into the protective copper-layer by the constant deliberations of the devout, who to this day, continue to gather the water seeping from the column, which is believed to make their wishes come true.

The Tribunes★★ – From the narthex, a large **paved ramp** leads to the tribunes, a splendid gallery around the nave. In the **northern tribune**, a mosaic represents Alexander, the ephemeral emperor who reigned for only a single year, in 912. The

Ayasofya, dome and crimson red walls of Byzantium

J.-F. Galmiche

western gallery, where the throne of the empress was located, offers a beautiful **view★** of the nave. However, it is the **southern gallery**, reserved for the Imperial family and the synods, where it is worth spending some time because it is here that the most beautiful mosaics of the basilica (and possibly of the world) are preserved. One of the rooms houses a remarkable **Deisis★★** (late 12C) which, even though heavily damaged, marvellously exemplifies the artistic renewal of the Palaeologi. Christ is surrounded by St John the Baptist and the Virgin, placed, unusually, on his left. The refinement of the facial features and the very human expression of the figure of Christ lend it a striking beauty.

The two **mosaics★★**, located on the wall at the end of the gallery, are equally superb. The one on the left (11C) represents Empress Zoe and her husband kneeling in front of Christ (the face of Constantine IX succeeded those of Romanus III and Michael IV, the previous husbands of the insatiable Zoe!). The **Theotokos★★** (Virgin in Majesty, on the right), which is almost a century older, follows more or less the same composition: Emperor John II Comnenus and his wife Eirene offering gifts to the Virgin Mary and the Infant Jesus.

Outside the basilica – The exit in the southwest corner is through a **bronze door** (9C). Prior to leaving the **vestibule**, be sure to turn around and look at the **Mosaic of the Donors★★** (10C), another splendid *Theotokos* which adorns the door: the Virgin, protector of Constantinople, is surrounded by Constantine and Justinian holding miniature models respectively of the city and the basilica.

Outside, notice the impressive **ablutions fountain** (1740) which sits majestically on the right. Opposite, the ancient Byzantine **baptistery** houses the ashes of Mustafa I and his nephew İbrahim I, whereas on the left, the three aligned **mausoleums** in the garden, all decorated with İznik tiles, hold the remains of Murat III, Selim II (Sinan's work) and Mehmet III.

It is well worth strolling around the basilica to appreciate it from all angles. It also provides an opportunity to discover **Soğuk Çeşme Sokak** (*behind the building*), a beautiful street flanked by **traditional wooden houses**, restored and transformed into hotels (*see "Making the most of İstanbul"*). At the easternmost end, the **Ahmet III Fountain** (1728), one of the city's most beautiful, marks the entrance to the Topkapı Palace.

The "Sunken Palace" (Yerebatan Sarayı) (Map II E4)

On Yerebatan Cad, near the Ayasofya. Daily, 9am-5.30pm. Entrance fee.

A visit to the extraordinary **Byzantine Cistern**, will fascinate you with its maze of 336 columns (8m high) which are reflected in the water and which give the impression of a sunken palace. Built by Justinian in the 6C, it is the largest underground cistern of İstanbul (140m by 70m), which the Ottomans used to supply Topkapı with water. In the 19C, the cistern was abandoned after the southwestern side was walled in. It was only in the 1980s that restoration work was begun. A wooden boardwalk allows you to move about in damp semi-darkness beneath the splashing drops of water. The shadowy effects and the discreet music which emanates from the columns creates a most unusual atmosphere. Notice the two columns resting on enormous inverted **Medusa heads★**, once part of an ancient temple.

For lovers of uncommon settings, you should know that another Byzantine cistern is hidden near the ancient hippodrome. The 224 partially submerged columns of the **Binbirdirek★** (D4), the "one thousand columns", in Turkish, bathe visitors in a bewitching atmosphere.

Water, a vital source of power
The city's water storage capabilities allowed Byzantium to face long sieges. The Byzantine emperors created a complex piping system which allowed the collection of water from the springs of the Belgrade forest via the Valens aqueduct, to supply the fountains of the capital and its numerous covered and exposed reservoirs.

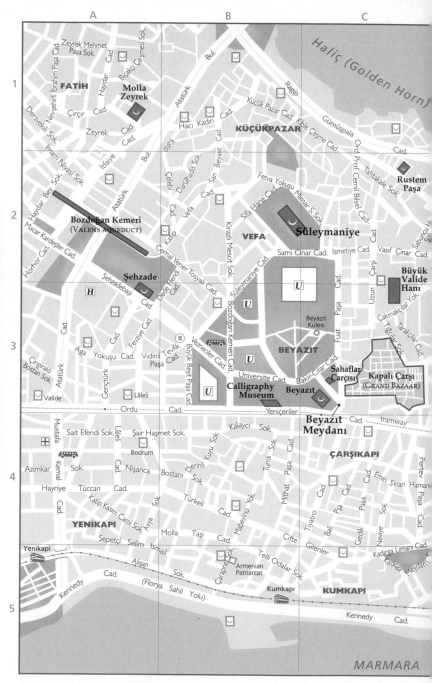

A

B

C

1

Zeyrek Mehmet Paşa Sok.
Zeyrek Mehmet Paşa Cad.
Bıçakçı Çeşmesi Sok.
Haydar Cad.
Nevşehirli İbrahim Paşa Cad.
FATİH
Çırçır Cad.
Molla Zeyrek
Zeyrek Cad.
Dersyekil Sok.
İmam Niyasi Sok.
Atatürk Bul.
Hacı Kadın Cad.
Katip Çelebi
Darülhadis Sok.
KÜÇÜKPAZAR
Küçük Pazar Cad.
Ragıp
Kible Çeşme Cad.
Gümüşpala
Ord. Prof. Cemil Bilsel Cad.
Tahtakale Sok.
Haliç (Golden Horn)
Cad.
Rustem Paşa

2

Haydar Bey Sok.
Atatürk
Bul.
Macar Kardeşler Cad.
Hornor Cad.
Bozdoğan Kemeri
(VALENS AQUEDUCT)
Cemal Yener Tosyalı Cad.
San Beyazit
Vefa Cad.
Fetva Yokuşu
Sıfa Hane Cad.
Kirazli Mescit Sok.
Mimar S Sok.
VEFA
Süleymaniye
Süleymaniye Cad.
Sami Onar Cad.
Ismetiye Cad.
Vasıf Çinar Cad.
Uzun Çarşı
Büyük Valide Hanı
Sabuncu
Çakmakçılar Yok.
Tarakçılar Cad.
Taşçılar Sok.

3

H
Şehzade
Şehzadebaşı Cad.
Dede Efendi Cad.
Fevziye Cad.
Aga Cad.
Yokuşu Cad.
Vidinli Paşa
Gençtürk Cad.
8
Tevfik Cad.
Büyük Reşit Paşa Cad.
Vezneciler Cad.
Bozdoğan Kemeri Cad.
U
U
U
Beyazit Kulesi
BEYAZIT
Fuat Paşa Cad.
Bakır-Cılar Cad.
Sahaflar Çarşısı
Kapalı Çarşı
(GRAND BAZAAR)
Universite Cad.
Calligraphy Museum
U
Beyazit
Cingiraklı Bostan Sok.
Atatürk Cad.
Valide
Lâleli

Ordu Cad.
Yeniçeriler
Beyazıt Meydanı
Cad.
tramway

4

Mustafa
Sait Efendi Sok.
Lâleli Cad.
Şair Haşmet Sok.
Bodrum
Kalayci Sok.
Kuyu Sok.
Tumli Sok.
Nişanca
ÇARŞIKAPI
Pertev Paşa Cad.
Emin Sinan Hamanı
Azimkar
Kemal Sok.
Hayriye
Tüccan Cad.
Katip Kasim Cami Sok.
Asya Sok.
Bostanı
Derinli Sok.
Türkeli
Cad.
Nabeyinçi Yok.
Mithat Paşa Cad.
Tiyatro Cad.
Bali Paşa Cad.
Gedik Paşa Cad.
Neviye Cad.
YENİKAPI
Molla Taşi Cad.
Çifte Cad.
Gilenler

5

Yenikapi
Kennedy Cad.
Sepetçi Selim İsmail Sok.
Alişan Cad.
(Florya Sahil Yolu)
Çarapnahor Yok.
Armenian Patriarcat
Telli Odalar Sok.
Kumkapı
KUMKAPI
Kadırga Limanı Cad.
Kadırga Meydanı
Kennedy Cad.

MARMARA

148

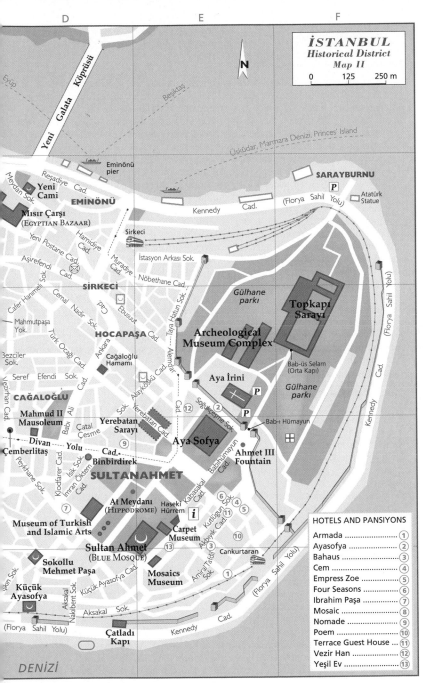

İSTANBUL
Historical District
Map II

0   125   250 m

D   E   F

N

Eyüp

Galata Köprüsü

Yeni

Beşiktaş

Üsküdar, Marmara Denizi, Princes' Island

Eminönü pier

SARAYBURNU

P

Atatürk Statue

Reşadiye Cad.

Meydan Sok.

Yeni Cami

EMİNÖNÜ

Mısır Çarşı
(EGYPTIAN BAZAAR)

Kennedy   Cad.   (Florya Sahil Yolu)

Hamidiye Cad.

Yeni Postane Cad.

Sirkeci

Aşirefendi Cad.

Muradiye Cad.

İstasyon Arkası Sok.

Nöbethane Cad.

SİRKECİ

Cafer Hanmet Sok.

Cemal Nadir Sok.

Ebusuut

Mahmutpaşa Yok.

Türk Ocağı Cad.

Ankara

HOCAPAŞA

Cağaloğlu Hamamı

Taya Hatun Sok.

Alemdar

Gülhane parkı

Topkapı Sarayı

Archeological Museum Complex

Bab-üs Selam
(Orta Kapı)

Bezciler Sok.

Seref Efendi Sok.

Nezirhan Cad.

CAĞALOĞLU

Mahmud II Mausoleum

Babı Ali

Çatal Çeşme

Alaykoşki Cad.

Yerebatan Cad.

Aya İrini

P

P

Sogukçesme Sok.

Gülhane parkı

Divan   Yolu

Çemberlitaş

Yerebatan Sarayı

Cad.

Aya Sofya

Bab-ı Hümayun

(Florya Sahil Yolu)

Kennedy   Cad.

Binbirdirek

SULTANAHMET

Babıhumayun

Ahmet III Fountain

Peykhane Sok.

Klodfarer Cad.

İmran Öktem Cad.

Işık Sok.

At Meydanı
(HIPPODROME)

Haseki Hürrem

i

Kabasakal Cad.

Kutlüğün Sok.

⑥

④

⑪

⑤

⑩

Museum of Turkish and Islamic Arts

Carpet Museum

⑬

Cankurtaran

Sultan Ahmet
(BLUE MOSQUE)

③

Adbiyik Sok.

Amiral Tafdil Sok.

(Florya Sahil Yolu)

Sokollu Mehmet Paşa

Mosaics Museum

①

Küçük Ayasofya

Aksakal Sok.

Nakibent Sok.

Küçük Ayasofya Cad.

(Florya Sahil Yolu)

Aksakal   Sok.

Kennedy   Cad.

Çatladı Kapı

DENİZİ

HOTELS AND PANSIYONS

Armada .... ①
Ayasofya .... ②
Bahaus .... ③
Cem .... ④
Empress Zoe .... ⑤
Four Seasons .... ⑥
Ibrahim Paşa .... ⑦
Mosaic .... ⑧
Nomade .... ⑨
Poem .... ⑩
Terrace Guest House ... ⑪
Vezir Han .... ⑫
Yeşil Ev .... ⑬

149

The Blue Mosque★★★ (Sultan Ahmet Camii) (Map II E4)

Access to the courtyard is free. Access to the Mosque is also free except during prayer hours. Women who are not dressed appropriately will be expected to wear head-scarves and long skirts provided at the entrance.

With its graceful architectural lines and its radiant interior, the Blue Mosque is a worthy neighbour to the Ayasofya. It owes its official name to its founder, Sultan Ahmet, and the name by which it is more commonly known to the 20 000 blue İznik tiles. Built between 1609-1616 on the site of the Byzantine Grand Palace by architect **Mehmet Ağa**, a student of the legendary Sinan, it was the last grand Imperial project undertaken in İstanbul.

The mosque with its six **minarets,** was the point of departure for pilgrims bound for Mecca in Arabia. It was modelled on the mosque in Mecca, which irked Arab religious authorities. To pacify them, a seventh minaret was added to the latter.

In front of the entrance, an army of multilingual shoe-shiners, cigarette, pen and postcard vendors awaits the visitor. Once inside, the luminosity and immense carpet-covered space of the **prayer hall**★★ is striking. The 43m-high **central dome** is supported by four enormous circular **pillars**★ known as "elephant paws". No fewer than 260 windows light up the walls covered with **blue İznik tiles**★. The original stained-glass windows, which have mostly disappeared, were cut in prism form in order to allow the same light to reach the faithful no matter where they were. Acoustics also play an important role in a mosque; here the faithful can hear the Imam from anywhere in the hall. Notice the **mihrab** and the **minbar** made of white Marmara marble as well as the wooden **doors and shutters**★ inlaid with mother-of-pearl, ivory and tortoiseshell.

The **courtyard**★, a vast quadrilateral framed by an elegant portico covered with small domes, is reached from the prayer hall. A magnificent **şadırvan** (fountain) stands regally in the centre. From here, the eye is drawn upwards to the sky and the magnificent succession of domes.

Around the Mosque

At the northeastern side of the mosque, an outside ramp leads to the *hünkar kasrı* (the Sultan's summer pavilion adjacent to his private quarters), which is home to the **Kilim Museum** *(still being renovated)*. The collections, which are poorly displayed, have suffered from the country's lack of interest, until recently, in this type of crafts-manship. The lower level houses the **Carpet Museum** and that is well worth a visit *(Monday through Friday, 9.30am-4pm, entrance fee)* because of its beautiful 16C to 20C mosque carpets from Anatolia, the Caucasus and Transylvania.

Skirting the southeast corner of the Blue Mosque, an avenue lined with many carpet-sellers leads to the **Museum of Mosaics** (Mozaik Müzesi) *(9.30am-5pm, closed Tuesdays)* where the extremely beautiful mosaics of the Grand Byzantine Palace are preserved.

The Ancient Hippodrome (At Meydanı) (Map II D4)

In the place that was once the prestigious Roman hippodrome, there remains an immense oblong field with a few obelisks. It is difficult to imagine that this was once a hotbed of political activity. To imagine the size of the site, one needs to see the fabulous chariot race in the movie *Ben Hur*. Septimius Severus had had the hippodrome constructed in 203, a few years after he had had the city levelled, perhaps to regain the favours of a people with a passion for races. In the 4C, Constantine extended it to the present Ayasofya Basilica to form a rectangle of 450x120m. The Imperial tribune, on the eastern side, was connected to the Grand Palace (*the Bucoleon*), while the space beneath the terraces held the stables and the charioteers as well as a large market. Pillaged in 1204 by the crusaders (who carried off the imperial tribune's bronze horses to Venice to decorate St Mark's Basilica), the hippodrome slowly fell into ruin, and the Ottomans used its stones until all the steps disappeared. Of the monuments which were situated in the middle of the track (*the spina*), only three survive. South of the square are the **Column of Constantine** (Örme Direk) (or "walled obelisk") and a modest pile of crudely cut stones, 32m high, probably erected under Constantine I. Constantine VII Porphyrogenitus covered the obelisk with bronze in the 10C, but the crusaders removed it and melted it down in the 13C.

More interesting, the **Serpentine Column** (Yılanlı Sütun or Burmalı) — formed by three intertwined snakes – is originally from the Temple of Apollo at Delphi. Eight metres high at its inauguration, it had already lost its golden tripod when Constantine brought it back. The serpants' fate was hardly better: their heads were were destroyed first by the Christians, and were further defaced by the Muslims, who saw in them the personification of the devil (only a jaw survives in the Museum of Antiquities).

The most beautiful monument, **Theodosius' Obelisk** (Dilikitaş), is Egyptian. It was raised by Pharaoh Thutmosis III in Karnak in the 15C BC before being transferred to Constantinople in 390. Damaged during transport, the piece lost its base. The visitor actually sees the upper third, 20m high, resting on four large bronze cubes. On the marble support slab, the Byzantine **bas-reliefs★** represent Emperor Theodosius I and his family observing a chariot race and the erection of an obelisk.

> **A Political Arena**
> The hippodrome (30 000 to 50 000 seats) saw the proclamation of the New Rome, on May 11 330. Some generals were acclaimed and emperors enthroned here, while others were executed; during the Nika Riot in 532, 30 000 people were massacred. The Byzantine emperors held ostentatious feasts until the 11C. To prove that hooliganism is not a recent phenomenon, the hippodrome was the theatre of battles between factions. The Blues and the Whites, close to the aristocracy and considered traditionalists in religious matters, were opposed to the Greens and Reds, who represented trade and craftsmanship, and were more sensitive to the eastern tendencies of the Church and closer to the people. The events taking place in the grandstands were as important as those on the field.

The Museum of Turkish and Islamic Arts★

(Türk ve İslam Eserleri Müzesi) (Map II D4)
10am-5pm, closed Mondays, entrance fee

The museum is housed in the ancient residence of İbrahim Paşa, the son of a Greek slave, who became the grand vizier (minister) of Süleyman the Magnificent. Surrounding a central garden, the rooms contain some splendid examples of **Islamic decorative arts** from the 11C onwards: porcelain, glassware, calligraphy, paintings and miniatures, from the Omayyads to the Ottomans. The room dedicated to Seljuk **carpets** shows the different stages of weaving.

A fascinating **ethnographic section** describes the way of life of various Turkish peoples in the 19C, with examples of a nomadic Yörük tent and the Western-style salons of İstanbul. The museum's well-stocked book shop is also worth a visit.

Toward the Sea

If you have time to spare, visit the charming **St Sergius and St Bacchus Church★** (Küçük Ayasofya Camii) (Map II D5) (*10.30am-5.30pm, 30min on foot from the Blue Mosque*). It owes its Turkish name "little Ayasofya" to its resemblance with the Ayasofya, its big sister. Begun under Justinian in 527, the first year of his reign, it was one of the most important Byzantine sanctuaries before being converted into a mosque in the

16C. The mosque rises at the end of a pleasant courtyard far from the urban bustle. It is pleasant to relax inside its half-darkened, soothing and calming interior. Furthermore, its irregular **architecture**★ reveals a period of increasingly innovative ideas: it consists of an octagon, covered with an eight-quartered dome topping a square room used as an ambulatory. The mosaics have long disappeared, but a few scattered remains make a pleasant if irregular floor covering.

A short distance to the north is a picturesque district where the streets are lined by wooden homes; the sound of children laughing and playing is often in the air. On Şehit Mehmet Paşa Sokak, you will find the small **Sokollu Mosque**★ (Sokollu Mehmet Paşa Camii) (Plan II D5), built in 1571 by Sinan. The entrance, an astonishing covered stairway, leads to the inner courtyard, embellished by the traditional *şadırvan*. In spite of its slender shape the prayer hall lies in semi-darkness, yet this does not diminish the impact of the beautiful **İznik tiles**★. A functioning medrese still exists and your presence may distract the children from their Koranic readings.

Topkapı Palace★★★
(Topkapı Sarayı) (Map II F3)

9.30am-5 pm, closed Tuesdays; tickets sold at the entrance to the second courtyard, additional fee to visit the harem. You will need half a day for the visit. There is a restaurant overlooking the Bosphorus located in the fourth courtyard.

Topkapı Palace (not to be confused with the Topkapı district) is likely to be one of the highlights of your trip, giving you a glimpse of the daily life of the Ottoman sultans. The atmosphere of the palace and the pomp of the sultans is illustrated by the luxury of the decor – porcelain, stucco, woodwork, stained-glass – and is further enhanced by the incredibly rich collections.

A Place of Power and Intrigues – Overlooking the Golden Horn, the Bosphorus and the Sea of Marmara, Topkapı is set in a dream location. It was here, approximately twenty years after the conquest of Constantinople that Mehmet II decided to build a new palace. All of the sultans were to live here, until the 19C, when the Dolmabahçe Palace was constructed on the shores of the Bosphorus. In spite of the many subsequent additions and the fires which on three occasions destroyed a large part of the original palace, its initial layout remains largely unchanged. It has been enriched by additional buildings, kiosks and small salons which transformed it into a luxurious labyrinth.

Topkapı, being the private residence of the Sultan and his relatives, was also home to the **Divan**, the country's main political structure, as well as various institutions which were linked to the court. Between 4-5 000 people lived in the palace.

The first courtyard, which was open to the public, included the Ministry of Finance and various services of the palace. The second courtyard, seat of the Divan, was only open to those appearing before the Council, while access to the third courtyard was permitted exclusively to important dignitaries. With its kiosks and gardens, the fourth courtyard was an area where the sultans could rest. Lastly, the harem, the women's quarter, was hidden away from the palace's public life.

The First Courtyard

The **Imperial Gate** (Bab-i-Hümayun) opens onto the "courtyard of the Janissaries"; the gate was built in 1478 and has been modified several times. The severed heads of dignitaries who had fallen from grace were displayed in the recesses located along its sides.

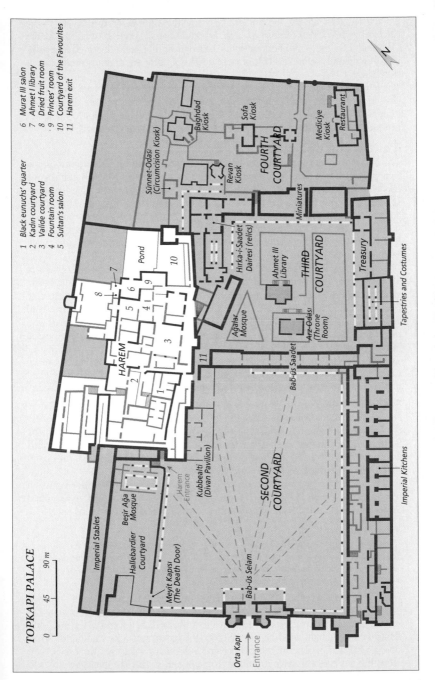

TOPKAPI PALACE

0 45 90 m

1 Black eunuchs' quarter
2 Kadın courtyard
3 Valide courtyard
4 Fountain room
5 Sultan's salon
6 Murat III salon
7 Ahmet I library
8 Dried fruit room
9 Princes' room
10 Courtyard of the Favourites
11 Harem exit

N

Imperial Stables

Hallebardier Courtyard

Beşir Ağa Mosque

Meyit Kapısı (The Death Door)

HAREM

Pond

Kubbealtı (Divan Pavilion)

Harem Entrance

Ağalar Mosque

Bab-üs Selam

Orta Kapı
Entrance

SECOND COURTYARD

Bab-üs Saadet

Imperial Kitchens

Arz-Odası (Throne Room)

Ahmet III Library

THIRD COURTYARD

Hırka-i-Saadet Dairesi (relics)

Miniatures

Treasury

Tapestries and Costumes

Sünnet-Odası (Circumcision Kiosk)

Baghdad Kiosk

Revan Kiosk

Sofa Kiosk

FOURTH COURTYARD

Mediciye Kiosk

Restaurant

153

On the left, lost among the foliage, is where the **Church of the Divine Peace (St Irene)**** (Aya İrini) (*occasionally open for classical music concerts*), was built under Constantine, in the 4C, to honour divine peace (*Irene*, in Greek). It served as a patriarchal cathedral before the Ottomans turned it into an armoury and later a storehouse.

The interior, consisting of stone and brick, has a sobriety and calmness all its own. The clergy would convene in the **apse,** located on the western side. It holds an example of a *synthronon*, unique in all of İstanbul. The only decoration is the apse's **mosaic** which consists of a large black cross on a golden background.

The Second Courtyard

The entrance to the "courtyard of ceremonies" is the **Gate of Salutations** (Bab-üs Selam) – or Middle Gate (*Orta Kapı*) – flanked by two towers which house a **scale model** of Topkapı. The long walkways shaded by cypress trees create a garden atmosphere in the courtyard. It has retained its original appearance: elegant white façades adorned with marble colonnades. This was the centre of the palace's public life, where the sultan reviewed the Janissaries; the ceremony was held, before thousands, in absolute silence. On their way to the Council, the viziers (ministers) had to walk by the decapitation stone, also known as the "warning stone".

The right wing of the courtyard is home to the **Imperial kitchens**, a succession of 10 vast rooms that were rebuilt by Sinan after the fire of 1574. They house an amazing collection of **Chinese porcelain***, the third in importance after those of Beijing and Dresden. Connoisseurs of porcelain, the sultans collected items from France (Limoges, Sèvres), Russia, and Saxony (Meissen). Even those visitors who prefer the convenience of disposable plates and paper cups cannot help but be impressed by the magnificent pieces on display.

The last two kitchens have retained the original **utensils** (plates, cups, ladles, bronze cauldrons) which seem designed for giants. Imagine the hustle and bustle when meals for 5 000 palace residents had to be prepared!

Further along, the very luxurious **Divan Pavilion*** (Kubbealtı) (*should be seen while you are waiting to visit the harem*) is adorned by the **Tower of Justice**. Four times a week, the Council of the Empire would meet in the first room (the second one was for the Secretariat), under the watchful eye of the Sultan who hid behind an iron-grilled window. The last council was held on August 30, 1876. It is here also that the Grand Vizier held gatherings to entertain ambassadors.

In the northern corner of the courtyard, the **Inner Treasury Chamber** houses a remarkable collection of Turkish, Persian, Mamluk, European, and African **arms and armour*** as well as the Sultan's ceremonial arms all inlaid with precious jewels.

The Harem**

10am-4pm, group visits of 40 to 60 persons every 20 minutes; tickets sold at the entrance. Beware, it is pointless to wait in a large group if closing time is approaching. For the Tower of Justice, you should purchase your ticket at the same time and inform your tour guide, who will escort you there at the end of the visit.

Only 30 of the labyrinth's 300 hidden rooms are open to the public (and they lack the original furnishings). The visit, accompanied by a fast-talking guide, is nonetheless fascinating. Constructed under the reign of Murat III at the end of the 16C, and almost entirely rebuilt after the fire of 1665; the harem was a later addition. Roxelana, a Christian of Slav origin who became Süleyman's wife, used the excuse of a fire at the old palace to have it built at Topkapı and so that she could be closer to the seat of power. Later, the harem began playing an increasingly important role in the affairs of the Empire. More than 500 people lived in its countless dark rooms which were often tiny and windowless. The area revolves around two patios: one for the eunuchs and one for the women, where the entertainment lounge and the Sultan's room are also located.

The entrance corridor, paved with pebbles, leads to the eunuchs' tiny cells. The rigour of their quarters was compensated by the beauty of the decor, which consists of beautiful Kütahya porcelain. As soon as the Sultan's voice was heard in the corridor, no woman was allowed to move about. The small **Kadın Courtyard**

The Harem, Desire and Confinement

Beside the wives and concubines of the Sultan, only Christian virgin slaves of great beauty had the honour of being secluded in the harem, a secret realm which was off-limits to men and guarded by black Egyptian eunuchs (completely emasculated, unlike the white eunuchs). Within the richly decorated blue İznik-tiled walls and in the hamams' vapour-filled white marble corridors, a strict discipline reigned. More than just a place for voluptuous debauchery, the harem was the seat of fierce battles and bloody intrigue between slaves, concubines and wives ("kadın") who often relied on the arbitration of the chief eunuch. The women's main goal was to provide the sultan with an heir in order for them to be promoted to the envied status of "haseki sultan"; then, in the event of the heir's accession to the throne, to the title of "valide" (Sultan's mother).

precedes the **Courtyard of the Valide**, nerve-centre of the harem which opens up to the **Sultan's Salon** (18C), the sovereign's entertainment area. On the gold-painted wooden balcony (16C), the female musicians played with their backs to the lounge and were not allowed to turn around.

Further along, we come to the **Fountain Chamber** (17C), where the sovereign greeted his favourites. The sound of water disguised the conversations as well as, no doubt, the frolicking. At the entrance, the set of small marble columns was supposed to detect earthquakes.

The highlight of the visit, the **Salon of Murat III**, is certainly the harem's most beautiful with its **İznik tiles** and bronze chimney. Wainscoting painted with bouquets of flowers and fruit adorn the charming adjoining **Fruit Room** where Ahmet III enjoyed relaxing while contemplating the gardens and pool below. The two **Princes' Apartments** with superb tiles were used for the young sultans' studies. These rooms were long known as *kafes* or golden prisons, where the young sultans lived as recluses for years hoping to someday accede to the throne. The visit ends in the **Courtyard of the Favourites**, where the upper apartments were inhabited until 1909.

The Third Courtyard

The **Gate of Felicity** (Bab-üs Saadet), leads to the Sultan's tile-decorated **Throne Room** (Arz Odası). The structure is from the period of Selim I but only the **throne's** canopy and the golden **chimney** survived the fire of 1856.

In the centre of the court stands the elegant **Ahmet III Library** (1718) (*closed to the public*), while on the left, near the harem's exit, rises the **Ağalar Mosque** which is entirely covered in İznik tiles. Inside, there is a remarkable Turkish, Arab and Persian **manuscripts collection**.

Be sure to see the **Tapestries and Imperial Costumes** collection which is located in the ancient hamams (*on the right when entering the court*). The blood-stained robe worn by Osman II when he was assassinated at the age of 19 is quite moving, as is the one worn by Abdülaziz, who died tragically in 1876.

İstanbul

There is always a queue waiting to enter the room containing the **Topkapı Treasury*****, located in the same wing. These rooms, which are among the most beautiful in the palace, have been uninhabited since the 17C. They bring together the incredible riches collected by the sultans, in particular four **thrones** inlaid with precious stones – that of Murat III, in solid gold, weighs 250kg; an enormous emerald weighing 3.26kg; an assortment of 50 diamonds, including the famous **Spoon-maker's Diamond** with its 58 facets (86 carats); numerous **priceless objects** which belonged to the sultans. These include carved daggers, an 18C golden cradle, rock-crystal vases, gold chandeliers weighing 48kg inlaid with 6666 diamonds, and reliquaries containing fragments of St John the Baptist.

In the centre of the north wing, the **Persian and Turkish Miniatures Room*** (*often closed*) overlooks the passage leading to the fourth courtyard. It contains a few 14C masterpieces and a gallery of the **Portraits of the Sultans**.

In the northwest corner of the court, the **Relics Chamber** or **Pavilion of the Holy Mantle** (Hırka-i Saadet Dairesi) houses the swords of the first four Caliphs as well as the **Relics of the Prophet** which are highly venerated by Muslims: hair from his beard, a tooth, a footprint, and his mantle, which Selim I brought back from Cairo in 1517 when he became Caliph.

A portico leads to a dazzling marble **terrace***, enhanced by a pond and a fountain, where the **view**** is enchanting.

Each side is flanked by an elegant pavilion, the **Circumcision Kiosk** (Sünnet Odası) and the **Revan Köşkü**, built in 1636 by Murat IV to commemorate the taking of Erevan (Armenia) from Persian control.

The Fourth Courtyard

This is a pleasure garden built on several levels and graced by a number of kiosks. In the northwest corner of the **Tulip Garden**, visit the luxurious **Bağdat Köşkü***, built by Murat IV to celebrate the conquest of Baghdad in 1638. The doors and windows are decorated with precious wood inlaid with mother-of-pearl. From the terrace, the **view*** over the Bosphorus and the Golden Horn is magnificent. The **Mustafa Paşa Kiosk** (or Sofa Köskü), a nice example of Turkish Rococo, contains a *brasero* (container for live coals), a gift from Louis XV to Mahmut I. The final addition to the palace, the **Abdülmahcid Kiosk** (Mecidiye Köşkü), was built by a Frenchman in 1840. It houses a pleasant **restaurant** on a terrace overlooking the Bosphorus (*see "Making the most of İstanbul"*). This is the ideal place for a well-deserved lunch break!

The Archeological Museums*** (Map II E3)

9.30am-4pm, closed Mondays. The Museum of the Ancient Orient is closed for restoration. Entrance fee. Allow 2hr for the two museums.

The Museum of Antiquities*** is one of the richest museums of antiquities in the world. A new wing was opened in 1991 for its centennial celebration. Unfortunately, several rooms are often closed because of a lack of personnel.

In the entrance stands a striking monumental **Roman statue of Beş**, from Cyprus, holding a small headless lion. The rooms on the left hold the heavy sarcophagi found in Sidon (Lebanon) in 1887. The most famous one, known as **Alexander's****, is the sarcophagus belonging to the Seleucid king Abdalonymus (4C BC), decorated with extraordinary bas-reliefs showing Alexander the Great on a lion hunt and fighting the Persians. Other beautiful works include the sarcophagus of the **Mourning Widows** (from the same period) and one belonging to **Tabnit** (6C BC) whose **mummy** is displayed.

On the right side of the entrance, the sculptures of the archaic, Persian, Greek and Greco-Roman periods are showcased. Noteworthy are the strikingly beautiful **Ephebos of Tralles★**, and the **Head of Alexander the Great**, a Roman copy of the Lysippus model, typical of the Pergamum style.

Upstairs, a room of the ancient building houses Ionian **terracotta** items. On the ground floor of the new wing, you can admire a reconstruction of the **façade of the temple of Athena of Assos** (6C BC) which includes original pieces.

The first floor is dedicated to **Anatolian civilisation** – Troy in particular – from prehistoric times and, in a big room on the left, a display case recreates the **tomb of Gordion**, the ancient capital of Phrygia.

The second floor covers Syria, Palestine and Cyprus, through sculpture and other objects, including the famous **Gezer calendar** (925 BC), the most ancient Hebrew text known to exist.

Slightly dusty and disorganised, the **Museum of the Ancient Orient** has nevertheless a collection of remarkable objects from Anatolian civilisations (Urartu, Hatti and Hittite), Arabia, Egypt (Sphinx, scarabs, funerary shields and mummies) and from Mesopotamia (many examples of writing on stone tablets). One of the most interesting pieces is the famous **Treaty of Kadesh** (found in Boğazköy) which was signed between the Hittites and the Egyptians in 1269 BC. The glazed bricks from the **Ishtar Gate** (in Babylon) represent bulls and dragons with snake heads, Babylonian god-figures, and the superb **passing lions★** which decorated the approach to the sanctuary at Marduk.

The **Ceramics Museum★** (Çinili Köşk) fills a charming 15C building originally included in the Topkapı seraglio. Its façade is enhanced with a beautiful white and blue calligraphic frieze. Often neglected, this little museum is worth visiting for its beautiful ceramics from İznik, Kütahya and Çanakkale (12C to 20C). The most interesting item is the **mihrab from the İbrahim Bey mosque★** in Karaman (1432).

Beyazıt★★
Allow one day on foot (see Map II, pages 148-149)

A stone's throw from Sultanahmet, this is Oriental İstanbul, noisier and messier, but also more spellbinding and bubbling with life in the bazaars, tea-houses, and caravanserais. The streets are a show of incredible human activity. Having rediscovered its role as crossroads, this neighbourhood, with its sidewalk stalls and opulent boutiques, attracts determined shoppers from around the world: you will cross paths with traders and bargain-hunters from Sofia, Damascus, Tashkent and Moscow, at the least. Here, there are few Byzantine vestiges, but imposing Ottoman architecture dedicated to the glory of Allah is omnipresent with the unavoidable Beyazıt, the majestic Süleymaniye or the little jewel of Rüstem Paşa. In the tight maze of little streets the traffic is so intense, that it is much easier to get around on foot, as well as far more rewarding.

The Divan Yolu (Map II D4)
This grand and busy street follows the line of the ancient *Mese*, a commercial artery which crossed the Roman and Byzantine city from west to east through the *Augusteon* (the forum). Traffic is forbidden between Çarşıkapı and Sultanahmet but a tramway line, used daily by 150 000 commuters, runs from Sirkeci to Aksaray (3.5km). Cross the road with care: unwary tourists have more than once been caught with a foot stuck between the tracks of the tram line!

On the right, at the corner of Türbedar Sokak, the **Mahmud II Mausoleum** (*9.30am-4.30pm, closed Mondays, free*), a small Baroque building (1839), sits regally in the middle of a humble cemetery alongside a café terrace.

The adjacent **Burnt Column** (Çemberlitaş), 35m high, is barely noticeable. It was however, the symbol of the Byzantine Empire: Constantine inaugurated it in the forum on May 11, 330, the day when Byzantium became the capital under the name of Constantinople. Beneath it, he placed pagan, Christian and Jewish relics in order to symbolise the unity of his Empire. In the 11C, the collapse of the statue which topped it killed several people. After the fire of 1779, it was encircled with iron.

Beyazıt Square* (Beyazıt Meydanı) (Map II C3)

To the west of Sultanahmet rises the third hill of Byzantium where the Ottomans built their first palace after their conquest. At the top of the hill, Beyazıt Square is a focus of both spiritual and intellectual life as well as of the commercial activity spilling over from the Grand Bazaar. Seat yourself in the vast shaded terrace located in the square and enjoy the show.

Dominating the area, the **Beyazıt Mosque's** sombre mass has been blackened by the city's dust. It is the only vestige of İstanbul's most ancient Imperial complex (1501-1505). Like many Ottoman buildings, in incorporates Byzantine elements, namely the green cracked columns of the courtyard and Imperial tribune (unusually located on the right of the *minbar*). The **Türbe of Beyazıt II** (the founder) is visible in the small cemetery behind the mosque.

The grand side grille leads to the **university**, a vast construction designed by a Frenchman, Bourgeois (1886). On the far side of the campus, rises a 50m-high **observation tower (Beyazıt tower)**; built in 1828, its function was to detect fires. West of the square, the ancient medrese of the mosque houses the **Museum of Calligraphy** (Türk Vakıf Hat Sanatları Müzesi) (Map II B3) (*9am-4pm, open Tuesday and Wednesday only, due to budget cutbacks. It is your responsibility to turn the lights in the display cases on and off*). In the former student quarters, old vibrantly coloured Korans and beautiful examples of calligraphy are displayed.

Behind the mosque, the **Sahaflar Çarşısı** (Map II C3) is a small, charming **second hand book traders'** market where you can find all sorts of cards, new and used books, in English and Turkish, as well as beautiful etchings and coloured prints. At the entrance, you might see a long-bearded man advertising his book, *Before I Die*. The Grand Bazaar is located just behind the book market.

The Grand Bazaar** (Kapalı Çarşı) (Map II C3)

9am-7pm in summer, 6pm in winter; especially busy between 10am and 6pm; closed Sundays. Allow 1hr to visit or a half-day if you plan to shop.

Although it is a cliché, this Bazaar truly is Ali Baba's cave, sparkling with a thousand lights and colours on the jewels and carpets. After all, this is the world's most famous market. In spite of the massive influx of tourists and consumer goods, it has not lost any of its authenticity. Juggling your time and your money is no easy feat. The ritual of bargaining requires skill and patience. Commerce overflows in all the *han* and alleys of the district. At closing time, the crowds make it almost impossible to move about. Porters carrying heavy loads of clothes on their backs or pushing trolleys overloaded with cartons, tea vendors with their little trays and vehicles stuffed with wares struggling in the little streets, are a constant threat to unwary toes!

The bazaar has been rebuilt several times since the first wood-covered market opened (1461). The current market rose after the earthquake of 1894 and was renovated after the fire of 1954. The heart of the Grand Bazaar is the **İçbedesten** (44mx33m). The **Sandal Bedesteni** was added at a later date and hosts auctions, three times a week, around 1pm. From here, the market spread outwards over a vast area, which, by the end of the 19C, held 61 streets, 4 399 stores, 2 195 work-shops, 497 stalls, 24 caravanserais, 12 depots, a hamam, a mosque and eight fountains. The most recent addition includes half a dozen restaurants, a post office, tea-houses, two banks and the tourist information office. People enter and exit through one of the 18 doors without realising it. Inlaid wood or marble, jewellery, carpets, copper, gold, ceramics, antiquities, clothes, leather goods, souvenirs, hookahs, water pipes are all there for purchase. Jewellery shops are located in the **Kuyumcular** and **Kalpakçılar** (main) alleys, while the antiquarians are in the İçbedesten, close to the carpets. The leather goods shops are mostly grouped on the right side of the main street.

To the southeast of the Bazaar, the **Nuruosmaniye Gate** leads to a pleasant pedestrian street with shops selling luxury goods and an 18C Baroque mosque.

J.-F. Galmiche

The vaulted alleys of the Grand Bazaar

The Caravanserais
(Map II C2-3)

Around the Grand Bazaar, there are approximately 30 han built between the 15C and the 20C. Their layout was designed according to the shape of the surrounding streets. Some have kept their original function, while others are used as workshops or depots which are in various states of disrepair but always buzzing with activity. The fief of jewellers, the **Zincirli Han** (*in the northeast corner of the Bazaar*) is undoubtedly one of the most beautiful and well preserved (late 18C). However, the most impressive is still the **Büyük Valide Hanı***(*north of the Grand Bazaar*). Built in 1651, it is İtanbul's largest caravanserai. Take the stairs on the left underneath the second porch at the end of the right gallery and then the second set of darkened stairs which lead to the roof. The **view**** is exceptional. The noise emanating from the tiny workshops which flank the long, dim corridors belongs to the weavers and their ancient craft.

Moscow-İstanbul-Moscow

Since the collapse of the USSR, historic trading routes have once again become active. Attracted by İstanbul's markets where everything is available and at bargain prices (underwear, jeans, coats, leather goods, shoes), the Russians are drawn like magnets and account for the majority of the population. They are known as the Chelnoki ("those who commute"). Women make up the bulk of these travellers, and prostitution is well developed: approximately 3 000 "Natashas", regularly shuttle to İstanbul. Local authorities tolerate this situation, although it is well known that the bulk of the profit feeds the coffers of Russian and Azeri Mafia organisations.

The Egyptian Bazaar* (Mısır Çarşısı) (Map II D2)
Go down Mahmutpaşa Yokuşu Cad until you reach Alaca Hamam Cad. Facing Eminönü Pier, 8.30am-6.30pm, closed Sundays.

Tourists flock here to stock up on Turkish delight and spices; the Egyptian Bazaar becomes a busy beehive in the late afternoon. Located inside a handsome U-shaped building (rebuilt in 1943), it consists of a collection of countless shops overflowing with large sacks of grain and coloured powders whose mixed vanilla, cinnamon and cumin aromas fill the air. The bazaar's trade dates back to the times when Genoese and Venetians came to sell perfumes, spices and drugs. However, the majority of the current 88 shops specialise more in woven baskets, jewellery, local crafts and food items (Turkish delight, pastries, and cold cuts). Observe the spectacle at a comfortable distance from the famous **Pandelı** restaurant (*see "Making the most of İstanbul"*) located on the first floor, above the entrance.

Not far from the Egyptian Bazaar, at the foot of the hill, stands the **New Mosque** (Yeni Cami) (Map II D2), begun in 1597 by the Safiye Valide and completed by Mehmet IV in 1663. To the northeast, the **Imperial Pavilion** (*hünkar kasrı*) is connected to the mosque by a vaulted portal, whereas the western side leads to a courtyard decorated with a beautiful octagonal **ablutions fountain*** covered with delicate blue **tiles**.

From the Egyptian Bazaar, go west along Hasırcılar Cad, a much quieter street.

The newly renovated **Rüstem Paşa Mosque*** (Map II C2) is 200m away (*access up a little stairway*).

This masterpiece was built by Sinan (1561) for the Grand Vizier and son-in-law of Süleyman the Magnificent. The sumptuous **İznik tiles**** of the façade and the interior – a wonderful variety of floral and geometric motifs – create one of the most beautiful collections of İstanbul.

To reach the Süleyman Mosque on the third hill, cross the Tahtakale district, home of iron-mongers, glass-makers and cabinet-makers.

The Süleyman Mosque*** (Süleymaniye Camii) (Map II B2)

Sinan dreamed of surpassing the Greek architects of the Ayasofya. With the Süleymaniye (which he considered to be his greatest work after the Selimiye in Edirne), the architect offered Süleyman a jewel worthy of the splendour of his reign. It is the largest of Sinan's mosques (built 1550-1557) set in a vast complex which includes five medrese, an *imaret*, a hospice, hospital and hamam. A true city within the city, the complex was financed by the Sultan and from the revenues of the hamam and the bazaar.

Flanked by four minarets, the **mosque**★★ is preceded by a **courtyard** shaded by a portico whose columns were formerly in the hippodrome. It is a sturcture of great elegance, in terms of both its architecture and decoration. Sinan deliberately emphasised the load-bearing elements of his buildings – bold cornices, free-standing pillars and well-defined arches – playing simultaneously with the effects of spherical and flat surfaces. The **prayer room** (70x60m) is covered by a 53m-high, 27.5m-wide dome resting on four pillars. The eye is drawn upwards by the complex geometry of Sinan's superstructure, illuminated by the daylight streaming through the 138 stained-glass windows. The **mihrab** and **minbar** in white marble, the walls covered in blue tiles and the wooden doors inlaid with mother-of-pearl and ivory are in perfect harmony with the surrounding space. The **galleries,** where the Court dignitaries were seated, are supported by porphyry columns (including the famous **column of Virginity**, originally in the church of the Holy Apostles).

In the **cemetery** behind the mosque, see the striking **Süleyman türbe** (*9.30am-4.30pm, closed Mondays*), an octagonal structure with a dome, decorated with İznik tiles, and the equally elegant one belonging to his wife, **Roxelana** (renamed Hürrem). Nearby, a **medrese** with an unusual layout contains 22 cubicles aligned along the garden. To the east, the mosque is flanked by Mimar Sinan Caddesi, an old *arasta* (market street) where you can find two identical **medrese** housing boutiques and workshops. Their arcades face those supporting the **terrace gardens** on the opposite side of the street (*accessible by a set of stairs*) where there is a very pleasant **view**★ of the district and the Golden Horn.

At the end of the street stands the **Mausoleum of Sinan**. In the northwest corner of the mosque, the **tabhane** (hospice), the **imaret** (kitchens converted into restaurants) and the **darüzziyafe** (hospital) are situated next to each other. Finally, to the southwest, the **Evvel and Sani medrese** were formerly the seat of the highly-reputed Tıp medical school. These two schools, separated by a narrow alley, house one of İstanbul's most famous libraries, containing 32 000 manuscripts. Shops and restaurants line the street up to the ancient **mektep** (primary school), to the southwest, which functions as a children's library.

From Süleymaniye Camii to Şehzade Camii

To the east, there is a popular residential district with cobblestone streets (*around the Şifa Hane Cad*), where a few beautiful **old wooden homes** survive. Next, the **Prince's Mosque** (Şehzade Camii) (Map II A3) (*under renovation*) appears. It is a vestige of Sinan's first Imperial İstanbul complex (1544-1548), which he considered to be part of his apprenticeship. The two octagonal **minarets**, with their balconies and geometric bas-relief are extremely elegant. Sinan decided to design a portico along the north and south façades to hide the buttresses which gave the building a heavy appearance. In the garden, the **türbe**★ of Mehmet, Rüstem Paşa and İbrahim Paşa are decorated with İznik tiles from the most beautiful period (16C), with noteworthy examples of *cuerda seca* ("dried rope", cloisonné enamel).

İstanbul

From the shade of nearby Saraçhane park, there is a beautiful **view**★ of the **Valens Aqueduct**★ (Bozdoğan Kemeri) (Map II A2), a sort of 800m-long dinosaur, which for the last 16 centuries has dominated the cityscape with its outline. It is the most eminent vestige of Roman İstanbul, linking the third and fourth hills, 26m above Atatürk Bulvarı. Damaged several times by earthquakes, it was always rebuilt because of its important role of providing water to the palaces. Unfortunately, an important element was destroyed in 1912 during reconstruction work around the Fatih mosque.

Underneath the aqueduct, take a look at the **Museum of Caricature and Humour** (Karikatür ve Mizah Müzesi) *(10am-5pm, free)* located inside the Gazanfer Ağa medrese (17C). The numerous drawings, some quite old, in this little museum illustrate the satirical and irreverent spirit of the Turks. A tradition which lives on, as you probably will notice on any street corner.

From St Saviour-in-Chora to the Fatih District★★

Have a taxi drop you off at St Saviour-in-Chora, and if you have 2hr to spare, walk down to Fatih (see Map I, p 142-143)

The district between St Saviour-in-Chora and Fatih displays another facet of İstanbul: Islamic around the Fatih mosque, Byzantine in the surrounding forgotten churches, and in all instances thoroughly working-class and deeply Anatolian. Laundry hangs from the windows of the decrepit buildings and the streets are awash with litter. You are likely to encounter a passer-by dragging a lamb or a man riding a donkey struggling up a small street.

Close to the Church of St Saviour-in-Chora, you can admire a portion of **Constantine's Wall**★ (Map I A3), a UNESCO World Heritage Site. It still delineates the landscape, and in some places continues to serve to define the city limits. The visible section was built in 413 by Theodosius II. Destroyed by an earthquake shortly thereafter in 447, when Attila's army was a threat, it was quickly rebuilt thanks to donations made by local citizens.

Near the ramparts, the **Palace of Constantine Porphyrogenetus** (Tekfur Sarayı) (Map I A3), is one of the rare examples of late civil Byzantine architecture (*a woman caretaker will eagerly await your arrival and ask you for a few coins*). It was built at the end of the 13C by the Paleologian emperors who lived there until their downfall. The inner courtyard serves as a children's playground. The white marble and red brick **façade**★ is an empty shell without a roof or floor. The windows are surmounted by a double-arched vault in marble and brick, and the wall is decorated with geometric motifs and the Paleologian monogram. Every level of the palace had only one room, which was vast and spacious.

The Church of St Saviour-in-Chora★★★ (Kariye Camii) (Map I A3)
9am-4pm, closed Wednesdays, entrance fee.

The church has one of the most beautiful sets of Byzantine mosaics in the world. Built at the end of the 11C, on the foundations of a 7C monastery, the church was converted into a mosque in 1511. Its importance grew in the 12C because of its proximity to the palace of the Blachernae, the residence of the emperors. In the 14C, **Theodore Metochites**, administrator of the treasury under Andronic II, added the triple gallery and the funerary chapel which he had decorated with mosaics, frescoes and marble.

G. Degeorge

The extraordinary **frescoes***** and **mosaics***** of St Saviour-in-Chora, contemporary to the works of Giotto, display the realism and sensibility of the Renaissance. Spirituality and naturalism also translate the aesthetic tendencies of the last golden age of Byzantine art and its enlightened spirit. The renovations undertaken in the 1950s have restored the beauty of these masterpieces: the dazzle of the gold and the vivid colours, the poetic painting of the faces, the finesse of their features, the realistic appearance of the clothing, the proliferation of picturesque details in each mosaic, are breathtaking. The works in the narthex and the exonarthex, where the less constraining order of the composition allowed the artists a free reign on their imagination, are superb. The mosaics of the **exonarthex** tell the story of the voyage of Joseph and Mary to Bethlehem, the life of Christ before his meeting with St John the Baptist, the Temptation and various miracles. In the **narthex**, other miracles of Christ are represented, accompanied by episodes of Mary's childhood according to the apocryphal Protoevangelium of St James. One of the domes shows Christ surrounded by the patriarchs and representatives of the 12 tribes of Israel. In another, the Virgin is surrounded by characters from the Old Testament, and above the door of the nave, Theodore Metochites offers the church to Christ.

Masterpieces of Byzantine art: the mosaics of St Saviour-in-Chora

The **nave** has lost a large part of its decoration, undoubtedly scenes of important religious feasts. Surviving are a **Dormition** (Assumption of the Virgin), a Madonna with Child *(on the right)* and Christ holding an open book *(on the left)*.

The well-preserved frescoes of the **paraclesion** surprise the observer with their vigour, beauty and sheer size. The artist, perhaps the same one who created the mosaics, displayed great originality in choosing themes which showed a wealth of knowledge of religious writings. In the first bay, the **Madonna with Child** appears, surrounded by angels. On the pendentives of the dome, portraits of four poets are featured, while the arches and medallions illustrate different episodes of the Old Testament. The main work of the second bay is the **Last Judgement*** overlooking a **psychostasy** (weighing of the souls) where naked sinners are dispatched to eternal torment.

A Byzantine Humanist

A humanist with an innovative spirit, Theodore Metochites represented the ideal Byzantine intellectual of the 14C, sensitive to the beauty of nature and human works, uniting moral qualities, universal knowledge and a desire to be involved in worthy causes. He was a diplomat, theologian, astronomer, poet and benefactor. Conscious of what was obsolete in Byzantine culture despite the fact that it was in a period of full renaissance, he felt above all that he was in charge of a legacy. The main advisor to Andronic II, Metochites fell out of favour with Andronic III. His palace was destroyed and pillaged by the people. He retired to the monastery of Chora, where he died in 1332.

In a more joyful spirit, the frescoes of the apse illustrate the theme of the **resurrection**, in particular one depicting Christ freeing Adam and Eve from the tomb. The lower paintings represent saints often wearing armour. A rare sight to behold, there are even angels bearing arms. All are there as a reminder of the Ottoman threat which exalted military virtues. The tomb at the back of the chapel belongs to Theodore Metochites.

Around the church of St Saviour-in-Chora, the **Kariye Meydanı** is a pleasant little shaded square whose renovated wooden houses have been converted to souvenir shops, restaurants and hotels, a change somewhat at odds with the otherwise impoverished surroundings. This initiative nevertheless conflicts with the humble means of the district's inhabitants.

On the way down to Fatih, take the time to visit the **Church of Theotokos Pammakaristos★** (Fethiye Camii) (Map I B3) *(ask the guardian in the courtyard for the key).* Set in an empty lot, today it functions as a mosque. Built between the end of the 12C and the beginning of the 14C, it was the seat of the Orthodox Patriarch until 1586. Its **paraclesion** (funerary chapel) preserves a remarkable collection of 14C **mosaics★★** on a golden background (brought to light during the 1960s by the American Byzantine Institute). On the pendentives of the dome appear the 12 prophets surrounding Christ in Majesty. His finely represented features express sorrow and joy. The conch of the apse is adorned with a **Hyperagatos ("All-Loving") Christ** while in a niche, on the left, stand the **Virgin Mary** and **St John the Baptist**. Among the other mosaics, the **Baptism of Christ** is the oldest *(on the right wall next to the choir).*

Continue along the Fethiye Camii Cad, then the Darüşafaka Cad.

The Imperial Complex of Fatih Mehmet★ (Map I B4)

This is one of the highlights of a visit to İstanbul because of the sheer size of the complex as well as the atmosphere of the deeply Islamic district in which it stands, far removed from the over-policed and tense Sultanahmet district. Most of the women here are veiled head to toe in black, revealing another aspect of Turkey. However, İstanbul is not Kabul: there is no need to fear animosity. It is sufficient to respect local customs by being properly clothed and waiting quietly for the end of prayers. Mehmet II had the complex built between 1463 and 1470. After the earthquake of 1766 had destroyed it, the mosque was rebuilt in the Baroque style. Of the old complex, only the courtyard, main entrance, mihrab, the base of the minaret, the southern wall of the cemetery and the adjacent door survive.

The decoration of the **mosque** is nothing exceptional, except for the **minbar**, an elegant Baroque structure in polychrome marble and the beautiful white marble **calligraphy** which decorates the western windows.

Spend some time in the **cemetery**, behind the mosque, where the striking **türbe of Fatih Mehmet★** (Mehmet II, known as the "conqueror", *see p 26*) lies regally. According to tradition, recently-enthroned sultans would gather here to find inspiration from their glorious ancestors.

Beyoğlu★★

Allow 2 days to visit. You are likely to spend most of your evenings here! (see Map III, p 167)

On the far bank of the Golden Horn stretches Beyoğlu, a district with a reputation as a gathering place for intellectuals, and an aura of glamour. This is the modern showcase which Turkey likes to present to the world, the side which allows it to claim its place among European nations. Utterly different from Sultanahmet, it is the essential complement to it. It is more than just lively, with its bars crammed full of local people (women as well as men) knocking back their rakı, conversing loudly, sing and dancing until the wee hours. Here, mosques give way to palaces, four-star hotels and the international boutiques which flourish around İstiklal Caddesi. Galata had long claimed its own distinct identity, and it was able to obtain, under the Genoese, the status of a separate city. It's on this side of the Golden Horn that the embassies and the central insitutions of Ottoman power were established in the 19C. In front of the Yeni Cami, the **New Galata Bridge** (Yeni Galata Köprüsü) (Map III A5) straddles the Golden Horn. It replaces the one that was ravaged by fire in 1991. Fishermen and illegal street vendors have wasted little time in claiming it, while the galleries along the water are still awaiting the planned fish restaurants.

The Galata Tower watches over Karaköy

J.-F. Galmiche

Istanbul

A small detour on the right after the bridge leads to the **Yeraltı Camii** (Map III B5), an **underground mosque** unique in its style, radically different from Sinan's works. The entrance is on Kemankeş Caddesi, just behind the Karaköy waterfront, a scene of constant activity. The mosque's low ceiling and its countless pillars give it a labyrinth-like appearance.

Galata Hill★

You can spare yourself the walk up the hill by taking the funicular. However, it would be a pity to miss the street activity on the little side streets. Many of them are specialised in a particular activity (musical instruments, antiques, second-hand books etc). Always clogged and bubbling with frenetic activity, Yüzbaşı Sabahattin Evren Caddesi, which becomes Tersane Caddesi, is a centre for the plumber's trade. Cars, trolleys, hand-carts, and pedestrians rival for every inch of space, but there is a method to the madness.

Drowning in this sea of humanity, the entrance to the **funicular** (*Yüzbaşı Sabahattin Evren Cad, departures every 5-10min until 10pm, tokens sold at the entrance*) is barely visible. The pride of İstanbul, this 560m underground line is the oldest in the world (1874) after those of New York and London.

On the left after number 51, the **Kurşunlu Hanı** (Map III A5), one of İstanbul's oldest caravanserais (1550) designed by Sinan, becomes visible. A wild grapevine has invaded its ruined walls, but craftsmen are busy toiling away in its many workshops. Next door, do not miss the **Galata Bedesten**, an appealing little covered market dating from the 15C.

Opposite, **Perşembe Pazarı Sokağı** ("Thursday Market Street"), climbs up the hills among the elegant 18C **brick and stone houses** with projecting upper storeys.

Turn left on Galata Mahkemesi Sokak to reach the **Mosque of the Arabs** (Arap Camii) (Map III A4), which owes it name to the Moors who settled in the district during the 16C. Tersane Caddesi is dominated by a tall red-brick belfry; which functions as a minaret. The square layout and the woodwork of this ancient 14C Dominican monastery give it the astonishing appearance of a Gothic mosque.

Nearby, the Camondo stairs lead to **St Peter Han** (*Eski Banka Sokak*), built in the 18C, by the French ambassador, on the site of the home and birthplace of the French poet André Chénier. Higher up, in Galata Kulesi Sokak, the **Catholic Church of St Peter and St Paul** (Map III A4) becomes visible. Restored in 1841, it has been administered by the Dominicans since the 15C.

At the end of the street, the **Galata Tower★** (Galata Kulesi) (Map III A4) appears suddenly, sombre and imposing, rising 68m above a little square (*9am-9pm, entrance fee*). A restaurant fills the last floor (*accessible by elevator*), a panoramic balcony with an impressive 360° **view★★** over the entire city. Built in 1348, it was the principal bastion of the Genoese fortifications. Later, the Ottomans removed the last two floors and used the tower as a prison and subsequently as a watch tower to guard against fires. Hezarfen Ahmet Çelebi flew off its summit in the 17C and reached Üsküdar with wings of his own making, and is considered to be the first man to fly. As compensation for his exploit, he received a gold coin from the sultan. However, he ended up in exile in Algiers.

On your way, take a look at the **Tekke of the Whirling Dervishes** (Map III A3), an ancient 15C monastery rebuilt in the 18C (*9.30am-5pm, closed Mondays, in Galip Dede Cad, between the Galata Tower and the terminus of the funicular*).The interior houses different objects related to the dervishes. Since green spaces are a rarity in İstanbul, you will appreciate a pause in the adjacent **small cemetery**, filled with tombstones crowned with Dervish turbans or hats.

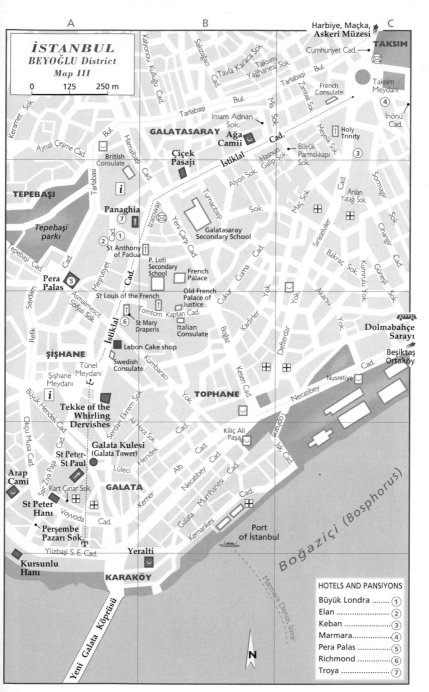

İSTANBUL
BEYOĞLU District
Map III

0   125   250 m

TAKSIM

Harbiye, Maçka,
Askeri Müzesi

Cumhuriyet Cad.

French
Consulate

Taksim
Meydanı

İnönü
Cad.

Holy
Trinity

Büyük
Parmakkapı
Sok.

Kahyonou Küllüğü Cad.

Sakızağacı

Tavla Karaca Sok.

Taksim
Yağhanesi Sok.

Bul.

Tarlabaşı Cad.

Mis Sok.

Zambak Sok.

Meşelik Sok.

Hasnun Galip Sok.

Keramet Sok.

Aynalı Çeşme Cad.

Bul.

Tarlabaşı

Tarlabaşı

GALATASARAY

Ağa
Camii

İmam Adnan
Sok.

İstiklal   Cad.

Sormagir

British
Consulate

Hamalbaşı Cad.

Çiçek
Pasajı

Alyon Cad.

Arslan
Yatağı Sok.

TEPEBAŞI

Tepebaşı
parkı

Panaghia

St Anthony
of Padua

Meşrutiyet Cad.

tramway

Turnacıbaşı

Yeni Çarşı Cad.

Galatasaray
Secondary School

Sok.

Maç Sok.

Sıraselviler

Bakraç Sok.

Çangir Sok.

Güneşli Sok.

Kumrulu Yok.

Tepebaşı Cad.

Cad.

Saydam

P. Loti
Secondary
School

French
Palace

Cuma Cad.

Yok.

Akarsu

Pera
Palas

St Louis of the French

Asmalımescit

Sofyalı Sok.

Old French
Palace of
Justice

Çukur

Kadirler

Yok.

Defterdar

Dolmabahçe
Sarayı

Beşiktaş
Ortaköy

Refik

İstiklal   Cad.

Tomtom

Kaptan Cad.

St Mary
Draperis

Italian
Consulate

Boğaz

Lebon Cake shop

ŞİŞHANE

Tünel
Meydanı

Şişhane
Meydanı

Swedish
Consulate

Kumbaracı

TOPHANE

Yok.

Kesen Cad.

Nusretiye

Necatibey

Büyük Hendek Cad.

Tekke of the
Whirling
Dervishes

Serdar Ekrem Sok.

Ali Hoca Sok.

Cad.

Kılıç Ali
Paşa

Tophane Cad.

İsk. Cad.

Okçu Musa Cad.

Galata Kulesi
(Galata Tower)

St Peter-
St Paul

Hendek

Lüleci

Altı

Cad.

Kemer

Necatibey

Cad.

Mumhanesi Cad.

Cad.

GALATA

Arap
Cami

St Peter
Hanı

Şair Ziya Paşa

Kart Çınar Sok.

Voyvoda

Cad.

Galata

Kemankes Cad.

Port
of İstanbul

Boğaziçi (Bosphorus)

Perşembe
Pazarı Sok.

Yüzbaşı S. E. Cad.

Yeralti

Kursunlu
Hanı

KARAKÖY

Yeni Galata Köprüsü

Marmara Denizi, İzmir

N

HOTELS AND PANSIYONS

Büyük Londra	①
Elan	②
Keban	③
Marmara	④
Pera Palas	⑤
Richmond	⑥
Troya	⑦

A   B   C

167

İstiklal Caddesi★ (Map III A3, C1)

The former Grand-Rue de Pera, remembered fondly by all who appreciated the cosmopolitan İstanbul of yesteryear, stretches 2.2km between the funicular (tünel) and Taksim Square. Returned to pedestrians at the beginning of the 1990s, it is travelled by a tramway reminiscent of San Francisco's cable cars. The district's children amuse themselves by hitching a free ride on the back. By the end of the 19C, the street had public lighting, pavements and a tramway, and took on the appearance of a Parisian or Viennese boulevard. In the years following World War II, rumour has it, it was out of the question to stroll there without being elegantly attired. İstiklal Caddesi has preserved some beautiful relics: old embassies, restaurants, palaces, covered galleries and bookstores, flanked by the tough competition of clothes stores and shops and stalls selling cassette tapes. The surrounding streets house İstanbul's night-life, pubs for trendy youths, bars where both old and young gather to sing and dance. On the right (*no 497*), behind an iron grille, the 17C **Swedish Consulate** is hidden behind a garden. Further on, the **Botter Building** (*no 495*), by the Italian architect Aronco, has a beautiful Art Nouveau façade.

On the corner of Asmalımescit Sokak, the Markiz Pastanesi (the former **Lebon Cake Shop**), with a pleasant Modern Style decor, was once very popular.

The little street descends toward the **Pera Palas Hotel★** (Map III A2) (*Meşrutiyet Cad 98*), a glorious landmark of late 19C İstanbul. The hotel's magnificent salons are worth a visit. The rooms have lost some of their lustre since Atatürk, Sarah Bernhardt, Agatha Christie, Zsa Zsa Gabor, Charles Boyer and nearly all of Europe's royalty stayed there (*see "Making the most of İstanbul"*).

Returning along the small Piremeci street, notice the eccentric **Suriye alleyway**, where five levels of access balconies criss-cross the narrow street.

Hold on tight on İstiklal Caddesi!

G. Boucher/TOP

The Marmara Region

On the right of Tomtom Kaptan Sokak, a small square is the setting of a Venetian palace with an elegant yellow façade housing the **Italian Consulate**. The building on the left, with the motto *"Lois, Justice, Force"*, housed the **Old French Palace of Justice**, which had the authority to prosecute foreigners in İstanbul. In the same block can be found the **Pierre Loti Secondary School**, the Church of St Louis of the French, the residence of the French Consul and the **Old Palace of France**, a

An Old Western Presence

France was the first major Christian nation to establish relations with the Ottomans. By creating an alliance with Süleyman the Magnificent, François I made a pact with the devil but warded off Charles V. In 1536, he installed a permanent ambassador to the Sublime Porte and obtained important commercial favours. The western embassies were virtual mini-states and had the capacity to try their own nationals. When chased by the police, a Western subject simply tossed his passport on the ground and stood on it by invoking extra-territoriality. This system disappeared with the proclamation of the Republic.

Louis-Philippe-style building (Nuri Ziya Sokak). A little haven of peace in the middle of the tumult, the astonishing **Panaya Greek Orthodox Church** (Panaghia) (1803) is concealed in Emir Nevruz Sokak.

Half-way up İstiklal Caddesi stands the **Galatasaray Secondary School**. Founded in 1868 to train the elite of the Empire in the art of French thought, its splendour has faded but it is very likely that any French-speaking guides you may hear have been schooled there. On the opposite side, the old **Post Office** is housed in an elegant 1875 marble building *(being renovated to house the new Postal Museum)*.

Equally known as the *Cité de Pera (left side)*, the **Flower passage*** (Çiçek Pasaj) (Map III B2) is a very busy area in the evening. It was built in the Rococo style in 1876. Above the shops, the floors were subdivided into luxurious apartments. Restaurants and "pubs" opened around 1940 and quickly became the watering holes of intellectuals and the powerful. The area, albeit somewhat invaded by tourists, has not lost any of its charm. Large numbers of small restaurants have opened up, featuring meze, cold cuts and spicy grilled mutton tripe *(kokoreç)* accompanied by rakı. Tradition held that a new restaurant's competitors should offer sumptuous flower wreaths, hence the name. The jolly atmosphere spills over into Sahne Sokağı, the **Fish market** street.

Just before Taksim Square, on the left, the **Institute of French Studies** (French Consulate) often displays art exhibits.

Taksim Square (Map III C1) (a distortion of *maksem*, the "reservoir"), around the Opera House is a vast esplanade lacking in charm, over-run with traffic. It is home to a large number of international hotels, including The Marmara.

Towards the North

(see Map I, p 143). Go up Cumhuriyet Cad, 1.5km until you reach Vali Konağı Cad, on the right.

A visit to the **Military Museum** (Askeri Müze) (Map I D2), if the time is right, will allow you to see the colourful **military band of the Janissaries** in costume *(Museum: 9am-5pm, closed Mondays and Tuesdays. Concerts 3pm-4pm, in front of the entrance)*. The opulence and sheer size of the museum give an idea of the importance of the Turkish army. Displays include the reconstruction of the Ottomans' plan of attack on Constantinople, fascinating miniature models and the obligatory profusion of all types of arms from all periods. Upstairs, a room has displays on Turkey's role in the Cyprus conflict of 1974. The **Imperial tents** should not be missed.

İstanbul

Halfway from Yıldız Park, the **Ihlamur Kasrı** (Map I D2) *(9.30am-5pm, closed Mondays and Thursdays)*, is a secret oasis. In this little Imperial summer palace of the 19C, surrounded by a lovely garden, Abdülmecid I received the French writer and statesman Lamartine. The pavilion in the back has a Rococo façade, enclosing an elegant salon whose ceiling is decorated with exuberant golden mouldings. You may find it hard to resist stopping for refreshments at the old ceremonial house, near the water basin.

Dolmabahçe Palace** (Dolmabahçe Sarayı) (Map I D3)

9.30am-4pm (3pm for the harem), closed Mondays and Thursdays. Entrance fee, extra for the harem. 45min guided tours, and 35min for the harem. Security check at the entrance. Visitors are requested not to wander away from the group.

An ostentatious palace with the allure of an Oriental Versailles, the Dolmabahçe symbolises the dying days of the Ottoman Empire. In the 19C, the sultans renounced the Topkapı residence, which they judged to be too sinister(!), falling prey to the siren song of European modernity and building a more Westernised palace in the Rococo style then in vogue in France. Built on an area of reclaimed land dating from the 17C (*dolmabahçe* means "filled garden"), the palace was begun in 1843 by the architect **Nikoğos Balyan** and his father, and completed in 1854. On the side facing the street, a high enclosure closes off the access to the park, whereas a simple grille protects its long façade (248m) on the sea-facing side. With a surface area of 15 000sqm, it includes 285 rooms spread over three sections: government, reception and harem. The heavy-handed decoration is the work of the Frenchman Sechan, who also decorated the Opera Garnier in Paris. The furniture and decorative accessories are extremely rich: Bohemian, Baccarat and Murano crystal chandeliers, Hereke wool carpets, porcelain and clocks from the entire world. When a sultan died, his successors would settle into a new section of the palace: the new sovereign would close off the old private rooms and open new ever more luxurious ones, as if this apparent abundance of wealth could erase the fact that the Empire was in decline. The palace has witnessed a number of historical events, starting with the expulsion of Abdülaziz in 1876. This is where the Republic of Turkey was declared in 1923 and where Atatürk died on November 10, 1938 at 9.05am (the city's sirens wail in his honour on this anniversary; the palace's clocks perpetually mark the hour of his death). His mortuary room is being restored.

With its salons, boudoirs and offices, the palace is an incredible labyrinth of marble, gold and crystal. Upstairs, the opulence of the **Grand Hall of the Reception of Ambassadors**** with its two elephant tusks at the entrance is striking. Created by French and Turkish craftsmen, the sumptuous 2.5-ton Baccarat crystal chandelier illuminates the gilding of the ceiling and walls. The piano is a gift from Napoleon III. In the back, on the left, is the private reception room of the ambassadors; all in red, symbol of the sultan's power.

The relaxation that the dream-like **baths**** provided can only be imagined. Made of rare Egyptian marble, they had the additional benefit of having a unique view of the Bosphorus.

From a gallery leading to the harem (behind the palace) the women could look down on the immense (2 000sqm) **Throne Room*** through the moucharaby without being seen. The **chandelier****, a gift from Queen Victoria, weighs 4.5 tonnes and has 725 light bulbs. It is the largest in the world.

At the back of the garden, on the left, is the **harem**. Here, everything is more restrained: no gilding and no Baccarat crystal. For anyone who has seen the Topkapı harem, this one will seem very modern in comparison. This difference was surely noticed by the women during their move (even though their cloistered life did not change). The eight **apartments** – of the official and non-official concubines, and the favourites – are set along a long corridor. Their layout does not vary: a bedroom, a bathroom, and one large and small living room. Besides the apartments, other rooms of interest are the **circumcision room**, the baby delivery room and the **apartments of the eunuchs** on the ground floor.

The **clock tower** (27m high) at the entrance of the park and the **Dolmabahçe Mosque** set by the water like the Ortaköy Mosque, were created by the palace's architect. Before leaving, enjoy a stroll in the palace gardens. (If you have a cup of tea on the esplanade, check the price list near the kiosk beforehand).

Further north, along the Bosphorus, the **Museum of the Sea and Caiques** (Deniz ve Kayık Müzesi) (Plan I D3) *(9.30am-4.30pm, closed Wednesdays and Thursdays; entrance fee)* contains ships' cannon, maps, ancient models, various objects having belonged to Barbarossa, as well as caiques, ancient princely boats of the Bosphorus and Golden Horn.

Yıldız Park (Map I E2)

Enter through Çırağan or at the top of Barbaros Bulvarı. Entrance fee for cars.

A vast space of greenery interspersed with lakes and kiosks, filled with rare scents, the park rolls down the hill towards the Bosphorus. Under Süleyman the Magnificent, hunting expeditions were held and in the 18C, İbrahim Paşa organised sumptuous annual galas to celebrate April's full moon.

At the top of the avenue which crosses the park, the many pavilions of the **Yıldız Chalet** (Yıldız Sale) *(9.30am-5pm, closed Mondays and Thursdays, entrance fee, group visit)* are an integral part of the palace bearing the same name. It was built in the 19C by Abdülhamid who did not feel completely safe in Dolmabahçe Palace. Seat of the declining Ottoman Empire for three decades, it later served to accommodate visiting foreign dignitaries. The chalet has a handsome red-storey yellow façade with white woodwork. The ground floor, housing the staff, is not accessible to the public. In the entrance, superb wooden **stairs** lead to the 60 rooms that were reserved for guests. They are decorated with Baccarat and Bohemian crystal chandeliers and **period furniture** (especially mother-of-pearl woodwork). The **Grand Throne Room**★, with a coffered ceiling covered with gold leaf, houses a carpet so big (406sqm) that a wall had to be knocked down to bring it into the room!

Refreshments are available in the park at the **Malta Köşkü** or the **Çadır Köşkü**, built under the reign of Abdülaziz. The **view**★★ over the Bosphorus is magnificent.

The Ortaköy District★ (Map I E2)

In the northeastern extremity of the city, between the Bosphorus and the coastal boulevard, this old fishermen's village retains a harmonious atmosphere rare in İstanbul. Flanked by its two minarets, the **Ortaköy Mosque** sits at the edge of the water with the backdrop of the majestic **Bosphorus Bridge**. It was built in the Baroque style, in 1854, by Nikoğos Balyan, the architect of Dolmabahçe Palace. The interior, which is bathed in light thanks to its large windows, is decorated with marble and gilding.

The many outdoor restaurants on the cobblestone square and in nearby streets of the **little port** create a quaint atmosphere with the added bonus of a view. The area is equally pleasant at lunch time or in the evening, for a meal, a drink or dancing in one of the night clubs.

İstanbul

Eyüp★ (Map I A2)

Map p 142. To reach the district, take a bus in Eminönü or Galata and get off at the stop by the Golden Horn, behind the Eyüp Mosque. Another possibility is to take a water taxi at the Eminönü pier, although the fare is usually exorbitant.

The Eyüp Complex★

Hidden right up the Golden Horn is one of the city's most venerated Islamic holy buildings after those of Mecca and Jerusalem. During the Ottoman period, several sultans came here to take hold of Osman's sword upon acceding to the throne. The whole area is imbued with a sense of spirituality and religious fervour.

The Eyüp Mosque (Eyüp Sultan Camii) rises over a shaded and recently renovated esplanade with souvenir shops and outdoor cafés. The original mosque was built in 1458 to honour the memory of Eyüp Ensari (Ayuub in Arabic), a companion of the Prophet, who died during the siege of Constantinople in 674. The site of the bones having been found (it seems he was already known and venerated under the Byzantines), Mehmet II decided to build a large mosque, which was completely rebuilt after the earthquake of 1766. Topped by a dome with an octagonal layout, the vast **prayer hall** does not lack elegance with its honey-hued light grey walls, its tiles, chandelier and huge blue carpet.

Birds chirp in the tree which has been growing in the small courtyard for two centuries; this courtyard connects the mosque with the founder's tomb, the **Eyüp Türbe**★ *(10am-4pm, closed Mondays)*. The tomb's remarkable **İznik tile panels**★ are the jewels of the complex. The mausoleum, which houses a footprint of the Prophet, is also a pilgrimage site: after a moment of meditation, the faithful retreat by walking backwards while reciting psalms until they reach the side corridor.

Also of interest is the **cemetery** on the side, filled with many lavish mausoleums of Ottoman dignitaries (Mehmet V, Ferhat Paşa, Sokollu Mehmet Paşa etc).

The Eyüp Cemetery

Set on the hillside along Silahtarağa Cad. Despite its wild vegetation and countless tombstones covered with lichen, this vast park filled with paths is a popular place to go for a stroll. The cemetery houses the tombs of ordinary people, as well as those of Ottoman dignitaries, who chose this site next to the Eyüp mosque for their ultimate resting place. The tombstones of men are topped by a fez, while those of women are sculpted with flowers, ornamentation forbidden by Atatürk as from 1926.

At the top of the street which crosses the cemetery, you will reach the **Pierre Loti Café**. The French novelist, a young officer at the time, was a regular customer. Several scenes of his book *Aziyadé* are set here. Since then, the two shores of the Golden Horn have seen the sprouting of many industrial buildings, but when the sun sets, the **view**★★ over the river valley remains enchanting.

Üsküdar (Map I E3-4)
Map p 143. Allow a half-day.
Boats depart from Eminönü, Kabataş, Beşiktaş (15min)

Asian İstanbul has not always shared the destiny of its European counterpart. In the 14C, the Bosphorus separated the two halves, each side an advanced post of a civilisation, one Christian, on the decline, the other Muslim, in full ascension. Avoid preconceived ideas: Üsküdar is not necessarily the most Muslim district of İstanbul, even if your visit there is likely to consist mostly of visiting mosques. It is also the place for a pleasant walk or a dinner after a romantic night crossing the Bosphorus, far from the hordes of tourists. If you have a car, Üsküdar is also the ideal starting point for exploring the Asian shore of the straits (Beylerbeyi, Kanlıca).

Boats arrive at Üsküdar İskelesi, in front of the Hakimiyeti Milliye Meydanı, the starting point for camel caravans bound in pilgrimage for Mecca in bygone times. Built on a terrace, the **İskele Camii** (1547-1548) is one of the two mosques created for the daughter of Süleyman the Magnificent. The entrance is preceded by a high porch harbouring an elegant square white marble **fountain**. A sundial decorates the southwest outer wall.

On the far side of the square where the **Ahmet III Fountain** stands, you reach the **Yeni Valide Camii** which was part of an 18C complex. The stunning wooden external structure has a direct view of the Imperial Loge. The inside encloses a part of the sacred cloth of the Kaaba. Near the entrance, the exquisite **türbe** of the *valide*, overgrown with roses, resembles an aviary.

In the street, on the left, a beautiful corner **fountain** in white marble is set against the wall of a caravanserai.

A small fish **market** keeps the nearby square busy. This is the starting point of **Hakimiyeti Milliye Caddesi**, the main commercial street of the district. Slightly further up, at the corner of Büyük Hamam Sokağı, is the **Sinan Hamam Çarşısı**, an old hamam converted into a **shopping arcade**.

All along the **docks**, there are men fishing; small craft serve as restaurants where you can sample the day's catch. Every weekend there is a village fair atmosphere as Turkish families with coal braziers cook their meals and entertain themselves by shooting at balls floating on the water. Nearby, the little **Şemsi Ahmet Paşa Camii**, another work of Sinan, remains aloof to this activity. It is true that Turks prefer to gather at the **Doğa aile çay Bahçesi** (*the other side of the street*), one of the taverns where they spend the afternoon drinking tea. This is a marvellous place for admiring the sun as it sets behind the domes and minarets of Sultanahmet. Approximately 100m from the shore, an unusual silhouette isolated in the middle of the water, the **Leander Tower** (Kızkulesi), sits atop an islet. A toll station in ancient times, in the 12C, it served as an anchoring point for a huge chain which closed off the Bosphorus and linked it to Seraglio Point. The islet was successively home to a beacon, a signal post (semaphore), a quarantine centre, and a customs station. The current building is from the 18C.

Take a taxi to continue the visit.

1.5km east of the disembarkation point, you will reach **Atik Valide Camii** (*being renovated*). It was part of a vast complex which included a prison. Preceded by a lovely courtyard, the mosque is one of Sinan's major works (1583), with a sophisticated layout consisting of a hexagon inside a rectangle. The **İznik tile** calligraphy is remarkable.

Due east, 500m away, in Valide İmareti Sokak, the **Tile Mosque** (Çinili Cami) (1640) resembles a Byzantine building with its stone walls and its red masonry. It too is decorated with superb blue **İznik tiles**.

From here, it is best to take a taxi to continue exploring towards the south.

A relaxing place to walk, the **Karaca Ahmet Cemetery** (Map I E5) (Karaca Ahmet Mezarlığı), is the largest in İstanbul, and also one of the oldest. It is possible to stroll for hours on end in this immense wooded park, peppered with hundreds of tombstones and mausoleums lost in the vegetation.

Finally, head north, under the Bosphorus bridge, by bus or taxi.

İstanbul

Beylerbeyi Palace★ (Beylerbeyi Sarayı) (Map I F2)

9.30am-4pm, 3pm in winter and on holidays, closed Mondays and Thursdays. Entrance fee. Guided tour.

This ancient summer palace, adorned in marble, rises up in the middle of a pleasant garden surrounded by small kiosks. As with the Dolmabahçe, a long pier flanks the Bosphorus which can be contemplated from the terraces above. Built in 1865 for Abdülaziz, it welcomed several famous visitors, such as Empress Eugénie of France. Its very eclectic style is a successful blend of Western influence and Ottoman tradition. It includes a **haremlik** reserved for women and **selamlık**, a private area for men.

Making the most of İstanbul

COMING AND GOING
Also see the Practical Information section for Turkey.

By air – Atatürk international airport is 20km west of the city centre, at Yeşilköy, near the Sea of Marmara. Buses (run by the Havaş company) depart from Taksim Cad, near the square, every hour from 6am-11pm (journey time: 30min to 1hr). The recently extended airport is under heightened security owing to the threat of terrorist attacks. Searches upon entry and scuffles are a regular occurrence, so it is advisable to arrive well in advance. The domestic flights terminal is 800m away and is served by a shuttle.
Airport:
information, ☎ (212) 663 64 00; reservations, ☎ (212) 663 63 63.

By train – There is no direct train from London and the journey takes about 70hr. Not only that, but it will cost you more than some return flights. Trains depart from London every day, with connections in Paris, Vienna, Munich or Bucharest, and arrive at **Sirkeci station** in İstanbul (Map II D2, E2). The station on the Asian side is **Haydarpaşa** (Map I, E5).

By bus – The vast new **Esenler bus station** is 7km northwest of Sultanahmet, on the road to Edirne, and is on a direct metro line (Hızlı Tramvay) from Aksaray. Most bus companies provide a shuttle service to the station and have agencies in the city-centre (İnönü Cad, near Taksim square, and at the top of Divan Yolu Cad in Sultanahmet). Most of the companies run services to the main cities in Turkey and Europe. Book in advance in summer. The Asian terminal is in **Harem**.

By car – İstanbul is approximately 3 000km from London by car; the northern route will take you across Belgium, Germany, Austria, Hungary, Romania and Bulgaria (visas are required for the last two countries), or, alternatively, you can follow the southern route via Italy, taking a ferry from Brindisi to Greece.

GETTING AROUND
The city of İstanbul has come up with a very convenient system involving a sort of magnetic pass, called an "akbil", which gives travellers access to all the city buses, boats, cable car, tramway and metro. This pass can be bought and topped up at bus ticket offices.

By bus – City bus tickets are on sale at bus stops and IETT kiosks. Monthly passes are available. Tickets are sold on board the private buses, which are orange and cream.

By shared taxi – As cheap as the buses, dolmuşes (shared yellow taxis) make numerous regular trips throughout the city. The price is fixed and is paid up front prior to departure. The famous American limousines of the 1950s are gradually being replaced by more functional vehicles, which are, sadly, less exotic.

By taxi – These are also yellow and equipped with meters (standard pick-up fare to be added). The night rate ("gece") applies from midnight-6am. It is 50 % higher than the daytime rate ("gündüz"). Taxis are convenient and cheap but it is advisable to have an idea of the route you want to take, unless you feel like taking a trip around the whole city! Make sure that the meter is working and that it is not set on the night-time rate during the day.

By tram – The İstiklal Cad tramway links Taksim to the cable car which goes down to Karaköy. Trams leave approximately every 15min. On the historical peninsula, the modern tramway goes from Sirkeci to the ramparts (Topkapı) via Beyazıt. It is quick and convenient and tickets are sold at the tram stops.

By metro – The new *Hızlı Tramvay* goes from Aksaray to the Esenler bus station in the northwest, then down to Yenibosna and Atatürk airport in the southwest. Another line is being built underground from Taksim to Şişli and Levent.

By ferry – This traditional form of transport in İstanbul enables all sorts of crossings between the banks of the Bosphorus, but is particularly convenient for travelling between the three extremities of the city: Sirkeci on the historical Eminönü peninsula, Beşiktaş more to the north of the Bosphorus, and Üsküdar on the Asian bank. Departures every 20min, on average.

By car – City traffic is anarchic and very tiring and it is easy to become lost. If you rent a car, use it for visiting the country rather than for getting around İstanbul itself.

By rental car – The international companies have agencies in the city and at the airport. The small local companies offer cheaper rates but do not give the same guarantees – far from it! They can be found near Taksim (Map III C1).
Avis, Cihangir Avis Otopark, Cihangir Cad, Taksim, ☎ (212) 249 79 41.
Budget, Cumhuriyet Cad 19-3, Taksim, ☎ (212) 253 92 00.
Europcar, Cumhuriyet Cad 47-2, Taksim, ☎ (212) 254 77 88.
Hertz, Cumhuriyet Cad 295, Taksim, ☎ (212) 241 53 23.

ADDRESS BOOK

Media – Local publications in English provide a mine of practical and cultural information. The annual *İstanbul*

Restaurant Guide lists almost all the establishments in the city. It contains a description of Turkish cuisine and wines as well as a very useful glossary. The bimonthly *İstanbul Guide*, which can be found in hotels, is an excellent source of general information. Lastly, the *Turkish Daily News* is a daily newspaper which is also summarised in the *Turkish Probe*.

Tourist information – Atatürk airport, ☎ (212) 663 07 04.
– Meşrutiyet Cad 57 K7, Galatasaray (Map III A2), ☎ (212) 243 34 72.
– Hotel Hilton Arcade, Harbiye (Map I D2), ☎ (212) 233 05 92.
– In Sultanahmet, between Ayasofya and the Blue Mosque (Map II E4), ☎ (212) 518 18 02.

Turkish Touring and Automobile Association (Türkiye Turing ve Otomobil Kurumu), Soğukçeşme Sok, Sultanahmet (Map II E3), ☎ (212) 513 36 60.

Bank / change – Currency exchanges offer better rates than the banks and hotels. They can be found in all the tourist areas and are often closed at weekends. Money can also be withdrawn by credit card, subject to a fixed charge of about US$5.

American Express, Koç American Bank, Cumhuriyet Cad 245 (Map III C1), ☎ (212) 241 02 68; and at the Hilton hotel (Harbiye).

Main post office – The *main post office* (Yeni Postane Cad, Sirkeci, open 24 hours a day) (Map II D2) has a poste restante service. Other post offices:
– Yeni Çarşı Sok, next to Galatasaray Secondary School (Map III B2).
– Cumhuriyet Cad (Taksim) (Map III C1).
– Grand Bazaar; Topkapı entrance (Map II C3).

Telephone – In public card-operated phone booths, calls are 5 times cheaper than in hotels. Calls can be made and faxes sent from the main post offices. The code for the European side of İstanbul is (0)212 and for the Asian side, (0)216.
Wake-up call, ☎ 135.
Information, ☎ 161.
Telegrams, ☎ 141.

Consulates – **British Consulate General**, Meşrutiyet Cad 34, Tepebaşı, Beyoğlu, ☎ (212) 293 75 40, Fax (212) 245 49 89.

American Consulate, Meşrutiyet Cad 104-108, Tepebaşı, ☎ (212) 251 36 02, Fax (212) 251 25 54.

Canadian Consulate, Büyükdere Cad 107 K3, Gayrettepe, ☎ (212) 272 51 74, Fax (212) 272 34 27.

Australian Consulate, Tepecik Yolu 58, Etiler, ☎ (212) 257 70 50, Fax (212) 257 76 01.

Airline companies – Air France, Cumhuriyet Cad 1, Taksim (Map III C1), ☎ (212) 256 43 56.

Austrian Airlines, Cumhuriyet Cad 6, Harbiye (Map I D2), ☎ (212) 231 28 51, Fax (212) 234 37 28.

British Airways, Cumhuriyet Cad 10, Elmadağ, ☎ (212) 234 13 00.

Cathay Pacific Airways, Cumhuriyet Cad 309/1, Harbiye (Map I D2), ☎ (212) 219 21 23, Fax (212) 234 49 99.

Delta Airlines, İstanbul Hilton Arcade, Harbiye (Map I D2), ☎ (212) 231 23 39 / (212) 233 38 20.

Gulf Air, Cumhuriyet Cad 213, Harbiye (Map I D2), ☎ (212) 231 34 50-4, Fax (212) 231 34 55.

Malaysia Airlines, Valikonağı Cad 9, Nişantaşı (Map I D2), ☎ (212) 230 64 31 / 59 68.

Olympic Airways, Cumhuriyet Cad 171a, Harbiye (Map I D2), ☎ (212) 247 301/2, (212) 246 50 81, Fax (212) 232 21 73.

Sabena, Cumhuriyet Cad 6, Elmadağ, ☎ (212) 232 22 00, Fax (212) 246 46 46

Swissair, Cumhuriyet Cad 6, Taksim (Map III C1), ☎ (212) 231 28 50.

Turkish Airlines, Cumhuriyet Cad 199-201, Harbiye (north Taksim) (Map III C1), ☎ (212) 225 05 56; Atatürk Bul 162, Aksaray (Map I B4), ☎ (212) 511 92 22.

Emergencies – Should a problem arise, contact the tourist police, whose agents generally speak English or French. Merutiyet Cad 57 (Galatasaray), ☎ (212) 245 68 75; Yerebatan Cad 2 (Sultanahmet), ☎ (212) 528 53 69.

Emergency police number, ☎ 155.

Medical service – Ambulances, ☎ 112.

International Hospital, İstanbul Cad, Yesilköy, ☎ (212) 663 30 00.

American Hospital, Güzelbahçe Sok 20, Nişantaşı, ☎ (212) 231 40 50.

German Hospital, Sıraselviler Cad 119, Taksim, ☎ (212) 293 21 50.

Laundry – Laundry services are available at the hotels and in various locations in the city.

Active Laundry, Doktor Eminpaşa Sok 14, at the top of Divan Yolu Cad (by weight) (Map III D4).

Süper Kuru Temizleme, Kalavi Sok, near the Büyük Londra Hotel (by garment) (Map III A2).

Dry cleaning at the **Marmara hotel**, Taksim Square, ☎ (212) 251 46 96 (Map III C1).

WHERE TO STAY

Prices indicated are for a double room in summer. They can often be negotiated, especially in winter (up to a 30% discount). Breakfast is usually included. There is a greater choice of accommodation in Eminönü than in Beyoğlu.

• **Sultanahmet** (Map II)

Under US$30

Pension Cem, Kutlugün Sok 30, ☎ (212) 516 50 41. A small guest house, basic but clean.

Pension Bahaus, Akbıyık Cad, Bayram Fırın Sok 11, ☎ and Fax (212) 517 66 97. In close proximity to Ayasofya, towards the sea. Some of the rooms have an en suite bathroom (with shower). A clean, inexpensive guest house offering a superb view from the roof terrace.

Pension Vezir Han, Alemdar Cad 5, ☎ (212) 511 24 14. ⁂ TV Near Topkapı.

Between US$30 and US$45

Pension Terrace Guest House, Kutlugün Sok 39, ☎ (212) 638 97 33, Fax (212) 638 97 34 – 6rm. ⁂ CC A small guest house with no particular charm, but it will do at a pinch.

Between US$45 and US$75

Ayasofya Pansiyonları, Soğukçeşme Sok, ☎ (212) 513 36 60, Fax (212) 513 36 69 – 57rm. ⁂ ⟋ ✗ CC A very charming guest house, set in one of the renovated old wooden houses in the alleyway running alongside Ayasofya (behind the basilica). Rococo decoration.

Hotel Poem, Akbıyık Cad/Terbıyık Sok 12, ☎ (212) 517 68 36, Fax (212) 517 68 36 – 21rm. ⌐ℓ 𝒫 CC Small but clean rooms with carpeting. Friendly, almost cloying welcome. Beautiful rooms offering views over the Sea of Marmara. The hotel is to be extended and a restaurant is planned. A good hotel, but still quite expensive for its category.

Hotel İbrahim Paşa, Terzihane Sok 5, ☎ (212) 518 03 94, Fax (212) 518 44 57 – 19rm. ⌐ℓ CC In an old, tastefully renovated house, within a stone's throw of the hippodrome. Panoramic view of the Sea of Marmara from the terrace bar. Rooms are small but charming.

☺ **Hotel Empress Zoe**, Cankurtaran, Akbıyık Cad Adliye Sok 10, ☎ (212) 518 43 60, Fax (212) 518 56 99 – 18rm. ⌐ℓ 𝒫 CC Small rooms, very tastefully decorated in a mixture of Byzantine and Ottoman styles, with kilims and icons. Very clean. Ask for a room overlooking the small garden (charming, and less noise filters from the street and the neighbouring mosque's 5am muezzin). Breakfast is served in the garden and a roof-terrace bar offers a beautiful view of the city and the Bosphorus.

Hotel Nomade, Ticarethane Sok 15, ☎ (212) 511 12 96 / 513 81 73, Fax (212) 513 24 04 – 15rm. ⌐ℓ 𝒫 CC Very friendly welcome. This very tasteful hotel is in a great location. Like the one above, the rooms are small. A disadvantage is that it is rather noisy.

Over US$75

Hotel Four Seasons, Tevkifhane Sok 1, ☎ (212) 638 82 00, Fax (212) 638 82 10 – 65rm. ⌐ℓ TV ✗ CC This highly luxurious establishment was opened by the Canadian hotel chain in a former prison, in close proximity to the Ayasofya basilica. The confined spaces of the fortress enshroud guests in an intimate atmosphere in which they can enjoy the elegantly refined decor. Excellent restaurant in the middle of a garden. There is also a bar and gym. Why not splash out on the last day of your trip?

☺ **Hotel Yeşil Ev**, Kabasakal Cad 5, ☎ (212) 517 67 85, Fax (212) 517 67 80 – 19rm. ⌐ℓ 𝒫 ✗ CC Between the Ayasofya basilica and the Blue Mosque.

Another well-renovated, beautiful wooden residence (19C decor). The restaurant, with its fountain and aromatic fig trees, is very pleasant.

Hotel Armada, Ahırkapı Sok, Sultanahmet, ☎ (212) 638 13 70, Fax (212) 518 50 60 – 110rm. ⌐ℓ 𝒫 TV ✗ CC Set in a historical residence at the foot of the first hill on the Sea of Marmara side. Traditional decor. Terrace bar.

• **Near the Grand Bazaar** (Map II)
Under US$75

Hotel Mosaic, Vidinli Tevfik Paşa Cad 21, ☎ (212) 512 98 50, Fax (212) 512 98 57. ⌐ℓ 𝒫 TV CC Lacking charm but clean and comfortable, near the Grand Bazaar. Caters for groups.

Over US$75

Hotel Merit Antique, Ordu Cad 226, ☎ (212) 513 93 00, Fax (212) 259 01 05 – 275rm. ⌐ℓ 𝒫 TV ✗ ⚎ CC Early 20C building, renovated. The hotel has several restaurants (Chinese, Turkish, Jewish and Italian). Numerous amenities: gym, wine bar, cake shop and boutiques.

• **Beyoğlu and Taksim** (Map III)
Between US$30 and US$55

☺ **Hotel Büyük Londra**, Meşrutiyet Cad 117, Tepebaşı, ☎ (212) 245 06 70, Fax (212) 245 06 71 – 110rm. ⌐ℓ 𝒫 TV CC An old establishment (19C) with somewhat faded charm, but still pleasant. Good but rather inconsistent level of comfort. Ask for the room with the balcony on the top floor. Friendly welcome.

Hotel Elan, Meşrutiyet Cad 213, ☎ (212) 252 54 49, Fax (212) 252 61 17 – 44rm. ⌐ℓ ▤ 𝒫 TV CC Good value for money at this modern hotel. Small but clean and comfortable rooms. A pity the welcome is not warmer.

Hotel Troya, Meşrutiyet Cad 107, Tepebaşı, ☎ (212) 251 82 06, Fax (212) 249 04 38 – 77rm. ⌐ℓ ▤ 𝒫 TV CC Rooms are clean and comfortable but with very poor soundproofing, especially near the lift. As in most hotels in the neighbourhood, breakfast is served in a gloomy room in the basement. Lounge bar.

Over US$75

Hotel Keban, Sıraselviler Cad 51, Taksim, ☎ (212) 252 25 05, Fax (212) 243 33 10 – 84rm. ⌐ℓ 𝒫 ✗ CC A luxurious but expensive establishment, only a few minutes away from Taksim square.

Richmond, İstiklal Cad 445, Tepebaşı, ☎ (212) 252 54 60, Fax (212) 252 97 07 – 106rm. ⌐ 📧 📺 ✗ Modern hotel, part of a chain. Professional and efficient welcome. Rooms are equipped with a safe and minibar.

Hotel Pera Palas, Meşrutiyet Cad 98/100, Tepebaşı, ☎ (212) 251 45 60, Fax (212) 251 40 89 – 145rm. ⌐ ℰ ✗ 📇 This famous old hotel (Agatha Christie and Mustafa Kemal stayed here) is rather expensive. The rooms overlooking the boulevard are noisy. Worth dropping in at least for breakfast or dinner to admire the magnificent reception and tea rooms.

Hotel Marmara, Taksim Meydanı, ☎ (212) 251 46 96, Fax (212) 244 05 09 – 410rm. ⌐ 📧 ℰ 📺 ✗ 📇 This vast luxury establishment dominates Taksim square. It offers all sorts of services, shops and a lounge bar with live music. Book in advance.

• **Camp sites**

Londra camp site, Londra Asfaltı, Çoban Çeşme, ☎ (212) 560 42 00, Fax (212) 559 34 38. Electricity and running water. Around US$2 per person per day.

Ataköy camp site, Rauf Orbay Cad, Ataköy, ☎ (212) 559 60 14, Fax (212) 560 04 26. Electricity (US$1 per day) and running water. Closer to the city than the one above. Around US$4 per person for a tent or caravan.

EATING OUT

In İstanbul you can eat at any time and very cheaply. Apart from the "meze", kebabs, "köfte" and other delights, the hot and spicy "kokoreç" (grilled sheep tripe) from the Çiçek Pasaj (once a flower market) are a veritable culinary experience. Certain restaurants do not serve alcohol. In the lively "meyhane", you can eat meze with rakı and in the "ocakbaşı", with their male clientele, long brochettes are cooked over a hot bed of coals in front of the customers. Many of these can be found near İstiklal Cad (open until around 11pm). Fish restaurants ("Balık Lokantası") abound in Kumkapı.

• **Sultanahmet**
Under US$8
Doy Doy, Şifa Hamamı Sok 13, behind the Blue Mosque (Map II D5). Beware, there are two restaurants of the same name (the smallest one is the best). Turkish cuisine (kebab and pizza), no alcohol.

Karasu, Akbıyık Cad 5, near the Blue Mosque (Map II E4-5). Very simple and standard (meat, salad, omelettes).

Vitamin, Divan Yolu Cad 16 (Map II D4). For a quick, convenient and cheap lunch. This place is rather like a canteen and is frequented only by tourists. Vegetables, chicken, omelettes and ratatouille are served here.

Around US$15
🍽 **Katishma**, Yeni Akbıyık Cad 26 (Map II E4-5), ☎ (212) 518 97 10. An original restaurant of modern design. Large bay window, exposed brick wall, cosy atmosphere with soft jazz music, mezzanine and magnificent terrace. The service is very friendly (the staff speak English). Try the "patlıcan kızartma" (tomatoes, fried aubergines, potatoes), the delicious "havuç sarmısaklı" (garlic, yoghurt, carrots) or the more classic leg of lamb.

Konyalı, ☎ (212) 513 96 96. In Topkapı palace (Map II F2), ideal for a lunch stop (closed in the evening and on Tuesdays, like the palace). From the terrace, there is a breathtaking view over the Sea of Marmara. It has both a restaurant and a cafeteria. The menu includes Turkish specialities (stuffed lamb, börek meat pastry, kebabs, brochettes). Expensive and a little impersonal, but good.

Rami, Utangaç Sok 6 (Map II E4), ☎ (212) 517 65 93. Soft lighting, classical music, wooden walls and view over the Blue Mosque. You pay for the setting, but the cuisine – Turkish – is good quality. Meze to start with and after-dinner fruit liqueurs are on the house. Closes at 11pm.

Over US$30
Sarnıç, Soğukçeşme Sokağı (Map II E3), ☎ (212) 512 42 91. Behind Ayasofya, open evenings only, reservation essential. Closed in July. Worth a visit, especially for the decor and atmosphere: the restaurant is set in a former Byzantine cistern, a large vaulted room in brick divided by beauti-

ful wrought-iron grilles. Dinner by candlelight with music in the background. Impeccable service. A pity the cuisine is nothing special (very westernised).

● **Beyazıt**

Darüzziyafe, Şifahane Sok 6, ☎ (212) 511 84 14, in the old outbuildings of the Süleymaniye (Map II B2). The setting is superb, clients dine inside, or under the arcades. No alcohol is served. Average welcome, frequented only by tourists. Turkish specialities (excellent meat balls). Reasonable prices.

Havuzlu, Gani Çelebi Sok PTT Yanı 3, in the Grand Bazaar (Map II C3), ☎ (212) 527 33 46. Closed in the evening and on Sundays. Ideal for a quick meal. The tables are set out in the little square in front of the restaurant.

Pandeli, Mısır Çarşısı 1, at the north entrance of the Egyptian Bazaar (Mısır Çarşısı) (Map II D2), ☎ (212) 527 39 09. Closed in the evenings and on Sundays. Superb ceramics. Quality Turkish cuisine, seafood. The speciality is aubergine börek. Open for lunch only.

● **Kumkapı** (Map II B4-5)

Formerly populated by fishermen, this neighbourhood with its vast terraces and waiters touting for business, is very lively and full of tourists (live music in every restaurant). It is difficult to recommend any one place in particular. Be careful to avoid being overcharged when paying the bill – the prices are not always indicated on the menu. This could be a good criterion when making your choice.

Yengeç, Telli Odalar Sok 6, Turkish clientele. Quite expensive.

Fırat, Çakmaktaş Sok 11 (Map II C5). A touch of originality on the menu (fish balls).

● **Beyoğlu**

Around US$8

Beyoğlu Pub, İstiklal Cad Halep Pasajı 140 (Map III B2). Very pleasant in summer because of its terrace (quite scarce in this area). Salads and grilled meats.

Gaki, Kameriya Sok 11. One of many eateries around Çiçek Pasaj (Map III B2). Meze ("hamsi", aubergine puree, octopus, spicy potatoes, melon) served with rakı. This new restaurant is attractively decorated with woven mats.

Han, Bankalar Cad Kart Çınar Sok (Map III A4). Extension work underway at the time of writing. Turkish cuisine. Set in the former residence of the Genoese podesta, built in 1312.

Kanguru, Tersahne Cad 2, on the corner of Perşembe Cad (Map III A4). A self-service restaurant used by workers in this district, below Galata. Quick and convenient.

Musa Ustam, Küçük Parmakkapı Sok 14, in a street running parallel to Büyük Parmakkapı (Map III C1). An excellent "ocak başı" where the brochettes are cooked in front of the customer. Lively atmosphere guaranteed on football match days!

Pera, Zambak Sok 9, on the right when coming from Taksim (Map III C1). Slightly faded decoration, elegantly picked out by pale neon lights. Try the "Pera kebap" (beef with aubergine ratatouille).

Refik, Asmalımescit Sofyalı Sok 10 (Map III A3), ☎ (212) 243 28 34. Run by a "Rum" (a Greek from İstanbul). Pleasant and not touristy. Try the "börek" (pastry stuffed with meat, cheese or spinach).

Teras Cafeteria, İstiklal Cad 365, behind the church of St Anthony of Padua (Map III A2). Entrance via a shopping arcade. View over the French Palace and the Bosphorus. Ideal stop for a sandwich.

Lades, İstiklal Cad Ahududu Sok 9 (Map III B1), ☎ (212) 251 32 03. 12noon-10pm. A good little no-fuss Turkish restaurant, for a quick but copious meal. Diners make their choice from the dishes in the kitchen.

Kallavi 20, Kallavi Sok 20 (Map III A2), ☎ (212) 251 10 10. A favourite spot for lunch with the local workers, and a "meyhane" for night owls after 8pm. Particularly lively atmosphere in the evening. 12noon-2am; closed on Sundays.

Between US$8 and US$15

Hacı Abdullah, Sakızağacı Cad 17, İstiklal Cad (Map III B1), ☎ (212) 293 85 61. Near the Aga mosque (Aga Camii). Customers choose their meals directly in the kitchen. House speciality: "komposto", fruit in syrup (quince, plums, cherries) preserved in multicoloured jars which provide an attractive decoration for the dining room. No alcohol served.

Making the most of İstanbul

Çiçek Pasajı, İstiklal Cad 172 (Map III B1-B2), opposite Galatasaray Secondary School, in the former flower market where several restaurants serve meze, grilled fish and meat at all hours of the day.

And don't forget the *Balık Pazarı*, the fish market (just next to the former flower market). In the first street on the right, Nevizade Sok, several restaurants offer good fish and succulent meze served with rakı. In the evening, gypsy musicians, accordionists, fresh almond and lottery ticket sellers pass among the tables, set out on the street in the summer months, in a good-spirited cacophony. The best places to go are the *Çağlar*, ☎ (212) 249 76 65, the *İmroz* (with its Greek proprietor), ☎ (212) 249 90 73 and the *Boncuk*, ☎ (212) 243 12 19, renowned for its famous Armenian "topic" (chickpea paste).

Cadde-i Kebir, İstiklal Cad, İmam Adnan Sok 7 (Map III B1), ☎ (212) 251 71 13. This pleasant restaurant, which is also a bar in the evenings, is decorated with old engravings and film posters. You can sample the delicious chicken in soy or curry sauce in a convivial atmosphere, while listening to good jazz music. Open every day from 10am-2am.

Over US$15
Yakup 2, Asmalımescit Sofyalı Sok 35, (Map III A3), ☎ (212) 249 29 25. A vast, brasserie-style restaurant with a lively and very friendly atmosphere. Difficult to find a seat. Try the excellent selection of meze.
Rejans, Emir Nevruz Sok 17, north of the Panaya Greek Orthodox Church (Map III A2), ☎ (212) 244 16 10. 12noon-3pm / 7pm-10pm. An institution set up by White Russians after the 1917 revolution, displaying plaques in honour of its famous and regular patrons. Try the beef stroganoff, served with lemon vodka, or the copious duck with apples, not forgetting the house speciality, chocolate meringue. Beautiful wooden dining room.
Four Seasons, İstiklal Cad 509 (Map III A3), ☎ (212) 293 39 41. The clientele, like the cuisine, is a mixture of Turkish and western. Very chic. Wide choice on the menu: chicken Kiev, steak tartare, fish, and a large variety of desserts.

• **Ortaköy** (Map I E2)
Çınar, one of the many restaurants facing the Bosphorus, with a vast terrace where you can eat meze in the sunshine or in the evening, among the crowds of young people. Very pleasant.
Bodrum, Sağlık Sok 4, right next door. In the same style, but the welcome is not as warm and there is less choice on the menu.

• **Üsküdar** (Map I E4)
Katibim, Şemsipaşa Sahil Yolu 53, ☎ (216) 310 90 80. Affords a magnificent view over the European bank from the terrace. This is an upmarket establishment serving good meze, kebabs and "içli köfte" (marinaded mutton).

• **Çengelköy**
On the Asian bank of the Bosphorus. To get to this district, take the Beşiktaş-Üsküdar boat, then a dolmuş.
Between US$15 and US$25
Çengel, İskele Meyd 20, ☎ (216) 321 55 04. You can sample fish, meze and fresh fruit on the waterfront terrace.
Çengelköy İskele, Cengelköy Vapur İskelesi Yani, 10, ☎ (216) 321 55 06. Not far from the one above, in the small village square, away from the traffic. Same style, but a little more expensive. Attentive welcome.

• **Kanlıca**
Körfez, Körfez Cad 78, ☎ (216) 413 43 14 / 413 40 98, closed on Mondays. To get there, take the restaurant's boat at Rumeli Hisarı. Book in advance. A chic restaurant with a luxurious decor and a view over the Bosphorus. Specialities: fish cooked in salt, crab, lemon sorbet.

• **Eyüp** (Map I A2)
Under US$8
Karadeniz Pide and *lokantası Eyüboğlu*, Kalenderhane Cad 51, ☎ (212) 616 56 09. Opposite Eyüp mosque. The specialities are "lahmacun" and "pide". Friendly welcome. On the first floor is a large dining room with 200 seats, reserved for families.

HAVING A DRINK
There is less choice in Sultanahmet than in Beyoğlu or Ortaköy, especially in summer. Avoid the tourist-trap cabarets

around İstiklal Cad. If there is a jovial tout out front, beware: it's a guaranteed rip-off. In the "gazino", a classic feature of İstanbul nightlife, the kitsch decoration is on a par with the bad taste of the shows.

Bars

• Beyoğlu (Map III)
Gramophon, Tünel Meyd. (A3), ☎ (212) 293 07 86. 9am-1am. A chic bar where good local jazz groups play every Friday and Saturday evening. You can also come here for lunch or dinner; the meal and concert together will set you back around US$15.
Kemancı Sanat Evi, Sıraselviler Cad (C2), ☎ (212) 251 27 23. Near the Belgian Consulate. A real hot spot for hard rock, spread over three levels, including the basement where the young westernised rockers can be found all dressed up in their leather gear and very much at home in all the noise and smoke. There is an endless succession of groups, each one different from the last.

• Harbiye (Map I)
Harry's Bar, in the Hyatt Regency hotel (D2), ☎ (212) 225 70 00. A trendy bar with a carefully styled decor, the lair of the city's jet set. Very good music (many foreign, especially American groups, perform here).
Kervansaray, Cumhuriyet Cad 30 (D2), ☎ (212) 247 16 30. Although quite touristy, this cabaret is one of the few with belly dancing. Make sure to check your bill before you leave.
Köy Cafe, Mis Sok, İstiklal Cad (B1). The decor, reproducing the interior of an Anatolian tent, is superb. Ideal for listening to Turkish songs in a lively atmosphere.
Fantasia Pub, Hasnun Galip Sok, parallel to İstiklal Cad, when coming from Tünel, on the right after the Galatasaray Secondary School (B1-2). Lively atmosphere: traditional songs and dances.
Hayal Kahvesi, Büyükparmakkapı Sok 19, near İstiklal Cad (C1). Jazz and rock groups perform live every night in an attractive decor of exposed stone. Rather "yuppie" clientele.
Roxi Bar, Aslan Yatağı Sok 113, next to Sıraselviler Cad, Taksim (C1). Classic haunt of İstanbul night owls. The bar, often full to bursting, has 3 rooms. Rock'n'roll style.

Cactus Bar, İmam Adnan Sok 4, near İstiklal Cad (B1). One of the trendiest spots of the moment. Bar with a very western, rather Parisian atmosphere.

• Sultanahmet (Map II)
Rumeli Cafe, Ticarethane Sok 8, Sultanahmet, opposite the Nomade hotel (D4). Closes at 1am. You can have a drink and listen to French music. Snacks are also served. Tables outside.

• Arnavutköy
Pupa's Bar, Birinci Sok 17, in Arnavutköy, on the European bank of the Bosphorus, ☎ (212) 265 65 33. Open every day, 2pm-2am. This is where all the basketball players and Rastas hang out, and the music is mainly reggae, Afro-pop and Cuban. Entry is free.

Cafés, tea shops – Lebon cake shop, İstiklal Cad 463-465 (Map III A3). Run by descendants of the founders of the Markiz. The pastries are prepared upstairs.
Sultan Pub, Divan Yolu Cad, Sultanahmet (Map II E4), ☎ (212) 528 17 19. In a good location, near the Blue Mosque and Ayasofya. A good place to rest your weary feet in a comfortable, vaguely English decor. You can stop here for lunch, or just for a milkshake or one of their delicious ice creams, and watch the comings and goings of the passers-by, shoe-shine boys and street vendors.

Live shows and festivals – İstanbul hosts numerous international festivals: music (between April and July), jazz (**Parliament**, in May and **Yapı Kredi**, end of June), cinema (between April and July), blues (Efes Pilsen, in November) and theatre (between May and June).
Atatürk Kültür Merkezi, east of Taksim square (Map III C1), ☎ (212) 251 56 00. Good quality classical music concerts, operas and ballets, mostly Turkish. Cheap.
Açık Hava Tiyatrosu (Maçka open-air theatre), behind the Hilton, (Map III C1) hosts several festivals between May and September.
Aksanat Cultural Centre, İstiklal Cad, (Map III C1), ☎ (212) 252 35 00. Classical music or jazz concerts, exhibitions and live shows.

OTHER THINGS TO DO

Excursions – In Sultanahmet, agencies offer tours of İstanbul lasting one or more days. If you fancy a cruise on the Bosphorus, you can also sign up directly at the harbour (see the following chapter).

Kirkit Voyage, Ticarethane Sok, İncili Çavuş Çıkmazı, Sultanahmet, ☎ (212) 512 05 47, above the Rumeli Cafe (Map II D4). Friendly welcome.

Adventure Tours, Şeftali Sok 12, Sultanahmet, near Ayasofya towards the southwest (Map II E4), ☎ (212) 526 61 94.

Turkish baths – These are not really traditional in İstanbul, but provide a good way to relax.

Cağaloğlu, Prof Kazım Gürkan Cad 34, ☎ (212) 522 24 24, 300m from the Ayasofya basilica (Map II D3). Open every day from 7am-10pm. Magnificent marble decor, but the establishment is expensive and the staff unwelcoming. Don't bother with a massage; too rushed (it should last at least 10min).

Çemberlitaş Hamamı, Vezirhan Cad 8, near the Çemberlitaş Column (Map II D4), ☎ (212) 522 79 74. 6am-midnight for men, 8.30am-9pm for women. Built in the 16C by Sinan and later altered, it is one of the most beautiful Turkish baths in İstanbul. Cheaper than the one above.

SHOPPING GUIDE

İstanbul certainly does not belie its commercial vocation. It taps all the fetishes of the consumer society as well as the crafts of the various regions of the country (jewellery, leather, carpets, kilims, ceramics, pottery). Haggling is, of course, a must!

Markets – Even if you have no intention of buying anything, you should take a look around the markets. They are scattered all over the city, but some are worth making a special detour. The *Çarşamba Pazarı* (Wednesday market) in the Çarşamba district (Map I B3), is one of the city's oldest and most famous, along with the *Salı Pazarı* (Tuesday market) in Kadiköy, further along the Asian bank of the Sea of Marmara. The *Çiçek Pazarı*, near the Egyptian Bazaar (Map II D2), specialises in flowers and animals (birds, parrots, puppies, fish, monkeys and even leeches!)

The *fish markets* ("balık pazarı") in Eminönü (Map I E4) and Galatasaray, near Çiçek Pasaj (Map III B2), are the oldest in İstanbul. On Sundays, the more recent *Russian market in Beyazıt* (Map II C3) is a good place to find cheap goods from central Asia.

Local delicacies – In the *Egyptian Bazaar* (Map II D2), you can find all sorts of spices, Turkish delight, almond paste, dried fruit, nuts, tea, oil, herbs etc.

For one hundred years, *Hacı Bekir*, in Sirkeci (Map II D2) and İstiklal Cad 127, in Beyoğlu (Map III B2), has enjoyed the reputation of making the best Turkish delight in İstanbul.

Carpets – The State runs an outlet in the former *Haseki Hürrem Turkish bath* (Map II E4) (9.30am-5.30pm, closed on Tuesdays) in Kabasakal Sok, between the Ayasofya basilica and the Blue Mosque. High prices.

Antiques, arts and crafts – In the heart of the Grand Bazaar (Map II C3), in İçbedesten, you can find Ottoman objects as well as a large selection of recent articles in gold, silver or wood, copper goods, ceramics etc, but the prices are high. You will be more likely to find a bargain at the *Horhor* flea market ("bit pazarı") at Şehzadebaşı, near the Valens aqueduct (Map II A2), or at the *Üsküdar* flea market in Hakimiye Cad (Map I E4).

Book shops – İstiklal Cad is littered with international book shops. Most of the national museums also have book shops which are well stocked in art books and postcards.

The major daily newspapers from abroad can be found the day after publication at the main hotels, the kiosks in İstiklal Cad and near the Ayasofya basilica. Before leaving, it is worth picking up a few issues of the luxurious biennial magazine *İstanbul* (in English), which deals with culture, history, economy, architecture etc, and is on sale in book shops.

Robinson Crusoe, İstiklal Cad 389 (Map III A2). A good selection of English-language books on Turkish civilisation.
Dünya Aktüel, İstiklal Cad 469, next to the Lebon cake shop (Map III A3). Newspapers and novels in English and French; this is, in fact, the French Hachette book shop ("Haşet" in Turkish).

Aslıhan Çarşısı, Meşrutiyet Cad 18 (Map III A2). Near İstiklal Cad. A shopping arcade full of old magazines and books in Turkish, English and French. Film posters and photos.
Sahaflar Çarşısı, a second-hand book market near the Grand Bazaar in Beyazıt (Map II C3).

The Bosphorus and the Galata Tower at sunset

Boivieux/HOA QUI

AROUND İSTANBUL★

THE BOSPHORUS

1- or 2-day trip, depending upon the chosen itinerary
Stay in İstanbul, Şile or the Princes' Isles

Not to be missed
The fortresses and the small fishing villages on the shores of the Bosphorus.
The wooded paths of the Princes' Isles. The beach at Şile.

And remember...
For the cruise, bring a sweater or light jacket.
For Şile and the Princes' Isles, bring a swimsuit.

In spite of İstanbul's uncontrolled growth, a few miraculously preserved havens of peace still exist in the areas surrounding İstanbul (but for how much longer?). There are many opportunities for catching a breath of fresh air and finding a quiet spot: fishing villages, forests, and boat excursions are all within reach of the city.

Cruise on the Bosphorus★★

Allow one day.
For details of boat trips, see "Making the most of the İstanbul region"

No trip to İstanbul would be complete without a cruise on the Bosphorus. It is the best way to experience the city and appreciate its wonderful natural setting. A narrow corridor between two seas and two continents, the Bosphorus (Boğaz) is an entity in itself. Throughout history, it has been considered either a bridge or a barrier, with a length of 32km and a width of 500m-3km at most. Its depth (80m) nevertheless allows the largest merchant ships to pass, bearing the riches of the Orient, Russia, and the Mediterranean.

In spite of the intensive urban growth on both shores, the Bosphorus has a special charm. Fishing villages and elegant *yalı*, luxurious wooden residences of the 18C and 19C, are built from the tops of the hills all the way to the shore. Spanning the strait, two suspension bridges cross the strait, a reminder of the modern era.

■ Before reaching **Beşiktaş** – on the European shore – you will have a beautiful **view★** from the boat of the façade of **Dolmabahçe Palace** *(see İstanbul)*, all in white marble.

Major strategic stakes
The Bosphorus is an international navigable waterway, under the Montreux Convention (1936) which authorises the passage of merchant ships but restricts naval vessels. It allows greater rights to the nations surrounding the Black Sea, Russia for one, as it is their only access to the Mediterranean. Since 1993, Russian development of an oil terminal for the pipelines of the Caucasus and Central Asia, has meant that additional tankers need to use the straits. Turkey is suggesting that a pipeline be built across its territory to avoid shipping accidents in the straits (in 1994, two ships collided, causing the death of 40 people as well as an oil spill).

After **Çırağan Palace★** *(just after Beşiktaş)*, the passage under the **Bosphorus bridge★** (Boğaziçi Köprüsü) is one of the high points of the cruise. Inaugurated in 1973, this was the first structure ever to link two continents. It is 64m high and the length between the two towers is an impressive 1 074m. At its feet, the lovely **Ortaköy Mosque**, rebuilt in the 19C by the Dolmabahçe's architect (Nikoğos Balyan), appears tiny in comparison.

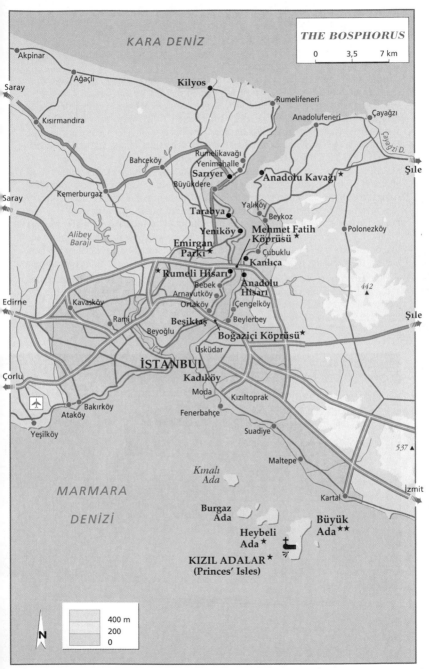

THE BOSPHORUS

0   3,5   7 km

KARA DENİZ

Akpinar
Ağaçlı
Kilyos
Rumelifeneri
Saray
Kısırmandıra
Anadolufeneri
Çayağzı
Çayağzi D.
Şile
Rumelikavağı
Bahçeköy
Yenimahalle
Sarıyer
Anadolu Kavağı ★
Büyükdere
Saray
Kemerburgaz
Yalıköy
Beykoz
Tarabya
Alibey
Barajı
Yeniköy
Mehmet Fatih
Köprüsü ★
Polonezköy
Emirgan
Parkı ★
Çubuklu
Kanlıca
★ Rumeli Hisarı
Anadolu
Hisarı
442 ▲
Bebek
Edirne
Kavasköy
Arnavutköy
Ortaköy
Çengelköy
Şile
Rami
Beşiktaş
Beylerbey
Beyoğlu
Boğaziçi Köprüsü ★
İSTANBUL
Üsküdar
Çorlu
Kadıköy
Moda
Kızıltoprak
Bakırköy
Fenerbahçe
Ataköy
Yeşilköy
Suadiye
537 ▲
Maltepe
İzmit
MARMARA
Kınalı
Ada
Kartal
DENİZİ
Burgaz
Ada
Büyük
Ada ★★
Heybeli
Ada ★
KIZIL ADALAR ★
(Princes' Isles)

400 m
200
0

N

185

Beyond, at the mouth of the stream known as the Sweet Waters of Asia (*Asian shore*), the small **Küçüksu (or Göksu) Palace***, also built by Nikoğos Balyan in 1857, has an elegant neo-Baroque, almost Rococo, façade which is reflected in the water. An old Imperial, then presidential, summer residence, it is now a museum (*9am-5pm, closed Mondays and Thursdays; entrance fee*).

On the same shore, the boat reaches the **Anadolu Hisarı**, a small fort whose only remains are four towers. Erected at the end of the 14C under Beyazıt I, it was to have been used as a base for attacking Constantinople. However, this project was delayed when Ankara was defeated by Tamerlane (1402). Fifty years later, Mehmet II reinforced its defences before launching the final assault. The eye is drawn to the European shore, with the towers and crenellated walls of the imposing **Rumeli Hisarı*** (1452); long serpentine walls run along the hillside (*9.30am-5pm, closed Mondays*). The fortress was built in only three months by the men of Mehmet II, in violation of the accords signed with the Byzantines. Its powerful cannon controlled navigation on the Bosphorus. After the fall of Constantinople, it served periodically as a prison, and currently hosts the annual İstanbul International Festival.

Beyond, rises the outline of the gigantic **Fatih Mehmet Bridge*** (Fatih Mehmet Köprüsü), the second suspension bridge over the strait. No less spectacular than the first one, it was built by the Japanese in 1991, and is located on the exact spot where Darius, the Persian king, crossed the strait on a floating bridge 2 500 years ago.

■ The first stop in Asia, **Kanlıca** is a charming fishing village with wooden houses and small restaurants on the water's edge. On a promontory to the north, the last viceroy of Egypt built a palace, the **Hıdır Kasrı** (1900), since converted into a luxurious hotel and restaurant.

R. Tixador/TOP

The boat continues its tranquil journey towards the Black Sea, reaching the greenery of **Emirğan Parkı**★ *(European shore)*, whose springs and streams and delightful **Tulip Gardens**★ attract visitors from near and far (not to be missed is the tulip celebration in April-May, a rainbow of colours). The regal Baroque mosque on the large square dates from the 18C.

■ The third European stop is **Yeniköy**, a picturesque village clinging to a hill covered with vineyards. In the northern part of the town, you will find the former summer residences of the Austro-Hungarian and German ambassadors. Farther along, beyond the enormous casino and the trendy **Tarabya**, İstanbul's summer resort, stand the residences of the French and Italian ambassadors.

■ The next stop, **Sarıyer**, is set on the hills in the background. This little fishing port, with a busy **fish market** and countless restaurants has become an important centre of tourism in the straits.

The quest for the Golden Fleece

Waiting for his son, Jason, to come of age and ascend the throne, old King Aeson of Iolcos, had bestowed power on his half-brother Pelias. Of course, when Jason reached adulthood and asked his uncle for his right, the latter refused, unless Jason managed to bring him the Golden Fleece, a gold-covered ram's skin kept in Colchis (Georgia). Pelias knew that such an exploit was impossible. However, Jason did not lose hope. He embarked on the *Argo*, a powerful ship constructed by Argos, a man endowed with several eyes. With his brave Argonauts, he crossed the strait and reached the Black Sea, where he managed to obtain the fleece, aided by Medea, a beautiful witch whom he married at once. In the Caucasus Mountains, there is a forgotten people, the Svans, who live from the gold of the surrounding rivers. To sift the gold they use a sheepskin — a custom as old as time.

Elegant *yalı* on the Bosphorus

■ The last stop on the itinerary, **Anadolu Kavağı**★ *(Asian shore)* enjoys a quieter atmosphere. Surrounded by a military zone and far from the capital, the village has been spared the voracity of land speculators. However, its location along the Bosphorus cruise route means that there are plenty of tourists, and they are eagerly awaited. The restaurants in the little port are nevertheless very enjoyable, and cheaper than in Sarıyer.

To the left *(heading towards the Otopark)* a small road climbs up to the **Genoese Castle** (1350) overlooking the straits. From the summit, the **view**★★ is magnificent and extends to the mouth of the Black Sea and the ancient Colchis, site of the exploits of Jason and his famous Argonauts *(see sidebar above)*.

The Princes' Isles★ (Kızıl Adalar)

One day excursion

A small archipelago guarding the entrance to the Bosphorus, on the Sea of Marmara, the Princes' Isles owe their name to the period when the Byzantine princes used to sojourn there. The Turks also call them **Kızıl Adalar**, the "red islands". At the beginning of the 20C, rich Armenians, Greeks and Jews built elegant *yalı* which are now home to İstanbul's jet set. It is a haven of peace bordered with bays, sprinkled with wooden houses hidden in the foliage, and where cars are banned in favour of horse-drawn carriages.

After a possible stop in **Kadıköy** (*leaving from Eminönü or from Kabataş*), the boat runs along the endless suburbs of the Asian side of İstanbul. Leaving **Kınalı Ada**, it stops in **Burgaz Ada** (1.5sqkm), home to two monasteries. Slightly larger, **Heybeli Ada★** is a very enjoyable stop where it is possible to relax at an outdoor café set among beautiful wooden residences.

Büyük Ada★★, the largest island of the archipelago, is the last port of call on this trip. The assembly of horse-drawn carriages on the small square on the left of the port is very picturesque, even if you do not plan to take the grand tour of the island (*1hr*) or the short tour (*35min*). You might prefer to rent a bicycle, or simply go on foot.

To the right of the landing stage, the elegant **residential district** is covered with pine trees and flowering shrubs. Beyond, approximately 3km away, the houses give way to the pine forest. From Birlik Meydanı (known as Luna Park), a small and very steep cobblestone road (1km) climbs the hill to the **St George Monastery**, where the **view★★** over the island and the sea is marvellous. The little restaurant-bar nearby is a good place to rest after the walk up the hill.

The descent towards the eastern side of the island leads to the **Convent of St Nicholas**. Directly opposite lies **Sedef islet**, a small private paradise reached by boat. From the convent, return to the port from the north.

On the Black Sea

A few oases of charm still hide on the shores of the Black Sea. Increasingly rare, such places attract large numbers of city folk in search of fresh air, peace and quiet.

Kilyos

20km north of İstanbul, on the European shore of the Black Sea. This is the nearest seaside resort to the city, a small town fringed by a beach which attracts a large crowd every weekend. It has plenty of restaurants, hotels and a lively night life.

Şile

70km from İstanbul, on the Asian side of the Black Sea. Set on a rocky promontory overlooking the sea, this charming fishing village is an ideal spot for spending a day outside İstanbul. Along the **main street**, the old residences house shops, restaurants and hotels; however the place is less crowded than Kilyos and the atmosphere more serene.

In the **port**, a small picturesque cove protected by a **Genoese tower**, it is possible to buy the fishermen's catch or simply observe them as they unload their boats under the watchful eye of all of the neighbourhood's cats. Şile is known for its embroidered cotton shirts and jackets, but especially for its surroundings and its beautiful **beach★** wedged between the rocks.

Making the most of the İstanbul region

COMING AND GOING

• Cruise on the Bosphorus
Boards from gangway 3 at the port of Eminönü (Boğaz Hattı, İstanbul). Daily departures at 10.35am and 1.35pm. Take your own drinks and sandwiches because prices on board are exorbitant. Good seats are hard to come by. The journey lasts 90min; return at 3pm and 5pm.

• Princes' Isles
About 10 departures per day from the port of Eminönü (Adalar, gangway 5). Journey time 1hr 40min. Some boats depart from Kadıköy. In summer, the hydrofoil from Kabataş to Yalova calls at Büyük Ada (1hr journey). Last return at 11.30pm on weekends and 9.45pm during the week.

• Kilyos
A 20min bus journey from Sarıyer.

• Şile
Buses depart from the bus station (near the Üsküdar jetty). Journey time: 2hr.

WHERE TO STAY

• On the Princes' Isles
Between US$45 and US$90
Hotel Splendid, 23 Nisan Cad, 71, Büyük Ada, ☎ (216) 382 69 50, Fax (216) 382 68 75 – 70rm. ⌘ ☞ ☴ ✕ ☰ ☱ With its high ceilings, this beautiful early 20C wooden house is steeped in a romantic atmosphere. Open from May to October.
Merit Halki Palace, Refah Şehitleri Cad, 88, Heybeli Ada, ☎ (216) 351 88 90, Fax (216) 351 84 83 – 45rm. ⌘ ☞ ✕ [cc] Tastefully renovated, this beautiful Ottoman residence offers not only everything you could possibly desire in the way of comfort, but also a real change of scene thanks to its location on the island with the fewest tourists. Open from May to October.

• In Şile
Beware, the hotels are in great demand at weekends and some are closed in winter.
Between US$15 and US$30
Hotel İtergen, Üsküdar Cad 150, Şile, ☎ (0216) 711 59 25, Fax (0216) 711 34 42 – 30rm. ⌘ [cc] Located in the town centre, this hotel boasts a very beautiful view over the bay, is clean, with a reasonable level of comfort, and has one family suite. Open all year round.
Over US$45
Hotel Kumbaba, ☎ (0216) 711 50 38, Fax (0216) 711 48 51 – 40rm. ⌘ ✕ ☱
On the beachfront at Kumbaba, 2km before Şile. Turn left just after the fuel station then first right, park your car and take a ferry across the little river. Bungalows with basic comfort, but clean. Closes at the end of October. Camping possible.

EATING OUT

• On the Bosphorus
You will find numerous fish restaurants at the harbour in **Anadolu Kavağı**.

• On the Princes' Isles
The restaurants next to the jetty are excellent, but you may prefer the tea rooms just opposite.
Birtat, to the left of the jetty; slightly more expensive than İstanbul, but the food and welcome are good.
Luna Park, Birlik Meydanı, 3 or 4km away to the right of the jetty. Beautiful view over the bay.

• In Şile
The main street is lined with terrace restaurants overlooking the sea.
Panorama, almost at the end of the village in a small street on the left. Wonderful view down over the fishing harbour.
Anamın Yeri, Üsküdar Cad, opposite the "otogar". Salads, "iskender kebab".

EDİRNE ★

Capital of Edirne Province – Map p 136
230km from İstanbul – Pop 100 000
Alt 84m – Cold and snowy winters, hot summers

Not to be missed
The Selim II mosque and the Beyazıt II complex.
Strolling in the busy city-centre streets.
A walk along the Tunca.

And remember...
Visit Edirne in June, during the Kırkpınar wrestling festival.

Edirne is a town of paradoxes and contrasts. A Turkish outpost in Europe, its elegant minarets and alcohol-free restaurants give it a distinct Ottoman personality. A university and garrison city – relations with neighbouring Greece and Bulgaria are tense – means that students and soldiers live side by side. The main city of eastern Thrace, Edirne nevertheless is built on a human scale and has practically no suburbs. It is wedged in an elbow of the Tunca, a tributary of the Meriç. The ancient Ottoman capital does not seem to take offence at the hurried travellers rushing through on their way to İstanbul. But, for those who take the time to explore the city, it opens up without reserve and unveils a thousand attractions. As well as busy shopping streets, lively outdoor cafés and the peaceful riverside, Edirne hides some fascinating masterpieces of Ottoman architecture.

Europe's last door

Ancient Adrianople (Hadrianopolis for the Greeks) owed its name to the Roman Emperor Hadrian who founded it in 125 AD. From its birth until the end of the 20C, its history was to be extremely rich: attacked by the Goths (378) and the Avars (586), pillaged by the Bulgars (814) then several times over by the crusaders in the 12C. In 1361, the city came under the control of the Ottomans, who thereupon severed Constaninople's links to the European hinterland.

Six years later, Sultan Murat I established his capital in Adrianople and renamed it Edirne. It was the beginning of a period of prosperity which reached its height under the reign of **Murat II** (1421-1451): Edirne endowed itself with many public and religious buildings and welcomed a court of wise men and writers. The transfer of the capital to Constantinople, in 1458, did not in the least affect the city, which remained an important strategic base for the conquest of the Balkans. The 19C was to mark another troubled era: after the treaty of Adrianople (1829) which granted independence to Greece and the opened the Straits, Edirne suffered severe damage during the Russian invasions (1829 and 1878). Later still, during the Balkan wars (1913), the Bulgars swept through the city after five long months of siege, only to cede it to the Turks the same year. Given to Greece in 1920, it was finally returned to Turkey by the Treaty of Lausanne (1923).

As strong as a Turk

Every year in June, the stadium of the **island of Sarayiçi** *(north of the city)* welcomes the **Kırkpınar Wrestling Festival** *(see "yağlı güreş" p. 90)*. During this week, the entire city is in a festive mood; a beauty queen is elected to preside and three days of wrestling matches conclude the celebrations.

This very popular tradition owes its origins to a legend that is several centuries old. In 1354, Orhan Gazi sent his brother to invade Byzantine Rumelia, on the other side of the Dardanelles. The latter left with 40 warriors, husky fellows, who in between battles enjoyed wrestling. But, one day, as they set up camp in Akirköy (in Greece), north of Edirne, the two most valiant engaged in a combat which ended only when both were dead. Their companions buried them were they had fallen, and were amazed to see a spring emerge at the place of burial.

Elbow grease
The wrestlers wear black leather breeches and smear their bodies with olive oil to avoid any possibility of being held fast. The only way of holding on to the adversary is by sliding the forearm inside the breeches (all ambiguous or malevolent moves are forbidden). After a short ceremony, the battle begins. The loser is the one "whose torso looks up at the sky", ie the one lying on the ground. In an overheated atmosphere, where the shouts of the fans mix with the deafening drumbeats, the wrestlers face each other in the overgrown grass. The winner of the finale is welcomed as a hero in the city.

In time, all of them were buried there according to their wishes. The place was named Kırkpınar, "the forty springs", and as the centuries passed, became the gathering place by default of all of the country's wrestlers.

The city
Edirne and its surroundings can be seen on foot in one day if the visitor concentrates on the main points of interest (allow a half-day for the city centre). City map p 195.

Few places offer such an array of Ottoman architecture, from its inception until its demise, in such a small space. Between the visits to the mosques and the promenade in the bazaar, take the time to relax in one of the lively outdoor cafés in the city centre, where students and families gather to drink tea.

Modern-day gladiators (Kırkpınar tournament, Edirne)

S. Faulkner/RAPHO

The Selim II Complex

At the top of a little hill, on the eastern side of the city, the **Selimiye Camii***** (C1), is the most important vestige of the Selim II Imperial complex (1575). The pride of the city, it is without question the highest achievement of Turkish Ottoman architecture.

The entrance is through a vast courtyard enclosed by a **portico** with 18 domes, the centre of which consists of an elegant octagonal *şadırvan* (fountain). Above the mosque, four immense minarets (71m) point to the sky, like rockets, visible for miles on end.

The mosque was conceived by the brilliant architect **Sinan** *(see p 49)*, who considered it his masterpiece. The dome, 31.5m in diameter, is 50cm larger than its equivalent in the Aysofya, built one thousand years earlier. The originality of the Selimiye resides in the conception of its space: Sinan abandoned the traditional Ottoman plan (with an inverted T) in favour of a centralised octagonal layout giving the impression of a single-shell structure. The **dome**** rests on an audacious double crown of alternating squinches and pendentives, which distribute the weight on eight massive pillars. This system allowed the architect to create an immense unified space which can accommodate up to 6 000 worshippers. It also permitted him to insert the windows around the dome without weakening the walls, giving the prayer hall an exceptional amount of light.

The decor is equally impressive: the marvellously chiselled white marble of the **minbar** and **mihrab*** underlines the harmony of the great edifice, as do the superb tiles and the **Imperial loge****(in the southwest corner)*.

To the the east, you reach the small **Museum of Turkish and Islamic Art** (Türk-Islam Eserleri Müzesi) (D1) *(8am-12noon/1.30pm-5.30pm, closed Mondays, entrance fee)* which occupies the complex's old medrese. It contains an array of handicrafts, 15C and 17C ceramics and furniture, as well as an exhibit dedicated to the legend of Kırkpınar.

Sinan's masterpiece, the Selimiye Camii at Edirne

G. Degeorge

Spend more time at the **Archeology and Ethnography Museum** (Arkeoloji ve Etnoloji Müzesi) (D1) (*8am-12noon/1.30pm-5.30pm, closed Mondays, entrance fee*) whose ethnographic section includes, in particular, beautiful Ottoman interiors. In the archeological section, it is possible to see several fossils millions of years old, Neolithic objects and Roman statues.

The City Centre

To the west, beyond the gardens below the mosque, you will cross the **Kavaflar Arasta**, a picturesque shopping arcade built under the reign of Selim III. Next, at the bend formed by Talatpaşa Caddesi, rises the 15C **Old Mosque*** (Eski Cami) (C2), built by the architect Hacı Alaeddin. In spite of its massive appearance – a huge square (50mx50m) – the work is nonetheless graceful. The little **minaret** on the left is probably original, whereas the second one, more elaborate, dates from the 16C. It is recognisable by its two balconies, supported by beautiful stalactite extensions. The interior space is divided into three naves each topped by a dome resting on four pillars. Gigantic black **calligraphy** decorates the walls.

After the completion of the Eski Cami, Mehmet I entrusted Haci Alaeddin with the construction of the **covered market** (bedesten) (C2). The walls – an elegant pattern of alternating white marble and red brick – support two rows of seven domes punctuated by windows. As the historical commercial centre of the city, the market harboured jewellery shops, armouries and a variety of shops supplying the mosque with considerable revenue. Renovated with care, it is currently home to paper-makers and shops selling clothes and shoes. As yet, it is not particularly busy, but this may change in time.

Behind the Eski Cami, is the **Rüstem Paşa Caravanserai** (Rüstem Paşa Hanı) (C2), designed by Sinan in 1571. The building includes two courtyards bounded by an arcaded gallery, creating two distinct caravanserais: the **Büyük Han** (big), on the left, and the **Küçük Han** (small), on the right. Since its restoration – awarded the Agha Khan architecture prize in 1980 – the latter houses a hotel (*see "Making the most of Edirne"*). The *han* flanks a pleasant little square where you can enjoy tea in an outdoor café. The record shops blasting music into the street will keep you up-to-date on the latest local hits, whether you want to be or not!

At a right angle to Talatpaşa Caddesi, **Saraçlar Caddesi** (C2) is the focal point of modern Edirne. There are all sorts of artisans and picturesque boutiques in the surrounding streets, as well as in the **covered Ali Paşa Market** (Ali Paşa Çarşısı), built by Sinan in 1569. This *bedesten* forms an interminable gallery running along the street for 300m, punctuated by marble arches and red bricks. Destroyed by a fire in 1992, it was renovated and reopened at the end of 1996, and now accommodates 130 shops.

To the south (*via Maarif Cad*) the shops disappear and the neighbourhood becomes more peaceful with closely-spaced elegant **wooden houses**, some painted in bright colours.

Return to the centre, go past the tourism office and head north, on the other side of Talatpaşa Cad.

A road leads to the magnificent **Sokollu Mehmet Paşa Hamamı*** (B1-2) (*see "Making the most of Edirne"*). On the way, you will pass the **Clock Tower** (Saat Kulesi), one of the rare vestiges of the Roman wall, built in the 2C under Emperor Hadrian. The hamam was designed by Sinan, for the grand vizier Sokollu Ahmet Paşa who wished to honour the city where he had been a young Janissary. The **marble** and the **fountains*** are original.

Nearby (*toward the east*), the **Three Balconies Mosque*** (Üç Şerefli Camii) (C1-2) was built thanks to the bounty gathered by Murat II during the taking of Smyrna (İzmir) (1447). It owes its name to the highest of the four **minarets** (67.65m), which has three balconies. Currently being renovated, this Imperial mosque was the largest of its period. It marks the transition from Seljuk style, still noticeable in the spirals of the minarets' decor, to an original Ottoman style, opting finally for a central plan topped by a large dome. The dome here measures 24.1m. It rests on a hexagonal drum on pendentives supported by six arches. Other innovations include the exterior buttresses of the drum and the arcades surrounding the charming **courtyard**.

Along the Tunca River

2km excursion, allow 3hr for the entire trip. From the main square (Hürriyet Meyd), go up Horozlu Bayırı Cad, then Imaret Cad until you reach the river (20min on foot). Walk westward along the river.

After the excitement of the city centre, take the time to take a country stroll along the river. It is also an opportunity to discover the other hidden treasures of Ottoman Edirne in a very pleasant setting.

Set along the banks of the Tunca, the **Beyazıt II Imperial Complex**** (Beyazıt Külliye) (A 1), seems hidden behind the embankment which protects it from flood waters. The light grey stone and the peaceful surroundings create a serene atmosphere. A mystic and a poet, Beyazıt II enjoyed inviting Dervishes there.

Completed in 1488, this complex is Edirne's largest, and also the most complete. For the **mosque**, graced with four elegant minarets, Hayrettin the architect chose the inverted T-plan. The building is preceded by the usual ablutions courtyard, bounded by a *midha* with domes resting on antique columns. The square-shaped prayer hall, is covered with a single 20m-diameter dome, directly set on the walls. The numerous windows bathe the interior in light, highlighting the elegant **Imperial loge.**

On both sides of the mosque, the **hospice** (*tabhane*) welcomed the Dervishes, or the poor who were allowed to remain for three days free of charge. Meals were served in the **imaret**, in the northeastern corner. The **medical school** at the western end had cells for 18 students and a vast domed classroom. The **hospital** (Darülşifa) and the **asylum** (*tımarhane*), were very distinguished: according to the wishes of Beyazıt II, musicians would perform for the patients.

Further along the Tunca, 2km to the northeast, are the ruins of the **Royal Palace** (Eski Saray). This residence rivalled for a time with the Topkapı in İstanbul. Begun under Murat II in 1450, it was severely damaged during the Russian invasions in the 19C. Only a portion of the kitchens remains, and it is difficult to imagine its past splendour. From here, Sarayiçi Island, seat of the Kırkpınar festival, is reached by the elegant **Bridge of Süleyman the Magnificent** (Kanuni Köprüsü) (Sinan's work), overlooked by a **tower of justice**.

Go east aross the bridge and walk 2km in the direction of the city centre until you reach the crossroads at Mimar Sinan and Muradiye Bay, on Sarayiçi Hill.

The Mosque of Murat II** (Muradiye Camii) (D1) stands at the edge of town close to the countryside. It is worth visiting even if it is just for the **view*** (*only open during prayer time*). Built by Murat II in 1436, it was originally a *zaziye* (a religious foundation) for the Whirling Dervishes. The crack in the mihrab dates from the 1953 earthquake which destroyed the minaret and the dome (since rebuilt).

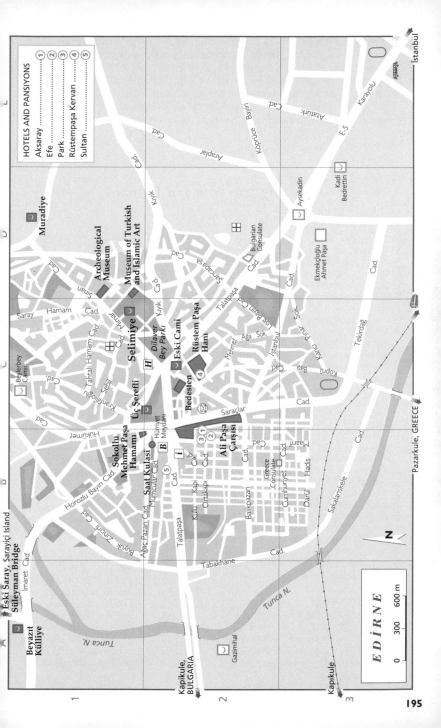

EDİRNE

0 300 600 m

HOTELS AND PANSIYONS

① Aksaray
② Efe
③ Park
④ Rüstempaşa Kervan
⑤ Sultan

Eski Saray, Sarayiçi Island
Süleyman Bridge

Beyazit
Külliye

Muradiye

Archeological Museum

Museum of Turkish and Islamic Art

Selimiye

Dilaver Bey Parkı

Eski Cami

Rüstem Paşa Hanı

Üç Şerefli

Bedesten

Sokollu Mehmet Paşa Hamamı

Saat Kulesi

Hürriyet Meydanı

Ali Paşa Çarşısı

Saraçlar

Bulgarian Consulate

Ekmekçioğlu Ahmet Paşa

Greece Consulate

Ayşekadin

Kadı Bedrettin

İstanbul

Pazarkule, GREECE

Kapıkule

Kapıkule, BULGARIA

Gazimihal

Tunca N.

195

The sultan was inspired by the Green Mosque, erected by his brother, in Bursa. On each side of the entrance, beautiful painted black **calligraphy** graces the walls. In the interior, the prayer hall is covered with two domes separated by a large arch, while the side wings housed the Dervishes' cells. Superb **İznik tiles** decorate the walls, topped by a frieze representing stylised Dervishes. Here and there, remains of polychrome calligraphy can be seen. The mosque is surrounded by a small abandoned **garden** and a cemetery where two Dervishes are buried (15C).

From here, the Selim II Mosque (10min on foot) is reached by taking Minar Sinan Cad.

Making the most of Edirne

COMING AND GOING

By train – Edirne is the first stop in Turkey for the old Orient Express and other trains coming from Europe. It takes longer to get to İstanbul by train than by bus (about 6hr, daily departures). Edirne has 2 stations, one south of the town which can be reached by taxi or dolmuş and the other at Kapıkule, on the Bulgarian border (west).

By bus – Take a dolmuş from the Rüstempaşa Kervansaray hotel (C2) to the bus station (Otobüs Garajı) (E3). Departures for İstanbul every 20min, journey time 4hr (230km). For Çanakkale, 2 buses leave in the morning and 2 in the evening, journey time 3hr 30min (223km).

Minibuses leave from the tourist information office for Kapıkule, the frontier post on the Bulgarian border, 18km from Edirne (open 24 hours a day). For Greece, a minibus will take you to the Turkish outpost of Pazarkule, 7km from Edirne, then you have to walk the last few hundred metres. On the Greek side (frontier post of Kastanies), the journey is made by taxi or on foot under escort (9am-1pm and 9am-11am at weekends).

By car – The E80 motorway links Edirne to İstanbul. Beware: fuel stations are few and far between.

ADDRESS BOOK

Tourist information – Hürriyet Meyd 17 (B2), ☎ (284) 213 92 08. 8.30am-6.30pm in summer, 5.30pm in winter.

Foreign newspapers – *ABC Kitabevi*, Orhisar İşhanı (at right angles to the post office) (C2), English press.

WHERE TO STAY

During the Kırkpınar festival in June, reservations should be made at least 1 month in advance. A great many hotels are located in the district around the post office.

Under US$15

Hotel Aksaray, Ortakapı Cad, ☎ (284) 212 60 35 – 15rm. An old and rather decrepit wooden house. Most of the high-ceilinged rooms only have a basin. Some charm, but a rudimentary level of comfort.

Between US$15 and US$30

Hotel Efe, Maarif Cad 13, ☎ (284) 213 61 66, Fax (284) 212 94 46 – 22rm. ⌑ ℰ TV Pleasant welcome. Adequate level of comfort.

Hotel Park, Maarif Cad 7, ☎ (284) 225 46 10, Fax (284) 225 46 35 – 60rm. ⌑ ℰ TV ✕ Impersonal welcome and decor, but clean and comfortable. Bar and discotheque.

Between US$30 and US$55

Sultan Oteli, Talat Paşa Cad 170 (B2), ☎ (284) 225 13 72 – 83rm. ⌑ ℰ TV ✕ A pleasant, well-run and tastefully renovated hotel.

⌑ **Hotel Rüstempaşa Kervansaray**, Eski Cami Yanı, ☎ (284) 225 21 95, Fax (284) 212 04 62 – 22rm. ⌑ ℰ TV CC Bar and billiard room. An amazing hotel set in an old renovated caravanserai with thick walls and a monastic level of comfort. Part of the establishment is reserved for students of a Koranic school, which has led it to be declassified by the Ministry of Tourism. Check the bill carefully.

EATING OUT

• In the town centre (C2)
Yeni Vatan, Kıyık Cad, Arasta Karşısı 28. Roast chicken, ratatouille, vegetable omelettes. Right next to the Selimiye Camii, handy for a quick, cheap lunch.
Üçler, Yeni Çarşı 12, behind the post office. Closes around 11pm, depending on the number of customers. Rice and chicken soups ("çorba"), lamb stock with potatoes ("kuzu haşlama"), alcohol. Local clientele and television tuned into sports programmes. Simple, good and cheap.
Serhad Köftecisi, Saraçlar Cad (B2), near Hürriyet Meyd. All the gourmets in town are familiar with its delicious "köfte" with yoghurt. A meal will set you back around US$3.

• Between the Meriç and the Tunca
This very pleasant place is difficult to find. Go south down Saraçlar Cad, turn right into Köprü Başı Cad (C3), go under the railway and cross the Tunca. Several restaurants are dotted along the riverside.
Yuva, Şaban Alabaş, ☏ (284) 225 20 67. Typically Turkish, with oilcloth, and sports on the television. Tables on the terrace or inside. Meze and rakı. Cheap.
Yuva ve Villa, Karaağaç Yolu, ☏ (284) 225 40 77. After the Yuva Restaurant, the road crosses the Meriç and turns right.

Large, rather pretentious, carpeted dining room. Meze, fish, alcohol. Expensive. Out front, an open-air café also belonging to the restaurant, serves grilled meats on the riverside, but watch out for the mosquitoes!
Lalezar, Karaağaç Yolu, just after the above restaurant, ☏ (284) 212 67 63. Vast white dining room specialising in banquets. Expensive.

HAVING A DRINK
The town centre is full of sunny pavement cafés, but some are for couples and families only and people on their own are not welcome. They do not serve alcohol. The nightclubs are open mainly in winter, when the students are around.
Malibu Bar, out of the town centre, next to the Yuva restaurant. Good for a drink.
Address Party, Belediye Karşısı Zemin Kat 1. A small street at the corner of Yapı Kredi and the post office (C2). 8pm-2am. Turkish, disco and rap music.

OTHER THINGS TO DO
Sokollu Mehmet Paşa Hamamı, Hükümet Cad, opposite Üç Şerefli Camii (B1-B2). 7am-11pm. Entry: US$5. This Turkish bath opens alternately to men ("erkekler kısmı") and women ("kadınlar kısmı").

İZNİK★

Bursa province – Map p 137
80km from Bursa – Pop 17 000
Alt 90m – Hot summers, mild winters

Not to be missed
The Ayasofya and the Green Mosque.
The Byzantine ramparts.
A walk around the lake.

And remember...
Enjoy a lakeside lunch.

For travellers arriving from Bursa, İznik appears suddenly at the turn of a bend. Wedged between the shores of Lake İznik and a row of hills – last buttress of the Köroğlu Dağları – the city seems lost in time, almost like a miniature from a medieval Book of Hours. Just as it was 1 600 years ago, it is surrounded by Byzantine ramparts, beyond which nothing has been built. Within the walls, a scattering of grey-tiled roofs rarely rises above the battlements. Two transversal axes – a vestige of the ancient city – create four equal-sized districts, crossed by small quiet streets barely disturbed by traffic.

Outside the walls, there are hedgerows of cypress, poplar and olive trees, casting their shadow over the prairies dotted with grazing sheep. Around the lake there are a number of restaurants with shaded, vine-covered terraces, good spots for enjoying both the scenery and the tasty grilled fish.

Capital of Empires

With the appearance of a sleepy town, far from the main thoroughfares, ancient **Nicaea** seems to ignore the events of the world. It was, however, once the capital of several successive empires and the seat of important councils.

The development of the city was placed under the auspices of two of Alexander the Great's generals: Antigonus who founded it in 316 BC, then Lysimachus, who took possession of it and gave it his wife's name, Nikaea. Nicaea became the capital of Bithynia, a status which Nicomedia (İzmit) forcefully removed in 264 BC. Nevertheless, the city continued to grow and experienced its first golden age under Roman domination, in particular under Hadrian who rebuilt it after the earthquake of 123 AD.

The Council of Nicaea

Nicaea was the seat of the First Ecumenical Council of the Catholic Church, convened by Constantine the Great in 325 to resolve the disciplinary and dogmatic conflicts which divided the Eastern Orthodox churches. The foundations of the Nicene Creed were defined (the Father and the Son are of the same substance) and Arianism was condemned. It was also in Nicaea that the council of 787 was held to resolve the Iconoclastic Crisis with the "Return of the Icons".

In the 6C, Emperor Justinian further embellished the town by building several monuments and restoring the ramparts, destroyed by the Goths and the Persians (3C). Nicaea resisted Arab attacks several times (8C) before falling in 1078, under the assaults of the Seljuks (who gave the place its current name). The crusaders wrested it from them in 1097, only to cede it to the Byzantines of **Theodore Lascaris**. Following the Crusaders' conquest of Constantinople (1204), the fallen Emperor established his headquarters making Nicaea the capital of the **Nicaean Empire**.

The Emperor prolonged his stay until 1261, when Constantinople recovered the status of capital as the Byzantine Empire was re-established.

This was an ephemeral episode, because the arrival of Orhan Gazi, in 1331, heralded the Byzantine Empire's death sentence. Transformed into the Ottoman capital, İznik was once again enriched with prestigious monuments and became highly prosperous. But not for long: successive earthquakes weakened it and the horror of the 1922 War of Independence was the final blow, yet İznik's old walls stubbornly continue to guard the glory of the past.

The City of Tiles

İznik owes its fame to the enamelled tiles and pottery, which have a central role in the art of Anatolian ceramics. This industry, whose origin dates back to prehistoric times, developed during the Roman period and continued throughout the whole Byzantine era. It was the Ottomans, however, who elevated its status to a prestigious level.

The oldest known tiles can be found in the Orhan Mosque (14C): green hexagonal ones covering the mihrab's niche. But it is the Green Mosque (1391) in İznik, which best exemplifies the development of this art with a magnificent combination of glazed bricks, sculptured tiles and mosaics. The red colour present in the beginning rapidly gave way to green and white as the technique evolved.

From the start of the 15C, İznik tiles quickly acquired an important reputation within the Ottoman Empire, adorning palaces and mosques in turquoise (the Blue Mosque and the Bağdat Köşkü in İstanbul's Topkapı, the Green Mausoleum in Bursa etc) before reaching Genoa and Venice. From 1514 onwards, Selim I had the best craftsmen brought in from Tabriz (Iran) in organised guilds under the protection of the sultan; the technique reached new heights and its apogee continued until the beginning of the 17C. Even though the kilns continued to function until the middle of the 18C, activity began to decline progressively. Since the 1980s, however, the tradition has seen a revival with the establishment of several workshops.

İznik

Ottoman tiles from İznik

P. Reimbold/HOA QUI

The City

Allow a half-day (on foot). The city centre is marked by the crossroads of Atatürk Cad (north-south) and Kılıçaslan Cad (east-west).

You can begin to explore İznik by visiting the **Ayasofya***, located in the centre of the city *(daily, 9am-5pm, closed Mondays; entrance fee. If the building is closed, ask for the key inside the museum).*

It is difficult to contain one's emotions when contemplating this time-worn edifice filled with so much history (it was here that the Seventh Council was held in 787). It is not an understatement to say that it has had a turbulent past, since three buildings have succeeded one another on this site. The first, dating from the reign of Justinian, was destroyed by an earthquake in 1065. The second church was converted into a mosque by Orhan Gazi in 1331, but burned down during the plundering of the city by Tamerlane, in 1402. Finally, it was reconstructed by Sinan in the 16C, to fall rapidly into ruins, until it lost its roof in the early 19C.

To the left of the entrance, the remains of the **minaret** serve as a sanctuary for storks whose nests are installed among the bricks. Beyond lies the nave, flanked by two bays and closed off by an apse which has retained its *synthronon* (clergy's steps), flanked since then by the Ottoman **mihrab**. Among the weeds invading the ground, a few beautiful **mosaics** are still visible. They are vestiges of Justinian's sanctuary and contemporaries of the pretty **fresco** decorating the northern wall, representing Jesus, Mary and St John the Baptist.

Just behind the Ayasofya, admire the splendid **Murat II Hammam** (Haci Hamza Hamamı) dating from the first half of the 15C. Since the room reserved for women is closed, the hamam is open on alternate days to both sexes.

About 300m from the central crossroads *(toward the east, on Kılıçaslan Cad)* rises the small **Hacı Özbek Mosque**. It is the oldest Ottoman sanctuary known to man (1332). The mosque's brick dome is covered with terracotta tiles. The portico was destroyed during the enlargement of the nearby street in 1939, but the interior retains its original appearance, exuding much charm.

Walk another 200m and take Müze Sokağı on the left.

The Green Mosque* (Yeşil Cami) is one of the city's most elegant, built by Hacı ben Musa (in 1492) for the Grand Vizier Çandarlı Kara Halil Hayrettin Paşa. The eye is immediately drawn to the superb tile-covered **minaret***, which gives the mosque its name (notice that some of the original tiles have been replaced by copies from Kütahya). Although the architecture betrays its Seljuk influence (small size and tile-covered minaret), the mosque retains a dome which is among the oldest in Ottoman art.

On the other side rises the **Nilüfer Hatun Imaret**, built in 1388 by Murat I to honour his mother (Nilüfer Hatun). The building was originally intended to be used as a *zaviye*, an establishment which welcomed wandering Dervishes and pilgrims. Its remarkable **walls** have brickwork in four different bands, resting on a stone base. A long porch precedes a long central hall, covered by a dome whose openings allow the outside light to fully illuminate the interior. The far end leads to the prayer hall, while the side rooms, each with their own *ocak* (chimney), house the dormitories and the kitchens.

The Imaret currently houses an interesting **Archeological Museum** *(8.30am-12noon/1pm-5pm, entrance fee)*, dedicated to the Hellenistic, Roman, Byzantine, Seljuk, and Ottoman periods. It includes very beautiful 14C and 15C **crockery****.

In a small side street *(south of the museum, next to the Imaret)*, admire the ruins of the small **Şeyh Kutbeddin Mosque** and its minaret, now inhabited by storks. Built by Grand Vizier İbrahim Paşa in the 15C, it was destroyed by the Greeks in the 1920s.

Around the Ramparts★★

Allow 2-3hr for a complete tour of the city. If you wish to see only the gateways the most interesting feature – 1hr is enough. Avoid climbing on the walls; they are very fragile in some parts.

More than the buildings and monuments, the ramparts are the city's most attractive feature. Forming an irregular 5km-long polygon, the double line of walls is pierced by four large gates (the main one, on the side nearest the lake, has disappeared) and 12 secondary ones. The inner wall, 9m high and almost 4m thick, has no fewer than 114 towers, just a little more than the outer wall, which is slightly lower and not as broad. A 15m-wide water-filled moat separates the two walls.

The inner wall was raised towards the end of the 3C AD under Emperor Claudius II, who retained parts of the 1C wall. It was renovated by Justinian in the 6C, then again in the 9C after the Arab invasions. In the 13C, when Theodore I settled in İznik, he had the wall raised and doubled it with an outside wall preceded by a moat. Since the Hellenistic vestiges have disappeared, only Byzantine, Roman and a few Ottoman additions are still visible.

The İstanbul Gate★ (north) is the most beautiful and the best preserved. This massive fortification, a triumphal arch with three openings between two robust towers, must have made a powerful impression on both the enemies and peaceable visitors passing through. The gate was built in the year 123 to commemorate Emperor Hadrian's visit. The arch itself connects the two walls. On the interior façade on both sides of the structure you can see two masks in relief, one of a woman, the other of a man, taken undoubtedly from the Roman theatre (which has since disappeared), while the marble bas-reliefs decorate the outer façade. Nearby, the battlement has unfortunately been pierced in order to allow traffic to pass.

To the south the **Yenişehir Gate**, built under Claudius II in 268, is framed by two 13C bastions. The work includes three bays leading to a small courtyard. It is the most damaged gate, since it is from here that the Seljuks attacked and that Orhan Gazi entered the city.

Like the İstanbul Gate, the **Lefke Gate** *(to the east)* is formed by a triumphal arch connecting the two walls. The façade of the inner gate is decorated with ancient murals representing the Romans fighting barbarians.

If you have time, explore the Byzantine vestiges located in the southeastern corner of the city. You will see a **sacred fountain** (Ayazma), which is actually a small, square Byzantine cistern *(ask for the key in the museum)*. The Hebrew inscription seems to indicate that it was formerly attached to a synagogue.

Next door *(in İstiklal Cad)*, take a look at the **Church of the Virgin** (Koimesis), the last remaining part of a 9C Byzantine monastery destroyed in 1922 during the war against the Greeks. The only remains are some walls and a few fragments of the floor mosaics. The building housed the tomb of the Emperor, Theodore I Lascaris, founder of the Nicaean Empire.

Continue west along Yakup Sokağı, 300m after Atatürk Cad.

A large grass-covered mound is the setting of the scattered and protruding ruins of the **Roman Theatre** where the local children love to play. Inaugurated in 113 AD by Pliny the Younger, governor of Bithynia, this theatre could accommodate

15 000 spectators. It was oriented to the north so that spectators could enjoy the summer's fresh evening breezes. The Byzantines used its stonework to construct various buildings. Excavations (now on hold) have revealed the stage, the side exits, the *orchestra* and the *cavea*. They have also brought to light the vestiges of a 13C Byzantine church and a cemetery, as well as sculptures, ceramics and pottery from different eras.

The Lake and its Surroundings

From the Lefke Gate, a short and rewarding trip gives you a view of the city in its setting. One hundred or so metres beyond the gate (*on the left*), stands the **Mausoleum of Çandarlı Halil Hayrettin Paşa**, a rich Ottoman born in 1387. Time-worn and a bit decrepit, it sits in a charming pine tree-shaded cemetery.

Beyond, the road runs along a vegetation-invaded Roman **aqueduct** which still serves to irrigate the fields. At the top of the hill, after 1.5km, you reach the **Tomb of Abdülvahap**, an Ottoman soldier who, legend has it, buried himself after his head was cut off during the siege of İznik at the beginning of the 14C. The site is especially interesting for its amazing **panorama**★★ of the lake and the plain, and an ideal place to observe the layout of the city and its ramparts.

İznik lake lies at the foot of the city, towards the west. The lake stretches out for 30km between two low mountain ranges, providing a lovely **view**★★. Picnic areas and restaurants are found along the shores. It is undoubtedly one of the most pleasant places for a lunch break. Swimming is allowed, if you are tempted, but the water is chilly even in summer.

Archeology enthusiasts will make the trip to the village of **Elbeyli**, 6km north of İznik, to see an impressive 2C AD **obelisk** consisting of five blocks of stone (originally six). It used to be topped with a statue of a bird.

Close by, an **underground cellar**, dug in the 4C, contains two tombs. The back wall is decorated with a **fresco** representing the combat of two peacocks, topped by a cross.

Making the most of İznik

COMING AND GOING

A return trip can easily be made in one day from Bursa.

By bus – Departures every hour from Bursa, 80km away (90min). The last bus back leaves between 6pm and 7pm. The journey to İstanbul lasts 3hr 30min. You can also take the bus to Yalova (75min) then a ferry (see "Making the most of Bursa").

ADDRESS BOOK

Tourist information – Belediye İşhanı Kat 1, 130-131, ☎ (224) 757 14 54, Fax (224) 757 19 33, 8am-12noon / 1pm-5pm. In Kılıçaslan Cad, opposite a small park, just after the Ayasofya basilica. Tucked away on the first floor of an arcade.

Main post office – Kılıçaslan Cad, west of the junction with Atatürk Cad. 8am-12noon / 1.30pm-5.30pm.

Bus station – Near the southern entrance to the town. ☎ (224) 757 14 18.

WHERE TO STAY

Most foreign visitors just go to İznik for the day and spend the night in Bursa. The town does, however, have a few establishments where you can find a double room for under US$15. Many Turks come to İznik for the weekend, so it is best to book in advance.

Under US$15

Hotel Kaynarca, Kılıçaslan Cad, Mah Gündem Sok 1, ☎ (224) 757 17 53 – 6rm. ☝ In the town centre. The rooms are small, but good value for money.

Between US$15 and US$25

Motel Burcum, Göl Kenarı, ☎ (224) 757 10 11 – 25rm. ☝ ✗ Basic but adequate level of comfort and the rooms are

clean. The hotel stands at the lakeside and some of the rooms afford a beautiful view.

Motel Çamlık, Göl Kenarı, ☎ (224) 757 16 31 – 32rm. ☝ ✗ Also at the lakeside, but more to the south, near the ramparts. The rooms are tiny but have a good view of the lake.

Hotel Şener, Belediye yanı H Oktay Sok 7, ☎ (224) 757 14 80, Fax (224) 757 13 38 – 21rm. ☝ ♪ 📺 ✗ In the town centre. More expensive and not as pleasant as the Kaynarca, but upmarket.

EATING OUT

The countless fish restaurants on the lakeside all have more or less the same menu. In the town centre there are also establishments which serve grilled meats, "köfte" and "pide". The prices are reasonable (US$6 all inclusive, with coffee).

Kırık Çatal, Göl Kenarı, ☎ (224) 757 29 90. Part of the Burcum motel. Diners eat among the olive trees, under the shade of a canopy of vines.

Savarona, Göl Kenarı. Also on the lakeside, slightly further to the north than the one above. This place is usually quite lively.

Konya Etli Pide Salonu, Kılıçaslan Cad. As you can probably guess by its name, this place only serves pide with a large choice of fillings. Cheap and copious.

Ottoman Restaurant, Kılıçaslan Cad 137. Grilled meats and dishes in a variety of sauces, at very reasonable prices.

SHOPPING GUIDE

Ceramics are, of course, the main speciality of İznik. Some boutiques can be found in Kılıçaslan Cad and near the museum. Several workshops were set up in the 1980s and a ceramics research centre was founded in 1995 to perpetuate the tradition.

BURSA ★★

Provincal capital – 240km from İstanbul
Map p 137 – Pop 1 100 000 – Alt 250m on average
Climate: hot and sunny summers, mild winters.

Not to be missed
The Green Mosque and the Green Mausoleum.
The Grand Mosque and the caravanserais of the city centre.
The Muradiye Complex.
The view of the valley and the Uludağ.

And remember...
It is best to use public transport since traffic is chaotic.
If you are on foot, begin your visit in the east to keep walking downhill.
If you go to Uludağ, bring along a warm sweater, even in summer.

Bursa, "the green city", stretches out along the side of a mountain in an idyllic setting on the lower slopes of the Uludağ. In winter, the Gökdere and the Çilimboz, the two streams running in deep ravines through the city from north to south may suddenly overflow with the melting of the snow. The Turks bestow an aura of spirituality on Bursa. For them, the city symbolises the first age of Ottoman culture, when there seemed to be no limit to the expansion of their empire, and when new forms of art, revealed by architectural marvels, emerged.

The Cradle of the Ottoman Empire
Founded by the King of Bithynia, Prusias I, at the end of the 3C BC, the former *Prusa ad Olympium* fell under the yoke of Rome in the 1C BC. Evangelised by St Andrew, the city enjoyed a prosperous era under the Byzantines (Justinian had a palace built) due to its thermal springs and the success of silkworm farming. From the 11C onwards, the Seljuks and the Byzantines fought bitterly over it until Constantinople was conquered by the crusaders in 1204. The Byzantine Emperor thereupon decided to use the region as a base for re-conquering the city.

The Silk City
The farming of the silkworm, which goes back probably to the period of Justinian (6C), was the foundation of Bursa's prosperity for more than a thousand years. Not only did the workshops produce the silk, but the caravanserais of the city welcomed all the caravans of the Orient transporting the most beautiful Persian silks. Bursa therefore became the biggest transshipment point of oriental merchandise destined for İstanbul and Eastern Europe, and many foreign merchants flocked to its markets. Through the centuries, Bursa became the largest raw silk production centre in the world, known also by the sultry French name of *Brousse*. Beginning in the 18C, its fabulous prosperity went into decline when Europe itself began producing silk (in Lyons), and İzmir stole its warehousing role.

But in 1326, the Ottoman sultan, Orhan Gazi, seized Prusa after a siege which lasted nearly 10 years. He renamed the city Bursa and made it the capital of his empire. Following the nomadic tradition and the call of military campaigns, the first sultans did not live in the city, but embellished it with numerous monuments and had themselves buried there (Osman Gazi and his five successors). In 1402, Tamerlane conquered the city, but it continued to play a major role in the Ottoman Empire, even after the capital had been transferred to Edirne. A city of commerce from the time of the Silk Road, Bursa remains an important economic hub for Turkey.

The ancient textile (including silk) industry has been enhanced by undertakings involved in processing foodstuffs, followed by the automobile manufacture in the 1960s (Renault and Fiat car factories). In spite of these activities, Bursa has managed to retain its human dimension with lively markets and old houses which punctuate the streets of the upper city (to the west). It is always a pleasure to wander around the colourful old neighbourhoods whose atmosphere recalls the golden years of the Ottoman era.

The Eastern Side of Bursa
Allow 2hr for the visit.

It is in this part of the city that the greatest monuments of Ottoman architectural masterpieces in Bursa are located. The **Beyazıt I Imperial Complex**★ (Yıldırım Beyazıt Camii) (F2), is located to the northeast. Upon arrival, the magnificent **façade**★★ of the mosque is striking, as is the equally elegant marble **portico**★. It is the most beautiful remnant of this structure, built in 1395. Besides the mosque, the Beyazıt I *türbe*, the medrese and the ruins of an aqueduct still stand in spite of repeated earthquake damage. The **mosque** was built according to an inverted T-plan, a regional variation of the classical Ottoman layout *(see p 49)*. A vestibule precedes the courtyard leading to a prayer hall whose entrance is through a large flattened arch. Both areas are covered by a dome. The slightly elevated side chambers in the courtyard house the **medrese's** study rooms.

Climb up to the small streets towards the south, for 1km, walking along the stream.

Renovated at the beginning of the nineties, the **Emir Sultan Mosque** (F3) stands next to a **cemetery** on a hill. From above, the **view**★ of the city and valley below is lovely (this is the resting place of Zeki Müren, a great star of Turkish popular music and film, who died in 1996). Completed in 1805, under Selim III, the mosque is located on the site of a 14C sanctuary. After the earthquake of 1855, the building was reconstructed in a Baroque style, in contrast to the usual austerity which typifies such a building.

The Mehmet I Imperial Complex
Set on a terrace on the edge of the city, the **Green Mosque**★★★ (Yeşil Cami) (F3) has fine minarets which rise from the midst of cypress trees. A jewel of white marble and ceramic tiles, it perfectly illustrates the refinement sought by the Osmanlı sultans. Ornaments, wreaths and rosettes create a fine lacework of stone around the doors and windows. Along with the Mehmet I mausoleum facing it, it is part of a large Imperial complex designed by the architect Hacı İvaz Paşa from 1413 to 1421. The building owes its name to the green tones of its **superb tiles**★★ (unfortunately some of the tiles disappeared during the terrible earthquake which shattered the city in 1855 and have been replaced with dull turquoise ones). Although it respects the inverted T-plan, typical of Bursa, the mosque appears to have been cut from a single block: instead of emphasising the dynamic balance of the building, the architect chose to hide the structural elements, giving the rather small-scale interior an austere appearance and contemplative atmosphere.

Past the vestibule – where you remove your shoes and women are asked to select a scarf from a dusty heap – enter the domed central hall, overlooked by the sultan's apartments leading to the nave. The nave creates a courtyard, embellished with the traditional *şadırvan* (fountain), covered by a **cupola** decorated with arabesques. On both sides, note the slightly elevated lateral wings, while a large arch leads to the prayer hall itself.

The 15m high **mihrab***** is a wonder, a true gate to paradise, with outstanding white enamel calligraphy on a blue background, the trademark of the masters from Tabrizi (Iran). The magnificent hexagonal **enamel tiles**** colouring the walls are from İznik (*see p 199*). Inspired by the Seljuks, they are star-shaped as if, in recreating the celestial vault, the artists had attempted to bring the sky within reach of the faithful.

Two sets of wooden stairs lead to the Imperial salons above the vestibule. In the centre, the **sultan's loge**** is a jewel-like space rich with carpets, a star-painted ceiling and a ceramic balustrade.

Another gem of the complex, the **Green Mausoleum**** (Yeşil Türbe) (F3) is an elegant octagonal building topped by a single dome (*8am-12noon/1pm-5pm, no charge*). The original green tiles which decorated the outside walls were replaced with turquoise-coloured ones in the 19C. Original features include the window **calligraphy**, and the tiles of the inner walls, which are of the distinctive green colour marking them as the work of Tabriz masters. Beautiful enamelled tile **mosaics*** embellish the dome, which is supported by fan-shaped pendentives. Everything is of the finest quality: the **mihrab***, with its fine calligraphy on a flowery background, the **stained glass*** of the windows, a delicate web of white marble sprinkled with multicoloured glass and even the smallest wooden panel whose engravings resemble lace.

Last but not least, admire the sultan's **tomb****, a marvel of refinement with yellow calligraphy traced out on a blue background surrounded by flower garlands. Mehmet "the fighter" was considered by his contemporaries to be a good and charitable sovereign. His death in Edirne, in 1421, was kept a secret until his son Murat arrived in Bursa. The other stone coffins belong to his children and his nurse.

Just below the mosque, the **Museum of Turkish and Islamic Arts** (Türk ve İslam Eserleri Müzesi) (F3) is worth the detour (*8am-12noon/1pm-5pm, closed Mondays; entrance fee*). Housed in the complex's old **medrese**, its rooms display beautiful wooden furniture encrusted with ivory, 19C bath accessories and all types of attire, materials and clothes, as well as arms and Karagöz puppets. You can also admire a beautiful reconstruction of an Ottoman café and a circumcision chamber (*sünnet odası*).

Exterior tiling of the Green Mausoleum, Bursa

G. Degeorge

In the little street around the museum are a number of beautiful **houses***, with projecting upper storeys, giving some idea of what Bursa must have looked like in the 19C before the earthquake devastated it.

The City Centre
Allow 2hr to visit

It is in the caravanserais, the markets and the shopping streets around the Grand Mosque that the heartbeat of Bursa can be felt.

Begin with the little **Orhan Mosque** (Orhaniye Cami) (D3), the oldest Imperial sanctuary of Bursa (1339), rebuilt in the 15C and again in the 19C. Unusually, its **mihrab** faces southwest and not towards Mecca. Solar discs and brick rosettes decorate the outer walls. A beautiful **portico** precedes the building, supported by elegant pillars and two 5C Corinthian columns. Inside, the *eyvan* were used to welcome the Dervishes of the Ahi brotherhood.

Outside the mosque is **Orhan Gazi Square.** The café tables set out around the fountain are inviting, and provide an excellent vantage point for watching the activity in the shopping arcardes and covered market.

On the other side of the square, surrounded by a few cypresses, rises the massive and impressive **Grand Mosque*** (Ulu Cami) (D3). The limestone walls, with beautiful shades of honey, pink and brown, come from the Uludağ. Only one of the two **minarets** withstood the earthquake of 1855.

According to legend, Beyazıt I made a vow, on the eve of a battle, to build 20 mosques in case of victory. Having won, he built the Ulu Cami (1399) which he covered with 20 domes (all collapsed during the earthquake, but the mosque was rebuilt). The centre of temporal and spiritual life in Bursa, the mosque was surrounded by three medrese, several caravanserais, a primary school, a hamam, a Dervish convent and a cemetery.

Some claim that the majestic **portal** is the work of Tamerlane who occupied the city in 1402-1403, even though the design of its frame betrays its Seljuk influence.

The **interior*** is a forest of columns and pillars bathed in light. In the middle, there is a 19C **ablutions fountain*** (*şadırvan*), while beautiful **calligraphy** surrounded by flower motifs covers the walls. However, the most beautiful feature of the mosque is the **minbar**** made of carved walnut and one of Turkey's most beautiful; its many different parts fit together without the benefit of glue or nails.

Behind the Ulu Cami, in the heat of a maze of shopping streets, lies the **covered market** (bedesten) (D2). Built during the same period and reconstructed after the earthquake of 1855, for centuries it remained the hub for all merchants. Today, its clientele is mostly Turkish and good deals can be made there.

East of the *bedesten*, is the **Eski Aynalı Çarşı** (D2), a picturesque market set in the ancient **Orhan Gazi Turkish Bath**, built in 1335. In the market is the Karagöz antique shop, which sells marionettes and stages puppet shows (the great heroes of Turkish puppet theatre, Kargöz and Hacivat, orignially came from Bursa) (*see "Making the most of Bursa", and also Karagöz, p 92*). Not to be missed!

The Caravanserais
The city centre is home to countless caravanserais, where merchants from the four corners of the Empire and beyond, sojourned while completing their transactions. It is interesting to imagine these vast inns during the period of the silk trade, bustling with activity, resonating with a hundred tongues, packed with horses and camels carrying heavy loads.

Attached to the Eski Aynalı Çarşı, the **Koza Hanı**★ (D3) ("of the cocoon", 1490) is one of the rare *hans* to have kept its original function, the farming of silkworms. In June and September the villagers of the region come to sell their harvests. The southern entrance *(on Gazi Camii Parkı)* provides direct access to the first floor, where travelling merchants lodged (shops and stables were located on the ground floor). A small octagonal **mosque** *(masgid)* stands in the courtyard alongside a large pool. Built in 1493, it was renovated by silk merchants in 1948, then by the Aga Khan in 1985.

No fewer than four caravanserais, more or less in good condition, surround the covered market *(bedesten)*. To the south, the **Emir Hanı**★ (D2) *(or Bey Hanı)* is the city's oldest (1340) caravanserai as well as one of the most beautiful, with an attractive **marble fountain**.

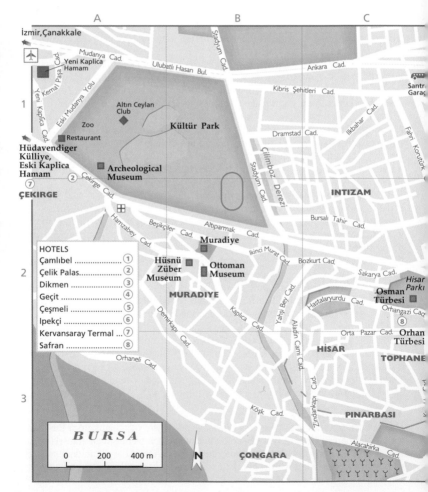

The Upper City

West of the city centre, Orhangazi Cad climbs up towards the Hisar district. Take a taxi or a dolmuş, since the attractions are far apart. Allow 3hr.

Byzantine ruins, Turkish baths, mosques, old Ottoman homes overlooking the bustling streets and their shops, the Hisar ("the fortress") district and the surroundings of the Muradiye Mosque reveal the soul of ancient Bursa. Take the time to wander about before relaxing in the greenery of the Kültür Park.

The Hisar District

Covering a hill west of the city centre, Hisar is Bursa's oldest district, still guarded by the remains of a Hellenistic wall. The maze of its streets hides some interesting rows of slightly decaying **Ottoman houses**★, with old-fashioned looking white or pastel

J.F. Galmiche

Old Ottoman houses

façades. From the entrance to **Hisar Park** (Hisar Parkı) (C2), a rampart of vegetation surrounding the hill, there is a very beautiful **view**★ of the city below and the outskirts. Facing the park entrance admire the **Osman and Orhan Gazi Mausoleums**, resting places of the founder of the Osmanlı Dynasty (d 1324) and his son, Sultan Orhan (d 1360). The two buildings were reconstructed after the earthquake of 1855 in the purest Baroque style of the Ottoman 19C. The Orhan *türbe* contains the fragments of the **mosaic** which covered the floor of the St Elias Byzantine Basilica.

The Complex of Murat II★★ (Muradiye) (B2)
2km west of the city centre. 8.30am-5.30pm, closed Mondays. Entrance fee.

Hidden in the middle of a delightful garden is one of the last Imperial complexes of Bursa, completed in 1426 by Murat II. The sovereigns who founded it rest in the sober and elegant mausoleums, dispersed among the cypress trees and flowers. The serene atmosphere makes it difficult to imagine the tumultuousness of the period when the hunger for power compelled members of the Imperial family to kill one another, only to ultimately lie in peace side by side.

Preceded by a portico with domes, the **Murat II Mosque** (also known as Hüdavendigar Camii) is built according to the traditional inverted T-plan. The interior has kept its beautiful hexagonal **tiles**★ (in a range of tones) varying from navy blue to turquoise to green, sprinkled with floral and geometrical patterns. Notice the marble **rosette** on the right of the entrance, the emblem of the Dervishes.

Nearby, the pink brick-walled **medrese*** – which serves as a dispensary – is the most beautiful in Bursa. The cells are laid out around a handsome square courtyard transformed into a garden. Only the **main study hall**, higher than the other rooms, is decorated with tiles.

Lost among the cypresses and the magnolias, 13 little pink-brick and white-stone **mausoleums*** house the remains of Murat II and a few members of the Imperial family (late 15C and 16C). The majority are decorated with magnificent blue enamelled İznik **tiles*** *(if closed, ask the guardian for the key).*

At the end of the avenue, the octagonal tower houses the **Tomb of Prince Ahmet**, the son of Beyazıt I. To the right, the **Murat II Türbe** (d 1451) is reached through a magnificent painted porch in sculpted wood, which contrasts with the austerity of the interior. Thanks to the opening in the dome, the tomb, beneath its simple earth mound, is watered by the rain, according to the sultan's wishes. Further along, we find the **Mustafa Türbe** (Şehzade Mustafa Türbesi), Süleyman's son, executed by his father in 1553. On the right, lies the **Djem Mausoleum***, Mehmet the Conqueror's youngest son, who fought over the throne with his brother Beyazıt II before dying as a captive of the Pope, in 1495. The inside of the tomb is decorated with enamelled tiles and superb paintings. Finally, there is the **Mahmut Mausoleum** *(behind, at the back of the garden)*, with blue tiles enhanced with gilding. Mahmut's father had him executed for rebellion in 1507.

A good place to recover from the contemplation of such violent history is the **Darrüzziyafe Restaurant**, inside one of the buildings *(in Murat Cad, see "Making the most of Bursa").*

On the little square in front of the complex, the **Ottoman Museum*** (B2) is worth a visit because it is housed in a beautiful, entirely renovated, 17C *konak* (Ottoman home). The interior gives an insight into the life of a well-to-do man of this period. *(Theoretically 8.30am-12noon/1pm-5pm, closed Mondays, entrance fee.)*

From Muradiye Camii, walk south along **Uzunyol Sokak*** (B2) where you will see another row of elegant pastel-coloured **Ottoman houses**. Before leaving the neighbourhood, have a look at the unusual **Hüsnü Züber Living Museum** (Hüsnü Züber Evi) (B2), housed in a residence dating from 1836, which once served as the Russian consulate *(10am-12noon/1pm-5pm, closed Monday, entrance fee)*. Hüsnü Züber – the owner – is a singular and eccentric man, a former lieutenant-colonel of the Turkish army, author of several works, illustrator and pyrographer. Under his strict authority you are shown the interesting rooms dedicated to the restoration of his home, his spoon collection, his pyrographies on wood and his series of yearly self-portraits from 1931 onwards!

The Kültür Park (A1-2)

North of the Muradiye. From Heykel, take a bus or dolmus (direct).

A haven of relaxation, the Kültür Park is much appreciated by the residents of Bursa. People come for a walk, to have tea at tables set up outside the cafés or lunch at one of the lakeside restaurants. Families bring their children to the **amusement park**, while the well-heeled meet in the Altın Ceylan Club *(see "Making the most of Bursa").*

The small **Archeological Museum** (A1) is set in the park, near the southwest entrance *(9am-5pm, closed Mondays)*. Not quite in the same league as the one in İstanbul, it nevertheless contains interesting items from the Hittite, Greek, Persian, Roman and Byzantine periods found in the region.

West of the Kültür Park, on the first street descending on the right, are the **Yeni Kaplıca Hamam** ("new baths"), built in 1555 *(see "Making the most of Bursa")*. Byzantine columns surround the marble pool, and the adjacent rooms are decorated with enamelled tiles.

Another hamam in the neighbourhood is the **Eski Kaplıca Hamam**, located in the heart of the enjoyable tree-shaded **Çekirge** district *(near the Kervansaray Termal Hotel)*. Recently renovated, it is Bursa's oldest bathhouse (14C).

The Hüdavendigar Complex (Hüdavendigar Külliye)

Designed by Murat I, "the creator of the Universe", Bursa's oldest Imperial complex (1366) has retained its **mosque**. While its layout is obviously Ottoman (the inevitable inverted T-plan), the architectural design reveals its architect's Italian origin: two-storey portico, façade gallery, ogival arcades and windows with delicate colonnettes recalling the Renaissance. Here and there appear Byzantine capitals removed from ancient monuments. Uniquely in Ottoman architecture, the **medrese** is located on the first floor. While theology students studied the Koran in all its orthodoxy, the Dervishes, defenders of a radically opposed mystic Islam, were housed in the ground floor *zavyie.*

Around Bursa

The Sea of Marmara is not far away, but it is not the ideal coastline for bathing. Facing the comings and goings of merchant ships, its concrete-lined shores are hardly an invitation to relaxation. In some sections, however, the coastal road is enjoyable, especially between Çınarcık and Gemlik; but do not expect to find an isolated Mediterranean-style cove or beach. **Çınarcık, Mudanya** and **Gemlik**, the beach resorts closest to Bursa, do not have any special appeal.

The region's attractions lie beyond, in the mountains overlooking Bursa to the south-west. In winter, the snow-filled slopes welcome skiers and in all seasons it is possible to take advantage of the hot water springs for which Bursa has been famous for centuries.

The Uludağ★

Dolmuş shuttles leave regularly from Bursa's bus station for the Uludağ (36km); however, the cable car (teleferik) is more convenient and comfortable. The station is on the eastern side of Yeşil Cami. In summer, the service is frequent but the wait can be long. The trip to Sarıalan lasts 30min. Allow a full day (or two) to take full advantage of the park.

Overlooking the city to the south, the peaks and slopes of the Uludağ (2 543m) are a wonderful asset for Bursa. One of the ranges given the name of Mount Olympus by the Greeks, it became a refuge for thieves who were more or less persecuted during the iconoclastic period. Today, city-dwellers flee here for the fresh air and the joys of skiing. Now a conservation area, the landscape will delight mountain ramblers.

At an altitude of 1 635m, **Sarıalan** hosts restaurants, souvenir shops and a camping site. From there, **walking trails** head deep into the mountain and its magnificent **scenery★**.

From Sarıalan, there is a 6km drive by *dolmuş* shuttle to the **Uludağ ski resort**, with a dozen hotels *(usually open during the ski season only)*.

From here, it is possible to reach the **summit** after an easy 3hr walk, through the superb **Uludağ National Park★** (11 000ha), rich in fauna and flora: olive trees, lavender, junipers, green oak, Byzantium hazel, lime trees, beech trees, oak; deer, bucks, wild boars, bears and wolves (rare), as well as mountain rams (at higher altitudes). The best period to visit is in the springtime when the park is covered in flowers, or from December to March, the ski season.

Making the most of Bursa

COMING AND GOING

By air – Direct flights from İstanbul and Ankara. The airport is northwest of the city, on the main road to Ankara. Two airline companies operate in Bursa: *THY*, Çakır Hamam Cad 16/B, ☎ (224) 221 11 67;

Sönmez Holding Hava Yolları, at the airport, ☎ (224) 246 54 45. Departures for İstanbul at 8.30am and 3pm from Monday to Friday, and at 9am on Saturdays.

By bus – *Ottomantur*, Cemal Nadir Cad Kızılay Pasajı (D3), Cakırhamam, near Ulu Cami, ☎ (221) 222 20 97. This company operates a service to Bursa airport. Buses for İstanbul every hour (journey time: 5hr).

By shared taxi – Departures for Yalova every 30min.

By bus and ferry – The bus station ("Santral Garajı") (C1) is at the end of Fevzi Çakmak Cad, on the main road to Ankara. The fastest route to İstanbul is by bus to Yalova (70min), then hydrofoil (1hr) to Kabataş, near Dolmabahçe, on the Bosphorus. The ferry is cheaper but takes longer (2hr 30min). The journey by land (4 to 5hr) is of no particular interest. Departures every hour for Ankara (5hr 30min), Çanakkale (5hr), and İznik (90min).

By ferry – Go to Eskihisar, in the Asian suburbs of İstanbul and embark for Topçular (13km from Yalova): this way you will avoid a long uninteresting detour via İzmit.

FINDING YOUR WAY

Lodged in the valley, between the slopes of Uludağ, the city stretches out in a long thin line. The great *Atatürk Cad*, runs through the city centre (shopping centre), which is known as *Heykel* (D2-3, E3) ("the statue") after the great equestrian statue (of Atatürk, of course) which has pride of place in the middle of the main square, Cumhuriyet Alanı.

GETTING AROUND

Traffic circulation, which is very heavy at rush hour, is further complicated by the one-way streets, which can cause long detours. It is really better to walk or use public transport. When you arrive in Bursa, park your car in an "otopark" and forget about it until you are ready to leave (be careful where you park, the police are very vigilant). Buses, taxis and dolmuşes are also very convenient for less accessible places, such as Çekirge, or the "otogar" (bus *no* 18).

ADDRESS BOOK

Tourist information – Orhangazi Altgeçidi 1, Heykel (D3), in the shopping arcade down below Atatürk Cad, in front of Orhan Gazi square, ☎ (224) 220 18 48. Friendly welcome.

Consulate – *British Consulate*, Ressam Refik Bursalı Cad 40, Zemin Kat, ☎ (224) 220 04 36, Fax (224) 220 03 31.

WHERE TO STAY

A wide range of establishments can be found in the city centre, but the luxury hotels are mainly in Çekirge, where they have their own thermal facilities.

Under US$15

Hotel Geçit, Celal Bayar Cad 175, ☎ (224) 254 10 32. A guest house with a basic level of comfort but in a quiet neighbourhood. One of the best places to stay near the bus station.

Hotel İpekçi, Cancılar Cad 38, to the north of Heykel, ☎ (224) 221 19 35. ⁋ Guaranteed peace and quiet, even though the place does not look very appealing.

Between US$15 and US$30

🏨*Hotel Çeşmeli*, Gümüşçeken Cad 6, Heykel, ☎ (224) 224 15 11. ⁋ 𝒫 TV A quiet, friendly establishment. One of the best value hotels in the city centre.

Hotel Dikmen, Maksem Cad, ☎ (224) 224 18 40 – 50rm. ⁋ 𝒫 TV Pretty indoor garden with fountain.

Between US$30 and US$75

Hotel Safran, Kale Sok, Tophane, ☎ (224) 224 72 16, Fax (224) 224 72 19 – 10rm. ⁋ 𝒫 TV ✕ CC In the Hisar district, opposite the park where Osman Gazi is buried. Very charming building. Small but comfortable rooms.

Hotel Çamlıbel, İnebey Cad 71, ☎ (224) 221 25 65. ⁋ This renovated hotel offers the advantage of a central but quiet location.

- **Çekirge**

Over US$75

Hotel Çelik Palas, Çekirge Cad 79, ☎ (224) 233 38 00 – 173rm. ⚏ 🖃 𝒫 📺 ✗ � A high-class establishment with every amenity (Turkish bath, discotheque). The decor is a tasteful combination of modern and traditional styles. Inaugurated by Atatürk in 1935, many famous personalities have stayed here, notably King Idris of Libya, who learnt during his sojourn that he had been overthrown by a certain Colonel Khadaffi!

Hotel Kervansaray Termal, Çekirge Meyd, ☎ (224) 233 93 00, Fax (224) 233 93 24 – 211rm. ⚏ 🖃 𝒫 📺 ✗ ⎓ � This luxury hotel opened in 1988 and houses the famous Eski Kaplıca Turkish bath. Numerous amenities (discotheque, gym). The same chain also owns two other establishments, one at Uludağ and the other in Bursa.

EATING OUT

It was in Bursa in the 19C that İskender invented the "döner kebab" in the restaurant which bears his name. His method of cooking lamb on a vertical skewer spread throughout the whole country. The Bursa kebab, served in many "kebapçisi", is a "döner kebab" on a slice of bread ("pide") with tomato sauce and a butter sauce. The other speciality is "İnegöl köftesi", a very tasty grilled spicy meatball.

Arap Şükrü Sokak, to the north of Hisar (**C2**) (go down Nadir Cad, turn left on Altıparmak Cad, then left a little further on into a small pedestrian street, which is very lively in the evening), ☎ (224) 221 14 53. The terrace is an ideal place to stop for meze with rakı.

Darüzziyafe, II Murat Cad 36 (**B2**), ☎ (224) 224 64 39. Set in one of the magnificent buildings of the Muradiye for "the preservation of the Turkish culinary tradition". Kebabs and "köfte", but no alcohol.

Cumurcul, Çekirge Cad (**A1**). One of the most chic restaurants in the city, set in an elegant residence on the edge of Kültür Park.

Oz Urfal Hacı Dayı, in the small Hisar park (**C2**). Serves "köfte" and "pide".

Yüce Hünkar, near Yeşil Cami. Rather like a tourist canteen, but a convenient place to go after your visit. Café and restaurant on 2 levels. Only serves pizzas and kebabs. Average welcome.

İskender Kebabçı, Ünlü Cad 7, Heykel (**E3**), ☎ (224) 221 46 15. Excellent "İskender kebab", with or without yoghurt. The waiter pours black butter sauce over the kebabs – delicious! Customers pay at the counter and the prices are low. Somewhat kitsch decoration.

Adanur Hacıbey, opposite İskender Kebabçı, in Ünlü Cad (**E3**), ☎ (224) 21 64 40. Plainer than the one above. Aubergine puree, "İskender kebab".

İnegöl Köftecisi, Atatürk Cad 48 (**E3**). The speciality here is meatballs ("köfte") with onions, cheese or grilled. US$6 per meal.

Çiçek Izgara, Belediye Cad 15 (**D3**), to the north of Koza Hanı. Excellent roast meat at very reasonable prices.

Ömür Restaurant, in the covered market of Ulu Cami (**D3**), offering a large choice of meats and salads.

HAVING A DRINK

In the small **Hisar Park** (**C2**), you will come across some very tempting outdoor cafés where you can stop for a drink (no alcohol) and admire the wonderful view over Bursa. From here, you can watch the concerts or football matches in the stadium down below. The **Sarayönü Çay Bar** has a small screen for film shows.

In the daytime, the shaded terraces of **Kültür Park** (**A1**, **B1**) also offer some welcome respite.

There is a more formal atmosphere at the bar of the **Altın Ceylan club**, which also has a nightclub.

Sera Bar, near the west entrance to Kültür Park (**A1**). In this large, dimly-lit bar, the young trendy set meet to have a drink and listen to groups playing local hits (8pm-1am, 3am on Saturdays).

Bello Bar, Kocaalizade Cad 17, near Atatürk Cad, overlooking the torrent (**D3**). Closes at half past midnight. You can have a drink and listen to rock music from the comfort of a wicker chair.

OTHER THINGS TO DO

Shadow theatre – Live *Karagöz* shows can be seen at the shop of the same name (see the "Shopping guide" section). Not to mention the festival, which takes place at the end of November.

Turkish baths – *Eski Kaplıca Hamam* (7am-11pm). In the Kervansaray Hotel. Water naturally at 42°C. Worth a visit especially to admire the sumptuous surroundings (the women's section is not as impressive). This is the most expensive one.

Yeni Kaplıca, after the Archeological Museum, at the exit of Kültür Park (A1). 5am-11pm.

Yeni Kaplıca Hamamı, Mudanya Cad 10 (A1), ☏ (224) 236 69 55. Be sure to take a look at this very old Turkish bath, opened in the Byzantine thermal baths renovated in 1522 by Rüstem Paşa, the Grand Vizier of Süleyman the Magnificent. Right next door are two other Turkish baths: the ***Kaynarca***, for women, and the ***Karamustafa***, for families, both open from 6am to 11pm.

Tarihi Murat Hamamı (8am-5pm), near the Muradiye complex (B2). Variable opening times and days for men and women. Less expensive than the ones above.

SHOPPING GUIDE

Antiques – There are some antique shops around Yeşil Cami and the ***bedesten*** (D2), the covered market which specialises in jewellery and clocks. ***Karagöz***, a boutique in Eski Aynalı Çarşı (D2) sells Karagöz marionettes as well as carpets, kilims, antique jewellery and embroidered goods.

Silk and clothes – *Koza Hanı* silk is of good quality (scarves), but the designs lack in originality. Woollen gloves, towels and towelling bathrobes can be found at the ***bedesten*** (D2) and Turkish baths.

Bookshops – *Dünya Aktüel Kitabevi*, Nalbantoğlu Cad, a shopping street just above Atatürk Cad (E3). Newspapers and books in English and French.

Making the most of Bursa

THE DARDANELLES STRAITS
(ÇANAKKALE BOĞAZI)
Length: 65km – Width: 1.3 to 8km
Map page 136

Not to be missed
The Eceabat Fortress. The Gallipoli Peninsula (Gelibolu).
The village of Gelibolu.
And remember...
Reserve your hotel in advance if you visit in March or August, when the Battle of
the Dardanelles festivities take place.

The Marmara Region

As you approach Lapseki, on the Asian shore, the European coast appears suddenly on the other side of the straits, as if within reach. It remains visible until the small city of Çanakkale, at the eastern tip of the passage. The sun-burnt land of the countryside bristles with cypresses and olive trees. On the European side, the Galipolli peninsula displays its brown and dark green hills, arid yet wooded in some areas. The canal resembles a busy river with the comings and goings of different ships. Nothing seems tragic in this dreary landscape which nonetheless was the site of one of the bloodiest battles of World War I.

The ancient Hellespont, a perpetually coveted site
The straits – the Dardanelles and the Bosphorus – are an outstanding strategic site and an exceptional commercial thoroughfare between two continents and three seas.

The Helle Straits
Hated by her mother-in-law who wished to see her dead, young Helle left the family home and fled with her brother to Colchis (Georgia), on the shores of the Black Sea, on the back of a flying ram covered in gold. Unfortunately, Helle fell from her saddle, plunging into the turbulent waters of the straits. In homage, the Ancients named the place Hellespont, the sea of "Helle". Legend has it that the beauty was saved from drowning by Poseidon who fell in love with her (they had many children together). The ram was less fortunate and was skinned; the famous Golden Fleece.

As early as 2C BC, these channels were highly coveted. The Greeks, following the capture of **Troy** (1200 BC) wished to ensure that wheat supplies from the Black Sea would not be interrupted. The straits saw the Persians of Xerxes who, during the second Greco-Persian war (481 C), crossed them using a floating bridge made of boats. Then came Alexander in 334 BC, followed by the Romans, the Byzantines and the Ottomans (14C). In the 18C, the rising power of the Russians, looking for an outlet to the Mediterranean, placed the straits in the middle of European geopolitics. The battle for control of these waters escalated during the Crimean War (1854-1856), and again during World War I (1915).

The Asian Shore

Çanakkale
Located at the narrowest point of the channel (1 270m), facing the impressive Kilitbahir fortress which guards the European shore, this main port of the Dardanelles for the last two centuries is simply a charmless city (pop 55 000). Only the never-ending ferryboat traffic, facing the pleasant **port promenade**, gives it a slight air of importance (it is the capital of the province, after all) reminding us of its strategic

situation. For the traveller, Çanakkale is a good point of departure to visit the Gallipoli (Gelibolu) peninsula and the legendary city of Troy. Hotels, restaurants and banks are located in the port area.

The city, like all of its surroundings, is profoundly marked by the memories of the Battle of the Dardanelles: all over, small monuments commemorate the deeds of Atatürk and, on the hill overlooking the port, the date *"18 mart 1915"* is written in huge white numbers, just like "Hollywood" in California. On the Euro-

Dardanus, the father of the Troyad
Zeus is at the origin of the history of the Dardanelles. Or to be more precise, one of his children, Dardanus, resulting from the union between the god and Atlas' daughter, Electra. Born in Samothrace, Dardanus had to flee his country on a raft following a violent deluge. He landed on the other side of the straits, where King Teucer warmly welcomed him, even letting his guest found a city, which the ungrateful Dardanus named after himself. Dardania, the future Troy, was born. When Teucer breathed his last breath, his guest set out to conquer the whole region, which he renamed "Dardania" (how original!).

pean shore as well, near the Kilitbahir fortress, a giant Atatürk is drawn on the side of the hill, an unusual silhouette surrounded by multicoloured stones.

If the story of the Dardanelles battle interests you, visit the **Çimenlik Military Museum** (Askeri ve Deniz Müzesi) housed inside the old **Sultaniye Fortress** (15C), close to the port in a southerly direction *(9.30am-12noon/1.30pm-5.15pm, closed Mondays)*. As well as numerous 14C and 15C cannons, you will see a mine-layer, the *Nusrat* (in the garden) as well as numerous photographs of World War I (in the side pavilion.)

Ancient history *aficionados* will want to visit the **Archeological Museum** (Arkeoloji Müzesi), south of the city *(on the left when going up the long Atatürk street; 8.30am-5.15pm, closed Mondays)*. Various objects – sarcophagi, ceramics – retrace the history of **Troy** and the Hellespont from the Bronze Age. The section dedicated to Dardanus' tumulus (4-1BC) is the most interesting (the tombs exposed outside originate from there).

The European Shore
One day excursion

■ **The Ottoman Fort of Kilitbahir** ★ – *From the port of Çanakkale take the ferry which runs every 15min (travel time: 25min). 8am-12noon / 1pm-5pm. Entrance fee.* Facing each other across the channel, the fortresses of Kilitbahir and Çanakkale (Çimenlik) played a pivotal role in the conquest of Constantinople (1453), and again during the battle of 1915. The Kilitbahir fortress is more beautiful than its Asian sister: extended by a curtain-like structure which leads to the second tower, it forms a cloverleaf, almost heart-shaped, overlooked by a massive **keep** set in the middle of the courtyard. It is also possible to climb up to the ramparts where the **view**★ of the straits is beautiful.

The Historic Park of Gelibolu

Transformed into a national historic park, the Gelibolu peninsula (or Gallipoli) will only interest military history buffs. Young Australians and New Zealanders come in large numbers to pay their respects to their ANZAC forefathers (the expeditionary corps of the two nations) who died here.

The **French Cemetery** is located at Cape Helles *(27km from Eceabat)*, where 15 000 men are laid to rest in a pine-tree setting. Visible from miles around, the **Turkish Memorial** (Çanakkale Şehitleri Abidesi Memorial) displays its tall pillars on a nearby promontory. From there, the **view**★ over the straits and the Aegean is

The Battle of the Dardanelles

In 1915, Churchill, first lord of the British Admiralty, was behind the creation of a French-British naval expedition in the Dardanelles in order to open a channel of communication with Russia. After a successful debarkation (25 February), almost a third of the fleet was destroyed by floating mines during the naval attack of 18 March. From April until August, the Allies attempted a series of ground operations in the Gallipoli peninsula and on the Asian coast. It was all in vain. They were pushed back by the Turks under the command of the German General Liman von Sanders and Mustafa Kemal, the future Atatürk. In late August, the Allies abandoned the operations and, in December, they retreated after failing to establish links with Russia. They left behind more than 100 000 dead (British, French, Indians, Australians and New Zealanders).

impressive. In the distance, the sea is speckled with Turkish vessels and submarines on the look-out for enemies.

2km to the west, it is easy to recognise **Seddülbahir** with its impressive **Ottoman Fortress**, built in the 16C during a war against the Venetians. Out at sea, the **island of Gökçeada** is visible. Returning towards the north, take a look at the little **Alçıtepe Military Museum**, set in a private home.

Farther north (*14km*), on the Aegean coast, **Kum Limanı** is reached; undoubtedly the best place to sojourn on the peninsula with its bungalows on a pleasant beach.

5km to the north, isolated in the middle of the hills, the **Kabatepe Museum** (*8am-12noon/1pm-5.30pm*) evokes the battle of 1915 and the fire which ravaged the peninsula. Numerous arms and objects fished from the sea are displayed, including a soldier's shoe with a single protruding bone covered with a worn sock.

Beyond, **Anzac Bay** is the tragic setting of the 1915 land operations. From the heights above, the battle fields are clearly visible and it is easy to imagine the amplitude of the drama which unfolded there. Remember to visit the **Lone Pine** (Kalı Sirt) cemetery and the reconstructed and invincible-looking **trenches**, to see how the Turks attacked the ANZAC soldiers below with relentless firepower.

■ **Gelibolu** – Situated at the northern entrance of the straits (*42km from Eceabat*), Gelibolu faces the Sea of Marmara. Last stop on the exploration of the peninsula, this charming little fishing port can be a pleasant stop on the way to İstanbul or Edirne.

Making the most of the Dardanelles

COMING AND GOING

● Çanakkale

Ferry links with Eceabat and the islands of Bozcaada and Gökçeada. From Çanakkale there are buses to Edirne, İstanbul, Bursa and İzmir.

For the Gelibolu peninsula – If you don't have your own transport, you will have to join a tour group at one of the agencies at Çanakkale. The trip lasts half a day and departs from Çanakkale.

For Troy – The town operates a bus shuttle service all day long to this site. Departures from the square opposite the harbour. Timetable available at the tourist information office.

● Gelibolu

Buses for Edirne and Çanakkale from Gelibolu (departure point near the harbour). Ferry for Çanakkale.

ADDRESS BOOK

● Çanakkale

Tourist information – İskele Meydanı 67, opposite the harbour. Monday-Friday: 8am-8pm, weekends: 9am-7pm.

Travel agency – Anzac House, Cumhuriyet Meyd, 61, ☎ (286) 213 59 69, next to the tourist information office. Organises a tour of the Gelibolu peninsula which ends in the evening with a film and documentary in English.

Next door to the agency, **Hassle Free**, ☎ (286) 213 59 69, also offers tours to Troy (departures at 8.30am and 12noon from in front of Anzac House), as well as guided one-day tours to the Gelibolu peninsula (all inclusive, with meal: US$6).

Bank / change – Emlak Bankası, Zübeyde Hanım Cad 2, behind Liman Meydanı. Monday to Saturday, 8.30am-12noon / 1pm-5pm, closed on Sundays.

Book shop – Orka, Yali Cad 5, behind the clock tower. Maps and newspapers in English.

WHERE TO STAY

• Çanakkale

Around US$8

Camp sites abound in the Dardanelles, and are all more or less of the same standard (3 at Gelibolu, 4 at Eceabat and 9 at Çanakkale). We will just suggest one at Gelibolu, the **Kabatepe**, ☎ (286) 814 11 28. It can be reached by dolmuş from the "otogar" or main square in Gelibolu.

Under US$15

Hotel Kervansarayı, Fetvahane Sok 13, near the clock tower, ☎ (286) 217 81 92 – 15rm. In a 19C Ottoman house with a rather kitsch decor. A very simple but very charming and cheap place.

Pension Avrupa, Matbaa Sok 8, near the clock tower, ☎ (286) 217 40 84 – 13rm. ⁂ ✕ cc An adequate guest house with simple but clean rooms. Café on the ground floor. Very friendly welcome. A pity the street is rather noisy (full of bars).

Between US$15 and US$30

Hotel Anzac, Saat Kulesi Meyd 8, ☎ (286) 217 77 77, Fax (286) 217 20 18 – 27rm. ⁂ tv Adequate standard of cleanliness and comfort. Good location. Not to be confused with Anzac House.

Over US$60

Hotel Akol, Kayserili Ahmet Paşa Cad, ☎ (286) 217 94 56, Fax (286) 217 28 97 – 136rm. ⁂ ▤ ✎ tv ✕ ⚓ cc On the quayside. Slightly to the north of the town centre, in a quieter area. Ask for a room with a view over the sea. Caters for groups, reservation required.

• Gelibolu peninsula

Under US$8

Hotel Hakan, Liman Meyd, ☎ (286) 566 24 24 – 18rm. Offering the very bare essentials, for small budgets. Extremely basic rooms (no private showers) and no breakfast. Friendly welcome.

Some guest houses can be found at Seddülbahir and there is a hotel south of Kabatepe:

Around US$45

Hotel Kum Limanı, ☎ (286) 814 14 66 – 56rm. ⁂ ✕ ⚓ The clientele consists mainly of groups of Australians and New Zealanders (reservation recommended). Accommodation in bungalows. Camp site, cafeteria and billiard table.

• Gelibolu

Around US$45

Hotel Yelkenci, Liman Meyd, ☎ (286) 566 10 22 – 20rm. ⁂ ✕ Beautiful view over the harbour. Basic level of comfort, but friendlier than the one above.

Hotel Yılmaz, ☎ (286) 566 35 95. ⁂ Good location, but basic standard of comfort and cleanliness. Quite expensive for its category.

EATING OUT

• Çanakkale

Temad, Gümrük Sok, at the end of the quayside. This upstairs restaurant is the liveliest one. Turkish clientele. For dessert, try the "peynir tatlısı", an excellent soft cheese.

Karakaş, Yalı Cad 47, ☎ (286) 217 61 40. cc A restaurant with a friendly, very Turkish atmosphere. Fish and seafood, meat and meze, salads and desserts.

Aussie & Kiwi, Yalı Cad 32, ☎ (286) 212 17 22. A tiny little restaurant, for tourists only. Meze, seafood and meat. Everything is English here, from the breakfast and desserts to the newspapers.

• Gelibolu

Numerous seafood restaurants around the harbour and on the seafront.

İmren, Liman Meyd, ☎ (286) 566 23 22. cc A little fish and seafood restaurant at the harbour, which also serves meat, meze, soup and desserts. Pleasant welcome.

• Kilitbahir

Sur, at the foot of the castle, ☎ (286) 824 53 75. A very friendly place on the waterfront boasting a large covered terrace. Fish and seafood, meat and meze, salads and desserts. English spoken.

İlhan, Liman Meyd, friendly welcome, fine cuisine.

Marina Cafe, next door. Has a very pleasant terrace, sheltered from the wind.

TROY★
(TRUVA)

Çanakkale Province – 25km from Çanakkale – Map p 136
Accommodation in Çanakkale (see p 219) or on the spot at Hotel Hisarlık

Not to be missed
Read or re-read Homer's epic to set your imagination going when you visit the ruins.

And remember...
Visit the site early in the morning or in the cool of the evening.
It is very hot indeed in the ruins in summer. Watch the video
before beginning your visit, it offers useful insights.

Of the mythical Troy immortalised by Homer, there is, to tell the truth, very little left, just a few portions of wall protruding from a small sunburnt hill. Nevertheless, a strange impression emerges from these enigmatic ruins, as if you were coming into physical contact with something from the pages of mythology. And even if it raises a smile, the huge wooden horse towering over the entrance to the site plunges the modern visitor irresistibly into a world of legend.

From Çanakkale take the coast road southwards. After 20km turn right at the yellow sign to "Truva" (5km). After the ticket office, carry on for 800m (small road lined with rose bushes) until you arrive at the site itself. Parking facilities on the left. There is a bookshop, water fountain and toilet facilities; refreshments before the ticket office. Minibuses provide a shuttle service (information and departure from the tourist office in Çanakkale).

The adventure of Heinrich Schliemann

Archeologists have always searched for Troy, like Indiana Jones for the Lost Ark! According to ancient writers, the famous city of Priam was to be found on a hillock overlooking the plain of Scamander, not far from the Hellespont Straits (the Dardanelles). But as to precisely which hillock, that was more difficult.

Then along came Heinrich Schliemann (1822-90), an amateur archeologist who from a tender age always had as his bedside book the Iliad, the wonderful epic story of Ilion – the Homeric name for Troy. Knowing all there was to know about Ancient Greek history, he was able to recite the *Adventures of Telemachus* off by heart. Self-taught, he perfected a method enabling him to learn all the European languages, Russian and Arabic in less than a year, and from being a modest clerk he became a banker, ending up at the head of the Imperial Bank of St Petersburg and an honorary citizen of the Russian Empire.

But at 46, he abandoned his career and decided to dedicate himself to his passion. He packed his case, set off for İstanbul and soon arrived at the site of Hisarlık, a hillock which researchers believe to be that of the legendary city. After one or two soundings, Schliemann started excavating in 1871 and carried on until his death. The architect Wilhelm Dörpfeld took up the torch in 1893 and 1894, but the first really scientific excavations only started in 1932, under the auspices of the eminent American professor Carl Blegen. The dig lasted for six years, during which time the Cincinnati team endeavoured to complete and correct the first conclusions drawn by Schliemann, who was apparently less keen on studying than on removing the treasure. Excavations were resumed in 1988.

Did the Trojan War really take place?

Does the site of Hisarlık really correspond to Homeric Troy? Even today the debate continues and excavation of the Karayur hillock, 7.5km to the east, is shedding some doubt on the data. Furthermore, no inscription uncovered in Hisarlık bears the name of Troy and nothing in the layout of the site corresponds to Homer's description (large ramparts, monumental Scoean Gate – large enough for the famous horse to pass through – sumptuous palace for Priam etc). Although prosperous, the Troy of that time was only a big village with a population of a few hundred, nothing like Homer's description, even allowing for the nature of epic poetry. On the other hand, discoveries from the Hellenistic era do point to the name of "New Ilion".

In fact archeologists now seem to agree that Hisarlık is indeed the site of ancient Troy. However the present issue is the revolutionary question as to whether the Trojan War actually took place. Myth or reality. Who knows?

The Trojan Horse

Gathered on Mount Ida (south of Troy) Hera, Athena and Aphrodite wanted to know which one of them was the most beautiful goddess. Under the auspices of Discord, a competition was organised. The prize – a golden apple – would be given to the winner by the handsome Paris, youngest son of Priam, King of Troy. But treacherous Aphrodite bought the young man's reply by promising him the love of the most beautiful woman, Helen, wife of Menelaus. Paris took her at her word and kidnapped Helen and brought her back to Troy, thus provoking the war. On one side, the Achaeans, led by Agamemnon, King of Mycenes and ally of Menelaus. On the other, the Trojans, aided by Aeneas, son of Aphrodite. The siege lasted nine years. The Trojans resisted stoically, so Agamemnon opted for a ruse: he made a gift to Priam of a superb wooden horse and hid inside it with his best men, Achilles, Ulysses and Ajax. The horse penetrated the city's defences, together with the enemy, and Troy fell.

Troy, Troy and Troy again

Troy is a very complex site, continually reshaped by the earthquakes and wars which mark its history. By digging 20m down, archeologists have uncovered nine different periods, each identified by a number, from Troy 1- the most ancient level – to Troy 9 – the most recent. Since then archeologists have discovered three new periods and there is still more digging to do.

Troy 1 (3000-2600 BC) was founded in the Bronze Age, a fortified fishing village. For unknown reasons, the city was suddenly decimated and the survivors had to rebuild it from scratch. The ramparts of **Troy 2** (2600-2300 BC) were more stalwart, reinforced with sturdy towers. The citadel was entered via large **paved ramps** and stone houses start to be built. The **potter's wheel** came into use here, together with the first *depas*, vases in many shapes and forms, sometimes anthropomorphic, which would become immensely popular later on. Troy 2 was involved in the bronze trade and controlled the shipping lines dealing in the tin needed to produce alloys (not available in Anatolia).

But another earthquake destroyed the citadel. Once again the population built it up again bigger and stronger. The walls of **Troy 3** (2300-2200 BC) were 10m thick and the first **megarons** were built within – vast rectangular houses, fronted with a porch (*see Lexicon page 58*). Alas, another earthquake ruined the city and the population fled in panic, leaving all their worldly goods behind them; this was the source of the **treasure** Schliemann discovered, and not, as he wrongly thought, Priam, which existed about a thousand years later.

The citadel declined into a long period of unrest, to judge by the traces left by successive fires. Trade diminished and **Troy 4** (2200-2050 BC) became more inward-looking, satisfied with more pastoral activities (spindle accessories, used for the weaving of wool, have been found).

Decline was followed by desertion. The people who had built Troy 1 left the citadel, and a new colony was established there; the horse was introduced to the region. (Was this where Agamemnon got the idea of building his Trojan Horse?) **Troy 5** (2050-1900 BC), a small town, came into being, and rapidly grew prosperous.

Troy

Troy 6 (1900-1300 BC) marked the golden age of the city. With the construction of new city walls, 550m long, Troy had never been so large. Trade was booming with Greece, (as demonstrated by the discovery of Mycenean pottery), and a new palace adorned the city.

But the earth was still rumbling and an earthquake again shook the walls. Renewed rebuilding, and on to **Troy 7** (1300-1100 BC), the **city of Priam**. The Trojan War can indeed be dated to 1250 BC, a period when the citadel seems to have undergone a siege. Was the enemy Agamemnon, come to retrieve Helen from the hands of Paris? A horde of pirates? Or was he one of the "Peoples from the sea", who came from the West and overran the whole of Anatolia? Nobody knows. Whoever the enemy, Troy emerged from the struggle much weakened, and was finally abandoned by the Trojans, leaving the city walls empty for the next four centuries.

The next occupants were the Aeolians – **Troy 8** (700-350 BC) – who would shortly relinquish Troy to the Persians in the 6C. The town was liberated by Alexander the Great (334 BC), who, by taking Troy, gained access to Asia Minor. Lysimachus, his successor in the region, rebaptised the town "New Ilion" – **Troy 9** (350 BC-400 AD) – and erected a temple to Athena Ilias ("Trojan"). Finally (85 BC) with Julius Caesar, who claimed to be descended from the hero Aeneas, Troy became a Roman city, with a theatre, a second temple dedicated to Athena, a gymnasium and a *bouleuterion*.

Archeological site
8am-7pm. Entrance fee. Allow 45min.

Just for an instant, slip into the sandals of Ulysses, Ajax or Achilles and climb inside the beautiful **wooden horse** standing guard over the ruins. Some 15m high, it is studded with little windows, allowing contemplation of the famous Trojan plain, the scene of epic combat.

Just behind, the **Archeological building** contains photos and documents as well as an interesting **video** (5min, available in English), which is worth watching before you visit the site.

The different interlocking levels are somewhat confusing. Luckily, little red signs indicate the main structures. The site is visited in a counter-clockwise direction. As excavations are underway, it is possible that some signs may have been moved, and new walls, as they are brought to light, may alter the tour. Therefore, the tour as described here is subject to change.

The visit starts by a climb on the right up onto the **city walls of Troy 6**, a thick fortification, 6m high, protected by a ditch and flanked by a large **square tower**, the base of which can be seen on looking down. On the right-hand side, inside the walls, notice the outlines of what remains of storehouses and several dwellings from the classical period (Troy 6 and 7). Continuing along the crest of the wall, you have a splendid **view★** (over the marshy plain and the area still being excavated).

This brings you to the remains of the **temple of Athena Ilias**, a modest rectangle of stones scarcely emerging from the ground, built over the razed walls of Troy 2.

The path continues alongside a new portion of **ramparts** (totally ruined), penetrated by a passage, flanked by two towers. On either side appear several **megarons** from Troy 1 and 2, just lines of stone amongst the grass.

Further on a fine **paved ramp★**, 21m long and 7.5m wide gives an idea of the entry into the city of Troy 2. Just on the left a large hole can be seen; that is where Schliemann discovered the famous treasure.

The ramp leads down towards the sacred part of the city, a vast **sanctuary** dating back to Troy 7 or 8, dotted with all sorts of rather enigmatic constructions, wells and (sacrificial) altar bases, partly rebuilt.

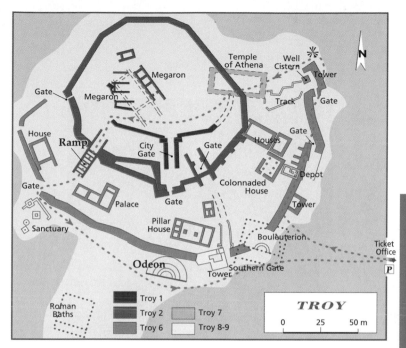

Along the way traces can be seen of mosaics and walls disappearing into the bushes, belonging to **Roman houses**. This is followed by the **odeon***, a small hemicycle of tiered steps from the Roman period (Troy 9), which has recently been meticulously restored. Currently it is the only building recognisable as such in the whole of Troy. On the other side of the path, fragments of columns and friezes lie hidden between the trees, romantic vestiges of a **Roman nymphaeum**.

Once past the odeon, push on a little further into the city *(to the left of the path)*. The ruins of the **south gate** to Troy 7 precede a broad **passageway**, previously covered, which crossed the town from north to south. The trench is very clearly cut, marked at intervals by the remains of some of the **water pipes** which ran through the town. On all sides there are haphazardly overlapping **houses** dating back to Troy 7. Some people think that the south (or Dardanian) gate is the one the Trojans enlarged in order to let in the famous wooden horse.

Making the most of Troy

WHERE TO STAY, EATING OUT
Visitors wishing to spend the night here will find suitable accommodation at the hotel Hisarlık, right at the entrance to the site (before the ticket office).
Hotel Hisarlık, Tevfikiye, ☎ (286) 283 01 26, Fax (286) 283 01 87 – 11rm. 📶 ✗ cc Just like in a motel, the rooms (upstairs) are all lined up in a row (each one is named after a Trojan hero: Paris,

Helen, Achilles etc). Although they are no longer in pristine condition, they are clean and afford a simple but adequate level of comfort. The very friendly proprietor, Mustafa Aşın, speaks English and French and will gladly share his extensive knowledge of the history of Troy with you. Currency exchange, post office and tourist information on the ground floor.

B. Brillion/MICHELIN

Sardis, the giant columns of the Temple of Artemis

THE AEGEAN COAST

From legendary Mount Ida, where the destiny of Homeric Troy was sealed, to the Castle of St Peter built by the crusaders on the shores of the Gôkova gulf, a total of 2 800 km of coastline faces the Aegean. Chiselled creeks, peninsulas, sandy bays, rocks and cliffs have seen generations of sailors pass by. Aegean Turkey turns its face to the sea, promising the riches of the Orient to the Western world beyond.

In the centre of this long coastline, at the base of a peninsula similar to an outstretched arm, the former Smyrna is the focus of nearly all of the area's commercial trading. The region's main centre, Turkey's second port after İstanbul, **İzmir** is a powerful trading city, through which most of the country's agricultural products pass: tobacco, cotton, olive oil, petroleum, not to mention the famous Smyrna raisins. But it is also an industrial centre, and possesses an important steelworks. From the 1960s onwards, the surrounding cities such as Aydın, Sôke and Denizli, have developed and taken advantage of a boom in agricultural products.

It is a fertile region with an amazing archeological heritage. Here too are the astonishing petrified waterfalls of **Pamukkale**, a geological phenomenon unique in the world – as if nature had wanted to build a castle as white as the surrounding ancient cities. Built of glittering marble, **Pergamum**, **Ephesus**, and **Aphrodisias** are among Turkey's most exquisite sites, which have given the world Heracleitus of Ephesus, Thales of Miletus, Herodotus of Halicarnassus, and any number of scholars and philosophers to whom are owed some of the greatest scientific discoveries.

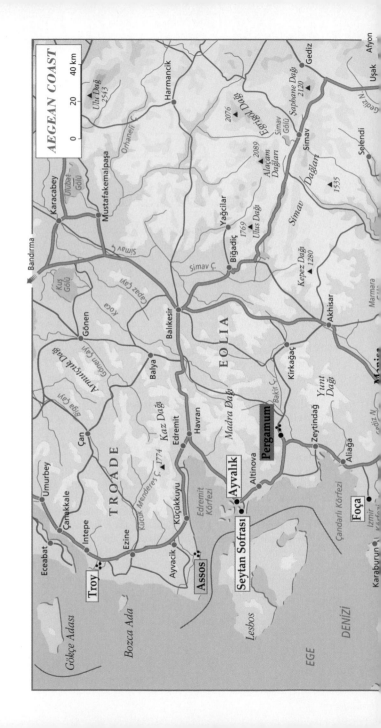

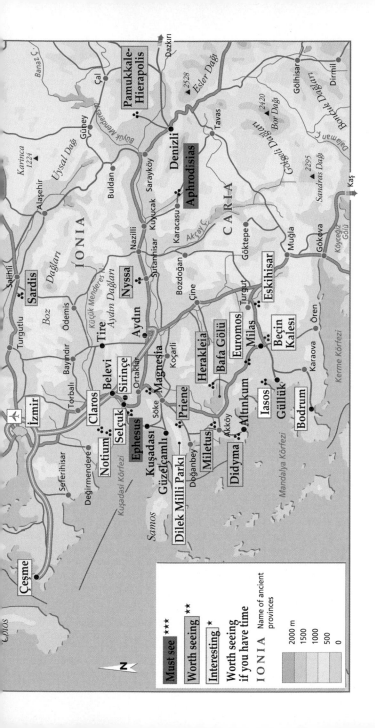

Greater Greece

The coast of Asia Minor attracted the Greeks as early as the Mycenian period (14C BC), but their colonisation intensified from the 11C BC. The **Eolians** settled in the north, the **Dorians** on the lands of ancient Caria, with the largest slice of cake going to the **Ionians** who settled along the whole of the Meander valley. Strength coming from unity, the cities of each region grouped themselves into a religious, military and economic confederation which reached its peak in the 6C and 7C. However, this equilibrium was severely disturbed in the 8C with the arrival of the Lydian named Gyges, who by stretching his entire kingdom out over the hinterlands, became a serious threat to the coastal cities. The situation worsened by the 5C BC when the Persians took possession of the territories conquered by **Croesus**, the legendary king of **Lydia,** who had expanded his Empire over almost all of eastern Anatolia.

The Seven Wonders of the World

Of the seven great works of architecture which the Greeks enjoyed categorising as wonders, two were located in Turkey on the Aegean coast: the temple of Artemis at Ephesus (4C) and the mausoleum of Halicarnassus (4C, Bodrum), today reduced to modest rock piles. Only one wonder of the world, which is strangely enough the most ancient, the 4 600-year-old Egyptian pyramid of Cheops in Egypt has survived. The four others were: the hanging gardens of Babylon, the statue in chryselephantine (in ivory and gold) of Olympian Zeus (the work of the sculptor Phidias, 5C), the Colossus guarding the port of Rhodes (end of 4C) and the lighthouse at Alexandria (early 3C), where archeologists are currently retrieving fragments from the bed of the harbour.

It was not until the arrival of Alexander the Great (334 BC), that the Aegean cities recovered their former independence. After the death of the conqueror, his successors, the **Seleucids**, imposed Hellenic culture on all of Asia Minor, propelling the cities into a new era of economic as well as intellectual prosperity.

A crossroads of different cultures, the Aegean coast could not fail to interest the evangelists, especially **St Paul**, who preached the gospel in Ephesus on numerous occasions. With the expansion of Christianity, Artemis gave way to Mary and churches were erected over the walls of ancient pagan temples. But Constantinople, which replaced Rome (496) and reigned over Asia Minor, overshadowed the coastal cities, not least because their harbours were silting up. Ephesus, Priene and Miletus began a slow death, and the first Arab raids, beginning in the 7C, only precipitated their downfall.

In the 12C, the Byzantines fought against the Seljuks for the region, and managed to conquer it for a while only to turn it over to Tamerlane's Turks, then to the crusaders. The troubled times of the region came to an end as Süleyman the Magnificent took Bodrum and the area in 1522. The Ottoman period was a breath of fresh air for Aegean Turkey. The plains were cultivated and the cities became trading centres for the products of the Empire. In the 19C, the Greeks attempted to create an enclave in this vast territory. However, İzmir, short-lived capital of Utopian Greater Greece, fell under the offensive of Mustafa Kemal in 1922 and the region became unmistakably Turkish. Only a few islands, facing the Turkish coast, remained Greek.

The land of green gold...

North of İzmir, the green plains of **Eolia** extend into the fiefdom of brilliant Pergamum, the city where the book was invented. Citrus orchards, vineyards, and cotton fields share the land; however, Eolia is really the land of the olive tree. The world's fourth producer of olive oil (*zeytin yağı* in Turkish), Turkey obtains three-quarters of its production from the olive groves of the region, the rest coming from the southern Aegean coast and the shores of the Mediterranean.

...and breeze block

However, olive trees and orchards are losing ground. Especially on the coast, which in the last 20 years has become the prey of real estate agents. Encouraged by increasing tourism, the cities have grown, the villages are surrounded by countless holiday homes and the hills are disappearing under breeze blocks. It is a real tragedy that has disfigured many natural and historical sites for which the coast was famous.

Luckily, a few portions of the coast have managed to escape the tender mercies of developers, in particular the Assos region, north of Edremit. This magnificent arid plateau with a rugged appearance has been disregarded by tour operators. Farther south, the coastline is much more frequented by tourists. However, the fishing ports of **Ayvalık** and **Foça** retain their roots: facing the hotels set up in old Greek residences, the fishermen busily work away in their multicoloured boats. If you have transport, you should travel inland as well. Right behind the hills, the modest villages reveal another facet of Turkey: serener, wilder and definitely more Anatolian.

An ancestral crop

Olive oil has made the Orient rich for the last 10 000 years. Needless to say, olive oil cultivation and pressing techniques are well developed. In fact, they have remained almost unchanged since their origins. The olive tree is fragile and its fruit does not tolerate mechanised picking. Knowing that an olive tree only yields fruit after five years, mistakes are not acceptable! Olive groves are handed down from generation to generation and patience is needed. After its fifth spring, the tree decks itself out with delicate light green flowers which give way to the precious green berries. As autumn approaches, the fruit turns to a red-orange colour, then brown, before it blackens completely as winter appears. This is the harvesting season, in which all the family participates. As soon as their tents are set up, the farmers proceed to gather the olives manually as has been the tradition for thousands of years.

Travelling up the Meander

South of İzmir, the land of ancient Ionia, the Meander (Büyük Menderes Nehri) traces a 584km line across an immense swampy plain, as flat as the sea. Cotton, olives, apples, pears, and vegetables are to be seen everywhere. Like Eolia, the Meander basin is very fertile, enriched by the sediment that the flood waters deposit along the entire length of the river. The river follows a tortuous course all the way to its mouth, its bends ("meanders") constantly changing as alluvium is deposited or removed. More sediments are discharged as it reaches the sea, which in consequence has been displaced more than 10 kilometres to the west. Ancient tradition has it that each of these meanders spells a letter of the Greek alphabet. However, the river has written its own language with numerous changing symbols.

Ancient Caria

At the southern tip of the Aegean coast, the province of Muğla marks the transition from the Aegean to the Mediterranean. It is the territory of the Carians, who had the reputation of being excellent seamen. But Halicarnassus, ancient **Bodrum**, owed its glory to the Persian satrap (ruler) Mausolus who built one of the Seven Wonders of the World: the first tomb called a "mausoleum". Looking out over the gulf of Gökova, Bodrum is today the departure point for wonderful cruises along the Akdeniz coast and one of the main holiday areas.

In spite of the invading concrete, the Aegean coast still retains an infinite number of treasures: the dark Assos stone, colourful streets of Pergamum, immaculate colonnades of Aphrodisias, the rocky peaks of Priene, seas of reeds on the Miletus plain, and the ochre sandstone of the hills of Bafa. And the further south, the blue the sea.

ASSOS★★
(BEHRAMKALE)
Çanakkale Province – Map p 226
95km south of Çanakkale – 89km from Edremit

Not to be missed
The Assos acropolis
and its splendid vantage point
And remember...
Spend the night in Kadırga:
it is very quiet, slightly cheaper than Assos,
and you can swim there as well.

Assos has a magnificent site. Perched on the summit of a rocky peak (238m) falling sheer into the sea, the ruins of its acropolis watch over the medieval village of Behramkale, leaning against the old ramparts. The old Ottoman mosque is distinguished by its light-coloured façade amongst the massive grey houses. At the foot of the mountain, an impressive **Seljuk hump-back bridge** (14C) crosses the river (avoid looking at the brand new concrete bridge flanking it). Beyond the bridge, the road splits. Towards the right it skirts the village and begins to descend in a series of vertiginous hairpin bends, eventually reaching the little hidden port of Assos, built on the site of an older settlement. Towards the left, it reaches the pretty bay of Kadırga, surrounded by a wild and hilly landscape.

Now designated as part of the national heritage, this section of the coast is a conservation area, and new construction activity is rare. The region's traditional architecture is taken into account: grey granite walls and red roof tiles blending into the earth's colours. It is a landscape of wild and stark beauty. Stop a while to contemplate it, for it is one of the last unspoiled stretches of the Aegean coast. Beyond Ayvalık, the coastline has been invaded by beach resorts and grim urban developments of all kinds.

Whereas the Assos acropolis has lost its name in favour of Behramkale, the port has retained the original Greek name. To visit the acropolis, therefore, follow directions for Behramkale. For the port, follow signs to "Assos".

Behramkale and the Assos Acropolis★★

Assos was founded in the 7C BC by Greeks from Mytilene, a city on the nearby island of Lesbos (*Midilli* in Turkish). In the 6C BC, it was first under the control of the Lydians, then the Persians, before joining the Athenian league of Delos. Subject in turn to the Sassanids, the Pergamenes, the Romans (2C BC) and the crusaders, it finally became Ottoman in 1330. Its only period of independence was in the 4C BC with the governments of Eubule, a rich banker, and the eunuch Hermeias, a disciple of Plato and admirer of Aristotle. The latter spent three years in Assos (from 348 to 345 BC) where he founded his first school of philosophy.

Visiting the site
Leave your car at the entrance of the village and climb up through the little streets to the summit. Entrance fee. Allow 1hr for the visit or more if you include time for contemplation.

Before exploring the ancient ruins, take a look at the village's little **mosque.** Erected by Murat I, c1360, it is one of the oldest Anatolian mosques to experiment with a dome-shaped roof. On the façade a cross is visible, a strange sight in a Muslim sanctuary, but it is simply part of the material taken from Byzantine buildings and used again here.

The **acropolis*** is all that remains of ancient Assos since the lower city has completely disappeared. Beyond the ticket booth, you climb instinctively towards the summit, the setting of the **Temple of Athena**** (530 BC). Between the slim Doric columns there is an exceptional **vantage point***** with views of the sea, the island of Lesbos and the surrounding mountains. You could spend hours sitting on one of the capitals resting on the ground. The sculptures that once adorned the building have been taken to İstanbul, Boston, or the Louvre.

On the south side of the acropolis below the temple *(towards the sea)*, is the **agora** (3C-2C BC), a vast plateau (111.5m long) with scattered blocks of stone. The square was surrounded by porticoes (or *stoa*), one (to the north) on two floors, another (south side) with three floors and two others facing the sea.

Farther down is the **theatre***. Currently being excavated, it has a very complete set of terraces undulating along the mountainside and facing the sea. Built in the 3C BC, it was later reconstructed by the Romans.

You may go up to the temple to walk around the ramparts before descending towards the ticket office.

Built in the 4C BC, the **ramparts**** protecting the acropolis are among the best preserved in the Greek world. They surrounded the upper city with a 3km-long defence. The main gate (adjacent to the mosque) has kept its two 14m-high towers.

The sheer extent of the fortifications and their great beauty is extraordinarily impressive, as is the extreme precision of the jointing of the blocks of stone from which they are built. Leaving Behramkale towards the port of Assos, the road skirts the foot of the walls, passing the splendid vaulted **gate**** with a trapezoidal arch.

The road leading to the port of Assos (half-cobblestone, half-tarmac) descends steeply. Be careful. Park your vehicle at the entrance to the village, which is reserved for pedestrians.

The Port of Assos**
Allow 30min

Wedged between the cliff and the sea, facing the island of Lesbos, the small port of Assos has a row of granite houses (almost all have been transformed into hotels) facing the gaily-painted fishing boats. Stroll along the quayside just below the road *(to the right of the main square)*. Among the prettiest façades is that of the police headquarters! Squeezed between the Nazlıhan Hotel and the Fenerlihan Restaurant are more fine houses with beautiful patios decorated with turquoise tiles.

Kadırga Bay
From Behramkale (4km), go down towards the sea from Assos (moving away), following the signs indicating the hotels and the beach.

Known mainly to Germans and locals, the Bay of Kadırga is still relatively tourist-free (but may not stay that way for long!). A few hotels have sprung up overlooking the grey pebble beach. All are built in the local style: granite walls enclosing a patio with greenery, and a shady terrace in front. The area is very peaceful and the setting enchanting, and there are no prettier or quieter beaches this side of Foça.

Making the most of Assos

COMING AND GOING

Dolmuşes shuttle between Assos and Ayvacık (18km) several times a day. Departures from the harbour outside the Behramkale hotel or from the village square in Behramkale. They will drop you off at Ayvacık bus station, where you will find numerous buses for Çanakkale, İzmir and Ayvalık **(Radar and Truva bus companies)**. Note: the bus to Ayvalık will leave you a few kilometres from the town, at the junction of the roads to Ayvalık and İzmir; walk or hitch-hike the rest of the way, it's not that far.

ADDRESS BOOK

Change / Post office – In an emergency, you can change money at the **Assos hotel**, but you will not get a good rate of exchange. If you can wait, it's better to go to **Ayvacık post office**, which is open until 7pm (small street to the right of the main road, before the crossroads with the road to Edremit), near the "otogar".

Fuel – On the road out of Ayvacık, after the **Mobil** station, there is a **Total** fuel station which accepts credit cards.

WHERE TO STAY

• Behramkale

Under US$15
Pension Eris, at the entrance to the village, ☎ (286) 721 70 80. Set at the end of an attractive terrace, this beautiful stone house overlooks the whole valley. The rooms are bright, simple and very clean. Bathroom facilities are on the landing.
Pension Sidar, in the small square where the dolmuşes park, ☎ (286) 721 70 47 – 6rm. ⚐ A small, very simple guest house with plans to expand. You will receive a friendly welcome from the proprietor, who speaks a few words of English, French and German and who rents out horses and motorcycles. A little expensive, but clean and adequate. Breakfast is taken at Cengiz, the restaurant just opposite.

Around US$25
Pension Konukevi, ☎ (286) 721 70 81 – 6rm. ⚐ ✗ Probably the most attractive and pleasant guest house in the village: a large, old stone house, attractively decorated with kilims and plants and set in a vast terrace garden. The

level of comfort is simple but modern, everything is very clean and well kept, and you will be warmly welcomed. The guest house is a little isolated (the entrance is at the end of a small cul-de-sac), but well signposted.

• Assos (the harbour)
Apart from the camp site, there are hardly any cheap places to stay in Assos. All the hotels are set in magnificent houses made of locally quarried stone. The rooms are fairly similar from one establishment to the next: comfortable, clean and plainly furnished (pine). In summer, half-board is a must.

Camp site
Assos camp site, at the very end of the village, on the left when facing the sea. ⚐ ✗ A tiny little waterfront camp site wedged between the hill and the sea, pleasantly shaded by fig and olive trees. Very simple but a pleasant place to stay, and cheap (under US$8 per pitch).

US$25 (US$45 for half-board)
Hotel Yıldız Saray, at the entrance to the village, set slightly back from the harbour, ☎ (286) 721 70 25 or 73 95, Fax (286) 721 71 69 – 8rm. ⚐ ✗ 🚿 cc Small, very simple rooms, with clean but rather dilapidated bathroom facilities. One of the rooms has a fireplace and there is a lovely terrace on the top floor. This hotel is mainly to be commended for its restaurant, which is very pleasant and serves excellent food (see the "Eating out" section). Very attentive welcome.
Pension Şen, behind the village, ☎ (286) 721 70 76, Fax (286) 721 72 09 – 14rm. ⚐ ✗ More of a hotel than a guest house, set in a large stone house in the heights of Assos. The top floor has a pleasant terrace swathed in kilims, with a bar where you can have breakfast or a drink while admiring the view of the sea. In the evenings there is an all-you-can-eat buffet (Turkish food). Quite expensive, but very good quality.

US$45 (half-board compulsory)
Hotel Assos Kervansaray, right at the end of the (natural) harbour, after the hotel Assos, ☎ (286) 721 70 93, Fax (286) 721 72 00 – 48rm. ⚐ 🎵 TV ✗ 🏊 cc For half-board, this place is slightly better value than elsewhere (and the food is good). It's therefore best not to dwell on

The Aegean Coast

the rather overdone decoration in the lobby, which tends towards the kitsch. 20 rooms have air conditioning. Being the last house on the shore after the harbour, the hotel boasts a small beach.

Hotel Assos, opposite the harbour, ☎ (286) 721 70 17 / 721 70 34, Fax (286) 721 72 49 – 36rm. ⁂ ▤ ✎ ⊡ ✕ [cc] The ground floor is a vast hall with exposed stone walls housing a bar, lounge and restaurant (very wide choice on the menu). You can have lunch outside, opposite the fishing boats. Very bright, pleasant rooms. Heating in winter. US$70 for half-board

Hotel Nazlıhan, İskele Mevkii, ☎ (286) 721 73 85, Fax (286) 721 73 87 – 37rm. ⁂ ✎ ✕ [cc] On the quayside, on the opposite side from the other hotels, after the police station (to the right when facing the harbour). This is one of the most expensive hotels in Assos, but it is the most beautiful and the most peaceful. The snug rooms have small bay windows with curtains which give onto the central patio and the bathrooms are decorated with blue Ottoman-style ceramics. The rooms without a view are less expensive. Warm welcome.

• **Kadırga**
Under US$8
Assos Sahil camp site, ☎ (286) 721 70 50, and **Hafızın Yeri camp site**, ☎ (286) 721 70 85. ⁂ ✕ Two almost identical camp sites, next door to each other and facing the sea, with large trees providing shade. Unfortunately, the level of cleanliness leaves something to be desired.

Since this is an isolated spot, all the hotels offer half- or full-board. Most are a little cheaper than in Assos.

Under US$40 for half-board
Hotel Yıldız Saray, ☎ (286) 721 72 04 – 24rm. ⁂ ▤ ✎ ⊡ ✕ ☂ 🐾 Small functional rooms with pine furniture. The cuisine is totally acceptable (good fish) and meals are served outside in the arbour. German is mainly spoken here. Travellers' cheques are accepted. Outside shower for bathers.

Over US$45
Hotel Eden Beach, ☎ (286) 721 70 39, Fax (286) 721 70 54 – 44rm. ⁂ ✎ ⊡ ✕ ☂ 🐾 [cc] A chic beachfront hotel, with a very refined decor. The rooms are on two levels surrounding a

garden which opens onto the beach. They all come with balcony and minibar, are spotless and tastefully decorated. The "business" category offers very charming little suites with office space. The restaurant offers 7 different menus. This hotel caters to a more international clientele than the Yıldız so the (friendly) staff speak English.

EATING OUT

• **Assos (the harbour)**
Under US$15
Yıldız Saray, this restaurant, which belongs to the hotel of the same name, is on a floating pontoon in the harbour. The location is pleasant and the food excellent, all very reasonably priced.

Fenerlihan, at the end of the quayside, just after the Nazlıhan hotel which owns it. Very beautiful dining area, all in stone, with a mezzanine and large fireplace surrounded by a sofa. Small terrace giving onto the harbour, in the quietest part of the village.

Nazlıhan, this harbourside restaurant belongs to the hotel of the same name, ☎ (286) 721 73 85 / 721 73 86. [cc] Seafood, fish, Turkish and western-style meat-based dishes, desserts. Live Turkish music every evening. Chic and quite expensive, but the food is good and the service friendly.

Assos, restaurant of the hotel of the same name, on the harbourside, ☎ (286) 721 70 11. [cc] Remarkable specialities of raw and unseasoned (except for salt) fish and "börek". Seafood (sometimes lobster), meat, meze and desserts. In winter, meals are served inside next to an open fire.

• **Behramkale**
Under US$8
Cengiz, in the square where the dolmuşes park, ☎ (286) 721 70 04. A quiet little restaurant in a pleasant arbour. Traditional, simple but excellent cuisine: "gözleme", "mantı", "börek", fish, meat, baklavas and tasty yoghurt. The proprietress, Asiye, and her son Ahmet, are charming.

Kale, set slightly higher up, near the old mosque, ☎ (286) 721 72 18. A quiet little unassuming restaurant, set in an arbour. "Gözleme", "mantı", "börek", meze, "köfte" and chicken. Good and inexpensive.

AYVALIK★

İzmir province – Map p 226
50km from Edremit, 150km from İzmir

Not to be missed
A stroll in old Ayvalık.
The sunset from the top of Şeytan Sofrası.

And remember...
Avoid Sarmısaklı; the beach is crowded and dirty.
For a swim, go to the Hotel Ozak beach near Şeytan Sofrası instead
(see Making the most of Ayvalik).

After the industrial plain of Edremit, it is a treat to stop in Ayvalık, a small but busy port filled with a Mediterranean air (avoid looking at the concrete shaft which disfigures the hill overlooking the port). The small streets of the **old city**★ are charming with their prim **corbelled houses** coloured with ochre, light green or blue. Near the mosque, children play inside the remains of an old but seemingly timeless American car, while cats sleep in various sun-drenched spots after snatching a few fish down at the harbour. Gas bottles are still delivered by mule-drawn carts, more practical than a cumbersome vehicle.

Facing the port, a group of islets acts as a Turkish land barrier hiding the large Greek island of Lesbos. Towards the south, **Alibey island**, the archipelago's largest, displays its arid hills which are slowly being overrun by the inevitable holiday homes.

Ayvalık is a very popular resort town and has been for quite some time. The 19C aristocrats have abandoned their elegant **villas** to berry bushes and rust, but **Sarmısaklı beach** to the south has become the playground of Turkish holidaymakers. A lovely stretch of golden sand which real estate promoters have permanently damaged, it is now a parade of large, hideous hotels creating a terrible racket with their beach discotheques after nightfall. Avoid it if you can! The only sanctuary for a swim and a sense of peace is the small **Hotel Ozak beach** (near Şeytan Sofrası). *(See the section below Where to stay)*.

Şeytan Sofrası★ (Satan's Table)

Towards the south, the road heads for Sarmısaklı, leaving to the right a wild and jagged coastline covered with pine trees. The section closest to the city has been transformed into a **nature park** (the **Paşa Limanı**), where you may picnic and even camp *(entrance fee, but very inexpensive)*. There is also a pleasant restaurant, the **Çamlık**, with a terrace under the pine trees *(at Ayvalık exit, near the park's entrance)*.

Farther along, the road skirts the base of the Şeytan Sofrasi promontory, its hillside plunging toward the sea and closing off Ayvalik bay. It owes its name (Satan's table), to the red light on the summit at dawn and at dusk, as if all the devils of Hell were convened around a table. The **view**★★★ over the islands and the sea is absolutely splendid. A violent wind sweeps the summit continuously, shaking the prickly bushes where "pilgrims" tie paper strips containing wishes which they hope will be granted (by Satan?!). Not long ago, the pinnacle was deserted. A snack shop has now opened and you must pay to park your car. The wonders of progress...

Making the most of Ayvalık

ADDRESS BOOK

Tourist information – In a tiny hut at the harbour. The documentation is quite meagre and the welcome rather frosty, but the staff speak English.

Bank / change – There are banks dotted around the harbour and a cash dispenser (Visa card) at *Yapı Credit télé 24*, on the main street (Cumhuriyet Alanı) right at the entrance to the harbour. Currency exchange next door at *Yapı ve Kredi Bankası* (9am-12.30pm, 1.30pm-5pm; closed at weekends).

Main post office – Atatürk Bul 49. Open every day, 8am-11pm. Currency exchange.

Car rental – *Avis*, Gazinolar Cad 67 (near the X Cafe Bar), ☎ (266) 312 24 26.

WHERE TO STAY

Around US$8
Ada camp site, on the Alibey peninsula (Cunda Adası). ⛺ ✕ ⚤ A beautiful location, which attracts many visitors (be sure to take a walk around the island and take a look around the little alleyways in the old village, up to the lovely abandoned church of St Nicholas). To get to the camp site from Ayvalık, take the "Alibey" bus (take the one which goes via Eski Yol – it's faster). Once you reach the terminus, you can either take a taxi or walk to the camp site.

Between US$15 and US$25
• In Ayvalık
🏠 **Bonjour Pension**, Marşal Çakmak Cad Sok 5, ☎ (266) 312 80 85 – 20 beds. In the old quarter of Ayvalık, go up Atatürk Bul until you reach the post office, then take the road opposite, Cumhuriyet Cad, up to Marşal Çakmak Cad, where the guest house is signposted. The guest house is set in a magnificent large 19C residence, decorated with beautiful wood panelling. The rooms are very spacious with queen-size beds and large armchairs. The downstairs lounge is reminiscent of the old family-run guest houses. One communal but immaculate bathroom. A large kitchen and laundry with washing machine are at the guests'

disposal. Everything is spotless. The shaded inner courtyard is a delightful spot for lunch. The guest house, built by French people (hence the name), is run by a Turk who will give you a very warm welcome.
Ayvalık Palas, Gümrük Meyd, ☎ (266) 312 10 64, Fax (266) 312 10 46 (next to the customs house to the north of the harbour) – 30rm. ⛺ 🅿 ⚤ A modern hotel, with no surprises, and a simple but adequate level of comfort. The rooms all have balconies, and the best ones, facing the sea, offer a magnificent view and are quieter than the ones on the street side where you can hear the noise from the discotheque.
Hotel Kaptan, Balıkhane Sok 7/9, a small street running parallel to Atatürk Cad (it is indicated by a large red sign). ☎ (266) 312 88 34, Fax (266) 313 00 00 – 15rm. ⛺ 🅿 ✕ ⚤ A modern hotel lacking in charm, but clean, functional and very quiet. Terrace overlooking the sea. Friendly welcome.

• In Şeytan Sofrası
On the road leading to Sarmısaklı, turn right at the roundabout before the town. Follow the signs to "Ozak Otel". If you don't have your own transport, take one of the numerous dolmuşes from the harbour. You will pass through a pine forest then a small residential area, behind which lies a quiet creek bordered by a few hotels. The area lacks charm but the **beach** is much cleaner and quieter than at Sarmısaklı.

Between US$30 and US$40
Hotel Ozak, Sarmısaklı Badavut, ☎ (266) 324 24 59, Fax (266) 312 25 74 – 28rm. ⛺ 🅿 ✕ ⚤ ⚤ Open all year round. Half-board possible. In a modern building. The rooms are spacious and very light with balconies overlooking the sea. Standard comfort. Small grocery and hardware shop right next door. Other hotels are under construction nearby.

EATING OUT

The harbour obviously attracts the most tourists, but is very pleasant. On the quayside, you will find many cheap little eateries where you can dine on meze and grilled fish under the vine canopies outside.

Under US$8

Gözde Pide Salonu, Talatpaşa Cad, Pınar Et Karşısı 46, ☎ (266) 312 24 49. Conveniently open 24 hours a day. A typical Turkish restaurant, simple, good and no-fuss: pide, "lahmacun", aubergine in every shape and form, soup, kebabs, pizzas and desserts. The welcome is friendly and the prices very attractive.

Around US$12

Kardeşler, Sahil Boyu, at the end of the harbour, ☎ (266) 312 60 44. cc This fish restaurant has very good seafood and some kebabs for those who don't like fish. Set menus (starter, main course, dessert, coffee and wine) for only US$9! Check out the kitsch pink decor inside.

Değirmen, Cumhuriyet Alanı 1, ☎ (266) 312 11 80. cc At the harbour, just before Sahil Boyu. For meat lovers: all the kebabs, döner, "köfte" and "şiş" of Turkey, as well as pide, pizzas and desserts, served in a large arbour facing the sea. Quite good and inexpensive. Rather impersonal welcome.

Gemi, on the "Mobidik", a boat which moors opposite the "Patisserie Cafe" every evening. Open every day, 12noon-6pm: lunch cruise for US$8. In the evening, dinner is served in the harbour (mainly fish and seafood). Wine at lunchtime, but only beer in the evening (your guess is as good as ours). Closes at 11.30pm.

HAVING A DRINK

Sokak Bar, Gümrük Cad 8, ☎ (266) 312 25 91. cc Behind Sahil Boyu, near Yapı Kredi Bankası. It's worth taking a look at this bar, if only for its extremely kitsch decor (just look at the façade...). A long room which opens out onto a terrace floating on the sea with a giant video screen. It is all rather impressive, but the music is unfortunately too loud.

OTHER THINGS TO DO

Boat trips – Many boats (wooden gulets) make day-trips to the islands of Lesbos and Alibey, with lunch on board. Departures for Lesbos are at 9am on Mondays, Thursdays and Saturdays, with a return at 4pm (2hr crossing).

Scuba diving – Information can be obtained next to the boats, from the captains or at the tourist information office. The **Ayvalık Palas** hotel, Gümrük Meyd, ☎ (266) 312 10 64, Fax (266) 312 10 46 (near the customs house next to the harbour) has a good centre where you can hire the necessary equipment, and an instructor will take you out on a small boat with room for about ten divers.

SHOPPING GUIDE

Sefa Cad and the surrounding alleyways (including Talat Paşa Cad) are part of a small but very lively pedestrian shopping area. You can find all sorts of things there, including a pharmacy.

Anatolia Bazaar, Gümrük Cad 3, ☎ (266) 312 97 46. A little boutique above the harbour, behind Sahil Boyu, where you will find a lot of beautiful copper objects, some hookahs and porcelain ware, little tables and wooden boxes inlaid with mother-of-pearl, etc. The prices are sometimes high, so feel free to haggle.

M.-P. Lejard/MICHELIN

In the streets of Ayvalık

PERGAMUM★★★
(BERGAMA)
İzmir Province – Map p 226
94km south of Edremit – 93km north of İzmir
Alt 68m – Pop 43 000

Not to be missed
The acropolis and the Asclepion.
A walk in the streets of the old city.

And remember...
Visit the acropolis at the end of the day, when the site is quieter and the
sunset lights up the ruins.
It is also the best time for the view (in the morning, the plain is often hazy).

The road to Pergamum runs across a withered plain and a long, dusty asphalt road
cluttered with dilapidated vehicles. Endless expanses of factories give the impression
of being in a desert which was sacrificed for industry's sake. The scene hardly begins
to improve inside the town itself; Pergamum has developed rapidly in recent years,
and the way into the centre is lined with jerry-built structures thrown up without
any concern for planning.

However, around Atatürk Square, the atmosphere is completely different: lively,
colourful and welcoming. Here too is the bazaar and the covered market equally
busy, with goods galore, including a wonderful array of ironmongery. Beyond is a
maze of narrow streets, bright with flowers; at the summit of the cliff-like hill overlooking the city, stand the ruins of the acropolis. The tall white columns sparkle in
the sunlight. The monuments of ancient Pergamum are well worth the detour, and
the old city is also enchanting.

The fief of the Attalids
Pergamum was a prestigious city, for many years a rival to both Rome and Alexandria.
In 301 BC, Lysimachus, one of Alexander the Great's generals, had a small fort built
to store the war booty won from the Persians during his conquest of Anatolia. His
intention was to dominate the region and found a dynasty. However, it is the name
of his great nephew, **Attalus I**, which has gone down in histoy, for it was he who
conquered the Seleucid territory and founded what was to become a brilliant capital.

The Roman alliance
However, in the late 3C BC, the small kingdom of Attalus I failed to blossom,
hemmed in as it was by Macedonia and Syria. Furthermore it had to free itself of
the yoke of Prusias I, King of Bithynia (237-183 BC). Pergamum therefore asked for
the assistance of Rome, which was pleased to oblige since this action allowed it to
increase its influence in the Orient. A price had to be paid. From 190 BC onwards,
Eumenes II, the son of Attalus I, saw his kingdom expand from the Hellespont (the
Dardanelles) all the way to the border of Cilicia by way of Cappadocia. Pergamum
in turn became one of the largest cultural and trading centres of the Hellenistic world.
With the assistance of Rome, **Attalus II** (159-138 BC) snatched the city from Prusias
II and ordered his assassination. However, his successor, **Attalus III** was far from
being such a clever strategist: he simply bequeathed Pergamum away to Rome (in
133) and therefore opened the gates to Anatolia. Graduating to the status of capital

of the Roman province of Asia, the city continued to prosper and was embellished with magnificent buildings which continue to be ranked among the ancient world's finest.

The age of decline

But by the 2C AD, Pergamum had lost out to Palmyra. In the 8C, the city fell to the Arabs closing in on Constantinople, and the inhabitants were forced to destroy the city's monuments in order to fortify the ramparts, since the Seljuks of Rum (Konya) were in turn a threat. The walls failed to resist the Ottomans of Orhan I, and Tamerlane's troops ravaged the city in 1402. So much for the prestige of the grand city of the Attalids. Mosques were built on the foundations of it ancient monuments, and the name of the city had ceased to resonate around the Mediterranean.

From papyrus to parchment

It is not common knowledge that parchment was invented in Pergamum? It is in fact the city which gave its name to this revolutionary invention (*pergamen* in Latin means parchment). In the 2C BC, the brilliant library of Pergamum was beginning to overshadow its great counterpart in Alexandria. In response, the Egyptian scribes reacted by blocking papyrus exports from the Nile to the city of the Attalids. However, the ingenious citizens of Pergamum soon found an alternative: tanned sheep (or goat) skin, which had the added convenience of being able to be used on both sides. However, since the hide was too thick to be rolled, it was cut, folded and bound, which was much more practical than the traditional roll (*volumen*). Alexandria could keep its papyri, the book (codex) was born.

In recent years, agriculture (cotton), the leather industry and tourism have pumped new life into Pergamum. However, it is a far cry from the grandeur and the beauty of long ago.

The lower city★

An entire day is necessary to explore the town and to visit the two archeological sites – the acropolis and the ruins of the lower city (Asclepion). Ideally, it is best to begin with a quick visit to the museum since it is located at the entrance of the city and then continue to the Asclepion; to finish your day, take a stroll in the old city before climbing up to the acropolis, glowing in the sun's last rays.

At the entrance of the city, behind the buildings straddling the right side of the main street, are two strange and perfectly conical hills – **tumuli** (funeral mounds) – an unusual sight amid the all-encompassing concrete. Further along on the left side of the avenue, is the pleasant museum **park**, set on a little hill.

The museum

8.30am-7.30pm; 5.30pm in winter, closed Mondays. Entrance fee. Allow 30min.
Given the richness and the beauty of the vestiges of the ancient city, you might suppose that the museum of Pergamum would contain priceless treasures. Unfortunately, this is not the case: Schliemann, the discoverer of Troy, was here in the 19C, and after him German archeologists took the most beautiful items to Berlin. Among fragments of friezes and capitals in the courtyard, is a beautiful **marble horse** (*under a portico*). It is just about the only component of the prestigious Zeus altar – jewel of the acropolis – which did not leave Turkish soil (2C BC).
Inside, beautiful Roman **glassware** shares the display cases with other architectural elements, including a fine **acroterium** displaying a *nike* (a winged Victory). You will see reproductions all over the city, for the statue has become emblematic.
On the right side of the courtyard, a small **ethnographic section**, attractively presented, displays exquisite objects representing daily life during the Ottoman period.

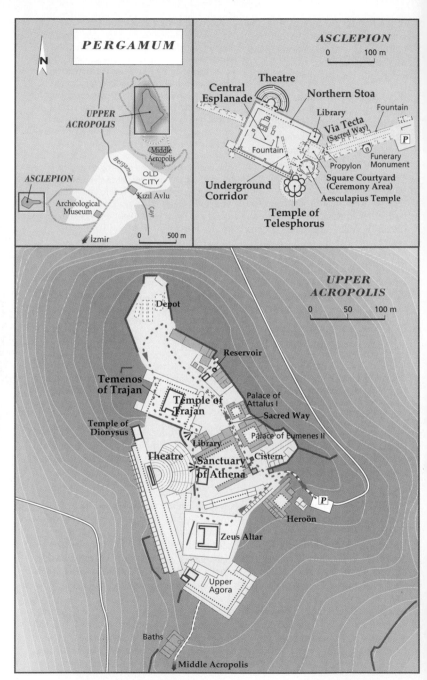

PERGAMUM

N

UPPER ACROPOLIS

Middle Acropolis

Bergama

OLD CITY

ASCLEPION

Archeological Museum

Kızıl Avlu

Çayı

İzmir

0   500 m

ASCLEPION

0   100 m

Central Esplanade

Theatre

Northern Stoa

Library

Via Tecta (Sacred Way)

Fountain

Fountain

P

Propylon

Funerary Monument

Underground Corridor

Square Courtyard (Ceremony Area)

Aesculapius Temple

Temple of Telesphorus

UPPER ACROPOLIS

0   50   100 m

Depot

Reservoir

Temenos of Trajan

Temple of Trajan

Palace of Attalus I

Sacred Way

Temple of Dionysus

Palace of Eumenes II

Library

Cistern

Theatre

Sanctuary of Athena

P

Heroön

Zeus Altar

Upper Agora

Baths

Middle Acropolis

240

The Asclepion★

Reached via a road on the left, after the museum (yellow sign), the site is wedged inside a vast military area which occupies the entire western side of the city, at the foot of the acropolis. Beware, it is strictly forbidden to take pictures of the military area. Focus your camera on the ruins and not beyond. 8.30am-7.30pm, 5.30pm in winter. Parking and entrance fee. Allow 45min for the visit.

The ancient remains of the lower city constitute an amazing health centre dedicated to the healer god **Aesculapius**, known in Greek as Asclepios. Most probably built in the 4C BC, this sanctuary acquired wide fame during the Roman era. It is here that the famous anatomist **Galen** welcomed the celebrities of the Empire seeking treatment. The guest list even included emperors such as Hadrian (in 123 AD), Marcus Aurelius (in 162) and Caracalla (in 214). The centre stopped operating in the 3C AD after a series of earthquakes damaged it.

A complete treatment

The Asclepion treated the physical as well as the mental: philosophy and medicine went hand in hand, according to the old saying: "a healthy mind in a healthy body". Baths, theatre and a library completed the sanctuary's facilities; the patients shared their time between massage sessions, sports activities, reading and music. However, the cure was not a sinecure, judging by the programme that was established by Galen for Aelius Aristides, one of his most loyal patients (he came to Pergamum for 13 years!): it included a fast; a late-night run, naked except for a whole-body mud-pack; cold baths and bitter potions made up of medicinal herbs. In addition, dream interpretation helped the priest-doctor to find the best treatment for each case. This was enough to restore the self-confidence needed by the patient for his next orgy in Rome.

Doctor Galen

Among the great figures of ancient medicine, the Greek Claudius Galen (131-201 AD) is considered the expert on anatomy. After studying medicine and philosophy, he served as a doctor in Pergamum and Rome. He acquired great renown for his research on the nervous system and the heart. As a result of animal dissection, he established a physiology based on the theory of humours (bodily fluids), a concept shared by Hippocrates which remained extremely popular until the 17C. Of the 16 volumes of his monumental writings, nine are known to us, and can be found in the library of every medical school. A doctor as well as a priest, Galen believed in the meaning of dreams and omens and his treatment included the use of remedies as well as placebos. The practice of combining psychology with other methods of healing has thus been used by doctors for centuries.

Visiting the site

The sanctuary is reached by way of the **Via Tecta**★ (Sacred Way), a beautiful marble avenue (820m long) formerly lined with elegant **Ionic porticoes**★ (many columns remain). Here and there, a few **honorific monuments**, fountains, and funerary stelae appear, while the centre of the avenue exhibits an intact **drainage system** still covered by marble slabs.

To the right, the route continues to the lower city's theatre (in a particularly ruinous state), at the foot of the acropolis, and then disappears across the military terrain (the mountain's flank bears an enormous Turkish flag with a white stone outline). To the left is the main complex, preceded by sober **propylons** (monumental gates). Next, a beautiful **courtyard** paved in marble has a little **altar** in the form of a base of a column. Decorated with snakes, it is the famous **emblem** of Asclepios (Aesculapius) and the medical profession.

The left side of the courtyard opens up to the **Temple of Aesculapius**, a large *tholos* formerly covered by a cupola. The adjacent **Temple of Telesphorus**★, is more interesting; it is a large round building with two floors which has kept its impressive lower level. Surrounding an enormous **central pillar**, a gallery leads to several **vaulted rooms**, most likely rooms for massages, baths (basins and fountains) and dream interpretation seances. Judging from the numerous terracotta **air ducts** in the wall, the space must have been rather steamy and damp, creating a relaxing atmosphere.

From here, visitors can follow in the footsteps of the former patients, reaching the theatre by way of the **underground corridor**★ crossing the central courtyard of the sanctuary, sheltered from the sun and the rain. This simple vaulted gallery, lit up by small windows, was once covered in marble. The corridor ends at the sanctuary's **central esplanade**★, next to a small Hellenistic **fountain** where water still flows. Only the **northern stoa**★★ of the surrounding porticoes survives. It consists of a magnificent row of Ionic columns hiding the **theatre**★. The latter has been restored, more or less successfully (the steps are fine, but the restoration of the stage seems clumsy). By skirting the *stoa* towards the square courtyard, you will pass in front of the **library**, a small square hall, covered in marble, where only a portion of the outer walls remains. The Via Tecta leads back to the exit. Blending into the countryside, the ruins of an old **Roman aqueduct** can just be distinguished as you exit the site.

Old Pergamum★

The narrow streets of the densely built-up old town on the slopes of the acropolis' hill are inviting. Above the **bazaar**, on the other side of a beautiful small bridge crossing the Bergama Çayı (ancient Selinus), discover an adorable little village, isolated from the rest of the town, and lost in time. The very modest homes are painted in all sorts of colours and some are hidden behind lush gardens as thick as a jungle, overflowing with flowers and the heady scent of jasmine and roses.

To the east is the road which climbs up to the acropolis (Bankalar Caddesi), the border between the old districts and modern Pergamum. There, facing the old carpet shops, rises an imposing building. Partially collapsed, the ruin of a 2C Roman temple, dedicated to Egyptian gods *(8.30am-5pm, entrance fee)*, it is named the **Kızıl Avlu**★ (the "red basilica"). It owes its name to the high brick walls (the marble cladding has disappeared). Two massive stone towers flank the sanctuary (one of them is a mosque). The **interior**★ of the temple, renovated during the Byzantine period, is very impressive with its immense sombre walls (260x100m) surrounding a large **podium** where the statue of the god Serapis must have stood. In the courtyard, fragments of **Egyptian statues** lie desolate among the tall weeds.

The acropolis★★

Car park at the top. 8.30am-7pm; 5.30pm in winter. Entrance fee.
Allow 2hr, or 3hr if you also visit the middle acropolis.

Although German archeologists stripped the site of its most beautiful pieces (almost all can be seen at the **Pergamum Museum**, in Berlin), the acropolis remains the highlight of a visit to Pergamum, because of the beauty of the standing buildings as well as the stunning view. From its 280m-high crag, it overlooks the entire plain. To the south, the hill descends in terraces towards the city, while to the north, it becomes a headland, barely 100m wide, whipped by a permanent wind.

On the way up to the top, the road winds through the **fortifications★**, elegant stone walls, reinforced haphazardly by towers. Below, towards the east, you can see an immense lake formed by a dam, a blue patch irrigating the surrounding crops.

The upper acropolis★★

Beyond the ticket office and the souvenir kiosks, a small **paved ramp**, still in excellent condition, leads to the site. Immediately below, on the left, observe the grey walls of a large rectangular building, a **heroön** (funerary monument), dedicated to the glory of the first deified kings of Pergamum.

The ramparts are reached through a doorway flanked by two large **square towers** (only the lower section remains). On the left, after the ruins of a **propylon** (on exhibit in Berlin), the **temenos of the Temple of Athena★** becomes visible (sacred area). It is made up of a vast windswept esplanade lined by the shafts of the columns which once surrounded it. On the east side is a well-made **drainage system**. From the end of the square, there is an extraordinary **panorama★★**, with the terraces of the amphiteatre hanging high above the plain.

On the other side of the path, stairs lead to the ruins of the royal palaces (those of Eumenes II and Attalus I), the stones of which are strewn among the weeds. Facing them, the **sacred way**, a lovely paved avenue, with the occasional step, crosses the whole site. To either side, people have made wishes by pinning paper streamers and bows to the flowering shrubs. Along the way, you will also see a pretty vaulted **cistern**.

A little detour to the east leads to the base of the look-out post dominating the site from its perch atop the **ramparts**. Excavated into the rock is a capacious **reservoir**, its centre graced by an unusual column.

A carpet shop

J.-F. Galmiche

Continuing towards the north, to the rocky spur *(the path is overgrown)* you will reach the **arsenal district**, a group of rectangular buildings (in ruins) protected by walls. Below, on the western side is the **Temenos of Trajan****, a magnificent esplanade of sparkling white marble leading into the void. From the majestic **portico**** which surrounded it on three sides, a portion of the eastern colonnade has been rebuilt. It includes a line of elegant columns formerly linked by a **balustrade** decorated with statues. In the centre of the sacred area stands the **Temple of Trajan****, erected by his son Hadrian (2C), a stately structure with its repositioned Corinthian columns of immaculate whiteness. A section of its fine **pediment*** has been reassembled on the ground. To the south, beside the temenos, rose the famous **library** of Pergamum, founded by Attalus I. During the time of his son, Eumenes II, it contained 200 000 volumes! Today, the sight of its razed walls challenges the imagination; it is difficult to believe that this library once rivalled Alexandria's.

From the terrace, the **view**** is splendid: around the town road, on the plain there are several **tumuli.** At this distance, the funeral mounds resemble mole hills.

The temenos of Trajan is supported by a remarkable **system of vaults****, in excellent condition, visible from below. There is a pathway (in fairly good repair) to the theatre below.

The theatre*** of Pergamum is undoubtedly Turkey's most impressive, dropping dizzily downwards. Its cavea is rather narrow, but very high. It consists of 78 **stepped terraces**** whose incline is nearly vertical, dropping from a height of 50m. From the top of the terraces (reached through one of the galleries), you will be lured irresistably towards the bottom. Below, the ruins of the **stage** form a narrow stone rectangle at the edge of the cliff. On the northern side *(to the right)*, notice the ruins of a small **temple dedicated to Dionysus**. As you leave the acropolis by road, turn to look back at the hillside: the view of the theatre is memorable. Further down, to the south, on the way back to the temenos of Athena, you reach the **Altar of Zeus** (or at least what is left of it). The Germans dismantled the entire building, stone by stone, to rebuild it in Berlin. Now only a few steps of the base remain (36x34m), where a pine tree has grown. Built by Eumenes II (197-159 BC), the altar formed a U-shaped portico perched on a podium. An immense frieze encircled it (now in Berlin), representing combat between giants and gods in homage to the victories of Attalus I against the Galatians.

The middle acropolis

There are other remains on the terraces at the edge of the lower city, below the Zeus Altar *(follow the blue lines painted on the rocks)*. This is a good excuse for a romantic walk among the ruins, with stops to admire the lovely **views***. The rectangular footprints of **agoras**, **gymnasiums** and **temples** stand out among the greenery. Remants of columns and white or grey marble statue bases worn by time, rest among the rocks while sets of stairs guide you towards a long-gone door or temple, summoning the imagination.

Further down, facing the southwest slope, is the **Sanctuary of Demeter***, a rectangular temenos punctuated by **altars**, set on a **terrace*** overlooking the city. Dating from the 3C BC, it is among the oldest structures of the acropolis.

A. Rossi/ALTITUDE

The vertiginous peak of the acropolis, Pergamum

Making the most of Pergamum (Bergama)

COMING AND GOING

By bus – The **bus station** is just after the stadium on the main road, more or less opposite the park at the museum. Buses run every day to İzmir (every 30mins), Dikili (likewise), Ayvalık and the north coast (roughly every 2hr, from 8.30am-3.30pm), and İstanbul (departures at 9am and 9.30pm).

GETTING AROUND

Most hotels, restaurants and useful addresses (museum, tourist information office etc) can be found on the main street, **İzmir Cad**, which comes out at Atatürk square, at the foot of the hill leading up to the acropolis. To the left, is the way to the Asclepion and, further up, the district of the bazaar and the old town. To the right, **Bankalar Cad**, a very busy road, leads up to the summit of the acropolis.

ADDRESS BOOK

Tourist information – Cumhuriyet Cad, ☎ (232) 631 28 51. At the very end of the main street, on the left after the museum. Friendly welcome, very helpful staff and good documentation.

Bank / change – Bankalar Cad is just the place to find a bank. After the fork, you will find a cash dispenser (Visa card) at the **Halkbank** (Monday-Friday, 8am-5pm, closed at weekends). There is a photo shop nearby.

Main post office – To the right at the entrance to Atatürk square. Open every day, 8pm-11pm.

Public toilets – The museum's toilets (just before the ticket office, on the right) are very clean and free of charge.

WHERE TO STAY

Camp sites

Caravan camp site, İzmir Cad, next to the Berksoy hotel. ☏ ✗ There are a few trees under which you can set up your tent, but this place, which is far from everything except the main road, is rather dismal. US$8 per pitch.

Around US$15

☏ **Pension Nike**, Talatpaşa Mah, Tabak Köprü Çikmazı 2, ☎ (232) 633 39 01 – 5rm. ☏ An adorable, attractively decorated guest house with an arbour concealing a garden awash with flowers where breakfast is served. The place is very calm, and the proprietress charming. This is probably the best guest house in town.

Pension Berlin, Ertuğrul Mah, Mustafa Yazıcı Cad 5, ☎ (232) 633 32 54 / 632 61 82 – 12rm. ☏ ✗ A large, very simple guest house, slightly down-at-heel but pleasant, with a vast covered roof terrace where you can take your meals. Both quiet and centrally located, near the "otogar", Archeological Museum and tourist information office. There is a bar on the ground floor and a hair salon next door.

Pension Akroteria, Bankalar Cad, next to the Çarşı Turkish bath, ☎ (232) 633 24 69, Fax (232) 633 17 20 – 14rm. ☏ ✗ A very inexpensive, but extremely rustic guest house. The rooms are on two levels surrounding a cool, flower-filled courtyard. Breakfast is served on a vast roof terrace. The Belgian proprietor is a very friendly chap, who will be delighted to supply you with all sorts of information on Pergamum, Turkey, Europe and the Belgians.

Pension Pergamon, Bankalar Cad 3, ☎ (232) 632 34 92 – 10rm. ☏ ✗ (See the restaurant of the same name). The rooms are spacious, but filled with an attractive hotchpotch of multicoloured material, eiderdowns and artefacts, which give them a rather old countrified feel. Guests sleep 3 or 4 to a room and the toilet facilities are very limited. Wonderfully quaint. But do make the most of the restaurant.

Pension Sayın, Zafer Mah İzmir Cad 12, ☎ (232) 633 24 05 – 18rm. (5 with shower-WC). This establishment, in one of the buildings on the main street, has no particular charm but is very well run. Small, comfortable rooms. The proprietor, Bruno-Hasan, is very amiable and knowledgeable.

US$40

Hotel Efsane, İzmir Cad 86, ☎ (232) 632 63 50, Fax (232) 632 63 53 – 24rm. ⁿ⌐ ℰ ⊤ⱽ ✕ ⫤ 𝖢𝖢 A small unpretentious hotel with spacious, clean rooms, and a tiny swimming pool on the roof. However, this out-of-the-way location on the edge of the highway is rather grim and very expensive.

Between US$40 and US$45

Hotel Asude, Fatih Mah İzmir Asfaltı 93, ☎ (232) 631 32 16, Fax (232) 632 05 12 – 50rm. ⁿ⌐ ✕ 𝖢𝖢 You can't miss its large red façade on the main street. Moreover, most of the tourist coaches pull up in front of it. The rooms are very comfortable and spacious (especially the bathrooms!). The basement bar is attractively decorated in the Ottoman style. Very friendly welcome.

Over US$45

Hotel Berksoy, right at the entrance to the town, on the left-hand side of the road, ☎ (232) 633 25 95, Fax (232) 633 53 46 – 60rm. ⁿ⌐ ℰ ⊤ⱽ ✕ ⫤ ✕ 𝖢𝖢 A would-be chic hotel, with spacious, attractively-decorated rooms and marble bathrooms. It is a shame that it was not planned out very well: the rooms face onto the road and breakfast (rather insipid) is served in a rather depressing room opposite the swimming pool terrace. Rather disappointing for the price.

EATING OUT

The most pleasant restaurants are on Bankalar Cad in the town centre.

Under US$4

☺ **Kahvaltı Salonu**, Talatpaşa Mah Değirmen Sok 4, not far from the red basilica and the little stone bridge. A tiny tea room serving enormous breakfasts at all hours of the day. Coffee, tea, milk, bread, cheese, jam, olives and yoghurt for just US$3. Very friendly welcome.

Around US$8

☺ **Pergamon**, Bankalar Cad 3, ☎ (232) 632 34 92. In a very beautiful Ottoman stone house, very tastefully restored by a team of young Turks with work experience in France and Germany. Also a guest house (see above). The restaurant is on the ground floor in a covered courtyard with an ornamental fountain. Attractive, good and inexpensive.

Sağlan, Bankalar Cad, near Cumhuriyet Meyd, opposite the mosque. Fish, kebabs, pide, "lahmacun", numerous meze and vegetable-based dishes. The delicious food is cooked over a wood fire and served in a pleasant shaded courtyard in the back. Not to be confused with Sağlan 02, in İstiklal Meydanı, which is not as good.

Meydan, İstiklal Meyd 4, right at the end of Bankalar Cad. Numerous excellent meze and meats (no fish), moussaka, fruit and desserts. However, the service is extremely slow.

SHOPPING GUIDE

Levent Güler, Bankalar Cad 17 . A tiny little boutique selling beautiful old kilims, mainly handmade and quite cheap. Open every day, 8am-8pm.

Tahsin Bayansal, Kınık Cad 9, opposite the red basilica. Beautiful kilims and carpets, copperware, hookahs, silver jewellery and glassware, at reasonable prices. The friendly proprietor loves to chat with the tourists.

FOÇA★

İzmir province – Map p 226
69km from İzmir – Pop 12 000

Not to be missed
A swim in one of the bays along the coast.
A boat ride.

And remember...
The best beaches are located north of Foça,
so don't be afraid of getting away from
the crowds and finding one for yourself.

From Pergamum, the road heading towards İzmir crosses an area of arid hills, now a vast industrial zone. For a breath of sea air before reaching Foça, make a small detour through **Çandarlı** *(from the main road, turn right at the sign)*, a pleasant town set on a peninsula, where little white houses and streets paved with large cobblestones surround a magnificent and perfectly preserved **Genoese fortress★★**.

The Phocaean Coast★

Back on the main road to İzmir, do not miss the sign on the right "Yenifoça-Foça" just before the "Opet" petrol station. After crossing another industrial zone, the road skirts an aircraft graveyard piled high with planes dating back to WW II.

At last, the sea is reached. The intense turquoise blue is set off by the white limestone cliffs along the whole **Phocaean Coast★★**, with its countless bays surrounded by pine trees. Beyond Yenifoça, especially, the beautiful scenery includes the stone **tower-houses★** and their narrow windows with massive white lintels. Built by the Greeks in the 19C, they are reminiscent of the Magna, a forgotten region of the Peloponnesus filled with fortified dwellings.

Unfortunately, the whole coastline and the surrounding hills have become the subject of a frenzy of development. Pine forests, vegetation and pebble beaches disappear every year to become holiday villages, indistinguishable colonies of small breeze-block shacks with no appeal. The unspoiled bays which created the beauty and reputation of the Phocaean coastline have become rarer and rarer. The remaining ones are often littered with rubbish.

However, there are still a few left, especially north of Foça. Those that are visible from the road are obviously the most crowded and therefore the dirtiest. To find a gloriously deserted little cove, all you need to do is leave the car by the highway and make your way down through the pine trees.

Foça Bay★

Despite the invasion of land speculators, Foça remains a very pleasant little port, relatively concrete-free, and gives an idea of what Kuşadası was like in former times. The city spreads along a bay split in two by a peninsula. On one side (to the north) it is called the **Küçük Deniz** ("small sea"), the area of the old city. On the other side (to the south), it is the **Büyük Deniz** ("big sea"), slowly being colonised by new hotels and holiday complexes. The liveliest area is of course the **port★** *(on the Küçük Deniz)*, where Turkish and international tourists mingle indistinguishably while cats observe the fishermen's every move.

The Aegean Coast

Facing the brightly-coloured boats huddled along the pier, **Greek houses** flaunt their white façades. Most of them have been renovated and transformed into hotels or restaurants, where fish features prominently on the menu.

The peninsula is guarded by the **Beşkapılar** Fortress ("five gates") where a portion of the walls has been rebuilt. Constructed by the Genoese at the beginning of the 14C, it was renovated by the Ottomans. Except for the fortifications, ancient Phocaea has been completely submerged by the modern city.

The Phocaeans of the sea
The Greek colonists who founded Phocaea, in the 7C BC, were great navigators to whom many Black Sea (Samsun), Aegean and Mediterranean (Marseilles) trading posts owe their existence.

The city of the monk seal

Amazingly, on the beach at Foça, you will not see the traditional statue of Atatürk but rather one of a seal! A monk seal to be precise *(monachus monachus)*, an endangered Mediterranean species. Foça enjoys claiming that the city is this mammal's last sanctuary. In 1991, the activities of the World Wildlife Fund (WWF) enabled the Phocaean coast to be declared a protected zone, in particular the **Mermaid Rocks**, at the northern tip of **Orak Island** (north of Foça), where a few seals have found refuge. Victims of large ships' fishing nets and especially of pollution, the monk seals number only approximately 300. If by an amazing streak of luck you should happen to see one, avoid approaching it in order not to frighten it, and inform the town hall. The sighting will quickly be relayed to the local WWF office.

Foça

The sea dances in the crystal-clear coves

M.-P. Lejard/MICHELIN

Making the most of Foça

COMING AND GOING

By bus – Buses leave for İzmir every 30min from 9am to 8.30pm. The municipal bus company also operates a shuttle service to İzmir 3 times a day (departures from Foça at 10am, 3pm and 8.30pm).

FINDING YOUR WAY

The harbour of Küçük Deniz, north bay, is the town centre. The main quay is called Sahil Cad. Most of the restaurants and hotels are gathered in this district. Where the quay meets the peninsula marks the beginning of Küçük Deniz Cad (or Fevzipaşa Mah). This is the town's second main road and leads up to the main square where you will find the bus terminal, taxi stand, post office, police station and tourist information office.

ADDRESS BOOK

Tourist information – 8.30am-6.30pm; 10am-1pm / 5pm-8pm at weekends. On the main square, at the end of Küçük Deniz Cad, ☎ (232) 812 12 22. A mine of information, and very good service. English spoken.

Main post office – At the end of Küçük Deniz Sahil Cad, almost opposite the tourist information office. Open every day, until 11pm in summer, 10.30am in winter. Currency exchange.

Bank / change – Türkiye İş Bankası, Küçük Deniz Sahil Cad 63, at the entrance to the harbour. Monday-Friday, 9am-12.30pm / 1.30pm-5.30pm, closed at weekends. Cash dispenser (Visa and Mastercard) outside.

Medical service – Sağlık Ocağı clinic, on the south bank of the peninsula, overlooking the bay of Büyük Deniz. Doctor Sedat, who works here, speaks English.

WHERE TO STAY

It's best to avoid the hotels near the main square since the noise in this area doesn't die down until 2am, then you will hear echoes from the surrounding nightclubs and, at dawn, the buses take over. It is preferable to stay in the small streets behind the quay, around İsmetpaşa Mah.

Around US$15
Pension Ensar, 161 Sok 15 Küçük Deniz, ☎ (232) 812 17 77, Fax (232) 812 61 59 – 18rm. 🍴 CC In a small street set back from the harbour. Quiet and pleasant. Very friendly welcome (the proprietor speaks English and a little French). Lovely roof terrace where guests can do their own cooking. Rooms are simple but pleasant and clean, all have a balcony.

Pension Siren, İsmet Paşa Mah 161 Sok, ☎ (232) 812 26 60, Fax (232) 812 62 20. Next to the one above – 14rm. 🍴 Same level of comfort as its neighbour, with terrace and balconies. TV room, bar and kitchen, with refrigerators on every floor. Travellers' cheques accepted. This guest house also organises excursions by car or minibus in the region. Very friendly welcome, and the proprietor's son speaks English.

US$25
Villa Dedem, Küçük Deniz Sahil Cad 66, ☎ (232) 812 28 38 – 18rm. 🍴 ℘ At the harbour. Very friendly welcome (the daughters of the family speak English and French), adequate service and spacious rooms with balconies overlooking the sea. Clean but, alas, rather the worse for wear.

Hotel Menendi, Fevzipaşa Mah Küçük Deniz Sahil Cad 28, ☎ (232) 812 24 20, Fax (232) 812 12 30 – 18rm. 🍴 ℘ 🍽 ✕ CC On the corner of the quay and the street which leads to the tourist information office. A pleasant and very well-run establishment. The congenial proprietor has lived in Germany and France and speaks English. The restaurant (lovely dining room and terrace) is a pizzeria. It's a shame that the rooms are so small. Travellers' cheques are accepted and safes provided. The proprietor also owns a bar and billiard room a little further up the street.

🕮 **Hotel Amphora**, İsmetpaşa Mah 206 Sok 7, ☎ (232) 812 28 06, Fax (232) 812 24 83 – 18rm. 🍴 ℘ ⤢ CC To get there, go along the harbourside on the right up to 169 Sok, a little street at right angles to the sea (the guest house is signposted) then take the first street on the right, running parallel to the quayside. In a beautiful 19C Greek house whose interior unfortunately retains nothing of its past (everything has been redesigned, and the decoration is not very attractive). However, the modern rooms are very good: bright, comfortable and clean (tiles). Breakfast is served on the terrace facing the swimming pool.

Sempatik Hotel Güneş, İsmetpaşa Mah 163 Sok 10, ☎ (232) 812 19 15, Fax (232) 812 21 95 – 16rm. ⌁ ⌁ ✗ cc
Not far from the Amphora. A good little hotel with well-kept, plain and comfortable rooms. Breakfast is served in an attractive arbour. Very good value for money.

US$40

Hotel Karaçam, Küçük Deniz Sahil Cad 70, ☎ (232) 812 14 16, Fax (232) 812 20 42 – 22rm. ⌁ cc An attractive old white house on the quay with a pleasant roof terrace. Small but bright rooms with high ceilings. Unfortunately the bathroom facilities are rather dilapidated.

EATING OUT

The quayside is very pleasant in the evening, and even though this area attracts a lot of tourists, dining there is enjoyable. Leave the **Foça** to the groups – there are so many other restaurants to choose from in the small side streets which are quieter and more picturesque.

Around US$6

Cafe, Küçük Deniz Sahil Cad, next to the Kordon restaurant. A tiny, pleasant little café at the harbour serving copious breakfasts, sandwiches and some meze. A good welcome and very cheap prices.

Pizza Milano, Küçük Deniz Sahil Cad 24/A, ☎ (232) 812 29 39. A small pizzeria in a pleasant arbour; good pizzas, "mantı", spaghetti, hamburgers, Turkish desserts and ice cream. Friendly welcome. No alcohol.

Under US$15

Bedesten, Küçük Deniz Sahil Cad, Aşıklar Yolu, at the harbour, ☎ (232) 812 25 17. cc A fish restaurant which also serves meat, hot and cold meze and quite a large selection of desserts. You can eat at the waterside or in the arbour. Reasonable prices, but the service is a little slow.

Celep, Küçük Deniz Sahil Cad 48, at the harbour, ☎ (232) 812 14 95. cc A large, often crowded restaurant specialising in lobster, fish and steak, and with about forty different meze on the menu. Also offering a wide selection of desserts, including a delicious chocolate soufflé.

Sedef, Küçük Deniz Sahil Cad, Belediye Meyd, ☎ (232) 812 22 33. A large terrace restaurant at the entrance to the harbour serving mainly meat (kebabs, şiş, köfte, grilled meats, pide, chicken), but also some fish, seafood and meze.

HAVING A DRINK

Balıkçı, Küçük Deniz Sahil Cad 50, at the harbour. A small but extremely popular bar, often full to bursting. Live music from 10.30pm every evening in summer. Mainly good quality Turkish music.

Dionysos, Fevzi Paşa Mah, 193 Sok 10. A quiet little bar set in an old, attractively decorated house, with a small shaded courtyard, away from the noise and bustle of the harbour. In winter, you can have a drink at the fireside and listen to Turkish music.

Kapı Dans Bar, Aşıklar Yolu 3. Across a pretty little courtyard in the shade of an arbour, in a very pleasant setting of stone and carpets, with a fireplace, you can listen to Turkish musicians playing traditional or modern tunes with jazz accordion. You can also dance here.

OTHER THINGS TO DO

Excursions – All along the quayside, numerous caiques await their next customers. Further information can be obtained from their captains at the harbour. Day-trips are from 10.30am to 5.30pm. The **tourist information office** also organises numerous excursions, including dinner cruises (7.30pm-11pm). It also offers treks on horseback (US$11 for 1 day) and tours to Pergamum (US$15), Ephesus and Pamukkale (2 days, all inclusive, US$60).

Beaches – To the north, between Foça and Yenifoça, some small creeks are still safe from developers. Minibuses leave for Yenifoça from the main square every 10min, stopping at the main beaches along the coast.

İZMİR

Capital of İzmir Province
Map p 255 – Pop 2 500 000
Very hot summers, mild and humid winters

Not to be missed
A walk in the cool and colourful bazaar.
The view of the gulf from the Kadifekale citadel.
Dinner in one of Alsancak's restaurants.

And remember...
To travel around, take a dolmuş or a taxi;
you will spare yourself stress and avoid parking problems.

The country's third largest city, İzmir is a sprawling metropolis which has developed considerably in the last few decades. Every year it devours more of the hills surrounding the once beautiful gulf of İzmir. The city's built-up area is now nearly 30km-long. In this immense labyrinth, where only the largest boulevards have names, traffic is constant, the noise deafening and the air is filled with dust. The shoreline is no less unattractive: the "Kordon" is an immense avenue flanked by sad façades filled with the reflections of a brown, or sometimes red, sea. The beautiful old Smyrna of old has left only a few traces: the *agora* (large square), a modest reminder of the ancient city and the Greek quarter of Alsancak, allow a glimpse of what the city was still like at the beginning of the 20C.

But modern İzmir does have its charms: hidden in the working-class districts (the Bazaar and Kadifekale hill), with inumerable shops, there are small, colourful houses and brisk hustle and bustle. Nearly all visitors to the region spend some time in İzmir, if only to visit the surrounding sights, the city is worth exploring in its own right. But most people will feel the urge to move on sooner rather than later.

Smyrna, the ancient İzmir

Throughout the ages, the city was a great port. Founded in the 8C BC by Eolian colonists, Smyrna was one of the great cities of Ionia. Like Ephesus and Miletus, its strategic location at the heart of important trade routes destined it for a prosperity which lasted longer than that of its neighbours, buried beneath the silt brought down by the floods of the Meander.

In 334 BC, Alexander the Great increased the size of the city by building a new district on the hills of Mount Pagus. The new Smyrna prospered during the Hellenistic and Roman periods until a terrible earthquake nearly destroyed it entirely (178 AD).

The golden age – The coming of Christianity revived the city. Smyrna was among the first places in Asia Minor to be evangelised: it participated actively in the spreading of the gospel of Paul and John, and soon became the seat of an important episcopate. The Arab invasion, from the 7C onwards, was to stifle its spiritual sparkle.

A cosmopolitan city – From the 10C onwards, Smyrna began to be coveted by its neighbours. It fell successively into the hands of Seljuks, Byzantines, crusaders, Genoese and Turco-Mongols, led by Tamerlane, before being annexed by the Ottoman Empire in 1424.

Jews and Levantines, the creators of prosperity

The population of Smyrna was long a kaleidoscope of ethnic minorities, which played a pivotal role in the economic and intellectual development of the city and in its trade with the Western world. The Sephardic Jews formed the oldest community, having found refuge in Smyrna after being driven out by Catholic Spain in 1492. Nearly a century later (1581), it was England's turn to do business in Smyrna. Thanks to a treaty between Murat III and Elizabeth I of England, the Levant Company acquired a 7-year franchise in Ottoman Turkey. The traders of this big merchant corporation were called Levantines. This term later came to designate all tradesmen of European origin – Genoese, Venetian or French. 1 500 Britons still reside in İzmir, in the Alsancak district.

This is when trade began to flourish, in particular under the reign of Süleyman the Magnificent. Smyrna became one of the Empire's largest ports, exporting all sorts of commodities (cotton, olives, grapes, figs, tobacco, textiles) bound for cities around the Mediterranean. Merchants flocked in from far and wide. Greeks, Levantines, Armenians, Jews and Westerners quickly made up more than half of the population and created a vibrant cosmopolitan society.

The last days of Smyrna

At the end of World War I, the Armistice of Mudros (1918) handed the Aegean coast to the Greeks as compensation for war damage. From that point onward, thousands of Greeks landed in Smyrna, promoted to the status of capital. An ephemeral status, however, since on September 9, 1922, Mustafa Kemal retook it during a determined attack: in a single day, the entire Greek population was expelled from the city which was ravaged by a gigantic blaze.

Smyrna was no more. Atatürk's victory meant the end of the Greek hold on Anatolia. It was a historical date for the young Turkish Republic, which local people have celebrated wholeheartedly ever since with great fanfare. It is undoubtedly in İzmir that the Turks' patriotism and loyalty to their "Father" is most strongly felt.

İzmir

Smyrna, the İzmir of yesteryear

ROGER-VIOLLET

İzmir, Turkish city

Upon the ashes of Smyrna, Atatürk founded İzmir. He wanted it to be a modern trade centre oriented towards the West. His wish came true, since today İzmir is Turkey's second largest port (after İstanbul). The city is also the seat of the general headquarters of NATO's ground forces for southeastern Europe. Every year *(at the end of August)*, it hosts the **International Industrial Fair**, a true symbol of Kemal's ambition. The exhibition is held in the **Kültürpark**, an immense space located in the heart of the city.

The City

A half-day suffices to visit İzmir's attractions.

The city consists of five main districts, from the north to the south: Karşiyaka (on the other side of the gulf), Alsancak (a pedestrian zone), the Bazaar district, the citadel (Kadifekale) and last but not least, the modern district of Konak (Clock Square). This itinerary ends in the quiet streets of Alsancak, a good place to eat before continuing.

From the citadel to the agora

Begin by seeing İzmir from above by climbing up to **Kadifekale** (C5) *(dolmuş on Konak square)*, the "Velvet Castle" *(no charge)*. Old houses huddle together in tight rows on the slopes of the hill (the Pagus) up to the base of the old fortress. Its partially destroyed walls give an impressive **view** of the city and the gulf (ideal for locating the different districts of İzmir). Between its Ottoman walls (raised on foundations dating from Alexander's period), a vast public garden spreads the shade of its large pine trees. Visitors come to relax and have a drink on the attractive terrace, while they overlook the sea and the hubbub of the city. Children play football (soccer), and in between goals, keep an eye on the cars they have agreed to guard. The women of the neighbouring houses, all wearing the countryside *şalvar* (scarf), come to peel their vegetables for the evening meal, while turbaned men sit in a circle on the ground to discuss the day's events. In a corner *(opposite the main entrance)*, the vaults of the ancient cisterns have collapsed, leaving gaping holes in the ground *(be careful where you step, it is not at all safe)*. No one could claim that the area is a model of tidiness, but a wonderfully relaxed and friendly atmosphere prevails.

A short detour on the way back down leads through the **Agora** (B4) *(9am-7pm; entrance fee)*, a solitary remainder of the ancient city. The ruins go back to the reign of Marcus Aurelius (161-180). Today, the square resembles an abandoned field; however, it has retained its **western portico** *(on the left)*, with elegant columns as well as the arches supporting its foundations. The southern edge of this wing was occupied by the administrative basilica; the central archstone of the entrance is decorated with a beautiful sculpted **head***. On the opposite side of the square, archeologists have laid out several lapidary pieces – statues, architecture fragments, antique sarcophagi – as well as beautiful Ottoman funerary stelae, originally from an ancient cemetery.

The Bazaar* (A4)

(8.30am approx., evening hours vary, closed Sundays.) Just north of Konak Square, the İzmir bazaar is typical of its kind: a tight maze of enclosed galleries and shaded alleys covered with grapevines. Relax and don't worry about getting lost, for there will always be someone to show you the way out!

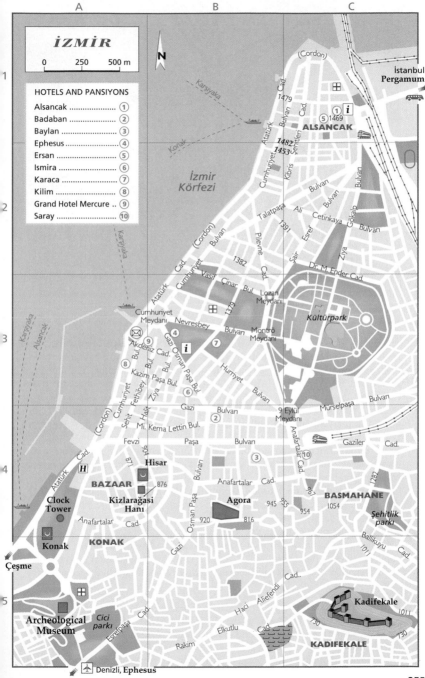

İZMİR

0   250   500 m

HOTELS AND PANSIYONS

Alsancak .... ①
Badaban .... ②
Baylan .... ③
Ephesus .... ④
Ersan .... ⑤
Ismira .... ⑥
Karaca .... ⑦
Kilim .... ⑧
Grand Hotel Mercure .. ⑨
Saray .... ⑩

İstanbul
Pergamum

ALSANCAK

İzmir
Körfezi

Kültürpark

Cumhuriyet
Meydanı

Lozan
Meydanı

Montrö
Meydanı

Hisar

BAZAAR

Kizlarağasi
Hanı

Clock
Tower

Konak

Çeşme

KONAK

Agora

BASMAHANE

Şehitlik
parkı

Kadifekale

Archeological
Museum

Cici
parkı

KADIFEKALE

Denizli, Ephesus

İzmir, relaxing in Kadifekale

This tightly packed group of shops hides three **caravanserais**, one of which has been restored: the **Kızlarağası Hanı*** (18C) recognisable by its magnificent pink-brick and white-marble walls, punctuated by elegant **moucharabies.** The immense square structure surrounds a courtyard accessible by four doors, one located on each side *(one of them at 21, Cevahir Bedesteni, another on the Hisar Mosque Square)*. Inside, a number of luxury boutiques (especially antiques, leather and gold) are housed in the **vaulted brick galleries** before reaching the courtyard where there is a pleasant café *(the Hisar; clean public toilets next door)*. The overdone restoration work has unfortunately altered the atmosphere; it has become the Bazaar's chic corner catering to tourists rather than Turks. Perhaps over time it will find favour with neighbourhood patrons.

On the way to the **Hisar Mosque**, you will reach a charming square **(Hisarönü)**, vibrant and lively. A **flower market** fills the centre, surrounding the mosque's ablutions fountain *(located on the left)*. The building forms an angle with the caravanserai while the other sides of the square lead to the alleyways of the Bazaar. Restaurants *(including the* Çevirme, *at the corner of street 902, and the* Baycigit, *next door)* have laid out their tables on the square and it is difficult to resist the temptation to relax under the cooling trees and observe the comings and goings of the faithful heading to the mosque to pray.

The Konak District

South of the bazaar is the **Clock Square** (Konak Meydanı) (A4), an immense windswept esplanade facing the sea. It is surrounded by charmless modern buildings and inhab-ited by flocks of pigeons. İzmir's emblem, the **Clock Tower** (Saat Kulesi), built in 1901, stands proudly in front of the town hall. It is one of the few remains of

The Aegean Coast

Ottoman buildings left in Smyrna, along with the little **Konak Mosque** (1748), located immediately next door, which has kept its pretty enamelled tiles. Images of the city of yesteryear create a feeling of regret.

Further to the south is the **Archaeological Museum★** (A5) *(9am-7pm; entrance fee)*, whose collections are worth a look. Unfortunately, the most interesting rooms are often closed *(officially for renovations, but more likely because of staff shortages)*. This is the case with the Hittite collection and the so-called treasury room, which contains the very beautiful **Bust of Demeter** (4C BC bronze, found near Bodrum). There are strange **painted terracotta sarcophagi**, original productions from the nearby city of Clazomene, as well as statues, mosaics and architectural elements primarily from the great coastal sites of Pergamum, Ephesus, Miletus and excavations of İzmir's agora. Next door, in the same courtyard, an **Ethnographic Museum** *(9am-1.30pm/2pm-5.30pm)* houses all sorts of traditional Turkish and Ottoman objects.

The Alsancak District★ (C1)

A stroll in the streets of Alsancak gives a glimpse of Smyrna's appearance at the beginning of the 20C; the area is one of the few districts not destroyed during the blaze of 1922. The neighbourhood is gradually being renovated and transformed into a pedestrian zone, but for the moment, only two parallel streets have been restored: **Muzaffer İzgü Sokak (1482)** and **Gazi Cadehlar Sokak (1453)** (B2, C2). You will discover bourgeois homes in a very refined Ottoman style: dainty residences with pastel shades, with one or two floors and elegant bow and sash-windows worthy of English homes. The surrounding streets also boast attractive houses which are waiting their turn for renovations. This pedestrian zone makes a welcome haven of peace. There are several restaurants and an interesting bookshop in the district *(see "Making the most of İzmir")*.

Making the most of İzmir

COMING AND GOING

By air – Adnan Menderes international airport. 18km south of the city. One of the largest in the country, operating services to most main European cities. **Havaş** operates a shuttle service by bus between the airport and the Büyük Efes hotel (journey time: approximately 30min; price: US$2). You can also take the train, which stops at the airport and goes to Alsancak station. There are many taxis, of course, but they are more expensive.

By train – İzmir has two stations which bear the name of the district in which they are located. **Basmahane station** (C4), ☎ (232) 484 86 38. For İstanbul. This station has a left-luggage office.

Alsançak station (C1), ☎ (232) 433 58 97. For Bandırma and Ankara.

By bus – İzotaş, the bus station, is outside the city in the district of Pınarbaşı, also known as Işıkkent. The easiest way to get there is by taxi, but the distance makes it an expensive ride. However, many bus companies offer a free minibus service to travellers who already have their tickets (departure from in front of the ticket sales offices). For the Kamil Koç bus company, for example, the shuttle leaves 30min before the scheduled departure time of the bus, from in front of the ticket office at 9 Eylül square, in Basmahane. Buses to İzotaş also depart from Şehit Fethibey Bul, in Alsancak.

At the bus station, you will find a bank, post office, restaurant (a rather grand word for it) and a bar, as well as all the major intercity bus companies: **Kamil Koç**, ☎ (232) 441 62 82 / 472 00 88.

Pamukkale, ☎ (232) 472 03 09 - 03 13.
Varan, ☎ (232) 372 03 89 / 03 90. Numerous services operate to all the country's main cities. For Ankara, 1 bus leaves every hour from 8am-midnight; for İstanbul, there is 1 bus every hour, 24 hours a day; for Denizli and Antalya, 1 every 30min, 24 hours a day, and for Marmaris, 1 every hour.

By boat – Ferry for İstanbul at 2pm on Sundays.

GETTING AROUND

In spite of its large main roads, İzmir is a labyrinth in which it is easy to become lost. The traffic is relentless and parking difficult. The best solution is to travel by dolmuş or taxi.

By shared taxi and bus – Most dolmuşes and (crowded) city buses depart from Konak Meyd (Clock Tower Square) (A4).

By taxi – It's no trouble to find a taxi. They are everywhere you look, especially near the main hotels, stations and shopping centres.

By rental car – Convenient for visiting Sardes, for example.
At the airport:
Budget, ☎ (232) 274 22 03.
Hertz, ☎ (232) 274 21 93.
Avis, ☎ (232) 274 21 72.
In town (Alsancak):
Budget, İsmet Kaptan Mah 22/1 Şair Eşref Bul (north of Kültürpark) (C2), ☎ (232) 482 05 05, Fax (232) 441 93 75.
Hertz, Hotel Etap Pullman, 138 Cumhuriyet Bul (B3), ☎ (232) 446 14 41, Fax (232) 446 10 81.
Avis, İsmet Kaptan Mah 18/D Şair Eşref Bul (C2), ☎ (232) 441 44 17, Fax (232) 441 44 20.

By boat – The main jetty is in **Konak** (Konak İskelesi) (A4), not far from the bus station, on Atatürk Cad. A ferry operates (via the gulf) between the Pasaport, Alsancak and Karşıyaka districts.

ADDRESS BOOK

Tourist information – On the ground floor of the Büyük Efes hotel, in Gazi Osman Paşa Bul (B3), Alsancak, ☎ (232) 445 73 90, Fax (232) 489 92 78.

Open every day in summer, closed at weekends in winter. As well as the usual maps and brochures, you will find information on the region and transport.

Airline companies – **Delta Airlines**, Cumhuriyet Bul 143, Alsancak. Information and reservations: ☎ (212) 231 23 39 / (212) 233 38 20.
Turkish Airlines, next to the tourist information office.

Travel agencies – The main ones can be found in the vicinity of the tourist information office, in Gazi Osman Paşa Bul. They have all sorts of excursions on offer.

Bank / change – There are currency exchanges and cash dispensers in most districts, but the greatest concentration can be found in Cumhuriyet Bul, the banking district (B2-3). **BNP Akdresdner**, 100m south of the post office, on Kâzım Dirik Cad, Meşhur Topçunun Yeri (A3).

Post office – **Main post office** (A3), Cumhuriyet Meydanı, just behind Pasaport. Open 8am-midnight all week. The post office has a currency exchange and cashes travellers' cheques. Other post offices can be found in Konak (near Eşrefpaşa Cad, a little further up 563 Sok) (A5) and in Anafartalar Cad (C4), not far from the NATO building.

Consulate – **British Consulate**, 1442 Sok 49, PK 300, ☎ (232) 463 5151, Fax (232) 421 29 14.

Medical service – **American Hospital**, 1375 Sok, Alsancak, ☎ (232) 484 53 60 / 40 14. **Alsancak Hospital** (SSK Alsancak Devlet Hastanesi) (B3), ☎ (232) 463 64 65. For dental problems, **Diş Hastanesi Konak**, in the Konak district, ☎ (232) 425 94 80.

WHERE TO STAY

It is very difficult to find accommodation in İzmir during the International Fair; all the hotels are full of tradespeople and manufacturers who have come to do business.

• **Alsancak**
Under US$8
Pension Alsancak, 1468 Sok 21 A, ☎ (232) 463 11 98 / 422 39 48. Next to the local tourist information office. No private bathrooms.

Pension Ersan, 1485 Sok 6, ☎ (232) 463 14 11 – 18rm. ⌁ In a little street running parallel to Kıbrıs Şehitleri Cad. A modest, but adequate guest house with a very simple level of comfort. Individual or shared showers, no breakfast, and only Turkish is spoken here. As a last resort.

Between US$30 and US$45

🍴**Hotel Kilim**, 1 Kâzım Dirik Paşa Cad, ☎ (232) 484 53 40, Fax (232) 489 50 70 – 90rm. ⌁ 🍽 🎱 TV ✗ CC On the seafront. A hotel with all mod cons right in the heart of Alsancak. The service is both courteous and efficient; the rooms are extremely spacious and bright with a lounge area and minibar. Bear in mind that breakfast is served on request only.

Between US$45 and US$75

Hotel İsmira, 28 Gazi Osman Paşa Bul, ☎ (232) 445 60 60, Fax (232) 445 60 71. ⌁ 🍽 🎱 TV ✗ CC A refined decor with warm colours that will make you feel at ease in this modern, comfortable and clean hotel. Rather expensive for the level of comfort provided, all the same.

Over US$75

Hotel Karaca, 1379 Sok 55 (Sevgi Yolu), ☎ (232) 489 19 40, Fax (232) 483 14 98 – 73rm. 🎱 ⌁ 🍽 TV ✗ CC Pleasantly located in a pedestrian street lined with very tall palm trees and packed with a multitude of stalls selling all sorts of things. The hotel, which overlooks the gardens of the Büyük Efes hotel, is both very quiet and centrally located. The rooms are spacious, simple and comfortable, all with a large balcony.

Büyük Efes Oteli (Grand Hotel Ephesus), Gazi Osman Paşa Bul, practically in Cumhuriyet Meyd, ☎ (232) 484 43 00, Fax (232) 441 56 95 – 446rm. 🎱 ⌁ 🍽 TV ✗ ⌂ CC In a large, cool flower garden. Very luxurious: vast, comfortable and immaculate rooms (overlooking the garden or the street), international press, currency exchange and a magnificent swimming pool. You can use the pool even if you're not staying at the hotel… for the outrageous sum of US$29!

Grand Hotel Mercure, 138 Cumhuriyet Cad, ☎ (232) 489 40 90, Fax (232) 489 40 89 – 168rm. ⌁ 🍽 🎱 TV ✗ CC A high-class luxury hotel dec-

orated in the Ottoman style with the added bonus of a non-smoking floor. Far too expensive.

● **Basmane**

Under US$15

🍴 **Hotel Saray**, Anafartalar Cad, ☎ (232) 483 69 46. More of a guest house than a hotel, with bathroom facilities on the landing. Nevertheless, it is comfortable and clean and the architecture is original: the rooms lead off from a long covered plant-filled patio, giving it a gentle Mediterranean feel.

US$25

Hotel Baylan, 1299 Sok 8, ☎ (232) 483 14 26 / 483 01 52. Next to the station – 33rm. ⌁ 🎱 TV ✗ You can't go wrong at this hotel, where you will find a friendly welcome and impeccable comfort.

● **Güzelbahçe**

Around US$8

Oba camp site, Çeşme Asfaltı, Güzelbahçe, on the road out of İzmir to Çeşme, ☎ (232) 234 20 15 – 28 bungalows. ⌁ ⌁ Nothing special: a few trees for shade, but with a large swimming pool. Cooking facilities. From İzmir, take bus no 80 from the Cordon (Atatürk Bul) in Alsancak direct to Güzelbahçe, or bus no 411 from Cumhuriyet Bul to Üçkuyular, then a minibus to Güzelbahçe.

EATING OUT

The most pleasant districts are the bazaar and the pedestrian quarter in Alsancak. Between Cumhuriyet Meydanı and the Basmahane district, the blocks of modern buildings conceal some picturesque little alleyways lined with small, unpretentious and very good restaurants.

● **Alsancak**

Under US$8

Meşhur Topçu 'nun Yeri, on the corner of Kâzım Dirik Paşa Cad and Cumhuriyet Bul (A3). A popular, typical Turkish restaurant with traditional meze, kebabs and brochettes served with yoghurt. Football fans can watch matches on the television set up outdoors.

Kemal'in Yeri, 1453 Sok 20/A (B2-C2). In one of the restored streets of the old quarter. The owner himself seats the clients and recommends the best fish of the day. Attentive service and excellent food.

Love's boat, in Atatürk Cad (seafront) (A3). The boat is moored opposite the Justy bar, close to the post office. Try the kebabs or fish, or just enjoy a cup of tea and relax to the gentle beat of the waves. Cheap and good.

Dört mevsim ve lokantası, 51A, 1369 Sok (A3). A definite must. All the locals know about it and the place is constantly full. You will discover a whole range of local dishes, such as "mahamara" or tasty "döner".

Hacıbey I, Akdeniz Cad 8F (A3), ☎ (232) 484 98 72. Near the sea and a stone's throw from Cumhuriyet Meyd, this little restaurant is of the most traditional sort: the house speciality is "manisa kebab", but you will also find "iskender döner", a variety of soups and a tasty rice pudding on the menu. Friendly welcome, speedy service, excellent and very cheap food. No alcohol. Closed in the evening and on Sundays.

Kırçiçeği, Kıbrıs Şehitleri Cad 83 (C1-2), ☎ (232) 464 30 90. Opposite the Italian cultural centre. Open every day, 24 hours a day. A very simple restaurant, rather like a canteen. Reasonable, traditional cooking at very low prices: kebabs, pide, "kiremitte", pizzas, "lahmacun", salads and soups. However, you won't find any alcohol (except the occasional beer), fish or desserts here.

Cafe Colette, 1391 Sok 1/3 B (B2), ☎ (232) 422 18 35. A nice little French-style café, named after the French author Colette. The proprietress, a cheerful lady with a good sense of humour, will give you a warm welcome. Quite refined food (meze, meat, a wide variety of vegetables, pasta, salads and desserts), very friendly service and a pleasant atmosphere. No alcohol. Closed on Sundays in summer.

Between US$8 and US$15

Reci's, 1382 Sok 31/A (C2), ☎ (232) 463 84 70. A very friendly, busy restaurant, attractively decorated with antiques. The western-style cooking (meat, crepes, pizzas, various salads, sandwiches

and cakes), is very good and inexpensive (no alcohol), and the proprietress is adorable. Closed on Sundays, and at 10pm during the week.

Karafaki, 1453 Sok 24 (B2-C2), ☎ (232) 463 83 68. CC An absolute must if you want to spend an evening in a typically Turkish atmosphere. In a pleasant pedestrian street lined with beautiful Greek houses, running at right angles to Kıbrıs Şehitleri Cad. Good, varied traditional cuisine: meze, meat, fish, salads, cheese, desserts and fruit, as well as a wide selection of alcohol. Diners eat out on the street in summer, and inside in winter, where they can listen to live music (on certain evenings) next to the open fire. Friendly welcome. Open every evening.

Between US$25 and US$45

1888, 248 Cumhuriyet Bul (B2), ☎ (232) 421 66 90 / 463 18 74. Set in an old, very tastefully restored Greek house, the 1888 combines charm and quality and serves a variety of refined specialities from all over the Mediterranean. A definite must, if only for the setting. Reservation recommended.

● **Basmane and Konak**

Under US$8

Cumhurun Yeri, Eşrefpaşa, Konak (A5). A cheerful little restaurant, like dozens of others in this neighbourhood, where you can eat for under US$3! Here the "fast food" consists of kebabs, grilled peppers and fresh (and clean) vegetables. At the end of your meal, the proprietor will sprinkle you with orange-flower water.

HAVING A DRINK

Nektar, Cumhuriyet Bul 285A, near the intersection with 1479 Street (B2). This is probably the most typical and friendly bar in İzmir, where you can settle down with the drink of your choice and listen to singers with the most beautiful voices backed by a small group playing traditional or contemporary Turkish music. Open every evening until all hours.

Ora, 1441 Sok 9 (C2), ☎ (232) 463 86 15, the third street on the right when going up Kıbrıs Şehitleri Cad. A little bar frequented by the young inhabitants of İzmir. From April to October, the tables are set in a little shaded courtyard, providing respite from the stifling heat of the city, and an ideal spot for a drink. Room on the first floor, and live music on certain evenings. Serves food (except on Sundays): meze, köfte, pasta, crepes. Friendly welcome and simple, reasonable and cheap food. Closed on Sundays in summer.

SHOPPING GUIDE

Avoid the boutiques in Alsancak if you can; they are all expensive and overrated. You will be spoilt for choice in the bazaar (B4), with its attractively-priced craftwork, hookahs and leather goods (slightly cheaper than in İstanbul). In September, don't forget to try the famous fresh figs.

• Alsancak

1001 Shop, 1379 Sok 37/1 C (B2), ☎ (232) 422 47 41. The only "antiques dealer" in Alsancak has some beautiful wares, including a large selection of "suzanı", superb embroidered wall hangings from eastern Turkey in iridescent colours, some kilims, old copperware, hookahs, cushions, books and furniture. It is quite expensive, but the quality is high. You will be given a warm welcome by the German proprietress, Charlotte, who speaks several languages, and her Turkish husband, Metin. Closed on Sundays.

D&R, Cumhuriyet Bul 209, near Gündoğdu Meyd (B2). A large variety of Turkish and international music, and some beautiful art books. Open every day 10am-10pm, and until 11pm at weekends.

Book shops – *Net Kitabevi*, Cumhuriyet Bul, between the French cultural centre and Cumhuriyet Meyd (B2). Here you can find beautiful Turkish art books (in English) and post cards.

Dünya Kitabevi, on the other side of the street, between the French Consulate and the İzmir cinema (B2). Offering very much the same sort of thing as the one above, but with some guide books and dictionaries on top.

İletişim Kitabevi, Kıbrıs Şehitleri Cad, 1443 Sok 48/A (in the pedestrian quarter of Alsancak) (B2-C2). Packed with beautiful books, records and postcards of İzmir in the 19C.

• Bazaar

For bargain hunting, the best place to go is to the caravanserai and the surrounding area, where, among other things, you will find magnificent kilims at very reasonable prices.

Önde-Turistik Eşya, 876 Sok 42 (A4), ☎ (232) 425 00 45, and 904 Sok 94 (A4), ☎ (232) 482 04 11. Very close to the caravanserai, but in this maze of narrow alleyways, it is best to ask the way rather than follow the street numbers, which are, moreover, often impossible to find. Two shops in close proximity to each other are full to overflowing with all possible and imaginable Turkish goods: ceramics, copperware, glassware, hookahs, backgammon boards, wooden objects inlaid with mother-of-pearl, articles made of bone or onyx, weapons, souvenirs etc. For all tastes and budgets (very reasonable prices in general). Closed Sundays.

Aykut, 871 Sok 18 (A4), ☎ (232) 484 64 13. Opposite one of the entrances to the caravanserai. Copperware enthusiasts will be in seventh heaven here: there are objects in all shapes and sizes to suit all tastes and at all sorts of prices, most of them modern but some older and therefore more expensive, including some extremely beautiful pieces. Also some wooden, porcelain, bone and onyx objects, but nothing extraordinary in this department. Friendly welcome. Closed Sundays.

Music – *Ejder Müzik Aletleri*, Anafartalar Cad Veysel Çıkmazı 35/P-8 Kapalı Çarşı, Konak (A4), ☎ (242) 425 37 54. Take a look around Ejder Güleç's shop. He is Turkey's greatest lute maker, probably one of the best in the world, and makes and sells lutes and "qanun", instruments which are as pleasant to the eye as to the ear.

SARDİS★★
EAST OF İZMİR

Manisa province – Map p 226-227
92km to Sardis, 140km via Manisa
Allow one day. Lodging in İzmir

Not to be missed
The temple of Artemis and the Imperial Hall of Sardis.
And remember...
Bring along some water and suitable clothing for Manisa.
Enjoy a picnic by the Temple of Artemis.

Northeast of İzmir, past the suburbs' last factories, the Manisa road heads deep into the beautiful countryside filled with rows of poplars and strewn with vineyards, and coloured with unusual patches varying from green to reddish brown. These vines are not grown to produce grapes, but raisins, specifically, the famous **Smyrna sultanas.** The grapes, picked when they are still green, are spread out on the ground where they dry for several days until they redden, then turn to brown.

Further north, the road climbs up the slopes of the Sipil Dağı, a vast forested massif which has recently become a protected nature park. Next, it descends towards the Manisa Plain before continuing east towards Manisa. Facing it, the endless Gediz expanse allows a bird's-eye-view of the patchwork of drying raisins. After Ahmetli, the mountains, which create a hazy rampart in the distance, are suddenly close. Some 20km from the site, the hills bordering the road are curiously shaped like Cappadoccia's "fairy chimneys": cones of porous rock whose eroded tips have formed strange hats.

Smyrna sultanas are spead out for sun-drying

B. Brillion/MICHELIN

■ **Manisa** – *33km from İzmir. Take the Ankara road out of town through the Basmahane district. Follow signs to Bornova, then Manisa (route 565).*

Once past the grey suburbs spilling onto the dusty plain, you reach the centre of Manisa (ancient Magnesia ad Sipylus), with its pretty square, **Muradiye Meydanı***, set on the slopes of the Sandık hills *(Sandık tepesi)*.

If the shoe fits …
On market days, Murat Caddesi is one of the city's busiest streets. Beware though, you will not find carrots or turnips, only shoes. By the ton! Small ones, large ones, slippers, boots, black ones, golden ones, everything under the sun, as long as it looks like a shoe. If yours have had their day, seize the moment!

A **bronze statue** of Sultan Murat III (1546-1595) gives the impression of lingering in the centre of the square. All around, there is a pleasant public garden shaded by palm trees where the local population gathers (especially women, most of them veiled). This is where the city's main gems are concentrated: two mosques with rose-brick and white marble, as well as the museum, set inside the remarkable buildings of a medresa (religious school) and an *imaret* (hospice) built by famous architect **Sinan** *(see p 49).*

The prettiest mosque, the **Muradiye Camii***, was built in 1583 on the orders of Murat III, to whom the city owes its golden age. The most interesting feature of the building (and its neighbour, the **Sultan Camii**) is the porch, consisting of elegant ancient columns. Step inside at an appropriate moment (not during prayer time), to experience the tranquillity of the place.

The **museum*** *(next to the Muradiye mosque, on Murat Cad., 8am-12noon/1pm-5pm, entrance fee)* consists of two parts, an ethnographic section *(on the left, in the medresa)* and an archeological one *(on the right, in the ancient imaret)*. The latter, well appointed, displays most of the items found in Sardis, including delightful **mosaics****.

Beyond the square *(past the museum, up one of the little streets heading to the city's heights)*, you reach the colourful homes of old Manisa. The village clings to the steep slopes of a hill. After a strenuous climb, you will arrive at the ruins of a **Byzantine citadel**, and a mosque, the **Ulu Cami** (1366). The mosque appears at the rear of a peaceful patio encircled by an elegant portico. Next door, a café has opened on a pine-shaded **terrace*** (a refreshing and cool place to catch your breath). From there, the whole city and plain are visible. For those who are not completely exhausted by the climb, proceed to the citadel, set in the middle of a magnificent **pine forest***.

Sardis** (Sart)

107km from Manisa (93km from İzmir). From Manisa, follow the Turgutlu road (71km). It connects with the Izmir-Ankara main road, which you follow towards the right (east). From there, continue straight on. From Izmir, take the Ankara raod through the Basmahane district, follow signs to Bornova, then Ankara again. As you leave the city, look for signs pointing to Afyon, then, after 10km, follow the Afyon-Turgutlu sign. The archaeological site is divided into two parts: the Temple of Artemis and the gymnasium. 8am-7pm. There is an entrance fee for both sites. Allow 2hr to visit the whole area.

Of ancient Sardis, only the city centre and the temple of Artemis have been excavated and restored to any significant extent. Yet the many vestiges scattered in the surrounding fields, on both sides of the road, make it easy to imagine the size of the ancient city. Today, the earth has covered the walls and rows of vines have replaced the colonnades. The farmers have even planted on the roof of a ruined building!

Sardis

The Aegean Coast

As rich as Croesus!

Sitting beside the River Pactolus, Heracles dreamt about beautiful Omphale while skimming stones on the water – except these stone were gold nuggets! When the demigod returned to his work, the Lydians picked up the precious bits. Their king, Croesus (561-547), had a foundry built at the foot of the mountain on a spot just before the river emptied its riches into the waters of the Hermos. Nearby stands the Temple of Cybele (later Artemis) who was held accountable for the purification of the metal. Coins, jewellery, statues for temples, and priceless treasures from Lydian workshops were exported to the whole of the ancient world. And thus did Croesus become a legendary simile!

A city of gold

Legendary city of the Heraclides – proud scions of Heracles and the Lydian queen Omphale – Sardis was founded around 1185 BC. However, the city never really developed until 685 BC, when a Lydian, Gyges, decided to establish the capital of his young kingdom here. Sardis became a rich city, drawing wealth from the gold which ran through the **Pactolus**, a small river flowing down the slopes of the Tmolos (the Boz Dağı, south of Sardis).

From Croesus to Cyrus – The prosperity of the city soon began to interest the Persians. Cyrus' camels made Croesus' horses flee (548 BC) and Lydia became a Persian province. A fallen yet prosperous capital, Sardis was transformed into the terminus of a new trade route linking Susa (Persia) to western Anatolia. The city could have continued its growth, but it chose instead to ally itself with the Ionian cities to fight off Persian domination (499 BC), and this led to its downfall.

It was necessary to wait for the victory of Alexander the Great, at the battle of Granica (334 BC), for Sardis to reclaim its freedom and rise from the ashes. The Romans integrated the city into their Asian province in 133 BC, the period which left most of the ruins still visible today. Later, St John the Evangelist included it among the Seven Churches of his *Apocalypse* and the city became one of the Byzantine Empire's largest bishoprics.

And the caravan moves on

A 2 500km-long trail links Susa to Sardis, a trip of several weeks for camel caravans. Royal messengers only took seven days. They slept on horseback, and transferred to another animal every 30km, at one of the relay stations set up along the way. During the Roman period, the royal trail was extended to Smyrna, where wheat bound for Rome was loaded. The present-day road linking İzmir to Ankara follows the same route.

A slow decline – Unfortunately for Sardis, a succession of attacks diminished its power: pillaged by the Sassanids in 616, occupied by the Turks at the end of the 11C, retaken by the crusaders, then annexed to the Ottoman empire in 1390, Sardis fell definitively under the assault of Tamerlane in 1402, never to rise again.

The Temple of Artemis★★

As you arrive in the hamlet of Sart, take the Hypaepa road on the right (yellow sign, a transport café is at the corner), which follows the course of the Pactolus (today's Sart Çayı). A car park is located on the left of the guard's booth.

Before reaching the temple, you will notice the ruins on the right-hand side of the road (*200m from the junction*). These are the remains of Cybele's altar and Croesus' **workshops** where the gold was smelted and refined. Nearby, archeologists have discovered the remnants of a rich Byzantine home, whose **mosaics** are now in the Manisa museum.

The 15m-tall columns of the Temple of Artemis rise at the back of a vast **natural amphitheatre**** surrounded by hills encircling it like the battlements of a castle. At the summit of one of them, the ruins of the **acropolis** are barely distinguishable in the haze. There is no escaping the feeling of grandeur which attaches itself to the site. The temple's size (46x99m, proportions comparable to those of the temple of Didyma or the Temple of Artemis in Ephesus) is colossal. Here and there, enormous Ionic **capitals** lie on the ground next to sculpted monoliths more than 4m long from the temple's architrave. In comparison, the adjoining diminutive **Byzantine chapel** (5C) at the foot of the temples' stairs seems positively Lilliputian.

Constructed in the 3C BC on the foundations of a Lydian temple dedicated to Cybele, the Temple of Artemis was divided in two by the Romans for the requirements of the cults of Jupiter and Rome. Beginning in the 6C, it was abandoned by the Christians, and later served as a stone quarry.

Take the main road on the right. The gymnasium is 1km away, on the left side of the road.

The Gymnasium**

The ticket office is located at the back of the gymnasium, whose entrance is reached by taking the Roman road skirting the highway, on the southern side of the buildings.

More than just a simple gymnasium, the Romans wished to create a bath, sports and cultural complex in the heart of the city, a kind of forum uniting political and social life. The entrance is reached through the **Marble Road**, one of the city's main thoroughfares in former times, bordered by cradle-vaulted shops (the visible ones date from the Byzantine era and cover the ancient layers). At the beginning of the street, *(below on the right)*, notice the **Byzantine latrines***, a marble bench pierced with holes and a trench below.

The **exercise hall** *(on the right, after the synagogue)* is an immense square structure with 80m sides, formerly decorated with marble plaques. On its western side there is an exceptionally imposing façade. This is the **Imperial Hall***** (or "marble court"), a prestigious vestibule preceding the thermal baths. Restored with much care by an American team, the walls rise on two floors, alternating brick and marble behind a row of columns. Begun in the 3C AD under Caracalla, and continued by Septimius Severus, this masterpiece of elegance testifies to the Romans' taste for the monumental, a symbol of their domination *(see sidebar p 282)*. A door on the left side allows a glimpse of the thermal rooms (in ruins), laid out in a symmetrical manner around the hall.

Go back towards the Roman road.

A **synagogue****, all in marble and mosaic, appears at the southern edge of the exercise hall. An annex of the Imperial complex, this long building was the city's gift to the Jewish community in the 3C AD. You enter through a small **atrium**** embellished by an ornamental pool. Surrounded by slim Ionian columns, the sides of this room were once covered. The **marble marquetries**** on the walls have been partially restored; the beige and pink tones echo those found on the floor **mosaics**. The **nave** of the synagogue is a long rectangular room closed off by the **apse**. Everything is sparkling white, from the marble floor slabs to the semicircular steps of the completely renovated chancel. Its decoration has been carefully studied down to the smallest detail. One example is the little drain spout next to one of the pillars, on the left, bearing a delicate rosette sculpted in a marble slab. The synagogue's most exquisite mosaics are housed in the Manisa museum.

Sardis

ÇEŞME★

İzmir Province – 89km west of İzmir (centre) – Map p 277
Very hot summers, mild and humid winters

Not to be missed
The Genoese fortress.
And remember...
Avoid Çeşme on weekends, all of İzmir's residents tend to be there.
Take the time to explore the old streets behind the castle.
For a swim, head for Altınkum.

Isolated at Turkey's westernmost tip, at the far end of a peninsula, Çeşme is İzmir's garden, its lung and escape hatch. On weekends, well-heeled city folks, dressed in their best clothes and mobile phone at hand, come here for a breath of fresh air on the beaches and to taste the fish from the restaurants in nearby villages. A well designed four-lane motorway has recently begun connecting İzmir to the resort town, which gives you an idea of the masses of people arriving every Friday evening. And since everybody needs to be lodged, the breeze-block homes sprout like mushrooms around the fishing villages in the north of the peninsula.

Nevertheless, Çeşme remains a small and quaint place, full of Mediterranean charm. It stretches along a narrow inlet guarded by an impressive Genoese fortress built of ochre-coloured stones. At the foot of the castle is the main square, extended by the quayside with its line-up of schooners. It is unfortunate that a large concrete cube – a hotel – has managed to disfigure the castle's surroundings. Behind the sea front lies the Çeşme of yesteryear, a maze of busy streets flanking elegant white façades with wrought-iron balconies.

Built by the Genoese in the 14C, the **Genoese Fortress★** owes its current appearance to the Ottomans who made many modifications in the 18C *(entrance on the right side, at the top end of an alley. 8am-12noon/1pm-5.30pm, closed Mondays. Entrance fee).* One of the towers houses a small **Marine Archeology Museum** *(9am -5pm).* The path along the ramparts *(beware, there are no railings)* offers a beautiful **view** of the bay.

Nearby *(on the left facing the sea),* a beautiful 18C **caravanserai** has been restored and transformed into a hotel. Even if you do not lodge there, have a look at the inner courtyard, awash in luxuriant vegetation.

The street leading to the heart of the old city *(İnkilap Cad.)* passes in front of an impressive building with narrow windows and a renovated façade which resembles a Baroque church. It is in fact a **Byzantine church** modified in the 18C, before it was abandoned. Temporary art exhibits held here offer the opportunity to discover the stucco embellishments inside.

The beaches of the peninsula

Not long ago, the Çeşme peninsula had a reputation for its beaches and charming fishing villages, such as **Dalyan**, whose fish restaurants are loved by İzmirites. Unfortunately, large-scale building has disfigured the coastline north of the city and has reduced the available seashore. The beaches are narrow, crowded in summer, and dirty. Luckily, those located in **Altınkum**, 8km south of Çeşme *(on the other side of the bay),* are better. Avoid the first one, which is the busiest. Continue farther on; the road turns inland to reach an open space filled with dunes dotted with pine trees and shrubs. Beyond is the "real" beach, the peninsula's wildest and least crowded.

A. Thévenart

Fish dressed up for dinner

The Aegean Coast

Making the most of Çeşme

COMING AND GOING

By bus – The bus station is at the entrance to Çeşme when coming from İzmir (1km from the centre), ☎ (232) 64 99. Services operate every day to İzmir at 20min intervals from 6am-9.30pm, and from 7am at weekends.

By shared taxi – Dolmuşes for Alacati, Altınkum, Ilıca and Ildır depart from İskele Meydanı, opposite the tourist information office. Departures for Dalyan (to the north of the peninsula) from the quayside opposite the post office.

GETTING AROUND

The town is not very large, so the best way of getting around is on foot.

By taxi – The taxi stand is on the main square, ☎ (232) 712 63 50.

By rental car – Avis, 11/1C, Cumhuriyet Meydanı, next to the Rıdavan hotel. Cars and scooters. Bus tickets for İstanbul, Ankara and the Black Sea can also be purchased here. There is another scooter rental agency on the road out of town to Ilıca, ☎ (232) 712 67 06, Fax (232) 712 70 29.

ADDRESS BOOK

Tourist information – 8 İskele Meydanı (main square), opposite the caravanserai, ☎ (232) 712 66 53. 8.30am-7pm (9am-12noon/1pm-5pm at weekends). Friendly welcome.

Bank / change – There is a small office in the main square, at the foot of the castle (to the left when facing it). Open every day, 9am-11.30pm.

Türkiye iş Bankası, next to the town hall, in Cumhuriyet square (the currency exchange is adjacent to the Avis agency). 9.30am-1pm / 5.30pm-9pm.

Main post office – Hürriyet Cad. Near the centre, along the quayside.

Medical service – Public hospital (Devlet Hastanesi). When coming into Çeşme from the direction of İzmir, turn left twice, ☎ (232) 712 07 77 / 78.

WHERE TO STAY

• **In the surrounding area**

Camp sites

Tursite camp site, at Altınkum beach, 9km south of Çeşme, ☎ (232) 722 12 21,

Fax (232) 722 12 92. Open every day in summer. Bungalow rental possible (very cheap). This camp site quickly fills up in summer, so it is best to call beforehand to check on availability. Dolmuşes shuttle between the camp site and the marina next to İskele Meydanı all day long. Around US$8 per pitch.

Vekamp camp site, at Paşa Limanı, 10km east of Çeşme, ☎ (232) 717 22 24. Offering the same facilities and rates as the one above, but with the added advantages of being located in a beautiful forest and having a thermal swimming pool. It is advisable to book ahead. Around US$8 per pitch.

• **On the seafront**

Around US$15

Pension Barınak, 16 Eylül Mah, Kutludağ Sok 62, ☎ (232) 712 66 70 / 712 79 60 – 14rm. A simple, clean and quiet guest house. 10 showers on the top floor, a large shaded roof terrace, a little beach nearby and a very friendly welcome.

Between US$25 and US$30

Hotel Maro, 16 Eylül Mah, Hürriyet Cad 68. An attractive, quiet establishment steeped in a gentle atmosphere. Simple, bright rooms.

• **In the old town**

Between US$8 and US$15

Pension Özge, Cumhur Kara, ☎ (232) 712 70 21 – 12rm. From the main road leading to the town centre, turn right into Uzun street, then take the fourth street on the right. This very well-kept guest house is hidden away in the heart of the old quarter, in a small, quiet and comfortable house. Spacious rooms, television lounge and bar. Breakfast is served in the garden.

Pension Tani, Musalla Mah, Tarhan Sok 15, ☎ (232) 712 62 38 – 6rm. Near the castle, above the caravanserai, high up in the old town. Although very simple, it is one of the nicest guest houses in town with its immaculate, cool rooms (very welcome in summer), shower facilities on the landing and a small flower-covered roof terrace where you can take breakfast and enjoy the view. Cooking facilities are also provided. The very attentive proprietress speaks a few words of English.

The Aegean Coast

Around US$15

🏨 **Hotel Sesli**, Nuri Alçimen Cad 39, ☎ (232) 712 88 45, Fax (232) 712 76 50 – 19rm. 🛏 📶 ✕ 🏊 CC A small, quite luxurious hotel in a very quiet street, with a little swimming pool, bar and restaurant in a courtyard full of flowers. The atmosphere is homely, the welcome friendly, the rooms immaculate, and the family speaks English and German. All of this for a very reasonable price. In short, a very good place to stay. Closed in winter.

Yalçın Hotel, Musalla Mah Şahinoğlu Sok 32, ☎ (232) 712 69 81. At the top of the street leading to the castle entrance (steep side) – 18rm. 📶 🛏 ✕ CC A small, quiet hotel, meticulously run by a friendly family. Rooms are small but bright, functional and clean. Breakfast and dinner are served in an arbour which opens out onto a little garden overlooking the harbour.

From US$70

Hotel Kerasus, Ayasaranda Koyu, ☎ (232) 712 05 06, Fax (232) 712 79 38 – 96rm and 95 suites. 📶 🍽 🛏 ✕ 🏊 🏋 CC 🍹 1.5km from the town centre by taxi or dolmuş. Set outside town in very pleasant natural surroundings, overlooking the bay of Ayasaranda, this luxury hotel boasts a private beach, sauna, Turkish bath, gym and discotheque (closed Mondays). Each room has a balcony overlooking the bay.

EATING OUT

• Çeşme

Under US$8

Biz Bize, 6 İnkilap Cad. At the top of the main street when coming from the castle. A popular little restaurant serving good food at reasonable prices.

Nil cake shop, İnkilap Cad 15/B, in the main street, ☎ (232) 712 64 11. You can sample quite good Turkish and "western-style" pastries, as well as Turkish delight, ice cream and all sorts of drinks.

Between US$8 and US$15

Kale Restaurant, on the terrace of one of the castle towers, with a view over the sea (particularly nice at sundown). Access is via the bar at the foot of the walls (the Kale Pub). Drop in for a "çorba" before enjoying the excellent fish.

Castle Barbecue, Musalla Mah, Beyazıt 8, ☎ (232) 712 63 01. CC At the foot of the castle, on the right. Below a large shaded terrace facing the sea. This is mainly a seafood restaurant, but they also serve meats, meze and desserts. Good welcome and moderate prices.

Star, Ertürk Sok 5, Kilise Yanı, ☎ (232) 712 94 44. CC Near the old church, in the main street. Pleasant shaded terrace, food cooked over a wood fire, meat, seafood, meze and cocktails.

HAVING A DRINK

Kale Pub, in the castle ramparts, facing the main square. The atmosphere here alternates between jazz and disco.

The Bar, Kısa Sok 11, ☎ (232) 712 71 23. Behind the old church, parallel to the main street. A jazz and rock bar with live music every evening, tables in the street and a trendy atmosphere; all the young holidaymakers from Çeşme come here. But the music, as usual, is often much too loud.

Os-To, Nuri Alçimen Cad 1/A, almost in the main street, ☎ (232) 712 08 66. A tiny little bar playing a mixture of Turkish pop, jazz and rock. Live music every evening in summer; a large selection of alcoholic drinks and cocktails.

Sultana, Nuri Alçimen Cad 9/A, ☎ (232) 712 08 66. Mainly Turkish pop music, in a rustic setting; tables in the street and a large selection of cocktails.

OTHER THINGS TO DO

Excursions – Most of the travel agencies are on the quayside. **Ertürk, Tourism & Travel Agency**, 7/8 zit Cad, ☎ (232) 712 67 68 / 712 68 76, Fax (232) 712 62 63.

SHOPPING GUIDE

İnkilap Caddesi, the big pedestrian street which leads to the town centre and castle, is lined with a myriad of boutiques: four of them, all very similar (rather expensive), sell beautiful kilims (don't hesitate to haggle); others offer ceramics, jewellery, souvenirs and typical local confectionery (jam, honey, Turkish delight). There are also a few shops selling leather goods and music, and one interesting and inexpensive onyx boutique, **Özer Onyx**.

SELÇUK★★

İzmir Province – Map p 227 and site map pp 278-279
75km from İzmir; 51km from Aydın, 18km from Kuşadası
Pop 20 000

Not to be missed
The ancient site of Ephesus nearby (see map pp 278-279)
The Basilica of St John and the archeological museum of Selçuk.

And remember
Stay in the İsa Bey mosque district, the quietest and most beautiful.

A rocky peak set in the middle of a plain, Ayosoluk Hill shoots up like a reef above a sea of olive and fig trees. As you arrive from the north, the view is magnificent. At night, the citadel on the hill resembles a beacon, attracting travellers from all over. Beneath its walls stretches Selçuk, a lovely town and interesting both for its ruins and for its proximity to Ephesus. The neighbouring hills, especially the Panayır Dağ (Mt Pion) and the Bülbül Dağ (Mt Coressus) are ideal for walks, and the city is an excellent base for exploring the region.

The city of St John

Tradition has it that St John the evangelist died in Ephesus around the year 100 and that he was buried nearby, on the hill overlooking the temple of Artemis. The apostle gave his name to the hill, then to the small town which was steadily growing during the Byzantine period. Until the beginning of the 20C, it was called *Ayosoluk*, the Greek contraction of Hagios Theologos, or St John the Theologian.

On what is presumed to be the tomb of the apostle, a first funerary monument was erected in the early 4C. It was later enclosed inside a prestigious basilica (6C), still visible today.

Scenting danger from the Arabs in the 7C and 8C, the inhabitants of Ayosoluk erected a citadel at the summit of the hill. They surrounded it with a mighty wall which protected the basilica of St John. However, the city fell to the Turks in 1304 and became the stronghold of the powerful emirs of Aydın, the Ollugari (1308-1390). The Christians progressively deserted the city to find refuge in Şirince, 7km to the north, where they built a new church dedicated to St John. Selçuk then continued to live, as it does to this day off of the agricultural resources of the plain and, for the last few decades, tourism.

The citadel★

The entrance is through the southern gate, reached by way of a pretty cobblestone lane (St John Sok.) linking the city-centre (to the east) to the İsa Bey mosque (west of the hill). Entrance fee. 8am-7pm. Allow 2hr.

The walls protecting the hill have no fewer than 20 towers. They were in part built with stones from ancient Ephesus, in particular those of the stadium, which the Christians were keen to destroy after the martyrdom of their colleagues. To the east, to the west and to the south, three doors flanked by towers pierce the bastion. It is through the last one, known as the **Persecution Gate**★, that you enter the enclosure. Above the arch, numerous stones can be seen. One of them (held in the Woburn Museum in England) showed Achilles fighting. It was thought to be a gladiator killing a Christian; hence the name of the gate.

At the summit of the hill, the **fortress*** *(closed)* seems to rest on a crown of stones. Its outer walls are well preserved and from the top of the embattlements, the view of the region is superb. Huge banners are often displayed (the national flag or the portrait of Atatürk) and can be seen from miles away.

The Basilica of St John**

However, the citadel's jewel remains the Basilica of St John which fills the entire width of the courtyard through which you enter the citadel. Instead of going directly there, climb up to the **atrium** on the left, a beautiful marble-covered terrace preceding the entrance. In this way you will be able to appreciate the layout of the building, find your way around, and you will also have a fantastic **view*** of the plain and the İsa Bey mosque, located just below at the base of the rampart.

Constructed under the reign of Emperor Justinian (527-565), then abandoned after the Turkish conquest, the basilica was carefully restored. The brilliant white marble lintels, columns and decorative features make a striking contrast with the redbrick walls. The building follows the traditional plan of the earliest Byzantine churches, consisting of three naves, a transept and an apse. The basilica which Justinian wanted had monumental proportions (145x40m) and a load-bearing structure well ahead of its time: the main body and the arms of the transept topped by four domes, supported by large square pillars and exterior buttresses worthy of Gothic churches. From the atrium terrace, enter the **exonarthex**, then the **narthex** leading to the **main nave**** and aisles. A majestic **two-tiered colonnade*** separates the latter from the nave giving

an accurate idea of the height and the magnificence of the building. Note the large side pillars which supported the cupolas.

In the centre, a ramp leads to the crypt *(no access)*, underneath the **transept** where the apostle's tomb was located. Its exact position is indicated by the **baldachin*** whose four charming marble colonnettes are still standing. An altar rose underneath, facing the steps of the *synthronon* where the priests would take their seats. The hemicycle separates the tomb – a site of worship – from the sanctuary proper (the **choir**), in which there remains a fragment of a wall painting.

In the northwest corner of the transept, a chapel, as narrow as a corridor, gives access to the **treasury**, a small circular room carved with

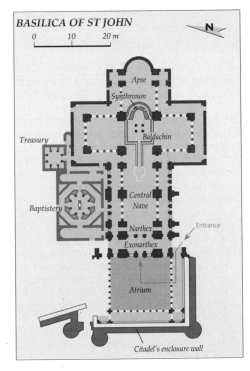

BASILICA OF ST JOHN

0   10   20 m

N

Apse

Synthronon

Treasury

Baldachin

Central Nave

Baptistery

Narthex

Exonarthex

Entrance

Atrium

Citadel's enclosure wall

seven niches. From there, you can reach the baptistery★★ (through the left) which occupies the northern side of the nave. In the centre of the room, covered in marble, there is a **baptismal pool** approached by two small lateral stairways.

As you leave the baptistery, you can reach the summit of the hill by a pretty marble-covered path leading to the fortress. On the way you will see a **miniature model of the basilica.**

In the city★

West of the ramparts, on the opposite side of the city centre, all the way at the end of St John Sok. Access via the western gate (at the opposite end of the ramparts) overlooking a square. Entrance fee.

The İsa Bey mosque★

As you descend the fortified hill. Recognisable by its red-brick minaret, this beautiful mosque was built in 1375 by İsa Bey★, the last descendant of the Ogullari dynasty, to belittle the basilica of St John. Enter through the magnificent **door with muqarnas★** of Seljuk inspiration. A simple lawn enhances the **courtyard**, surrounded by tall walls which formerly supported the roof of a colonnaded portico (a few columns are still standing). A second **door**, unfortunately in a poor state, faces the rampart side.

On the right side (south), the prayer hall forms a vast rectangle divided in two by four massive pink granite columns which sustained the roof's two domes. Like most of the materials used for the construction of the mosque, these columns were from Ephesus, used as a quarry since the Byzantine era. A few beautiful fragments of glazed tiles can be seen in various parts of the walls.

Archeological Museum★★

Facing the Tourist Office on Kuşadasi Cad., 8.30am-12noon/1pm-7pm. Entrance fee).

Opened in 1964, it houses most of the discoveries made in Ephesus and should not be missed. Miniature replicas and drawings give one an improved perspective of the most ruined buildings of the ancient city.

The first room's main theme (as you enter on the left) is daily life. In addition to the reconstruction of scenes (which leave a lot to be desired!), there are a few fragments of Roman era **frescoes** and various objects found in the terraced homes. The room also displays the famous statue of the god Priapus (with the oversized phallus), seen on all the local postcards, but you will probably be more interested in the small **bronze dolphin★** ridden by Eros, or the beautiful **Bust of Socrates★** (marble, 1C AD).

The second room assembles several elements from the monumental fountains of Ephesus. The group of statues decorating the **Pollio Nymphaeum** (Ulysses fighting the Cyclops Polyphemus) can also be seen.

Before reaching the atrium, an open courtyard cluttered with capitals and sarcophagi, cross a small hall which includes theatre masks, beautiful **golden palms** and a stirring burnt **ivory frieze**. Farther on, a few drawings retrace daily life during the Hittite period. Then you enter Room 5, dedicated to Artemis. The famous statues★★ of the goddess found in the enclosure of the Prytaneum are displayed here. These are copies of the ones which decorated the Artemision. The visit ends with the Roman room, where several marble busts of emperors are shown along with, in particular, the original frieze of the temple of Hadrian★★ representing the legend of the foundation of Ephesus.

COMING AND GOING

By train – The station is in the town centre. Daily services operate to İzmir (7 departures, from 6am-8pm, for about US$2), Denizli (3 trains between 10am and 8pm), Afyon, İsparta and Söke.

By bus – Selçuk is the point of departure for countless destinations in the region and to the country's main cities. The "otogar" is near the tourist information office, opposite the hospital, at the entrance to the town when coming from Kuşadası. Buses leave every hour for İstanbul, Antalya, Marmaris, Fethiye, Bodrum, Denizli, Konya and Pamukkale.

By shared taxi – The dolmuş stand is adjacent to the bus station. Dolmuşes leave regularly for Bodrum, Marmaris, Aphrodisias and Denizli.

GETTING AROUND

The town is not very large and can be visited on foot. Parking is relatively easy, except in the town centre, which is reserved for pedestrians.

By taxi – Next to the bus station and dolmuş stand. It is a good idea to hire the services of a taxi for a day to visit the sights near Selçuk.

By rental car – Probably the best way to explore the town and its surroundings is by scooter. Rental agencies can be found in Namık Kemal Cad or in the pedestrian street which runs alongside the museum. **Budget**, Atatürk Bul 5, Belediye Pasajı, ☎ (232) 892 22 26.

ADDRESS BOOK

Tourist information – In the "bungalows" of the small shopping centre opposite the museum. 8.30am-12noon / 1pm-5.30pm every day in summer, closed weekends in winter, ☎ (232) 892 63 28 / 892 69 45, Fax (232) 892 69 45.

Bank / change – **Ziraat Bankası**, Cengiz Topel Cad 16. Cashes travellers' cheques and converts cash. The post office offers the same services.

Main post office – On the corner of Cengiz Topel Cad and 1006 Sok, ☎ (232) 892 64 50. Open 24 hours a day.

Medical service – **Public hospital**, 20, Atatürk bul, ☎ (232) 892 70 36 and 892 67 73. There are pharmacies scattered all over the town centre.

WHERE TO STAY

Selçuk is full of guest houses, offering generally highly satisfactory services at prices often lower than elsewhere (the prices are in fact directly controlled by the town council).

• Near the İsa Bey mosque
Under US$8
Pension İsa Bey, Atatürk Mah, 1054 Sok 2, ☎ (232) 892 49 81 – 9rm. (24 beds). Opposite the mosque. This guest house has a terrace where you can have breakfast while admiring the fortress and olive groves. Internet service.

Between US$15 and US$25
Hotel Akay, Atatürk Mah, 1054 Sok 3, ☎ (232) 892 31 72, Fax (232) 892 30 09 – 16rm. ⁎️⃝ ✗ This peaceful hotel with its plain decor surrounds an attractive little rose garden. The rooms are clean and simple (pine furniture). Meals are served on the terrace, from where you can enjoy a lovely view of the neighbourhood and the mosque. Free minibus service to Ephesus.

• Near the basilica of St John
Camp sites
Garden camp site, behind the castle, ☎ (232) 892 24 89 / 892 61 65, Fax (232) 892 24 97. ⁎️⃝ ✗ A pleasant, peaceful site, with bungalows scattered among the fruit trees. Around US$8 per pitch.

Around US$30
Pension & Cafe Nazhan, 1044 Sok 2, ☎ (232) 892 87 31, Fax (232) 892 40 11 – 5rm. ⁎️⃝ A tiny little guest house with bags of charm and a sitting room and garden crammed full of unusual objects, just like Ali Baba's cave. The rooms are very cosy, comfortable and tastefully furnished. However, this all comes at a price.

• Town centre (market)
Under US$15
Pension Monaco, Atatürk Mah, Kubilay Cad 28/A, ☎ (232) 891 21 18 – 5rm.

🖋 A new and modern guest house where you will be greeted with a smile. The proprietor will gladly get his map out and tell you all about the region's historical and geographical background.

👜 **Pension Barim**, Müze Arkası Sok 1, ☎ (232) 892 69 23 – 10rm. On the left after the museum. Here you will discover a very attractive, typical Ottoman house (18C), set around a small garden with a fountain. The welcome is warm and the rooms immaculate. The only drawback is that they are rather small.

Pension Southern Cross-Errol, İsabey Mah 2003 Sok 9, ☎ (232) 892 21 99. 🖋 ✗ A large guest house in a quiet little street running parallel to İzmir Cad. The rooms are comfortable and spacious, and there is a vast, covered roof terrace where you can eat, have a drink at the bar or tea on the sofas. Beautiful view of the castle and mountains. Free transport to Ephesus. English, French and German spoken.

Pension Eyüp, Atatürk Mah, Tahsin Başaran Cad 19, ☎ (232) 891 22 78. A simple guest house with the main advantage of being very close to the bus station and market.

Pension Vardar, Atatürk Mah 7, Şahabettin Dede Cad, ☎ (232) 891 49 67, Fax (232) 891 40 99. Presents the same characteristics as the one above. Large, pleasant roof terrace. Clothes washing facilities. Nothing is too much trouble for the friendly young proprietress where her guest house and clients are concerned.

Between US$30 and US$45

Hotel Cenka, Atatürk Mah, Kubilay Cad 24, ☎ (232) 892 31 30, Fax (232) 892 34 90 – 54rm. 🖋 📶 🖵 TV ✗ CC Fans of modern hotel comfort will not be disappointed, but this hotel is devoid of any particular charm.

From US$30

👜 **Hotel Kale Han**, on the road out of town to İzmir, ☎ (232) 892 61 54, Fax (232) 892 21 69 – 52rm. 🖋 🖵 ✗ 🛎 CC Once you have stepped inside, you will completely forget the noise from the road: the rooms are at the back, at the end of a magnificent garden with a swimming pool. The hotel is a veritable museum, furnished with beautiful old pieces, wardrobes, locks and crockery recovered from ruined houses, and is very tastefully decorated throughout. Family accommodation is provided in 4 delightful Ottoman-style bungalows which stand to the side of the garden. Several languages are spoken here, and you will find a friendly welcome, courteous service and refined cuisine. Excellent value for money, and charm to boot.

● **Behind the railway station (on the small hill)**

Under US$15

Pension Pamukkale, 14 Mayıs Sok 1, ☎ (232) 892 23 88 / 892 31 76 – 8rm. 🖋 ✗ A delightful, peaceful guest house: very simple but immaculate rooms, with a small garden in the shade of fruit trees where the ladies of the house serve the meals in the arbour, while the jovial proprietor sings, dances and plays the saz. On the roof is a terrace and kitchen to which clients have access, and there are clothes washing facilities. Very warm welcome, attentive service and good-natured atmosphere. The only drawback here is that it is rather out of the way and the climb up to the guest house is quite steep.

👜 **Hotel Artemis**, Atatürk Mah, 1012 Sok 2, very near the station, ☎ (232) 892 61 91 / 892 61 91 – 18rm. 🖋 🌊 ✗ A good little place to stay, with comfortable and very clean rooms, TV room, Internet, and an attractive garden with a hut for hookah smoking and barbecues, which are prepared by the proprietor, who speaks several languages. Free transport to Ephesus, good documentation on Turkey, laundry, 5 different kinds of breakfast. What more could you ask for?

👜 **Pension Cheerful**, Zafer Mah, Çimenlik Sok 3, ☎ (232) 892 27 32 – 9rm. An adorable guest house with a lovely garden shaded by fruit trees. Very comfortable, immaculate rooms. Beautiful view of the town and fortress.

Pension Nur, Zafer Mah, 3004 Sok 16, ☎ (232) 892 65 95 – 6rm. The charming proprietress, Nur, will bring you here by taxi and make you feel very much at home.

EATING OUT

• Town centre

The pedestrian town centre is full of restaurants offering simple fare consisting of the usual kebabs and "pide" (Turkish pizzas).

Under US$5

Okumuşlar, Namık Kemal Cad 18b. In a street running parallel to the one in which the post office stands, a little further down towards the basilica. A small, simple restaurant, which serves delicious "pide" prepared over a wood fire.

Between US$5 and US$8

Köşem-Döner & İskender, Belediye Eski Binaları, ☎ (232) 891 43 96. A stone's throw from the post office, on a shaded terrace right in the heart of this lively district. Friendly welcome and very attentive service.

Between US$8 and US$15

Seçkin Bizim Ev, Atatürk Mah, Cengiz Topel Cad 26, ☎ (232) 892 90 66. [CC] A nice restaurant in the town centre with tables in the street and a roof terrace. Numerous excellent vegetable- and yoghurt-based meze, and dishes prepared with aubergines, mushrooms and rice; meat, fish and desserts, all carefully prepared by the proprietress. Good and inexpensive.

Firuze, opposite the one above, ☎ (232) 892 79 95. [CC] A tiny, unpretentious and very good restaurant serving breakfast, "gözleme", "şiş kebabs", meze and fruit.

Okumuş, Atatürk Mah, PTT Karşısı Eski Hal Binaları 4, ☎ (232) 892 61 96. Near the post office, in a peaceful little shaded square, this restaurant serves a large variety of meze, such as moussaka, "börek", stuffed peppers, and all sorts of meat, fish and seafood, accompanied by a wide selection of wines. Friendly welcome, attentive service. Cheap.

Eski Ev, Atatürk Mah, 1005 Sok 1/A, a small street running parallel to Cengiz Topal Cad. This quiet, pleasant restaurant-café-bar serving meze, omelettes, burgers, meat and desserts is set in an attractive courtyard shaded by fruit trees. In winter, customers sit in a little room decorated with kilims.

OTHER THINGS TO DO

Excursions – The local travel agencies offer tours of the surrounding sights by minibus. You can sign up for a day-trip to Miletus, Priene and Didyma, with lunch included, for a ridiculously low price. You may also be tempted by a trip to Pamucak, a black-sand beach stretching over 15km, and only 15min away by dolmuş. Departure from the bus station.

Camel Wrestling Festival – A spectacle not to be missed, which takes place every year in January.

SHOPPING GUIDE

In the town centre, near the basilica, you will come across many boutiques which are less expensive than in Bodrum or Kuşadası and where you can unearth very beautiful kilims and carpets. You will have no trouble haggling here.

Carpets – At the lower end of St John Cad, you will find a small boutique brimming with modestly priced carpets. The shop assistant will offer you tea and give you plenty of useful information on the region.

Book shops – 4, Uğur Mumcu Sevgi Yolu. In the pedestrian street running alongside the museum. International press.

Music – Turcu Music, Cengiz Topel Cad 16. A record shop selling a great variety of music at unbeatable prices. Watch out for copies which may have found their way in among the originals.

Celsus Ceramic, Cengiz Topel Cad 21/B, an attractive boutique mainly selling ceramics, from the most kitsch to the most refined. Some beautiful backgammon boards in inlaid wood, and some onyx objects. The proprietor speaks good English, and his wife is an artisan herself. Very moderate prices.

EPHESUS ★★★

İzmir Province – Map p 227 and site map p 278-279
75km from İzmir; 51km from Aydın, 18km from Kuşadası
Pop 20 000

Not to be missed
The traditional music festival (in summer) inside the ancient theatre.
And remember...
Visit Ephesus as soon as it opens
before the sun gets too strong and the crowds arrive.

The city of Artemis ★★★

Ephesus is undoubtedly Turkey's most visited ancient site, in summer as well as winter. In the last few years, more than two million visitors have walked among its ruins. Needless to say, you will not be alone; it won't be unlike the time the city had a population of 250 000 inhabitants, in the 2C AD. Ephesus is one of the best preserved ancient cities. Archeologists have been working here ever since 1869, and most of the city's streets and buildings are exposed to view. Everything is here: city hall, houses, shops and even public toilets. A city of white marble sparkling under the sun, a book in stone, Ephesus tells the story of what life was like in the times of the Greeks and Romans.

The port of the Aegean

Ephesus is set in an exceptional location. Equally distant from the Hellespont (the Dardanelles) and Lycia, it faces Greece and was the last stop on the Persian royal road, an important trade route traversing all of Anatolia.

The legendary home of the Amazons, the original Ephesus was probably founded by the Carians around the 12C BC, on top of the walls of a Hittite city named *Apasa*. The mouth of the Cayster (the Küçük Menderes, "small Meander") around which the city developed was then at the foot of Ayosoluk Hill overlooking Selçuk. This is where the Carians erected a temple to their goddess **Cybele**, followed by one dedicated to Artemis.

The real development of Ephesus did not begin until the 10C AD, with the arrival of the Ionians. It was the advent of an important dynasty of financiers, who would rule the region for four centuries. As the "General Treasury of Asia", Ephesus rose to the top rank of the 12 cities of the **Ionian Confederation**. The motherland of Artemis, it attracted numerous pilgrims and became a great centre of intellectual activity, channelled through the Ionian School and the philosopher **Heracleitus** (576-480BC).

Alexander and the new Ephesus – The fame of the city's wealth soon attracted envy: the Lydian king, **Croesus** *(see p 264)* conquered the city in 560BC and 50 years later, **Cyrus**, the Persian, completed his conquest of Anatolia here. The city regained its freedom under the rule of Alexander, in 334BC. This period marked the advent of a new city: with the passing of the years, the silt deposited by the Cayster had transformed the region into a marshland, filling the port of Ephesus and pushing the sea back by 3km. When **Lysimachus** succeeded Alexander, he moved the city to where the sea had retreated, at the foot of Mt Pion and Mt Coressos. The newly-formed well-sheltered bay was ideal for creating a new harbour.

The Aegean Coast

The Roman apogee – In 129 BC, Asia Minor became a Roman province and the Ionian cities were forced to pay heavy taxes. **Revolt** followed soon thereafter and the denizens of Ephesus massacred 80 000 Roman citizens in a single day (88 BC). In an act of revenge, General Sulla reduced the city to ashes. It did not recover until 27 BC, when Octavian, who became the August Emperor, decided to make it the capital of the province, to the detriment of Pergamum. This new status propelled the city to the rank of Asia's most important city. From that point on, Ephesus began constructing prestigious monuments and buildings with plumbing, baths, gymnasiums, a library and even public lighting.

A fish and a boar
Upon the death of his father, the Ionian prince, Androcles, decided to establish a colony in Asia Minor, leaving Athens in the hands of his brothers. Prior to his departure, he consulted the oracle of Delphi who told him that a fish and a boar would reveal the ideal location to him. When they landed near Ephesus, Androcles and his sailors cooked a fish on the banks; but the flames set fire to the nearby bushes forcing a boar to run out. Discovering the animal, Androcles understood the meaning of the prophecy and took possession of the city.

Saint Paul's epistle to the Ephesians – Ranked as the third most important port in the ancient world (after Rome and Alexandria), Ephesus had become a cosmopolitan city, where all ideological and religious influences mingled under the benevolent presence of Artemis. However, the advent of Christianity dislodged the goddess and the cult of the idols. In 53 AD, the apostle **Paul** landed in Ephesus and began preaching for three years. Little by little, his following grew, and he founded an important church (one of the Seven Churches of the *Apocalypse*). Upon Paul's death, **St John**, who had come to Ephesus in the company of the **Virgin Mary**, took up the succession of the bishopric. It was in Ephesus that he wrote his gospel, and on his death was buried on Ayosoluk Hill, not far from the temple of Artemis.

From Ephesus to Selçuk – The relentless withdrawal of the sea heralded the city's decline: Lysimachus' port silted up in its turn, creating marshy and unhealthy conditions. Starting in the 4C, the population, mostly Christians, left the area to be closer to St John's tomb, which was already attracting numerous pilgrims. The small Byzantine city of Ayosoluk (today's Selçuk) was built on the site of the first Ephesus, established five thousand years earlier by the Carians. The two **councils** held in Ephesus in the 5C, in the Church of the Virgin, marked the end of its importance. The Roman city sank deeper into neglect and its buildings were quarried to construct the city of St John.

The site

There are two entrances: one at the bottom of the site, the other – recommended – at the top, through the Magnesian Gate. From Selçuk, take the Aydın-Denizli road, as soon as you leave the city, turn right at the yellow "Efes-Meryem Ana" sign. The entrance is 2km, on the right. Ideally, you should be dropped off at the top (by bus or taxi) and picked up at the bottom. This itinerary allows you to descend towards the library before its esplanade is invaded by tourist groups. It also saves you from backtracking at the end of your visit. 8am-7pm. Entrance fee. Allow half a day.

The city seen today is Roman Ephesus, as most of its monuments were built during Augustus' reign. It is laid out in two main districts. The upper city corresponds to the administrative district, with city hall (Prytaneum), the civil basilica and the odeon aligned on the northern part of the State agora. The lower city, which faced the port, encompasses the religious and cultural buildings: library, theatre and stadium. The homes of the notables (currently being excavated and restored) are found on the slopes of Mount Pion and Mount Coressus, on both sides of the Curetes Way linking

Ephesus

277

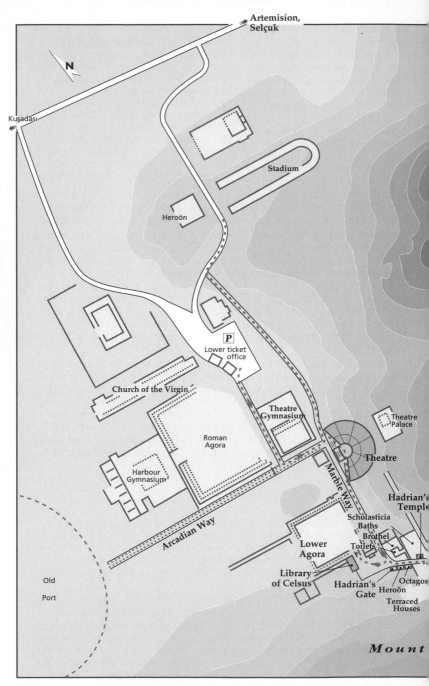

Artemision,
Selçuk

N

Kuşadası

Stadium

Heroön

Lower ticket
office

Church of the Virgin

Roman Agora

Theatre
Gymnasium

Theatre
Palace

Theatre

Harbour
Gymnasium

Marble Way

Hadrian's
Temple

Arcadian Way

Scholasticia
Baths
Brothel
Toilets

Lower
Agora

Library
of Celsus

Hadrian's
Gate

Heroön

Octagon

Terraced
Houses

Old

Port

Mount

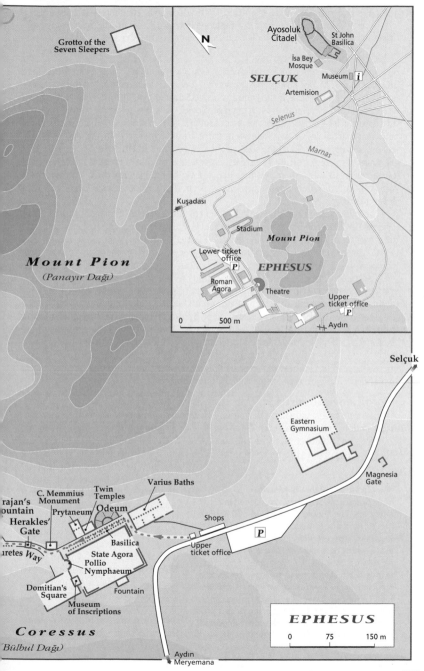

Grotto of the
Seven Sleepers

N

Ayosoluk
Citadel

St John
Basilica

İsa Bey
Mosque

SELÇUK

Museum ☐ **i**

Artemision

Selenus

Marnas

Kuşadası

Stadium

Mount Pion

Lower ticket
office

P

EPHESUS

Roman
Agora

Theatre

Upper
ticket office

P

0   500 m

Aydın

Mount Pion
(Panayır Dağı)

Selçuk

Eastern
Gymnasium

Magnesia
Gate

C. Memmius
Monument

Twin
Temples

Varius Baths

rajan's
ountain

Prytaneum

Odeum

Shops

Herakles'
Gate

P

uretes *Way*

Basilica

Upper
ticket office

State Agora
Pollio
Nymphaeum

Domitian's
Square

Fountain

Museum
of Inscriptions

Coressus

(Bülbül Dağı)

Aydın
Meryemana

EPHESUS

0   75   150 m

the city's two districts. A large portion of the decorative elements – statues, friezes, etc. – are still in place, but the most precious ones are stored in the Selçuk museum. Imitation mouldings (which look realistic) can be seen at the site.

The administrative district★

Beyond the ticket offices at the Magnesian Gate (whose name comes from the ancient neighbouring city, *see p 288*), are the **Varius Baths**, a large building with impressive arcades. To the left stretch the remains of the **State agora**, an immense rectangle of greenery (160x56m) strewn with marble blocks. This was a sacred and administrative forum (the Roman emperor was considered to be a god), in which the political and religious affairs of the State were carried out. A portico ran the entire length, encompassing a temple which was probably dedicated to Augustus.

The northern stoa, skirting the street, was transformed at the end of the Augustan period into an **administrative basilica**, a long building with three narrow naves whose beautiful **colonnades★** can still be seen. Their capitals were decorated with **bulls' heads**.

On the other side of the street, the **odeon** (or **bouleuterion**), a small theatre, leans against the flank of Mt Pion. Built in 150 AD, it was used as a concert hall and meeting place for the senate (the *Boule*). Formerly covered, it could accommodate 1 400 spectators. The western side of the odeon contains the ruins of the **twin temples** which Augustus had erected to honour the divinity personifying Rome as well as Julius Caesar, elevated to divine status by the Roman senate.

Farther down, away from the road, rise two tall Doric columns covered with inscriptions. They are the remains of the **Prytaneum** (3C BC), the building which housed the sacred fire of the city, which was kept by the Prytaneis. The building stood in front of a small square courtyard with a portico. Hidden behind the columns of the façade was a large room dedicated to Hestia, the goddess of the home, who is shown with the features of Artemis. A stone altar stood in the centre, the tabernacle of precious flames. Two **statues of Artemis polymastros★★** ("with multiple breasts") were unearthed. They are now in the Selçuk museum.

Domitian's Square★

To the west is a small triangular square. Nearby is a lovely *Nike* (winged victory), a bas-relief from the Heracles Gate *(see below)*. Leaning against a fountain in the "square's" northern corner, the **monument of Caius Memmius★** (4C) is a tribute of Ephesus' Roman citizens to General Sulla's son. Unfortunately, the restoration, which relies heavily on concrete, blemishes the beauty and understanding of the building, a sort of tall baldachin with refined adornments.

To the south *(on the left)*, the square widens and becomes a vast terrace which held the **Temple of Domitian**, completely ruined (two columns have been set up again). The **Pollio Nymphaeum★** (97 AD) is a monumental fountain whose imposing arch stands out above the wall of the agora. Sextillius Pollio had an aqueduct built which fed the city with water.

The Ephesian administration

The government of the city was divided into two chambers. The "Boule" made up of 300 councillors formed the consultative assembly (Senate). It gathered together the city's notables. The "demos", which held meetings in the large theatre, represented the people. Only men would participate. Each chamber was managed by a secretary and by a registrar known as a "grammateus." The two assemblies would meet under the auspices of the Prytaneis, magistrates who were selected from among the most important men and women of the city. The Prytaneis were also dedicated to the cult and upkeep of the city's sacred flame, the emblem of its perpetuity.

The supporting arches of the western side of the "square" house the **Museum of Inscriptions*** *(almost always closed)* where archeologists have gathered the majority of the engraved marble plaques found during their digs.

Return to the square and go down to the lower city.

The Curetes Way**

Beyond the square is the Curetes Way, flanked by two **stelae** representing the god Hermes. They precede the **Heracles Gate***, a once vaulted passageway, erected in the 5C AD, with elements dating from the 2C. The two elegant **pillars***, with a carved effigy of the demi-god, remain.

The roadway was paved with marble during the Roman period. In places, striated markings were carved in the stone to prevent horses from slipping. The Curetes Way was the sacred way *(Embolos)* which led to the Temple of Artemis. All the processions used it, which explains the abundance of stelae, statues, fountains, and temples on its northern side (the southern side was reserved for shops selling votive offerings).

Among the buildings of particular interest is **Trajan's Fountain***, erected at the beginning of the 2C AD. Its restoration, in concrete, is unfortunately something of a disaster which does not replicate its proper proportions (it should be imagined much taller with a pediment supported by columns). Numerous fragments of statue which decorated it are kept in the Selçuk museum, where an enlightening drawing of the building in its original form can be seen. Right after the fountain, a narrow street on the right climbs up towards the hilltop. This is a good opportunity to escape the crowd and enjoy a beautiful **view*** of the lower city. The viewpoint also overlooks the Baths of Scholasticia *(directly below)*, giving a good understanding of their layout.

Hadrian's Temple

Dusart / PIX

The Curetes, Artmesis' attendants

The Curetes were high officials of the temple of Artemis. This brotherhood of six, (later nine), priests was responsible for the cult's administration. Its main task consisted in organising the drama festival which celebrated the anniversary of the birth of the goddess. Initially attached exclusively to the Artemision during the Augustan period, the Curetes had a second headquarters in the Prytaneum, which explains the road's name.

Back on the Curetes Way, do not miss **Hadrian's Temple**★★, an elegant little gem which is also very well preserved. Built under Hadrian's reign (117-138 AD), it is made up of a Corinthian porch (*pronaos*) preceding a small square room (*naos*). The beauty of the building lies in the design of the two façades: the semicircular pediment surmounting the entrance to the naos is set exactly in the porch's central arch. The arch's keystone is decorated with a beautiful head of Tyche, goddess of fortune. On the frieze running inside the vestibule (*the 3C original is in the Selçuk museum*), is the figure (*on the left*) of Androcles, the legendary founder of the city, chasing a boar, as well as a group of Amazons (*on the right*), the mythical figures of Ephesus' history.

The **Scholasticia Baths**★ (*access from either side of Hadrian's temple*) form a large U around the temple. Built around the 1C AD, the baths owe their name to a wealthy Ephesian woman, Scholasticia, who enlarged them at her expense in the 4C. Entry is through a vestibule used as a changing room, before reaching the baths proper (*large arcade at the back, then on both sides*). Since their floor has disappeared, the entire hypocaust heating system (*see p 53*) is visible. On the walls, the **terracotta pipes** through which the warm air circulated (*tubuli*) are still visible. The visit ends in the cold room (*frigidarium*), recognisable by its large central **pool** in the shape of an ellipse.

A passageway (once vaulted), on the western side of the baths, leads to the **brothel** (*at the end of the lane on the left*), the "sanctuary" of Priapus, god of fecundity. The building consists of several small rooms with pools and **mosaics**. A statuette with an oversized phallus was found here (*Selçuk museum*). The brothel is located next to the **public toilets**★ (*at the corner of the two streets*), a small courtyard decorated with a central basin and surrounded by a portico. Along the length of the four sides runs a marble bench pierced with holes and with a drain below flushed by running water. The **southern side of the street** (*left*) is filled with the remains of **shops**. They open onto a long **gallery**★, once covered, which has retained part of its colonnade as well as beautiful **mosaics**★ with geometric decorations. Behind, the **Terrace Houses** of the wealthy citizens can be seen. The excavated area (*unfortunately closed to the public*) is only a small portion of this residential district which stretched all the way to the esplanade of the Temple of Domitian. The Selçuk museum authorities, to whom the ugly roofs topping the houses can be attributed, prefer to complete the restoration of the entire sector before opening it up to the public. This is unfortunate, since some of the houses have magnificent paintings as beautiful as those found in Pompeii.

The architecture of power

The will of the Romans to impose themselves as the conquerors of the East is reflected in the development of a particular architectural style, known as "tabernacle". The principle involved facing a façade with decorative elements – columns, small triangular and semicircular pediments and statues – which protrude slightly. This gave the effect of a baldachin, a direct reference to the one which topped the throne of Eastern kings. The Romans used this symbol of power in their monumental fountains, since the force of water was associated with the power of the emperor. On the façade of the library of Celsus, the power of the elements is replaced by that of knowledge, personified by the statues of Wisdom, Science, Virtue and Thought. So this is where Michelangelo got his ideas...

Farther down (*still on the left*) is a funerary monument known as **Octagon**, a Byzantine fountain and a **heroön** (a tomb of the Augustan period), and finally **Hadrian's Gate**★ (*right before the esplanade of the library*). Recently re-erected, this Corinthian gate gave access to the district south of the library (*currently being excavated*).

The library of Celsus★★★

The façade of the library overlooks a small trapeze-shaped square giving access to the lower agora. It marks the meeting-point of the city's two main streets, between the upper and lower districts. Everything seems to converge on it. With 12 000 scrolls, the Ephesus library constituted one of the ancient world's most important centres of information, after those of Alexandria and Pergamum. This cultural treasure disappeared in a fire, in the 3C AD. The Byzantines transformed the façade (the only remaining portion) into a nymphaeum. Restored by a team of Austrian archeologists, the **façade**★★★ is an architectural gem which gives some idea of the city's great beauty in its glory days. The play of niches and columns are an excellent example of the architectural style developed in Ephesus during the Roman period (*see photograph below*). The library was built in 114-117 AD by the consul Julius Aquila in memory of his father, governor of the province of Asia. His tomb, intact, is preserved underneath the central niche of the reading room. Other niches, on each side, were used to store scrolls. The walls were separated by a 1m-wide gap to protect the works from humidity. Today the room houses an interesting exhibition on the history and restoration of Ephesus' monuments.

On the northern side of the library, the **lower agora**★ is reached through **the Gate of Mazeus and Mithridates**★ (also known as the Gate of Augustus), an elegant triumphal arch with three bays, erected to honour Augustus and his family by two slaves who had been freed by the emperor. Located near the port, the lower agora was the city's market. Laid out during the Hellenistic period, it owes its current dimensions (110m on each side) to a 3C rebuilding. It was surrounded by a portico housing many shops. The south and east wings are the best preserved, with an upper floor accessible from the Marble Way.

The jewel of Ephesus: the library of Celsus

B. Brillon/MICHELIN

The Marble Way★

Named after the superb white marble slabs which were used to resurface it in the 5C AD, it leads to the theatre and to the Arcadian Way, which led to the port. Beyond, it continues through a narrower street all the way to the stadium. A portico sheltering pedestrians ran on both sides. Before the theatre, there is (*on the left*) a

door which gave access to the upper floor of the agora *(north-east corner of the square)*. A small **platform** gives a view over the whole of the square. Nearby, a message in the form of a puzzle is engraved on one of the street slabs. A footprint, a coin, a female head and an arrow indicated the way to the brothel, a source of great amusement to guides and visitors alike!

The theatre★★★

The theatre is reached via a side ramp. Erected by Lysimachus, it was enlarged during the Roman period to become one of the ancient world's largest theatres. Its **stage wall**, which should be imagined as richly decorated in the manner of the Celsus library façade, is no less than 18m long. Unfortunately little remains, but the system of vaults formerly supporting the stage is clearly visible. The **cavea**★★, forming a half-circle with a diameter of 154m, could accommodate 24 000 spectators. From the uppermost terrace, at a height of 38m, there is a splendid **view**★★ of the city and the plain which the sea left behind (today 8km away). The outline of the ancient harbour can be seen, in the shape of the area of greenery at the end of the Aracadian way.

Here too, restorations have been crudely carried out, especially on the orchestra floor. Nevertheless, it allows the theatre to accommodate the annual summer **Festival of Traditional Music** giving it something of the life it used to have.

G. Dagorge

Artemis,
the goddess of nature
(Selçuk Museum)

Towards the stadium

Leaving the theatre by way of the garden *(right)*, you walk along the **Sacred Way**, the extension of the Marble Way. The paving is the same as that of the Curetes Way, as is the underground pipework which fed the fountains. Like the other streets of the city, the Sacred Way was lined with shops sheltered by a portico. The Sacred Way reached the Artemision by passing in front of the **stadium**★ *(on the right, open only during festivals)*. The structure is 230m long and 30m wide. Nothing is left of the stands, except their slope, one part of which was built into the side of the hill. Only the circulation galleries have been preserved, as well as the enormous bays facing each part of the entrance. Once the scene of chariot races and gladiator fights, nowadays the stadium hosts the very popular **Camel Wrestling Festival** *(January)*.

Towards the port

To the right at the corner of the Marble Way and the Arcadian Way, stretch the ruins of the **Theatre Gymnasium**, a vast sports complex awaiting excavation. Only the base and the steps leading to the palestra can be seen.

The Arcadian Way★★, a superb avenue covered with marble, led to the port. Built by Lysimachus, it was embellished and lit with lanterns by Emperor Arcadius (395-408), who gave it its name. Some 600m long, it was flanked by shops shaded by a portico (numerous columns can still be seen).

On the right, beyond the gymnasium, an attractive pine tree-lined path leads to the car park at the site's lower entrance.

On the left side of the path, in the distance, are several ruined buildings with walls of brick hidden by tall grass. They are the **Harbour Baths and Gymnasium**, another important city institution. Behind the ruins are the walls of the **Church of the Virgin**, also known as the Church of the Councils (*see above*). The first church of the East to be dedicated to the Virgin Mary (Mary died in Ephesus, as did John, the apostle), it was the scene of two councils, in 431 and 449, which set out some of Christianity's main principles.

Around the site

The Artemision*

As you leave Selçuk, on the right, on the road to Kuşadası. 8.30am-5.30pm. Entrance fee.

It is difficult to imagine that one is standing in front of one of the Seven Wonders of the World. A pile of shapeless rocks is all that remains of the prestigious Temple of Artemis which once attracted crowds of pilgrims. Only one column has been re-erected, which, together with a few fragments of stone, give an approximate idea of the building's former height. Actually, there was not enough to rebuild it completely: it measures only 14m in height, to which four metres need to be added to reach the level of the architrave (whose weight is estimated at 24 tons). The diameter of the columns was 1.2m and the base of the building created a rectangle measuring 105x55m. It was indeed a building of colossal scale.

The best way to get an idea of the beauty and the grandeur of the Temple of Artemis is to see the one belonging to her brother, Apollo, in Dydima (*94km to the south, see p 326*).

The present ruins are those of the fourth and last temple completed around the 3C BC. When Lysimachus moved the city to the west (287 BC), the isolated sanctuary of Artemis became prey to plunderers. The fatal blow came later when the Christians, who had set up a church within its walls, used the stone from the temple to build the basilica of St John, as well as Constantinople's Ayasofya.

From Cybele to Artemis

A mother goddess of generous proportions, which she inherited from the most ancient Anatolian peoples, Cybele is the source of the cult of Artemis, whose multiple breasts (unless they are eggs or testicles) symbolise the life and fecundity of the earth. According to legend, Artemis had commissioned a bee to wake up the sun god who slept inside the darkness of a cave. The insect stung the lazy god who sprang out of his den; and then there was light! The Ephesians turned the bee into the symbol of their city. It is found on coins, buildings and in the unusual head attire of the goddess, where fruit, flowers and animals appear as figures of an abundant nature. It was therefore natural that Artemis' sanctuary, the Artemision, rose on the foundations of Cybele's: to her daughter, the mother goddess gave her home, which mere men transformed into a marvel.

The Grotto of the Seven Sleepers

As you leave Ephesus through the lower entrance, turn right before the Kuşadası-Selçuk road, then follow the yellow signs. Coming from Selçuk, take the Kuşadası road for 700m, turn left at the yellow sign, then left again. The site has been closed to the public due to the danger of collapse, but it is possible to get some idea of the site from the outside.

Legend has it, that seven young men persecuted for their Christian faith under Emperor Decius (249-251), found refuge inside a cave near Ephesus. Their persecutors walled in the entrance to the cave and the prisoners fell asleep to wake up two hundred years later (during the reign of Theodosius II), when Christianity had become the law of the State. Upon their death, the "Seven Sleepers" were buried in the grotto where they had hibernated. It became a pilgrimage site; a small church (5C) was built nearby and a necropolis developed all around. Visible on the far side of the barbed wire surrounding the site are the ruins of the **funerary chapels**, with their **tombs**, dug in the walls or in the ground.

AROUND EPHESUS★

İzmir Province – Map p 227
Accommodation in Selçuk

Not to be missed
Şirince and Claros.
Sunset over the ruins of Notium.
And remember...
Taking a picnic on day trips will allow you to stop wherever you want.
If you are travelling to the coast, do not forget your bathing things.

Izmir Province – Map p 227

Rather than wandering around Kuşadası, it is a good idea to concentrate on the attractions in the area around Ephesus. The best way of discovering them, without getting too tired, is to use Selçuk as a base. Leave behind your luggage for a few days and escape, with the bare essentials, to discover the region's four corners. Hikes, archeological visits combined with a swim or walks in the narrow streets of beautiful villages – everyone will find something to suit their needs.

The attractions in each of the excursions described below are shown in order of their distance from the starting point – from the nearest to the farthest. Practical information – accommodation, restaurants, etc. – are in the "Making the most of Selçuk" section, in the preceding pages.

West of Selçuk

Conquering Lysimachus' ramparts

Walking tour. 3km west of Selçuk, along the paths departing from the two roads leading to Ephesus (Aydın and Kuşadası roads). Leave early in the morning, when it is cool, with a picnic and a bottle of water and, if you have one, a compass (there is no map of the area).

The hills overlooking ancient Ephesus make a very enjoyable hiking area, far from the crowds. From Selçuk, it is easy to reach Panayır Dağı (Mt Pion); several paths lead to it, starting from the Grotto of the Seven Sleepers *(see p 285)* or from the Aydın road. Ideally, follow the ruins of Lysimachus' ramparts (8km) which run like a long scar along the crest of the hills, from north to south. From here, there is an exceptional **view**★★ of Ephesus. To the south, further along the flanks of Bülbül Dağı ("Mount Nightingale", in Turkish) towards Meryem Ana, the vegetation becomes denser and the path runs in the shade of pine trees. A good spot to picnic off olives, tomatoes, feta and soft bread.

Meryemana (The house of the Virgin Mary)

8km southwest of Selçuk via the Aydın road. Easy to get to by group taxi. 1km after leaving the town, turn right towards the upper entrance to Ephesus. Keep on past the entrance, through the mountainous terrain. At the summit, there is a checkpoint, where the (very expensive) admission charge is paid. The car park is a little further on. Daily 8am–7pm.

While most apocryphal texts agree that the Virgin died in Jerusalem, some versions say that she left the Holy City and went to Ephesus, in the company of St John, after the Crucifixion (between 37AD and 45AD). She is said to have spent her last days here, in a small isolated hermitage on the heights of Mount Coressus (Bülbül Dağı), away from the city. Nothing is mentioned in the Scriptures, but the exact location is said to have been identified by a German nun, Anna Katharina Emmerich (1774–1824), known in her time for her unusual visions.

Whatever the case may be, since 1951 the Meryemana site has been officially recognised by the Vatican and the Eastern Orthodox Church. Pope John Paul II came to meditate at the beginning of his pontificate and the house has become a major pilgrimage site. Thousands of faithful (including an important Muslim following) crowd into the minuscule **Byzantine chapel** (6C) erected on the presumed foundations of the Virgin's home. Below, a sacred water source (now distributed through a series of taps!) attracts the pilgrims who come to fill their plastic canisters.

A drinks stand, restaurant, souvenir shops and sellers of holy water, not to mention the car park hacked out of the pine grove, have made Meryemana more of an amusement park than a sacred site.

North of Selçuk

Şirince*

7km northwest of Selçuk. Leave Selçuk via the İzmir road. Just before leaving the town, turn right at the yellow sign, then, slightly further on, turn left. Continue to the junction and head right. Then straight on. Allow 45min. Numerous daily dolmuşes.

After passing by Selçuk's last house, the road traverses a beautiful valley filled with olive and fig trees. It then climbs up the hills to the village, where lovely white houses stand out like so many cubes lined up against the dark green of the hillside. Şirince owes its uniqueness to the Greek community which lived here until 1924, when the population exchanges between Greece and Turkey took place.

First impressions are disappointing: a makeshift car park *(fee)* has been set up at the village's entrance and the first streets have been invaded by souvenir shops. The inhabitants also sell a local speciality, something akin to cider with a very sour flavour, which they will press upon you. But higher up, the village atmosphere of former times reappears, even if visitors are pestered to visit an – *"Antique house! Antique house!"* – for a few notes. This is one alternative; another is to stroll peacefully at one's own pace in the charming streets. The **houses*** of Şirince are very characteristic: the upper floor contains the living room and the bedrooms, overlooking the kitchen on the ground floor. Large windows with wooden frames, blackened by time, create a domino pattern on the white façades. Every now and then there is a little terrace overlooking the valley. It is a pleasant scene: luscious bright pink bougainvillaeas caress the walls, peppers dry in the sun in an iron pot, an old man wearing a cap passes by with his donkey and a woman wearing a *şalvar* removes pistachio shells on the steps of her house.

A small pink patch in the middle of the white houses, the **Church of St John** raises its modest bell tower above the roofs. Its doors are topped with an engraved white marble lintel. The interior has been restored and retains a few (rare) fragments of **Byzantine frescoes**, apostles with chiselled faces.

From Şirince, you may choose whether to continue further north to visit the pretty little town of Tire.

Tire

30km northeast of Selçuk. Take the İzmir road for 14km, then turn right at the yellow sign. Then, straight on. You can also reach Tire from İzmir. Allow 30min to 1hr.

Far from the main tourist routes, Tire is a small and very lively town, with a typically Turkish atmosphere. After the ugliness of the modern suburbs which devour the plain, it comes as a great relief to discover, up in the hills, a village where time seems to have stopped. The more one climbs, the more the alleyways become sinuous, narrow and steep. It is easy to get lost between the multicoloured façades of the old Ottoman houses, which face the street with elegant **moucharabies**. There are delightful surprises along the way; the porch of a minuscule mosque, with a tile roof, or a small cobblestone square, where little girls skip.

Below the old city, the bazaar is housed inside an ancient caravanserai, restored with much care. Like İzmir's, it has walls of alternate pink brick and white marble. This is a good opportunity for shopping in a much more authentic atmosphere.

On the road to Aydın

Magnesia ad Maeandrum (Magnesia of the Maeander)

25km southeast of Selçuk on the Aydın road. In Ortaklar (21km from Selçuk), turn right at the yellow "Magnesia" sign. The site is 4km from there. Entrance on the right, in a bend. 8am-7pm. Entrance fee.

Since the excavations are still not very advanced, Magnesia ad Maeandrum will only interest archeology enthusiasts, especially since the surrounding plain does not have much to offer. The latest digs however, are very promising. In addition, Magnesia has a very beautiful theatre*, which, unusually, was never finished, allowing the visitor to discover its structure. *At the entrance of the site, take the path on the left after the ruins of a small mosque.* The work is hidden behind a hill which has to be climbed on foot *(800m)*. At the end of the path, the terraces of the theatre appear, laid out on the slope of the hill opposite. A narrow **gallery** runs all around the orchestra and was used as a backstage. The gallery was faced in marble, and it is still possible to make out those parts of the stonework on which bas-reliefs would have been carved. There are very beautiful **griffin paws*** carved at the ends of the rows.

The penultimate stop along the Persian royal road (which terminated in Ephesus), Magnesia ad Maeandrum was a very prosperous city. Founded undoubtedly in the 11C, it was conquered by the Persians in 530 BC, before falling under Roman dom-

The Church of St John and the Greek houses, Şirince

M.P. Lejard/MICHELIN

ination (2C BC). The moods of the Maeander River obliged its inhabitants to move, leaving the hills (where the incomplete theatre is found) to settle further north, around the site's current entrance.

There, archeologists have unearthed a part of the **agora**, an immense marble quadrilateral (partially excavated) surrounded by very elegant **Ionic columns**. Some have been restored to their upright position. In a cabin located north of the agora, all types of carved marble blocks can be seen – capitals, parts of frieze– which are all excellent examples of the master-masons' skill. This can only mean that other treasures lie below.

Facing the entrance to the site, on the other side of the road, the ruins of Roman soldiers' barracks border the cotton fields.

Along the coast

To the north, the coast is sparsely populated and the scenery is particularly beautiful. An afternoon is sufficient to visit Claros, Notium and Teos (the latter really only for the keenest of archeology enthusiasts, since it is the farthest). Ideally, begin with Claros, continue with a stop at the nearby beach, and end the day by contemplating the sunset from the top of the acropolis at Notium.

Claros★

18km northwest of Selçuk by the coast road. From Selçuk, take the Kuşadası road, then turn right at the roundabout. Next, skirt the sea until you reach the Sahileveri-Claros intersection (at the Notion Restoran). There, turn right heading inland, and 200m on the right, a small path leads to the site. If you visit it at the end of summer, you will be able to see archeologists at work. Free access.

Surrounded by high hills, the ruins of Claros stretch out among the poplars and fig trees, on a small and narrow marshy plain leading to the sea. The ground water here is very high and constantly submerges a portion of the excavated buildings, obliging the archeologists to pump the water out before each dig.

Blood, sweat and tears – A sanctuary dedicated to Apollo, Claros was among the most renowned oracles after Delphi. Its origin goes back to the 8C BC, but the oracle acquired its notoriety during the Hellenistic period. It depended upon Colophon, an important city established 15km to the northwest (hardly anything remains). Its fate was often linked to that of the city and, when Lysimachus destroyed Colophon (294 BC), the sanctuary fell into disrepair. It experienced a new golden age in Roman times (2C AD), when a number of the excavated buildings were constructed. With the spread of Christianity (4C), the site was abandoned, and the river succeeded in burying the walls with its repeated floods. Resurrected by archeologists, Claros is today a unique example of a complete oracle, with sacrificial area, altars and sacred crypt.

The sanctuary is entered through the **propylaea** (100 BC), a square (11x11m) monumental gate, decorated with four columns on its façade. The right side is enhanced by a very beautiful **exedra★**, with a small semicircular marble bench. Beyond the propylaea lies the **sacred way** leading to the heart of the sanctuary. Both sides are lined with **commemorative monuments**, stelae and columns once surmounted with statues, which speak highly of the oracle's renown; all are covered with inscriptions – tributes, prayers, dedications to the gods – left there by the numerous pilgrims. Further down, on the left, another **exedra**, straight this time and in excellent condition, can be seen.

The exedra adjoins the **Temple of Apollo★**, whose colonnade (Doric) lies on the ground in an impressive heap of fluted **drums**. Built in the 3C BC, the building was enlarged by Augustus (1C AD) creating a rectangular edifice measuring 40x26m. It seems that an earthquake caused the columns to topple, since they all fell in the same direction (north), as if under the effect of a brutal lateral jolt which aligned their drums like salami slices. The fact that they are on the ground allows visitors to appreciate their great size. The **fragments of statues★**, scattered alongside the building, are equally impressive (they were nearly 9m tall).

Among the ruins is the complete vaulted substructure of the temple, its arches reflected in the water. This underground space housed the **sacred crypt★**, the oracle's inner sanctum. The remarkably well-conserved room was divided in two. One half was for the priests and the scribes in charge of transcribing the divine messages, while the other, more secret, was reserved exclusively for the medium. The priest would come into contact with the god at the source of the sacred spring. The northern side of Apollo's temple is filled with the ruins of a small Ionic temple dedicated to Artemis, the god's sister.

The sacrificial area – Each temple had an altar, erected on the other side of the sacred way. The most largest is **Apollo's altar**, no less than 19m long. Between the temples and their altar runs the sacrifice area, where the **hecatomb or ox-slaughter festival** would take place (the Greeks call it the "sacrifice of the one hundred oxen"). When it is not too flooded, it is possible to see four rows of stone blocks, each with a ring, it is here that the animals were attached before being immolated. The extent of the area (26x15m) is evidence of the great scale of the sacrificial ceremonies held in Claros, which took place every five years (in ancient Greek, *claria* meant five). Dance, music and libations in honour of the gods accompanied this giant barbecue which brought all the pilgrims together in a celebration lasting all night.

In addition to the excavation itself (geophysical tests have revealed the presence of a stadium, a gymnasium and an odeon), the objective of the archeologists is, in the long term, to raise the columns and the colossal statues of the Temple of Apollo.

Notium★ (Notion)

Pronounced "no-tea-uhm". Near Claros, by the sea. You may park your vehicle in the Notion restoran car park. The site is located at the top of the hill facing the restaurant. Allow 15min to climb up (the climb is steep, but not very long). Ahmetbeyli Beach, at the end of the road, is quite pleasant and not very busy. Take advantage of it, since decent beaches are quite rare on this stretch of coast.

Manto's tears

In spite of the floods which regularly buried the site under tons of alluvium (4m of soil separated the 7C surface from the Roman level), the oracle at Claros remained active for centuries, a measure of its importance in the ancient world. Legend links the founding of Claros to the tears of a woman: Manto, the daughter of a famous Boeotian seer, had been offered as a gift to Apollo of Delphi, along with the wealth of her conquered land. When she recovered her freedom, she returned to her country on the arm of the husband promised her by the oracle. During her journey, she stopped in the plain of Colophon; her voyage was nearly over. She was overcome with emotion thinking about the fate of her conquered land. She cried so much that a spring began to flow at her feet, around which Claros was founded. Ever since, Manto has not ceased to cry and the plain is still flooded.

The acropolis at Notium fills a vast isolated and windswept plateau sitting atop two hills which drop sheer into the sea. The site is actually more interesting for its beautiful surroundings than for its ruins. These are scattered around an area 1km across, covered in pines and shrubs and with a magnificent **view★★** of the coastline. To the north, the **Colophon** hills are covered with cluster pines, producing colophony (or colophonium), a rosin (hence the name of the ancient city), overlooking the plain where the white ruins of Claros, surrounded by trees, can be seen.

Founded in the 5C BC, Notium was the port of Colophon. The site has hardly been excavated but the digs carried out by archeologists from the museum at Selçuk promise interesting discoveries ahead. For now, only a few portions of the **ramparts** as well as the ruins of a **temple** dedicated to Athena can be seen. Further along the plateau, there are two **agoras**, immense squares whose limits can be guessed by looking at the ground. Further down is the **theatre** (2C AD), a truly romantic sight with its pink stone terraces undulating between the pine trees. In the evening, when the sun has tinted the trees orange, it is simply amazing.

The city of colophony or colophonium or rosin

Colophony, colophonium or rosin, a resin which is a by-product of the distillation of the essence of turpentine, has been used for centuries in the production of soap, glues, printing inks and varnish. Violin, violoncello or double bass players also use it to polish their bows to make them glide smoothly over the strings. The ancient city of Colophon, which produced and sold this resin, gave its name to the pines from which it is extracted.

Making the most of Şirince

WHERE TO STAY

Between US$8 and US$15

Pension Halil, at the top end of the village, near the church, ☎ (232) 898 31 28 – 3rm. A tiny guest house, with a very simple level of comfort (1 very clean bathroom for the whole house), but charming and well kept by an adorable grandmother who speaks only Turkish. Breakfast is served in the courtyard under the trees, and guests can make their dinner with the family.

Şirince Evleri, in the centre of the village, opposite the mosque, at no 6 in the street, ☎ and Fax (232) 898 30 99 – 6rm. ⚌ ℰ ▤ A real gem! Two magnificent Greek cottages, which have been entirely restored and very tastefully decorated in 19C Ottoman style. Wood panelling, wainscoting, old furniture, beautiful materials, cushions, crockery and a fireplace create an intimate, quaint and warm atmosphere. Such refinement obviously comes at a price... Book well ahead, the hotel is always full. The reception is in the "Motif" boutique, a stone's throw from the mosque, at the top end of the street.

EATING OUT

Between US$8 and US$15

Ünal Pide Salonu, in the centre of the village, ☎ (232) 898 30 42. The most typical Turkish restaurant in Şirince. Pide, Kiremitte, çöp şiş, gözleme and meze. The food is simple, good, cheap and cooked over a wood fire. Very friendly welcome, in a rustic, warm setting.

NYSSA★★

Aydın Province – Map p 227
87km from Selçuk – 32km from Aydın – 98km from Denizli
Lodging in Selçuk (see p 273) or Aydın

Not to be missed
The theatre and its bas-reliefs.
The agora in its olive grove setting.

And remember...
Have a picnic among the olive trees near the ruins.
Wear sturdy shoes: the tunnel and some paths are rocky.

The long road east from Selçuk towards Aphrodisias and Pamukkale (*see following chapters*) is crowded with trucks and buses, it crosses the immense fertile plain of **Büyük Menderes** (the "great Meander"), a long blue ribbon twisting endlessly between the cotton fields, the olive groves and the orchards. The trip seems endless, especially in summer, when the sun beats down on the plain and the horizon becomes a dancing mirage.

But, halfway are the ruins of ancient Nyssa, hidden in the mountain, in the middle of a superb olive grove. It is a pleasure to wander in the peaceful shade, far from the tumult of the plain. Neglected by tourist buses, Nyssa is an oasis of silence and beauty, which leaves its few visitors spellbound.

City of Science and Literature

Nyssa has left behind beautiful remains, and every year, the continuing excavations reveal more and more of its treasures. During the Hellenistic and then the Roman periods, the city was a brilliant intellectual centre, enlivened by prestigious schools. Probably founded in the 3C BC by the Seleucid king, Antiochus I, it prospered thanks to its proximity to an important sanctuary dedicated to Pluto, attracting many pilgrims. The city's golden age was during the Roman period (most of the ruins date from that time), before it was overshadowed by Tralles (modern day Aydın). In the plain, closer to trade routes, Tralles progressively attracted all of the local population and Nyssa fell into neglect.

The site

From Selçuk, take the Aydın and Nazilli road to Sultanhisar. At the sign, turn left, to go up to the village. Go through the village towards the mountain (straight on after the main square with the bust of Atatürk). The site's entrance (a quaint small stone house) is on the bend before the theatre. Toilets and soft drinks are available. There is an entrance fee if the warden is present. The ruins are spread out and guides will offer to take you from place to place (no charge, but tip appreciated). Allow 1hr, (excluding a picnic and a nap!).

The ruins of Nyssa are scattered around on both sides of the road, on a hill overlooking the steep **gorge**★ of a stream (*dry in summer*). Skirting the edge of the ravine towards the theatre, you will notice regular outlines of the **stadium's** terraces, clinging giddily to the sheer drop! Farther along, the broken arch of a **Roman bridge** lies amid the shrubbery.

Above the road, the **theatre**★★ spreads out like a fan among the olive trees. Built into the hillside, its terraces are well preserved and the whole structure is very impressive (if you avoid looking at the concrete buttressing holding up the topmost terrace). The **stage wall**★★ is especially worth a detour: it has retained all of its magnificent marble **bas-reliefs**★★ depicting the doings of Dionysus. It is unfortunate that they can only be looked at behind bars.

The Aegean Coast

At the foot of the theatre, further along the road, a narrow path descends steeply into the gorge *(on the right side)* and leads to the entrance of an impressive 150m-long **tunnel***, dug by the Romans to channel the waters of the stream to avoid floods *(it can be crossed when the riverbed is dry)*. The tunnel bends toward the east and is lit, halfway, by a large air vent into the vault *(No need for a torch, but be careful where you step. The ground is covered with fallen rocks)*. The sounds emanating from the clusters of hanging bats contribute to the somewhat creepy at-

The Father of Geographers
It was in Nyssa that the Greek geographer Strabo (58 BC – c 22 AD) studied history and geography. As soon as he was qualified, he began writing two long essays: "Historic Memoirs" and "Geography" (only the latter has come down to us). Not well known in his time, his work was rediscovered during the Renaissance (a genius such as Leonardo da Vinci could not fail to be interested). Although it is two millennia old, Strabo's "Geography" is still very relevant for its writings on the origins of peoples, the history of empires and especially the relations between man and his natural environment.

mosphere. Once out of the dim light of the tunnel, the road leads to the east of the theatre. The fine series of vaulted openings on the right once housed a row of **Roman shops**. Farther along, the road bends again leaving a red dirt path on the right-hand side, disappearing under the olive trees. The path leads to the **bouleuterion***, a charming semi-circle in marble, covered in former times, and whose terraces have been restored with much care.

East of the bouleuterion is the **agora** *(when facing the steps, you should head right)*. The extremities of this vast esplanade are lost in the olive grove. The ground is littered everywhere with stone blocks. Then, suddenly, behind the foliage, a magnificent row of **Ionic columns**** appears. These were part of the square's eastern stoa, the whole sub-structure of which has been brought to light.

Making the most of Nyssa

WHERE TO STAY
The only suitable hotels to be found on the road between Selçuk and Pamukkale are in Aydın.

• **In Aydın**
US$20
Hotel Sedef, Hükümet Bulv. 12 Sok 29, ☎ (256) 212 37 72, Fax (256) 225 60 79 – 29rm. 🍴 In the town centre, near the pedestrian streets (from the roundabout marking the entrance to the town, go straight on to the second roundabout and turn left). The rooms are simple, but comfortable and clean. Very attentive welcome. The proprietor speaks English and a little French.

US$70 for half-board
Hotel Turtay, Muğla Karayolu, ☎ (256) 213 30 03, Fax (256) 213 03 51 – 72rm. 🍴 🅿 🗏 📺 ✕ 🛋 🍽 🐎 📇 At the entrance to the town, on the road to Muğla (towards Çine). A luxury hotel

with a rather kitsch decor, equipped with Turkish bath, sauna, weight-training room, discotheque etc. Rooms are bright and comfortable; marble bathrooms. Dinner is served around the swimming pool, which is very pleasant. The menu, however, is not up to the same standard.

EATING OUT

• **In Aydın**
Sarıoğlu Lokantası, Hasan Efendi Mah, Mimar Kemalettin Cad 11, near the Sedef hotel. Simple dishes made with lamb, haricot beans and aubergines, as well as köfte, kebabs and desserts. No alcohol. Friendly welcome, but only Turkish is spoken here.

• **In Nazilli**
On the road to Denizli. **Çağdaş Lokantası**, in the square where the town hall stands. Very friendly welcome, delicious "pide" and kebabs for only US$3!

PAMUKKALE-HIERAPOLIS★★

Denizli Province – Map p 227
268km from İzmir, 192km from Selçuk, 19km from Denizli, 441km from Konya
Alt: 364m (Denizli)

Not to be missed
The sunset on the travertine basins.
The theatre and the ancient necropolis of Hierapolis.

And remember...
Avoid the on-site hotels; they are an affront to the natural beauty of the area.
Avoid swimming in the pools advertising "thermal waters":
the water has passed through the hotels at the summit and is far from clean.

A strange cliff, white as snow, appears among the bare hills. As one gets nearer, it is seen to be made up of a myriad of sparkling basins filled with light blue water. No deeper than dinner plates, they are piled up above each other, creating a giant staircase on the rocky wall. Pamukkale, "cotton castle" in Turkish, is an extraordinary geological oddity, given added interest by the presence of a remarkable archeological site. The Romans, who were always partial to the pleasure and the benefits of bathing, established the spa city of Hierapolis here, whose golden ruins glow among the cypress trees, above the immaculate basins.

The waters of Pamukkale are warm, as warm as the human body and are saturated with mineral salts. Flowing from the inside of the mountain, they reach the plateau in countless small steaming springs. As they evaporate, the salts are deposited on the flanks of the cliff and petrify. This explains how the incredible "castle" of supernatural whiteness was formed. As long as the water continues to flow, the masterpiece will not cease to evolve, giving birth to other basins.

A sacrificed site

If the Romans beautified the site, the same cannot be said of the local developers. Dozens of hotels have been built on the plateau, between the ruins and the travertine basins, disfiguring the landscape and threatening it seriously: diverting the mountain's water, their swimming pools dry up natural basins which gradually lose their whiteness. Worse still, fake concrete basins, painted in white, have recently been recklessly cut into the cliff, which was recklessly cut! As if this were not enough, huge car parks have been constructed on both sides of the site, flanked by a shopping gallery with all the elegance of a motorway toll booth.

Encouraged by Unesco and the World Bank, the Turkish authorities have designated the area a natural park, the **Pamukkale Örenyeri**, and, since 1992, there has been talk about razing all of the surrounding modern constructions. For the moment, nothing has changed and the damage increases yearly. Anyone with any sensitivity should boycott the park's hotels in favour of the ones at the foot of the cliff in the old farming village of **Pamukkale Kasabası.** Adapted for tourism, it has a good range of accommodation and a view of the travertine basins.

B. Morandi/DIAF

The "cotton castle", Pamukkale

The site

Two choices: at the foot of the cliff, at the entrance of the town, the road splits; on the right, it leads to the southern entrance of the site (Güney girişi), and ahead, to the northern entrance (Kuzey girişi, in the direction of Karakayıt.) The suggested itinerary is via the southern entry. The ancient city stretches along 2.5km. It is best to explore it on foot, avoiding the road which flanks the cliff and is subject to heavy traffic. Entrance fee, car park and museum, additional fee. Open 24hr (except the museum, 8am-12noon/1pm-5pm) because of the hotels. Allow at least a good half-day to visit the whole complex.

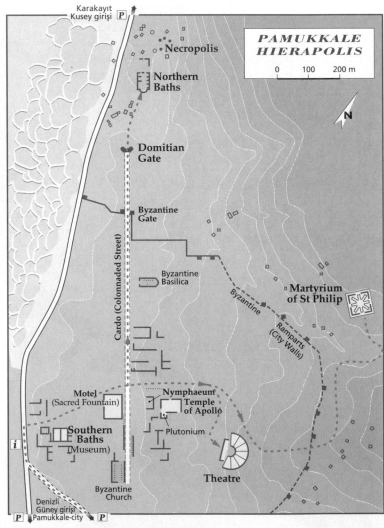

The Aegean Coast

A Roman spa

Founded by the King of Pergamum, Eumenes II, in 2C BC, Hierapolis developed thanks to the wool industry and especially because of the hot springs. Except for the necropolis, its oldest remains – Roman – date from the 1C AD, a period in which the city was rebuilt after a violent earthquake (60 AD). It is also the time when it was evangelised under the authority of St Philip who was crucified here in 80 AD. Because of the spread of Christianity, the Byzantine era brought in a new breath of life to the city. However, the decline of Ephesus in favour of faraway Constantinople, spelled trouble for Hierapolis, starting in the 11C. In addition, a series of earthquakes, especially violent in 1334, contributed to the inhabitants' decision to definitively abandon the city.

The southern quarter

From the southern car park, a little path leads through the remains to the road flanking the cliff. It skirts the ruins of a large **Byzantine church** (on the right) then links up to the **southern baths** (2C AD) housing the **museum★** (8.30am-12noon/1.30pm-5pm; entrance fee). The lovely vaulted rooms, the frigidarium and the caldarium cause the building to resemble an aircraft hangar. Inside, there is a beautiful collection of **glassware** and **sculpture★**, found during the excavations.

To the right on leaving the museum, you see the very elegant **Motel Pamukkale** built upon the ruins of a large **sacred fountain**. The hotel's main appeal is its **pool**, the sacred pool of classical times. The water flows at 37°C and one swims among countless fragments of columns. It is undoubtedly the most unusual pool in Turkey! A fee is charged to non-residents.

Leave the motel on your right and go up the path leading to the theatre.

The heights

Along the way is another **nymphaeum** and the **Temple of Apollo**, with fragments of the pediment, frieze and columns lying around in the grass at the base of the building.

Above the Temple of Apollo is the **theatre★★**. Built under the reign of Septimius Severus (193-211), it is undoubtedly one of Hierapolis' finest buildings. It is entered via the wings, then beneath the stage, and finally

The vapours of hell

The lower level of the Temple of Apollo, the Plutonium, housed an oracle dedicated to the god of hell, Pluto, served by eunuch priests. Inside, a spring giving off deadly vapours could only be approached by priests without fear of death: which of course delighted the faithful! Was it a requirement, therefore, to be a priest or a eunuch to survive the vapours of hell? More rationally, Strabo concluded that the servants of the oracle simply held their breath! The spring still exists nearby. Access is of course forbidden since the gases are still active.

into the orchestra at the foot of the terraces. The **cavea★★**, with a capacity of 7 000 spectators, built in ochre-coloured stone, is particularly fine (notice the **central exedra**, where the city's governor would sit).

Even more remarkable are the **bas-reliefs★★** decorating the base of the stage wall. A marble frieze of immaculate whiteness illustrates the story of Dionysus and Apollo (unfortunately, they are viewed through a grille). The conches and twisted colonnettes of the podium's **niches★★** are masterpieces of skilful carving recalling the prestigious school of Aphrodisias (see the following chapter). Since the stage floor has disappeared, its arcaded substructure is clearly visible though its appearance is hardly enhanced by the concrete soft-drink stand.

From the theatre the climb continues, heading north *(taking the path on the right of the theatre)* up to the **Martyrium of St Philip***. Built in the 5C, this astonishing tomb (or cenotaph, the body of the apostle was never found) was an important pilgrimage site during the Byzantine period. It consisted of a large octagonal chapel covered by a wooden cupola, encircled by a large portico with arcades. A massive portion of its walls are still standing, and from here, a beautiful **vantage point**** gives a view of the site and the surrounding landscape.

Go back to the motel and then head north, taking the path on the right, parallel to the road. It follows the track of the ancient "cardo", the city's main axis.

Along the cardo

To the north, the ancient **main street** is marked by several buildings and **Byzantine churches** still proudly displaying their beautiful walls. The avenue, paved with marble slabs, was lined by a colonnaded portico housing small shops. The excavations, still in progress, constantly reveal new portions, regularly revealing a column or the base of a wall.

Further down are the **Byzantine ramparts**, pierced by a **gate** surmounted by an arch and a broad monolithic **lintel,** apparently ready to split in two! It precedes the **Domitian Gate*** – entrance to the ancient city (82-83 AD) – a beautiful triumphal arch with three openings flanked by two large **round towers**.

Beyond the gate are the **northern baths*** *(on the right)*, an impressive and ornate building, whose tall blond **arches*** hide behind a row of cypresses. Built at the beginning of the 3C, they were converted into a church in the 5C. In spite of the baths' massive walls, as thick as the ramparts' themselves, successive earthquakes have created impressive cracks which seem to make some sections as unsteady as a house of cards. It may be best not to linger too long under the arches!

By contrast, the last of the site's attractions is its best, and it is worth taking one's time to fully appreciate it, especially as the surrounding cypresses offer some pleasant shade. The Hierapolis **necropolis**** is among the most remarkable in Turkey. Approximately 1 200 tombs (many belonging to weavers) have been counted (2C BC-3C AD). Quite apart from its landscape and peaceful setting, the necropolis is worth a visit because of the diversity of its tombs: circular *tumuli* covered with a flattened dome, houses or little temples with pitched roofs scattered all over the slopes to the very edge of the cliff. There, an **isolated tomb*** has fallen prey to calcareous sediments, seemingly floating like a small boat on a petrified sea, as white as foam. This makes for a spellbinding scene at **sunset*****, when the whole cliff is magically transformed.

For a few minutes, as the sun begins to set, the pools take on the sumptuous look of stained glass, lent an additional aura by the shadowy silhouettes of the last visitors. Then as the sun finally disappears, Pamukkale reclaims its peace and grandeur of former times.

COMING AND GOING

By bus – A minibus shuttle runs to Pamukkale every 30min from the bus station at Denizli. Last departure from the site is at 11.15pm. Some companies offer a day-trip to *Pamukkale-Aphrodisias*. Departure at 9.30am from Denizli station. The trip, including lunch, will cost you only around US$15!

The *Denizli bus station* is very large and all the major companies can be found there. Buses to İzmir (via Selçuk) leave every 30min from 5am until sundown (journey time: 4hr). For İstanbul: 15 departures per day (mostly at night), operated by 3 companies (journey time: 10hr). For Konya: 22 departures per day (journey time: 6hr), operated by numerous companies. The best 3 are Isparta, Kontaş and Haş. For Antalya: the Pamukkale company operates 3 services per day, every 90min (journey time: 5hr). For Ankara: Kamil Koç, Pamukkale and Köseoğlu each have 3 departures per day, which means there is one departure roughly every 90min starting from 9am (journey time: 6hr 30min).

ADDRESS BOOK

Tourist information – *Denizli tourist office*, in the railway station, across from the bus station. Very good service and accurate documentation.

The *Pamukkale Örenyeri tourist office* is much less interesting; a mere cabin tucked in between two hotels, opposite the museum, ☎ and Fax (258) 272 20 77. 8am-12noon/1.30pm-7pm, 5pm in winter (in principle). Another small office can be found below the south entrance. No better.

Bank / change – Three banks in the vicinity of the town hall, in the town centre, and several currency exchanges on the site.

Beware, there is no cash dispenser in Pamukkale itself; consequently, if you need money, make sure you take some when you pass through Denizli; the *Garanti Bankası* is very close to the "otogar", at Atatürk Bul 2, with a Visa and Mastercard dispenser outside, which operates 24 hours a day.

Post office – Several little kiosks on the site, and a post office in the village (8.30am-12.30pm / 1.30pm-5pm).

WHERE TO STAY

As soon as you set foot in Denizli, you will be besieged by hordes of hotel touts on scooters. Stay polite, but don't give in! In Pamukkale, every hotel establishment, down to the smallest guest house, has a swimming pool. But beware: few of them are clean, most of them being filled with water from the site which has already passed through the swimming pools of the hotels standing on top of the cliff! All our addresses are in Pamukkale Kasabası, the little town located below the site.

• In Denizli

For those who have a bus to catch early in the morning, or if there is no more room in Pamukkale:

Hotel Ben Hur Yıldırım, Santral Garaj Üstü Sok 13, ☎ and Fax (258) 263 35 90 – 42rm. 🍴✗ Just above the bus station. A large modern building, lacking charm and rather dilapidated. However, the rooms are ordinary, clean and comfortable. Reasonable welcome (English spoken). Still a little expensive for its category (around US$15).

There are other places to stay nearby if this one is full (unlikely) or if you don't like the look of it (more likely), such as the *Laodikia hotel* next door, the *Şubasıoğlu hotel* and the *Yıldız guest house*, a little further away.

• In Pamukkale

Around US$10

Pension Venüs, ☎ (258) 272 21 52 – 15rm. 🍴⚒ Set in the tranquillity of the lower end of town, reached by an alleyway leading down to the left from the main road. Run by a friendly young couple. Rooms are very simple but functional. Meals served in a small arbour (good home cooking). Give the swimming pool a miss – it's not very clean. Travellers' cheques accepted. Free bus service to the town centre.

Pension Öztürk, ☎ (258) 272 21 16, Fax (258) 272 28 38 – 17rm. ⁿ⃠ ✗ ⤒ In the peace and quiet of the lower end of town, set at the far end of a beautiful, rose-covered courtyard. The swimming pool is more of an ornamental pond. Breakfast is served under the willows in a lovely little spot next to a pond containing a few trout (for dinner!). Friendly welcome and very simple but clean rooms.

🏠***Motel Mustafa***, ☎ (258) 272 22 40, Fax (258) 272 28 30 – 16rm. ⁿ⃠ At the top end of town, on the main road. The proprietor, a jovial character who is extremely proud of his enormous stomach, will welcome you with open arms. The rooms, tiled and furnished in pine, are clean and pleasant, and there are very cheap dormitories on the roof. The atmosphere at the reception desk downstairs is very friendly. The proprietor's wife does the cooking (see the "Eating out" section). Very luxurious for the price.

🏠***Hotel Allgau***, Hasan Tahsin Cad 19, ☎ (258) 272 22 50, Fax (258) 272 27 67 – 23rm. ⁿ⃠ ✗ ⤒ A little outside the village, set back on the right-hand side of the road when coming from Denizli. This quiet hotel is set in the countryside, far from the noise, and has a large swimming pool, restaurant, small camp site and car park. The charming proprietress speaks English and German and is a good cook. Very simple but clean rooms, and meals are served on the tables dotted around the peaceful garden.

Ali's Motel, Değirmen Sok, right at the end of the village, at the foot of the travertine deposits, ☎ and Fax (258) 272 26 07 – 28rm. ⁿ⃠ ✗ ⤒ A large yellow guest house, set in a quiet flower garden. It's a pity that the swimming pool, fed by water cascading down over the travertine deposits, is too near the road. The rooms and bathroom facilities are clean but a little precarious. Friendly welcome; English is spoken here, and if you call ahead, you will be picked up from the bus.

Between US$15 and US$25

Hotel Koray, on the other side of the village from the cliff, ☎ (258) 272 23 00 / (258) 272 22 22, Fax (258) 272 20 95. ⁿ⃠ ℓ ✗ ⤒ cc A delightful large hotel with comfortable, clean and modern rooms and bathrooms with bathtubs. You can relax in the vast flower garden, at the poolside (unfortunately not always very clean) or at the bar. Or you may prefer to smoke a hookah in the spacious lounge looking out over the travertine deposits. You will be given a friendly welcome and picked up from the bus if you call ahead (at all events, there is no escaping the moped-riding hotel touts). The evening meal consists of a buffet in the garden. Very good value for money.

US$30 for half-board

🏠***Motel Yörük***, ☎ (258) 272 21 02, Fax (258) 272 20 73 – 58rm. ⁿ⃠ ℓ ✗ ⤒ cc In the centre of the town, near the town hall. This large motel, which is pleasing to the eye, caters to a lot of groups (large dining room). It is very well run. The rooms, spacious and comfortable, are set around a beautiful and very clean swimming pool. Excellent value for money.

Hotel Traverten, ☎ (258) 272 21 54, Fax (258) 272 20 04 – 57rm. ⁿ⃠ ℓ ✗ ⤒ cc Right at the bottom end of town. Exactly the same kind of establishment as the one above, but a little less well-kept. The difference can be measured in the decor, which is rather dull, the slightly out-of-the-way location, and the price, which is a little more expensive. All the more reason to negotiate a better price! Closed from October to March.

US$45

Hotel Hal-Tur, ☎ (258) 272 27 23, Fax (258) 272 22 51 – 12rm. ⁿ⃠ ℓ ▤ �📺 ✗ ⤒ cc Standing at the foot of the cliff, on the road to the site. You will spot it right away thanks to its rather kitsch castle-style façade! The decor is not in the best of tastes, but the hotel is probably the best run in the whole town, well built, spotless and very comfortable. Rooms and bathrooms are spacious and tiled, with balconies giving onto the cliff. Here you don't need to think twice about using the swimming pool. Sauna, gym and bar.

• In Karahayıt

This little village is overcrowded in summer. Hence a myriad of guest houses, almost entirely frequented by Turks. It is very noisy, but although it is preferable to avoid sleeping here, it is a pleasant place to stroll around and for dining out, especially in the bustling and colourful main street. All the same, here are the best places to stay:

Between US$15 and US$25

Pension Yıldız, at the entrance to the village when coming from Pamukkale, ☎ (258) 271 40 25 – 25rm. ⌂ ✕ ⌕ A large, fairly attractive guest house, with plants on the balconies, garlands of dried peppers and kilims in the restaurant. Comfortably seated on cushions, you can sample the food prepared in front of you on hotplates by the ladies of the house. Clean, pleasant rooms, an attractive arbour, a small thermal swimming pool, sauna and a friendly welcome. English and German are spoken (albeit badly).

Pension Ömer Albay, in the centre of the village, in the main street, ☎ (258) 271 42 53, Fax (258) 271 42 53 – 32rm. ⌂ ✕ ⌕ cc A large, rather noisy guest house. Give the very down-at-heel rooms at the back a miss; the ones on the street side are noisier, but they are modern and have been freshly decorated and equipped with air conditioning. You will receive a reasonable welcome, but don't expect more than that.

EATING OUT

The best solution is to take your meals at the hotel. The countless little tourist cafés on the site at the top of the cliff are expensive and of very mediocre quality.

Gürsoy, in the centre of the village, opposite the Yörük hotel, ☎ (258) 272 22 67. cc A very large selection of hot and cold meze, kebabs, fish, "köfte", "gözleme", moussaka and desserts, served in a pleasant arbour to the gentle strains of music.

Mustafa, the restaurant of the hotel of the same name, ☎ (258) 272 22 40. Very good and very copious traditional fare, prepared by the imposing and jovial proprietress; many vegetable-based dishes, some fish and meat, and Turkish desserts. Attractively decorated with kilims and copperware around the fireplace.

Han and **Pamukkale**, Cumhuriyet Meyd. Two very similar little restaurants facing each other, with covered terraces in a quiet little square. Serving breakfast, hot or cold meze, meat, omelettes, sandwiches and desserts.

• **In Karahayıt**

Sinan, in the main street in the centre of the village, ☎ (258) 271 43 69. A very pleasant restaurant with tables set out in a tree arbour with a refreshing fountain. There is an Ottoman room for the long winter evenings. Frequented only by Turks. Kebabs, chicken, fish, meze, soup, salads. It's a pity the welcome is rather cold. No alcohol.

SHOPPING GUIDE

A rather unusual crafts product of Pamukkale are the terracotta or glass bottles, covered in the same white limestone as the bowls on the site. They are left in the course of a spring until they become covered in sediment, after which they are polished.

Making the most of Pamukkale

APHRODISIAS★★★

Denizli Province – Alt 600m – Map page 227
105 km from Pamukkale, 86km from Aydın, 138km from Selçuk
Lodging in Geyre, the village adjacent to the ruins

Not to be missed
The theatre, odeon, stadium and Tetrapylon.

And remember...
Visit the ruins early in the morning or at sunset,
when the site is quiet and a soft light allows good photography;
then end your visit with the museum.

Arriving from Denizli (Pamukkale), take the scenic Antalya road (E87) heading south. After 31km, turn right (yellow sign) in the direction of Tavas. In Tavas, turn right and take the Nazilli road (the site is indicated). If you are coming from Selçuk, turn right, 13km after Nazilli. In Karacasu, turn left toward the city centre (yellow sign). Past Nazilli, signs indicate the way to the site.

The road to Aphrodisias runs across green countryside, a vast plain with a scattering of poplars, cotton fields, vineyards and fig trees. It stretches out at the foot of the Akdağ chain, overlooked by the imposing dome of **Baba Dağı** (2 308m), a big white bonnet which emerges above a layer of clouds.

Until the last minute, the ruins of Aphrodisias remain invisible because of the flatness of the plain. Along the road, the outline of the stadium is barely visible in the middle of the fields. When the ruins do finally appear they are even more striking. Aphrodisias merits its name: the city of Aphrodite is the essence of beauty. The image retained is one of an immaculate city of white marble tinged with blue. The excavations, still in progress, are not as far advanced as those of Ephesus. However Aphrodisias' remarkable ruins are as important and fascinating as those of the city of Artemis. In addition, the serenity and pervasive bucolic atmosphere make the ruins particularly magical.

The city of Aphrodite

The first archeological surveys undertaken on the acropolis (above the theatre) revealed that the site was inhabited as early as the third millennium BC. However, it was in the 7C BC that the city developed with the birth of the cult of Aphrodite which gave it its name. The cult flourished, bringing prosperity to the city, just as Artemis had done for Ephesus. Aphrodisias became an important pilgrimage centre as well a prestigious intellectual sanctuary: capital of Caria during the Roman period, it had a philosophy school and in particular, an important school of sculpture, established next to the important Baba Dağı marble quarries (an ancient quarry is still visible next to the site). Its artists developed an original style, with fluid and graceful lines, which was successful throughout the Roman world. However, the coming of Christianity signalled a period of decline. In the 4C, the Byzantines found it difficult to dethrone the goddess in favour of Christ. They renamed the city *Stavropolis*, the "city of the cross", transformed the temple into a church and made the city a bishopric. To erase the memory of the goddess, Constantine IV (337-361) did not hesitate to destroy the most beautiful ancient monuments with the excuse that he needed them to build city walls. But the efforts were in vain, since they were unable to stop the onslaught of the Selçuks, then of the Turks, who swept through the region starting in the 11C. The city emerged weakened, and Tamerlane dealt the final blow in 1402.

Built on the ancient ruins, the little village of Geyre was destroyed in 1956 by an earthquake. This was a disaster for the inhabitants but a blessing for archeologists, the village was rebuilt farther west, far from the ancient ruins, and the excavations could begin.

Visiting the site

8.30am-7.30pm, 5pm in winter (the museum closes at 6pm). Entrance fee.
Allow 3hr. Soft drinks, telephones, toilet facilities and postcards are available.

The ruins extend over 520ha and the excavations are far from complete! However, the official tour, restricted to main monuments, is quite frustrating since many of the remains cannot be approached: the walk is among the ruins, rarely inside the buildings. A few adventurous visitors go under the thin protective ropes which officially close off the edifices, while the rest of their hurried tourist group presses forward. Shortly before the site are the ruins of the **Tralles Gate** (formerly known as Aydın), let into the city wall.

The theatre district ★★★

From the little square in front of the museum, the path heads left toward the theatre district (*south*). It runs along the side of the excavation depots, behind which hides the **Sebasteion**★, a very beautiful processional way built in the 1C AD and dedicated to the glory of the Roman emperors (in Greek, *sebastos* means "august"). A portico on two levels (only the first level is seen) ran on both sides of the way and was interspersed with marble busts (now in the museum).

Further along is the entrance of the **Theatre Square**★ (or **Tetrastoön**), a vast quadrilateral paved with marble slabs and fringed by an elegant colonnade. In the centre stands a strange circular base, all that is left of a fountain or small temple. Surrounded by the theatre (to the west), the baths and the basilica (at the back, to the south), this square was a very popular gathering place. One can perhaps try and imagine how it must have looked.

The Tetrapylon, gateway to heaven

M.-P. Lejard/MICHELIN

The square is not accessible, however, it can be viewed from the top of the terraces of the **theatre★★**, a sparkling white marble hemicycle built on the slope of the hill, once crowned by the (now completely destroyed) acropolis. The theatre was laid out in the 1C BC by Ioulos Zoilos, a slave freed by Octavian, who became the city's magistrate (an epigraph in his honour, in Greek, runs along the frieze of the stage wall). The Romans modified the building at the end of the 2C, creating the orchestra to accommodate the more popular games: such as gladiator fights and wild animal hunts. Then, the Byzantines transformed it into a fortress, filling the cavea and building an enormous tower over it to protect the acropolis. When the archeologists began their excavations, no less than 42m of debris covered the terraces! Underneath, they found the nearly intact **cavea★★**, still with its first row of seats – with backrests – reserved for the city's notables. The **stage★★**, with its floor intact, has a backdrop of Doric columns. Moveable panels were used to decorate and hide the backstage, a row of small vaulted cells reached by five doors in the back wall. The theatre could hold 10 000 spectators. Here and there on the terraces are engraved initials which allowed regulars to find their seat.

From the top of the acropolis, there is a fine **view★★**. Leave by the right side of the stage to see some of the buildings around the theatre. This leads to the square and then to the **basilica★** (also known as the Imperial hall of the baths), a building with three naves whose beautiful **Corinthian colonnades★** rise from a superb **floor★** of black and white marble slabs. The basilica is linked to the square through a door whose remains include magnificent **engaged piers★★** sculpted with foliage scrolls, in the purest style of the Aphrodisias school.

Close by are the well-preserved **Theatre Baths★★**. Their walls, almost 10m-high, hide two beautiful rooms, still with their pools. In the first one (the *frigidarium*), a large **hexagonal swimming pool** can be seen, while the second (the *caldarium*, located behind) has a small rectangular pool which was once surrounded by bathtubs set in the niches. The floor is still completely intact and in an adjoining room, **board games** are drawn on the ground in an *opus sectile*, made up of small squares of black and white marble.

Around the agoras★★

The path now passes by the remains of the **Great Basilica** (*on the left*), whose columns are lost in the undergrowth. On the opposite side of the path runs the **Tiberius Portico★★**, a magnificent Ionic colonnade of the 1C AD which enclosed the **South Agora★**. The square's entire surface is hollowed out, forming an astonishing oblong **basin★★**, 200m-long, surrounded by steps where people could relax or watch a sporting event. It is a kind of mini-stadium, located in the city centre. At the eastern extremity (*towards the theatre*), the agora's **Monumental Gate** was transformed in the 4C into a nymphaeum with the addition of a basin intended to contain the flood waters when the river was in spate.

To the west, the agora leads to **Hadrian's Baths★**, constructed during the Emperor's reign (117-138 AD). This complex is even better preserved than the theatre baths and is accessible. All of the rooms can be seen – including the atrium (vestibule), exercise room, bath rooms – with their hypocaust heating system and beautiful marble floors. The consoles and the sculpted friezes of the bas-reliefs decorating their walls are exhibited in the Archeology Museum in İstanbul.

The path swings to the north, leaving on its right side the vegetation-covered ruins of the **North Agora**, parallel to the Tiberius agora. Then it reaches the **Episcopal Palace** (Bishop's Palace), built in the 4C or 5C. The palace still has its beautiful **peristyle courtyard★** whose blue-grey marble columns have been re-erected.

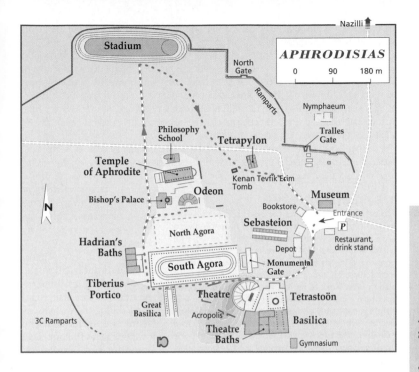

On the wall contiguous to the Odeon *(hidden behind the palace)*, a **sarcophagus** sits in the centre of a small circular platform (possibly a heroön or the tomb of a local celebrity?).

On the southern side, a narrow street leads to the **Odeon****, in excellent condition, undoubtedly one of the site's most attractive buildings. Built at the end of the 2C AD, it was restored by a rich citizen in the 4C. Its hemicycle has an almost intimate scale, though it must be remembered that it was twice its present height, was roofed in and had a second set of stepped seating. It faces a small stage with a number of beautiful marble pedestals (the statues which stood on them are now in the museum). Except in summer, the **orchestra** is regularly flooded by the ground water, creating a romantic setting. This was already the case at the time of its foundation, and the Romans transformed the space into a pool, covered with a beautiful *opus sectile* floor (under restoration). All of the restoration is extremely refined: with steps decorated with lion paws and with dolphin-shaped elbow rests.

The northern part of the city

The path leading to the northern part of Aphrodisias skirts the grand **Temple of Aphrodite***, an impressive Ionic peripteral structure built during the reign of Augustus (1C BC), to which the Byzantines, in the 5C, added an atrium, a narthex and an apse to convert it into a Christian basilica. Only 14 of the original columns which surrounded it are still standing, but they give an idea of the monument's grandeur.

Beyond, still on the right hand side, the ruins of the **Philosophy School** are a collection of small buildings made of stone and brick.

Finally, at the northern extremity of the site, is the **stadium****, an amazing work, 262m long and 60m wide (the track's dimensions are 250x34m). It is Turkey's largest stadium and one of the best preserved along with the stadium at Perge (*see page 441*). Its 20 rows of terraces are laid out in the form of an ellipse, which allowed each of the spectators – nearly 25 000 in all – to have an unobstructed view of the action. Later on, the Romans set up a **circular arena** in the eastern hemicycle (the walls can still be seen) for gladiator fights.

The visit ends with the superb **Tetrapylon*****, a monumental gate (with four pillars, hence the name) erected during the reign of Hadrian (*see photograph on the preceding page*). It held the ancient temenos (sacred area) of the Temple of Aphrodite. It is a true masterpiece with elegant columns, some twisted, some fluted or smooth, plus the finely-sculpted relief of its pediment.

The Herald of Aphrodisias

Near the Tetrapylon rests the body of Kenan Tevfik Erim, the archeologist who dedicated his entire life to the revival of Aphrodite's city. Born in İstanbul, Erim left to study classical literature in the United States. Soon he oriented his field of study towards archeological research and, in 1958, was given a professorship in New York. One day, he came to study some sculptures found in Aphrodisias. It was love at first sight! Erim instantly decided to fine tune an excavation project which began in 1961. His mission lasted 30 years, and brought to light one of Asia Minor's loveliest cities. The work accomplished was considerable and the discoveries spectacular, leading Erim and his team to be awarded several prizes. In November 1990 he died from cancer and was buried near the temple of Aphrodite. This was the city's goddess' last tribute to her discoverer.

No one should leave Aphrodisias without visiting the **museum***. It is small but interesting – and has many items found during the excavations (from the archaic to the Byzantine period): portraits of emperors and luminaries, statues of gods, figurines of acroteria from the theatre, magnificent sculptures, each one more graceful than the last, illustrating the great talent of the local artists. Not to be missed is the **Zoilos Frieze****, a magnificent bas-relief which once decorated the monument erected in honour of this great benefactor of the city (the building itself was not found). Zoilos himself is shown in the company of gods and some of the Virtues. Each figure, standing, is a pure marvel. The sculptural detailing is superb, particularly the light and flowing folds and the faces with their subtle smiles and their hair as soft as waves. In the **Aphrodite Room***, admire the statue of the goddess, wearing her cult gown which resembles the one worn by Artemis of Ephesus and especially, a fine **Apollo Head*** with androgynous features (found in Hadrian's baths).

Making the most of Aphrodisias

COMING AND GOING

It is difficult to get to Aphrodisias if you don't have a car. The best solution is to use one of the coach companies in Denizli, upon leaving Pamukkale. They offer day tours to Pamukkale-Aphrodisias (as do the agencies in Selçuk). Departure at 9.30am from Denizli station. The trip, including lunch, will only set you back around US$8!

By bus – From Denizli, daily bus services run to Nazilli, where a minibus shuttle will take you to Karacasu, 10km north of the site (journey time: 1hr). From there, Aphrodisias is only a 30min dolmuş ride away. If you are planning to return by bus that same evening, make sure that you ask the price before leaving on the outward journey. Selçuk-Aphrodisias: direct by minibus; further information at the tourist information office or at the bus station in Selçuk. To return to Selçuk: 1 bus per day, in the morning (further information at Denizli bus station).

WHERE TO STAY, EATING OUT
US$12
Pension Chez Mestan, on the roadside near the stadium, 400m from the entrance to the site, ☎ (256) 448 80 46,

Fax (256) 448 84 82 – 6rm. ✗ Very simple rooms with showers, WC on the landing. Rudimentary but very clean, and friendly welcome. The proprietor will invite you to drink a çay in his little Ottoman-style sitting room, swathed in carpets and surrounded by a comfortable wall-sofa. He has an impressive stock of magnificent carpets, kilims and saddle-rugs, and he certainly has all the banter down to a fine art. Try out your haggling skills: the prices are attractive and the merchandise is good quality. The food is excellent here, so it is also an ideal place for dinner.

US$20
Hotel Aphrodisias, on the roadside, 400m from the one above, ☎ (256) 448 81 32, Fax (256) 448 84 22 – 27rm. ⌂ ✗ Car park. This is the most upmarket place to stay in the area, and is run by Mestan's French wife. It is a small, simple building but the rooms are bright and well kept and have balconies overlooking the surrounding countryside. There is a pretty arbour out front where breakfast is served, and a terrace restaurant on the roof. It is also possible to camp out in the garden. At sundown, you can hear the crickets and the bells of the kid goats grazing in the hills. A wonderful lullaby…

KUŞADASI
DİLEK NATIONAL PARK★

Aydın Province – Map p 227
21km from Selçuk. 68km from Aydın
80km from İzmir by motorway
Pop 32 000 – Mediterranean climate

Not to be missed
A swim at one of the Dilek Park beaches.
And remember...
Don't spend too much time in Kuşadası.
It is better to stay in Güzelçamlı, near the Dilek Park.

Kuşadası, it is said, used to be a pretty fishing village with beautiful beaches. Visitors could be forgiven for thinking they have come to the wrong place. The village has become a large town, whose character continues to change as a result of the activities of speculators and developers. The expansion has been worse than elsewhere on the Aegean. Here, even nature has been modified: areas have been flattened for building, hills have been remodelled to accommodate enormous hotels which, seen from the hinterland, form a more or less continuous concrete screen. Kuşadası and Kadınlar, another village on the coast located 2km away, are now a single city, linked by an endless stretch of hotels and holiday homes. The beaches have been reduced to thin strips of crowded and dirty sand.

Kuşadası is a victim of its proximity to Ephesus: most tourist groups prefer to sleep here rather than in Selçuk which is too far from the coast. Old Kuşadası, reserved for pedestrians, is suffocating because of the T-shirt shops, the discotheques and tourist restaurants which have completely spoiled the atmosphere of its little streets. It is noisy, loud and the shops are expensive and mediocre.

The only attractions of the place are the **caravanserai**, a battlemented building facing the port and the **Pigeon Island Fortress** (Güvercin Adası), isolated on a peninsula overlooking the bay. Carefully restored, the caravanserai houses a luxury hotel with rooms surrounding a magnificent and deliciously refreshing inner courtyard garden, where it is a treat to have a drink. Another haven of greenery is the square located in the heart of the Ottoman fortress. Some of the towers along the ramparts have been converted into open-air restaurants with fine views.

The Dilek National Park★ (Dilek Milli Parkı)

The main point of interest lies farther south, 26km from the town. It is the Dilek National Park, a vast forested zone pointing toward the Greek island of Samos. Here, there is no concrete, only unspoiled nature, with the all variety of its fragrances and fauna. Trees line tranquil pebble **beaches,** with a few showers, wooden deck chairs and wicker parasols. Some have a snack stand for food and drinks. The flanks of Dilek Dağı, however, belong to the lynx, bears, Anatolian leopards, eagles, and avid trekkers seeking peace and the natural countryside.

For a small fee (*approximately 65 US cents*), this domain is yours for the entire day. A pleasantly shaded road links the various areas of activity: foot paths (especially in the **Sarıkaya canyon★**), sporting facilities and beaches (İçmeler,

Aydınlık, Kavaklı and Karacasu) accessible on foot or by car on good dirt roads. Beyond the last beach, the road stops and gives way to an area reserved exclusively for wildlife.

To take advantage of the park, it is best to sleep in **Güzelçamlı**, a small seaside resort located near the park's entrance. The town has no special appeal but it is quiter and less expensive than Kuşadası. The Güzelçamlı beach is quite pleasant (not too crowded) but the surroundings are not as beautiful as the park.

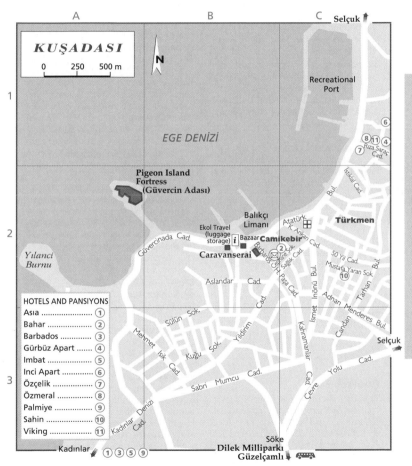

Making the most of Kuşadası

COMING AND GOING

By bus – *The bus station* is to the south of the town, about 1km from the centre by way of Ismet İnönü Bul, and can be reached by dolmuş. Intercity services are fairly frequent and numerous: Ankara (every 2hr), Bodrum, Fethiye-Marmaris, İstanbul and the other main towns in the region. All the major companies have agencies here. ***Kamil Koç***, ☎ (256) 614 84 16.

By shared taxi – You can travel by dolmuş (departure from the bus station) to Söke, Selçuk, Davutlar, Güzelçamlı, Kadınlar, Aydın, Sahilsiteleri, Soğucak and Seferihisar. Departures every 15min. Prices vary from US$1 to US$2.

GETTING AROUND

Since the town has grown considerably, cars and public transport have become indispensable. In the town centre and on the quaysides, however, it is best to get around on foot (parking is difficult and there are some pedestrian-only zones).

The main road in Kuşadası is Barbaros Hayrettin Paşa Cad (B2-C2), a long pedestrian street full of shops, which starts at the harbour.

By rental car – *Avis*, 26/A Atatürk Bul (C2), ☎ (256) 614 46 00, Fax (256) 614 14 75.

Dinamik, 38/3 İsmet İnönü Bul (C2), ☎ (256) 612 11 51, Fax (256) 612 26 47.

Budget, 58 Sağlık Cad (C2), ☎ (256) 614 49 56, Fax (256) 614 98 24.

ADDRESS BOOK

Tourist information – Liman Cad 13, opposite the harbour. Very professional welcome, and efficient service, ☎ (256) 614 11 03, Fax (256) 614 62 95. Open 7 days a week in summer, closed weekends in winter.

Bank – Numerous cash dispensers and currency exchanges in the vicinity of the post office, which has its own currency exchange (travellers' cheques accepted). ***Garanti Bankası***, Türkmen Mah Atatürk Bul Belvu Center A Blok 2/6.

Main post office – 23, Barbaros Hayrettin Paşa Cad, ☎ (256) 614 15 79. Currency exchange and phone booths.

Medical service – *Public hospital*, Atatürk Bul, near the pedestrian quarter.

WHERE TO STAY

• In the town centre

Between US$15 and US$25

Pension Bahar, 12 Cephane Sok, ☎ (256) 614 11 91. Near the post office – 20rm. ⌘ ✆ ☯ CC A small, very pleasant hotel right in the town centre, in the pedestrian quarter. Unfortunately, the noise sometimes penetrates from outside.

Hotel Özmeral, Türkmen Mah, Cennet Bahçesi Mevkii, ☎ (256) 614 51 65. In a very peaceful location, near the town centre – 13rm. ⌘ CC A simple, but well-run hotel. Several little grocery stores nearby, in case of need.

Pension Şahin, Cumhuriyet Mah, Mustafa Varan Sok 1, ☎ (256) 614 68 31 – 16rm. ⌘ Near the Belediye Çarşısı (large covered market) in a centrally located but quiet quarter. A simple, peaceful and immaculate guest house, with a little covered garden full of flowers in summer, where breakfast is served.

Between US$30 and US$45

🕮 ***Gürbüz Apart***, Türkmen Mah, Gürbüz Sitesi 11, ☎ (256) 612 64 39 – 10 apartments. ⌘ ▤ ✆ ✕ ⊠ CC If you want to spend a few days in Kuşadası and are looking for somewhere quiet, comfortable and clean, this is the place for you. The hotel has small, very well-equipped apartments (2 rooms), which open out onto a small garden (a pond serves as a swimming pool). It also has a laundry. You must book at least two months ahead. Closed in winter.

Hotel Özçelik, Atatürk Bul, Yat Limanı Karşısı, ☎ (256) 614 44 90, Fax (256) 614 45 05 – 70rm. ⌘ ✆ ✕ ⊠ ☯ CC This hotel certainly deserves its 3-star rating: the welcome is friendly and efficient, the establishment very well-equipped, the location quiet, and the rooms (with balcony) overlook the sea. What more could you wish for?

İnci Apart, Türkmen Mah, Gürbüz Sitesi 15, near Gürbüz Apart, ☎ (256) 614 39 28, Fax (256) 614 12 42 – 17rm. 🍴 𝒫 ✕ ⊻ cc Identical to Gürbüz Apart, and run by the same family. Quiet, modern, very comfortable and not too expensive. It is, however, a little out of the way, but there are several grocery stores in the vicinity. Closed in winter.

Between US$45 and US$60
Hotel Viking, Rıza Saraç Cad Yat Limanı Karşısı, ☎ (256) 612 70 91, Fax (256) 612 54 60. 🍴 ▤ 𝒫 ✕ ⊻ ⚘ cc A stone's throw from the Özçelik hotel. This new establishment has all mod cons and a very pleasant blue and white Mediterranean decor, which gives it a very restful atmosphere.

• **Between the town centre and Kadınlar**
Between US$10 and US$15
🍴 **Pension Asıa**, Yılancı Burnu Mevkii, ☎ (256) 614 22 83 – 10rm. 🍴 𝒫 ✕ Out of town, perched on a hill overlooking the sea, this guest house is a haven of peace and greenery. It is not easily accessible, so is really only for travellers with their own transport (the guest house is hidden away at the end of a lovely shaded path at the end of a track).

• **In Kadınlar (Ladies Beach)**
US$25
Hotel Palmiye, ☎ (256) 614 70 49, Fax (256) 614 74 80. 🍴 ▤ Small modern hotel with no particular charm, but comfortable and run by a friendly family. Car park. Terrace and view of the sea.

Over US$60
Hotel Barbados, ☎ (256) 614 46 10, Fax (256) 614 46 14 – 88rm. 🍴 ▤ ✕ ⊻ ⚘ ♨ cc Further away from the noise and bustle. A pleasant hotel with a plain yet refined decor. The welcome is friendly and the rooms spacious and comfortable. A television can be installed in your room upon request.
Hotel İmbat, ☎ (256) 614 20 00, Fax (256) 614 49 60. Right at the end of Kadınlar beach – 310rm. 🍴 ▤ 𝒫 ✕ ⊻ ⚘ ♨ 🌙 cc A luxury hotel built in a very beautiful, traditional style and boasting a private beach, casino, sauna, Turkish bath, shops and even a doctor's surgery.

EATING OUT

• **Town centre**
Between US$8 and US$15
🍴 **Captain's House Restaurant-Bar**, 66 Atatürk Cad (C2), ☎ (256) 612 12 00. Excellent fish and an equally delicious aubergine caviar ("hünkar beğendi") are served in this restaurant with its marine-style decor (blue and wood), which opens onto a pleasant terrace.
🍴 **Paşa**, Camikebir Mah, Cephane Sok 20 (C2), ☎ (256) 612 22 92. cc This little corner of paradise is tucked away in one of the many alleyways in the old town centre. Meals are served in a very attractive and peaceful little shaded garden, decorated with kilims and old objects. Bar. Good, cheap, traditional Turkish fare; breakfast.
🍴 **Sultan Hanı**, Camikebir Mah, Bahar Sok 8 (C2), ☎ (256) 614 63 81. cc In the old centre of town, near to the one above and with the same characteristics: a small, tree-filled courtyard, decorated with plants and kilims. Traditional cuisine, mainly seafood. Occasional live music with oriental dancing.
Çam, Balıkçı Limanı, in front of the caravanserai, opposite the harbour (B2), ☎ (256) 614 10 51. cc The tiered layout of this restaurant, with its large veranda and several terraces facing the sea, sets it slightly apart from the noise and bustle of the harbour. Turkish cuisine, fish and seafood. A little expensive, but good.
Türk Mutfağı, Türkmen Mah, İsmet İnönü Bul 6/3 (C2), ☎ (256) 433 92 50. cc In the main street leading down to the harbour. If you're looking for a simple, traditional restaurant with speedy service, this is the place to go. The decor is not up to much, but the food is good and there are no surprises: kebabs, stuffed peppers and aubergines, soup, meze. Open 24 hours a day, convenient for night owls.
Güvercinada, on the quayside, next to the market (B2), in close proximity to the caravanserai. A very simple little restaurant, like all the others which line the quayside. Food and drink are served all day long. Reasonable service.
Ali Baba, 5 Turistik Çarşısı (B2), ☎ (256) 614 15 51. At the harbour. This restaurant specialises in fish, which are presented on a bed of ice for customers to make their own choice.

HAVING A DRINK

Hasan Usta, Türkmen Mah, İsmet İnönü Bul 27 (C1). A tea room specialising in milk-based desserts: chocolate pudding, ice cream, rice pudding, typical Turkish puddings and, last but by no means least, mouth-watering caramel custard. However, the decoration and neon lights slightly spoil the enjoyment.

Café Central, Belediye Meyd, in front of the caravanserai, opposite the harbour (B2). An authentic Turkish bar, full of kilims and musical instruments, where you can have a drink and listen to a group playing traditional music while the customers dance and clap along. The only drawback is that the music is really too loud and since the bar next door is just as noisy, it's a real cacophony!

SHOPPING GUIDE

Kuşadası attracts many visitors, mainly on account of its shops, in particular the *leather* shops. Jackets and bags are indeed slightly cheaper than at the İstanbul bazaar. However, avoid shopping in the pedestrian quarter, where the prices are all much higher.

Star Leather Shop, Camikebir Mah, Bahar Sok 6 (B1), in the old centre of town, next to the Sultan Hanı restaurant.

Leather clothes to suit all tastes. The friendly proprietor speaks a little English, but beware, he has the gift of the gab; don't hesitate to haggle (with a little diplomacy, of course).

OTHER THINGS TO DO

Excursions – The local travel agencies organise all sorts of excursions to the neighbouring islands (Chios) and the region's archeological sites. Bookings can be made at the agencies at the harbour.

Ertürk, Tourism & Travel Agency, Mehmet İzik Cad 7/8 (B2), ☎ (232) 712 67 68, Fax (232) 712 62 63.

Bars and nightclubs – *The Temple Club*, at the entrance to the town, in Atatürk Cad, opposite the Özçelik hotel (C1). This club combines a restaurant, café, fast-food restaurant and a swimming pool. At night, it is the trendiest discotheque in Kuşadası.

Bar Street, right in the heart of the pedestrian quarter. This street is literally jam-packed with bars and discotheques (open-air) and when night falls, it turns into a living hell! The neon lights and decibels rage out of control. You won't believe your eyes – let alone your ears. Another discotheque has been set up in the fortress on *Pigeon Island*.

⸺ Making the most of Dilek (Güzelçamlı) ⸺

COMING AND GOING

From Kuşadası, Güzelçamlı can be reached by the coast road, via Davutlar. Frequent dolmuşes from Kuşadası (see below).

FINDING YOUR WAY

The town has two main roads: Milli Park Cad, which brings you into town and ends at the entrance to the park, and Özer Türk Cad, which runs perpendicular to Milli Park Cad, going from the town centre to the beach.

ADDRESS BOOK

Tourist information – *(Bridge Tours)*. In the town centre, at Özer Türk Cad 35/C (turn left at the roundabout when coming from the main road). The staff are very

welcoming and helpful. This tourist information office provides the same services as the one in Kuşadası (car rental, trips to Samos, tours of the regional archeological sites), and has all the information on activities in Dilek National Park.

Main post office and change – Özer Türk Cad, a little further up the pavement opposite the tourist information office.

WHERE TO STAY

Güzelçamlı is much cheaper than Kuşadası and you will sleep much more peacefully here.

Around US$15

Park Pansion, Başçeşme Cad, ☎ (256) 646 13 59. In the town centre a little further up the street after the tourist information office (after the roundabout) – 16rm. ⌂ ✗ A well-run family guest house (the proprietors used to work at the Club Med in Switzerland). The son is the French-speaking agent at the tourist information office. Good, traditional Turkish food. Breakfast is served on the delightful, shaded terrace with its canopy of vines (do taste the delicious grapes).

Saray Pansion, Atatürk Mah, Liman Cad, ☎ (256) 646 15 03. In the third big street to the right of the main road, towards the sea – 11rm. ⌂ ✗ A recent guest house, all white and spotlessly clean, run by a Dutch proprietress. Beautiful roof terrace. The very low-ceilinged rooms on the top floor were not designed for tall people.

Pension Moustache, Başçeşme Cad 51, set in the higher part of town, ☎ (256) 646 18 69 – 7rm. ⌂ ✗ A very pleasant place to stay, with a beautiful kitchen garden full of flowers, fruit and vegetables which you can sample. Meals are taken in the arbour in the company of the proprietor, who is very proud of his impressive moustache. His wife is a very good cook, the atmosphere is homely and the rooms simple and clean. On the roof is a terrace and kitchen to which guests have access, and there is also a small car park. The proprietor will come and pick you up from the "otogar" if you give him advance warning of your arrival.

Pension Valley, Atatürk Mah, Zeus Cad 27, ☎ (256) 648 18 70 – 7rm. ⌂ This small guest house stands in yet another delightful setting in the countryside just outside the village, at the entrance to Milli Park. The only noise you will hear comes from the birds and cicadas in the garden, which is full of the proprietor's carefully tended fruit trees. The cool, silent rooms are pleasant and spotless. Since the guest house is far from the "otogar", the proprietor will come and pick you up if you give him advance warning of your arrival.

Hotel Dört Mevsim, on the road to Milli Park, ☎ (256) 648 16 95, Fax (256) 648 23 87 – 18rm. ⌂ A small, modern and comfortable hotel, with no particular charm, but with a little garden and set in a good location, on a fairly quiet road very close to the entrance to the park. The proprietress runs her establishment with great care, but only speaks German. Closed in winter.

Around US$30 (for half-board)
Hotel Özmen, in the town centre, in Özer Türk Cad, ☎ (256) 646 17 95, Fax (256) 646 17 94. Just before the tourist information office – 53rm. ⌂ TV ✗ ⌖ CC This modern upmarket hotel offers spacious, simple (pine furniture), clean rooms (ask for one overlooking the swimming pool at the back – it's quieter). Minibar in each room.

Hotel Club Solara, take the first street on the right (towards the sea) at the entrance to Güzelçamlı, just after the fuel station, ☎ (256) 646 10 04, Fax (256) 646 14 83 – 90rm. ✍ ⌂ ✗ ⌖ ⌖ CC Very homely. A row of pavilions with 1 or 2 storeys, containing double rooms, some with a mezzanine for children's beds. They are all spacious, very clean and well equipped. The pavilions are set around a pleasant garden with a swimming pool. Caters to a mainly German clientele. Meals at set times (large buffet), and organised entertainment in the evening. Fortunately, this never carries on very late (after 10pm, it's lights out for children), unlike in the neighbouring hotels. Open from April to October.

EATING OUT

Sarazena 2, Özer Türk Cad 30/A. ☎ (256) 646 22 67. A little restaurant with a covered terrace in the village square, next to the "otogar". Meat, squid, prawns, "böreks" and spaghetti; there is not a great amount of choice, but the food is good and inexpensive and the proprietor friendly.

Beyaz Saray, Adnan Menderes Cad 25, near the main square, ☎ (256) 646 18 91. A traditional, unpretentious "Pide & Kebab Salonu". Simple, good and cheap food, but no alcohol is served here. Friendly welcome.

OTHER THINGS TO DO

Beaches – Güzelçamlı has its own beach, which is pleasant and never crowded. However, it's not a patch on the beaches of **Dilek National Park**, of course, which are in a completely natural setting.

Treks – Treks on horseback or on foot are organised in the **Sarıkaya canyon**, in Dilek National Park. Further information can be obtained from the tourist information office.

PRIENE★★

Aydın Province – Map p 227
39km from Kuşadası, 18km from Söke, 140km from Bodrum – Alt 150m
Accommodation in Altınkum (south of Didymes, see p 329)

Not to be missed
The Temple of Athena and the Theatre.
The vantage point overlooking the plain from the Temple of Demeter.

And remember...
Wear sturdy shoes if you plan to climb up to the higher parts of the town.
Bring along some water (no drinks at the site)
and enjoy a picnic among the pine trees.

If you do not have private transport, dolmuş shuttles link Söke and the site from in front of the city hall. Alternatively, travel agencies and the tourist offices in Selçuk, Kuşadası and Söke organise tours which allow you to visit Priene, Miletus and Didymes in one day.

Priene is a grandiose site; emotion-filled memories are likely to linger for some time. Granted, the ancient city is in a more ruinous state than either Ephesus or Aphrodisias; however, the setting is one of breathtaking beauty. The city is located on a tiered terrace on Dilek Dağı (ancient Mt Mykale). It is overlooked by an enormous wall-like crag with a flat summit which seems to have been sliced out by the sword of a giant. The omnipresent cliff rises from the endless green plain left behind by the sea as it receded. Beautifully set among the pine trees, the ruins have an appeal which is further enhanced by these striking, almost hypnotising, contrasts in the landscape.

The city of Bias
Before Priene, there was another Priene elsewhere. The first city, founded in the second millennium BC, developed slightly to the west of the current site, close to a small port called Naulochos. It grew rapidly, thanks to its relations with Greece and Crete, taking advantage as well of the success of the Panionion sanctuary (dedicated to Poseidon), located north of Dilek Dağı. Priene flourished as a member of the Ionian league, economically as well as intellectually; according to ancient historians, this is where Bias lived, one of the Seven Wise Men of Antiquity, an eminent lawyer and legislator who marked the city's most brilliant period (6C BC).

The Seven Wise Men
Seven being the number of wisdom, the podium which gathered together the wisest men of Antiquity had to number seven. According to the 6C Greeks, the Seven Wise Men were the most eminent philosophers of the period (philosophers then included all men of literature and science) whose pronouncements had become actual proverbs. The list of these wise men varies according to historians. However, it most often includes Thales of Miletus, Bias of Priene, Pittacus of Mytilene, Cleobulus of Lindos, Periander of Corynth, Chilon of Lacedemone and Solon of Athens. Seven geniuses, just as there had been Seven Wonders. The figure Seven occurs over and over again in principles and formulas of many kinds. One only has to think of the Seven Deadly Sins, Seven League Boots or Seventh heaven. And of course God, who created the world in seven days.

However, the arrival of the **Persians**, at the beginning of the 5C BC was to draw the city into a turbulent period. Together with its neighbours, Priene tried to revolt, but the Ionian fleet foundered by the island of Lade (which today is surrounded by dry land south of Miletus) and the Persians destroyed the city.

R. & S. Michaud/RAPHO

The temple of Athena, Priene
and the rock of the acropolis

Nevertheless, Priene rose from the ashes, but its rebirth was brief because nature decreed otherwise: the floods of the Maeander (the Büyük Menderes) kept pushing the sea further and further away and the ports of Priene and Naulochos became silted up and ultimately unusable.

The new Priene

Only one solution was left: rebuild the city elsewhere. And so it was. In 350 BC, a new Priene rose on another promontory, to the east, away from the coast but above the river's meander which linked it to the sea. It was the chance to apply a plan by a man named **Hippodamus of Miletus**. His principles had been very much in fashion ever since their first application, in Miletus, a century earlier. Despite the uneven terrain, it is in Priene that the **Hippodamian plan** can be best understood, since the streets of Miletus have disappeared. However, on a sloping and uneven site such as the one found in Priene, the Hippodamian type of layout does not appear to be the most appropriate. In fact, its adaptation required enormous levelling work and the creation of multi-tiered terraces. Certain axes of the city are more like steps than avenues (there is a 40m difference between the northern and southern edges,). While the citizens of Priene probably never got lost, they would certainly have needed sturdy legs!

The ideal city

For Hippodamus of Miletus, philosopher and urban planner, the ideal city needed to include an orthogonal map grid, perfectly regular and oriented according to the cardinal points. All the rectangular blocks had the same surface area (in Priene: 47.20x35.40m), on which several houses were built. Public buildings could occupy an entire block, or more, according to their importance. The residential quarters surrounded the agora (the Romans' forum), headquarters of political, trade and religious life in the city. Only the ramparts followed the irregularities of the terrain, for improved efficiency. Spread by Alexander the Great, the Hippodamian plan had a considerable following in the Hellenistic world, before attracting the Romans who adopted it for a while in many of their colonies.

With Alexander the Great (late 4C), Ionia was Hellenised and prosperous Priene was embellished with a new Athena Temple, financed by the conqueror. The city later came under Seleucid control, then Attalid (the kings of Pergamum), before falling to the Romans who integrated it in the Roman province of Asia in 129 BC.

Unfortunately, the golden age was ephemeral since the new city was to meet the same fate as the old one: the floods of the Maeander continued their work. The riverbed had progressively moved, leaving behind a silted-up port which was further and further from the sea (8km from Priene in the 1C AD, it is now 15km away). Priene's fate was sealed. The Byzantines nevertheless established a bishopric, but in the 14C the Turks found a modest village almost emptied of its population.

Visiting the site

By car: from Söke, take the road to Bodrum for 2km. Turn right toward Güllübahçe (yellow Priene sign). As you leave Güllübahçe, turn right until you reach the village of Priene (11km). There, a small road bends right, then left, and climbs up to the car park (very steep for 200m). 9am-7.30pm. Entrance fee. Allow 2hr, without the walk, the picnic and the nap under the pine trees.

To the left of the ticket booth, a small path climbs up along the promontory and ends up at the entrance to one of the city's main avenues. Rather than following this way to the city centre, it is more interesting to go towards the stadium and the

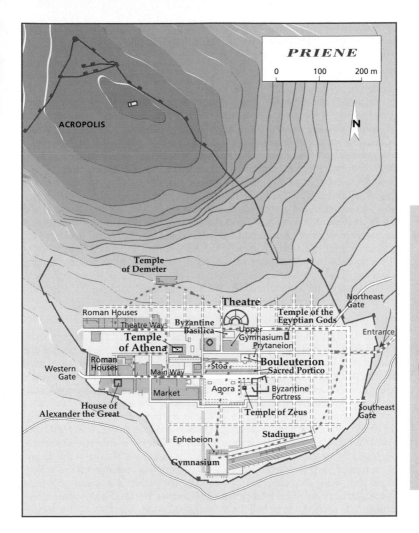

gymnasium on the edge of the plateau. The **stadium** (2C BC) has lost nearly all of its terraces which are covered by shrubs and bushes. The outline of the 190m long track, however, is still easily distinguishable (at the western edge, notice the **stone blocks** which indicated the starting positions).

At the other end of the stadium stood the **gymnasium**, a huge square-plan building surrounded by a portico. The complex's northern wing housed an **ephebeion** (a school for boys), whose back wall, leaning against a boulder, is covered with **graffiti** engraved by the school children (this is not a modern phenomenon!). Looking at the Greek inscriptions, one almost has the impression of hearing the children playing in the courtyard. The other rooms in the gymnasium were dedicated to physical activities, with changing rooms and a **water closet**, where there are still a few intact **basins★**, fed with water by beautiful gargoyles shaped like lion heads.

The heart of the city

The centre of Priene is to the north. Its **agora** *(north)* is a vast terrace whose ruins are lost among the overgrown grass. Besides the view, the square itself is of no particular interest. It was however, the heart of the city where political, commercial and cultural life was concentrated: to the west was a food **market**, to the east, the **Temple of Zeus** (its walls disappeared under those of a small Byzantine fort, also in ruins). The northern side was reserved for the administration: a **sacred portico** (late 2C BC), a prestigious 115m-long double-colonnaded gallery ran the entire length and housed a number of rooms reserved for VIPs. One of the rooms was dedicated to the cult of the emperor, hence the name "sacred portico".

This stoa separated the agora from the **Prytaneion** (magistrates' headquarters) and the **bouleuterion★**, seat of the citizens' assembly. The building (2C BC), one of Priene's best preserved, has an unusual layout rarely seen in Turkey: instead of the traditional hemicycle – which allowed the room to be transformed into an odeon (for concerts) – the **tiered seats★** are located on three sides of the building, forming a U with right angles. The orators' tribune (no longer there) faced the 640 members. In the centre of the orchestra stands the **altar** dedicated to the gods, permanent witnesses to men's decisions.

The west and the city heights

From the agora, the **main avenue** leads west: a beautiful thoroughfare still paved with slabs and with a **drainage channel**. The street heads towards the pine trees, in the heart of one of the residential districts. On both sides, are **Roman houses** whose walls are lost among the pines which line the path. Before the western gate, on the left side of the street is **Alexander's house**, a grouping of square rooms surrounding a courtyard. This is where the Macedonian supposedly lived before it was converted into a sanctuary dedicated to his memory; a tribute from the city to the one who financed the construction of the Temple of Athena (a statue of Alexander was unearthed here). The streets at right angles to the avenue lead to the **Temple of Athena★** on a terrace supported by a remarkable **rusticated wall★**. The great care taken with the corners of the masonry is particularly noticeable. Five superb **Ionic columns★** stand in front of the cliff, facing the immensity of the plain. They are in a way the emblem of Priene, gloriously enhanced by their setting. Alexander the Great, who wanted a masterpiece, had ordered it to be built by the architect Pythius, the creator of the famous Halicarnassus Mausoleum (ancient Bodrum). The statue of the goddess, 7m-tall, was a smaller version of the work he had done for the Parthenon in Athens.

A short way up, beyond the temple, a broad avenue on the left descends slowly through pine trees to the west. This is a good opportunity for an enjoyable walk among the ruins of additional **Roman houses.** Since their walls have been razed, the floor plans are clearly visible. Each house, often two storeys, included an atrium, a small patio leading to the other parts of the house, living rooms, bedrooms and communal areas. The more luxurious ones were built of stone, the other ones of brick (long gone), except for the basement.

More energetic visitors – and all those who are spellbound by the scenery – will want to climb up to the **Temple of Demeter**, high above, almost at the foot of the cliff on which the acropolis was built *(the slope is very steep and rocky, but fortunately* *well-shaded)*. Almost nothing is left of the city's old temple (4C BC), but the **view***** from above is fabulous. The panorama takes in the whole of the ruined city, complete with its hallmark columns of the Temple of Athena standing out sharply against the background of the plain. This could be the perfect moment to unwrap the feta and the tomatoes and afterwards to take a nap under the pine trees, as the crickets chirp their lullaby.

The eastern district

A descent to the east leads to Priene's **theatre***. Better preserved than the bouleu-terion, this small 5 000-seat building is a real jewel with its **proedrium** (first row of seats) punctuated by five superb **marble thrones**** with lions' feet. The stage was raised up somewhat in the 2C AD, and this new front row was placed on top of the old one, ensuring that the local notables continued to have a good view.

On the other side of the **Theatre street**, notice the remains of a small **Byzantine basilica**, the seat of a 6C bishopric *(adjacent to the upper gymnasium)*. In the centre of the nave, the pulpit still stands, its beautiful little steps adorned with foliated ornament.

Further on, towards the east, the street passes in front of the remains of a **temple dedicated to the Egyptian gods** (in ruins), which the inhabitants built to please the Egyptian merchants who traded with Priene.

Finally, the exit is reached. Those who cannot resolve to leave right away can always climb up to the peak's summit (375m), to the **acropolis** *(by following the red markings on the rocks)*. The climb is strenuous and nothing is left of the citadel. However, up there, it is almost like being on top of Mt. Olympus.

On the way from Priene towards Miletus *(Yenihisar road)*, there is a wonderful view back to Priene. Below the rocky buttress, the city's **ramparts** are easily distinguishable, formidable and elegant walls still adorned with a few large square towers. Priene's rock becomes smaller and smaller and the road penetrates further and further into the plain, as if absorbed by this immense marshland, with its reed beds and cotton fields. Alongside the road, makeshift plastic tents shelter farm workers who have come to work in the region during the harvest. All of the plain south of the Dilek massif is part of the national park of the same name *(see p 308)*, a protected zone where building is prohibited and where hundreds of species of birds live in a green paradise.

Priene

MILETUS ★★

Aydın Province – Map p 227
59km from Kuşadası – 23km from Priene – 115km from Bodrum
Lodging in Altınkum, south of Didyma

Not to be missed
The theatre and its galleries.
The small İlyas Bey mosque.

And remember...
Climb to the top of the theatre
within the walls of the Byzantine fortress that overlooks it;
it is the ideal spot to admire the entire city and its layout.
Avoid sandals, the terrain is a bit muddy.

At the foot of Dilek Dağı and the great cliff above Priene lies the plain of Balat **(Balat Ovası)**. The immense marshland was left behind by the sea as it retreated, conquered by the floods of the Maeander. The river loses itself in the immensity of the plain as it twists and turns among reedbeds and cotton fields. Suddenly, a huge white rock marks the horizon like an island set in a tranquil sea; a strange promontory which seems to float away. To the traveller, the Miletus theatre resembles an enormous fortress standing on a lonely hill, sparkling like a lighthouse in a green sea. In fact, at the time of its splendour, it ruled over the sea since it lay at the tip of a peninsula, a small stretch of land barely 2.5km long, guarding the entrance of a gulf (today's Lake Bafa). Since then, the silt brought down by the river has covered everything, pushing the sea back 10km. Hidden at the base of the plain, the remains of the city appear only at the last moment, just as you stop in front of the monumental façade of the theatre.

The theatre at Miletus

M.-P. Lejard/MICHELIN

From Priene, cross the plain; then turn left at the yellow sign. A small road leads to the foot of the theatre where you will find a car park shaded by a row of poplar trees. Souvenirs and drinks are available. The museum is further down the road on the right (towards Didyma).

A major Ionian power

Miletus was founded during the Mycenaean period (1400 BC) through an alliance between a Carian population and Cretan immigrants. In the 10C, the Ionians who colonised the entire region gave it a homogeneity, allowing Miletus to flourish. The city grew spectacularly, becoming one of the most powerful members of the Ionian confederation. Besides the fertility of the surrounding land, its wealth was derived from maritime commerce and its four ports (one to the east, the other three to the west – the Port of Athena, the Port of Lions and the Port of the Theatre, site of the current car park). These facilities meant that it ranked among the principal centres of mercantile trade between the Orient and the Mediterranean. Beginning in 670 BC, the city established several trading posts, (Pliny counted 90!) on the Sea of Marmara and the Black Sea.

But in 546 BC, Persian domination put a brutal stop to this prosperity. The entire region was subdued and the traffic between Miletus and its trading posts (also under Persian control) was blocked. The city was therefore the first to foment the **Ionian Revolt** (494 BC), a bungled initiative which was to lead Ionia into real disaster: the Persians destroyed the Ionian fleet near the island of Lade (today a hill in the plain, visible to the south of the site), devastated the city and deported the population of Miletus to the banks of the Tigris (Iraq).

The new Miletus – The region had to endure the first Persian defeats, in 479 BC, before the city could dream about freedom. Its reconstruction was assigned to the philosopher Hippodamus, who had the opportunity of experimenting – successfully – with his famous Hippodamian plan *(see p 316).*

A city of wise men

Not content with being the richest city of Ionia, Miletus, starting in the 7C BC, attracted attention by becoming an intellectuals' haven. Its philosophy school acquired a reputation throughout the Greek world, whose alphabet it standardised. It was in Miletus that the most famous of the Seven Wise Men (see p 314), the mathematician Thales (640–546), lived: a true genius of geometry with a theorem named after him. His student, Anaximander (610–546) was famous for his geography and for establishing the first maps (he was one of the first to imagine that the universe was infinite and the earth a disc lost in space). Also worth mentioning are Hecataeus (540–480), historian, geographer and traveller, precursor to Herodotus, the urban planner Hippodamus (5C) and, during the Byzantine period, the no less famous Isidorus of Miletus, architect of Ayasofya in Constantinople.

With the arrival of Alexander the Great (4C BC), Miletus found new life which continued during the Seleucid reign, then under the Attalids (kings of Pergamum), before reaching its golden age during the Roman era beginning in 133 BC. Rather than integrate it into the province of Asia, Rome preferred to leave the city independent in order to maintain their excellent relations.

The advent of Christianity saw several apostles passing through Miletus, including St Paul who preached the gospel in the entire region. The city also became an important archbishopric during the Byzantine period.

However, the moods of the Maeander were to condemn it as well as its neighbours Ephesus and Priene, covering progressively all of the ports with silt. Reduced and less powerful than before, the city survived nevertheless for a while, but the attacks by the Seljuks (1071), the Turks, and then the crusaders only served to further weaken it. At last, the Emir of Menteşe, **İlyas Bey**, gave it new life in 1279: he restored one of its ports, built mosques and hamams and renamed the city *Palatia*. In 1424, Murat II took possession of it and *Balat* became Ottoman. But this signalled the death of the city: the port was irreversibly silted up and, in the 17C, the city was permanently abandoned. Only the little village of Balat survived but it too disappeared in 1955 following an earthquake. Its inhabitants moved 1km further south, leaving it to the trowels and brushes of the archeologists.

The site

8.30am–7pm. Entrance fee. Allow 2hr30.

From the 17C onwards, the city was the subject of numerous reports and the first excavations began in 1899, under the leadership of the German archeologist, Theodor Weigand. Work continues today under the direction of a German team.

The theatre★★★

The most striking thing on arriving in Miletus is the sheer size and magnificence of the theatre. One can only guess at the impression it must have made on a merchant arriving in the port (now the car park) for the first time. He would be faced by the immense structure, concealing the cavea, a formidable wall 140m long and an imposing, 30m-high, rampart, pierced at both ends by two large black openings, the *parodos* (entrances). Today, although the wall has mostly crumbled, the scale of the building is no less striking. Originally constructed in the 4C BC, it was enlarged and restored by the Romans, capable of accommodating 15 000 spectators.

Entry is by the stage whose floor has disappeared. Facing it, the immense **cavea★★** unfolds like a giant fan, a cascade of tiered terraces marked by the two columns of the **Imperial tribune**. Although in ruins, the **stage** building, 34m long, has kept beautiful **bas-reliefs**, visible at the sides.

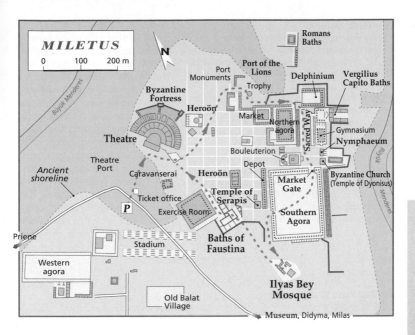

Particularly astonishing are the **parodos**★★, the internal corridors used by the spectators to reach their seats *(enter via the left stairs)*. Their proportions are monumental – as if designed for giants – and they are in perfect condition. One of them goes around the hemicycle at the halfway point of the cavea, while the other gives access to the upper row (ambulacre). The scale of the vaults is amazing. The splendour of the structure, enhanced by the sunlight pouring through the windows set at regular intervals is simply grandiose.

A Byzantine fortress (8C), largely constructed with stone taken from the terraces of the theatre (notice numerous pieces in the walls), sits proudly on the hill. The building is ruined and is of no particular interest, except for a row of shops with oblique vaults. But it makes an ideal **viewpoint**★ for beginning to understand the complex layout of the site as well as enjoying the panorama over the plain.

From the Port of Lions to the sacred way

The best way of exploring Miletus is now to do as visiting merchants once did, after they had disembarked at the Port of Lions behind the theatre. On the way there, the route passes in front of a pretty **heroön**, a small mausoleum isolated at the foot of the hill. Inside on the back wall, there are five niches, used as receptacles for sarcophagi.

The **Port of Lions**, whose name originates from the two feline statues which guarded the entrance, has become a shapeless marshy terrain. The only reminder that this was a harbour is the **monument** which overlooked the anchorage, a circular feature erected to honour the naval battle of Actium which Octavian (the future Augustus) had won against Anthony and Cleopatra. The monument, with its flame burning in a great basin – was decorated with a frieze representing the sea divinities (two sections are still intact and a triton's tail is visible on each one).

İbrahim's women

If you are a member of the female sex or if one of its representatives accompanies you, İbrahim will not fail to salute you by waving his shapeless cap. The old toothless man, voiceless and ageless, has an unusual hobby: to have his picture taken next to every nice-looking woman who visits the site. These pictures, sent to him by the women on their return home, overflow in all of his pockets. They are stacked in large dog–eared and yellowed piles which he will invite you to admire. All of them are the same: İbrahim proudly holding next to him a nymph in shorts and T–shirt. There are hundreds of them, the oldest dating from the seventies. Once the picture is taken, copy the address written on the rumpled envelope he will hand you and send him the picture to add to his collection. It will make his day.

Towards the east (*on the left*), are the imposing walls of the **Roman baths** (1C AD), a vast complex which contained five rooms surrounding an exercise room.

Then comes the **Delphinium**, undoubtedly one of the site's most romantic spots. Not much is left of the sanctuary dedicated to Apollo of Delphi except for a flooded open space in which the clumps of tall grasses and herbs are reflected. Nearby, a few cows graze peacefully under the watchful eye of İbrahim, a cowherd who seems to have been here forever, almost invisible among the ruins. In the centre of the *temenos* (the sacred courtyard of the sanctuary) rose a *tholos*, a small circular temple whose foundations can just be made out beneath the surface of the water.

Along the sacred way

A beautiful 30m-wide avenue, the city's processional way leads southward, flanked on each side by an **Ionic stoa** housing shops (1C AD). One of them (*east side*) has been re-erected, giving an idea of its elegance, even if the cement pointing is completely out of place. The avenue stretches for 100m to the southern agora, then on beyond the city to the sanctuary of Didyma, 19km away.

Behind the eastern stoa are the **Vergilius Capito Baths**, a beautiful 1C AD building named after the governor of the city who had them built. On the other side of the avenue, the **north agora** ran all the way to the Port of Lions by way of an important **market** surrounded by shops (all in poor condition).

Further along the avenue, are the ruins of a 2C **nymphaeum**, a monumental fountain originally on three levels, of which only the arches of the first level have survived. The elegant colonnaded façades of the Ephesus library or the Imperial hall of Sardis give an idea of the original appearance. The nymphaeum was adjacent to the **Temple of Dionysus**, a pagan building converted by the Byzantines into a **church** at the beginning of the 7C. Its mosaics and a part of its wall, protected by a stone building, are visible through the grilles of the openings. Lastly, you come to the hemicycle of the **bouleuterion** (very ruinous) which linked the northern and southern agoras. A few grass-covered steps are still partially visible.

Around the southern agora

The next stop, the southern agora – the city's main square – is a vast marshy esplanade, 196x164m. A portico ran along the four sides (little of which is left), facing the processional way through a magnificent propylaeum with three arches, the **Market Gate**. Only the foundation, half-covered by water, remains in place. The rest of the building, as beautiful as the Ephesus library, was dismantled by German archeologists to create one of the most beautiful rooms of the Pergamum Museum in Berlin, next to the Zeus Altar, from Pergamum. It is this very beautiful façade which features on the tickets issued at the site's entrance.

The western wing of the agora was flanked by a **storage building**, a long structure whose remains include the bases of the walls and the columns lying in the grass. Before continuing the visit through the ancient city, take a millenary leap in time by looking at the **İlyas Bey Mosque***, a delightful little Seljuk building hidden behind an olive grove, southeast of the agora. The spot is full of serene charm: the mosque, attributed to the Emir of Menteşe (1404) stands at the end of a small Ottoman cemetery whose white marble stelae are lost among the tall grass. Now disused, it has lost its minaret which was destroyed in the earthquake of 1955. Patches of grass cover its small tiled dome like the hair growing on a baby's head. Although the building is of modest size, its detailing is very refined, in particular the **portico***, whose three arches in two kinds of marble, are closed off by stone *claustrae*.

Go back and head west (left) to the theatre.

To the west of the storage building, the **Temple of Serapis** (3C) honoured Helios Serapis, a Romanised Egyptian divinity. Its face appears crowned with a solar halo in the centre of the pediment which has been rebuilt on the ground.

Not far from the temple are the remains of the **Faustina Baths**, a vast spa complex built by Marcus Aurelius' wife (161–180 AD). Along with the theatre, they are among the best preserved and most interesting buildings on the site *(ideally, it is best to visit them by following the same route that the bathers used in the past: begin in the north, by going all the way to the back of the buildings and then come back through the complex to the southern end, on the same side as the mosque).*

Its high stone walls, partly hidden beneath debris brought down by the river, hide a succession of very spacious rooms – especially the hot rooms – where portions of the vaults can still be seen. From north to south, the first room is the **apodyterium** (changing room), a long gallery punctuated by niches where bathers undressed and prepared themselves for the baths. To the north, a small **room of muses**, with an apse, held the statues of the gods and city's divinities. On the right side *(west)*, an **exercise room** (or gymnasium) was intended for sports activities (ruins covered by thistles are all that remains).

On the left side *(east)*, three **frigidaria*** succeed each other. In one of them (the cental room), a statue of the god Maeander guards the pool (copy, the original is in the museum). Then, the hot rooms are reached, followed by the sweating room *(sudatorium)*, adjacent to the great hall of the **tepidarium**.

Before leaving the site for Didyma, the **museum** is worth a brief visit. It is located on the right-hand side of the road, shortly after passing the İlyas Bey Mosque *(9am–5.30pm, entrance fee)*. It houses a beautiful lapidary collection, a few mosaic fragments and winged griffin statues.

Miletus

DIDYMA★★
(YENİHİSAR)

Aydın Province – Map p 227
19km from Miletus – 77km from Kuşadası – 125km from Bodrum
Accommodation in Altınkum (4km to the south)

Not to be missed
Strolling among the colossal ruins of the temple,
particularly at the rear of the building.

And remember...
If the weather is good, wait for the sunset;
the sun's rays on the columns will make them even more beautiful.

Didyma is not the name of an ancient city; just a temple. And what a temple! If this colossal structure had not remained unfinished, it would have been among the Seven Wonders of the Greek world, a tough competitor for the Artemision of Ephesus, its twin in many ways. The two sanctuaries are the work of the same architects – Paionios of Ephesus and Daphnis of Miletus – and they are dedicated to the two most famous twins of Olympus: Artemis at Ephesus and Apollo at Didyma (*Didyma* is supposed to mean "twins"). The only survivor of the story is the Didymaion.

The third temple of the Greek world

As with numerous ancient centres of worship, the Didymaion owes its origin to the presence of a spring which gushed at the edge of a grove of laurel trees, Apollo's favourite tree. The inhabitants of the region quickly turned the site into a shrine, dedicated to the son of the old Anatolian mother goddess, Cybele.

When the Greeks reached the coast of Asia Minor, in the 7C BC, they set up a sanctuary, with temple, altar and sacred spring, whose remains were found underneath the walls of the current temple. Initially reserved for advice on affairs of state, the oracle of Didyma was later opened to more personal requests, and the shrine quickly attracted all sorts of pilgrims. Furthermore, its *temenos* was a place of asylum, where anyone could be sheltered without fear of reprisal. In time, the Oracle's renown grew and a bigger temple (6C BC)

N. F. Carteret/HOA QUI

The furious Medusa
of Didyma

The Aegean Coast

was built. However, as soon as it was completed, it was attacked by the Persians (early 5C) in reprisal for the revolt of the Ionian cities *(see p 321)*. Legend has it that, at that moment, the spring dried up, and only began to flow again with the arrival of Alexander the Great, who was to give Didyma the same renown as the oracle of Delphi. The new sanctuary requested by the conqueror (332-331 BC) had to be gigantic, worthy of the oracle which, two years before, had predicted his victory against the Persians. In fact, Alexander's Didymaion was indeed an enormous temple, ranked third in the Greek world by its dimensions (109x51m) and the extent of its peristyle: a double Ionic colonnade with 120 columns.

An unfinished temple – However, the construction work dragged on for 150 years well into the Roman period and several columns were left unfinished without their fluting. The advent of Christianity put an end to the cult of Apollo, and the Byzantines transformed the temple into a basilica. A violent fire swept through it in the 10C, followed five centuries later by an earthquake which toppled all of the colonnades. The temple became a pile of rocks, and a quarry for the nearby villagers. Until recently, the Didymaion was in the countryside. Since then, hotels and souvenir shops have replaced the goat herds. A small town has grown up around the temple, depriving it of its majestic qualities. In addition, the ruins are below street level. But, once inside, the magic and sheer size are still inspiring.

The temple

9am-7.30pm. Entrance fee. Allow 30min.
In the inner courtyard, a pane illustrates the original appearance.

The Didymaion is unusual in that it is a hollow temple: instead of the usual cella (or naos), there is a vast open courtyard, an adyton hidden behind high walls. This is where the sacred spring was located, sheltered inside a small temple – the naiskos – where Apollo's statue was enthroned. Only the priests were allowed to penetrate this courtyard, the sacred seat of the god and his prophetess, the Pythia. Unlike the pilgrims, modern visitors are privileged to penetrate this inner sanctum.

At the foot of the steps, two enormous **Medusa Heads★** rest on the ground, impressive fragments of the frieze which ran atop the colonnade. Among the shapeless mass of stone blocks, it is possible to distinguish the wells and the circular base of the altar where the soothsayers sacrificed the animals. The route followed the pilgrims led them up the steps of the **pronaos★**, a large vestibule crowned with 20 massive **columns★**, as broad as ancient oaks. Only the bases are left, all decorated during the Roman period with palmettes, foliage patterns, and wonderful marble plaques sculpted with **bas-reliefs** (no two are alike).

Coded messages

The pilgrims going to Didyma disembarked in Miletus, from where they would reach the sanctuary on foot by following the processional way (see p 324). Every spring, processions would leave the Delphinium, the sanctuary of Apollo of Delphi, for the Didymaion. Once there, the pilgrims would wash in the water of the sacred well to purify themselves. Then, they had to find out if Apollo was available. The priest would find the answer in the entrails of a goat or sheep which had been immolated on the altar. One by one, the pilgrims would climb the steps of the pronaos. There, they would ask a question to the priests who would pass it on to the Pythia, secluded in the temple of the sacred courtyard. The answer that the god would whisper to the prophetess was often enigmatic. The priests would then translate it into simple language, in the chresmographeion, before giving it to the pilgrim who had remained patiently at the entrance of the temple.

These guardians of the sanctuary would stand high above the supplicants, framed in the doorway of the **chresmographeion**, a small elevated room separating the pronaos from the sacred courtyard (*access is forbidden*). It is in this "prediction hall" that they would read the god's response to the pilgrims in a solemn and glacial tone. On both sides of the chresmographeion's door, two small intact **vaulted corridors**** slope down gently toward the **adyton***, a vast rectangular courtyard, 54x22m. This secret heart of the temple, reserved exclusively for priests and servants of the cult, has a striking austerity, and the dim light lends it a great air of mystery. 4.5m below the level of the peristyle, it is surrounded by 8m-high walls interspersed with simple pilasters. The only decor, a **frieze*** with griffins and lyres (Apollo's attribute), can be seen in several portions at the foot of the walls.

On the northeast side of the courtyard, a **monumental staircase*** leads to the chresmographeion. On the opposite side, at the back of the courtyard, the outline of the **naiskos** appears on the ground, a small temple which housed Apollo's statue and the sacred spring, the domain of Pythia. Subject to a fast during each oracle, she was happy to chew laurel leaves, a sacred food thought to help her enter into a trance in order to communicate with the god.

Once out of the adyton, walk around the temple along the **peristyle***, beginning with the south side where two gigantic columns have been restored to their upright position. But the sheer scale of the temple becomes even more apparent through looking at or even feeling those parts of it now on the ground. There is foliage moulding from an entablature with stems as thick as jungle creepers, ovolos as big as ostrich eggs. The bases of each column seem even larger when they are missing their shafts, and one feels Lilliputian standing beside them. At the back of the building, there is a striking chaos of drums, capitals and giant pieces of frieze, an entire section of the temple lying shattered on the ground.

Besides the Temple of Apollo, Didyma has no other features of interest. Altınkum, a small beach resort, 4km to the south used to be one of the most attractive beaches of the Aegean coast. Unfortunately it is now nothing more than a convenient place to stop overnight.

Making the most of Altınkum

COMING AND GOING

By bus – The Kamil Koç, Hakkiki Koç and Pamukkale bus companies are all at the corner of Altınkum Cad and Karakol Cad, at the entrance to town, opposite the large shopping centre.

ADDRESS BOOK

Main post office – Altınkum PTT Merkezi, almost at the corner of Yalı Cad and Çiçek Sok. Open every day in summer, 8.30am-11pm. Currency exchange.

Medical service – Sağlık Merkezi, Altınkum Cad, next to the large pink shopping centre. Open 24 hours a day. The competent staff speak a little English.

WHERE TO STAY

Hotels abound in Altınkum (rooms around US$15). All offer the same standard comfort (good beds, bright rooms with pine furniture, small bathrooms with varying degrees of finish). There's no need to waste time making up your mind, just take the first one whose façade or surroundings appeal to you. It is, however, worth bearing in mind that the seafront (Yalı Cad) is very noisy (discotheques). If you're looking for quiet, you're more likely to find it at the ends of town. Around the temple in Didyma, you will also find a few guest houses and restaurants which are much quieter than those in Altınkum.

US$15

Pension Çamlık, Çamlık Mah, Çiçek Sok (opposite the Han Han motel), ☎ (256) 813 10 58, Fax (256) 813 22 36 – 10rm. ⌐| A very quiet little guest house with a shaded garden where breakfast is served. The rooms are simple but clean, the welcome friendly and the neighbourhood quiet. There is a little grocery store next door in case of need. If this guest house is full, try the **Tules guest house**, a little further up the street (same style). **Han Han Motel**, Çiçek Sok, ☎ (256) 813 13 74, Fax (256) 813 22 51 – 34rm. ⌐| ✗ ⌐ Behind the post office, set back from the beach. On entering the town, take the street on the right after the large pink shopping centre. The hotel is set below street level in a quiet area surrounded by a pine grove. Rooms are very simple, tiled and clean, with beautiful bathrooms. Meals are served on the roof terrace, facing the sea. Laundry right next door. Give the swimming pool a miss (unappealing). However, you will receive a very warm welcome (the jovial proprietor speaks English and there is a very youthful atmosphere). Travellers' cheques accepted. Open from May to October.

US$40

Apartotel Güçlü, Yalı Cad 40, ☎ (256) 813 72 21, Fax (256) 813 72 25 – 45 apartments, from 1 to 3 rooms. ⌐| ⌐ ✗ ⌐ [cc] At the east end of the beach (turn left when you arrive in Altınkum). A chic new hotel. All the apartments are very spacious, functional and spotlessly clean. Lovely large swimming pool. Rather expensive, but you can do your own cooking. This set-up may be of interest to those who want to stay here for a few days and use it as a base to visit the region.

• **Mavişehir**

A tranquil village, 2km from the site and from Altınkum, and 800m from the beach. **Pension Orakçi Tesisleri**, Madarinen Garten, ☎ (256) 825 64 65, Fax (256) 825 94 53 – 12rm. ⌐| ⌐ ✗ ⌐ Sometimes

closed in winter. In a garden dotted with mandarin trees, this little guest house is carefully kept by a Turkish-Swiss couple. The rooms are simple, bright and comfortable, breakfast and lunch are served on a large terrace, and there is a small swimming pool and even a marble Turkish bath where you can have a massage.

EATING OUT

After visiting the temple, you can dine out at Didyma: excellent little fish restaurants are hidden away in the small surrounding alleyways. If you want to eat well in Altınkum, avoid the restaurants on the seafront.

• **Didyma**

Aşık is a good fish restaurant, standing opposite the entrance to the temple.
Genç Urfa and **Meşhur Tekirdağ**, Yunusoğlu Sitesi, Yunuslu Park, behind the large pink shopping centre in Altınkum Cad. Two unpretentious but pleasant little restaurants serving traditional Turkish fare, which is simple and cheap, especially for this place. "Güveç", moussaka, "köfte", kebabs and soup. And the gentlemen can always go upstairs for a shave at Raymond's barber shop afterwards, should they feel so inclined.
White Garden, Altınkum Mah Yalı Cad Deniz Sok 4, ☎ (256) 813 16 73. Just below the Haltur hotel. Small restaurant set on a terrace above a leafy alleyway. Meals are served in an arbour to the gentle strains of good Turkish music. The young, relaxed atmosphere is very friendly. The English proprietress is charming, and her husband, who is very much in touch with his country's culture, offers some traditional dishes, such as the "Ottoman Dish" or "Hüntar Beğendi", tasty lamb stews with vegetables and spices, which you will rarely find elsewhere. Very good and inexpensive.
Rich Star, next to the post office, access via the beach. Recommended by the proprietor of the one above; of a similar standard and in the same vein. Try the "mantı", delicious Turkish ravioli. Good but expensive.
Hakan cake shop, Deniz Sok 7, on the same side of the street as the White Garden, a little further up. A large cake shop with a somewhat off-putting decor but plenty of good Turkish and western-style desserts, as well as hot and cold drinks.

HERAKLEIA AND LAKE BAFA★★

Aydın Province – Map p 227
63km from Söke – 41km from Milas
Lodging in Kapıkırı

Not to be missed
Hiking in the mountains
among ancient and Byzantine ruins.

And remember...
Spend 2 or 3 days in Herakleia (Kapıkırı)
to take advantage of the atmosphere and the beauty of the site.
For hikes, wear comfortable shoes,
bring along drinking water and binoculars.

It is pleasant to relax on the shores of Lake Bafa (also called Çamiçi lake, *Çamiçi Gölü,* in Turkish.) Silence reigns and space is abundant. After the buzz of the beach resorts, this is the place to recover, in the midst of a wild landscape of great beauty with numerous vestiges of the ancient world. The villages of Bucak and Kapıkırı, today's Herakleia, are tiny white spots in a chaotic landscape of grey sandstone and red earth shaded by olive trees. Every village has its minaret, as thin as a match stick, its little zinc roof sparkling in the sun like a diamond. Overlooked by Mount Latmos (1 375m), named **Beş Parmak** ("five fingers")
by the Turks because of its shape, the sur-rounding hills roll down to the shores of the lake where they flatten out to become green marshes. This is where the villagers grow cot-ton and watermelons. Donkeys graze quietly and migrating birds meet during the mating season. An enchanting scene.

The peaceful shores of Lake Bafa

On the main road from Söke toward Milas, turn left toward Herakleia-Kapıkırı (white "Herakleia" sign) in the village of Çamiçi. A minor road (10km) skirts the lake via Bucak – the first village perched on the right – and ends in Herakleia.
For those without transport, buses from Söke and Milas serve Çamiçi. From here, the only way to get to the village is to hitch a lift, unlikely to be difficult.

Shortly before Çamiçi *(approximately 1km before the village)*, to the left of the road, are the tow-ers of a beautiful **castle** emerging from the olive trees, next to a rocky peak. There is no path, but it can easily be reached by walking through the olive grove. From this ancient observation post, there is a superb **view★** over the lake.

The kingdom of birds...
Lake Bafa (7 000ha, 15km long, 5km wide) is located in the heart of a national park of 12 280ha which includes a large portion of the Latmos massif. Until the 1980s, fish was abun-

dant (perch, carp, *kefal*, a type of mullet) and the fresh water allowed the inhabitants to irrigate their fields. Unfortunately, increasing salinity and intensive fishing have ended up nearly destroying this bounty of nature. In addition, the hundreds of thousands of migrating birds who wintered here have fled.

Now a designated nature reserve, closed off by a dam, the lake is slowly being repopulated and the birds are returning to its shores. Ducks, cormorants, pink flamingos and 250 different species come here

The monk's perch

Once upon a time in the 4C, there was a Syrian hermit, known as St Simeon Stylites, originally from Antioch (Antakya). To isolate himself from the world without ceasing to preach to the pagans, he had the ingenious idea of setting up a platform the top of a column. From above he could harangue the crowds on a daily basis. He went from city to city, converting many pagans from the top of his column. The success of his endeavours created a following of disciples all over the known world: the Stylites, from the Greek "stylos", column. One of them, Paul the Young (10C) chose to create a home on a rocky peak in the Latmos massif. The monastery of Latmos was built around this peak.

every winter (68 species mate here.) The most numerous are the **Dalmatian pelicans**, an endangered species (only 2 000 left in the world); the lake is their third largest colony, a hopeful sign!

...and monks

Until the Roman period, Lake Bafa was connected to the sea. It was a deep bay (the Latmos Bay) which the silt deposited by the Meander (Büyük Menderes) slowly closed off. Towards 1000BC, Carians settled at the inland end of the bay, in the

M.-P. Lejard/MICHELIN

hills, away from the pirates who scoured the coast. They founded a fortified city: Latmos. In the 4C BC, under the auspices of King Mausolus, they abandoned their citadel to establish a settlement on the shores, further west, where they built the port of Herakleia. The new city experienced its golden age during the Hellenistic period, endowing itself with the most beautiful monuments, until the Meander finally closed off the bay.

A Christian city – After being isolated from the sea, Herakleia lost some of its importance. However, the spread of Christianity permitted it to revive: with the arrival of 300 Egyptian monks, expelled from the Sinai by the Arabs (7C), the city became an important bishopric. Three centuries later, it acquired exceptional fame and influence with the advent of St Paul the Young, a monk who was faithful to the philosophy of Simeon the Elder. Mount Latmos became a sacred mountain: numerous hermits and monks found shelter in caves dug in the rock or by building monasteries. The mountain and the islands of the lake remained a realm of monks for more than six centuries, until the Turkish conquest (1280), Herakleia's death knell.

Herakleia (Kapıkırı)
Allow approximately 1hr30min.

Today, the ruins of the ancient city play hide and seek with the white houses of Kapıkırı, and it is difficult to imagine the magnitude of the ancient city. The finest ruins are those of the **ramparts*** *(the best preserved portion is north of the village)* built

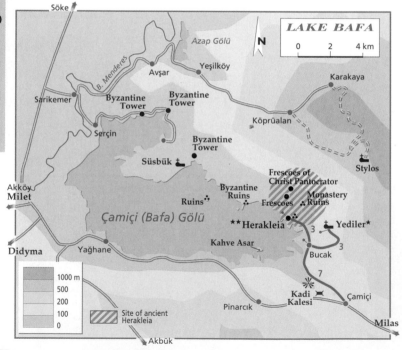

by Lysimachus in 287 BC, at the same time as those of Ephesus. They encircled the city with a 6.5km perimeter which snaked its way across the crests of the surrounding hills. A few **square towers** of the original 65, still stand proudly along the lake and among the rocky heights.

The village school now occupies the site of the **agora**, whose southern wall can still be seen from the school's courtyard. *A map of the site is available.*

Nearby, towards the lake shore, is the **Temple of Athena** (3C BC). Its dark walls stand on a small promontory, like a lighthouse overlooking the lake. It has a fine **view***★ over the marshes and hills.

Among the rocks plunging into the lake is a large number of **Carian tombs**, dug in the rock. A few emerge like small islets, others are filled with water, like strange bathtubs. Careful scrutiny reveals dozens more scattered around the edges of the lake, in the marshes and in the middle of the fields. They are part of the **Necropolis of Latmos**★, a cemetery (cut in the rock) of incredible magnitude: the archeologists have catalogued more than 2 500 tombs. The finest examples are in the mountains, in the place where the Byzantine monks would later seek refuge to pray.

Following in the footsteps of the monks
Walking tours around Herakleia.

If you wish to explore the ruins of Latmos and the Byzantine monasteries up in the hills, it is best to take a guide (*see "Making the most of Herakleia"*). It is in fact impossible to find your own way around the chaos of rocks, except for the Yediler Monastery (the track leading to it is quite clear). With a guide, you are sure not to miss anything, and to find your bed come sunset!

In search of ancient Latmos★★★
(northeast of Herakleia; allow at least 1hr30min on foot from the village).

Today, the stones of the monasteries are mingled with those of ancient Latmos. One of the most beautiful sites to explore is the **Necropolis***★★★. Silence reigns among the jumbled rocks, broken only by the call of a nomadic shepherdess to her goats. A dignified, solitary figure, she seems to belong to another time altogether, and when she vanishes, it is almost as if she had been a ghost, wandering among the rocks and tombs. The tombs seem numberless. The whole mountain is full of them. The majority were dug in the rock, sarcophagi which are sometimes lined up four at a time when the rock is big enough. Others are burial vaults covered with enormous **monoliths**, reaching 4m in length and of unimaginable weight.

Here and there, a few steps are visible. They are part of a road – among the rocks – which once ran through the city of Latmos. Other surprises include a few fragments of the **ramparts**, including an **observation tower**, which is only apparent at the last moment, so deeply has it

The sleep of Endymion
The wild beauty of the hills of Latmos imposes respect and silence. Walking among the rocks or along the shores of the lake, it is easy to understand why many monks and hermits chose it as a retreat. Before them, the Carians and the Greeks had not been unmoved by this strange landscape which inspired numerous legends; such as the one about the young shepherd Endymion. Zeus, overcome with love, preferred to put Endymion into eternal sleep, in the depths of a cave, rather than see him grow older. Every night, Selene, the moon goddess, comes to visit him. So, be quiet and walk by without making any noise!

disappeared into the landscape. It overlooks the ruins of a small **fortified monastery*** (with a forgotten name), built on a rock. From the top of its walls, the **view***** over the mountain and lake is magnificent.

Not far from here, closer to the tower (toward the north), another wonder awaits you, a rock unlike any other. Hollowed out like a vault, it hides a **Byzantine fresco** (8-9C) representing Christ in Majesty. This explains the name: the **cave of the Pantocrator**. The work is badly damaged but still amazing to behold.

Several frescoes are hidden in this manner in the mountain, especially near the **Monastery of Yediler*** *(near the village of Bucak; allow 2hr to go there and back; an easy climb)*. Near the ruins, a rock hides **paintings*** telling the story of Christ, from his baptism to his Resurrection.

Of the monastery itself, which had no fewer than four churches, there only remains the little battlemented citadel atop a large round rock. Yediler (or Kellibara), was the second largest monastic complex in the region, after Stylos (*Araphavuzlu* or *Arabavlı*, in Turkish). The latter, heavily damaged, is much farther to the north (35km away) and the path leading to it is long and very difficult.

The monastery of the islands

(Access by boat from near the restaurants.) A few monasteries (now in ruins) were founded on the lake's islands. The best preserved is on **Kahve Asar island** *(from the Çerinin Yeri restaurant, take the path on the left of the Söke-Milas main road, slightly before arriving in Çamiçi; the crossing only takes a few minutes)*. Still standing are the beautiful brick and marble walls of a chapel and church.

Making the most of Herakleia

WHERE TO STAY

Herakleia-Kapıkırı is a tiny village with only two modest guest houses providing food and accommodation. The first, the **Herakleia Pension**, stands on the lakeside and can be reached by a small road going off to the left, just before the village. The second is right at the entrance to the village and is the one we prefer.

Around US$15

Agora Pension, ☎ (252) 543 54 45, Fax (252) 543 55 67 – 11rm and 3 bungalows. ✕ ☂ Guests have lunch in the arbour from where they can enjoy a view of the countryside. In the evening, dinner is served in a very convivial little room inside. Access to the rooms is behind the restaurant, via another arbour with large hanging gourds. Furnished with old wardrobes and warm carpets, the rooms are spacious and comfortable. 2 rustic but clean bathrooms are reserved for the use of guests. The 3 wooden bungalows outside are equipped with camp beds and have access to a small and very basic communal bathroom. Good food and very friendly welcome (homely). The staff speak fluent English and German. Guaranteed peace and quiet (once the neighbour's donkey has gone to sleep).

EATING OUT

Two or three small unpretentious restaurants stand on the lakeside, next to the Herakleia Pension, down below the village (access via the little road which leads off to the left before the village). On the menu: traditional meze and good fish, as in the restaurants at the two guest houses.

OTHER THINGS TO DO

Walks and treks – Spring is the best time of year to visit Lake Bafa (especially April and May), when the flowers are blooming and the temperature is still warm. Mustafa Yıldırım and his cousin, who co-manage the **Agora Pension**, organise exciting treks in the mountains and around the lake, lasting half a day, a whole day, or even several days, with tent accommodation.

Further information can be obtained at the guest house or from the village's young imam who will welcome you upon your arrival and who has been trained as a guide by Mustafa. The prices are high, however (fixed rate of about US$45 for the trek to the fortified monastery and for the one at Yediler); but the more of you there are, the cheaper it is, since the price is split between the whole group.

THE ROAD TO MİLAS ★

115km from Herakleia to Güllük (one day)
Map p 227 – Accommodation in Milas or Güllük

Not to be missed
The view of the sea from Iasos Hill.
The little-known ruins of Stratonicia.

And remember...
If you have time, take a boat to Iasos from Güllük.

The road from Söke to Milas crosses a marvellous countryside of arid hills, covered with wild olive and pine trees. Hidden away are a few unrecognised archeological sites, whose interest does not reside alone in the often exceptional beauty of the ruins. The area also provides a fantastic variety of scents and atmosphere, far from the crowds of the more popular sites. This is a good way to continue your trip after visiting Herakleia.

■ The Temple of Euromos ★

On the road to Milas, a sign on the left indicates the temple, 150m away on a dirt track (visible from the road). 8am-7pm. Entrance fee, but you can also see the temple outside opening hours, as it is not fenced off. 15min visit.

On the fast road to Milas, it is easy to miss this beautiful Roman temple, which is only sign-posted at the last moment. The only visible remnant of the city of Euromos (still waiting to be excavated), it seems to stand in the middle of nowhere. Built in the 2C AD for Jupiter, it is among Turkey's best preserved

Ruined fortifications on a rocky spur

classical temples. Sixteen of its **columns★**, with fluted shafts and Corinthian capitals, have been restored to their upright position. Four of them have plaques with inscriptions, signatures of the donors.

■ Iasos★ (Kıyıkışlacık)

30km north of Milas and 40km from Bodrum. 3km south of Euromos, take the track on the right (good condition) going down to the sea. The site can also be reached by boat from Güllük: departure every day at 11am, returning at 4pm. The boat is moored just in front of the Çiçek restaurant.

Past Euromos, the track descending towards Iasos reveals a magnificent **view★★** of the sea before entering an immense pine forest.

After 14km, take the little road on the left leading to the sea. At the entrance to the village of Kıyıkışlacık you will see the ruins of an impressive domed building. Continuing straight on, you reach the museum and the centre of the village. Head left towards the port, a beautiful small bay between two hills. On the right, a few restaurants are lined up on the shore.

In Antiquity, the hill at Iasos was an island, separated from land by a narrow isthmus. A small prosperous city, living from fishing and its good trade relations with Athens, it did not fare well under the domination of Mausolus who took control of it in the 4C *(see p 342)*. The city was only revived with the arrival of Alexander the Great, an era in which it became famous for its music and theatre festival. The Byzantines transformed the city into a bishopric before it slowly fell into neglect.

The site

Entrance on the left of the car park. Entrance fee (warning, you can visit the site with the museum ticket; but the converse does not apply. If you purchase your ticket in the museum, you will also have to pay the entrance fee to the site!) Allow 2hr.

M.-P. Lejard/MICHELIN

Go straight on beyond the ticket office, head straight (try to avoid the goats) to reach the **agora***, which stretches at the foot of the hill. A Mycaenian era **necropolis** has been rediscovered beneath the surface of the agora and archeologists have transformed the square into a piece of Swiss cheese. However, the outline of the ancient esplanade is still visible as a large number of **porticoes** are still standing.

The southeast corner of the square has a small building with a large arch, known as the **Caesareum**, the main hall marking the entrance to the sanctuary of Artemis, whose temple was located immediately behind (in ruins).

The south side of the agora faces the **bouleuterion****, the best preserved building in Iasos with beautiful marble steps, all quite successfully restored.

From here a climb leads up to the summit of the hill topped by a **Turkish fortress**. Now a ruin, it is of no particular interest except for the magnificent **view**** over the bay. The remains of the harbour walls which protected the entrance to the port, can easily be distinguished. The Byzantines built a small bastion here. Unfortunately a large white hotel is set on the heights, on the other side of the bay.

Descending from the fortress to the east *(facing the bay)*, you will discover the remains of the **theatre**, on the slope of the hill facing the sea. Only the hemicycle, its fine lines of grey stone lost among the olive trees, is distinguishable. Here too, the **panorama**** of the coast is superb.

The entrance to the site is reached by going south along the side of the hill and around the rock. Along the way, are the ruins of a **Roman villa** containing numerous **mosaics** (protected by a layer of sand) and a few traces of frescoes which decorated the walls. The owner of the villa knew what he was doing when he chose this location.

Finally, before reaching the ticket office, the path traverses the ruins of a few **Byzantine churches**, located near the well-preserved **ramparts**.

If there is time, visit the **Lapidary Museum** *(8am-12noon/1pm-7pm, entrance fee)*, located inside a caravanserai built around a beautiful **Roman mausoleum**.

After the museum, return to the car park and take the narrow road on the left which follows the coastline. On one side is the sea, fringed by pink marble rocks; on the other, a superb panorama over the plain. At the next village, turn left after the strange red and white milestone in the middle of the road.

A tea break among the carpets

J.-F. Galmiche

■ Milas

Except for its famous carpets, Milas is a town of no particular interest, and if it were not at the intersection of a few beautiful sites, it would be a pleasure to avoid it. Of its past – it was after all the capital of Caria, then of the Emirate of Menteşe (1300-1426) – almost nothing is left, and the few remains are not displayed to their fullest advantage. For example, the **Gümüşkesen Mausoleum** is thought to be a replica of the mausoleum of Halicarnassus: this marble "model" dating from the Roman era (1C AD) stands in the middle of a run-down square at the edge of the town.

■ Beçin Kalesi★

6km from Milas, on the road to Muğla, turn left as you leave the town, then right at the round-about (Beçin, yellow sign). After 1.5km, turn right at the second yellow sign. The road climbs up to the entrance to the castle (parking). Allow 1hr.

East of Milas, the buttresses of the Batı Menteşe mountains form an imposing cliff, preceded by a rocky spur which has detached itself. A perfect site for a **fortress★**, which is exactly what the Emirs of Menteşe chose to build in the 14C (on the remains of an ancient acropolis). Except for the still very impressive walls, the interior is in ruins but has a fine **panorama★** over Milas and the plain.

However, Beçin Kalesi is not only a castle. On the plateau facing the ramparts, there are other remains of the same period, including a small **medrese** built in 1375. Its **iwan** (*eyvan*) has the tomb of the founder, Ahmet Gazi, which attracts a few pilgrims. A few families come to picnic on the grass surrounding the **ruins** of the residences of the governors of Milas.

On leaving the plain around Milas for the heights, the **road★** runs through a magnificent forest of oaks, beeches and chestnuts which in places give way to small pine forests. In September, the bee-keepers of the region come to sell their **honey** at the side of the road, close to the **restaurants** tucked away in the forest.

■ Stratonicia★ (Eskihisar)

26km from Milas, via the Muğla road, the site is at the end of the modern village of Eskihisar, by the side of an enormous coal mine. Take the small road on the left which descends towards the site. Keep right and stop in front of the old village's abandoned mosque. Free admittance; follow the arrows. There is a kiosk in front of the mosque, but the guardian is usually at the excavation building, at the back of the site. You can ask him to give you a guided tour. Allow 1hr.

The village of Eskihisar has not concealed the ancient city, but has blended into it. Here, Ottoman houses are located next to ancient buildings and the streets are still paved with marble. The place has a surreal beauty, and the past seems within reach. The atmosphere is even more spellbinding due to the total silence of the village: it was completely abandoned after the earthquake in 1957 and rebuilt slightly further away, on the road to Muğla, leaving the area to Turkish archeologists.

A Carian city, Chrysaroris traded in its name for Stratonicia, the name of the wife of Antiochus I (281 BC), the Seleucid king who gave the city its golden age. During the Roman period, Hadrian embellished it with many monuments (early 2C) and the city continued to flourish up until the Byzantine era. But, by the time it came under Turkish control, it had dwindled into a modest township, which then became Eskihisar.

The few ancient ruins which have been excavated reveal a city of great size, a potential rival in beauty to Ephesus or Aphrodisias. However, to resurrect Stratonicia, Eskihisar would have to be destroyed. A difficult choice, since the village is charming. Will the small wooden **mosque** guarding the village's entrance need to be destroyed? All around it, archeologists have dug a ditch revealing the walls of a Byzantine basilica.

The paved roadway through the village leads past a number of Ottoman houses, prettily built in pink brick with marble dressings. Then the road skirts a small field where, curiously, a marble **doorway** stands alone amid the tall grass. It was the entrance to the **bouleuterion**, whose ruined hemicycle is nearby *(from the road, access is through the small staircase on the left)*.

The building marked the centre of the city at the crossing of its two main axes, large avenues paved with marble. The decumanus leads west to the **theatre**, adjoining a hill covered with fig trees (if it is the season, stock up, the figs are delicious). The steps of the theatre are well preserved, as is the stage wall, decorated with a pretty **frieze of masks** (3C AD).

At the opposite end of the path *(back towards the east)*, is the **gymnasium★**, undoubtedly the most beautiful building in Stratonicia. This 2C complex is one of the largest known today; moreover it is in excellent condition (only part has been excavated as yet). Four aligned rectangular rooms form a setting for a semi-circular one. All of them have retained their sparkling white marble cladding. The gymnasium, flanking the **stadium** (in ruins) to the south, which stretched all the way to the theatre.

■ Güllük

The last place on this itinerary, or a stopping-off point on the road to Bodrum, Güllük is an attractive little port, with **naval dockyards** where wooden sailing ships, *(gület)*, continue to be built for the needs of tourism.

The best place to use as a base for visiting the region is Milas, although the hotel infrastructure there is primitive and the atmosphere not very friendly. Güllük is another possibility.

COMING AND GOING

By bus – To get to the "otogar" from the town centre, wait for a dolmuş at the roundabout between the Sürücü and Turan hotels, in front of the newspaper seller, or take a taxi, if you can find one. From Milas: buses for Söke, Bodrum, İzmir, Didyma and Altınkum, changing at Dalyan and Güllük (beware, in Güllük, the buses leave from the town centre, not from the bus station).

WHERE TO STAY

• **Milas**

US$12
Hotel Turan, Cumhuriyet Cad 26, ☎ (252) 512 13 42 – 30rm. ⚞ In the town centre. Access is often through the breakfast room, to the left of the reception area. A very modest but clean establishment.

Around US$20
Hotel Sürücü, Atatürk Bulv, ☎ (252) 512 40 01 / 512 32 27 – 22rm. ⚞ ⚟ 📺 ✘ When leaving the town on the way to Muğla. A supposedly very chic 3-star hotel, but whose hour of glory has been and gone… It is all very spacious, but now very much the worse for wear. Nevertheless, the service is still adequate and the rooms are pleasant. Good cake shop on the ground floor.

• **Güllük**

US$8
Pension Mandolya, Atatürk Mah 173, ☎ (252) 522 26 42 – 4rm. Set back from the harbour, towards the dolmuş stand, in a small quiet street. Tiled rooms with good beds (19 in all), with 2 spacious and very clean bathrooms to share. Roof terrace overlooking the harbour. Small café on the ground floor. Extremely cheap, very reasonable and friendly.
Hotel Kordon, at the end of the harbour on the right when coming from the dolmuş stand. ☎ (252) 522 23 56 – 13rm.

⚞ ✘ A very simple hotel, but very well run by a friendly Turkish family. Spacious and peaceful (the harbour in Güllük is not a noisy place). Meals are served on the quayside.

US$21
🏨 **Hotel Özer**, Çamlık Mevkii, ☎ (252) 522 27 41, Fax (252) 522 27 21 – 37rm. ⚞ ⚟ ✘ ⚞ ⚟ On the road out of Güllük to Bodrum. A large white building concealed by trees, set on the rocks on the seafront. The rooms are immaculate, spacious, comfortable and very bright (marble tiles). Good welcome. Terraced garden above a small private beach. Very good value for money.

EATING OUT

• **Iasos**
In the bay, opposite the entrance to the site, you will find several fish restaurants. The tables are set in floating arbours. Very pleasant and peaceful, and the food is good.

• **Milas**
Kalbur, Atatürk Bul 66, not far from the Sürücü hotel. 💳 A large dining room, attractively decorated but a little cold, with a pleasant terrace on the boulevard. Reasonable, cheap food (meze, kebabs, "börek", chicken etc). The choice is rather limited, but there is not much else in Milas. On your way out (or in), take a look at the lovely bourgeois houses next door.

• **Güllük**
Kordon, the restaurant of the hotel of the same name, ☎ (252) 522 23 56. A variety of meze, seafood, fish and kebabs, all prepared by the proprietor. Meals are served on a large covered terrace facing the sea. Good and inexpensive.
Eski Depo, at the harbour, ☎ (252) 522 27 90. Meze, fish, seafood, meat. Vast covered terrace facing the sea, attractive but slightly antiquated decoration, and discreet Turkish music. The neighbouring restaurants are all very much in the same vein. If you prefer pide and soup, try the alleyways behind the harbour.

BODRUM★

Muğla Province − Map page 227 − Pop 25 000
167km from Marmaris − 157km from Ephesus − 254km from İzmir

Not to be missed
The Castle of St Peter and the views of the bay.
A boat excursion in the Gulf of Gökova.
And remember...
Walk around the town in late afternoon, when the sun's rays are less fierce!
Rent a scooter, take along a picnic basket and enjoy a day on the Bodrum peninsula.

Those who visited Bodrum in the 1980s will probably be disappointed by how much it has changed. What was once a pretty fishing village nestling in a turquoise bay has transformed itself into a large tourist town which is continuing to expand over the surrounding hills. But it is far from being another Kuşadası. Nowhere do the abominable concrete blocks deface the coastline. In Bodrum, local architecture has held its ground and the traditional white cube-shaped houses, with one, or at the most two storeys, serve as a model for the village-like hotel complexes with their profusion of bougainvillaeas and oleanders. It is true that the atmosphere has changed, but it is still pleasant to get lost in the quayside alleyways beneath the Castle of St Peter. The fortress's dark walls are a contrast to the dazzling whiteness of the city. Isolated on its peninsula in the middle of the bay, as if laid on the sea, the crusader stronghold watches over the marina's numerous sailing boats and the comings and goings of the ferries.

The city of Mausolus and Herodotus
Founded by the Dorians toward the beginning of the first millennium BC, **Halicarnassus** became one of the richest Dorian cities. In 480 BC, Xerxes, the Persian, took control of it but Queen Artemisia's influential relations with the conquerors enabled the city to continue developing. Halicarnassus in turn joined the confederation of Delos. The Greeks then ceded it once more to the Persians and the Satrap of Caria, **Mausolus** (377-353 BC), who made it the capital of his province. It was the golden age of the city and ranked among the greatest maritime powers of the Aegean. It was embellished with fortifications and prestigious buildings such as the Palace of Mausolus (since disappeared), and especially, the funerary monument that the king had built for himself − one of the Seven Wonders of the world − the name of which (mausoleum) lives on into posterity.

After the apogee, the decline: with the death of Mausolus, the political and economic power of Halicarnassus ended. In 334 BC,

The father of travellers
It was in Halicarnassus that Herodotus (484-425 BC), the Greek historian, was born. Cicero considered him to be the "father of history". A historian and great traveller, he was one of the first to roam the planet, from the Pillars of Hercules (Gibraltar) to the banks of the Indus, by way of Siberia and the deserts of Libya (Africa). His work, *History* (the only one to have reached us), is the oldest travel writing known, historical but also ethnographic. It constitutes an exceptional account of daily life in the ancient world, the beliefs and morals of different peoples, but also of the greatest monuments of the period, whose descriptions have been of great assistance to archeologists. The whole work is written in a simple and congenial style, full of enthusiasm and humour. It is a model of its kind, and one that has never aged.

the city refused to subject itself to Alexander the Great, who set fire to it. When it joined the Roman province of Asia, it was nothing but a small town which had long lost its strategic role.

At the beginning of the 15C, the city's appearance changed with the arrival of the crusaders: the ruins of the acropolis and the Palace of Mausolus became the foundations of an imposing fortress – the Castle of St Peter – (whose Latin name, *Petrum*, gave rise to Turkish *Bodrum*). To build it, the crusaders did not hesitate to use the legendary stones of the mausoleum, destroyed a century earlier by an earthquake. In 1522, it was the turn of the city's last vestiges to be used by the citizens of Rhodes to reinforce the ramparts, to block Süleyman's advance towards their island and the Carian coast. In vain: Halicarnassus was conquered in 1523 and the whole shore handed over to the Ottomans.

The town

Allow at least a half-day,
dedicating most of your time to the Castle of St Peter.

Set in the middle of the bay, the Castle of St Peter divides Bodrum in two. Beyond its walls, to the east stretches the old city's maze of alleyways, the centre of commerce and night life. Restaurants, night clubs, souvenir and handicraft shops have invaded the whole area all the way to the pebble beach where the café tables on the cobbles face the reflections of the medieval walls. In the evening, this seems to be the gathering place of the entire population of Bodrum. A mass of fluorescent T-shirts, provocative shorts and mini skirts en route to the trendy *Halicarnas* discotheque.

To the west (the port), beyond the garland of *gület* squeezed along the quayside, lies the far quieter residential port of Bodrum. Houses and small flower-bedecked hotels huddle around the Halicarnassus Mausoleum, between two grocery shops

The Castle of St Peter watches over the schooners

B. Morandi/DIAF

Bodrum

The mausoleum of Mausolus

Inspired by the tomb of the Nereids, long the glorious symbol of the city of Xanthos (later to become the pride of the British Museum, see p 389), the tomb which Mausolus undertook to build for himself, in 355, was to be Halicarnassus' most prestigious monument. Built on a podium of 38x32m, it consisted of an immense Ionic colonnade supporting a pyramidal roof of 24 stars. Crowning the summit, Mausolus and his wife Artemisia held the reins of four bronze horses. The whole structure measured 55m from top to bottom. The colossal monument remained Halicarnassus' emblem for more than 16 centuries until an earthquake destroyed it in the 14C. In 1402, the crusaders dismantled it to build the Castle of St Peter, followed by Rhodes (1522) which plundered its funerary chamber. Newton saved a few modest elements of this jewel of architecture: a frieze and some funerary furnishings now in London.

and a hardware store. The more exclusive hotels are located on the heights, at the western extremity of the city. Almost nothing is left of the monument which was the glory of the Carian city. Today, the **Mausoleum of Halicarnassus** (B1) *(8am-12noon/1pm-5pm; free entrance)* is simply a pile of uneven rocks, in spite of the honourable efforts of Swedish archeologists. It is however possible to get an idea of the size of the building from the traces left by its walls. In the little pavilion to the left of the entrance, there are two **models**, one of the ancient city, the other of the mausoleum. The adjoining portico also houses several elements of the **lower frieze★★** which ran around the monument (three are originals, the others are mouldings. The discoverer of the mausoleum, English archeologist Charles T. Newton, transferred the rest to the British Museum in 1857.)

The Castle of St Peter★★ (Bodrum Kalesi)

8am-12noon/1pm-5pm. Entrance fee. Two tours are possible: one short (in green), the other long, (in red). It is best to take the second one, allowing a complete tour of the castle.

Erected by the Knights Hospitallers, or Knights of St John of Jerusalem, the Castle of St Peter is the last crusader castle on Turkish soil (1402). Strolling amidst its walls is a real pleasure. The battlements are well preserved and give magnificent views over some of the world's greatest sailing ships moored in the bay. Furthermore, the castle also hides the remarkable **Underwater Archeology Museum★★**, with a collection of wrecks of ancient vessels and their cargoes.

Unfortunately, several rooms are closed, due to a lack of personnel, and certain re-enactments are reminiscent of a wax museum: for example the **Gatineau Tower** (which served as a prison), where one's descent into the dungeon is enlivened by red lights, pre-recorded moans and wax hands stretching out through the iron bars! There is an additional fee to visit the more interesting rooms, making this an expensive visit compared to other Turkish sites.

Despite all this, the castle is well-worth the trouble. It is entered via a narrow ramp between the walls of the building's outer perimeter. This leads to the **lower courtyard**, a vast esplanade enlivened by a drinks stand and a few craftsmen (glass-maker and potter wearing period clothing). On the left, a portico housing large jars runs the length of the wall, while on the right stands the **Chapel of the Hospitallers★**, an attractive building restored in 1519 which encloses a beautiful collection of objects – copper bars, plates, jars – found in a pair of 2 500 year old shipwrecks.

One of the castle's most interesting rooms is one which houses the remains of a 10C **Fatimid shipwreck★★** *(entrance fee)*, raised with its cargo of broken glass and amphorae. This ship was carrying a cargo of glass shards towards the Balkans and

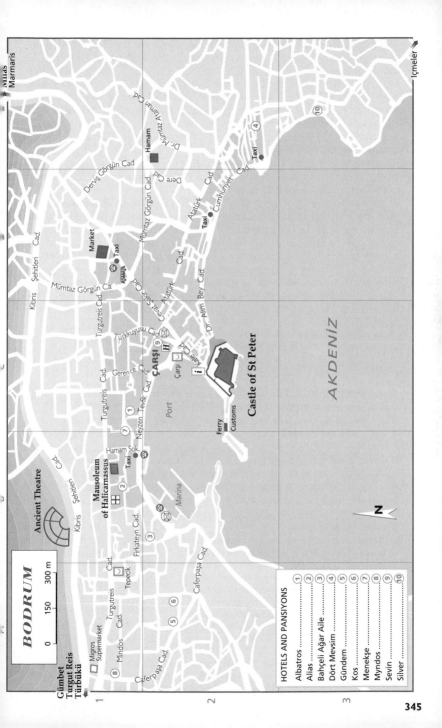

BODRUM

0   150   300 m

Ancient Theatre

Mausoleum of Halicarnassus

Castle of St Peter

AKDENİZ

Port

Marina

Gümbet
Turgut Reis
Türbükü

Milas
Marmaris

İçmeler

Migros Supermarket

Market

Hamam

Hamam

HOTELS AND PANSIYONS

Albatros	①
Alias	②
Bahçeli Ağar Aile	③
Dört Mevsim	④
Gündem	⑤
Kos	⑥
Menekşe	⑦
Myndos	⑧
Sevin	⑨
Silver	⑩

345

southern Russia, where glass recycling techniques were known. The intact glassware *(in the display case at the back of the vessel)* was transported in the wicker baskets, which are visible in the hold.

On the left of the chapel, another ramp and a series of steps lead to the **upper court-yard**. Overlooked by the **Tower of France*** and the **Tower of Italy**, its walls are partly built from stones originally belonging to the mausoleum. The Tower of France *(Glass Hall)* assembles another superb collection of glassware found in a 10C wreck. Unfortunately, the darkness protecting the colourful objects is a bit too dense, and it is difficult to see anything very much.

The two towers are linked by a curious pavilion in grey marble, added in the 16C, hiding a pretty **rib-vaulted room****. It opens out onto a terrace which has a beautiful **view**** of the Bay of Bodrum.

At the southeast point of the peninsula rises the large **Tower of England**, the farthest one from the castle. Notice the **coat of arms** sculpted on the façade and the unusual **statue of the lion** embedded in the wall on the right. Inside, a medieval dining hall has been recreated, with all of its furniture – tables and bulky chairs, window benches, etc – where visitors are invited to taste some wine. Although it is somewhat anachronistic, the reconstruction is authentic.

From here, the lower courtyard is reached by the **sentry walk**, toward the north. On the way down, there are several **ancient anchors** (large stones pierced with holes) assembled at the foot of the wall that is supposed to be the only visible remains of Mausolus' palace (4C BC).

The Bodrum Peninsula

One day excursion,
including lunch break, a nap and a swim.

If you wish to swim and see the Greek windmills which straddled the hills of the region, you should explore the Bodrum peninsula, going either west or north *(the following selects the latter)*. The state of the road following the coastline is quite uneven, but you will not encounter any particular difficulty, whether travelling by car or moped.

It is best to travel in the interior of the peninsula, which is less urbanised than the coast. On the crest of the barren hills, a few windmills, painted white and without sails, appear scattered in geometric patterns among the circular tombs of the Ottoman era, similar to Roman tombs. On the coast, the proliferation of concrete is making the villages and the beaches lose a bit more of their charm every year. However, the atmosphere is pleasant and it is a welcome change from the tumult of Bodrum.

■ Beyond **Türkbükü** and its small white houses is the broad **bay of Gündoğan**, one of the peninsula's most beautiful beaches. A fine place for a swim, even if a pontoon, where pleasure boats dock, divides the beach in two.

Sponge "fishing"

At the beginning of the summer, in the small ports of the peninsula, it is still possible to see the docks covered with sponges laid out to dry by divers. Until 1986, the sponge (*sünge*) was their main source of revenue and had been since Classical times. However, a disease ravaged the sponge beds, forcing the divers to rent their *tirandil* to tourists for sea excursions. A less lucrative profession, but less dangerous. Sponges, which live 10-70m below water, are not fished but picked. The sponge "fisherman" is a diver, linked to an air pump by a simple hose which the Turks have named a "water pipe". Risking his life, he spends 2-3 hours underwater.

■ Farther away, the pleasant village of **Turgut Reis** stretches out at the foot of the mountains with their scattered windmills. A few flower-decorated hotels line the beach with their woven willow sunshades. Brightly-coloured fishing boats slumber in the harbour, while the wooden caiques wait patiently to take passengers on pleasure trips.

■ Finally, **Ortakent** is quite appealing. Its old **Greek houses** are shaped like towers, their golden stonework set off by white window-frames. The prettiest are in fact outside the village, on the flanks of the hills.

■ Bodrum is reached by way of **Gümbet**, a Las Vegas-on-sea, Turkish style, with more casinos and night clubs packed together than anywhere else in the country. A fine wall of pine trees protects the beach, the place's only interesting asset.

Making the most of Bodrum

COMING AND GOING

By bus – The bus station is very central, a few minutes away from the harbour and shopping district (D1). It has a left-luggage office. For İzmir via Selçuk: one bus per hour 24 hours a day (journey time: 4hr). For İstanbul via Bursa: 4 buses between 12noon and 10pm (journey time: 13hr). For Fethiye via Dalaman: one bus every two hours. For Antalya: one bus in the morning, another in the evening. **Pamukkale Turizm**, ☎ (252) 316 06 50 / 316 66 32. **Varan**, ☎ (252) 316 78 49 / 316 30 08.

By shared taxi – Dolmuşes run from the bus station to the airport, Gümbet and the villages on the peninsula.

GETTING AROUND

Bodrum is a dense maze of small alleyways which it is very difficult to get around by car. It is also important to bear in mind that a large part of the harbour is pedestrian-only. The best means of transport is by scooter or moped, which is also a good way to visit the peninsula.

Renting a bike – Several rental companies hire out scooters and bicycles at the harbour, towards the castle and in Atatürk Cad (D2).

By rental car

By rental car – All the car rental companies are in Neyzen Tevfik Cad (C2). **Nezoz Tour**, Neyzen Tevfik Cad 232/B (C2), ☎ (252) 316 80 74 / 316 14 98. Also organises yacht cruises. **Budget**, 86/A, ☎ (252) 316 73 82, Fax (252) 316 30 78. **Avis**, 92/A, ☎ (252) 316 19 96, Fax (252) 316 58 80.

ADDRESS BOOK

Tourist information – At the harbour, very near the castle, adjacent to the police station (C2). 8am-12noon / 1pm-5.30pm. You could not wish for a better reception (all languages spoken), but the documentation leaves a lot to be desired. ☎ (252) 316 10 91, Fax (252) 316 76 94.

Bank / change – Several banks and currency exchanges in Kale Cad, the shopping street which starts from the tourist information office and runs parallel to the quayside. At no 7 in this street, **Bodrum Döviz** offers very good rates. Open every day in summer, closed on Sundays in winter. Two banks next door: **Vakıf Bank** and **Y. Kredi Bank** (opposite).

Main post office – Cevat Şakir Cad (in the street running from the town centre to the harbour) (C2-D1). Converts currency and cashes travellers' cheques.

Medical service – Public hospital, Turgut Reis Cad. Behind the mausoleum. **Medicare clinic (Bodrum Medical Center)**, 4 Hamam Sok. On the corner of Neyzen Tevfik Cad and Hamam Sok. Open 24 hours a day, English spoken, ☎ (252) 316 70 51.

Consulate – British Consulate, Kıbrıs Şehitleri Cad, Konacık Mevkii 401/B, ☎ (252) 317 00 93 / 94, Fax (252) 317 00 95.

Airline company – Turkish Airlines, Neyzen Tevfik Cad 202. Reservations and ticket sales.

Laundry – Minik Laundry, 236/C Neyzen Tevfik Cad (C2). Near the entrance to the marina and a few metres away from Hertz; you can leave your laundry and pick it up 3 hours later. Around US$8 per load.

WHERE TO STAY

The quietest places to stay are in the west of town and in the hills to the east.

• In the west
Between US$15 and US$25
Pension Bahçeli Ağar Aile, 1402 Sok 4. Take the street at right angles to Neyzen Tevfik Cad, near no 190, ☎ (252) 316 16 48. ᵃ⅂ ✕ A very attractive house surrounded by greenery, where the pleasant atmosphere is matched by the hospitality of the proprietors. Guests have access to a kitchen.
Pension Alias, Neyzen Tevfik Cad Saray Sok 12, ☎ (252) 316 31 46. ᵃ⅂ ⤵ Reached via an alleyway running at right angles to Neyzen Tevfik Cad near the Kocadon restaurant. This quarter is a real labyrinth, so make sure you remember the way. Spacious, well-equipped guest house with a sun-drenched terrace.
Pension Menekşe, Menekşe Çıkmazı 36 (from Neyzen Tevfik Cad, take the alleyway near Lowry's Pub, where it is signposted), ☎ (252) 316 58 90, Fax (252) 316 69 34 – 7rm. ᵃ⅂ cc Tucked away in a maze of alleyways, this guest house is right in the heart of town, and perfectly quiet despite its central location. Smothered in greenery, the garden contains an arbour covered in grape vines. Simple, immaculate rooms. The very friendly proprietor organises scuba diving trips out to sea.
Pension Sevin, Çarşı Mah, Türkkuyusu Cad 9, near the mosque, ☎ (252) 316 76 82 / 316 06 00 – 27rm. ᵃ⅂ ✕ A very pleasant place, both central and quiet. The immaculate, quite comfortable rooms are set around a garden shaded by a creeping vine, where all the meals are served. Attractive decoration, roof terrace, laundry, post office next door, very friendly welcome and very reasonable prices.
Hotel Albatros, Çıkmak Sok (first street after Lowry's Pub, in Neyzen Tevfik Cad), ☎ (252) 313 70 70 – 17rm. ᵃ⅂ ⤵ A small, very quiet and well-kept hotel but breakfast is not served here. Quite cosy atmosphere; peaceful and clean, with comfortable rooms, but the welcome, although not at all unpleasant, is very scant.
Around US$30
Hotel Gündem, Eski Çeşme Mah, Caferpaşa Cad 6, ☎ (252) 316 23 42 / 316 99 60, Fax (252) 316 18 21 – 70rm. ᵃ⅂ ✕ ⤵ Very close to the Kos hotel (below), the Gündem has the same qualities as its neighbour, at a much better price.
Around US$60
Hotel Kos, Eski Çeşme Mah, Caferpaşa Cad 3, ☎ (252) 316 81 43 / 44, Fax (252) 316 81 46 – 70rm. ᵃ⅂ ▤ ⤵ ✕ ⤵ cc A short walk from the marina, but in a peaceful spot. A spotlessly clean establishment, combining the standards of a hotel with the nonchalance of a holiday home.
Hotel Myndos, Mindos Cad, near the "Migros" supermarket, ☎ (252) 316 30 80, Fax (252) 316 52 52 – 71rm. ᵃ⅂ ⤵ ✕ ⤵ cc A very pleasant and well-planned hotel, consisting of attractive white houses set around a vast swimming pool. Everything is very trim: the wooden window shutters, the trees and the flowers decorating the walls. Likewise, the welcome is efficient and very friendly (young English-speaking staff). The rooms are comfortable and spacious (immaculate bathrooms). It is a real pleasure to take breakfast on the terrace, under the laurel trees which shade the swimming pool. Good but very much out of the way.

• In the east
Around US$15

🏨 **Pension Dört Mevsim**, Zeki Müren Cad 23, ☎ (252) 316 27 43. 🍴 In a quiet spot, 100m from the Halikarnas discotheque. A very pleasant guest house, opening onto a flower-covered terrace where you can enjoy the view of the sea over breakfast.

Over US$25

🏨 **Hotel Silver**, İçmeler Yolu 116, ☎ (252) 316 12 34 / 316 26 39, Fax (252) 316 12 34 – 18rm. 🍴 📧 🔌 ✗ 🆑 🔌 Perched on a small hill overlooking the bay, 50m from the quayside opposite the castle, this small hotel enjoys the advantages of the town centre without any of the disadvantages. It is run by a very friendly family, and if you're looking for quality, this is the place to go.

• Gümbet
Camp sites

There are no less than 5 camp sites on the Bodrum peninsula, but we will only recommend one of them: **Zetaş camp site**, in Gümbet, ☎ (252) 316 22 30. 🍴 ✗ 🔌 Located 3km from Bodrum, it can be reached by dolmuş from the "otogar" (in the direction of Gümbet, get off at the terminus). Spacious site, well shaded, fairly green and overlooking the sea. This place naturally attracts many visitors, so it is quite noisy. US$8 per pitch.

Between US$15 and US$25

Hotel Amca, 8 Büyük İskender Cad, ☎ (252) 316 10 20 / 316 97 19 – 24rm. 🍴 📧 🔌 Near the Gümbet dolmuş stand. This quiet hotel, with its clean rooms (and mosquito nets) and pleasant service, is ideal for small budgets. (Beware: soap and towels are not provided).

Between US$25 and US$45

Hotel Siesta Aparts, Değirmenler Altı, ☎ (252) 316 97 55, Fax (252) 316 97 53. 🍴 📧 ✗ 🔌 🆑 🔌 Next door to the Club Hotel Flora (below). Set out like a local village. Access to rooms is via little bridges surrounded by greenery. A very pleasant and restful place.

Hotel Paloma, Zümbül Sok 60, ☎ and Fax (252) 316 56 70 / 316 03 96 – 50rm. 🍴 📧 🔌 ✗ 🆑 Same concept as the one above. Attractive rooms opening onto a well-kept garden.

Between US$45 and US$60

Club Hotel Flora, ☎ (252) 316 82 00, Fax (252) 316 44 99. Near the Amca hotel – 56rm. 🍴 📧 🔌 ✗ 🆑 🔌 🔌 🆑 Away from the hustle and bustle of the seafront, this very comfortable, well-equipped hotel (with Turkish bath) is a good place to relax.

EATING OUT

The narrow shopping streets of the town centre are lined with little restaurants offering the classic menu of kebab-pide-salad at unbeatable prices. They are all open almost 24 hours a day.

Between US$8 and US$15

Mausoleion, Neyzen Tevfik Cad Tepecik Camii Yanı (C2), ☎ (252) 316 54 94. For a large meal or just a sandwich, depending on your appetite. On the menu: pizzas (Italian style), döner kebabs, omelettes, pasta and hamburgers.

Mystic Pizza, 140 Neyzen Tevfik Cad (C2), ☎ (252) 313 09 90. A large choice of Italian dishes and pizzas. Pleasant terrace and speedy service.

Captain Hiko, 196/A Neyzen Tevfik Cad (C2), ☎ (252) 316 17 69, Fax (252) 316 72 85. Pide and kebabs are served by attentive waiters in a pleasant orchard, or in the tastefully decorated inside dining area.

The Garden, Cumhuriyet Cad 80 (D2), ☎ (252) 316 56 38. Go through the rather noisy dining area and you will come out onto a vast terrace with a breathtaking view of the castle. There are even tables on the beach. The service is friendly and efficient, the menu varied and very satisfying (grilled fish, vegetable gratins etc).

Over US$15

🏨 **Şalvarağa**, Şalvarağa Cad, ☎ (252) 316 83 11. Perched on the hill to the east of the town, at the end of a short track (signposted), this restaurant has a superb terrace overlooking the bay. On the menu: tandir-style fish, which you can sample while admiring the view. The sunset over the bay is a breathtaking sight not to be missed!

🏨 **Kocadon**, 1 Saray Sok, behind the boutique of the same name which sells very tasteful furniture and objects (this is rare enough to deserve a mention...) (C2), ☎ (252) 316 37 05. Slightly set back from Neyzen Tevfik Cad. The atmosphere is refined and the delicious food (traditional dishes) is served in a pleasant wooded garden. Book ahead. Only open in the evening.

Çobanyıldızı, Neyzen Tevfik Cad 172, opposite the marina (B2), ☎ (252) 316 70 60. cc A very pleasant and peaceful restaurant (quite a rarity in Bodrum) set in a very simple old house and decorated in a rustic, plain and tasteful style with kilims, beams and fireplaces. Diners can enjoy fine traditional Turkish food on the harbourside terrace to the gentle strains of soft music.

Bodrum Köftecisi, Çarşı Mah, Türkkuyusu Cad 4 (C2), not far from the mosque, ☎ (252) 313 92 03. A tiny, simple and charming restaurant, far from the noise and bustle of the harbour with two terraces, one above the other, set around a large tree. "Köfte", chicken brochettes, yoghurt with cucumber, rice. Little choice, but good and very cheap, especially for Bodrum. Closed on Sundays.

HAVING A DRINK

Bars / nightclubs – *Halikarnas*, to the east of town, near the castle, facing the bay (D2). One of the best-known nightclubs on the whole coast. Clubbers dance in the open air on a vast terrace surrounded by antique-style columns. An original setting and a good atmosphere.

Küba, Neyzen Tevfik Cad 62 (C2), ☎ (252) 313 44 50. cc "The" trendy bar in Bodrum, full to bursting every night, with a sort of garden raised above street level where you can dine (expensive). Rock, jazz and Latin-American music. You will not receive a very warm welcome, but there is a lively atmosphere.

Lowry's Pub, Neyzen Tevfik Cad 82 (C2), ☎ (252) 313 06 10. cc A big Irish pub with a warm decor and cosy little lounge area at the back. Rock, house and Turkish pop music; friendlier welcome than at the Küba.

West Side, Neyzen Tevfik Cad 54 (C2), ☎ (252) 316 94 29. A little bar with live music in the evening. Rock, jazz, reggae and Turkish pop music. Small covered terrace. Crowded and quite expensive, but a nice place to go.

OTHER THINGS TO DO

Boat trips – Bodrum is the departure point for many excursions (to Kos, Karaada or the beaches along the coast) and the famous "Blue Voyage" in the gulf of Gökova. Information can be obtained from the agencies at the marina or directly from the captains of the gülets moored along the quayside. The prices can always be negotiated, and the more of you there are, the easier it is.

Hi Tour, Otel Sami Karşısı 33/D, ☎ (252) 316 46 15, Fax (252) 316 65 18.

Scuba diving – *The Aegean Pro Dive Center*, 174/C, Neyzen Tevfik Cad, ☎ (252) 316 07 37, Fax (252) 313 12 96. Underwater adventures to suit all tastes: for beginners or more experienced divers, short-and-sweet or all day long (with picnic lunch on the boat). The centre provides all the equipment and has qualified instructors. Very attractive prices.

Karting – *Kart*, on the main road to Gümbet which passes to the north of Bodrum, near the "Migros" store (A1). The staff are very friendly. Rather expensive (around US$25 for 30min), but thrills guaranteed.

SHOPPING GUIDE

Carpets – *Orhan's Place*, Neyzen Tevfik Cad 40/B (C2), ☎ (252) 316 45 71, at the harbour. A little shop selling kilims and carpets. Generally quite expensive, but the goods are beautiful and good quality. Sayın Burku, the English-, French- and German-speaking owner will give you a warm welcome.

Galerie Anatolia, Çarşı Mah, Kale Cad 2 (C2), ☎ (252) 316 24 68. cc Also Alim Bey Cad 13 (C2), ☎ (252) 316 15 85. cc Two addresses near the mosque for this shop run by two brothers. Here you will find beautiful carpets and kilims, all supposedly hand woven, and lots of pretty cushions. Prices range from very cheap to very expensive. Try your hand at a bit of good-natured haggling in English or Italian.

M. P. Lejard/MICHELIN

Bodrum Bay

The bay of Ölüdeniz

E. Valentin / HOA QUI

THE MEDITERRANEAN COAST

The southeast coast is an orchard, a sun-filled garden. The climate is mild, the rays of the sun are intense, the plains and the slopes are green and the sea is a beautiful turquoise. Some of the ancient world's most beautiful cities were founded here, and maybe the brilliant white stone gave rise to the Turkish word for "Mediterranean", **Akdeniz**, which means quite simply the "white sea".

The **Taurus** (Toros Dağları), a huge barrier of mountains rising between the sea and the Anatolian plateau, stretches the entire length of the Mediterranean Sea, from the Aegean to the banks of the Euphrates. Like a rocky scarf warding off the winds of the open sea and the rigours of the Anatolian winter, the mountains protect a 1 075km-long seaboard sculpted with creeks, gulfs, caves and golden beaches. They protect the coast, but also contribute to its isolation: from Antalya to Antakya, only five main roads cross the mountains to the lands of central Anatolia. For long periods, the Taurus range was the impenetrable refuge of bandits, the unruly and all of those who fled the authority of the rulers. It is still the territory of the Yörük *(see sidebar, p 428)*, nomads who for years have lived among the rocks, and as time goes by their customs are changeless.

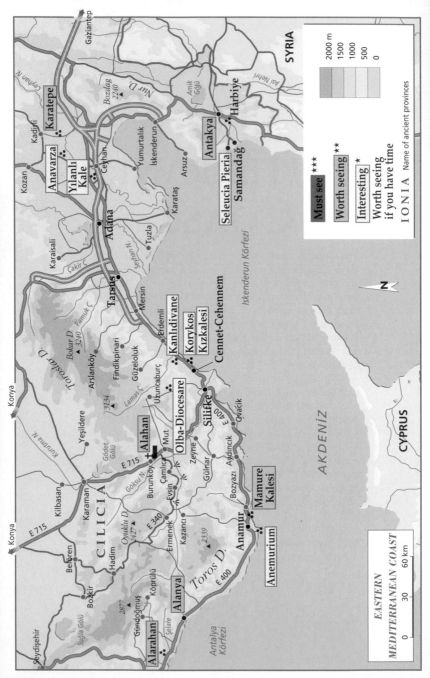

EASTERN MEDITERRANEAN COAST

0   30   60 km

SYRIA

Karatepe
Anavarza
Yılanlı Kale
Antakya
Harbiye
Seleucia Pieria
Samandağ

Gaziantep
Kadirli
Kozan
Bozdağ 2240 ▲
Nur D.
Amik Gölü
Ceyhan N. (Ceyhan N.)
Ceyhan
Yumurtalık
İskenderun
Arsuz
Asi Nehri
Karataş
Tuzla
Karaisalı
Adana
Tarsus
Mersin
Çakır Ç.
Seyhan N.
İskenderun Körfezi

Kanlıdivane
Korykos
Kızkalesi
Cennet-Cehennem

Erdemli
Fındıkpınarı
Güzeloluk
Bokar D. 3240 ▲
Pamuk Ç.
Arslanköy
Toroslar D.
Konya
3134 ▲
Lamas Ç.
Uzuncaburç

Olba-Diocesare
Alahan

Mut
Yeşildere
Gödet Gölü
E 715
Kurtma N.
Silifke
E 400
Ovacık
Aydıncık

Mamure Kalesi
Anemurium
Anamur

Burunköy
Çamlıca
Göksu N.
Zeyne
Gülnar
Bozyazı
Evsin
Kazancı

AKDENİZ

CYPRUS

Kilbasan
Karaman
Belören
Bozkır
Sugla Gölü
2877 ▲
Gündoğmuş
Şelale

Alarahan
Alanya

Oyuklu D. 2427 ▲
Ermenek
E 340
2339 ▲
Toros D.
E 400
Antalya Körfezi

Seydişehir

CILICIA

IONIA Name of ancient provinces

Must see ★★★
Worth seeing ★★
Interesting ★
Worth seeing if you have time

2000 m
1500
1000
500
0

N

354

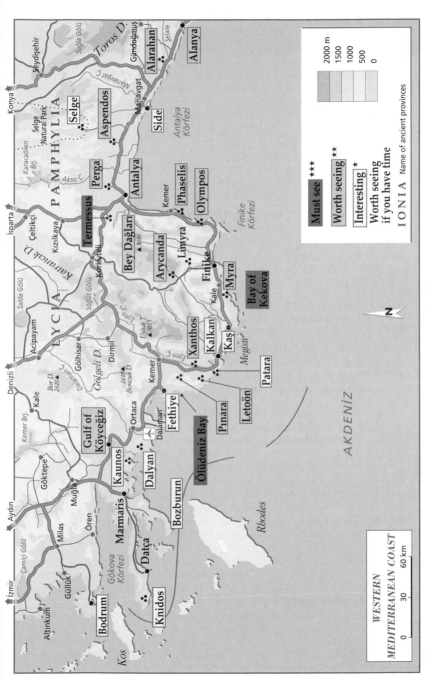

WESTERN MEDITERRANEAN COAST

0   30   60 km

Must see ★★★
Worth seeing ★★
Interesting ★
Worth seeing if you have time

I O N I A   Name of ancient provinces

2000 m
1500
1000
500
0

N

AKDENİZ

Rhodes

Kos

LYCIA

PAMPHYLIA

IONIA

Toros D.

Alarahan
Alanya
Şelale
Gündoğmuş
Seydişehir
Sugla Gölü
Konya

Selge
Aspendos
Side
Manavgat
Selge Natural Park
Karacaören Brj.

Perga
Antalya
Termessus
Phaselis
Olympos
Antalya Körfezi
Kemer

Bey Dağları ▲3086
Arycanda
Limyra
Finike
Myra
Kale
Bay of Kekova
Finike Körfezi

Isparta
Çeltikçi
Kızılkaya
Korkuteli
Söğüt Gölü

Kâtrancık D.
Eşen Ç.
Uyluk T. ▲3015

Xanthos
Kalkan
Kaş
Patara
Letoön
Pınara
Megisti

Salda Gölü
Acıpayam
Gölhisar
Dirmil

Denizli
Kale
Kemer Brj.
Bor D. ▲2430

Gölgeli D.
2418 ▲ Boncuk D.
Daleman Ç.
Kemer
Ortaca
Dalaman
Fethiye
Ölüdeniz Bay

Gulf of Köyceğiz
Kaunos
Dalyan
Bozburun

Muğla
Göktepe
Marmaris
Datça
Knidos

Aydın
Ören
Milas
Gökova Körfezi

İzmir
Güllük
Altınkum
Bodrum
Çamiçi Gölü

Manavgat Ç.
Aksu Ç.

Agriculture and tourism

To the west, between Marmaris and Alanya, is the land of tourism. In summer, foreign visitors and Turkish vacationers flock to the Lycian coast, which boasts more than 60% of the country's hotel capacity. Antalya is the meeting point of all travellers, whether they come by land or sea. At the gates of Lycia and Pamphylia, with some of the most beautiful archeological sites in Turkey, the city is the starting point for the many excursions to be enjoyed here, and its harbour is replete with schooners waiting to hoist their sails and set off on a **Turquoise Cruise** *(see "Practical information", p 118-119).*

The agricultural Mediterranean begins east of Alanya. From the fertile delta of Anamur to the plains of eastern Cilicia, the coast is an immense oasis, a kingdom of fruit and cotton. This part of the coast is one of the country's richest: oranges and lemons from Alanya, bananas from Anamur, and cotton from Çukurova. Every year, the area attracts more and more farmers and nomads seeking work.

From Neanderthal to Mustafa Kemal

It was on the Mediterranean coast, in **Karain** (north of Antalya), that the remains of a 100 000 year old Neanderthal individual were found. From the second millennium onward, several small kingdoms began to appear along the coast. Trade with the Mediterranean was born and Greek, the language of trade, spread throughout Anatolia. But with trade also came war: in the 6C BC, the Persians swept down the coast, expelling the Ionians, Hittites, Assyrians, and other colonisers to become masters of Asia Minor. The Mediterranean cities fought among themselves to retain their spheres of influence, alternating their fights against Persians or Greeks according to the opportunities of the moment. The arrival of **Alexander the Great**, in 333 BC, put an end to these conflicts with the Hellenisation of all of Asia Minor.

Pirates ahoy! – Unfortunately, his premature death created new troubles. Fortresses and citadels rose everywhere to protect against belligerent neighbours. Taking advantage of the rivalries isolating and weakening the largest cities, **pirates** began pillaging the entire coast.

The arrival of the valiant Roman general, **Pompeius** (67 BC) forced the buccaneers to disarm and their fleets were sunk in front of Alanya, their stronghold. After Alexander, the Romans were therefore the first to reunify Asia Minor. The coastal cities, now opened to the West, began to enter their golden age, covering their streets with sumptuous buildings to the glory of Rome.

Another day, another invader – Prosperity continued during the entire Byzantine period. The decline of all of the Mediterranean cities began with the attacks of the Arabs in the 7C, who were followed by Turks. Taking advantage of this weakness, the audacious pirates returned to further destabilise the Byzantine Empire.

From the 11C onwards, the coast entered into a long period of instability. Highly coveted, it was subject to the attacks of the Franks (crusaders), Turks, Seljuks, Armenians and lastly Byzantines, yet only the Armenians were able to constitute a small empire, from 1198 to 1375, covering eastern Cilicia. However, the assaults of the Karamanids and the Mamelukes of Egypt ruined the Mediterranean coast. In 1515, the Ottomans inherited a tired and spent land, ravaged by years of wars.

The agricultural revival – During the entire Ottoman period, the region plunged into lethargy. Its fortunes recovered only at the beginning of the 19C with the arrival of a new population: Arabs, Kurds and Egyptians settled on the shores and began exploiting the land. Agriculture developed and was further encouraged by Atatürk. From this point onwards, the face of Cilicia was transformed: the marshes became huge cotton fields and even the virgin and unruly flanks of Cilicia, not farmed for more than two millenia, began to be covered with bananas, figs, olives and vegetables. Today however tourism and the petroleum industry of the east (where Iraq's oil pipelines terminate) should be added to the list.

The negative effects of progress – Home to the writer Yaşar Kemal, the plain of Çukurova has become the symbol of this renewal. It has also created some serious side effects: urban sprawl and pollution brought about by the concentration of people in search of employment. The proliferation of concrete on the entire coast, apartments or vacation homes, as well as the growing number of pleasure boats in the waters of the Akdeniz, is detrimental to the environment and to the beauty of the region.

Armenia Minor
At the beginning of the 11C, Armenia, then Byzantine, was attacked by the Seljuks, the Mongols and the Turcomans who dangerously threatened the territory. Led by Prince Ruben, the population fled to Cilicia to found Armenia Minor (1080). The young kingdom prospered and experienced great growth with Leon II (1187-1219) by becoming a vassal state of the Byzantine Empire. "The Magnificent" and his successors turned Little Armenia into a brilliant land of exchange, a crossroads of cosmopolitan ideas and tolerance. Turned towards Europe and France in particular, the Armenians gave asylum to the crusaders heading for Jerusalem, where they also assisted them. The last dynasty was in fact French (the Lusignans). The kingdom fell in 1375 under the attacks of the Mamelukes.

Millenary provinces

Lycia, Pamphylia, and Cilicia; the map of the Mediterranean coast is filled with the Greek names of all those ancient provinces, reminiscent of Hellenic expansion, from the first Greek colonisers to the last Byzantines.

West of Alanya

To the west of the Taurus, at the meeting point between the Aegean and the Mediterranean, **Lycia** – the "land of wolves"– owes its name to sailors ("sea wolves"), fierce warriors of the Aegean who colonised it in the 8C BC. Few traces remain of their cities since the Romans, and then other conquerors, often totally erased them. The only testimony to their history and their way of life are the cities which they built for the dead. Lycians gave more importance to the afterlife than to terrestrial life – the tragic proof lies in the woeful history of their capital, Xanthos *(see p 388)*. This explains the existence of the monumental rock tombs, extraordinary façades of houses, palaces and temples sculpted on the walls of cliffs (such as Myra or Kaunos), inscribed forever in the rock. Even the sarcophagi resemble little houses with their roof-shaped lids; unless they represent the underside of a boat, which would evoke their origins.

East of Antalya stretches the great plain of **Pamphylia**, the "land of all people", whose lush shores attracted numerous colonisers, including Greeks, Persians and Ottomans. More than 40 cities prospered: Perge, Side and Aspendos, without forgetting the magnificent Termessos, suspended high up among the summits. With Ephesus and Aphrodisias, they are among the best preserved cities of Asia Minor, which rival without doubt those of Greece.

Pastoral and rugged Cilicia

Undoubtedly, the Lycian coast has the country's best beaches and its antique sites rank among the most significant for their memorable ruins and setting. Cilicia reveals many marvels: medieval fortresses rising in front of the sea (Anamur, Kızlakesi), a hermitage forgotten in the heights of the Taurus (Alahan), not to mention the omnipresent mountains. Sharp peaks, rocky plateaux, velvet valleys, ravines, the Taurus range has many facets; as do its stones, varying from the whitest limestone to the sombre basalt of the volcanoes.

The Cilicia of the cliffs – Past Alanya, the mountainside edges brutally towards the sea. This is where Cilicia begins and stretches for a further 700km. Less known to tourists, it nevertheless boasts some of the most sumptuous mountain scenery. Two Cilicias flank each other. The first one, rugged and harsh, is *Cilicia Tracheia*, a mountainous region, steep and impenetrable. Here, the mountains advance to the shore, a sombre wall which plunges into the sea. It is so intimidating that Alexander the Great chose to take the longer route inland to reach the eastern plains. The land was also awash with pirates, plunderers and slave traders making the region a perilous plan. Today, pirates have disappeared and the development of agriculture has given the region a more welcoming appearance. However, adventure is not lacking: between Alanya and Silifke, the road crosses ravines, hangs over steep hills, rides through the winding flanks of the cliffs and by-passes wild creeks. A never-ending waving line which stretches for nearly 300km. Since Alexander's army never moved about at night, avoid trying it for yourself! It could be very dangerous and it would be a pity to miss the scenery which is among Turkey's most beautiful.

The Cilicia of the fields – Beyond the delta of the Lamos (today's Göksu Nehri) lies *Cilicia Campestris*, gentle and pastoral. The mountains move away from the coast, allowing room for a swathe of fertile land, the cradle of fruitful economic and cultural exchanges. It has always been a region which has attracted the envy of its neighbours, Phoenicians, Romans, Mamelukes, up to the Ottomans.

Past İçel, the **Çukurova**, an immense marshy plain, spreads out at the foot of the Taurus. Modern technology has transformed it into the kingdom of cotton. This industry has overwhelmed Adana, a small city which has spread its tentacles in less than 20 years with the arrival of farmers in search of employment. It is also the land of forts – remnants of the ephemeral Little Armenia – majestic crenellated crowns set on the surrounding hills.

The Hatay

To the south, the Hatay region is one of Turkey's most industrialised areas and home to the refineries which collect the black gold from the Iraqi deserts. The last city before Syria, Antakya (Hatay), ancient Antioch, is almost as cosmopolitan as İstanbul because it is at the cultural crossroads of the East and the Mediterranean.

From the cape of Knidos to the gates of Syria, the Mediterranean coastline is filled with treasures, historic ruins and natural landscapes of unparalleled beauty. The unusual and the spectacular appear wherever you look. Follow in the footsteps of Darius, Alexander, Pompeius, and *Mehmet the Thin*, the falcon of the Taurus, to name but a few.

F. Levillain

Daylan, Lycian tombs

KNİDOS★
AND THE DATÇA PENINSULA

Muğla Province Map p 355
Datça: 75km from Marmaris
Alt 350m – Accommodation in Datça

Not to be missed
"Old" Datça.
The view overlooking the Knidos site and the peninsula's small creeks.

And remember...
Reach Knidos by boat from Datça or Marmaris.
Bring along drinking water and your swimsuit.

West of Marmaris, the Reşadiye Peninsula, also known as Datça, stretches like a long finger (90km) between two seas – the Aegean and the Mediterranean – pointing towards the Greek islands of Kos, Nisyros and Tilos. From Marmaris, the road crosses a tormented landscape offering beautiful **views★★**. It follows the crest of the peninsula, a cliff rising between the blue waters of the gulfs of Hisarönü and Gökova. Farther down, it dips into a dark green valley, flanked by two impressive mountains (over 1 000m). Then the hills become smooth and dry as the grass turns to straw and rocks level the ground. Past the last hamlet, the road turns into a dirt track that is long, dusty and bumpy. It runs by the sea whose waves break against the rocks all the way to the end of the peninsula. The weather is dry and hot. The small creeks below the sides of the trail entice the visitor to stop for a swim but unfortunately they may only be accessed by boat.

At the far end of the track, the ruins of the city of Knidos cling to the windswept hills. In the ancient port, schooners drop anchor while their passengers dip in the cool waters before going for a stroll through the ruins. In the car park, vehicles pant like old horses as they sizzle in the sun. This is when you realise that it would have been wiser to come here by boat!

Datça

Set in a bay overlooking the Gulf of Hisarönü, Datça is a small, quiet and unpretentious seaside resort with barely 5 000 inhabitants. It is here that people come to rest from the hectic pace of Marmaris. Since it is always windy, it is the ideal place for those wishing to sail. This explains the large port and the busy marina: bars and seafood restaurants share the space, catering mostly to Turks spending their holidays with their families. For foreign visitors, the main reason for coming to Datça is to use it as a starting point for a visit to Knidos, preferably by boat.

If you are travelling by car, be sure to visit **Eski Datça***, "old Datça", lost among the hills overlooking today's port. Depopulated in former times, this delightful hamlet of old stone houses and flowers is little by little being restored by rich Turks from İstanbul or İzmir who come here in search of peace and quiet.

Knidos*

38km from Datça. 8am-7pm in summer. Entrance fee. Allow 2hr to visit.

By car:

leaving from Datça (or Körmen, the disembarkation point north of the peninsula), there is a paved road for 24km, followed by 11km of a poor and rather rocky track. An ordinary vehicle is adequate but it is slow and troublesome (1hr trip). If you take the ferry back to Bodrum, allow enough time from Knidos (1hr also to the Körmen embarkation point).

By boat:

one day cruises are organised from Marmaris, including the visit of Knidos (departure around 9.30am, returning around 6.30pm.) However, it is wiser to depart from Datça; the trip is shorter and you will have more time to enjoy yourself, swimming and visiting the site (and the boats are much smaller!). Depart in the morning, return around 5pm. Information available at the Datça Tourist Office.

Isolated at the tip of the peninsula, the ruins of Knidos stand in a magnificent setting. They face **Cape Tropium***, a small island with a white lighthouse resembling a church. Since ancient times a dike has linked the land to this islet, creating a narrow isthmus which can be crossed in order to climb up to the lighthouse. From the top, the **view**** of the sea, the rocky coast and the terraced ruins lying in the sun-bleached grass is stupendous. In September, a cloud of white flowers covers the hills which the wind blows away like a swarm of fireflies.

Cnide, marble vestiges on the shore

M. P. Lejard/MICHELIN

A dividing issue

To protect their city from Persian invasion (546 BC), the people of Knidos had the idea of digging a trench between the continent and the Datça peninsula, in the area where it is narrowest (less than 1km), therefore isolating it like an island. However, the oracle did not agree, arguing that Zeus would have done it himself if he had judged it wise. The project was therefore abandoned and the entire peninsula fell to the Persians. The decisions of the gods are sometimes unfathomable.

A grand Dorian city

The last stretch of land extending into the sea before the shores of Africa, Knidos was a convenient stopping point on the route linking the Aegean to Egypt. Founded by the Dorian Greeks in the 7C BC, the city rapidly became a very active port, developing exchanges between the cities of the Mediterranean and the Egyptian coast.

In the 1C BC, the city was under Rome's tutelage before being conquered by the Cilicians who invaded the peninsula. From then on, the prosperity of Knidos gradually declined. The Byzantine period marked a brief renewal, as the remains of numerous churches can testify. However, the Arab invasions led to the definitive fall of the city. Reduced to a modest village, Knidos was completely abandoned at the beginning of the 20C. The current population comprises: the site's guard, the cook and the waiter of the (uninspiring) restaurant flanking the ancient port.

Aphrodite's city

Knidos is nothing more than a vast field of ruins, and it is quite difficult to imagine its original appearance. Only the size of the site helps you to picture its extent. In this labyrinth of stones, the main buildings are identified by a sign, but it is the beauty of the site that will make your visit truly enjoyable.

The isthmus created by the people of Knidos between the island and the peninsula has separated the canal into two small perfectly sheltered bays, housing on one side the **trading port** (to the south) and the **Trireme port** (warships) on the other. The latter has retained impressive remnants of the defensive **towers**.

As you arrive by boat, anchor is dropped in the bay of the ancient trading port, where the ruins of the old docks were levelled but now submerged. From there, you can see the city's terraced profile, due to the unevenness of the terrain.

Once you disembark, pass in front of the base of the **Temple of Dionysus**, which flanks the **agora**, completely invaded by weeds.

At the other end of the agora (*heading back towards the left*) a **Byzantine church** was erected. Only the base of the walls survives. Clear away some of the sand on the ground and you will discover, almost intact, floor **mosaics⋆** consisting of black patterns on a white background – a magical surprise which makes you want to take a broom and sweep the rest of the sand away!

Following the ramparts, you reach the extremity of the peninsula and a superb **panorama⋆** of the sea spreads out before you. Further up, on the right, the **Temple of Apollo** displays the modest remains of its colonnade and fragments of sculptures. On the right of the wall, the path continues to climb through the ruins of houses whose razed walls and floors are visible through the weeds. Finally, you reach the

The charms of Aphrodite

Inside the Temple of Aphrodite stood the famous masterpiece of the sculptor Praxiteles (4C BC), the "Aphrodite of Knidos", the first statue of a nude woman in Greek sculpture. The artist had created two copies, one dressed, the other not. The city of Knidos made the wise choice of purchasing the second one, offering its temple extraordinary fame, especially among visiting sailors! Unfortunately, the work disappeared in a fire, but two copies remain from the Roman period, one in the Louvre and the other in the Vatican.

last terrace, home of the **Temple of Aphrodite**, a white marble tholos where the only remains are the beautiful steps of the base. The **view**** over Cape Tropium is even more attractive than from below.

Returning over land to the trading port, you will pass in front of the ruins of a Doric gallery before discovering a **sundial** created by the Knidos' scholar, Euxodos (4C BC), a mathematician, physician and philosopher. Nearby, the **bouleuterion** (or odeon) spreads out its ruined steps before the blue waters of the trading port.

Another interesting ruin, a second **Byzantine church**, is concealed nearby (*towards the left*) and its shape is still discernible. This is a true treasure for those who are attentive: the ground is covered with beautiful **mosaics** and quantities of sculpted stones lie around. Last but not least, you reach the **lower theatre***, one of the site's best preserved buildings. Its 34 steps could accommodate 4 500 spectators.

Making the most of Datça

COMING AND GOING

By boat – You can go to Datça from Bodrum or Marmaris. Your best bet is to take a ferry in Bodrum that will leave you north of the peninsula in Körmen, 9km from Datça. From there you can take a shuttle to Datça. The Bodrum ferries (9 cars) make the trip daily at 9am, returning at 5pm (2hr crossing). One way ticket: approximately US$10, return ticket: US$15. You can also take the hydrofoil (45min crossing) but the hours are less desirable (departs late morning).
Bodrum Ferry Boat Association, in Datça, ☎ (252) 712 21 43, Fax (252) 712 42 39. Two shuttles daily to Bodrum at 9am and 5pm. There are also crossings to the islands of Kos, Rhodes and Simi.

By bus – Buses depart Marmaris hourly (trip: 2hr). The road, however, is long and difficult and the bus terminal in Datça is 1.5km out of town. In Datça, the company **Pamukkale**, ☎ (252) 712 31 01 / 712 33 02, operates 11 departures daily for Marmaris between 6am and 6.15pm. Two buses depart at the end of the afternoon for İstanbul, two depart for Ankara in the evening and three for İzmir, also in the evening. You'll find similar service at **Kamil Koç**, ☎ (252) 712 34 85.

By shared taxi – From Datça to Mesudiye, departs from the railway station (across from Hotel Soytok). The dol-

muş for Palamut Bükü departs from Yalı Cad, in town, in front of the entrance to Pamukkale agency.
By car – About 90min by car from Marmaris on a rather bad road, although in a very beautiful setting.

ADDRESS BOOK

Everything is centred around İskele Mah, the main street which cuts through the town.

Tourist information – Like the post office, the tourist information office is in the centre of town, in İskele Mah, ☎ (252) 712 31 63, Fax (252) 712 35 46. 8am-7pm in summer, 8am-12noon / 1pm-5pm in winter. Good welcome. The staff speak fluent English and a little French.

Post office – İskele Mah 1 Yalı Cad. Open 8am-midnight in summer, 8.30am-12noon / 1.30pm-6pm in winter.

Bank / change – *TC Ziraat Bankası*, 8.30am-12noon / 1.30pm-6pm. An automatic cash dispenser is available at **İş Bankası**, in İskele Cad (next to the Soytok hotel).

Market – Every Friday in the street next to the post office. You can find virgin olive oil, honey, basketry and local handicrafts here.

WHERE TO STAY

Most of the hotels are in the town centre, in İskele Mah. Some give directly onto the beach, but these are the least attractive.

The best guest houses can be found right at the end of the town, around the harbour (to the west).

• In town

Under US$9

Pension Tuna, Atatürk Cad, ☎ (252) 712 39 31 – 18rm. 🛏 If there is nobody there, try the grocery store next door. Set in a large building, devoid of charm, right in the centre of Datça, with direct access to the beach. Guests make their own meals, including breakfast. The rooms, double or triple, are very simple (tiled) and have small balconies. Ask for one of the rooms facing the sea – they are less noisy and more pleasant.

Around US$15

Pension Huzur, İskele Mah, ☎ (252) 712 33 64, Fax (252) 712 30 52 – 17rm. 🛏 In the quietest quarter, at the other end of town. A small, pleasant hotel with cool, tiled and spacious rooms. Breakfast is served in an arbour. The proprietor is planning to add a terrace overlooking the sea.

Hotel Soytok, İskele Mah 1 Yalı Cad 5, at the entrance to the town's main square, ☎ (252) 712 38 87, Fax (252) 712 30 65 – 40rm. 🛏 In a building lacking in charm but very well kept. Ask for a room on the top floor, with a view of the sea. All the rooms are spacious, full of light and clean. Bar on the ground floor. Open only in summer.

Between US$15 and US$45

Hotel Club Dorya, İskele Mah Esenada, ☎ (252) 712 35 93 / 712 36 14, Fax (252) 712 33 03 🏧 🛏 ⚏ ✕ ⚑ cc To the left of the port on a small peninsula. This hotel complex is very guiet, away from the noisy bars. Its well-kept, refreshing and charming atmosphere makes it an ideal place for total relaxation.

• In the area surrounding Datça

Camp sites

Ilica camp site, on the beach west of town. You can rent a bungalow (for approximately US$10 per day) or a tent (US$3 per day), breakfast included.

Camp Amazon, north of the peninsula. After Hisarönü (heading towards Datça), go right at the sign and follow the road 9km. ☎ (252) 436 91 11 /

436 91 59, Fax (252) 436 91 60, www.campamazon.com ⚏ ✕ ⚑ Open from May to late September. A washing machine and small supermarket are available for campers' use. This campground is far from everything and borders a pleasant wooded area. It's near a river that leads to a delightful little beach that is well protected from the wind. For tents and campers, expect to spend US$3 a day, and US$25 for a bungalow. The price for children ages 12-18 is only US$2 a day.

Around US$15

Badem Motel, in Palamut Bükü, ☎ (252) 725 51 83 / 725 52 86. Across from the large pebble beach. This simple and unpretentious hotel offers basic but clean comfort.

UCPA, in Hisarönü, ☎ (252) 466 63 32, Fax (252) 466 63 33. 🏧 ⚏ ✕ ⚑ ⚓ Close to a lovely – although windy – beach surrounded by mountains. The centre can accommodate up to 120 persons in double, triple or quadruple rooms. There are also many activities offered daily or weekly, such as sailing in catamarans, windsurfing, hikes, mountain biking. A "multi sport" package costs approximately US$200 a week full board. Open April to mid-October.

US$90

Golden Key Bördübet, 35km from Marmaris, on the road to the Amazon campground, ☎ (252) 436 92 30 / 436 90 88, Fax (252) 436 90 89. 🏧 🛏 ✕ 📺 ▤ ⚑ ✖ cc This sophisticated luxury hotel is located in an exceptional setting. For those who enjoy playing "paşa" there is nothing better than this nest hidden under the trees.

EATING OUT

There are a lot of little restaurants in İskele Mah and at the harbour, where you can eat well (simple cooking) and cheaply.

Under US$10

Imren Restaurant, İskele Mah, behind the dolmuş station, ☎ (252) 712 45 12. Well-ventilated terrace. Turkish pizzas ("lahmacun"), grilled meats and pide, all for a modest price. Clean and practical.

Between US$10 and US$15

Akdeniz Restaurant, ☎ (252) 712 38 84, at the harbour. Kebabs and a good selection of meze across from the gülets.

Emek Restaurant, Captain Place, Yat Limanı, Atatürk Cad, ☎ (252) 712 33 75 / 712 32 79. This family restaurant serves all sorts of meze and grilled fish. Acceptable service.

Yasu Bar, see below in the section "Having a drink".

• **In the area surrounding Datça**

A number of restaurants line the main road that runs along Palamut Bükü's large pebble beach. At **Dostlar** and **Liman**, meals cost around US$8. **Dolphin** and **Hadi Dedim** serve crayfish (expect to spend around US$46 a kilo), and **Kardeşler** offers grilled fish and meat.

HAVING A DRINK

Stop for a drink at the **Cafe Dadyadost**, to the right of the main street when going towards the harbour. It is set in an old stone house at the end of a small passageway and also serves as an art gallery. **Eclipse Bar**, across from the sea, on the corner of Atatürk Cad, ☎ (252) 712 43 10. Here you can listen to good funk, rock or reggae music. The bartender prepares your drink while he's dancing and there is always a festive atmosphere.

Bambu Bar, Yat Limanı. Calmer. Also provides Turkish and English breakfasts for less than US$3 as well as cruises to Rhodes and Simi.

At the **Turtle Bar**, on the north beach. Guitar music and Turkish songs are given priority.

Yasu Bar, İskele Mah Neyla Okyay Cad, ☎ (252) 712 28 60. This is the place the sailors come to, located in the higher reaches of town overlooking the harbour. Every evening there is a band that plays Turkish and western music. Also a restaurant.

Perched even higher, the **Koliba** will please those who love disco music.

OTHER THINGS TO DO

Excursions – Şeker Tours, Uslu Pasajı, facing the sea next to Bambu Bar. In summer, ☎ (252) 712 24 73 / 712 87 89, Fax (252) 712 84 27. In winter, ☎ (252) 712 30 17, Fax (252) 712 24 70. Organises cruises to the Greek islands.

Live shows – Concerts take place some evenings at Datça's amphitheatre, located on the point of the peninsula. Information available on site.

SHOPPING GUIDE

On the road to Cnide, take a left to go to **Çeşme Köy** (after the fork in the road towards Kumyer Mah). Some of the roads are still paved as in former times in this typical village. You can purchase virgin olive oil, honey and fresh almonds direct from the locals' homes.

Making the most of Datça

MARMARİS
AND THE BOZBURUN PENINSULA★
Muğla Province – Map p 355
167km from Bodrum – 128km from Fethiye – 96km from Dalaman airport
Pop 16 400 – Pleasant climate all year round

Not to be missed
Taste the delicious honey of the Bozburun mountains.
A boat excursion.

And remember...
Compare the prices of cruises and boat excursions.
Avoid the port and beach restaurants which are not only expensive
but mediocre too.

Marmaris nestles behind a deep bay, closed off by a large peninsula and rocky islets. A few decades ago it was still a modest village inhabited by sponge divers. Since then, the tourist industry has colonised the entire seafront west of the old port. Hotels, restaurants and discotheques have propagated along the beach creating a concrete land wall which the palm trees try to conceal with much difficulty.

Marmaris nevertheless retains some charm. A last vestige of its past, the Ottoman fortress overlooks the red tile roofs of the old city, a small maze of merchant streets where a walk is always enjoyable.

Around Marmaris, nature reigns supreme. Beyond the white cubes of the hotels (unfortunately more and more numerous), are a magnificent bay, creeks surrounded by primeval pine forests, clumps of oleander and prickly pears creating a wonderful blend of colour and fragrance. And all accompanied by a chorus of crickets.

A few traces of history
Nothing is left of the old city, the ancient Physcus, founded in the third millennium BC by Ionians arriving from Rhodes. It was, however, a busy port during the Carian period, and its prosperity endured during the Seljuk domination (13C) until the city was annexed to the Ottoman Empire. The small **fortress** dates from this period. Erected by Süleyman the Magnificent in 1522, it was used as a military base in his campaign against Rhodes. Today it houses a museum (*8am-12noon/1pm-5.30pm, closed Monday, entrance fee*). The **view** from the top is quite beautiful. Below, the old city (a pedestrian area) boasts a busy **bazaar** with boutiques huddled around the **İbrahim Paşa Mosque** (1783).

The bay of schooners
For a simple excursion lasting a few hours, including a swim, or for a cruise with friends over a few days, take a schooner. This is the best way to enjoy the attractions along the coast since many sites (including the best **beaches**) are not accessible by road.

Marmaris has become the country's most important harbour for pleasure craft, a departure point for all cruises (more so than Bodrum), where hundreds of sailboats gather. In summer, the city's population rises tenfold, and the streets become the theatre for some sort of incredible cacophony – echoes of discotheques and radios pulsating from the boutiques and restaurants.

Those who seek tranquillity and want to get to bed early will have to exile themselves in İçmeler and Turunç, smaller seaside resorts for the well-off and set at the
entrance of the bay *(10-15km west of Marmaris' centre)*, or even Datça, 75km away, on
the other side of Hisarönü Bay. There at least, they will be able to sleep without
having to endure the thumping sounds of techno music!

The Bozburun Peninsula★
One-day boat excursion. (See p 355)

Southwest of Marmaris, the Bozburun and Datça (or Reşadiye) peninsulas form
two long, almost perpendicular stretches of land, and enclose the great bay of
Hisarönü. The Bozburun peninsula points towards the Greek island of Rhodes (to
the south), while the Reşadiye – the longer one – stretches westward, towards the
island of Kos. Their jagged coasts hide the Mediterranean Turkey, more authentic
and imbibed with seemingly eternal serenity. The boat sails from village to village,
dropping its anchor in bays concealing ancient ruins. It is a real pleasure to explore
these coves, not so much for their ancient stones, but rather for their setting, wild
and peaceful, just right for a stroll or a swim, and far from the bustle of Marmaris.
The first stop, **Amos** *(allow 1hr on foot after the boat has docked)*, is a small site, located
at the entrance to the bay of Marmaris. Remains of an acropolis, a theatre and a
temple are visible, but most of all the spot offers a splendid **view★★** of the coast.
The boat continues its journey to **Çiftlik** *(second stop)*, a charming little hamlet set
near a very beautiful **beach★**, before reaching **Loryma** *(third stop)*, an ancient port
isolated at the tip of the peninsula, still retaining the ruins of a small 3C BC citadel.
Past Cape Kara, the boat continues along the coast towards the superb **Hisarönü
Bay★** *(fourth stop)*, now a conservation area. This is a perfect opportunity for a stroll
or bicycle ride in the surrounding pine forest.

Marmaris, a popular marina

C. Bolvieux/HOA QUI

The Cedar Islands (Şehir Adası)

One-day boat excursion. Departure from Taşbükü, 20km north of Marmaris. Head to Akçapınar and Gökova, then, after 10km, take the small road on the left, heading for Gelibolu (Çamlıköy) and Taşbükü.

In the deep bay of Gökova, the largest of the three Şehir islands, **Cleopatra Island** (or castle island), is a strip of land of 800x300m, covered with olive and pine trees concealing the ruins of the Hellenistic city of **Cedrae**.

Behind the walls (5-4C BC) still flanking the shores, you can see a small, well-preserved **theatre** as well as the columns of a **temple** and the apse of a Byzantine church. All around stand the ruins of a few houses together with their cisterns, whereas in the north of the island, the docks of the ancient port are just slightly beneath the water, only a few strokes away from the beach.

Cedrae was one of the many places where Cleopatra made legendary visits: this is where she is supposed to have fallen madly in love with Anthony and the latter is said to have filled the western beach with sand from the banks of the Nile. Its name? Cleopatra of course, the prettiest beach on the island.

But the legend (and the charm of the place) has turned Şehir into a somewhat overcrowded destination. Avoid public holidays, and come early in the morning or in the evening. That being said, in high season it is always crowded!

Making the most of Marmaris

COMING AND GOING

By bus – To get to the *bus station*, which is about 1km from the harbour, follow the signs to the "Otobüs Terminali". The main bus companies represented there are the following: *Kamil Koç*, ☎ (252) 412 29 91 / 412 29 92 in Marmaris, and ☎ (252) 455 20 69 in İçmeler. Services to İstanbul (7 departures per day), Ankara (1 departure in the morning and 3 overnight services which leave in the evening), and İzmir (every hour, 24 hours a day, US$8). *Varan*, ☎ (252) 412 09 79 in Marmaris and ☎ (252) 455 49 60 in İçmeler: services to İstanbul (3 departures per day) and Ankara (1 departure per day). *Pamukkale*, ☎ (252) 412 55 86 / 412 49 31, operates services to İstanbul (4 per day), Ankara (4 per day) and İzmir (1 per day).

Minibus services operate to the neighbouring villages: *Metro*, ☎ (252) 413 55 42 / 43, Fax (252) 413 03 85. Fethiye: every hour from 7.30am to 10pm. Köyceğiz, Dalyan, Dalaman, Göcek: every hour from 7.30am to 6.30pm. Antalya and the neighbouring towns: 4 departures per day between 9.30am and 10pm. Muğla, Milas and Bodrum: 3 buses in the morning, 2 in the afternoon.

By shared taxi – The dolmuş stand is adjacent to the marina (just opposite the *Kamil Koç* sales offices). Services to İçmeler and Armutalan only. 1 departure every 15min. Price: 50 cents!

By boat – The docks are at the entrance to the town. For Venice, it will cost around US$150 per car, US$15 per person and US$45 in taxes (price does not include cabins).

GETTING AROUND

Marmaris stretches out along the coast. It is easy to get around on foot, especially since the district around the old harbour is the only area worth visiting.

By rental car – Avis, 30 Atatürk Cad, ☎ (252) 412 27 71 / 412 64 12, Fax (252) 412 46 07.

Hertz, İskele Meydanı Anıt Apt 41/2, ☎ (252) 412 25 52 / 412 95 91, Fax (252) 412 31 15.

Budget, Kemeraltı Mah Ulusal Egemenlik Bul Girginç Apt, ☎ (252) 412 41 44, Fax (252) 412 57 74.

Europcar, Ulusal Egemenlik Bul Datça Yolu Kavşağı, 16, ☎ (252) 412 20 01 / 412 86 89, Fax (252) 411 29 60.

ADDRESS BOOK

Tourist information – At the harbour, 8.30am-7.30pm, 7 days a week, ☎ (252) 412 10 35.

Bank / change – Countless banks in Ulusal Egemenlik Bul, one of the main streets, exchange foreign currency and have automatic cash dispensers: **Esbank, Garanti, Pamukbank, İşbank, Yapı Kredi** and **Egebank**. Some offices are open until 11pm in summer. There is also a currency exchange at the point where this boulevard joins the seafront (Atatürk Cad).

Main post office – In the bazaar, ☎ (252) 412 19 51. Open until 8pm. Phone cards, currency exchange, travellers' cheques. Phone booths outside.

Medical service – Public hospital, on the road out of town in the direction of Datça, ☎ (252) 412 10 29. **Private hospital**, ☎ (252) 413 14 15.

Laundry – In the street with all the bars, opposite the Begonya hotel (see below).

Consulate – British Consulate, c/o Yeşil Marmaris Turizm ve Yat İşletmeciliği A.Ş., Barbaros Cad 11, Marina, ☎ (252) 412 64 86, Fax (252) 412 45 65.

WHERE TO STAY

Marmaris is a very noisy town in summer, unbearably so in places. The village of Armutalan, situated to the west and now engulfed by the suburbs of Marmaris, is more sheltered from the noise of the nightclubs. But if you're in search of peace and quiet and more charming surroundings, you will be better off in İçmeler or Turunç.

• Marmaris

Camp sites

Ziraatçılar Tatil Köyü, 5km south of Marmaris, ☎ (252) 411 00 23. ✕ ☉ Rents out small apartments, bungalows and tents for US$6 per day or US$8 with half-board.

Pekuz camp site, 20m from the one above, on the seafront, ☎ (252) 411 23 24. ☼ ✕ ☉ Rents out rooms and tents for US$9 and US$7 per day, respectively. Electricity and refrigerator. Every evening there is a concert of Turkish music in the restaurant, where clients can sample wild boar and grilled fish, and play billiards. The camp site has its own minibus to take clients into the city. Open from March to September.

Under US$15

Interyouth Hostel, Tepe Mah 42. Sok 45, ☎ (252) 412 36 87, Fax (252) 412 78 23. ☎ ☂ Washing machine. Terrace bar. In a very convenient central location, not far from the marina. Organises excursions to the bay of Marmaris and the island of Rhodes.

Between US$15 and US$30

☺ **Hotel Nergis**, Kemal Seyfettin Elgin Bul, ☎ (252) 412 66 68 / 412 66 69, Fax (252) 412 12 04 – 100rm. ☎ ▤ ☎ ✕ ☴ ☼ cc Although right in the centre of town, this recent hotel is very pleasant. It is well laid out and you will find all the comfort and quality of service of a major hotel. The naval-style architecture works rather well.

Hotel Yavuz, Atatürk Cad 34, ☎ (252) 412 29 37, Fax (252) 412 41 12. ☎ ☎ ✕ ☴ ☴ ▤ cc A hotel with no particular charm, but well run. A little noisy in the evenings on the side overlooking the avenue. Dinner consists of a very reasonably priced buffet on the terrace.

Between US$30 and US$45

Hotel Begonya, Kısayalı, Hacı Mustafa Sok 101, ☎ (252) 412 40 95, Fax (252) 412 15 18 – 10rm. ☎ ✕ TV ▤ cc A charming hotel with an inside courtyard and garden, wood panelling and lace curtains. A pity it's in the street with all the bars, where there's no escaping the noise.

• In Turunç

About 20km north of Marmaris, this little town is much quieter and more attractive than İçmeler, despite a few new buildings in the higher reaches. The seafront is home to a host of charming little restaurants. From Marmaris, you can get here by dolmuş or boat.

Under US$15

Çardak Pansiyon, Turunç Köyü, ☎ (252) 476 70 47 / 476 71 99. ⁌ ✕ A few metres from the sea. Friendly welcome and facilities for doing your own cooking.

Between US$15 and US$30

Hotel Malmen, Turunç Köyü, ☎ (252) 476 74 69 / 214 17 21. ⁌ ✆ ▤ ☒ A modern hotel, lacking in charm but well run, and located 20m away from the beach.

• İçmeler

Under US$15

Pension Eren, 4, Atatürk Cad, ☎ (252) 455 21 20. ⁌ A very clean guest house, run by a welcoming family. This guest house has the dual advantage of being in a quiet area but not far from the more lively districts. There is a constant stream of dolmuşes in the street, which is, in fact, the main highway between Marmaris and İçmeler.

Pension Podium, opposite the Pension Eren. Slightly smaller but with a similar atmosphere. Shower facilities on the landing.

Between US$30 and US$45

⊕ **Hotel Alinda**, 8, İstiklal Cad, ☎ (252) 455 33 16, Fax (252) 455 24 40 – 60rm. ⁌ ✆ ✕ ☒ CC Out of the way, almost isolated. With its attractive decor and wooden furniture, this hotel is rather like a chalet. Flawless service.

Hotel Navy, 14, İstiklal Cad, ☎ (252) 455 48 10, Fax (252) 455 48 11. ⁌ ▤ ✕ ☒ ✿ CC Open from April to October. A quiet hotel, set slightly back from the beach.

Hotel Mar-Bas, 91, Kayabal Cad, ☎ (252) 455 33 68, Fax (252) 455 33 69. Clean and comfortable, but no particular charm.

EATING OUT

• Marmaris

The rather mediocre quality and high prices make it very difficult to recommend a restaurant in Marmaris. Give the restaurants at the harbour a miss, and even more so the ones along the seafront, which are squeezed in between the sand and the impenetrable barrier of hotels. However, the best ones in the district are the **Hillside** and the **Kartal, at the harbour**. On the corner of the street with all the bars and the seafront, you can also sample what is reputedly the best **döner in town**. Lastly, in Gözpınar Cad, in the district around the bazaar, you will find some good, cheerful restaurants:

Palme, Tepe Mah 16, Gözpınar Sok. Lively atmosphere guaranteed. Closes very late. Very varied choice of meats: a must for kebab fans.

• In İçmeler

The street which runs parallel to Atatürk Cad is lined with several nice little restaurants.

Under US$15

İstanbul Restaurant, Kemer Altı Cad 4, ☎ (252) 413 45 23. In the old town, on the way up to the castle. This cheap and homely little restaurant, set in a lop-sided house away from the noise and bustle, is run by a lady from İstanbul.

• Towards Turunç

After İçmeler, on the road to Turunç, you can stop at the **Turkish House**, a completely isolated restaurant, perched on top of the hill. The food is rather frugal, but the setting makes it really worth a visit.

• Çetibeli (on the road to Muğla)

15min away from Marmaris by car or scooter, you will find several establishments offering excellent food in an idyllic setting.

Milli Parklar Genel Müdürlüğü, 10km from Marmaris, next to natural springs, on the edge of the forest. Very pleasant.

A little further on, a second **restaurant** (next to the police station, signposted) stands near a waterfall. A very attractive location.

HAVING A DRINK

• In Marmaris

There are countless bars and places to go out at night in Marmaris. If you want a peaceful place to go and relax, try the *Bar Panorama* in the old town (near the museum), ☎ (252) 413 48 35, which has a charming terrace offering a sweeping view of the harbour. Open until 1am.

In Barlar sokağı (the street of bars), you will be spoilt for choice, and there is no shortage of originality: in the *Downtown Club*, decorated like an old windmill and fitted with black light, you will be greeted with soap bubbles; or you can mingle with a crowd of young Turks in the *Ambiance Bar*; the party never stops in the *Irish Bar*; or if you're after a more intimate atmosphere, try the *Petit Bar*.

Ice cream – The city is full of traditional ice cream sellers offering ice cream made with gum arabic ("sakız"), but *Mado*, in Egemenlik Cad, really stands out from the crowd on account of its delicious Italian ice creams.

• In Turunç

Bob Bar, in Cumhuriyet Cad, ☎ (252) 476 78 13, Fax (252) 476 78 14. This bar is not just for night owls: it also offers paragliding, water-skiing, windsurfing, scuba diving (all certificates) and car rental.

OTHER THINGS TO DO

If you are in Marmaris in October, don't miss the *International Regatta*. It's a wonderful opportunity to see some very beautiful sailing boats.

Cyber café – *Kahve Evi*, Garaj Karşısı, Yat Limanı, ☎ (252) 413 72 37. On the seafront. Drop in for a coffee and cake while you surf the Web for US$4 an hour in an air-conditioned room equipped with 6 computers, a camera and printers.

Turkish bath – *Sultan Hamam*, Ulusal Egemenlik Cad Taşlık İş Merkezi, ☎ (252) 413 68 50 / 412 41 42. Opposite the statue of Atatürk. Sauna and fitness centre. Rather expensive (US$10 without the massage, US$15 with), but clean. Separate and / or mixed sessions for men, women and families.

Boat trips – The agencies around the harbour area have numerous packages on offer. However, since the boats are very large, they cannot really get very close to the sites. For Kaunos, in particular, the best solution is therefore to take a small boat from Dalyan; the smaller boats can drop you at the foot of the site (see p 372 and 373).

From Marmaris, you can take a trip to the Greek island of Rhodes (3hr journey, departure at 9am). A day-trip is probably the best idea, otherwise you will have a long wait at customs, and the taxes are high.

Insu Tour, *Anadolutour* next to the tourist information office, ☎ (252) 415 32 14.

Estun Tour, 50, Atatürk Cad, ☎ (252) 412 89 14 / 413 08 81.

Other excursions – In Turunç, *Muyara Tour Travel Agency*, ☎ (252) 476 78 36, Fax (252) 476 75 66 in summer, (252) 476 73 38 in winter. muyaratour@hotmail.com / safarileader@superonline.com: organises one-to three-day trips to Ephesus, Pamukkale, Dalyan or Rhodes, as well as blue cruises. Also offers scuba diving, rafting, and motorcycle and car rental.

Scuba diving – Diving enthusiasts will find all sorts of packages in the above agencies, for beginners and experienced divers. The marine depths around Marmaris are among the most interesting in Turkey.

Beaches – Don't swim in the sea at Marmaris itself. The surroundings are unattractive and the water not really clean. The beaches at İçmeler and Turunç are better and have facilities for various water sports. It is also worth bearing in mind that the boat trips often schedule a beach stop to give you a chance to swim and relax. Not a bad alternative for those not lucky enough to be able to go hunting for deserted creeks in their own boat!

SHOPPING GUIDE

The region is renowned for its *honey*, which can be found at the bustling *bazaar* in Marmaris, or – and at a much better price – at the roadside, where beekeepers often set up shop. Marmaris is also renowned for its sponges but intensive fishing is damaging the natural coastline. It is perhaps a good idea, therefore, not to encourage this trade too much.

In town, the big *Tansaş* supermarket in Ulusal Egemenlik Bul is open every day 8am-11pm.

THE GULF OF KÖYCEĞİZ★★
KAUNOS★
One day boat excursion departing from Dalyan
Map p 355
Dalyan (Kaunos) is 86km from Marmaris – 61km from Fethiye

Not to be missed
Facing Dalyan, the cliffs and their rock tombs.
The theatre of Kaunos – İztuzu beach.
And remember...
Bring along your swimsuit if a mud bath entices you.
Avoid walking barefoot (snakes!).
Bring along binoculars to get a closer look at the rock tombs.

A gulf? No. An immense marsh surrounded by mountains with blue slopes. It is an infinite maze of islets covered with tall grass, floating on the waters like a group of small clouds hovering above the sky's reflection. The gulf of Köyceğiz is dying: as the sea has receded over the years it has locked the gulf behind a barrier of golden sand curving between two waters. At the foot of the mountains, the marshes make way for a lake fed by rivers such as the Dalyan Çayı. The river finds a way through the marshes and forms meander after meander among the reeds, until it finally reaches the sea.

Marshes and shellfish
With fish from fresh or brackish waters, small blue crabs, wild duck and geese, the marshes of Köyceğiz abound with life. The gaily coloured boats of the local fishermen glide silently through the tall grass, in the maze of canals. The gulf can only be visited by boat; and the hidden treasures which lie about cannot be reached any other way. The ruins of Kaunos, an ancient Lycian city established on a small plateau overlooking the river's winding course, await you. Step aboard one of the small boats in Dalyan huddled along the dock (the *dolmuş boats*) and as you sit comfortably under the sheltering canopy, begin exploring the river, marshes and ruins.

■ **Dalyan**★ – *From Marmaris, take the road to Muğla, then take right turn heading towards Antalya. Past Yangı–Köyceğiz, turn right at the Dalyan sign. If you are coming from Fethiye, turn left at Ortaca (Dalyan sign).*
If you are sailing, you can go up the river with your boat. However, there are motorised dinghies which can pick you up at sea and take you to Dalyan, Kaunos and the İztuzu beach, through a wonderful itinerary across the marshes (impossible with a sailboat; see following paragraph).

Isolated on the southeastern side of Lake Köyceğiz, the peaceful village of Dalyan slumbers among the liquidambars, oleanders and orange trees. Its white houses and sidewalk cafés along the riverside make a charming sight, even if tourism has left its mark. Dalyan is the ideal point of departure for exploring the gulf and visiting Kaunos, concealed a little farther downstream.
However, Dalyan has its own treasure: a surprising **cliff** rising on the other side of the river, facing the village. From the steep bank, the eye is instinctively drawn upwards to the **Lycian tombs**★★ sculpted in the rock face – an unusual alignment of small façades in the shape of temples or houses. As the boat sails along the river, the sight of the necropolis becomes even more striking: the cliff is literally riddled with tombs, often simple niches (Carian tombs), alternating with groups of façades

(4C BC), sometimes incomplete, yet mastered like fine jewels. Imagine the stone-cutters of the period, ancient Tarzans dangling on primitive scaffoldings, with tools in hand! Equipped with binoculars, you will be able to see the decor of the upper tombs, often the most beautiful.

■ Kaunos★

Can be reached by boat from Dalyan, or, for those arriving by sailboat from the sea, by heading up the river from the İztuzu beach (see further on). Allow 15–20min of navigation and 1hr for the visit. 7am–8pm. Entrance fee.

The high point of your boat trip, the ancient city of Kaunos is as exciting for its ruins as it is for its scenery. Surrounded by mountains guarding the river, the ruins are lost among the rocks and the tall grass, and offer beautiful views of the gulf from many points.

The boat will leave you at the foot of the site, near a fish pond filled with bass and mullet *(arriving from Dalyan, be sure to be dropped off at the fish ponds and not before; there is actually another way of reaching the site by way of the acropolis, but it is almost inaccessible and less practical).*

A rich city of Caria

Kaunos was founded by the 10C BC at the latest. According to Herodotus, it was founded by the Carians, a local people, before being invaded by the Lycians who colonised the western part of Anatolia. In the 6C BC, the city attempted, in vain, to resist the advances of the Persians who partially destroyed it. It regained its freedom in the 4C BC, a period in which the Carian King **Mausolus** (377–353) surrounded it with a powerful network of fortifications (several portions are still visible in the upper sections, to the west).

Greek, then Roman occupation transformed the appearance of the city and marked a period of great prosperity, thanks to the salt curing and the slave trade. However, the city

Ancient joke

Built on the edge of a gulf which the floods slowly filled, Kaunos has always been surrounded by mosquito-infested lagoons which gave rise to widespread malaria among the population. A "green complexion", is an old joke (Hellenistic) which claimed that the climate in Kaunos was so healthy that even the dead walked about in the streets!

was progressively condemned by the silting up of its port and was finally abandoned at the end of the Byzantine period. The excavations, in progress since 1967, are led by Turkish archeologists.

Visiting the site

From the disembarkation point, a 100m path skirts an elevated area *(on the left)* containing **rock tombs**, hidden behind thick bushes. Past the hill, you reach a small marshy pond, the **Leeches' Pond**, modest remains of an ancient port mentioned by Strabo, now home to turtles and frogs.

Continuing higher up on the right, you reach the **Roman Theatre★**, an imposing hemicycle built in the Greek manner, accessible by two **side galleries** with cradle vaults (still visible). The stage building has almost disappeared, allowing a beautiful **view★** over the port and the remainder of the site. Admire the scenery by sitting on the steps of the **cavea★** (76m diameter), in the shade of the olive trees which create a somewhat romantic setting.

From the theatre, return to the pond to explore the heights of the north shore, filled with the remains of a **tholos**, a circular temple whose **dome** was found by the archeologists and reassembled on the ground. Further up, there rose a 95m-long

Noah's ark
One of the characteristics of the Kaunos site is the abundance of animal life: besides the pond's turtles, frogs and leeches, the river's fish and the herds of goats grazing among the ruins, numerous bird species can also be observed. Snakes live among the old rocks, and the stoa is periodically home to wasps and bees, whose continuous buzzing makes them easy to detect and avoid. Therefore, be careful, watch where you place your feet and hands!

Hellenistic **stoa** (eroded), an elegant colonnaded portico formerly decorated with statues overlooking the port. It was closed off to the east by a **Roman nymphaeum** dedicated to Emperor Vespasian (69-79 AD), still visible. Its southern façade bears a long **Greek inscription**: Port's customs.

From here, take the former main avenue – a **stairway** climbing up to the city's heights. Along the way, you will notice on the left the base of a small circular temple preceding the ruins of an **exercise hall**. The path then continues beside a pretty **Byzantine church**★, a pleasing 5C building which has retained part of its vaults and openings.

Lastly, further north *(on the left)*, rise the **Roman baths**★, one of the site's best-preserved buildings. A few fragments of the floor are still visible through the openings, as well as its heating system and a very beautiful **exedra**★. Its high, thick **walls** are a result of the transformation of the building into a stronghold during the Byzantine period.

Behind the baths, a path leads through cotton fields towards the north to the foot of the necropolis hill. It is therefore easier to see the rock tombs up close (however, the spectacle is much more captivating from the boat).

Finally, the athletically-minded can climb up towards the east, to the **acropolis**, perched on the summit of the hill overlooking the theatre. Nothing is left today, except a few meagre sections of its **Byzantine fortifications**, but it is worth the effort for the superb **panorama**★★.

■ **İztuzu Beach**★★ (İztuzu plajı) – *Access to this beach is by boat from Dalyan (1hr), or by car on a 15km-long winding road across the marshes.*

Past Kaunos, the boat continues its journey towards the river's estuary, a marshy delta closed off by an immense sand bank. The site is stupendous: a strand of golden sand forming a 7km-long strip of desert dotted with a few wooden cabins built by Turkish holidaymakers. The sea is warm and not very deep...it is hard to resist the temptation of a swim! Be careful, the site is protected: this is where the caretta turtles *(Caretta careta)* lay their eggs. They are an endangered Mediterranean species, which was threatened a few years ago with extinction and is today rigorously protected.

■ **Towards the lake**★★ – Returning to Dalyan, the boat heads back into the heart of the marshes. The maze of canals, barren islands

Caretta caretissima
During June and July, the caretta turtles come ashore on the İztuzu beach to lay their eggs (more than 200 each!). They proceed by digging a hole in the sand, which they cover up before returning to the sea. A long battle by ecologists has allowed the beach – a magnificent site – to be protected from the real estate promoters who have always coveted it. Since the turtles lay their eggs at night the beach is off limits between 6pm and 9am; and during the laying season an entire swathe of sand is protected. Bathers can cross it, but spreading out your beach towel or sticking a beach umbrella in the sand is forbidden!

and clumps of reeds conceal birds and probably fishermen and their multicoloured boats busily catching blue crabs. It is a strange world of water and plants, from which you feel there is no escape.

Fortunately, the boat navigates the river again and heads upstream towards **Lake Köyceğiz****, beyond Dalyan, revealing a stunning landscape of greenery: meadows and groves of trees reminiscent of the countryside rather than the Mediterranean. It is customary to stop on the western shore of the lake, in **Selimiye**, to take a **sulphurous mud bath**, greyish clay reputed for its curative effects. Even if you are not tempted, the spectacle of visitors adorning the water's edge, busily smearing themselves with mud is quite amusing! Once they are covered in mud, they strut around in the sand waiting for their "mask" to act before rinsing off under the showers which have been installed on the shores. The odour of sulphur permeating the area is not very pleasant, but the baths are very refreshing, as long as the overcrowding and the organised-tour feeling don't bother you!

One last dip in the fresh, cool waters of the lake, and the boat heads back to Dalyan at sunset, where the excursion ends. This is the time to enjoy good fish at one of the open-air restaurants scattered around the harbour while watching the rock tombs disappear in the twilight.

Making the most of Dalyan

COMING AND GOING

By bus – From Marmaris, take the bus for Ortaca (via Akçapınar). From there, dolmuşes leave every 15min for Dalyan (14km).

By shared taxi – From Atatürk square, the dolmuşes of the **Minibüs Kooperatifi** run a shuttle service to İztuzu beach every day: the outward journey can be made up to 3pm, with the last return at 7pm.

ADDRESS BOOK

Main post office – At the entrance to the town. 8am-midnight in summer; 8.30am-12noon / 1.30pm-6pm in winter. Phone booths and currency exchange.

Banks – In the town centre near Atatürk square, **Yapı Kredi** and **İş Bankası** exchange foreign currency.

Car rental – **Europcar**, Kaunos Tur, PTT Karşısı, ☎ (252) 284 28 16 / 284 41 29, Fax (252) 284 31 57. **Aktan Turizm**, Maraş Cad, ☎ (252) 284 38 02, Fax (252) 284 34 96. Also hires out motorcycles for US\$15 per day (US\$75 per week), and jeeps for around US\$45 per day.

Renting a bike – **Kardak Turizm**, in the main street (pedestrian) which runs alongside the river.

WHERE TO STAY

The hotel establishments in Dalyan are, on the whole, very pleasant. The guest houses on the riverside are a little more expensive, on account of the spectacular panorama. But what wouldn't you give to have breakfast overlooking the boats and the tombs of Kaunos!

Camp sites

Dalyan camp site, Maraş Mah, at the end of the avenue which runs alongside the lake. ✖ ♀ Rents out bungalows, caravans and tents (around US\$8 per pitch). Also has a discotheque.

Around US\$8

Sahil Pansiyon, Göl Kenarı, Maraş Mah, ☎ (252) 284 21 87, Fax (252) 284 33 28. ⌐ ✖ A peaceful, pleasant place to stay, with a lakeside terrace. The friendly proprietors organise day trips to Kaunos and Ekincik for their clients (departure at 10am, return at 6pm).

Under US\$15

Pension Zakkum, Maraş Mah, ☎ (252) 284 21 11. A very simple, but very clean guest house. Constant hot water and a magnificent view over the river.

Pension Aktaş, Near the lake, ☎ (252) 284 22 73, Fax (252) 284 43 80. ⌐ One of the most recent guest houses. The welcome and service are faultless.

Pension Çınar Sahil, ☎ (252) 284 21 17 – 17rm. ☂ A charming guest house, also overlooking the river and the Lycian tombs.

Between US$15 and US$25

Beyazgül Motel, Maraş Mah Balıkhane Sok 26-28, ☎ (252) 284 23 04 – 4rm. ☂ ✗ A pleasant establishment, set in a charming wooden Turkish house, on the shaded banks of the river.

Hotel Caria, Maraş Mah, Yalı Sok 82, ☎ (252) 284 20 75, Fax (252) 284 30 46 – 20rm. ☂ In close proximity to the lake, at the end of the village, this very comfortable establishment offers rooms equipped with mosquito nets and balconies.

Between US$25 and US$45

Hotel Binlik, Sulungur Sok 16, on the road to İztuzu, ☎ (252) 284 21 48 / 284 22 80, Fax (252) 284 21 49. ☂ ☰ ✗ ⎓ cc Beautiful wood panelling gives this place a warm atmosphere and the rooms are very simple and spacious. One of the best hotels in this price range.

Hotel Caretta Caretta, near the jetty, ☎ (252) 284 33 01. ☂ ⌂ ⎓ cc Built by a young architect, this hotel, with its original and tasteful decor, is very pleasant. The quality is also superb (flawless service and immaculately clean) and the breakfast copious. Good value for money.

Over US$75

Hotel Assyrien, ☎ (252) 284 32 32, Fax (252) 284 32 44 – 34rm. ☂ ⌂ ✗ ⎓ cc A very elegant establishment, which respects the traditional local architecture and has been decorated with great care. The swimming pool is set in a lovely garden and the quality of service is faultless. You cannot fail to fall under its spell.

Hotel Dalyan, Maraş Mah, Yalı Sok, ☎ (252) 284 22 39, Fax (252) 284 22 40 – 20rm. ☂ ☰ ⌂ ✗ ⎓ ☼ cc Although very different from the Assyrien hotel, this one has an equally distinctive character, with its original and refined decor. Facing the Lycian tombs.

EATING OUT

Dalyan is jam-packed with restaurants, snack bars and fast-food restaurants, most of which are to be found on the waterside. The fish specialities here are simply delicious.

On the terraces here you can sample grilled bass and mullet, and little crabs in blue shells, said to be the only ones of this colour in the Mediterranean. You will also find a mullet egg pâté on the menu, ambitiously called "fish caviar". Beware of the more crowded restaurants – they tend to serve warm beer and charge unrealistic prices. Excellent kebabs and pide can be found near the post office, in the main shopping street.

Riverside, Maraş Mah, ☎ (252) 284 42 62 / 284 31 14. Despite the English name, the food is unmistakably Turkish: deliciously seasoned fish dishes. Concerts every evening.

Adonis, Çarşı İçi, ☎ (252) 284 32 38. Excellent traditional food. Copious brochettes and perfect kebabs.

The *Dalyan Café* in Balıkhane Sok Maraş Mah makes good "gözleme" (Turkish crepes filled with cheese or minced meat). In Atatürk square, the *Mulberry* has set menus at US$9 and US$13; the *No Name* has menus at US$5 and the *Pizzeria Carretta* offers breakfasts at US$3 and meals at US$5.

The *Ceyhan Restaurant*, İlkokul Arkası, Nehir Kenarı, is run by Yaman, who comes from İstanbul, and prepares the fresh sea bream and eels himself. A true nature lover who highly values peace and quiet, he also organises bike rides, crab fishing expeditions and Optimist sailing on Lake Köyceğiz.

HAVING A DRINK

At the end of the harbour, towards the Meltem guest house (Gülpınar Mah), you will find a pleasant open-air *jazz bar*.

Or you may be tempted by *Ike's Bar*, also known as the *Secret Garden*, with its entirely wooden decor, warm carpets and inviting divans. But then again, you may find the terrace or garden a better place to relax.

For a completely different atmosphere, try the *Crazy Dancing Bar*, where you can listen to rock and funk music in a psychedelic decor.

OTHER THINGS TO DO

Boat trips – Nothing better for exploring the delta's labyrinth of channels. Boat trips on the lake and river, including a trip to Kaunos and a mud bath in the lake, are organised by the hotels, guest houses and fishermen.

Spas – A spa has been set up in Selimiye, on the northwest side of the lake, where you can unwind for a few days (information from the tourist information office).

Massages – Ask Yaman, the proprietor of the Ceyhan restaurant, for *Elga's* address; originally from Germany, she has been living in Dalyan for several years and is renowned for her relaxing massages.

Outdoor pursuits – The local agencies offer activities such as *rafting* in the gorges of the Dalaman Çayı or *cycling* in the beautiful countryside around Dalyan. Take your pick!

Making the most of Köyceğiz

About 50km to the east of the turn-off to Marmaris, why not call in at Köyceğiz, a little town set on the lakeside. Tranquil, charming, and less touristy than Dalyan, you can stop and relax at one of the terrace restaurants in the main square, under the shade of immense eucalyptus trees.

COMING AND GOING

By shared taxi – Marmaris-Köyceğiz: 14 return journeys per day. Fethiye-Köyceğiz: 17 return shuttle services per day.

By boat – Boats for Dalyan leave from the lakeside at Köyceğiz as soon as they are full.

ADDRESS BOOK

Tourist information – Atatürk Kordonu (in the village square), ☎ and Fax (252) 262 47 03. Warm welcome. A mine of historical and tourist information.

WHERE TO STAY

Camp sites
Köyceğiz Belediyesi Kulak Mesire Yeri, ☎ (252) 262 40 90. ⚑ Located to the west of the village, near Halk beach (Halk Plajı), this is the municipal camp site. Well run and with lots of shade, it only costs US$3 per person per day.

Under US$8
Çiçek Pansiyon, in the village square, ☎ (252) 262 30 38 – 6rm. ✗ Showers on the landing. In an old Ottoman house with corbelling and moucharaby, run by a cheerful and efficient proprietress.

Between US$15 and US$25
Hotel Alila, Emeksız Cad, ☎ and Fax (252) 262 11 50/51. ⚑ ✗ ⌷ 🖹 CC A recent hotel, lacking charm but well run, quiet and set in a good location facing the lake.

EATING OUT

The *Alila hotel's* restaurant has delicious and very reasonably priced trout on the menu. The countless little restaurants and snack bars in the main square serve meat, fish, sandwiches and salads of acceptable quality.

OTHER THINGS TO DO

Outdoor pursuits – *The Panorama hotel*, Ulucami Mah Cengiz Topel Cad 69, ☎ (252) 262 37 73, Fax (252) 262 36 33, offers surfing and Optimist sailing on the lake. 1hr of surf: US$6, 4hr: US$15. 1hr Optimist sailing: US$6.

Excursions – Boats leave from the lakeside (Köyceğiz Gölü) for excursions of one or more days to Kaunos, Dalyan and Selimiye.

FETHİYE ★

Muğla Province – Map p 355
294km from Antalya – 50km from Dalaman
Pop 48 500 – Hot summers

Not to be missed
The rock tombs of Fethiye – The island of Gemili.
The view from the acropolis of Tlos.

And remember...
If you take a dolmuş to the Ölüdeniz beach and back,
avoid taking the last one (6pm), as it is bound to be packed.
If you visit Gemili, wear good shoes and bring drinking water.

A small town with a peaceful atmosphere, Fethiye is hidden at the back of a cove opposite the gulf named after it. The town stretches out at the bottom of the imposing buttresses of the Babadağı (1 969m), in front of a string of islets floating on the turquoise water. This charming site's appearance has obviously changed since the development of tourism; concrete hotels, old traditional homes and antique remains mingle, forming a not always happy mixture. However, Fethiye has been able to unite the past and the present with more success than in many other coastal towns: here, there are no tall buildings and no rows of beach hotels. It is always a pleasure to stroll in the city centre's market streets, between the little white houses still bathed in the perfumes of the old Mediterranean. The elegant sailboats in the marina offer a memorable sight from the quayside restaurants. Fethiye is an excellent starting point to explore the area and enjoy some of the region's most beautiful beaches.

Telmessos, ancient Fethiye

The gateway to Lycia, Telmessos was a prosperous city from the 5C BC. A member of the league of Delos, then the Lycian Confederation, it was among the most important cities of the region, ranking among the metropolises. The city prospered until the Arab invasion in the 9C, a period in which it was reduced to a modest village, taking on the Turkish name of Fethiye in the 19C.

The city retained the traces of its past for a long time. Unfortunately it experienced two violent earthquakes, one in 1856, the other in 1957, which destroyed a large number of Ottoman houses and most of the ancient buildings. Only a few ruins remain – noble sarcophagi scattered around the city – and in particular a superb rock necropolis cut in the side of a cliff.

The city

Allow 2hr to visit the main sites.

At the edge of the port, to the west, the **small theatre** can still be seen (Telmessos had another larger one which disappeared). Its lower steps were recently cleared. However, take a look at the side streets with their discreet beautiful **Ottoman houses** and white façades with flowered windows, surrounded by dark wood frames. Go back to the **main street**, filled with numerous craftsmen, then turn right on **Kayaköy Yolu Caddesi**, a charming residential quarter populated by spinners wearing headscarves. Sitting in front of their doorsteps, they will invite you to have a look at their creations. From there, climb up the hill, south of the city, which overlooks the **medieval citadel of the Knights of St John**, in ruins. The climb is especially interesting for the **panorama★** of the bay of Fethiye, particularly at sunset.

The most remarkable ruins are the extraordinary **Lycian Tombs**★★ (*8am-7pm*) in the cliff bordering the city to the southeast (*from the citadel, go down towards the hill and take the little road immediately on the right which skirts the cliff, at the foot of the tombs*). Façades of temples or houses – traditional depictions of the residences of gods or the deceased – are sculpted in the rock. Pediments and colonnettes protrude from the sheer wall. The most beautiful is undoubtedly the **tomb of Amyntas**★★, a celebrity of the city who lived in the 4C BC (*access from the road by a staircase with 150 steps*). The pediment, surmounted by an acrotera, is supported by two Ionic columns and two pilasters *in antis*. Behind it is a heavy stone door with four sculpted panels. The bottom right panel, a loose one, disappeared during the pillaging of the tomb.

Continuing along the road, at the foot of the cliff, another 20 **tombs**★★ are set in the rocky wall. The view consists of an impressive series of temples or houses chiselled with care, or simple rectangular niches known as "pigeon holes".

From here, return to the port by taking Atatürk Caddesi, to stop at the **museum** (*8.30am–12noon/1pm-5.30pm; closed Mondays; entrance fee*) which houses a few beautiful statues found in the city and the region. You will see the **stela** found in Letoön (*see p 391*), engraved with a text in three languages – Greek, Lycian and Aramaic. Dating from 338 BC, this text states the rules of the cult dedicated to the gods Kaunios (Leto's father) and Arkesimas, and the list of sanctions which the disrespectful would incur.

Around Fethiye
Allow at least one day.

For those who love beautiful scenery, the area surrounding Fethiye contains some real treasures. If you enjoy boats, take a **tour of the islands**★ in the bay of Fethiye. Most of them are still unexplored.

The Gorge of Saklıkent★★
17km after the junction. The site is open to hikers from April to October, 8.30am-7pm.
Enthusiasts of rafting or nature walks will head for the Gorge of Saklıkent, an impressive canyon carved by a tumultuous stream. After walking on hanging bridges, muddy paths and hiking in the rocks, your legs will be well stretched, and you will feel refreshed! At the entrance to the gorge, the restaurant owners have established **trout farms**, where visitors can tuck into a tasty dish of fish at the water's edge, seated on comfortable cushions strewn on the rocks (*see Making the most of Fethiye*).

Kaya Köy★
8km south of Fethiye, head towards Ölüdeniz (numerous taxi services) and turn right after 6km (a second dolmuş completes the trip from the intersection). Bring water and a hat. Entrance fee. Allow 1hr.
An unusual site: Kaya Köy is an abandoned village whose ruined homes cling to the flank of a hill like stone ghosts. Its inhabitants – Greeks – left it in 1923 during the population transfers between Greece and Turkey. Every house has kept its walls, but the roofs have disappeared, as if to allow the spirits of the souls of the inhabitants to fly away. The area is bathed in a strange, melancholy atmosphere. The almost deserted streets of not long ago have given way to a number of shops, cafés and restaurants which local holidaymakers invade as soon as the sun sets.

The **church**★ (*at the edge of the village*) still contains beautiful painted and stuccoed vaults. Still intact, is a splendid **pebble floor**★ in black and white, with geometric and fish motifs. This unusual type of decor can also be seen in another church at the entrance to the village.

The Bay of Ölüdeniz★★★

12km south of Fethiye (dolmuş every 10min). From Kaya Köy, access to Ölüdeniz via a well-marked path (allow 3hr on foot).

At the foot of the Babadağı, hidden in the curve of the gulf of Belcekız is a lagoon surrounded by pine trees and isolated from the sea by a bank of white sand, lapped by turquoise water. The bay of Ölüdeniz ("dead sea" in Turkish) is a protected site of stunning beauty (*see photograph p 352*). Unfortunately, the surrounding area is overrun by motels and camping sites and in the summer, the beach is packed. Two solutions: visit outside peak season, or pay to enter the natural reserve, the **Ölüdeniz Tabiat Parkı** (very inexpensive) and enjoy a portion of the beach which is part of the protected zone. It is less crowded, with fewer boat engine noises, and the sea is just as inviting.

You can also swim at **Çalış beach** (*north of Fethiye*), a slightly less attractive setting, but quiet and uncrowded.

The island of St Nicholas★★ (Gemili Adası)

20km southeast of Fethiye, via the Kayaköy road, 2km south of the present village, a path leads to the Gemili bay. The island is opposite, separated from the coast by a narrow 200m canal. It is easy to reach by boat, from Fethiye (going round the cape of İbliz) or from the beach of Ölüdeniz. Until recently, the island's population consisted of two donkeys; today, a team of Japanese archaeologists lives on the island to explore the site and a warden is posted at the site's entrance.

A forgotten Byzantine city – Gemili consists of a small rocky hill (barely 1km wide) in the sea. Steep paths wind their way through the chaotic rocks, bushes and ruins covering the whole island. On Gemili, basilicas, dwellings, tombs and cisterns are the astonishing Byzantine religious remains of a city devoted to the worship of St Nicholas. Many items are still waiting to be discovered and the adventure is not only reserved for archeologists, hikers can also play their part.

The first tomb of St Nicholas? – Historians believe that the saint, highly popular in the area, was originally buried on the island of Gemili, before his body was transferred to the church of Myra (*see p 408*). The four churches built on the island, the processional path linking two of them and the many cisterns, all indicate a highly popular pilgrimage site. The dates themselves seem to confirm this: the first churches of Gemili are thought to have been built around the 4C, after Nicholas' death (in 340) and the island seems to have been evacuated in the 7C when Arab fleets threatened the coast. The relics were transferred to Myra during the same period.

Following in the pilgrims' footsteps – Starting from the little port to the west and following the path traced on the hillside are the meagre remains of a first **church**, surrounded by numerous structures – walls, watchtowers and cisterns leading to a second **church**★, in better condition. The apse has retained its **synthronon** and on its walls a few touching traces of **frescoes** can still be seen. Further up, a few hundred metres on, another **church**★ stands near the cliff, with a magnificent **view**★ of the bay. Its walls are covered in fragments of **mosaics** and sculpted decor.

Behind the western apse is a stunning **vaulted passage**★★, partially collapsed, connecting it to the neighbouring church, 300m away. Inside are scattered remains of frescoes and one halfexpects to encounter a procession, with a perfume of incense and myrrh in the air. An unusual construction for the region, this passage allowed the monks and pilgrims to move about in the shade between the main churches. It leads by successive gates to the island's last church – highly damaged – also surrounded by cisterns, sarcophagi and various buildings.

Y. Travert/DIAF

Kaya Köy, ghost town

Tlos★

37km from Fethiye, via the Antalya road. Past Kemer (26km), take the road to Korkuteli (northeast), then turn right and follow the road skirting the Xanthos, straight towards the south. Continue for a dozen kilometres until you reach the village of Güneşli, then turn left (east) towards the hamlet of Kale (Kaleköy), 5km on. The site is next door. For those without private transport, the dolmuş will drop you off at the intersection of the Güneşli and Kaleköy–Tlos roads and you will have to walk the remainder of the way. Entrance fee. Allow 45min for the trip, and another 45min for the visit.

High on a steep hill overlooking the green valley of Xanthos (the modern Eşen Çayı), the acropolis of Tlos watches over the river, seemingly unaware of the blue crest of Ak Dağları rising behind it at over 2 000m. At its feet, the ruins of the city extend through the middle of fields, shaded by poplars and olive trees. The overgrown shrubs and bushes make it seem romantic.

It is difficult to imagine that Tlos, so ruined today, was one of the most powerful cities of Lycia. In the 2C BC, the city was among the six cities of the Lycian Confederation, along with Telmessos, and it became a bishopric during the Byzantine period. It is also one the region's oldest cities, some of the objects found on the site are nearly 4 000 years old.

The site's most interesting area is undoubtedly around the **Ottoman citadel** *(from Kaleköy, take the road to the site where a path climbs on the right, towards the citadel)*, on the walls of the ancient **acropolis** and on the **Byzantine ramparts**. There is a lovely **view★** over the corn and aniseed fields blanketing the valley. Climbing towards the summit, on the right, is a series of **rock tombs★**, small façades of Lycian homes or primitive niches dug into a cliff, on the northeast flank of the hill. They are not easily accessible but are worth the effort: several tombs (accessible) have retained beautiful **bas-reliefs** – heads of animals protecting the city and, especially, a depiction (unfortunately quite worn) of **Bellerophon riding**

381

Pegasus, arm upraised to kill a chimaera. Half-man, half-god, this valiant young hero was the talk of the town in Lycia, and the citizens of Tlos liked to think that they were his descendants. *(See sidebar p 418).*

Go back to the road and continue right towards the theatre.

At the foot of the hill, on the right, the **stadium** contains a few remaining traces of terraces leading into the field. On its sides are the ruins of a strange **building**, 150m long and equipped with three two-level naves. Archeologists have been unable to determine its function: gymnasium, market or civil basilica? Further down, on the same side of the road, the ruined walls of a large **Byzantine basilica** stand out above the invading vegetation, which has already covered the entire esplanade of the neighbouring **agora**. Behind the basilica *(towards the south)* are the **baths*** – one of the site's most beautiful remains – a building whose **vaults*** and **windows*** face the sky and the valley.

Last but not least, on the other side of the road, continuing towards the east, is the overgrown **theatre*** (2C AD). The shrubs on the **terraces*** have replaced the spectators, but the structure is well preserved, particularly the supporting **vaults**. From the top of the cavea, there is a wonderful **view**** of the acropolis.

Making the most of Fethiye

COMING AND GOING

By bus – The **bus station** is at the entrance to the town (1km from the centre), at the junction of the roads to Muğla, Antalya and Ölüdeniz. The following companies are among those operating services from here: **Kamil Koç**, ☎ (252) 614 19 73 / 612 02 66, Fax (252) 614 38 31. The main destinations are İzmir via Selçuk (1 departure every 2hr), İstanbul (3 departures in the evening), Ankara (10pm and 11pm), Bodrum (3.30am and 3.30pm) and Kaş (6am, 9.30am and 3.30pm). **Pamukkale**, ☎ (252) 612 37 67 / 614 14 51. İzmir (every 2hr), İstanbul, Ankara, Konya, Antalya, Kalkan, Kaş, Marmaris, Bodrum. **Metro**, ☎ (252) 612 08 42. Ankara and İstanbul, 2 departures in the evening (cost around US$15). **Ulusoy**, ☎ (252) 612 37 37. Departure for İstanbul at 9pm, Ankara at 10pm and Antalya at 4pm. **Uludağ**, ☎ (252) 612 35 79. Operates services to İzmir, Ankara,

Bursa, Bodrum and Alanya. **Öz Habur Tur**, ☎ (252) 614 80 66. Connection to Antalya every day at 4pm.

By shared taxi – The dolmuş stand is in the town centre, next to the post office and police station. For under US$2, you can take a dolmuş (making various stops in town) to the beach at Ölüdeniz, Yanıklar, Katrancı, Günlüklü, Esenköy, Kemer, Eşen, Ören, Kumluova, Karadere, Hacıosmanlar and Gölek. In short, they go everywhere!

By taxi – ☎ (252) 614 33 33 / 614 43 43 / 612 25 20. Next to the bus station. Convenient for getting to the town centre.

ADDRESS BOOK

Tourist information – At the harbour, 8am-7pm in summer, 5pm the rest of the year, ☎ (252) 614 15 27. Just to the left of the tourist information office, drop in at the **Fethiye Tourism Association**, which provides good advice, ☎ (252) 614 10 51, Fax (252) 612 30 96.

Bank / change – In Atatürk Cad: *Garanti Bankası*, *Yapı Kredi*, *Ziraat Bankası* and *İş Bank* (opposite the post office), *Akbank* towards İskele, *Koç Bank* next to Europcar, and *Esbank*, in Çarşı Cad.

Main post office – In Atatürk Cad. Currency exchange, ☎ (252) 614 14 98. Open 8am-midnight in summer.

Internet – Atatürk Cad 18, next to Koç Bank. US$4 per hour.

Medical service – *Public hospital*, Atatürk Cad, a few hundred metres from the post office, ☎ (252) 614 12 25 / 614 12 26.

Car rental – *Avis*, Fevzi Çakmak Cad 1/B, ☎ (252) 614 63 39 / 612 13 85, Fax (252) 614 63 39.

Budget, Karagözler Mah Karagözler Yokuşu, ☎ (252) 614 61 66, Fax (252) 612 24 01.

Europcar, Atatürk Cad 40, ☎ (252) 614 49 95/614 19 91, Fax (252) 614 93 62.

Public toilets – Near the Budget car rental agency.

Laundries – *Segem Laundry*, Çarşı Cad, at the end of Hamam Sok, in the town centre. *Güneş Laundry*, in Kordon Boyu, and *Laundry Captains*, next to the Status hotel, in the vicinity of the marina.

WHERE TO STAY

Fethiye is a small, fairly quiet town which comes alive in the evening. We prefer the western quarter, at the very end of the bay (towards the theatre).

• In the bay of Ölüdeniz

Under US$15

Ideal Pansiyon, Zafer Cad 1, ☎ (252) 614 19 81 – 20rm, 13 of which have a view over the bay of Fethiye. ⚑ ✕ The level of cleanliness is mediocre, but you will find a warm welcome and good home cooking. Breakfast is served on the panoramic terrace. Half-board possible. "Quiet time" from 11pm to 8.30am.

Hotel Aramis, ☎ (252) 617 00 21, Fax (252) 617 02 25 – 27 bungalows, 54 beds. ⚑ A 10min walk from the sea. A delightful little hotel, consisting of comfortable wooden bungalows scattered around a charming, shaded garden full of flowers. The copious breakfast is served in an arbour laden with vines. Excellent value for money, with charm to boot.

Between US$15 and US$30

Hotel Status, Yat Limanı Sok 8, ☎ and Fax (252) 614 10 68 / 614 33 96. ⚑ ♪ ▤ ⚄ An impersonal but modern and well-run hotel, with bright rooms. It's only a pity that it's near the rather noisy Marina nightclub.

Pension İrem, 1 Karagözler Mah 45, ☎ (252) 614 39 85, Fax (252) 614 58 75 – 7rm. ⚑ Open all year round, this guest house is run by a very welcoming and highly attentive family. The atmosphere here is very warm, and breakfast is served on a flower-filled terrace overlooking the bay, a veritable haven of peace. There are also a few little bungalows set back from the beach.

Pension Polat Aile, 1 Karagözler Mah 43, ☎ (252) 612 23 47 – 8rm. ⚑ A pleasant house covered in flowers and set against the hill, overlooking the bay. Breakfast is served on the terrace.

Hotel Horizon, 1 Karagözler Mah, ☎ (252) 614 63 93 / 614 63 90 – 32rm. ⚑ ✕ ⚄ cc The hotel certainly lives up to its name: clinging to the rock which towers over the bay, it has an unparalleled view over the sea which can be admired from the balconies in every room.

Hotel Hobby, 1 Karagözler Mah Gençlik Yolu, ☎ (252) 614 36 39, Fax (252) 612 36 47 – 25rm. ⚑ ♪ ▤ ⚄ ✕ ♥ cc This very well-run, bright and quiet hotel opened 4 years ago. The proprietress speaks good English. Panoramic terrace.

Hotel Doruk, Yat Limanı Karşısı, ☎ (252) 614 98 60, Fax (252) 612 30 01. ⚑ ♪ ▤ TV ✕ ⚄ cc Minibar and discotheque. A modern, clean hotel with very attentive staff.

• Towards Çalış

The hotels at Çalış have the advantage of being near the beach, but the disadvantage of being quite far from the town centre. Fortunately, dolmuşes shuttle between the two every 30min.

• In Kaya Köy

Çavuşoğlu Motel-Restaurant, a few metres from the site of the abandoned town, ☎ (252) 616 67 49, Fax (252) 616 67 51. ⚞ ⚟ ✕ ⚟ A family hotel with well-kept rooms and a warm welcome. The vine-laden arbour is a godsend in the hot season, and the food is simple but carefully prepared.

EATING OUT

The narrow alleyways in the pedestrian quarter are packed with restaurants. There are also some on the quaysides facing the boats. The cuisine cannot be described as highly refined, but it is copious and cheap.

Park Çay Café, Fethi Bey Parkı Yanı Liman Civarı, ☎ (252) 614 58 56. Opposite the yachts in the marina.

Pizza 74, Gezi Cad, at the end of the quayside. The pide are very good, and the atmosphere youthful and very pleasant.

Cuisine Restaurant, Hamam Sok. Good Turkish and foreign cuisine served on a spacious split-level terrace, with a beautiful cascading fountain. Reasonable prices.

• In the bay

Cim Restaurant, Yat Limanı, Gümrük Arkası, ☎ (252) 413 78 16. 200m from the Status hotel. A charming restaurant with a terrace and a vine-covered arbour. The house specialities are meat and squid casseroles and vegetarian dishes. Rather expensive, but good.

• In Saklıkent

Kanyon Restaurant, on the first ramp at the entrance to the site. This open-air restaurant is set on pilings among the rocks strewn over the river bed. Here, seated on cushions and carpets, diners can sample the delicious grilled trout.

River Restaurant, on the second ramp. This restaurant offers the same type of menu and setting, but with the added bonus of little individual terraces on pilings above the water. This place would be so much more relaxing if only the bar would turn off the music. Also serves as a camp site.

HAVING A DRINK

Otantik Bar, Paspatur Mevkii, Hamam Sok, ☎ (252) 612 28 70. This is where Fethiye's young people hang out. Small dance floor where you can dance to the latest Turkish hits.

Yes Bar, Cumhuriyet Cad 9, ☎ (252) 612 42 39 / 614 92 89. Very friendly atmosphere. You can also dance here, but to more western music.

Yasemin Bar, in the town centre, behind the tourist information office. In an old traditional house, where you can listen to Turkish music.

Car Cimetery Bar, Hamam Sok. Offering a wide variety of coffee from all over the world.

Music Factory, Hamam Sok 29. Very warm and cheerful atmosphere.

Bar Deep Blue, in the same street; just follow the waves of rock music, and you'll find it.

OTHER THINGS TO DO

Turkish bath – Old Turkish Bath, Hamam Sok 2, ☎ (252) 614 93 18. Open every day until 11pm.

Beaches – Ölüdeniz, 12km south of Fethiye, is Turkey's most beautiful and best-known beach, and one of the most crowded. The quietest part of the beach (equipped with showers and toilets) is in the national park (entry fee). Dolmuş shuttle service every 10min. The beach at **Çalış** is just as pleasant and can be reached by dolmuş (1 every 30min) and by town buses.

Scuba diving – European Diving Center, 12/1 Atatürk Cad, ☎ (252) 612 32 81 / 614 97 71, Fax (252) 614 97 72. The marine depths of the bay of Fethiye are renowned for their natural riches and beauty. Whatever your level of experience, you are sure to find something here.

Excursions – In Kordon Boyu, which leads to the 1 Karagözler Mah district (the bay area), there are countless tourist agencies offering rafting, paragliding (US$90), tours of the twelve islands (US$8 per day, 9am-6pm), scuba diving (US$55 for two 30min dives, including lunch) or cruises to Ölüdeniz and Rhodes.

Libtour, ☎ (252) 614 69 52/53/54, Fax (252) 612 06 88, libtour@exite.com, near the marina, organises blue cruises lasting several days.

Windsurfing – On the long windswept beach at **Çalış**, a little seaside resort much loved by Turkish families, a windsurfing centre provides equipment for around US$13 per hour. You can reach Çalış by water-taxi: connections to Fethiye every 20min, from 9am until midnight.

Rafting – In **Saklıkent**, you will have the opportunity to go tubing (going down the river on large inner tubes). US$11 per person for a 45min descent.

Market – At the junction of Belediye Cad and Hükümet Cad. Here you will find fresh fish, spices and also a Turkish fast-food restaurant serving soup, grilled liver, meat brochettes and sandwiches.

Making the most of Ölüdeniz

ADDRESS BOOK

Tourist information – *Ölüdeniz Turizm Geliştirme Kooperatifi*, ☎ (252) 617 04 38 / 617 01 45, Fax (252) 617 01 35. This office provides detailed documentation on each establishment, which is extremely helpful in choosing between the 70 hotels and 6 camp sites available here.

Motorcycle rental – *Safari* agency, ☎ (252) 617 06 65.

WHERE TO STAY

Camp sites
Ölüdeniz camp site, ☎ (252) 617 00 48, Fax (252) 617 01 81. ✘ ♥ You can stay in an individual tent or bungalow for around US$4 per person per day.

US$25
Hotel Türk, ☎ (252) 617 02 64 / 617 04 44, Fax (252) 617 03 73. ⌂ 🍴 🍽 ✘ ♥ ♨ CC Among the incredible

multitude of hotels which has sprung up on the beach and site, this one, in an attractive setting fragrant with jasmine and honeysuckle, offers good quality service. Open from May until the end of October.

EATING OUT

Around US$10
Ying Yang Restaurant, a Chinese restaurant in the street where most of the hotels are to be found. Good value for money.

OTHER THINGS TO DO

Outdoor pursuits – *Wise Tours*, ☎ (252) 617 05 51, Fax (252) 617 05 52, offers rafting, horse riding, scuba diving and paragliding.
Easy Riders, Han Camp, ☎ (252) 617 01 14 and *Sky Sports*, Deniz Camp, ☎ (252) 617 05 11, Fax (252) 617 0324: paragliding for US$90 per person.

FROM FETHİYE TO KAŞ★★
PINARA – XANTHOS – LETOÖN
112km tour – 1 to 2 days – Map p 355
Lodging in Patara, Kalkan or Kaş

Not to be missed
The rock tombs of Pınara.
The pillar tombs of Xanthos and the views of the valley.
The buried theatre of Patara.

And remember...
Bring along binoculars to observe the tombs of Pınara,
good walking shoes and a bottle of drinking water.
Stay in Kalkan, the ideal starting point for tours.

Beyond Fethiye, the road climbs slowly inland to the banks of the Esen Çayı (the ancient river Xanthos), which it follows sinuously into the mountains. Here, numerous ruins are hidden, remnants of ancient Lycian cities. Approaching the coast, the road crosses quiet hamlets to reach other ancient sites, a sea of sculpted stones scattered among the fields. Then, the immense blue sea appears. Continue along the coastline, with its ruins, sleepy villages and endless beaches to the gates of Kas, which guards the bay of Kekova. The road takes visitors through villages as if it was taking them on a journey through time: from Lycian dwellings to Ottoman houses, it travels across 2500 years of history, under the unchanging glare of the sun.

■ Pınara★★

47km from Fethiye and 30km from Kalkan. On the main road from Fethiye to Kaş, on the right before the hamlet of Gülmez, take the small road on the right which leads to Minare (5km). Right before the village, on the left, a small 2km long dirt track leads to the site (poorly sign-posted). For those without transport, the dolmuşes frequently travel from Fethiye; however, they drop you off in Gülmez and you have to hitchhike or walk the rest of the way. Ask for a guide; they are available at the Tourist Office in Fethiye or at the site. Open all year round. Entrance fee. Allow at least 2hr.

Clinging to the flanks of **Baba Dağı**, the ruins of Pınara merge into the rocks, drowned in the scrub filled with bushes, prickly plants (long trousers are advisable) and wild olive trees covering the hills and peaks. The only inhabitants of the area, brown and black goats, pass by in flocks, piercing the silence with the tinkling of their bells.

Shrubs and rocks
The ancient city covers an extended (and steep) area, laid out in terraces on three hills (the highest rises to 715m), set one behind the other from east to west like the steps of a giant staircase. The uneven ground and dense vegetation make the visit tiring and the remains are sometimes hard to depict. But it is this tormented setting which renders the site beautiful and its discovery picturesque. One can almost imagine what Charles Fellows, a 19C English traveller and enthusiast who "discovered" the site in 1840, experienced.

The history of Pınara is relatively unknown. Legend has it that the city was born during the Trojan war, but it was probably founded in the 5C BC by colonists from Xanthos. In any event, Pınara ranked among the Lycian Confederation's most important cities. After swearing allegiance to Alexander the Great in 334 BC, it underwent an important revival during the Roman period and later became the seat of a bishopric. However, the successive earthquakes (especially those of 141 and 240) weakened it and its inhabitants abandoned it for good in the 9C.

From necropolises to acropolises

On arrival the eye is instantly drawn towards the impressive peak which rises on the western side of the site, an abrupt 500m-tall cliff. Entirely riddled with tombs, this **rock necropolis**** resembles a honeycomb with a multitude of cells. No less than 13 000 tombs have been counted, as well as 786 sculpted tombs, imitating the façades of temples or houses. The only way to explore the tombs is with binoculars, since they are inaccessible.

The **first necropolis** is reached via the car park, along the dirt track which crosses the stream. This group of rock tombs is known as the **royal cemetery***. Behind a thick curtain of trees and shrubs are some beautiful tombs decorated with bas-reliefs engraved in the rock at eye-level. Visitors can enter and admire the engravers' work: one of the tomb's pediments is decorated with the horns and ears of a bull; another one has four eyes on the façade. The **"royal" tomb***, the most interesting, features very beautiful bas-reliefs in its vestibule, representing Lycian cities.

Two hundred metres further down are the ruins of a Roman **bath complex** (2C AD), with three rooms, one of which is closed off by an apse. From here, a ramp leads to the terrace of the **acropolis** (*northern extremity*). Here are the vestiges of a **Roman temple** known incorrectly as Aphrodite's Temple because of a bas-relief depicting a phallus (*on the ground, nearby*). Further south is the outline of the base of a great **funerary monument**. Some 100m away are the remains of a **Lycian gate**, an impressive wall segment lost in the vegetation, and the administrative district of the city, a vast terrace occupied by the ruins of the **agora**, whose surrounding colonnades and shops can easily be seen. On the eastern side, a small hemicycle building marks the site of the **bouleuterion** (or odeon), the seat of the municipal assembly. The edge of the terrace overlooks a steep hill with a **view of the western necropolis**** (the highest) and approximately 100 tombs.

Go back and down the ramp and continue towards the eastern valley.

At the northern extremity of the valley, the beautiful grey terraces of the **theatre** stand out on the dark green flank of the hill (*reached by crossing the fields in the valley*). In Greek style, although probably built during the Roman period, it is quite well preserved and has recently been cleared of the vegetation which covered it. It could hold 35 000 spectators.

For the more adventurous, brave enough to cross other valleys and rough terrain, the ruins are quite numerous: towards the west (*returning to the car park, beyond the royal cemetery*) are the remains of a **Byzantine church** and

Good or evil eye

Bull horns, eyes and phallus, these items are, in various degrees, "amulets" designed to ward off the evil eye. The phallus, far from being an erotic or obscene representation, is the symbol of true strength able to combat all maledictions. It does not, therefore, designate temples dedicated to Aphrodite or brothels as some guides say. The eye, through which evil comes, is the best defence: it protects by creating fear. It is often found on vases, shields, jewellery and tombs throughout Antiquity. This belief is still very much alive in Turkey, and you will see numerous "göz" eyes made of glass paste on stalls. Turks also hang them in their cars, at the entrance to their homes and in hotels.

a **large solitary sarcophagus**. Further still is the **first acropolis**, set on the highest hill. The sheer flanks of the latter are also filled with countless **tombs★** dropping off into the void.

Finally, for the most energetic, continue on to the **southern necropolis★★**, perhaps the site's most beautiful, due to its setting and the diversity of its tombs, clinging to the face of a dizzying cliff *(reached by crossing the car park toward the south. From there, a little path leads to a steep incline. Allow at least 20min for the difficult climb)*.

Climbers are met with a vast dried-up **plateau★★**, a marvellous barren stretch of land, which the wind sweeps relentlessly. Take this opportunity to catch your breath before setting off again! At the edge of the plateau, the **cliff★★**, as abrupt and as sheer as the plateau is flat, contains a gigantic wall riddled with **tombs★★**, which immediately command your attention. Here too, take the time to discover the countless details of their façades with binoculars.

Near Pınara

If time is available, take a short stop in **Yakabağ**, a little village located less than 4km south of Pınara *(toward the sea)*. Stairs, cut in the rocks, lead to the village where, the ruins of an ancient **Lycian rock tomb sanctuary** are adorned with **bas-reliefs** displaying warriors and divinities sitting in the company of children and goats.

■ Xanthos★★

25km from Pınara, 62km from Fethiye and 19km from Kalkan. On the road from Fethiye to Kalkan, turn left at the village of Kınık. The site is 5km from here. A car park and a drinks stand await the visitor. Dolmuşes run from Fethiye, Patara, Kalkan or Kaş. 8.30am-7pm. Entrance fee. Allow at least 1hr.

Surrounded by the arid hills, covered with shrubbery and wild olive trees, the valley of Xanthos was the cradle of Lycia. Up in the hills, 8km from the sea, the city bearing its name was the capital and the most important city of this part of Asia Minor. It used to face the sea, before its port became silted up and the sea retreated 8km. Xanthos is listed among UNESCO's World Heritage Sites, as is neighbouring Letoōn. Both have been excavated since 1950 by French archeologists who are on the site in August and September.

A tragic history

Xanthos' first archaeological traces go back to the 8C BC. The city remained independent and prosperous until the conquest of Asia Minor by the Persians, in 545 BC, which brought Xanthos to its ruin: according to Herodotus, the Xanthians preferred to sacrifice their site rather than abandon it to the enemy, not hesitating to burn their women and children before dying, in turn, in combat.

One hundred or so years later (between 475 and 470 BC) the city, rebuilt and repopulated, was once again destroyed during a campaign related to the Peloponnesian War. Rebuilt again and affluent, it came under the control of Alexander the Great (333 BC) and then that of his followers, before being handed over to Rhodes. It recovered its independence in 167 BC and propelled itself to the top ranks of the Lycian Confederation.

In 43 BC, it was attacked and taken by Brutus, and the Xanthians were once again massacred after having seen their women and children burnt (this second massacre, identical to the first, may in fact have been imagined by the historian Appian copying the master Herodotus). As a Roman city, Xanthos regained its wealth and became a Byzantine bisphopric. Its decline, between the 7C and 10C, is attributed to successive Arab attacks.

A complex site

Xanthos is a vast and complex site, still only partially excavated, and somewhat incomprehensible for the uninitiated. There are

A despoiled city

Charles Fellows visited the site in 1838 and returned two years later to prepare for the retrieval of the visible sculptures and a few architectural items. The transport was undertaken in 1842 by a detachment of the Royal Navy. He created the grand Lycian rooms at the British Museum. Afterwards, Xanthos found relative peace, until 1950 when a French archeological mission, headed by Pierre Demargne, undertook the scientific exploration of the site. The research and consequential revival of Xanthos continues to this day.

nonetheless numerous items which relate the splendour of this Lycian metropolis. The wild setting bathed in the fragrance of sage bushes will make a walk very enjoyable.

Shortly after leaving the village, on the road leading to the entrance of the site, is the **southern gate** of the city, preceded by a **small Roman triumphal arch** dedicated to Vespasian. On the right, 50m away, is the base of the famous **tomb of the**

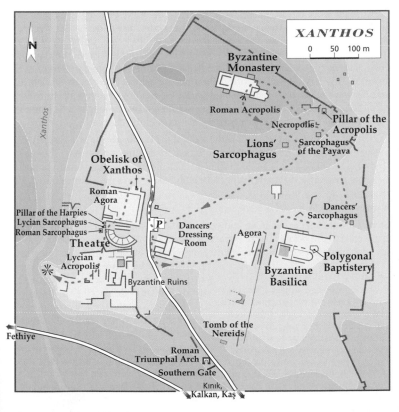

Nereids (5C BC). Its splendour is difficult to imagine: the monument is a magnificent tomb shaped like a temple which served as a model for the Halicarnassus Mausoleum *(see p 342)*, known today as one of the jewels of the British Museum (a few fragments are exposed at the Antalya museum).

The road (which corresponds to the Roman way) crosses the site, in the middle of the ruins, gives the impression of walking through an archeological park. It divides the city into two distinct areas: on the left, the oldest part and heart of the Lycian city is terraced on a steep hill all the way to the shores of the Xanthos *(this is where the visit begins)*. On the right, the area is flatter and drops down to a gentle slope toward the south, where the vegetation claims its rights. This part is more specifically Byzantine.

Leaving the car park, you see the **Roman agora** (2C and 3C), a large square which has retained part of its portico. In the northeast corner is the **Xanthos obelisk***, a massive pillar, 4m high, covered with archaic Lycian inscriptions which have not been completely deciphered. A Greek poem is engraved as well, probably the translation of a Lycian text which relates the accomplishments of the Xanthians during the taking of the city in 475-470 BC. This monument held a funerary chamber whose sculptures, representing combat scenes, are now preserved in the Archeological Museum in İstanbul.

South of the agora is the **Roman theatre***, a pretty hemicycle whose uneven terraces are the work of earthquakes. The western side of the building is overlooked by **three funerary monuments**, heavy stone sarcophagi shaped like houses perched on a pillar. One is **Roman** (1C), heavily damaged, the other, decorated with a cracked arch, is **Lycian** (4C BC), while the third one, called the **Pillar of the Harpies** *(today in the British Museum)*, sheltered the remains of a Persian satrap (governor of a province) who died around 475 BC. The latter monument was almost 9m tall. It owes its name to the bas-reliefs which decorate the top portion of the pillar *(copies; the originals are in London)*: mermaids, winged women who were thought to be harpies, transport small female figures symbolising the souls of the deceased.

The tiers of the theatre are set against the walls of the **Lycian acropolis**, a vast terrace strewn with blocks of stone, sitting on a promontory dominating Xanthos. The ruins of several Byzantine buildings lie to the east. On the opposite side, a narrow platform juts out over a stream, revealing a beautiful **view*** over the plain below.

To continue the visit, return to the car park, and go up the site on the right bank, the "Byzantine" side, by beginning in the south.

Go past the unidentified building known customarily as the **dancers' dressing room** to a second **agora** before a **large Byzantine basilica*** with three naves containing a few remaining geometric **mosaics**. On the outside, left of the central apse is the little **polygonal baptistery***, recently excavated, which has retained part of its marble paving. Similar in form to the paleo-Christian baptisteries of the West, it is an exceptional monument for the region. *(The baptistery and the basilica, currently being renovated are surrounded by barbed wire and closed to the public; but local guides will take you there with pleasure, if asked.)* Northeast of the basilica is the cover of the **Dancers' Sarcophagus**,

Snatching harpies

In Greek mythology, harpies ("kidnappers" in Greek) are winged genies who steal children or the souls of the dead and clasp them in their claws. These she-vultures operate in groups of two (sometimes three according to different sources). Their names evoke the flight of birds: Aello signifies Gust, and Ocypete, Fly-fast.

decorated with elegant hunting and dancing scenes. Continuing toward the north you come to yet another **necropolis**. Lost in the vegetation, its most remarkable tombs are the **Sarcophagus of Payava** (*bas-reliefs at the British Museum*), still sitting on its pedestal, and the **Pillar of the Acropolis★** (6.40m high).

The courageous will continue to the **Roman acropolis**, in the middle of which are the beautiful remains of a **Byzantine monastery★**. Here, the **panorama★** of the site is beautiful.

Perched tombs
The ancient tombs of the region are of two types, be they rock tombs or stand alone: they evoke the residence of the gods and men (tombs in the shape of temples or houses), or more strictly those of the dead (sarcophagi equipped with a roof-shaped lid, sunken rock tombs, niches, etc). The tombs of Xanthos display a very original variant of the Lycian tradition: pillar tombs. The funerary monument is itself supported by a 4-5m (or more)-high pillar, placing the deceased in the "spotlight", allowing passers by to recall his memory, meditate or simply admire his tomb.

Lastly, to reach the starting point, take the pleasant little path in the shade of olive trees that is strewn with numerous remains, including the **Lions' Sarcophagus★**, where a depiction shows two felines devouring a bull.

Letoön★★

5km from Xanthos, 20km from Kalkan. 1km after the village of Kınık returning toward Fethiye, turn left in the direction of Karaköy. The site is 4km away. By dolmuş, ask to be dropped off in Kumluova and continue on foot. On the way, children sell small packs of sage. They know the area well; ask them to guide you around. 8.30am-7pm. Entrance fee. Allow 30min.

South of Xanthos is a vast, fertile alluvial plain, which the sea left behind as it retreated. The Esen Çayı terminates its run here as it scatters itself over the numerous meanders irrigating the surrounding orchards.

Set on a small rocky plateau in the middle of cotton fields, Letoön is a difficult site to excavate: a thick layer of alluvia covers the remains, and the archeologists have to regularly pump the rising ground water. The most flooded areas (to the north and south) have become home to numerous frogs!

The refuge of Leto

Letoön was the federal sanctuary of the Lycians, a place of high pilgrimage dedicated to Leto, mother goddess of Anatolian origin and to her two children, Apollo and Artemis. It attracted pilgrims from the entire confederation, who were welcomed spiritually, culturally and materially.

The most ancient remains go back to the 8C BC. There still exists a **double portico** (*visible from the north of the car park, as you leave towards the left*) from this period, whose rows of columns stand in the middle of a large pool. It is thought to be a primitive sanctuary.

To the southeast, the bases of **three temples** sit next to one another. The first building (the largest: 31x16m) was dedicated to **Leto**. Built in the 2C BC, it was built on the foundation of a Lycian temple dating from the 4C BC, whose foundations were found under the stone slabs. The numerous items of the second temple which were cleared from the area – column drums, Ionic capitals, etc. – will someday permit a partial reconstitution.

To its side, the smallest of the three temples was undoubtedly dedicated to **Artemis**. It is the most ancient and this is confirmed by the base, found in front of the entrance, engraved in a bilingual text (Greek-Lycian) dating from the 4C BC.

Leto and the wolves

Zeus' mistress, Leto, was pursued by the wrath of Hera, the jealous wife of her divine husband. She sought refuge in Delos where she gave birth to her twins, Apollo and Artemis. Then she continued her flight, wandering until she reached Anatolia. One day, as she wanted to bathe her children in the waters of a river, she was prevented from doing so by shepherds, whom she quickly transformed into frogs. Wolves came to her rescue and guided her to Xanthos, where she was able to bathe the children and quench her thirst. In recognition, she dedicated the river to her son and baptised the region Lycia, from the Greek word lykos: wolf. In the gardens of Versailles, in France, you can admire a beautiful statue of Leto, in the middle of the Latone basin.

The third building, of Doric order, was dedicated to **Artemis** and **Apollo**. A small **mosaic***, preserved on the ground of the cella, represents the attributes of two divinities: a lyre for Apollo, a bow and quiver for his twin sister, goddess of the hunt. A **stela****, from 385 BC, engraved in three languages (Greek, Lycian and Aramaic) was found near the cliff which flanks the temple. Now in the museum of Fethiye, this Lycian "Rosetta stone" was a precious discovery for linguists.

South of the temples (*opposite them*), the site is almost constantly flooded, to the delight of ducks and frogs – undoubtedly the descendants of Leto's shepherds. Here an important **Roman nymphaeum*** was erected in Hadrian's honour. It can be recognised by its base, a large hemicycle with a 27m diameter, formerly surrounded by a beautiful portico with columns. It received water from a spring which could have been that of the primitive cult. The nymphaeum is opposite a Hellenistic grouping comprised of a small vaulted niche resembling an artificial grotto.

To the east, the nymphaeum gives way to the remains of the sanctuary's most recent monument: a **Byzantine church** (5-7C) testifying to its take over by Christianity. At the site's northern extremity is the **Hellenistic theatre***, a beautiful hemicycle clinging to the hill with two side-access galleries. The northern one features a beautiful **frieze*** of masks. Beyond the theatre, a few sarcophagi were recently cleared.

■ Patara**

23km from Letoön, 47km from Kaş. On the road from Fethiye to Kalkan, 5km after Kınık, turn right. The site is 8km away, near the village of Gelemiş, better known as Patara (if asking for directions, ask for "Patara" only). Dolmuşes leave from Fethiye, Kalkan or Kaş. Entrance fee for the beach and the site (pass valid for one week). The beach is closed to the public after 8pm when it becomes the home of the carretta turtles which come to lay their eggs. Allow 1hr.

Lost in the marshes and sesame fields, close to the sea, the Patara site was completely deserted until not long ago. Unfortunately, the creation of a holiday village – **Gelemiş** – near the ancient ruins, increasingly threatens its charm. The site is nevertheless breathtaking: behind the dunes lining the coastline, the strewn ruins protrude from the tall grass, prickly bushes and sand to create a romantic landscape. Beyond the dunes, an immense swathe of white sand – a 20km- long beach – flows towards the north to the other side of the Xanthos plain. It is impossible to resist the temptation of swimming, especially since the setting is so peaceful. Nonetheless care is required, since the beach faces onto the open sea and currents can be strong.

The city of sand

Patara was an important city, belonging to the Lycian Confederation with the same rank as Xanthos. However, it was always considered an extension of the latter. Most likely founded by colonists from Xanthos, it was the city's second port. It also housed the oracle of Xanthos, that of Apollo, which only spoke in winter. The city was organised around an immense port, 1600x400m. It remained active until the 12C, before silting up.

Before reaching the car park, you will see a discreet little **triumpal arch*** *(on the right)*, built in the 1C by the governor of the province, Mettius Modestus.

Right behind it lie the ruins of **Roman baths**, shaded by palm trees, then those of a **Christian basilica** *(at the far edge of the road)*. Beyond the car park *(on the right)*, other **baths, known as Vespasian's**, open their arches and windows toward the sky.

But Patara's most beautiful building is without question the **Roman theatre**** (1-2C), set on a steep-sided hill rising from the dunes *(300m from the car park on the left, towards the dunes)*. Its terraces are in the middle of the bushes, covered in the sand which has invaded the entire orchestra and its access galleries. A landscape that would enthuse romantic painters!

Rather than going back down, explore behind the theatre, in the dunes, following the coastline towards the northwest. In this way the marshes, the area of the ancient port which the sand has separated from the sea, can be avoided. There is also a stunning **panorama*** of the coast, up to the ruins of the **lighthouse**.

To the north stand the **granaries***, an imposing mass of stone emerging from the reeds, built in 129-130 during Hadrian's visit. They form a long building, 70m by 30m, composed of eight communicating sections. The **agora** stood to the west of the granaries *(no longer exists)*, while to the north, the ruins of a **necropolis** can still be seen, including a **large tomb** shaped like a temple.

■ Kalkan*

17km from Patara and 28km from Kaş. Also see "Making the most of Kalkan".

A small fishing port clinging to the mountain, Kalkan is in a tranquil bay of turquoise waters. Above the marina, the narrow alleyways of the old village climb among the white houses, all covered with bougainvillaea flowers and decorated with pretty wooden balconies (woodwork is the local craft). Kalkan is a haven of easy living and charm, a restful change from the other coastal resorts. Its beautiful Ottoman houses are home to many small hotels or cafés, whose terraces are an ideal spot for contemplating the bay.

Kalkan is an excellent starting point for visiting the region's surrounding sites and to go swimming. Some 4km to the east *(toward Kaş)*, there is a superb creek named **Kaputaş***, accessible from the road by a set of stairs *(several dolmuşes go there)*. Hidden between two cliffs, it hides a beautiful pebble beach lapped by turquoise waters. It can be crowded in season.

Kalkan, a small port with a typically Mediterranean atmosphere

L. Barret/PIX

Making the most of Patara (Gelemiş)

COMING AND GOING

By bus – Departures every day at 9pm from the centre of the village, to İzmir, Fethiye, Ôlüdeniz, Kôyceğiz, Antalya and Trabzon.

By shared taxi – From the stand in the centre of the village, services operate to Patara every day, to Xanthos, Letoön, and Saklıkent from 10am to 4pm, Fethiye on Tuesdays, Kalkan on Thursdays and Kaş on Fridays.

ADDRESS BOOK

Main post office – 8am-2pm. Stamps, phone cards, currency exchange and travellers' cheques, ☎ (242) 843 52 25.

Car rental – **Light Tour**, in the main street, ☎ (242) 843 52 05. Car and scooter hire.

Kırca Tours, in the centre of the village, ☎ (242) 843 52 98, Fax (242) 843 50 34.

WHERE TO STAY

Avoid the centre of the village at all costs – it is rife with bars and nightclubs. It's worth going a little further out into the surrounding hills. You won't regret it!

• Near the site and the beach

Under US$15

Motel Ekizoğlu, ☎ (242) 843 50 45. ☜ On the road to the beach. Adequate.

Between US$15 and US$25

☜ **Hotel Merhaba**, near the entrance to the site. The hotel is signposted, ☎ (242) 843 51 99 / 843 51 13, Fax (242) 843 51 33 – 10rm. ☜ ✕ ☙ Perched on top of the hill, with a sweeping view of the beach, this magnificent house with its oriental decor is a haven of peace. The rooms are very clean and spacious, and the beds are shrouded in beautiful white mosquito nets. Laundry facilities. Run by a delightful family: the father is a retired doctor (and now village doctor on the side), and the mother, a university lecturer, is a real cordon bleu cook. They treat you so much like a houseguest that you may forget you have to pay!

• In the village

Camp site

Medusa camp site, next to the bar of the same name. Cheap but noisy due to its central location.

Under US$15

Hotel Pataragate, just as you enter the village, ☎ (242) 843 51 68 – 20rm. ☜ ☙ ☙ CC You will receive a friendly welcome at this hotel, which stands at the entrance to Patara. The only disadvantage for travellers without their own transport is that it is the one furthest away from the centre of the village, the archeological site and the beach. Very good value for money.

Pension St-Nicolas, on the left just before you enter the village, ☎ (242) 843 50 24 / 843 51 54. ☜ You will receive a very cordial welcome in this guest house bordered by flowers, with giant bougainvillaea and clusters of red geraniums.

Golden Pansiyon, ☎ (242) 843 51 62 – 15rm. ☜ ✕ The proprietor speaks English and French. Friendly, personalised welcome.

Between US$15 and US$30

Hotel Delfin, on the road into the village, on the left, ☎ (242) 843 50 91, Fax (242) 843 51 69 – 30rm. ☜ ✕ ☙ ☙ CC This hotel, set slightly above street level, is very clean and has a lovely flower garden.

• On the hill

Between US$15 and US$30

Three rather expensive, but clean and welcoming guest houses:

Pension Zeybek 1, ☎ (242) 843 51 32 – 16rm, **Pension Zeybek 2**, ☎ (242) 843 50 86 – 15rm, **Sülo Pansiyon**, ☎ (242) 843 50 70 – 15rm. ☜ ☙

Over US$45

Hotel Beyhan, west of the village, ☎ (242) 843 50 98, Fax (242) 843 50 97 – 30rm. ☜ ☙ ✕ ☗ ☙ ☙ CC Turkish bath, sauna. A charming hotel, much more luxurious than the others. Access is difficult, but largely compensated for by the bird's-eye view of the valley.

EATING OUT

Florya, in the village square, ☎ (242) 843 50 33. A little restaurant where you will be greeted with a smile.

The White Dolphin, in the village square. Try the fish: this is what really sets it apart.

Manos has a pretty terrace where you can sample grilled trout for US$5.

Aspendos: the setting is rather nondescript, but the food is excellent and the menu very varied: "lahana sarma" (cabbage leaves stuffed with meat), "cacık" (cucumber with yoghurt), grilled fish, stuffed vine leaves, soup, and rice pudding.

Patara, on the road to the beach. Cheap and unpretentious, a handy place to stop on the way back from the beach.

HAVING A DRINK

Vitamin Bar, in the centre of the village. The bar gives directly onto the street. This is where all the globetrotters hang out, but the liveliest bars in the area are the **Lazy Frog** and the **Tropic**, with "happy hours" between 7pm and 9pm.

OTHER THINGS TO DO

Walking, hiking and swimming: what more could you ask for when staying on a hill covered with woods next to a stretch of white sand 20km long and 500m wide?

Excursions – The **Kırca Tours** agency, ☎ (242) 843 52 98, Fax (242) 843 50 34, organises canoe trips on the Xanthos (departure at 10am, return at 4.30pm), trekking in the mountains around Gömbe (departure at 9.30am, return at 6.30pm) and trips to Saklıkent (departure at 9.30am, return at 5.30pm).

Next to the post office, **Han Horse Riding** organises rides along the beach (in the morning from 7am to 12noon and in the afternoon from 4pm to 9pm). Around US$15 for 1hr, US$25 for 2hr and US$30 for 3hr.

Making the most of Kalkan

COMING AND GOING

By bus and shared taxi – The **bus station** is at the crossroads at the entrance to the village. Two companies operate services from here: **Kamil Koç**, ☎ (242) 844 31 11. Minibuses for Marmaris, Denizli, Pamukkale, Bodrum, Antalya, Kaş and Fethiye, and luxury coaches for İstanbul, Ankara, Selçuk, İzmir, Dalaman and Ortaca. **Pamukkale**, ☎ (242) 844 51 21 / 844 37 77 (İzmir, İstanbul, Ankara, Bodrum, Marmaris, Antalya, Fethiye, Dalaman, Ortaca, Köyceğiz and Kaş).

For Antalya, Fethiye, and Kaş: over 12 buses or minibuses per day. For the other destinations: at least 2 or 3 buses per day.

By boat – The marina, which is very well equipped, is only open in summer, from April to mid-November. Cost of mooring: around US$15 per day.

ADDRESS BOOK

Main post office – At the entrance to the village, turn left towards the centre, ☎ (242) 844 32 30. Open until 8pm, phone booths outside.

Bank / change – At the **post office** or at the harbour, opposite the fuel station. **Ziraat Bankası**, next to the post office: currency exchange and automatic cash dispenser.

Car rental – Enes, Yat Limanı, Pirat Oteli Dükkanları, ☎ (242) 844 39 61 / 844 38 07, Fax (242) 844 38 07.

Laundry – At the harbour (US$4 per load). Showers and toilets next door.

WHERE TO STAY

Set in beautiful Ottoman houses, the guest houses in the village are, for the most part, very pleasant and attractive. Make sure to book well in advance; the best ones are always in great demand.

Under US$15
Akın Pansiyon, YaliBoyu Mah, ☎ (242) 844 30 25 / 844 29 10, Fax (242) 844 20 94 – 11rm. Depending on the room, showers are available on the same floor. This is the oldest guest house in the village, set in an old Ottoman residence which has kept all its rustic charm (parquet floors and lace curtains).

Between US$15 and US$25
Pension Eski Ev, in the centre of the village, set slightly above street level, ☎ (242) 844 31 29. ⌁⌁✗ Run by a Turkish-Norwegian lady, this guest house is spacious, clean and has a pleasant garden where guests can take breakfast.

Pension Patara Stone House, slightly to the east of the harbour, on the coast, ☎ (242) 844 30 76. This old fisherman's abode is now a very pleasant guest house, managed by a young, dynamic and friendly team. Laundry facilities.

Between US$25 and US$30
Pension Balıkçı Han, Yaliboyu Mah, at the harbour, ☎ (242) 844 30 75 / 844 36 40, Fax (242) 844 36 41. ⌁⌁✗ In an old house, very tastefully decorated with traditional objects, furniture, carpets and hookahs, and a beautiful fireplace. It is a little more expensive, but the setting is delightful, and the terrace is a wonderful place for a drink.

Hotel Dionysia, high up on the hill, ☎ (242) 844 36 81. ⌁ A very clean, new and efficient hotel.

Between US$30 and US$45
Hotel Zinbad, Yaliboyu Mah 18, ☎ (242) 844 34 04 / 844 34 75, Fax (242) 844 39 43, www.kalkan.org.tr/kalkan/zinbad – 20rm. ⌁⌁ ⌁ ▤ ⎅ In a pedestrian street shaded by bougainvillaea. This place would be very peaceful if only the mosque weren't so close. Clean, bright rooms and a charming proprietress.

Kleo Pansiyon, Yaliboyu Mah, ☎ (242) 844 37 76, Fax (242) 844 21 65. ⌁⌁ ⌁ ▤ ✗ ⍨ Minibar. Next to the one above. Vast, clean rooms. The proprietor speaks English.

Over US$45
Hotel Kalkan Han, ☎ (242) 844 31 51, Fax (242) 844 20 48 – 16rm.

⌁⌁ ⎅ A beautiful building reminiscent of the façades of Ottoman residences. The rooms are very bright (everything is white and very clean) and simply but tastefully furnished. The magnificent roof terrace, facing the sea and surrounded by flowers, is the ideal place to relax over a drink and watch the sun set over the bay. An absolute must!

Hotel Pirat, at the harbour, ☎ (242) 844 31 78, Fax (242) 844 31 83 – 140rm. ⌁⌁ ⌁ ▤ ✗ ⍨ ⎅ The hotel is set out in small blocks of four rooms with balconies overlooking the harbour. The service is faultless and the setting original and very refined.

• **On the road to Kaş**

Camp sites
There are two seafront camp sites with bungalow accommodation 2km away from Kaş:

Olympos camp site, ☎ (242) 836 22 52 – 25 pitches.

Can camp site, ☎ (242) 836 15 41 – 20rm. ✗

EATING OUT

• **Kalkan**
Han, Yat Limanı 5, ☎ (242) 844 21 00 / 844 22 00. At the harbour, like the restaurants below. Fish and traditional Turkish dishes.

Korsan, (also a guest house), ☎ (242) 844 36 22. Like its neighbours, it serves good fish in a very warm atmosphere.

Doy Doy, Yalı Boyu Mah, at the foot of the Balıkçı guest house, ☎ (242) 844 31 14. Sweeping view of the harbour. The salads and meze are excellent and the fish delicious.

Akın Restaurant, belonging to the guest house of the same name. Its vine-covered terrace (feel free to pick the grapes) offers a sweeping view of the harbour and part of the village.

Chinese Restaurant, next to Korsan, at the harbour. Offers good set menus for 2 people for between US$18 and US$30.

• **On the road to Kaş**
Kaputaş, 3 or 4km from Kalkan. A very pleasant restaurant perched on the hill overlooking the road.

3km from Kaş, at Akçagerme, you may be glad to stop at this picnic area and restaurant after a long haul on the road.

OTHER THINGS TO DO

Boat trips – *Kahramanlar*, at the harbour, ☎ (242) 844 21 01, Fax (242) 844 38 95. For next to nothing, you can hire a magnificent, fully equipped and very comfortable sailing boat (for 5 to 8 people), for 1 day or 1 week. It will cost you around US$8 per person per day for a week-long cruise, all meals included, in twin cabins, to Kaş, Kale and Fethiye. An opportunity not to be missed! The agency also organises helicopter rides to Cappadocia, Pamukkale and Ephesus.

The ***Ada*** restaurant also offers sea trips in small boats.

Scuba diving – *Dolphin Scuba Team*, at the harbour, ☎ and Fax (242) 844 22 42 (office), ☎ (252) 844 22 65 (home). All levels of experience. Departure every day at 10am and return at 5pm. (US$30 for the whole day).

Barracuda Diving Center, at the harbour. Organises dives every day (departure at 9.30am, return at 4.30pm). For PADI and CMAS certificates.

Water sports – *Blue Marlin Watersport*, at the harbour, ☎ (242) 844 39 55, Fax (242) 844 35 40. Water-skiing, jet-skiing, windsurfing etc. Rather inflated prices.

Beach – Except for a small strip of well-kept sand to the left of the harbour, there is not really any beach at Kalkan to speak of. Instead, go 4km towards Kaş, to the place where the Kaputaş torrent flows out onto a magnificent beach. But you have to go down 180 steps to get there!

SHOPPING GUIDE

The alleyways in the village are lined with dozens of shops selling souvenirs, clothes and craftwork (carpets, copperware etc) and sometimes interesting antiques. Here are two good addresses, right in the heart of the shopping district:

Arts and crafts – *Türkmen*, Yalı Boyu Mah, ☎ and Fax (242) 844 20 97. Henriette Muheim, who is Dutch, and her Turkish husband, Aykut Dumlupınar, will enthusiastically recount the history of carpets. They have some very beautiful pieces on offer (carpets and kilims of all sizes and reasonably priced) and provide very good advice.

At ***Bouquet***, in the same alleyway and very near the one above, ☎ (242) 844 23 32, you will find some remarkable copperware (trays, vases, teapots etc), worked with a master's hand by a young, very friendly artisan, who is so attached to his works that he sometimes finds it hard to part with them!

Market – The permanent bazaar in Kalkan is behind the Akın guest house.

Making the most of Kalkan

KAŞ★ AND THE BAY OF KEKOVA★★★

Antalya Province – Map p 355
112km from Fethiye – 48km from Myra (Kale)
Kaş: Pop 4 600

Not to be missed
A boat excursion in the bay.
A walk in the streets of Kaş.
The small port of Kaleköy.

And remember...
For the bay of Kekova, take a boat from Andriake or Üçağız,
much more practical and enjoyable than the larger tourist boats in Kaş.

A charming little town nestling at the foot of the impressive Taurus Mountains, overlooking the sea, Kaş guards the entrance of a small peninsula as fine as an eyebrow (*kaş*, in Turkish). Its ancient remains, scattered throughout the town, are an invitation to a pleasant stroll. Walking up from the port, you see narrow streets lined with beautiful Ottoman houses with flowered balconies and heavy painted doors. In the evening, the city sparkles with a thousand lights and in the outdoor cafés the conversations of locals and holidaymakers mingle. A relaxed, lively atmosphere (particularly in the evening) and as yet sheltered from the frenzy of the large resorts.

Phellus and Antiphellus

Phellus and Antiphellus, you can't have one without the other. A small city in the mountains, approximately 15km north of Kaş, Phellus ("rocky terrain" in Greek) was founded in around the 6C BC, making it one of Lycia's most ancient cities. However, it was during the Hellenistic period that the city experienced its greatest growth. The prosperous expansion of its port, Antiphellus, was responsible for it becoming a capital during the Roman period. Antiphellus became a major trade centre, minting coins and living off the commerce of wood and sponges. A Byzantine bishopric, Antiphellus changed its name to Kaş when the Ottomans arrived and it subsequently went into decline.

Almost nothing is left of its rich past. In an alleyway climbing up on the left-hand side of the Tourist Office, stands a **Lycian tomb on a pillar** (4C BC) underneath a tree. A few remains are scattered around the city up to the isthmus. To the west, the **theatre** is still visible (*accessible on foot by the coastal road*) and its terraces overlook the sea, revealing a **beautiful view★** of the islands of Bucak bay.

The narrow path behind the theatre leads to **rock tombs** lost among the olive trees. One of them, the **Doric Tomb★**, displays a beautiful house-shaped façade. In the funerary room, a bench runs along the length of the wall, surmounted by a (barely visible) frieze decorated with dancers.

Excursions from Kaş

The **Kaş Peninsula** boasts innumerable small creeks, many of which are still unknown (but without beaches) and numerous **vantage points★★** overlooking the sea and the cliffs surrounding the coastline. The tour can be made by car but it is much more enjoyable by boat. Enquire among the fishermen in the port; for a small fee they will be happy to oblige.

In the mountains

Take the Antalya road. 11km from Kaş, turn left toward Kasaba-Elmalı. The road climbs up the mountain through lovely scenery.

North of Kaş, the **Taurus**★★ form an impressive wall of peaks and snow-capped summits with **Kızlar Dağı** (3 086m) and **Akdağ** (3 030m). Charming **villages** are hidden in the hillsides folds, clinging to the flanks or lost in the niches of valleys, far from the modern world. As the last examples of traditional rural life, they are worth exploring. The heights of the **Gömbe region** provide a refreshing walk *(70km from Kaş; first go towards Antalya. At the first traffic light, follow the signs to Elmalı. The winding road crosses a Lebanese cedar forest. At Gömbe, turn left after the bridge to climb the mountain)*. Apple orchards line the road and shade the open air restaurants serving goat's meat *(see "Making the most of Kaş")*. The mountains are also popular among hikers (care should be exercised in winter due to the snow) and trips can be arranged in Kaş.

Cruise in the Bay of Kekova★★★

One-day boat excursion (see "Making the most of Kaş")

A small natural cove, protected by the island of Kekova and a string of islets, the Bay of Kekova contains numerous remains: stone ghosts lost among the rocks, the shrubbery and the marshes, or drowned in the transparent waters of the bay. One way to take full advantage is to take a boat, not forgetting your swimsuit for a few impromptu swims. The smaller the boat, the more accessible everything becomes. For example, visit the "pirates' cave", before moving on to the islet of Burçi, where at the foot of a castle you can enjoy tea as you dip your feet in the sea.

■ **Andriake**★ – The excursion's first stop is the ancient port of Myra *(see p 408)* completely silted up and whose ruins emerge from the sand and the marshes like lonely reefs. On the western bank of the river, easily crossed in summer (due to a dry bed), a **nymphaeum**★, monumental fountain, appears with its two remaining beautiful arcades. On the left, a modest fountain dug in the rock undoubtedly marks the site of a primitive cult.

Warning, danger!
Next to the large cistern, the ground is covered with pieces of ancient ceramics which are undoubtedly the remains of a potter's workshop. Avoid the temptation of picking them up: Turkish legislation concerning the export of antiquities (anything older than 100 years) is very strict and searches are commonplace in airports. In addition to immediate confiscation, you would also face a heavy fine and a lot of difficulties.

The site's most interesting part is located on the eastern bank, 200m inland *(towards the south, crossing the dunes on foot)*. Go past a zone of houses and pools formerly used as shelter for boats, in order to reach an impressive building carefully constructed with rectangular and polygonal shapes. It was a **merchandise warehouse★★** *(horreum)* completed during Hadrian's visit, in 129-130. It is the most remarkable example of utilitarian Roman architecture to be seen in Asia Minor. 69m long and 39m wide, it is made of up of eight loges of uneven sizes and two small pavilions at the edge of the façade. Retaining all of its height (more than 8.5m), it has kept the truncated pediment that decorated its main façade. On its walls are the **busts of Hadrian and his wife Sabina**, **bas-reliefs** displaying arms', the Egyptian divinities Isis and Ser-

The fortress of Kaleköy watches over the blue waters of Kekova

M.-P. Lejard/MICHELIN

apis, Greek inscriptions and in particular, the Emperor's large dedication **epigraph**, in Latin. The building is surrounded by the remains of another fountain, a **large cistern** and several storage rooms.

■ **Kaleköy**★★ (Simena) – A small fishing port facing the island of Kekova, Kaleköy is an ideal stop for lunch. A few restaurants line the shore, and in complete isolation in the sea, a **Lycian sarcophagus**★ *(on the right, facing the sea)* emerges. In spite of the influx of tourists, Kaleköy has retained its charm. Facing the coloured boats aligned in the port, the old houses are terraced on the slope among the Hellenistic ruins. Climbing up the alleyways you see beautiful **vantage points**★★ overlooking the bay and Kekova island – a clutter of white rocks strewn with shrubs and olive

The business touch

In Kaleköy, a poor village, small businesses do well: in the summer, small children will offer to guide you around (hastily) and they will not fail to show off their new school. They will sell you traditional scarves decorated with small shells, while on street corners, their grandmothers sell sachets of aromatic herbs. It is also possible to have a pair of Turkish trousers tailor-made while sipping the seamstress' tea on a terrace in one of the villager's homes.

trees above the transparent waters. A steep incline leads to the **Byzantine fortress***
(*entrance fee*) whose beautiful battlemented walls still survey the village. Built on the
site of the ancient acropolis, it hides a small hemicycle, barely 15m wide, cut into
the rock. Contrary to what most guides say, it is not the "smallest ancient theatre",
but rather a **bouleuterion**, the municipal assembly room. Higher up, a group of
Byzantine houses is visible, with a large stone **mortar**.

At the top of the citadel is (*access via a narrow path below*) a Hellenistic and Roman
necropolis whose heavy stone tombs are scattered among the olive trees.

■ **The island of Kekova*** – Opposite the port is the island of Kekova, 7km long,
which almost encloses the whole bay. History and nature have composed a beautiful landscape: with the surrounding islets which encircle it, Kekova was used as a
quarry throughout Antiquity and it is covered by a multitude of remains lost among
the shrubs. Most have not been excavated and therefore are not visible, except near

the shore to the west of the island (*on
its northern coast*). Here, under a few cen-
timetres of water, are numerous
remains of dwellings and the docks of
a **Lycian port*** (*swimming and diving forbidden*). Isolated near the southwest tip
of the island, the apse of the Byzantine
church of **Tersane** seems to guard the
boats which disappear into the
distance.

Submerged ruins

Along the coastline, ruins of cities which have
been "swallowed" are visible and whose history local guides often embellish with apoc-
alyptic events or earthquakes. In fact, this
phenomenon is simply due to the slight increase in the Mediterranean's water level
which has submerged the remains of ancient
port installations and houses that were located on the shore.

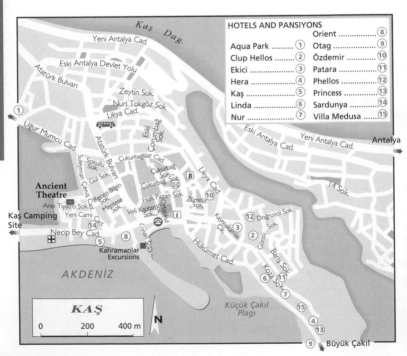

HOTELS AND PANSIYONS

		Orient	⑧
Aqua Park	①	Otag	⑨
Clup Hellos	②	Özdemir	⑩
Ekici	③	Patara	⑪
Hera	④	Phellos	⑫
Kaş	⑤	Princess	⑬
Linda	⑥	Sardunya	⑭
Nur	⑦	Villa Medusa	⑮

▪ Teimiussa ★ – On the return journey, a short visit to the north of the village of Üçağız, on the other side of the bay is well worth the time. There are lines of beautiful **Lycian sarcophagi** facing the shore, forgotten amidst the bushes and the rocks. One of them (4C BC) is decorated with a **bas-relief** representing a young man. These are the remains of the necropolis of Teimiussa, a completely submerged Antique city.

Making the most of Kaş

COMING AND GOING

By bus – The bus station is at the entrance to the town, 1km from the centre. **Antalya Tours** operates services to Olympos, Demre, Finike, Patara, Fethiye and Kemer. **Kamil Koç** goes to İstanbul and Ankara. **Pamukkale** has connections to İstanbul, Ankara and İzmir. **Uludağ** goes to Bursa and Antalya.

By shared taxi – From the bus station, the dolmuşes of the **Minibüs Kooperativi** depart for Patara, Phellos, Kalkan and Gömbe every 30min, as well as to Demre (Kale) and the beautiful beaches at Kaputaş.

ADDRESS BOOK

Tourist information – At the harbour, opposite the statue of Atatürk. A very pleasant welcome, precise information, a detailed map: without a doubt this is the best tourist information office on the coast! Open from May to September, 8am-7pm during the week, 9am-7pm at weekends. Beware: it occasionally closes from noon to 1pm. ☎ and Fax (242) 836 12 38.

Bank / change – Ziraat Bankası, opposite the post office. **Yapı Kredi Bank**, Hastane Cad (on the road to the theatre). There are also other banks to be found in the main street (Elmalı Cad), such as **İş Bankası**.

Main post office – 7am-11pm. Currency exchange. Phone booths outside.

Internet – Café Net House Computer Center, Çukurbağlı Cad, ☎ (242) 836 40 73, Fax (242) 836 39 38, nethousecafe@superonline.com. US$4 per hour.

Car rental – Alibaba, Hastane Cad 42, ☎ (242) 836 25 01 / 836 13 54, Fax (242) 836 32 25. **Bougainville**, Çukurbağlı Cad 10, ☎ (242) 836 31 42, Fax (242) 836 16 05.

Medical service – Public hospital, to the west of the town, opposite the antique theatre, ☎ (242) 836 11 85 / 836 14 68.

Laundry – At the harbour or in Süleyman Topçu Sokağı street. **Laundry Rose**, in the town centre, a few metres from the Chez Evy restaurant.

WHERE TO STAY

Owing to the great surge in tourism in Kaş over the last few years, hotels and guest houses have been sprouting up here, like everywhere else. However, if you avoid the harbour, where decibels rocket sky-high in summer, the town is a very pleasant place and you can easily find somewhere quiet to stay. There are 3 distinct sectors: the town centre, based around the harbour area, the administrative quarter (police station) to the east, and the antique theatre district to the west.

• East end

Among the establishments which line the coast, 3 are run by the same manager and present the same excellent standards of cleanliness and efficiency:

US$15

⊛ **Pension Patara**, Küçük Çakıl Mevkii, ☎ (242) 836 13 28 / 836 17 88, Fax (242) 836 17 88 – 8rm. ⌂¶✕ A very pleasant guest house with a shaded terrace (like most of the neighbouring guest houses). The rooms are very clean, with pretty curtains and little balconies offering a view of the mountains or sea. Friendly welcome.

Nur Pansiyon, Küçük Cakıl, ☎ (242) 836 12 03 – 15rm. ⌐¶ Clean, bright rooms with balconies overlooking the sea.

US$20

Hotel Linda, Küçük Çakıl Mevkii, same telephone number as the one above – 20rm. ⌐¶ ♪ cc Same characteristics as the Pension Patara but on a larger scale: the building is bigger, as are the rooms, and the establishment is more upmarket.

US$25

Hotel Rhea, Küçük Çakıl Mevkii, ☎ (242) 836 13 28 / 836 30 84, Fax (242) 836 17 88 – 20rm. ⌐¶ ♪ ▤ cc There is no notable difference in comparison with the one above, apart from the air conditioning.

Under US$25

Hotel Ekici, slightly to the east of the police station, ☎ (242) 836 14 17, Fax (242) 836 18 23 – 60rm. ⌐¶ ♪ ✗ ⌒ cc A little out of the way, but without being isolated, very simple but functional, clean and very well run, the Ekici hotel is one of the best in its price range.

Around US$30

Hotel Aqua Princess, on the beachfront at Küçük Cakıl Mevkii, ☎ (242) 836 20 26 – 42rm and 9 suites. ⌐¶ ♪ ▤ ✗ ♥ ⌒ ✿ cc Minibar. A luxurious multi-storey hotel, with a rather effective Mediterranean decor, all in blue and white, with spacious rooms. The only (small) drawback is that there is no lift. Reasonable value for money.

Over US$60

Hotel Medusa, Küçük Çakıl Mevkii, ☎ (242) 836 14 40, Fax (242) 836 14 41 – 80rm. ⌐¶ ♪ ▣ ▤ ✗ ⌒ ✿ cc

Hotel Hera, Küçük Çakıl Mevkii, ☎ (242) 836 30 62, Fax (242) 836 30 63 – 46rm. ⌐¶ ♪ ▤ ✗ ♥ ⌒ cc Minibar. Also has a jacuzzi, Turkish bath, sauna and nightclub. A fake Greco-Roman temple as kitsch as it is pretentious.

● **Town centre**

Under US$15

⊛ **Özdemir Pansiyon**, İlkokul Sok 30, ☎ (242) 836 10 54. ⌐¶ ✗ A very pleasant, clean and charming little guest house run with care. Warm, quiet rooms (at-

tractive wooden decor with rustic charm), away from the noise of the bars. Breakfast is served up above on the shaded terrace, which is always lovely and cool. Pure heaven!

Between US$15 and US$25

Hotel Oryant, Elmalı Cad 7/1, ☎ (242) 836 15 45 / 836 15 46, Fax (242) 836 24 13 – 20rm. ⌐¶ ♪ ✗ cc Right in the town centre, on the main road linking the bus station to the harbour. Typically Turkish, tasteful decoration, and unbeatable value for money.

● **Towards the theatre**

Camp site

Kaş camp site, 400m from the Kaş hotel. With plenty of shade and a good location, not far from the theatre. Very reasonable rates (US$8).

Under US$15

Hotel Sardunya, Hastane Cad, ☎ (242) 836 30 80 / 836 30 81, Fax (242) 836 30 82 – 16rm. ⌐¶ ♪ ✗ cc Everything is spacious: the rooms and balconies (with view of the sea), and the restaurant, whose terrace takes up the entire roof. You will receive a cheerful welcome in this peaceful oasis.

US$15

⊛ **Kaş Hotel**, Necip Bey Cad Hastane Yolu, ☎ (242) 836 12 71 – 16rm. ⌐¶ ✗ ♥ ⌂ ✿ Even better than rooms, this hotel has lovely concrete bungalows, basic but clean, which open out onto a small beach set among the rocks. A large terrace in the style of a ship's deck opens out over the sea, above the bar (the Elit) which is run by the sociable Savas.

Over US$45

⊛ **Hotel Club Phellos**, Doğru yol Sok Cad, ☎ (242) 836 19 53 / 836 13 26, Fax (242) 836 18 90 – 81rm. ⌐¶ ♪ ▤ ✗ ⌒ ✿ cc A beautiful hotel with a simple and tasteful decor, offering a breathtaking view of the sea, and a notch above the other establishments in town. The swimming pool is very clean (self-cleaning system) and the food excellent.

● **In the area around Kaş**

Between US$30 and US$45

Aquapark Hotel, Çukurbağ Yarımadası, ☎ (242) 836 19 01, Fax (242) 836 19 92 – 78rm, 21 suites, 24 apartments. ⌐¶ ♪

▤ TV CC Minibar. If you're planning to stay for a while, or just for a day. Free for children under 6, half price for 7- to 12-year-olds. Half-board possible. Set on the peninsula, 6km from Kaş, in a very pretty spot surrounded by the sea, this holiday village is run by a dynamic young man. Activities are organised every evening and various outdoor pursuits are on offer: football, volleyball, golf and scuba diving. Open from 15 May to 15 October. Three daily bus services run between the village and Kaş.

Hotel Otağ, on the other side of the bay, ☎ (0532) 563 14 07 – 23rm. ☜ ♗ ▤ ✗ ♟ ♙ Minibar. The only way to get there is by the hotel shuttle, which will pick you up at the marina. If you want to book a room and shuttle, ask for the manageress, Ms Fayka. Since the hotel owners choose not to work with the tour operators, you are guaranteed peace and quiet and a personalised service. Clients can even choose when they eat. From the hotel's private beach you can admire the view of the whole bay of Kaş, and the garden leads up to a nomad's tent. You can come here just for the day, but why not take a break from urban life and spend a week in this haven of peace and quiet?

EATING OUT
Good restaurants abound in Kaş, and, like the bars, they are all to be found in the old town. The fish is often very well prepared and served with fresh vegetables, and the competition is steep, which works in the customer's favour. But a word of warning: the terrace restaurants in the main square in Kaş are not all of the best quality or the most honest when it comes to the bill.
Our choice:
Under US$15
Marina Restaurant, Cumhuriyet Meyd 9, ☎ (242) 836 16 40. Good pizzas.
Bahçe Restaurant, in the town centre, near the Lycian tomb. Tasty meze.
Also in the centre, you can dine at the **Blue House**, in an attractive Mediterranean decor (a meal will set you back around US$15) or at the **Belle-Vue** for around US$10.

The **Turkmene Restaurant**, in Süleyman Sandıkçı Sok, does not serve alcohol, but you can sample traditional Turkish dishes at very reasonable prices: "yayla" (yoghurt soup), Turkish ravioli ("mantı") or "gözleme" (Turkish crepes).
Gökkuşağı, Hükümet Cad, ☎ (242) 836 19 37. A fish restaurant which also has crayfish (around US$55 per kilo) and good meze on the menu.
Küçük Çakil, opposite the Pension Patara, on the seafront. More-than-adequate traditional food served in a restful setting.
Around US$15
Chez Evy, Terzi Sok 2, in the pedestrian centre, ☎ (242) 836 12 53. Open from May 1 until the beginning of November. For a change from Turkish cuisine, try this remarkable French restaurant, expertly run by Evy, an eminent cordon bleu chef who is also very kind. This restaurant is set in a pretty little house with an inner courtyard full of jasmine and honeysuckle and decorated with half-Andalusian, half-Anatolian azulejo tiles. As for the food, everything is simply delicious, for example, the memorable squid à la provençale, fillet of beef with béarnaise sauce, and crêpes Suzette (the real thing), prepared by Evy herself, for whom nothing is too much trouble when it comes to her clients.
Eriş, Cumhurriyet Meyd Gürsoy Sok 13, ☎ (242) 836 21 34, Fax (242) 836 10 57. Open all year round. The proprietor pampers his clients. The specialities served here are fish cooked in salt or grilled, prawns, crayfish, octopus and meze.

• **On the road to Gömbe**
Müdürnü Yeri, ☎ (242) 831 48 79. In the shade of the poplars, you can savour delicious goat's meat (around US$9 per kilo), served with onions, peppers and slices of toast. The proprietor himself cooks the meat on a "mangal" in front of his clients.

HAVING A DRINK
Habessos Bar, overlooking the harbour, just below the Köşk guest house. You can drink Turkish coffee here and listen to live music. After midnight, Turkish

classical music is played. The atmosphere is very relaxing and the proprietress welcoming and helpful.

Déjà vu, at the harbour, opposite the one above. If you fancy a change from Turkish music, you can come here for a dose of good modern western-style music: jazz, jazz-rock, pop and rock.

Sun Café, Hükümet Cad, ☎ (242) 836 10 53, Fax (242) 836 19 24. A western-style, open-air jazz bar, which also has a restaurant serving good Turkish fare in the garden.

Elit Bar, the bar of the Kaş hotel (see the "Where to stay" section). The view of the sea is definitely worth a look.

The Reggae Bar, Hükümet Cad 10, ☎ (242) 836 28 32. True to its name, this bar plays only reggae (or ska upon request). You have the whole night to try out its 500 different varieties of cocktails!

SHOPPING GUIDE

The Kaş **market** takes place on Fridays in a street running at right angles to the main road (Elmalı Cad) just behind the fuel station.

Magic Orient, in the shopping centre next to the tourist information office. Wide selection of carpets and kilims.

OTHER THINGS TO DO

Boat trips and scuba diving – *Kahramanlar*, at the harbour, ☎ (242) 836 30 42 / 836 10 62, Fax (242) 836 24 02 / 836 20 97. Various types of cruises available to the surrounding islands and bays, on board magnificent gülets.

Bougainville Travel, Çukurbağlı Cad 10, ☎ (242) 836 31 42, Fax (242) 836 16 05. Scuba diving and trips to the island of Kekova.

In Küçük Çakıl Mevkii, to the east of town, several agencies offer scuba diving

initiation and certificates. The **Nur guest house** also has a scuba diving centre.

Dolce Vita, Cumhuriyet Meyd A3, in the square where the tourist information office is located, ☎ (242) 836 22 67, Fax (242) 836 16 49. Offers all sorts of attractively-priced packages for boat hire and cruises, from 3, 7 or 14 days, half- or full-board on gülets with 4 or 6 cabins equipped with showers, a kitchen and breakfast bar. This agency also offers scuba diving packages.

Kekova bay cruise – You can embark for this trip in Kaş, but the boats are big, often overloaded and it's a 5hr journey by sea. The best solution is to set out from Andriake, where the boats are much smaller (8-10 places). Some of the guest houses in Kale (Demre) organise a shuttle to the harbour and some even have their own boat. However, the best point of departure still remains the village of **Üçağız**, to the west of the bay, or **Andriake** (our option).

Beaches – There are two good beaches at Kaş: **Küçük Çakıl**, in the district of the same name, near the Ekici hotel, in the east of town; and **Büyük Çakıl**, 4km east of Kaş, on the road to the Aqua Princess hotel. A beautiful little bay with pebble beaches and clear, cool water. You can rent a parasol for a modest sum and take some refreshment at one of the five little bars and "lokanta" set up on the beach. In the bay of Kaş, opposite the town, there are also some unspoiled sand and rock beaches, which you can reach by water-taxi (from the harbour, below the sign "Liman Beach Service"). These boats also go to the Otağ hotel and the village of Üçağız.

Festival – At the beginning of summer each year (end of June / beginning of July), the international festival of Lycia plays host to folk dancing groups from all over the world.

Making the most of Üçağız

This tiny fishing harbour, which was still very much isolated only a few years ago, has recently been swept up in the tide of the tourist industry, and its inhabitants are all now turning their hand to the hotel and restaurant trade and organising boat trips in Kekova bay and the surrounding area.

COMING AND GOING

Üçağız can be reached from Kaş by car, dolmuş or boat. A footpath links Üçağız to the port at Kaleköy (around 45min walk).

ADDRESS BOOK

Tourist information – Smart Tourism, in the centre of the village, ☎ (242) 874 20 40 / 874 20 38, Fax (242) 874 20 39. Leyla Hanım, who speaks English, will supply you with a mountain of historical and tourist information on the village and region.

WHERE TO STAY

Under US$15

It is possible to camp on the beach, north of the village, after the Kekova restaurant. **Pension Onur**, ☎ (242) 874 20 71, Fax (242) 874 22 66, onurpension@yahoo.com, www.come.to/onurpension – 8rm. Onur and his Dutch wife, Jacqueline, will give you a warm welcome in their pleasant wooden house with a terrace on the seafront. The price of the room includes breakfast and 30min Internet connection time per day (use this to check out their Web page, in 5 languages, which recounts the region's history). In the evening, there is a meze buffet for around US$4. Clients without their own transport can arrange by telephone to be picked up at the crossroads with the road to Antalya.

It is also possible to rent a room in one of the local's houses, in particular with **Leyla Hanım**, ☎ (242) 874 20 38, Fax (242) 874 20 39, a cheerful and dynamic lady who speaks English and also works at the tourist information office. Her house has 3 rooms, with a shared shower on the landing, a terrace and garden. Breakfast is a real Pantagruelian feast!

EATING OUT

Don't be fooled by the apparent popularity of the two restaurants on the seafront in the centre of the village: they are very touristy and it's advisable to check your bill carefully. Instead, why not try the restaurant of the **Onur guest house**, which serves good fish and squid at very reasonable prices.

It is also worth bearing in mind that if you are staying in one of the local's houses, you can also come to an arrangement for your landlord to provide the meals of your choice at a set price.

OTHER THINGS TO DO

Several establishments (guest houses, restaurants, private individuals) organise boat trips to **Kekova**, **Kaleköy**, **Batikent** (the "sunken" city) and **Tersane**. Go for the most simple form of transport, the fishing boats, which are not only cheaper than the gülets but also much quieter. Ask for Halil Bey (at the Onur guest house) who will gladly take you out for a 2hr trip, for US$6 per person.

MYRA★★
(KALE, DEMRE)
Antalya Province – Map p 355
43km from Kaş – 149km from Antalya
Pop 14 500

Not to be missed
The Church of St Nicholas in Demre.
The rock tombs of Myra.

And remember...
If you do not have a car, choose a hotel which can offer transport
around the area, since public transport is non-existent.
Bring along binoculars to appreciate the details of Myra's rock tombs.

Demre, recently renamed Kale, is an ordinary little town of no particular interest, except for its very beautiful church dedicated to St Nicholas and the amazing rock tombs of Myra, the ancient city located nearby. It is also the ideal starting point for visiting the Bay of Kekova and neighbouring islands *(see previous chapter)*, a superb site best explored by boat. Of course, do not leave without biting into one of Demre's specialities: tomatoes grown in local greenhouses.

The Church of St Nicholas★★
200m from the city centre in the direction of Myra.
8am-7pm in summer and 8am-5.30pm in winter. Entrance fee.

Did you know that St Nicholas, Father Christmas' twin brother (?), came from Turkey? Born at the beginning of the 4C AD in Patara, Nicholas converted to Christianity under Diocletian before embarking on a long journey to Palestine. Upon his return, he became Myra's first bishop and undoubtedly participated in the Council of Nicaea, in 325. He died around 345, and was probably buried on the island of Gemili *(see p 380)*, before his remains were transferred to the church in Myra, later dedicated to him. In 1087-88, his relics were stolen by pirates and deposited in Bari, the Italian city on the Adriatic Sea, where he became the patron saint. Since then, his body has been dispersed between Bari, Venice, Russia and the Antalya Museum which preserves the Myra shrine.

The patron of children and pirates
The account of his merits and miracles rapidly made Nicholas one of the Eastern world's best known saints, before he was adopted by all of Europe. Originally patron of sailors – Myra was a very large port – Nicholas also became the patron of pirates, who stole his relics. However, he is especially famous for being the protector of children, hagiographical literature having quickly credited him with numerous miracles in their favour. One of the best known is the resurrection of three young boys whose bodies were discovered by the saint in a butcher's salting tub in Myra.

In northern Europe, Nicholas became Claus (Santa Claus) and as he was celebrated on December 6, in the middle of winter, popular devotion imagined him with a sleigh, a cape and furs. This is how Nicholas, saviour and saint of children from warm climes, replaced Father Christmas of snowy northern regions (he is also the patron of Holy Russia), where he distributes gifts to deserving children.

Venerated by Christians as well as Muslims, celebrated in the four corners of the world, Nicholas is undoubtedly the most ecumenical and international of saints!

A labyrinth of chapels

On the outside of the town, the church of St Nicholas proudly displays its old grey walls amid the orchards. Although its size remains modest, the complex layout was designed in the 8C around an older plan which itself had been altered over time. The church underwent extensive excavations and a major restoration in 1989.

As you enter, you are immediately struck by the majesty of vaulted rooms with their barren stones bathed in golden light. The visit begins through a small **gallery** paved with **mosaics**★ where you can admire beautiful **capitals**. Thereafter, the first **chapel**★ (12C), lit through an elegant window with **three bays**, leads to a gallery on the left where several **ancient sarcophagi**★, reused during Byzantine times, have been laid. Returning to the chapel, you reach two **rooms with apses**. They are the church's oldest and have been incorporated into the Byzantine building. A very beautiful 11C **opus sectile**★★ (marble marquetry) decorates the floors of the three chapels.

The first room with an apse leads to a narrow gallery filled with an imposing **sarcophagus** thought to be that of **St Nicholas**. In fact, the tomb was reconstructed in the Middle Ages using older remains. Nevertheless, it is likely that this gallery, illogical in Byzantine architecture, may have been the saint's original burial place. The light unveils the remains of beautiful **frescoes** representing a stylite and two saints.

Myra, the Lycian tombs

E. Valentin/HOA QUI

Myra

Next, enter the main body of the church (8C), the **central nave****, originally topped by a dome. Your eye is immediately drawn to the **main apse**** (the *bema*), the mosaics, the elegant columns rising in front of the altar (they were used to support a canopy) and the white marble steps of a *synthronon*, a small hemicycle where the choir stood.

The northern apse (the *prothesis*), where mass was prepared, leads to the **side aisles** and to an entire network of rooms. These areas were built over various periods and belong to a convent added in the 11C.

Enter the **endonarthex** (inner vestibule) to the west where you can see 11C **frescoes** representing the emperor and a series of saints and archbishops.

The visit ends with the **exonarthex**, a modern component dating from the restoration undertaken by Czar Nicholas I and begun in 1862, seven years after his death. It opens onto the **courtyard**, a vestige of the former convent, decorated with a fountain and a funerary recess *(to the south)*.

Myra, the ancient city**

2km from Demre. A small car park is located 100m from the theatre and the first group of tombs. 8am-7.30pm, 6pm in winter. Entrance fee. Allow 2hr for the visit.

Built at the foot of a steep hill, and facing the plain of Andriake, Myra displays the most impressive group of rock tombs in all of Lycia. Upon arrival, you are struck by the array of tombs sculpted in the cliffside and the majestic theatre below.

A great metropolis

The existence of Myra is attested to by the monuments and inscriptions from the 5C BC onwards. However, it experienced its greatest development during the Hellenistic and Roman periods. It was among the six main cities of the Lycian Confederation, minting coins, and was equipped with one of the coast's finest ports *(Andriake, see p 399)*. In the 4C the city became an important centre of Christianity thanks to St Nicholas (bishop). Emperor Theodosius II made it capital of Lycia in the 5C. With Arab invasions beginning in the 7C, the city began to decline and the silting up of its port led the inhabitants to move away in the 12C.

Partially built into the mountainside, the **theatre**** is the finest vestige brought to light. In Hellenistic style, it was in fact reconstructed during the Roman era, after the earthquake which destroyed it in 141. Its **cavea***, nearly complete, has retained its 38 steps which could accommodate 8 000 persons, and a portion of the stage building's façade still stands. Several decorative items lie about the orchestra: fragments of **friezes*** embellished with theatre masks, the eagle of Zeus and heads of Medusa. You can enjoy yourself by looking for the inscription of a merchant of the time, who had reserved a section to sell his goods to the spectators.

A protected site

Along the little path leading to the theatre you will notice slopes made of mud, gravel and sand. These are the traces of the general silting up of the site and the floods which it endured over the years. This layer of alluvia (reaching 10m in some areas) has protected – and continues to protect – practically all of the ancient city. Archeological digs would enable the discovery of all of its treasures.

Immediately west of the theatre is the first part of the **"maritime" necropolis**. It constitutes an exceptional ensemble of **Lycian tombs***** carved in the cliffside, imitating the façade of a house or a temple. Among the bas-reliefs, notice a funerary banquet and a gladiator fight.

At the foot of the cliff, the ground is littered with numerous frieze and capital fragments, whose decorations – ova, interlace (wreaths), foliage and acanthuses – are always overlooked by visitors.

Walk around the hill from the east. Less than 1km away, you reach the **"fluvial" necropolis**, so called as it skirts the Myros Andriakos (the current Kokar Çayı or Demre Çayı), whose bed has since shifted. Here lie several other beautiful **tombs***, with decorations or inscriptions. The pediment of one of them depicts the combat between a lion and a bull. Another one carries a frieze representing a funerary banquet, whereas a third one *(in the median level)* shows full-sized figures.

Finally, the more athletically-minded may climb up to the **acropolis**, perched on the summit of the rocky peak, by following a small path heading towards the eastern side of the valley (in former times, access used to be by way of steps carved in the rocks). It is the only place where one can explore the (meagre) remains of the Lycian city: fragments of ramparts, a gate and remnants of houses.

Making the most of Kale (Demre)

COMING AND GOING

By bus – Antalya Tours, ☎ (242) 871 21 59 / 871 44 23 / 871 35 96 operates services to Finike, Kaş, Antalya (every 30min), Kalkan, Olympos, Patara, Fethiye (every 30min), İstanbul and Ankara.

By taxi and shared taxi – Travellers without their own form of transport can get to the ancient site of Myra, 2km from Demre, by taxi or dolmuş (around US$5 per ride). Taxis also go to Andriake, the harbour at Demre, 3km from the town centre.

ADDRESS BOOK

Banks – İş Bankası, in Müze Cad, opposite the church of St Nicholas. 9am-12.30pm / 1.30pm-5pm. Cash dispenser and currency exchange.

Main post office – Lise Cad, 8am-6.30pm. Currency exchange also possible here.

WHERE TO STAY

All sorts of guest houses can be found at Kale, most of them in the vicinity of the post office.

Between US$8 and US$25
Pension Kekova, İlkokul Karşısı, Çarsı İçi, ☎ and Fax (242) 871 22 67. In the little street to the right when facing the post office. A friendly guest house, run by a young team who organise excursions to Kekova bay. Full-board is compulsory, but the home cooking is very good.

Hotel Kıyak, Merkez Girişinde, ☎ (242) 871 45 09 / 871 20 93. At the entrance to the town, next to the school. This is more of a guest house than a hotel, with its small rooms and homely welcome. Unfortunately rather noisy.

Hotel Kekova, almost opposite the post office, ☎ (242) 871 34 62. A modern hotel with no particular charm. Once very popular, but those days would appear to be long gone.

EATING OUT

Güneyhan, next to the church of St Nicholas. A pleasant, shaded terrace, which is unfortunately often overrun by coach loads of tourists who have come to visit the monument. Set menu at US$6.

Akdeniz Restaurant, Müze Cad 9, ☎ (242) 871 54 66. Simple and cheap: "döner", pide and salads.

THE HEIGHTS OF FİNİKE ★

Antalya Province – Map p 355
29km from Kale – 120km from Antalya
Pop 20 000 – Very mild climate, year round

Not to be missed
The funerary monument of Xantabura, in Limyra.
The entire site of Arycanda.

And remember...
For a picnic, buy your groceries in the colourful Arif market
and enjoy fresh tomatoes as you admire the scenery in Arycanda.

Surrounded by the tallest summits of Bey Dağları, a rocky crest running between
Finike and Antalya, the Akçay Valley (ancient Arycandus) reaches the sea in a vast
plain covered with cotton fields and orchards. Protected by the mountains, the site
is blessed with a particularly mild climate, which has led to the success of Finike, a
quiet fishing port at the mouth of a river. Completely rebuilt after an earthquake,
the small town (pop 10 700) today has no charm except for its modern marina surrounded by restaurants and nearby pebble beaches, home to Turkish holidaymakers.
The advantage: its proximity to the archeological sites of Limyra, and especially
Arycanda the ruins and setting of which are extraordinarily beautiful.

Limyra

*10km from Finike. Take the road to Elmalı towards Turunçova, where you will turn right
heading for Kumluca. The site is 3km from there. For those without private transport, a bus
serves Turunçova (departure in front of city hall). The final kilometres are made on foot. Allow
1hr for the visit, 2hr if you climb up to the acropolis.*

Limyra is not an exceptional site, but its quiet, slightly romantic atmosphere makes
it a very enjoyable excursion. The Lycian city stretches at the foot of Mount Tocat
(1 215m), an imposing hill dominating the plain. The ruins enliven this small haven
of greenery and freshness, an "Arcadian Garden", irrigated by the waters where sheep
and goats come to drink. At the top of the hill, the walls of the acropolis (in ruins)
grip the barren rocks, affording a beautiful view the plain, an immense green blanket
rolling towards the sea.

Lycian capital

Limyra first appears in history in the 5C BC. A prosperous city in spite of the Persian occupation, it lived through its golden age in the 4C, when Prince Pericles made
it the capital of the Lycian Confederation. It became Roman in 167 BC and continued to develop until an earthquake completely destroyed it. Its renaissance was due
to Opramoas, one of the city's wealthiest citizens, who restored the theatre. During
the Byzantine period, Limyra became a
major bishopric and continued to prosper
until the arrival of the Arabs, when it was
abandoned.

Fortune-telling fish
Pliny said that there existed a sacred fountain in Limyra with fish that could be questioned like oracles. If the fish ate the food
tossed to them, it was a good omen. If they
did not, a sombre future was in store.
Therefore, it was wise to feed them
scrumptious morsels!

The road leading to the site crosses the
modern village – a modest hamlet – to
reach the **theatre** *(on the left side)*, a small
building seating 2 500, and sitting on the

side of the hill like a large armchair. Reconstructed in the 2C and restored by arche-ologists (Austrian), it is the site's best preserved building, even if it has lost its stage wall and part of its cavea. Above the topmost step, notice the holes dug at regular intervals: **large awning stakes** were used to stretch an immense piece of fabric to shelter the spectators from the sun. The side access galleries serve as storage areas for sculptures and frieze fragments found during the excavations.

The hill is home to several **necropolises** ★ – groups of **sarcophagi** or **rock tombs** ★ with sculpted façades – lost on the slopes, east and west of the theatre. Behind the theatre, a series of niches (4C BC) housed the statues of Lycian gods. Nearby, 100 metres to the east *(by way of a path)*, a superb **Lycian sarcophagus** ★★ rises above the rocks and the shrubs like a lonely and rigid silhouette. It enclosed the remains of Xantabura, Pericles' brother. On its frontispiece, notice the bas-relief representing the judgement of the dead.

The ascension towards the **acropolis** *(from the village rather than from the theatre)* is reserved for those who have the stamina and are not bothered by the heat. All that remains are portions of the walls protecting it, as well as the bases of a **temple dedicated to Pericles**, and a **Byzantine church** surrounded by **cisterns**. The remains are certainly meagre, but the **panorama** ★ is worth the effort, and up above, you feel so exhilarated.

At the foot of the hill, on the other side of the road, you reach the **lower city**, whose remains are lost in the greenery, half submerged by the ground water. The whole city lies in ruins, but the spectacle of stones below the sparkling water is quite enchanting.

The **city walls**, still partially upright, protected two districts set on both sides of the main stream: on the west bank, the Roman city (currently being excavated) and on the east bank, the episcopal centre constructed during the Byzantine era (5C). The entrance was through a **monumental gate**, flanked by two powerful towers *(at the extremity of the ramparts)*. This was where of the **cathedral** rose. The three naves of the vast basilica are still distinguishable and were once decorated with sumptuous mosaics which have since disappeared.

Arycanda ★★

29km from Finike on the road to Elmalı. In the village of Çatallar, head towards Antalya on the right, then turn at the yellow signpost. A rocky track, 1km long, will lead you to the site (20min on foot). For those without private transport, buses leave every hour from Finike (towards Elmalı). Get off in the village of Arif. 8am-7.30pm; entrance fee. Allow 2hr for the visit.

Lycian Delphi

Arycanda resembles Delphi in Greece. Isolated in the mountain far from the crowds of the coastal sites, the Lycian city is perched at an altitude of 750m, on the terrace of a rocky promontory overlooking the snow-capped summits of **Akdağ** (3 030m) and **Kızlar Sivrisi** (3 086m). A beautiful vertiginous landscape, the ruins are lost among the pine trees whose scent embalms the whole mountain. As you progress, the views become more and more dazzling. Undoubtedly the Ancients knew how to choose their site and had the art of organising the location to its fullest advantage: you will quickly notice that all the public buildings – baths, stadium, theatre and agora – were designed with the panorama in mind, always facing the spectacle of the mountains. This is a good lesson in urban planning and the art of good living.

The coins minted with Pericles' effigy, from the 5C BC, are the oldest traces of man discovered in Arycanda. Nevertheless, the Anatolian suffix *anda* leads us to believe that the city already existed in the second millennium BC. In any event, the city shares more or less the same history as all of its Lycian neighbours: it was liberated from the Persian stranglehold by Alexander the Great before falling under the control of Rhodes. Then it experienced its greatest development in the 2C BC by joining the Lycian Confederation. The Romans, starting in 43 AD breathed new life into it, but the city was progressively abandoned from the 11C as people moved southwards.

Visiting the site

From the car park, take the path on the right.

On the left side, the walls of a great **Byzantine basilica** are outlined on the ground, surrounding pretty **mosaics**★; a moving testimony to the building's lost splendour. The choir is also distinguishable with a few fragments of the **altar's step** still in place.

Further away, on the right *(not far from the map of the site)*, the path overlooks the **grand baths**★, an imposing building which aligns its large rooms in front of the valley. From their pools, the bathers could contemplate the landscape through the windows. Imagine the pleasure! Nearby, a few ruined walls indicate the location of the adjoining **gymnasium**.

The other side of the path is the domain of the dead: a Roman period **necropolis**★ occupies the entire flank of the mountain, above the baths. Elsewhere, there are all sorts of **mausoleums**, small temples or simple tombs housing a sarcophagus. One of the most beautiful is undoubtedly the **"Grand Tomb**★**"** *(near the baths)*, a temple-mausoleum pierced by a very beautiful door: its lintel is decorated with the head of a bull surrounded by winged divinities. Notice the beautiful masonry of the inner walls – a polygonal structure whose stones, although irregular, are neatly joined.

Return to your map and take the stiff ascent towards the upper terraces, heading north (take your time, it is steep!)

First you reach the **agora**, a small rectangular esplanade outlined by the base of the three porticoes surrounding it; three, not four, which open up the square to the absolutely superb **scenery**★★. On the opposite portico *(north)*, three gates lead to the **odeon**, a small building surrounded by scrub, whose steps were once plated with marble.

Behind the odeon, stairs climbs up towards the **theatre**★★, one of the site's most beautiful buildings. Its steps spread out with grace among the pine trees, facing the valley and the crest of the surrounding mountains. The **cavea**★★, of Greek design, exceeds the hemicycle.

The **stage building**, modified during the Roman period, is still visible. Behind the theatre, turning your back to the valley, notice the long **support wall**★, which seems embedded in the face of the mountain. It sustains the **stadium**, reached by a small staircase left of the wall. The **track** stretches among the pines for 90m, a dimension twice as small as it would be in a Greek stadium, leading us to believe that part of the site was buried under the rocks closing off the western side. A few rows of recently cleared steps run along the north side. The **view**★★★ of the surroundings is extraordinary. Silence envelops you except when the wind rustles a few leaves in the trees. It is a true delight.

The brave-hearted and those who love beautiful panoramas should continue on to the **bouleuterion** – seat of the municipal assembly – set on a terrace northwest of the stadium *(on the right, as you face the valley)*. You will discover the steps carved directly in the rock at the extremity of the ruins of a **stoa**, an immense 100m-long portico plunging into the valley. It is obviously the most beautiful and breathtaking **view***** of the site and its surroundings. Far away from everything, this is the ideal moment to unwrap the feta and olives, before taking a little nap.

Or as you leave the site, stop for lunch in one of the restaurants along the road, the **Özçoban** or the **Altıntaş**, where trout is served next to the roaring stream.

Making the most of Finike

COMING AND GOING

By bus – Antalya Tours, ☎ (242) 855 15 66 / 855 31 12 / 855 15 10 operates services to Elmalı, Kale and Olympos. **Finike Kooperatifi** and **Fethiye Kooperatifi** have connections to the surrounding area.

By taxi and shared taxi – Dolmuşes depart for Elmalı from the bus station in Yayla Cad every 30min. You can also make a return journey to Arycanda by taxi, with a 1hr stop to visit the site (around US$20).

WHERE TO STAY

Under US$8
Pension Paris, Eski Mah, ☎ (242) 855 14 88. ⌐ In a good location, high up in the old town, not far from the Turkish bath. Simple but clean.

Between US$8 and US$15
Pension Şendil, Atatürk Parkı Karşısı, ☎ (242) 855 16 60. ⌐ ▤ In the same part of town as the one above. The guest house has a minibus which takes clients to the beach, and is conveniently located next to a small supermarket.

EATING OUT

Petek Restaurant, Liman Girişi, at the marina, ☎ (242) 855 17 82. Offers a US$5 buffet, including drinks, in a typically Turkish atmosphere.

OLYMPOS★★

Antalya Province – Map p 355
93km from Antalya – 51km from Finike
Food and lodging in Finike or Tekirova (see Phaselis)

Not to be missed
The entire site!

And remember...
Bring along some drinking water if you are walking,
and your swimsuit for the beach, after your visit.

*From Finike, take the road to Antalya. After Beşikçi, turn towards the sea at the "Olympos"
sign. If you are travelling by bus, have the driver drop you off at the intersection; you will
have an additional 15km to go on foot or by hitch-hiking! It is also possible to turn earlier,
immediately to the right after exiting Kumluca, and follow the small road to Beykonak (very
picturesque but in a deplorable state) which leads to Olympos (31km).*

The ruins of Olympos, an ancient Lycian city, owe a great deal to their setting: a small forgotten vale surrounded by tall hills and leading to a magnificent beach. In the middle of the vale flows a river with fresh (and very cold) water originating in the mountains and thereafter spreading among the marshes, pink oleander forest and gorse from which the ruins emerge.

Far from the roads and tourist trails, Olympos seems cut off from the world and the site is bathed in a sort of romantic serenity. A few Robinson Crusoes landed here in the 1970s and built modest, makeshift tree houses near the ruins. The comfort is basic but the point is to blend with nature. The river's fresh water, the sunny beach, the fragrance of the oleanders provide enough reasons to set up your own tree house!

No relation to the gods
No need to look for the dwelling of the gods in Olympos. In ancient Greek, "olympos" simply means "mountain" and more than 20 sites around the Mediterranean bear this name. The Lycian city owes its name to Tahtalı Dağı (2 375m), the ancient Olympia of Lycia, a mountain rising between Olympos and Phaselis. The only residence of the gods is Mount Olympus of Thessaly, in Greece. Its summit is permanently snow-capped, an exceptional phenomenon in the region.

The pirates' cove

The city's history is not very well known. Founded in the 3C BC, Olympos was an important, if turbulent, member of the Lycian Confederation, alternating regularly between respectable city and pirates' hideout. The last occupants, Venetians and Genoese, were chased out by the Ottomans in the 15C who neglected it. The city was simply abandoned. A **Venetian Fortress** (in ruins) perched on a hill closing off the beach to the south, is the only remnant of this period. On the other side of the river, topping the nearly inaccessible summit of a rock, the ancient acropolis continues to guard the port, now lost among the vegetation of the marshes.

Romans to starboard!
During the 1C BC, the southern coast of Anatolia was the prey of numerous pirates. The most famous among them, Zeniketes, had installed his command post in Olympos. He ruled over the entire sector until 78 BC, when the governor of Cilicia, Servilius (appointed by Sylla) put an end to his career after a laborious naval battle. He was hit and sunk.

The Mediterranean Coast

Visiting the site

From the car park, follow the path which flanks the river up to the beach (less than 10min). You will be welcomed by an "official" guide, armed with a rusty colt and wearing a captain's hat. If he is not there, the entrance is free! The site can be visited at all hours. Allow 1hr30min for the site and a half day if you extend your visit to Chimaera.

The site has never been excavated and the ancient city's secrets are still well kept. Although they are periodically cleared, the protruding ruins are regularly covered with the vegetation which invades the site. This is another chance to feel like an explorer. From the beach, the path skirts the river. It leads into the greenery where the piles of a ruined **Roman bridge** as well as two **Lycian sarcophagi** are hidden among the shrubs. One of them, recently excavated, is decorated with the head of a **Gorgon** (Medusa) and – a rarer motif – a **ship**. As you head deeper into the forest, on the right of the path, you will discover the ruins of an **ancient aqueduct** which snaked its way through the city at ground level.

Further away, on the right, a small path, half erased by the shrubs, leads to the front of a striking **door★** with a sculpted frame, 5m tall, pierced in an imposing wall. An unusual sight, it opens up to the chaos of the brushwood as if it were a rampart erected in front of the lush vegetation. It is in fact the entrance to the cella of a great Ionic temple, long gone, which according to the inscriptions found nearby, was built (or restored?) during the reign of Marcus Aurelius (161-181).

Rising less than 100m away *(towards the right)*, you will note the walls of the **Byzantine baths★** (7C). They are still covered by minuscule **domes** and a few pretty **mosaics** consisting of geometric patterns.

The Olympos beach, an endless stretch of sand

B. Brillion/MICHELIN

Returning to the banks of the river *(50m to the left)*, you will recognise the traces of the river's ancient layout: you can clearly make out the design of a polygonal **dock** in the shrubs.

A path leads to the river crossing (which is easily crossed in summer. It is much more difficult in winter when the river is flooded!).

On the other bank

The path follows the river towards the west before climbing up the hill where the **Roman theatre**, barely excavated, is located. The entrance is through one of the two side **galleries**, a large cradle vault.

Those who wish to know more will climb up to the **necropolis** which clings to the hill overlooking the theatre to the southwest. Dotting the slope are numerous **tombs** with simple square openings pierced by trees. Lastly, returning to the beach by way of the river, you reach the ruins of several buildings, including those of a **Byzantine basilica**★ still sporting elegant **arcades** by the waterfront. From here you can make out the remains of the walls of the **acropolis**, perched on the hill dominating the other bank. Returning to the **beach**, there is only one thing left to do: swim. The setting is wonderful, wild yet calm. Olympian. Furthermore, you can rinse off in the river's fresh water (the site is protected and therefore perfectly clean). This is truly a delight!

Chimaera★

5km to the northwest of Olympos. Allow 30min on foot (one way).

If time allows, continue your exploration all the way to Chimaera (also called **Yanartaş**, in Turkish: "rock on fire"). The very picturesque site is interesting for its ancient ruins as well as its geological phenomenon.

Chimaera can be reached by taking the main road towards Antalya, then by turning right towards the village of Çıralı. From there, a 5km-track descends towards another track which heads left into a narrow pass. Once there, you must leave your car and continue on foot along the path which leads up the mountain.

Bellorophon and the Chimaera

A hero of the Iliad, Bellorophon was a handsome, proud and courageous young man. His charm attracted the jealousy of the king who wished to distance him from his wife and therefore sent him off to his friend, Lobates, King of Lycia. The latter asked him to kill the Chimaera – a mission which he thought would be fatal – whose fires ravaged the harvests and forests of the region. Bellorophon rode on his winged horse, the famous Pegasus, and from above the clouds threw his lance into the creature's mouth. The Chimaera perished and returned to the entrails of the earth where its fire breath has never ceased to blaze. Lobates nevertheless did not give up. He sent Bellorophon to Termessus, a 100km flight by horse, to attack the fierce Solymes, indomitable mountain thieves. Once again, Bellorophon managed the challenge unscathed and Lobates finally recognised the young man's divine character.

However, the simplest way of getting to the site is to leave from the Olympos beach: the ingenious locals supply tourists (for a few dollars, of course) with trailers pulled by old tractors which snake their way through the orange groves and family "pansiyons" and drop you off at the foot of the rock. A mule service has also recently begun!

At the top of the stiff ascent (350m), where traces of the old road can still be seen, you reach a small rocky plateau where unusual **live flames** flare up among the rocks. The methane emanations ignite spontaneously as they come into contact with the air. This astonishing spectacle, visible in ancient times, made this one of the Chimaera's dens, a mythological fire-breathing monster with the head of a lion, a goat's body, and a dragon's tail.

The Ancients also associated it with the cult of Hephaestus (the blacksmith-god, the Roman Vulcan). The debris of a **grand temple** was found in a forest surrounding the site along with Greek dedications near the flames.

Recent excavations have revealed other Roman buildings *(a few metres away)*, in particular a **monumental fountain**, where the incoming and outgoing plumbing is still visible. Lastly, the pretty ruins of a **Byzantine church*** confirm that the site was still sacred in the Middle Ages. The building has retained a few **frescoes** from the iconoclastic period, in the half-dome of the choir (8-9C).

Making the most of Olympos

WHERE TO STAY

• In Olympos

Between US$5 and US$20

Kadir's Yörük Top Tree House, near the site and the beach, ☎ (242) 892 12 50, Fax (242) 892 11 10, treehouse@superonline.com.tr – 22 bungalows with showers and 40 tree houses (communal bathroom facilities). ✗ ⍭ A bungalow will set you back US$18, a tree house US$14, and a night in the dormitory US$6, for half-board. This very original and convivial place attracts a lot of globetrotters. The proprietor organises boat trips and excursions to Chimaera. A bus departs for Göreme, in Cappadocia, at 8am every Saturday.

• In Çıralı

3km from the Olympos site. All the guest houses are at the crossroads.

Between US$8 and US$15

Pension Bermuda, ☎ (242) 825 72 74 / 825 71 13. ⍭ ✗ ✗ Bright little rooms, set on a level with the garden.

Pension Orange, ☎ (242) 825 71 28. ⍭ ✗ A peaceful, well-kept place, closer to the site than the one above, and near an orange grove.

Pension Çıralı, ☎ (242) 825 71 22. ⍭ ✗ A slightly more upmarket guest house with very reasonable rates, set in a quiet garden.

• In Çavuşköy

Numerous guest houses have been set up along the riverside, 13km from the site, in a location which is much quieter and more rural than Çıralı. They all have a restaurant on pilings, standing above the river, where you can sample grilled trout and seafood casseroles (around US$8 per meal per person).

US$15

Motel İkizler, at the beach (Adrasan Plajı). ⍭ ✗ Wooden bungalows, camping possible.

Between US$18 and US$21

River Garden guest house and **Golden River guest house**; the **Gelidonia guest house** is slightly more expensive.

EATING OUT

Between Olympos and Phaselis, the road to Antalya cuts deep into the pine forest and rocks which conceal a few very simple but pleasant restaurants. Among them (on the left-hand side of the road, just before Phaselis), the **Yarıkpınar** is a favourite with Turkish truck drivers, drawn here by the delicious roast chicken. Meals are served on a shaded terrace overlooking a fresh-water spring and if you order an omelette, you may well witness the chef running off into the rocks to gather the eggs which are hidden there.

PHASELIS★★

Antalya Province – Map p 355
59km from Finike – 61km from Antalya
Food and accommodation in Tekirova or Antalya

Not to be missed
The main avenue and the view from the acropolis.

And remember...
Bring your swimsuit along.
To avoid the crowds, visit the site early in the morning
or at the end of the day.

The Antalya road flanks the **Olympos Natural Park★★** (Olimpos Milli Parkı), an immense pine forest straddling the rocky buttresses of the Bey Dağları. It encompasses the sites of Olympos *(see p 416)* and Phaselis, extending to the edges of Antalya. The pine forest covers the entire area, from the hills to the coves which line the coast, shading dozens of little grey pebble beaches. Overlooked by **Tahtalı Dağı** (2375m) – the ancient Olympia of Lycia – Phaselis lies on a small rocky promontory covered with maritime pines. It is separated into two large bays surrounded by turquoise waters. The fragrance of resin is embedded in the rocks; you swim near the sunken vestiges of the dikes; and you stroll across the acropolis, on the beautiful avenue which seems to end up in the sea. Phaselis is a site full of charm where it is a delight to roam about, especially when the hordes of visitors are not there!

Phaselis, between sea and pine forest

E. Valentin/HOA QUI

The Mediterranean Coast

On the road from Fethiye to Antalya, slightly before the village of Tekirova, turn right heading for the sea (signpost). If you are travelling by dolmuş, have the driver drop you off at the junction. Continue on foot for 2km (shaded path) until you reach the site. You can also take a boat from Kemer or Tekirova (numerous shuttle boats). In the summer it is overrun: the beach is invaded with visitors embarking or disembarking. Avoid the rush hour at all costs!

A trade centre

According to ancient and Byzantine historians, Phaselis was founded around 690 BC, a date which is confirmed by the traces of dwellings uncovered by archeologists. Phaselis quickly became a large and important trading port: during Greek domination, the city paid a tax which was almost as high as that of Ephesus, which gives an idea of its importance. The wealth was due to the pragmatism of its inhabitants, able merchants, greedy and unscrupulous, whose proverbial dishonesty earned the city a poor reputation.

This mercantile spirit guided all of its political choices. The city voluntarily accepted Persian control which in turn gave it access to Egyptian and Oriental trading posts. It even regretted being liberated by Athens in 469 BC and quickly returned to its old conquerors until the arrival of Alexander the Great who defeated them in 334 BC. After his victory, the Macedonian remained in the vicinity for six months to ensure that his control would take root.

Like the whole region, Phaselis was subjected to the wrath of the local pirate, Zeniketes *(see sidebar p 416)*, who was eliminated by the Romans in 78 AD. From then on, the city began a period of great prosperity (until the 3C AD), reinvigorated by the Byzantines in the 7C and 8C. However, the repeated invasions of the Arabs weakened it and the Seljuks, who took the city in the 11C, finally abandoned it in favour of Antalya.

Visiting the site

Since the site is incorporated inside a protected park, camping and picnicking are theoretically forbidden. In spite of this, the beaches are usually littered with refuse and the site ought to be better maintained.

The itinerary suggested below is for those travelling by road. If arriving by boat, you should follow the itinerary in reverse: begin with the southern port, then the city itself and end with the northern port. 7.30am-7pm from May to October, 8am-5.30pm from November to April. Parking and entrance fees. Allow 1hr for the visit or more if you decide to take advantage of the beach!

Three ports for one city

Phaselis had three ports, interconnected by the main avenue, the backbone of the city. The central "port" – the smallest one – was set in a creek on the eastern shore of the promontory, while the other two were located in the coves at the city's extremities.

The road leading to the city reaches the **north port**, an enchanting little bay which will undoubtedly appeal to swimmers! Nothing is left of its structure except the **dike** which rose in between the two islands, in the middle of the bay. Submerged today, a long white line is visible under the surface of the water.

Flanking the bay, a **Roman aqueduct**★★ – one of the region's best preserved – struts its high stone arches among the pine trees and the scrub, before it disappears into the forest. A truly romantic picture which would have inspired the paintbrush of an Impressionist.

Phaselis

As you go deeper into the pine forest, you will reach the **necropolis** (Byzantine period, mostly) – a chaos of sarcophagi – forgotten in the rocks and the shrubs. On the way, you will encounter a **small building**, most likely Byzantine, whose walls are almost entirely constituted of **ancient column drums** (recycling is not a recent phenomenon!)

Backtrack and head for the city centre on the peninsula.

Firstly, you will skirt the **central port**, a rocky circular creek, with a very narrow opening (the channel is only 18m wide) formerly protected by a fortified dike. Apparently, it was a military port which could also host ships of small tonnage.

The heart of the city★

Enter the city by following the **main avenue★**, a superb 10m-wide road, preserved for 270m. Going towards the sea from the right side *(towards the southwest)*, you will cross the ruins of an ensemble of **Byzantine houses**. They are adjacent to the Roman **grand public baths** filled with beautiful fragments of geometrical polychrome **mosaics**. Farther away, the **agora**, also known as *tetragonos* ("four sides", in Greek), is an almost perfect square partially laid out under the reign of Hadrian (circa 130 AD). A **basilica,** whose apse is still clearly visible, was constructed during the Byzantine period (6C). Around the agora, the main avenue becomes a **triangular plaza★**, still marble-covered, flanked on its left side by **small baths**, recognisable by the groups of small circular piles lining the floor of some of the rooms. Just behind, a small **staircase** in a corner leads to the **theatre** (2C AD), whose steps are hidden in the middle of the pine trees and the tall grass. From the top of the cavea, there is a magnificent **vantage point★★** over the pine trees coating the landscape all the way to the mountains. Of very modest size (1 500 seats), the building is tiny in comparison to the theatres of Aspendos or Ephesus, which could accommodate ten times the number of spectators. Were Phaselians only interested in commerce?

As you go deeper into the forest by taking the small path behind the steps, you will reach the **acropolis** located at the tip of the peninsula. Almost nothing is left of the high city, except for some elements of the land **walls** (Hellenistic), but you will enjoy a superb **panorama★★** of the site, Tahtali Dağı and the sea.

Towards the south port

Past this square, the main avenue crosses diagonally towards the right to flank the **Agora of Domitian** (69-79 AD), a vast esplanade whose contours have since disappeared in the pine forest. It used to be closed off in the south by the large **warehouses** (heavily eroded) stretching all the way to the shore.

Lastly, you reach the **south port** *(southwest bay)*, the city's most important, facing the open sea. Enter through **Hadrian's Gate** (ruined), whose sculpted blocks are aligned on the side of the road, possibly awaiting rebuilding. All that is left of the port is a beautiful beach sliding into the transparent waters making its amplitude difficult to imagine. An obligatory stop on the trade route between Greece and Syria, it managed to shelter the largest trading ships, which ranged up to 100 tonnes. Today tourist shuttle boats serve the site; a revival of sorts.

In the area

Some 4km from Phaselis, on the road to Antalya, you can stay in **Tekirova**, a small seaside resort stretching along a 5km-long **beautiful fine-sand beach**. The setting, still peaceful, is much more enjoyable than Kemer (uninteresting) for accommodation as well as swimming. You will find **a few good hotels** that are modern but with pleasant architecture. Some are quite refined and have pretty gardens.

Making the most of Phaselis (Tekirova)

The site of Phaselis is right next to the small town of **Tekirova**.

ADDRESS BOOK

Car rental – *Ödil Rent a Car*, PTT Karşısı, ☎ (242) 821 40 84 / 821 47 80. Also sells phone cards. Car rental also possible at the Öz Barış hotel, below.

Main post office – Opposite the bus station. 8.30am-11.30am/ 1.30pm-5.30pm.

Bank / change – Next to the bus station, *Garanti Bankası* has an automatic cash dispenser. Currency exchange at the big crossroads with the main highway.

Shopping – The ***Elegan Shopping Plaza***, an enormous shopping centre with little squares, terrace bars and luxury boutiques, has just recently opened here.

WHERE TO STAY

Camp site

Yıldırım camp site, to the right of the town, next to the beach, 200m from the road. A pleasant camp site set in the shade of maritime pines. US$5 per day per person.

US$15

🏨 **Pension Uraz**, in an avenue running parallel to the main street (turn right at the crossroads with the taxi stand), ☎ (242) 821 44 48, Fax (242) 821 43 99. 🍴▤♨ New, spotless and set in a beautiful garden. The rooms are large and full of light, and there is a left-luggage office.

Pension Aykut, ☎ (242) 821 41 12, Fax (242) 821 41 09. 🍴▤♨ Not far from the one above. Small, clean rooms with balconies overlooking the swimming pool.

Between US$40 and US$45

(half-board compulsory)

Hotel Öz Barış, at the end of the town, on the right, ☎ (242) 821 42 62, Fax (242) 821 42 63 – 8rm. 🍴♪✕♨ In the same style as its neighbours, but more upmarket. Everything here is bigger, more comfortable and more attractive, including the architecture. The hotel also hires out all kinds of vehicles (cars, jeeps, bicycles and scooters). Closed from December to March.

US$150!

Hotel Phaselis Princess, ☎ and Fax (242) 821 40 70. 🍴♪▤✕♨☼ 🎾 CC For wealthy travellers or those wanting to give themselves a (very big) treat. The Phaselis Princess is a big holiday village made up of small houses dotted around a magnificent garden, offering boundless luxury and all the sporting activities you could ever wish for.

ANTALYA★★
Provincial Capital – Map p 355
469km from İzmir – 413km from Konya – 553km from Adana
Pop 603 000 – Mild winters and very hot summers

Not to be missed
The Archeological Museum is a must
if you plan to visit the archeological sites in the area.

And remember...
Avoid weekends at the Düden falls when it is very crowded.
If you go mountain hiking, bring warm clothes.

On the shores of a vast gulf, Antalya is a highly esteemed Turkish beach resort and very popular with international travel agencies. The site has everything: an exceptional climate with record sunny weather (300 days per year) and a choice location between the turquoise sea and the snow-capped mountains. Even in

Antalya, sunshine on the bay

B. Morandi/DIAF

springtime, it is not rare to see snowy peaks while swimming in the already warm sea. Perched on a rocky promontory overlooking a small creek, old Antalya and the maze of tortuous alleys shaded by century-old homes is definitely worth the detour.

A city with tentacles

Of course, the city has spread considerably in the last 10 years. Old Antalya (Kaleiçi) is now simply the historical and protected district of a megalopolis. Its tentacles stretch along the entire coastline, devouring beaches, villages and orange groves all around. Endless avenues lined with buildings surround the entire periphery. However, it is pleasant to stroll about, especially around the **Clock Tower Square**, the meeting point of **Cumhuriyet Caddesi** and **Atatürk Bulvarı**, the two large arteries marking the border between the old and new cities. It is the heart of Antalya, swarming with people and besieged by endless traffic. You can find everything, from modest traditional shops – barbers, hardware shops, workshops or women sorting cotton – to the luxurious display windows of boutiques selling clothing and perfume.

Antalya

Capital of Pamphylia

Since Antiquity, Antalya has been the capital of Pamphylia, a vast agricultural plain bordered to the west and the north by the Taurus range, and to the east by the course of the Manavgat (the ancient Melas). A very fertile region, protected by mountains and facing a quiet gulf, Pamphylia has always been coveted by its neighbours – Pisidians, Lycians and Cilicians, without forgetting the pirates who at one time made Antalya their strategic base. Occupied by the Greeks, then by the Persians, the region was transferred to Alexander the Great, then the Seleucids, before becoming one of the possessions of the King of Pergamum, Attalus II, in the 2C BC.

It is to the latter that the foundation of Attaleia (hence "Antalya") is owed. The city rapidly became a prosperous port. In 133 BC, Attalus allied his States to Rome, and Pamphylia joined the Roman province of Asia. The region regained its senatorial province status under Hadrian (135 AD), who undertook the construction of Antalya's ramparts (still standing in parts). Consolidated by the Byzantines in the 7C and 10C, the city walls resisted the assaults of the Arabs and protected the crusaders en route to Palestine. In 1207, however, they failed to resist the offensive of the Seljuks who later ceded them to the Ottomans (14C).

Constant development

After World War I and the division of Turkish territories under the Treaty of Sèvres, Antalya was handed over to Italy until 1921. It was the beginning of incredible growth which has continued ever since. In the 1960s, the population of Antalya quadrupled. The orchards and the surrounding fields attracted many farmers looking for work. Today, the city does not live off tourism alone: besides its industrial activity linked to regional agriculture, it is an important commercial port, one of the country's premier export centres along with İzmir.

Kaleiçi, old Antalya★★

Allow half a day. In summer the district is a tide of humanity.

The old city coils itself around a minuscule cove, closed off by two dikes which almost isolate it completely from the gulf. Behind the ramparts protecting the port, the red roofs huddle together, allowing here and there a palm tree or a cypress tree to emerge. Its maze of alleys hides many 18C and 19C **Ottoman houses★**, beautiful white façades or stone walls decorated with dark wood-framed windows and balconies. In 1988, the site was declared a protected area and an important restoration campaign was undertaken to preserve the district. The restoration proved to be a bit too energetic at times and Kaleiçi lost some of its soul, since most of the houses were converted into hotels, guest houses or souvenir shops. However, a few forgotten buildings remain, and the result is magnificent. Kaleiçi is also a rare example of what an Ottoman village on the Mediterranean looked like. Do not hesitate to push open the gates to the houses which often hide green **patios★**, filled with the fragrance of oranges or jasmine.

Facing the **Clock Tower** (a remodelled Roman vestige), the **Yivli Minare★★** (B1) pierces the air like a lighthouse above the roofs. Built in 1230, this superb red brick-and-blue tile minaret with a grooved cylinder (*yivli* in Turkish), has become the city's emblem. Some 39m tall, it is also a good landmark for finding your way around. At its feet, the six domes of the **Alaaddin Mosque** (1372) seem Lilliputian in comparison. The spacious interior sometimes hosts handicraft shows. Each dome is supported by fine columns decorated with beautiful capitals.

From there, enter the colourful streets of Kaleici. Along the way, do not miss the unusual **Truncated Minaret*** (Kesik Minare) (B3) flanking the Cumanun (or Korkud) Mosque. Set up near the ruined walls of a Byzantine basilica, built on the foundation of a Roman temple, the mosque has taken a few **capitals** from the primitive building as well as an elegant **lintel of a carved door** *(western wall)*. The largest part is nevertheless Byzantine (5C and 7C). The minaret, added in the 14C, lost its tip in 1896, during a fire which ravaged the entire building (hence the name).

Going up Hesapçı Sokak all the way to the end, you will reach **Hadrian's Gate*** (C2), a majestic propylaeum of white marble rising on the side of Atatürk Bulvarı (the road is higher than the ancient level, slightly overpowering the monument, unfortunately). Erected during the visit of the Emperor in 130 AD, this gate is one of Antalya's oldest vestiges (entirely rebuilt). 14m tall, it opened up inside the wall of the city's enclosure, flanked by **two observation towers** (you can go up inside one of them for a **lovely view***over the bay and the roofs of the old city).

Towards the southeast, the boulevard follows the **remains of the ramparts** up to **Karaalioğlu Parkı***, a very beautiful botanical park set at the tip of the promontory of the old city. Stroll among the royal poincianas (flamboyants), date trees and hundreds of Mediterranean and tropical species. A welcome oasis after exploring the city which seems to melt in the heat. The very restful atmosphere entices you into taking a little nap, or simple contemplation. The **view**** of the mountains and the bay is magnificent, especially at sunset. Below the terrace, a large Roman tower – **Hıdırlık Kulesi*** – seems to watch over the port. It was probably the city's lighthouse.

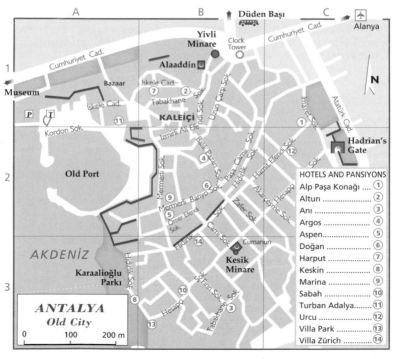

HOTELS AND PANSIYONS
Alp Paşa Konağı .... ①
Altun .... ②
Anı .... ③
Argos .... ④
Aspen...................... ⑤
Doğan .... ⑥
Harput .... ⑦
Keskin .... ⑧
Marina .... ⑨
Sabah .... ⑩
Turban Adalya........ ⑪
Urcu .... ⑫
Villa Park .... ⑬
Villa Zürich .... ⑭

End your day in the **old port***, dominated by the battlements of the ramparts *(which you should cross)*. Renovated with care, the ancient fishing port harbours sailboats and you can have dinner in one of the little restaurants set on the pier. It is Antalya's most tourist-laden district, very busy in the evening, but very enjoyable for dinner.

The museum★★

On Konyaaltı Cad, more than 3km from the city centre,
in the direction of Kemer, by way of Cumhuriyet Cad.
Dolmuş service from the centre,
tramway stopping at: Müze; 8am-4pm, closed Monday.
Entrance fee. Allow 2hr.

The Antalya museum is an indispensable stop for those wishing to visit the region's ancient sites (in particular Perga, since all of the sculptures that were found during the excavations are displayed here). The richness of the collections, the clear explanations and the adjoining buildings (air-conditioning, cafeteria etc) render the visit highly instructive and very pleasant. The modern museum is housed inside a former mosque (on the left side as you enter, notice the beautiful *türbe* of the Seljuk era). The current buildings surround an attractive lapidary garden where capitals, column fragments and friezes are stacked up. It includes part of the frieze which decorated the tomb of the **Nereids of Xanthos** *(see p 389)*.

The first room, dedicated to the region's **prehistory**, assembles the objects discovered inside the **cave of Karain**, a Paleolithic site (100 000-15 000 years before our era) situated 27km northwest of Antalya.

Next, the **Phrygian rooms**** (circa 8C BC) house a superb collection of plates and silver and bronze jewellery. Among other interesting items, you can see a bronze banner formed with a stylised bouquet of phalli, and especially two magnificent **statuettes*****, one in silver, 12cm high, the other in ivory, barely taller (17cm). The former represents a priest wearing a tiara and a long pleated robe; the second – more moving – shows a woman smiling, holding a young girl by the hand and a baby over her shoulder.

The Yörük

As you visit the heights of the Taurus, you might perhaps cross paths with a Yörük shepherd, one of these nomads who comes from the large family of the Oğuz Turks. The Yörük populate the mountains north of Antalya and the Çukurova plain. In summer, they lead their goat herds across the Taurus' high plateaus (*yayla*). In the winter, they seek refuge in the villages surrounding the coastal plains or in the ridges of the valleys. Even if many of them leave the mountain in search of work on the coast, the majority is against sedentary life. In spite of their Islamic faith, they continue to respect their animist beliefs, dominated by the idea that all of nature – animal, plant, rock, or stream – is living and thinking. Is it for this reason that their embroideries and kilims are so beautiful?

The **Greek section**** displays beautiful collections of vases, jewels and objects related to daily life, as well as sculptures, including a **Lycian bas-relief** from a Kaş tomb, representing the 12 gods of Olympus accompanied by as many dogs!

The next three rooms – undoubtedly the museum's most interesting – are a gathering of the objects found in **Perga**: busts, **sarcophagi**, reliefs and in particular, the great statues which decorated the city's monuments. Many of them are Roman copies of Greek originals, but pure Roman creations are also on display. The first series of statues represents the gods: Zeus, Apollo, his sister Artemis, **Hermes** lacing his sandal, and **Aphrodite** armed with her shield.

After the gods, men: the second series gathers the important figures of history with the full portrait of a few emperors and **Plancia Magna**, Perga's most famous female citizen *(see sidebar p 442)*. Do not miss the **Dancer★★**, a beautiful bacchante found in the southern baths. 2.25m tall, she is sculpted from two different marbles, white for the body, black for the clothing and hair adding to her graceful attitude.

The visit continues with the **Christian room** where a few Paleo-Christian sculptures and numerous 19C **icons** are exhibited. In one of the display cases, you will be able to see a few presumed relics of the very popular **St Nicholas** – modest bone fragments found in the tomb of the Church of St Nicholas, in Kale *(see p 408)*. Spend some time as well in front of the **Roman mosaics★** and the stunning stone **game table** – a primitive type of backgammon – found in Perga's main street.

Last but not least, visit the **ethnographic section★** where urban and nomadic **dwellings★** are reconstituted in an intelligent manner (in particular that of the famous **Yörük**), **clothing**, remarkable **carpets** from the neighbouring village of Döşemealtı, and various objects illustrating daily life during the time of the Seljuks and Ottomans.

Between plain and mountain★★

Only if you have a car.

Antalya is also a perfect base for visiting the surrounding archeological sites – Termessos, Perga and Aspendos – which are among Turkey's finest *(see the individual chapters)*. The region is also ideal for countless excursions, in particular in the neighbouring mountains where the pleasant temperatures are a welcome change from the torrid coast. It is very easy to reach the site of **Selge★** set in the heart of a superb **natural park★★** *(see "Making the most of Antalya", p 430)*. Devotees of nature walks, old forgotten villages and wild landscapes, get your shoes ready!

Climbing the Bey Dağları★★

Hiking excursions from Antalya. Information and arrangements at the Tourist Office or in the city's travel agencies.

In winter, the snowy peaks of the **Bey Dağları★★**, a chain running below the eastern side of the Taurus, welcomes many skiers (**Saklıkent**, the ski resort closest to Antalya, is only 50km away). However, it is in the spring that the mountain is at its most beautiful, when it is covered with flowers and young green tips. It is the ideal season for hiking, before the summer's heat arrives.

Countless itineraries can be chosen. Among them, two are truly exceptional. The first leads to the **heights of Kızlar Sivrisi★★**, the tip of the Bey Dağları, southwest of Antalya. It is best to take the Elmalı road *(via Korkuteli)* – which is also marvellous. Ten kilometres or so before Elmalı, a small road on the left heads toward the **valley of Çamkuyusu★** climbing up the flanks of Kızlar Sivrisi across a magnificent forest of beeches several centuries old.

Another delightful path leads to the **ascension of Tahtalı Dağı** (2 375m), the summit overlooking the site of Phaselis. You enter the **Olympos Natural Park** (Olimpos Milli Parkı) by way of the beautiful village of **Yalakuzdere★**, before discovering the amazing **view★★★** of the coastline and the Lycian mountains.

The waterfalls of Düden... and Düden

Beware! There are two sites with the same name, both of them on the **Düden**, a tumultuous river that flows into the sea near **Lara beach**, 12km east of Antalya. But "flow" is too mild a word for this river which plunges and falls – the **Düden Çayı** – from the height of a cliff. The falls can be seen by taking a small excursion boat from Antalya.

The other waterfalls, the **Düden Başı**, are found upstream, in a small green park (*9km north of Antalya, along the Korkuteli and Burdur road. Dolmuş service available. Entrance fee.*) A haven of freshness only minutes away from Antalya, the site is cherished by the local inhabitants who invade it on weekends, with picnics and hammocks. Do not expect to find the Turkish Niagara Falls; these falls are not as impressive (8m-high, no more) and the riverside is quite commercialised: cafés, restaurants, picnic areas, small bridges (quite pretty to look at) have erased part of the natural charm. The site nevertheless remains very pleasant, and it is a treat to walk around the park and savour excellent freshwater fish under the plane trees.

Making the most of Antalya

COMING AND GOING

By air – *Antalya international airport*, 8km east of the city on the way to Alanya. Services operate to numerous European destinations via İstanbul. Turkish Airlines runs a bus shuttle service (departing from Cumhuriyet Cad).

By bus – The vast **bus station** is located at the entrance to the motorway in the direction of Denizli. All the major companies are represented, including *Kamil Koç*, ☎ (242) 241 92 92 / (242) 241 93 13 and *Pamukkale*, ☎ (242) 247 16 00 / (242) 241 61 88. For Ankara: 3 buses in the morning and 4 in the evening (journey time: 10hr). For İstanbul: 1 bus in the morning and 4 in the evening. For Denizli-Pamukkale- İzmir: 1 bus every hour from 6am to midnight. There are also numerous bus services to Fethiye-Dalaman, Marmaris, Adana, Gaziantep, Side and Manavgat.
Varan, ☎ (242) 331 11 11/12, operates services to İstanbul, Ankara and several European cities.

By shared taxi – The *main dolmuş stand* is in Ali Çetinkaya Cad. Dolmuş services operate to the surrounding areas (Termessos and Perga) and also to towns further afield, such as Kemer. Departures every 15 to 30min. Many dolmuşes make a stop in the Clock Tower Square (**B1**), or at the junction of Adnan Menderes Bul and Mevlana Cad.

By boat – The **jetty** is at the entrance to the city when coming from Kemer (to the west), 5km from the centre. Connection to Venice.

Türk Denizcilik, Büyük Liman, ☎ (242 242 08 60. Ferry-boat connections to Alanya, İzmir and Venice; connections to Girne (Kyrenia, northern Cyprus) on Mondays and Fridays. Hydrofoil ("Deniz otobüsü") connections to Alanya and Girne.

GETTING AROUND

By bus – One of the most convenient and cheapest ways of getting from one end of the city to the other, for example for getting from the museum to the beach.

By shared taxi – Handy for getting around the city centre. They are cheap and everywhere you look.

By taxi – To be avoided during the day because of the constantly heavy traffic. Even if it means being stuck in a traffic jam, take a dolmuş instead (cheaper).

By tram – The ideal solution. The line runs along Atatürk Cad and Cumhuriyet Cad, then continues up to Konyaaltı beach, with a stop at the museum ("Müze"), opposite the Clock Tower. Tickets (50 cents!) are purchased directly in the tramcars.

By rental car – *Avis*, Fevzi Cakmak Cad Talya Apt 67/B, ☎ (242) 248 17 72 / 248 17 73, Fax (242) 248 17 19. At the airport, ☎ (242) 330 30 73 / 330 30 08, Fax (242) 330 34 30.
Budget, Gençlik Mah Fevzi Cakmak Cad 27/C, ☎ (242) 243 30 06, Fax (242) 242 50 46. At the airport, ☎ (242) 330 30 79, Fax (242) 330 31 28.
Europcar, Demircikara Mah Dr. B. Onat Cad Körfez Apt 53/3, ☎ (242) 312 83 94, Fax (242) 312 83 99. At the airport, ☎ (242) 330 30 88, Fax (242) 330 30 68.

ADDRESS BOOK

Tourist information – Cumhuriyet Cad 90, Özel İdare İş Hanı, ☎ (242) 241 17 47. Next to the municipal theatre (Devlet Tiyatrosu) (A1). The tourist information office occupies the ground floor of a large government building *(Özel İdare İşhanı)*. 8am-5.30pm, every day in summer. The welcome is rather cold and unprofessional, and information is supplied very sparingly.

Bank / change – You will find automatic cash dispensers and currency exchanges all over the city. **Şeker Bank**, opposite the tourist information office, changes foreign currency, as do **Koç Bank**, **Finans Bank**, **Ziraat Bankası** and **Pamukbank** in Atatürk Cad and Cumhuriyet Cad. **Akbank**, Kazım Özalp Cad. There is also a currency exchange in Cumhuriyet Meyd, next to the Internet café.

Cash Points are open 24 hours a day and take all cards. Several addresses: Konyaaltı Cad Cem Apt 38/A-B, or 55 Anafartalar Cad.

Main post office – Near the corner of Anafartalar Cad (at no 9) and Cumhuriyet Cad (beware: Anafartalar Cad is also known as Güllük Cad). Open 7 days a week. There is another post office in Tuz Kapısı Sok at the harbour, near the Turban Adalya hotel (A1).

Medical service – *Emergency Ambulance Service*, ☎ 112, Antalya State Hospital (next to the museum), ☎ (242) 243 50 60. *Mediterranean University Hospital*, ☎ (242) 345 08 00. *Private Antalya Hospital*, ☎ (242) 335 00 00.

Consulates – *British Consulate*, 1314 Sokak 6/8, Gençlik Mahallesi, ☎ (242) 244 53 13, Fax (242) 243 20 95.

Airline company – *Turkish Airlines*, Cumhuriyet Cad 90 (A1), ☎ (242) 243 43 82 / 243 43 87 (information and reservations). Next to the tourist information office. Open from Monday to Friday, 8.30am-8pm; Saturday and Sunday, 8.30am-5.30pm.

Laundry – Tabakhane Sok in the old town, next to the Anı guest house (B3).

Turkish bath – *Sefa Hamamı*, Barbaros Mah Kocatepe Sok 32, Kaleiçi (C2), ☎ (242) 241 23 21, not far from the Urcu hotel. Entry: US$9, including massage.

Public toilets – In Cumhuriyet Meyd and in Karaalioğlu parkı (A3).

WHERE TO STAY

In addition to the hotels, there are many good guest houses in Antalya, where you can stay for under US$8.

• In Kaleiçi
Under US$15

Villa Park, Kılıçarslan Mah Hesapçı Sok 69, ☎ (242) 248 63 09. ⌘ ▼ A quiet, family guest house, opposite Hadrian's Gate (Hıdırlık Kulesi). Rather basic, but convenient for small budgets.

Pension Keskin 2, Kılıçaslan Mah Hıdırlık Sok 35, ☎ (242) 242 39 41 / 241 28 65. ⌘ Recently renovated, this modern guest house offers pleasant, clean and quiet rooms overlooking a garden.

US$25

Hotel Urcu, Barbaros Mah Hamit Efendi Sok 6, ☎ (242) 243 67 00/01/02, Fax (242) 247 09 31 – 12rm. ⌘ ✒ ▤ ▼ ⎅ Two old, identical houses, carefully restored and offering spacious, comfortable and warm rooms. Pleasant bar on the roof terrace.

Between US$15 and US$30

⌂ **Pension Anı**, 26 Tabakhane Sok (in the south of this district; be careful, there is another street with the same name in the north), ☎ (242) 247 00 56 / 247 86 54 – 12rm. ⌘ Away from the busy shopping streets, in a quiet spot. A modest but charming little guest house. The rooms are very bright and decorated in wood. Breakfast is served in a flower-filled courtyard.

Pension Sabah, Kılıçaslan Mah, Hesapçı Sok 60, ☎ (242) 247 53 45, Fax (242) 247 53 47 – 10rm. ⌘ ▤ Less character than the one above, but it is clean and you will receive a warm welcome. Here again, breakfast is served in the garden.

Hotel Altun, Selçuk Mah, ☎ (242) 241 66 24 / 243 04 12. Clean, with a pleasant patio and nice terrace.

Hotel Villa Zürich, Kılıçaslan Mah, Hıdırlık Sok 18, ☎ (242) 243 93 49 – 24rm. ⌘ ▤ ▣ ⎅ In the heart of the old town, a large, new building with all mod cons. The rooms are charming, well equipped and immaculate (the owners used to live in Switzerland, hence the hotel's name). Breakfast is served in the garden, under the shade of palm and fruit trees.

Between US$30 and US$45

Hotel Harput, Selçuk Mah, İskele Cad, Tabakhane Sok 1, ☎ (242) 248 55 45, Fax (242) 248 55 44 – 10rm. ⌐] TV ✕ ⌂ CC Set in a tastefully restored Ottoman house, this hotel has retained a very warm atmosphere and offers the best in comfort. A boutique on the ground floor sells leather products and souvenirs.

Hotel Argos, Atatürk Ortaokulu Karşısı, ☎ (242) 247 20 12 / 247 20 13, Fax (242) 241 75 57 – 15rm. ⌐] ☰ TV ✕ ⌐ ⌂ CC This luxury hotel occupies a 100-year-old house, decorated with very beautiful Ottoman wood panelling. A successful combination of old-style charm and modern comfort.

Between US$45 and US$75

Hotel Doğan, Kılıçaslan Mah, Mermerli Banyo Sok 5, ☎ (242) 241 88 42, Fax (242) 247 40 66 – 28rm. ⌐] ☰ TV ✕ ⌐ ⌂ CC The rooms are attractively decorated (faience and wood), and are set around a pleasant garden. Excellent value for money.

⌂ **Hotel Turban Adalya**, ☎ (242) 243 47 55-56, Fax (242) 243 47 51 – 28rm. ⌐] ☰ TV ✕ ⌐ ⌂ CC Near the harbour in Antalya, not far from the fortress. Set in a big old building, tastefully restored and decorated with magnificent wood panelling. The rooms are spacious and decorated in the Ottoman style. The cuisine is also highly refined, and you can enjoy a panoramic view of Kaleiçi.

Alp Paşa Konağı, Barbaros Mah Hesapçı Sok 30-32, ☎ (242) 247 56 76 / 243 00 45, Fax (242) 248 50 74, info@alppasa.com / reservation@alppasa.com, www.alppasa.com ⌐] ⌐ ☰ TV ✕ ♥ ⌐ CC In a splendid 19C konak, consisting of two elegant wooden pavilions with elaborate corbelling, set in a garden with swimming pool.

Over US$75

Hotel Marina, Mermerli Sok 15, ☎ (242) 247 54 90 (7 lines), Fax (242) 241 17 65 – 42rm. ⌐] ☰ TV ✕ ⌐ ⌂

CC A hotel with all mod cons and a Mediterranean decor. Located in the heart of the old town, it affords a superb view over the harbour and bay.

Hotel Aspen, Mermerli Sok 16/18, ☎ (242) 247 05 90, Fax (242) 241 33 64. 200m from the old harbour – 40rm. ⌐] ☰ TV ✕ ⌐ ⌂ CC Take the soul of the ancient residences of Kaleiçi, the colours of the Mediterranean, the best in modern comfort, and you will get the Aspen hotel. You can admire the ramparts while taking a stroll under the bougainvillaea in the garden.

EATING OUT

There are two specialities which you absolutely must try: "patlıcan reçeli", a tasty aubergine chutney and "tandır kebap", mutton cooked in a potato.

• In Kaleiçi

Under US$8

Sırrı Fish, Uzun Çarşı Sok 25 (B2), ☎ (242) 241 72 39. Near the ramparts, opposite a jazz bar, this little establishment serves delicious fried fish.

Tropic Pansiyon, Hesapçı Sok 44, next to Kesik Minare (B3), ☎ (242) 243 79 79. Good home cooking served in a garden. Very friendly welcome.

Between US$8 and US$15

Kırkmerdiven, Selçuk Mah Musalla Sok 2 (B2), ☎ (242) 242 96 86. Meals are served on the terrace or in the air-conditioned dining room, to the gentle strains of Ottoman music. A choice of four set menus.

Turban, at the harbour. Like most of the restaurants set on the quayside, here you will find fish, meze, salad and pide.

Around US$15

Alp Paşa Konağı, the restaurant belonging to the hotel of the same name (C1). The tables are set around the swimming pool, in the centre of the shaded courtyard. Attentive and polished service. This place is very popular, particularly with the British, so it is advisable to book ahead.

Alaturka's, Uzuncarsı Selçuk Mah 48 (C1), ☎ (242) 243 16 06 / 241 79 71. A "fazıl" (Ottoman classical music) orchestra plays on the terrace from 9pm every evening in summer. The menu offers a large choice of fish and meat (we recommend the delicious "Ottoman kebab", prepared in a casserole). You can also lie back on the sofas and smoke a hookah.

🍴 **Han**, Paşa Cami Sok 34 (B2), ☎ (242) 248 60 81. Quality and refinement are the key words here. A mini-concert is given every evening. Book in advance.

🍴 **Hisar Tesisleri**, Cumhuriyet Meydanı (A1), ☎ (242) 241 52 81. Set in the ramparts, the terrace has a sweeping view over the bay. The food is both refined and copious, and there is a bar for night owls.

Mermerli, Selçuk Mah, Mermerli Banyo Sok 25 (A2), ☎ (242) 248 54 84. A terrace restaurant at the harbour, set slightly above street level. On the menu: the fish of the day, grilled, fried or in sauce, the choice is yours!

• **At the harbour**

Under US$15

Anfi, Kaleiçi Yat Limanı (A2), next to the amphitheatre, ☎ (242) 243 20 73/74, Fax (242) 242 34 59. This is a very popular Turkish restaurant with a permanently festive atmosphere. On a vast terrace facing the citadel, you can sample grilled sea bream and meze served with rakı.

Ceneviz, Kılıçaslan Mah Hıdırlık Sok 12/B (B3), ☎ (242) 247 52 15. A small, very cheap restaurant serving only a variety of meze and drinks.

HAVING A DRINK

If you feel like a "çay" in an airy spot, go to Cumhuriyet Meyd, to one of the numerous **Çay Bahçesi** which tower above the citadel and the harbour.

Bars – Matawit Ali Baba Rock Café, Uzuncarşı Sok 24 (B2), ☎ (242) 243 49 37. True to its name, this is essentially a rock bar.

Gece Bar, Tuz Kapısı Sok (A2), near the post office at the harbour. A very lively place, where the crowds spill out onto the street.

Kale Bar, Mermerli Banyo Sok 2 (B2), ☎ (242) 248 65 91 / 248 64 78. More upmarket than the ones above. Set on the ramparts of the old town, its terrace, which dominates the harbour, is an ideal spot for a drink.

Disco Allı, an open-air bar 100m from the Harput hotel (B1). This is where all the trendy young Turks hang out.

Disco Olympos, in the Falez hotel, Yüzüncü Yıl Bulv., outside the old town.

Internet café – Naturel Internet Café, Cumhuriyet Meyd, ☎ (242) 243 87 63, Fax (242) 243 87 64, yvural@antinter-cafe.com.tr. Air-conditioning. US$3 per hour.

OTHER THINGS TO DO

What better place for a stroll at sundown than **Karaalioğlu Parkı** (A3), with its panoramic view of the bay of Antalya, its neat flower beds, paths bordered with palm trees and countless exotic plants. It is very popular with Turkish families, who come here to relax and make the most of the children's playgrounds and the roller-skating ramp.

Turquoise cruise – Antalya is one of the main ports of call on the turquoise cruise, where boats come to stock up (see p 117-118).

Beaches – The beaches closest to Antalya are at **Konyaaltı** (2.5km west of the centre) and **Lara** (10km east); of limited interest.

Water slides – Dumlupınar Bul, towards Konyaaltı beach.

Excursions to the Taurus Mountains – The local travel agencies organise day-trips by car to Köprülü Kanyon and Selge (see p 447), as well as treks (1 day or more) in the Bey Dağları massif. They also offer 4wd tours. But nothing beats walking if you really want to make the most of the mountains!

Cinema – At the beginning of October, Antalya hosts a Film and Art Festival, **Altın Portakal** ("Golden Orange"), which is becoming more international each year.

SHOPPING GUIDE

Bazaar – In the old town, from Cumhuriyet Cad to the marina (A1). This is a classic bazaar selling all the usual Turkish craft products.

TERMESSUS ★★★
Antalya Province – 34km northwest of Antalya
Map p 355 – Alt 1 050m – Lodging in Antalya

Not to be missed
The theatre.
The southern and western necropolises.

And remember...
Wear sturdy shoes and bring water, and in winter, warm clothing.
Try to arrive early in the morning, before the masses of tourists.
Watch out for the numerous open cisterns in the ground.
Picnic in the natural park at the site or near the gorges of the Güver.

Termessus is a site of powerful, natural and wild beauty, the discovery of which will undoubtedly be a memorable one. Surrounded by the summits of Güllük Dağı, the ancient city is laid out on a steep plateau wedged between two mountains, drowning in a thick forest of pine and olive trees and fragrant bushes. A true jungle where the ruins seem to emerge like reefs and where the views of the surrounding scenery are extraordinary.

Located next to the Yenice valley, the site is in the heart of the **Güllük Dağı Natural Park** (Güllük Dağı Milli Parkı), a protected territory with a surface area of 6 700ha. A beautiful jewellery box which is the setting of equally amazing ruins. In spite of the invasive vegetation, Termessus is one of Turkey's best preserved ancient cities, and the region's rugged terrain adds an adventurous touch. Between the steep hills and the paths which disappear among the scrub the hike will be strenuous, and exceptionally charming!

An ephemeral city

The origins of Termessus have been lost in time. According to Strabo, the city was founded by a people who had arrived from Pisidia, a small mountainous region north of Lycia. Its inhabitants, mentioned in the *Iliad* for their valour, called themselves Solymians. However, the city only began to appear in history as of 334 BC, during Alexander the Great's passage when he supposedly placed it under siege without ever being able to conquer it. The Hellenistic period marked its first golden age. Then, after being the ally of the Syrian king Antiochus III against the Romans (189 BC), the city sided with them to fight Mithridates, the Pontic king. Thereafter, Termessus remained faithful to Rome, to the point that it was considered "a friend of the Roman people" by the Senate. This distinction permitted it to retain a large portion of its autonomy, including the right to create its own laws which sparked a new era of prosperity. Later, the city simply faded and was abandoned from 5C AD.

Termessus was rediscovered in the middle of the 19C by British and German travellers. Nevertheless, the city has never really been excavated, and many treasures lie hidden in this site, which is already exceptional.

Fierce warriors
Little is known about the origins of the people of Termessus, the Solymians. Their name is supposed to come from an Anatolian divinity, Solym, to which the mountain flanking Termessus, the Solymus (now Güllük Dağı) would have been dedicated. They lived off the harvest of olives and at times by plundering. Tradition has especially classified them as a bellicose people who attacked Bellerophon (in vain), the mythical hero who killed the Chimaera (see sidebar p 418).

Visiting the site

The site is unfortunately neither served by bus nor dolmuş. Those without private transport can nevertheless take a dolmuş to Korkuteli, which will drop them off at the intersection where taxis will be waiting (in summer). Another solution: use the services of a travel agency, in Antalya, to join a group excursion. Ideally, an inexpensive option allowing extra flexibility is to negotiate a set fare with a taxi driver.

From Antalya, take the Burdur road (towards the north), then, after 11km, follow the road on the left in the direction of Korkuteli. After 14km, turn left again at the "Güllükdağı Termessus Milli Parkı" sign. You pay at the park entrance, where the information centre (equipped with a cafeteria) has a local flora and fauna exhibit. The archeological site is 9km further on. Thanks to the fact that it is inside the park, it is fairly well maintained: useful directional signs and the main monuments are identified with signs. The visit is therefore facilitated; however it is nonetheless long and tiring due to the uneven terrain. Allow 2hr to see the main sites, or half a day for a complete visit. 8am-7pm; 5.30pm in winter. Entrance fee.

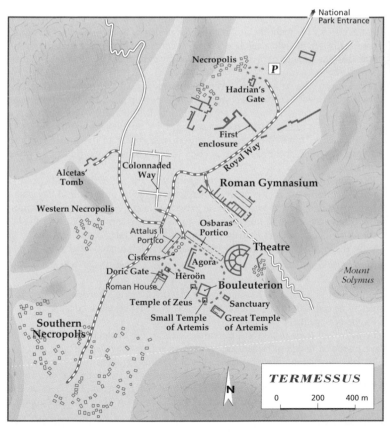

National Park Entrance

Necropolis

P

Hadrian's Gate

First enclosure

Royal Way

Alcetas' Tomb

Colonnaded Way

Roman Gymnasium

Western Necropolis

Osbaras' Portico

Attalus II Portico

Theatre

Cisterns

Agora

Doric Gate

Hèroön

Roman House

Bouleuterion

Mount Solymus

Temple of Zeus

Sanctuary

Southern Necropolis

Small Temple of Artemis

Great Temple of Artemis

TERMESSUS

0   200   400 m

N

As soon as you cross the car park you are in the midst of a chaos of rocks, ruins and shrubs which are all intermingled. Towards the right *(west)*, a small **necropolis** spreads out on the flanks of a hill, hiding a multitude of **sarcophagi** broken up by the vegetation. The majority were already pillaged several centuries ago, as the crude holes piercing their covers will attest.

Returning to the southeast, do not miss **Hadrian's Gate**, an unusual marble frame, with a height of 4.5m. It rises above a few steps covered with fallen rocks, a view of the mountain affording. This is all that remains of the small Ionic temple erected in 130 AD to honour the emperor. Next, take the **"royal" way** *(the marked path on the right)*, a modest incline whose polished marble slabs were nevertheless walked upon by Alexander the Great! It crosses the **first enclosure** – the one which blocked off the conqueror – an impressive grey wall built during the Hellenistic period.

Less than 300m away, a small path on the left leads to the **Roman gymnasium★★** (2C), a large building whose **walls★**, very well preserved, are pierced by large shrubs. Windows decorated with elegant pilasters punctuate the façade, which is no less than 91m long (14m wide).

The agora district
Return to the main path and climb towards the left.

On the edge of the path, the 2m deep **water drainage system** appears among the gaps. Nearby on the right a **colonnaded way** is concealed in the vegetation; this small 100m axis, the remains of one of the city streets, was enclosed by porticoes and their shops.

Further down, the path climbs towards the **agora**, a vast rectangular esplanade invaded by weeds. Of the four **stoas** (porticoes) surrounding it, only the one dedicated to Attalus II (king of Pergamum from 159 to 138 BC) remains. It is a long Doric-style gallery which rose over two levels, the lower one opening up to the outer slope, towards the west. The northeast corner of the square has also retained the ruins of the **Osbaras portico** (a local benefactor), built during the Roman period.

Continuing toward the south across the agora, you will notice the round openings of several **cisterns**, which were very numerous in the city. Further still, at the agora's southern extremity, an impressive **Doric gate★**, 6m high, protrudes from the shrubs. It marks the entrance to a **Roman house**, today in ruins. An inscription on the left post of the door indicates that the owner was the "founder of the city", in other words, the benefactor to whom the city owed many important works.

Return to the agora and the path which traverses it to continue to the right (toward the east).

On the right side of the path, stairs among the rocks lead to a **heroön**, a stone mausoleum pierced with three niches and adjoined by a small **exedra**, housing the tomb of some personality of the day.

The path then leads to a group of temples next to the **bouleuterion★**, Termessus' best preserved building (Hellenistic period): its embossed **walls★** still rise 10m and alternate with elegant pilasters. The inside of the building, once covered with polychrome marble, has not been unearthed yet. Underneath the stone blocks covering it, the hemicycle steps remain hidden. They could accommodate 600. Its size and the probable existence of a cover indicate that it was most likely used for concerts (odeon).

To the west, in the middle of the shrubs, you can still see part of the **temple of Zeus Solymeus**, then towards the southeast, the first **sanctuary dedicated to Artemis**. Well preserved, it has retained its **inscription** on the door's lintel indicating that it was built by a female citizen of Termessus, Aurelia Armasta. Immediately behind, the meagre remains of the **Grand Temple of Artemis** can be seen. The city's largest, it was built by the Antonines (138-192 AD). A dedication to Artemis was found on the temple. Beside it (to the north) rose the **fourth sanctuary**, built upon a podium.

From there, taking the path towards the right, you will reach the **theatre★★★**, the city's highlight. Perched on the city's heights, it looks down onto a deep valley, facing the steep slopes of Mt Solymus. From the well-preserved steps, the **view★★★** of the summits and the valley is extraordinary. The theatre, a vast 66m-diameter hemicycle, could hold up to 4 200 spectators. Built during the Hellenistic period, it was modified during the 2C by the Romans who added a stage building. Of the latter, only the façade remains, pierced by three elegant doors opening up to the grandiose decor of the mountains. This is a good opportunity for a break, as you sit on the steps and contemplate the surroundings, before bravely enduring the ascent to the southern necropolis.

Return and cross the agora to the main road which you will take on the left.

The southern necropolis★★★

To the extreme south of the site stretches Termessus' largest necropolis (one of three). Clinging to the steep flank of a mountain, several hundred **sarcophagi★** are concealed among the shrubs and the rocks. Some are standing, like superb stiff silhouettes, whereas others are half toppled as a result of earthquakes or pilferage. A multitude of **rock tombs★**, with **façades★** in the shape of houses or temples, riddle the summits with strange alveoli. All are of Lycian or Roman style, decorated with **bas-reliefs** with various themes – family life, war figures etc, which you discover with each step like treasures hidden in the jungle. Climb to the summit (1 220m) and enjoy the **superb panorama★★** of the site.

On descending, take the path on the left to reach the **western necropolis**, where the remains of the **rock tomb of Alcetas** are to be found. The bas-relief shows this Roman general (of Alexander the Great) on a horse with his armour.

From there, return to the main path which will take you to the foot of the site.

If you have the time, complete your discovery in the heights with a small tour along the **gorges of the Güver★** (Güver Uçurumu), close to the Termessus ruins, in the natural park *(6km after the site returning toward Antalya; a sign indicates the starting point of the excursion).* The road follows the ravine dug by the river by crossing a large **deer reserve**. It is here that you will discover the dizzying **views★★** of the summits and depths of the gorges, at times 100m deep.

The sad story of Alcetas

After Alexander's death, his generals fought over his empire: especially Antigone and Alcetas, who sought control of Lycia. Vanquished, the latter found refuge in Termessus. It was not a smart decision, since the city Elders decided to return him to his adversary. The younger warriors opposed this, but the Elders found a fallacious excuse to send them to combat Antigone and took advantage of their absence to foment betrayal. Feeling defeated, Alcetas preferred to kill himself. The Termessians, who were furious, furnished Antigone with a heavily-mutilated body which was left without burial. The young warriors who were ashamed of the Elders' act, recovered the body, performed a grandiose funeral service and a burial which was worthy of his rank.

PERGA ★★

Antalya Province – 20km from Antalya
Map p 355 – Accommodation in Antalya

Not to be missed
The stadium, the theatre (if it ever opens),
the Hellenistic gate and the baths.

And remember...
Bring drinking water and a hat, to protect against the glare and scorching heat!
Visit the Antalya museum beforehand,
where most of the statues which lined the streets of Perga can be seen;
this will give you an idea of the city's beauty.

Perga is undoubtedly one of the most interesting archeological sites of the southern coast. While the city does not possess the romanticism of Pınara or Termessus, it nevertheless has the advantage of enabling you to understand the layout of a typical Roman city in Asia Minor. As you stroll among its ruins, it is very easy to imagine the daily life of the inhabitants. A heavily-populated city, given the impressive number of shops and the importance of its public buildings, Perga is also striking due to the number of infrastructures related to water – canals, baths, countless fountains, sacred or utilitarian. Water, which was of capital importance to the Romans, was the symbol *par excellence* of prosperity and power; it therefore had to reach the entire city, to beautify and refresh it. Visiting the site on a summer afternoon allows you to instantly understand its beneficial effects!

A privileged location

Tucked away between two slopes, Perga stands against a small hill which is as large as a plateau – the site of the acropolis — stretching its sand-coloured ruins in the middle of cotton fields and orange groves.

The city owes part of its prosperity to its geographical position, which facilitated its political and commercial role: on a map, it appears in the heart of the great fertile plain of Pamphylia, near the banks of the Kestros (the current Aksu Çayı), linking it to the sea. To the north, the Taurus raise their majestic crests, protecting the plain from the strong winds, whereas to the south, the coast is 12km away, keeping it safe from the many invaders who swept through along the shores.

From the Achaeans to the Romans

The inhabitants of Perga liked to believe that they descended from the mythical heroes of the Trojan War, such as Mopsus, mentioned regularly in local inscriptions. However, the city, founded in the third millennium, was most likely colonised by the Achaeans in the millennium which followed. Herodotus tells us that Perga then passed to Croesus, King of Lydia from 560 to 547 BC, who had to cede it to the Persians in 546. The city was then part of the first satrapy (province) of Ionia and remained under Persian domination until the arrival of Alexander the Great (334 BC), who was greeted with open arms by the population.

The titles of Perga
Like most large coastal cities, Perga minted coins, especially under Roman control. On the city's coins can be seen its proud titles: "Hiera" (the sacred), "Lamprorate" (the most brilliant), "Endoxos" (the illustrious), "Prote" (the first, the capital), "Neocoros" (the city of the new Imperial cult), or "Metropolis Pamphylias." It is true that Perga was in the heart of Pamphylia, the centre of its world.

The Mediterranean Coast

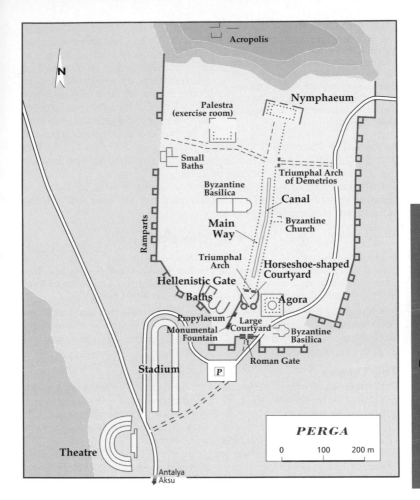

PERGA

0   100   200 m

Perga remained faithful to the Seleucids, including Antiochus III (223-187 BC) who fortified it. Later, it came under Roman control, like all the other cities of the province. Roman domination was to mark an important era of prosperity, in spite of the terrible pillage of the quaestor (Roman treasurer) Caius Verres, slightly before 70 BC: in his orations, Cicero reported that the bandit went so far as to remove the gold plaques covering the statue of the city's patron, Artemis Pergaia.

Reconstructed and embellished, Perga pursued its growth until the 3C AD. It received in the meantime (in the middle of the 1C), a visit from St Paul who preached and founded one of the region's first churches.

After the 4C, Christianity won over the cult of Artemis, by associating the goddess with the Virgin (as shown by the column which carries the effigy of Artemis, in the narthex of a Byzantine church).

From Artemis to Mary
In a city where the cult of Artemis was especially strong, the switch to the cult of Mary was favoured by an iconographical particularity: in Perga, the pagan goddess was represented with a luminous crown, thereby resembling the Christian nimbus. A coincidence which singularly eased recycling!

However, the city entered into competition with Side for Christian pre-eminence in the region, until Pamphylia was split in two. Each city was then represented by a different archbishop after the 6C. Antalya became in turn the main religious centre and the capital of the region but Perga began to decline and was further weakened by the attacks of mountainous tribes and the Arabs. The city nevertheless endured under the reign of Constantine VII Porphyrogenitus (10C), then sank rapidly before being almost entirely abandoned in the 12C, occasionally being occupied by Turks.

The city was excavated by Turkish archeologists starting in 1946 (necropolis). It continued in the 1950s (Hellenistic Gate and main way), and since 1967, the rest of the site has been regularly explored.

Visiting the site

From Antalya, take the Side-Alanya road. After 18km, in the village of Aksu, turn left. The site is 2km away. For those without private transport, minibuses leave from Antalya. Take a taxi for the remaining 2km. 8am-7pm, 5.30pm in winter. Entrance fee. You can exchange money at the post office, next to the ticket office. Allow 2hr for the visit.

It is through the entertainment district, outside the city walls, that you enter Perga. Before reaching the parking lot at the city gates, the road passes between the theatre and the stadium, skirting the city's two largest monuments. Their sheer size and excellent state of preservation will impress you.

The Theatre★★

Once you have parked your vehicle, return to the theatre, a superb hemicycle with almost perfectly proportioned steps, standing against the western slope *(if the building is closed, you can explore the interior by climbing up the hill)*. Built essentially in the years 110-120 AD, it was constructed according to the Roman plan, although its **cavea★★**, which exceeds the half-circle, has Hellenistic references.

With a capacity of 14 000 spectators and a diameter of 114m, it is not the region's largest nor best preserved *(see Aspendos)*. However, the hundreds of stone blocks stacked on the stadium's track should allow for an almost complete reconstruction. In the meantime, the main interest of the theatre resides in its decor, a refinement which expresses the taste of the period. Notice the **orchestra parapet**, containing a series of good-luck *hermes*; then, admire the 10 superb panels making up the lower portion of the **stage wall★★** *(frons scaenae)*. In friezes, they represent several episodes of the myth of Dionysus (the Roman Bacchus), god of theatre and wine. He can be seen leaving Jupiter's thigh *(second panel)*, where he was incubated due to his premature birth. On the fourth panel on the right of the central niche, you can see the grooming of the divine child, whereas the tenth panel – the best preserved – depicts one of his trips in the company of the Maenads *(bacchantes)* and the god Pan, half-man half-ram. The other panels are displayed in the Antalya museum, with the countless statues which decorated the façade. On the outside, the **stage building** must have been richly decorated: the ruins of a monumental fountain still appear at its base. Apparently it was composed of several basins and pierced with statue-bearing niches.

The stadium**

On the other side of the street you reach the stadium (2C AD), an immense structure with arcades on its outer perimeter. As you enter (the wall enclosing it, which included the main entrance, is completely destroyed), you will be surprised by its proportions and the extraordinary perspective of the stands. Perga's stadium is Asia Minor's largest and best preserved along with the one in Aphrodisias: its impressive size (234m long, 34m wide) enabled it to accommodate 15 000 spectators. Entirely built on a flat surface, its **stands*** stood on a series of **barrel-vaulted galleries*** facing the exterior. These rooms were used for the stadium's services or rented to shopkeepers whose names are sometimes engraved on the walls.

Return to the parking lot and continue to the north to visit the city itself.

The city gates*

Beyond the car park rise the **city walls** and their beautiful rectangular **towers**. They were erected at the end of the 2C AD to protect the growing city. They are reached through a **Roman gate** surrounded by two mighty square towers, one of which is still standing. You then enter a **large trapezoidal-shaped courtyard**, strewn with stone blocks. Immediately to the right *(east)*, notice the ruins of a **Byzantine basilica**, which seems isolated from the rest of the city.

The remains of a **monumental fountain**, built during the reign of Septimius Severus on the site of an ancient sacred spring are to the left side of the courtyard. The vast rectangular **basin**, carved with two **exedrae** can still be seen along with the base of the **façade.**

Further down stood the **propylaeum** (in ruins), a monumental gate decorated with eight columns leading to the city's largest **baths***. A large portion of the walls are still upright and their general appearance, together with the **large pool-filled rooms**, ranks them among Turkey's best-preserved Roman baths. This is a perfect

Perga, the masks of the ancient theatre
(frieze fragment)

A. Thévenart

opportunity to discover the technical aspects related to bathing establishments of this period. The hypocaust system, which ensured the heating of the structure, can be observed in *"flayed"* style: the *suspensura*, a cement floor of piled bricks resting on **small piles**, the *tubuli* rising along the walls; the various **pools** – cold, warm and hot – and the **hearths** which heated them in the basement *(see "Architecture", p 53)*. Past the **palestra**, an exercise courtyard surrounded by a portico, you saunter from room to room, from the coldest to the hottest. Beautiful **mosaic or black-and-white marble floors** covering the ground appear haphazardly.

In the heart of the city★★

What strikes you as soon as you enter the city *(on the left as you leave the baths)*, is the might of the two powerful circular **towers** of the **Hellenistic gate★★** – a remnant of the city's first enclosure (200 BC) – rising at the other end of the courtyard. With a height of nearly 12m, they were Perga's largest towers, a veritable symbol which the Romans chose to keep as they enlarged the city. Impressive in spite of their state of disrepair, they guard the entrance to the **horseshoe-shaped courtyard★**, originally oval, surrounded by high walls. The Romans transformed it into a main courtyard, covering the walls with marble and piercing it with **large niches** housing the statues of the city's protective divinities *(in the Antalya museum)*. Towards 121 BC, a rich citizen, Plancia Magna *(see below)*, further embellished it by adding a **triumphal arch** to its northern edge (heavily ruined), and thereby reducing the surface by half.

Beyond is the city's main way and immediately on the right, the **agora★**, or market place, a perfect square (75x75m). The **colonnade** of the portico which surrounded it has been partially raised and a large number of its shops are still visible. The regular alignment of **marble doors** faced the square and the neighbouring streets. Fragments of the **mosaic** floor can be seen, and in the centre, the base of a **tholos**, a circular temple.

Return towards the triumphal arch.

The city's **main way★★**, a veritable boulevard (20m wide) covered with marble and lined with **porticoes**, stretches for more than 300m. It is so well preserved that you can easily imagine a Roman coming to do the shopping. Divided by a 2m-wide **canal★** where refreshing water flowed, the street was the domain of horses and carts (a few traces of the wheels can be seen on the slabs), whereas the pedestrians walked in the shade of the porticoes, home to various types of shops and offices. A few of them have retained fragments of **mosaics★** indicating the name and profession of their owner. For example, the mosaic of the 39th shop from the gate, on the eastern side, indicates a doctor's surgery.

150m after the gate, still on the eastern side, the four ancient **columns** belonged to the narthex of a **Byzantine church** built over the shops.

Further on, the road crosses the city's main east-west artery which is perpendicular. The intersection, currently being restored, was marked by an elegant **triumphal arch**.

Important Pergans

Among its citizens, Perga had several notables, such as the philosopher Varus (2C AD), and the mathematician and astronomer Apollonius (3C). The latter – very advanced for his time! – made the deduction that since the moon rotates around the earth, the latter in turns rotates around the sun. An implacable truth which took a very long time to be accepted! Perga's most illustrious citizen however, was a woman named Plancia Magna, daughter of the proconsul of Bythinia. She dedicated her life and her wealth to the beautification of the city, undertaking large remodelling projects during Hadrian's reign. Her grateful fellow citizens elevated her to the rank of tutelary divinity of the city. Her tomb (in ruins) stood in front of the Roman gate, near the car park.

The main way ends at the foot of the acropolis where a large **nymphaeum**** stands – one of Perga's most important buildings. It collected the waters from the neighbouring heights and fed the central canal. It contains two levels, flanked by two arches and two side wings. The whole structure was decorated with numerous **statues**, such as the one of the god Kestros (Perga's river), set in front of the main body of the central building. At its base lies a large **basin** where the water from the hill would cascade before draining away on a set of small stairs leading to the canal. Still standing (almost entirely), it remains a monumental decorative work closing off the main road and demonstrating the city's wealth and power.

You could easily end your visit of Perga here and head for the entrance to cool off under the oleaster (Trebizond date) trees. Those who are fascinated by the site can continue towards the west by taking the street perpendicular to the main way, starting at Demetrius' arch. They will discover the remains of a **palestra** and **small baths** *(at the end of the street)* and, along the way, those of a large **Byzantine basilica** *(towards the south)*.

The **acropolis**, the city's most ancient area, perched on the hill situated behind the great nymphaeum, is almost inaccessible and retains only a few meagre Byzantine remains.

ASPENDOS★★
Antalya Province – Map p 355
50km from Antalya – 37km from Side
Lodging in Antalya or Side

Not to be missed
The aqueduct and the theatre.
Antalya's art and film festival (October)
held in the theatre.

And remember...
Come early and start by visiting the theatre,
before the crowds arrive.
Bring a bottle of drinking water.

Like Perga, Aspendos developed away from the coast, in green Pamphylia, near the tranquil shores of a river (the Köprü Çayı, the ancient Eurymedon). Its ruins stretch on a small grassy plateau, a promontory rising above the plain, among the fields of wheat and cotton stretching all the way to the bluish foothills of the Taurus Mountains. A beautiful countryside setting, which includes a jewel: the Aspendos theatre, one of the Ancient world's best preserved. It alone is worth the trip.

Long-lasting prosperity
The foundations of Aspendos are very old: the site was undoubtedly inhabited from 1000 BC, and on its first silver coins (minted in the 5C BC) the city bears a name derived from a Hittite king who lived in the 8C BC.

Sports, a lucrative business
The silver coins minted in Aspendos during the Hellenistic period are among the most interesting series from the Ancient world. Their theme consists of sports combat, the emblem of the city's fighting spirit. On one side, men wielding slingshots accompany the name of the city surrounded by various symbols, whereas on the other, two naked wrestlers practise several types of hold. A treasure of 196 of these coins was discovered near Aspendos in 1971 (several of them can be seen in the numismatic room in the Antalya Museum).

A member of the Athenian Maritime League, Aspendos quickly became prosperous. In 468 BC, it was the port of the Persian fleet which sailed up the Eurymidon, navigable at the time. The city was later handed to Alexander, who demanded an annual tax of 100 gold *talents*. Since a *talent* weighs 26kg, it gives an idea of the city's wealth!

This was a period in which the city was completely transformed, producing a wealth which continued under Roman domination. The Romans built a new Aspendos which left nothing of the original city.

Its power hardly ever wavered in the periods which followed. In the 13C, the Seljuks took it from the Byzantines and began its restoration. It is to these people that the theatre owes its exceptional state of preservation. The city began to decline with the arrival of the Ottomans in the 14C.

Visiting the site

On the road from Antalya to Alanya, turn left at the "Aspendos" yellow sign. The site is 4km from there. 7.30am-7pm in summer, 8am-5.30pm in winter. Entrance fee. Allow 30min for the theatre and 90min for the rest of the site.

Aspendos, Turkey's best-preserved theatre

Some 2km from the site, the road crosses the Köprü via a magnificent **Seljuk bridge*** (13C), built upon the piers of a Roman bridge, much wider but in ruins. This forced the Seljuk architect to base his arches on what was left of the bridge. It was not a simple task!

Shortly before arriving at the site, the road skirts the vestiges of **Roman baths**, large walls of brick and stone facing the fields. Further on, a **large gymnasium**, built in the 3C AD, retains its vaultless walls in the middle of the fields.

The theatre***

Farther still, the road leads to the car park, located at the foot of the theatre (*on the other side of the road*), on what was once the theatre garden. Enter through one of the two original entrances flanked on both sides by the almost intact **stage building****. As soon as you enter the building, you will be captivated by the majesty of the site. The nearly perfect state of the building makes the structure of a Roman theatre easier to understand, its own world closed off from the rest. The

445

spectators were not distracted: while Greek theatres allowed views of the countryside, Roman theatres had a single focus, an immense **stage wall***, which should be imagined covered in marble, columns and pierced with niches harbouring statues (the façade of the library in Ephesus is a good example of the richness and elegance of these decorations).

The Aspendos theatre follows the classical Roman plan *(see "Architecture", p 53)* although its cavea extends slightly beyond the half-circle. You can also note that although it is flanked on the side of a hill like most Greek theatres, the **cavea**** rests entirely on substructures built with cradle vaults. The latter (95m diameter) could accommodate up to 20 000 spectators. A record! Above the last step runs the **ambulacre****, a corridor surrounding the hemicycle with an imposing **row of arcades**** on columns. From there, enjoy the **view**** of the stage wall and all the steps.

All masterpieces should be signed and dated: an inscription in the city's ruins informs us that the architect was named Zeno, son of Theodore, who lived during the reign of Marcus Aurelius (161-180 AD).

The city*

In comparison to the theatre, the city is a bit dull. Nevertheless, proceed to the impressive **stadium** *(approximately 300m north following the path which climbs up alongside the theatre, then turn slightly to the right)*, even though it is more of a ruin than that of Perga.

Backtracking about 100m, you will enter the city, established on a neighbouring plateau *(take the path which flanks the western side of the theatre)*. From there, the **view**** of the building and the plain which unfolds at your feet is breathtaking.

Once you have crossed the ruins and the **eastern gate**, a small path takes you to the **Roman aqueduct**** leaving the city's centre on the southern side *(left)*. At the edge of a small plateau invaded by tall grass, you reach the ledge of a cliff where you can see the entire plain (very beautiful **panorama****). The aqueduct's tall **arches**** carried water from the neighbouring hills. 850m long, the Aspendos aqueduct is the region's best preserved, along with the one in Phaselis: it has retained the two **pressure towers***, impressive works which are 30m high and are located at the extremities of the bridge.

Reaching the centre of the ancient city *(200m towards the south)*, you come to a **large building** equipped with an apse, the function of which is unknown. A gigantic **wall*** isolates it from the agora*, a "screen" measuring 15m in height and 35m in length. It rises on two levels pierced with niches, and in some areas retains elements of the frieze whose white marble stands out against the ochre-coloured stone. This forms the façade of an imposing **nymphaeum***, a monumental fountain which closed off the **agora*** to the north. A series of **shops** (in ruins) were aligned on the western side of the latter, whereas the east is filled with an immense **administrative basilica** (2C AD), 105m long. The building is joined by an **"annex"** *(northern extremity)*, an impressive square tower, 15m high, later transformed into a turret. Last but not least, to the south, the agora is closed off by a **high wall** pierced by a large **exedra** of brick and stone. Many guides claimed that this was a conference room for philosophers and orators, although there is no proof.

The Selge road**

57km from Aspendos. From the site, return to the Alanya road and continue for 5km before turning left at the "Selge" sign. In Beşkonak, the paved road becomes an adequate 20km track (beware, in areas it is a bit rocky).

If you have time, continue your day by taking the road to **Altıkaya**, a charming village established on the ruins of ancient **Selge***. The **view**** along the road is grandiose. The snow-capped summits of the Taurus Mountains overlooking the Pamphylian plain are memorable!

Lost in the heights of Pisidia, in the heart of the magnificent **Köprülü Canyon Park**** (Köprülü Kanyon Milli Parkı), Selge's ruins are scattered throughout the forest. The **theatre**** is the only monument in good condition, a true jewel of marble turned grey over time. It offers spectacular **views**** of the surrounding landscape which is simply breathtaking! The play needed to be extremely captivating in order not to distract the 9 000 spectators from the enchanting view of the mountains!

⎯⎯ Making the most of Aspendos (Belkıs) ⎯⎯

EATING OUT

Numerous little restaurants are to be found on the riverside around the site itself, where you can sample the excellent "güveç", meat, fish or prawn stews prepared in earthenware casseroles.

OTHER THINGS TO DO

Concerts – *Classical music* concerts are given in the theatre during one week in July every year.

Festival – In October, Antalya's Film and Art Festival makes for a lively atmosphere at the monument.

Making the most of Aspendos

SİDE★
(SELİMİYE)

Antalya Province – Map p 355
74km from Antalya – Pop 11 550
Mild climate all year round

Not to be missed
The museum located inside the Roman baths.
The temples of Athena and Apollo.

And remember...
Visit Side in the off-peak season, between November and March;
in summer the city overflows with people.

Ancient Side is set on a small, totally flat peninsula, a headland surrounded by the blue waters of the Mediterranean. The first thing you see as you arrive is the theatre, a magnificent semicircle of grey stone rising like a rampart at the gates of the peninsula. Behind, the modern city of **Selimiye** has unfortunately overrun the surrounding remains with an army of hotels, souvenir boutiques, bars and discotheques (Side is undoubtedly the most popular spot on this part of the coast). This invasion extends all the way to the coastline, where the majestic temple of Apollo raises its elegant white marble columns next to the limpid waters of the sea. In summer, the ruins are mobbed with people and the streets filled with the usual cacophony of the summer's hit songs. However, once the summer season is over, Side is once again quiet, and its former charm suddenly reappears. It becomes a pleasure to stroll and explore its ruins (the entire city is a pedestrian zone).

From the Greeks to the Turks... of Crete

Archeological discoveries reveal that the city was founded in the 7C BC, probably by Greek colonists who had come from Smyrna. Their dialect became the language of all of Pamphylia (replaced by Greek once Alexander the Great arrived in the 4C). The usual conquerors succeeded one another – Persians, Macedonians, Seleucids – and the city reached its apogee during the Roman period between the 2C BC and the 3C AD. During the interval in which it was a Byzantine diocese, Side enjoyed its last golden age in the 5C and 6C, before enduring Arab attacks in the 8C. It was abandoned in the 12C in favour of Antalya. The current city, once a charming village, was founded by Turkish refugees from Crete, who landed on the peninsula at the end of the 19C after the insurrection of 1896.

A pirates' den
Its unusual layout – a peninsula easily accessible by sea – made Side a favourite haunt for the pirates who terrorised the coast during the 1C BC. The city became a centre for a sinister commerce: slave traffic and auctions of pillaged bounties. This gave the city a terrible reputation, which the Romans had a hard time rehabilitating.

Visiting the city
Allow 90min for the visit,
or more if you plan to walk on the beaches.

Just before entering the city, the road passes by a large **nymphaeum** (C2) *(on the left)* the façade of which is no less than 52m long (only the first level, whose niches were once filled with statues, has survived). Thereafter you cross the meagre remains of the **city gate** (C2), in the Hellenistic walls. It was a tall, concave horseshoe-shaped portal, flanked by two imposing towers. After the ramparts, on the right, a few arcades of the **aqueduct** which supplied the city with fresh water are still visible. On the opposite side, an ancient way disappears between modern-day houses and leads to a large **Byzantine basilica** and the **bishop's palace** (heavily damaged).

Straight on, the harbour road follows the trace of the **ancient main artery** (*Liman Cad*). It crosses the heart of the city, all the way to the agora. Just before reaching it, two small 2C BC **houses with peristyles** can be seen on the left.

The ancient centre

Beyond this point, you need to leave your vehicle in the car park (*on the right, on the side of the theatre*), as the remaining vestiges and city may only be explored on foot. Begin by returning to the agora (facing the theatre) and the museum.

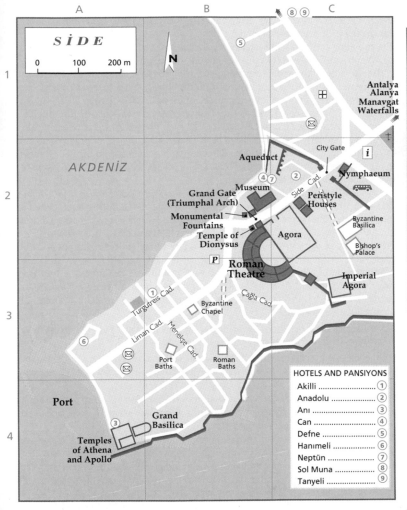

Side

HOTELS AND PANSIYONS

Akilli	(1)
Anadolu	(2)
Anı	(3)
Can	(4)
Defne	(5)
Hanımeli	(6)
Neptün	(7)
Sol Muna	(8)
Tanyeli	(9)

You will pass under the beautiful arcade of the **Grand Gate** (Triumphal Arch) (B2), cut out of the **enclosure** built in the 7C to protect the southern side of the city. It was radically modified at the end of Antiquity: notice the countless column drums which make up the *piedroits* (the recycling of ancient pieces was quite common). Immediately on the right, resting against the arch, notice the splendid façade of the **temple of Dionysus**. The other side of the gate is flanked by a group of **monumental fountains**★. The largest one contained three basins.

Further down, on the left side of the road, you reach the **museum**★★ (B2) *(8am-7pm in summer, 8am-12noon/1.30pm-5.30pm in winter; closed Mondays. Entrance fee)* ingeniously laid out inside the Roman baths of the 5C AD. This is a great opportunity to explore a bathing complex in excellent condition, paved with mosaics and marble, in addition to an interesting collection of miscellaneous items. Change your identity for a few moments and pretend you are a Roman notable going to the baths to relax (even though the path does not follow the original one).

The museum encloses a rich collection of sculptures discovered during the city's excavations, undertaken between 1947 and 1966. The most important items include a **Victory**, a delightful group representing the **Three Graces**, statues of **Hercules**★ and **Hermes**, as well as a large **sarcophagus** decorated with a frieze of cupids. The majority of these works are Roman marble copies of Greek originals.

As you leave the museum, cross the road to reach the **agora** – seat of the administrative and commercial life of the city – a vast quadrilateral of 100m on each side, strewn with stone blocks which have been neatly stacked by the archeologists. In the centre notice the base of a **tholos** (circular temple) dating from the 2C, whereas in the southwest corner, against the theatre, a building decorated with a large central niche houses the **public latrines**.

On the southern side of the agora, the **Roman theatre**★★ *(currently closed for restoration; otherwise, same hours as the museum, entrance fee)* displays its superb steps between the ramparts. The immense hemicycle – 119m diameter – could accommodate 15 000 spectators. Constructed in the 2C AD, it is nonetheless Hellenistic in style. From the top of the last row of steps, there is a beautiful **view**★★ of the sea and the coast.

After the theatre, you can follow the **land wall** towards the east up to the **Imperial agora**★ (C3), flanked by the ruins of an elegant building, probably a **library**★. Its façade is adorned with fine Corinthian columns and pierced with niches (one of them still houses a statue).

Backtrack and cross the agora again all the way to the road. Pass the Grand Gate (Triumphal Arch) to enter the city.

On the left, discover the remains of an **ancient way** that led to the tip of the peninsula. It ran past another **Roman bathing establishment**, today lost among the modern houses.

Following the main street *(Liman Cad, straight on towards the port)* – the current city's main shopping street – pass by the ruins of a **Byzantine chapel** *(on the left)*, then those of the **port baths** *(also on the left)*.

Right at the end, you reach the modest **port**★. It does not compare to the splendour of the ancient port! The spot is nevertheless enjoyable with its beautiful wooden homes, built in the regional Ottoman style (building codes in this district are very strict). It is a pleasure to end the day in one of the numerous pavement cafés lined up along the front waiting for the sun to set.

An American benefactor
One of the people responsible for the success of tourism and culture in the city, was the American journalist, Arthur Friendly (Pulitzer Prize) who became chief editor of The Washington Post and who lived the last years of his life in Side, in the sixties. His widow created a well-endowed foundation which helped restore many of the city's monuments, especially those in the port.

As you skirt the sea toward the east (*on the left*), you reach a vast esplanade which is home to the principal sanctuaries of the city, the **temples of Athena and Apollo*** (A4). Between the immaculate columns of the temple of Apollo (five have recently been raised), there is a splendid **view**** of the horizon.

Adjacent to the terrace, the 5C **Grand Basilica** erected by the Byzantines can still be seen. The nave houses a small church built in the 9C. Facing the basilica, notice the remains of an unusual **temple** with a semi-circular apse erected on a podium. Built in the 2C BC, it was dedicated to the moon god Men.

On the road to Antalya*

The Manavgat waterfalls (Manavgat Şelalesi)

4km northwest of Side. Dolmuşes depart from the "otogar". Neglected by the tourists who concentrate on Side, **Manavgat** is a charming little town, very lively and business oriented, located along the banks of the Manavgat. Rather than shop in Side where the boutiques rarely sell any local products, shop here; and, at the end of the day, have excellent grilled fish in one of the restaurants along the river.

From Manavagat, visit the falls of the same name (*4km from the town, on the right of the Şıhlar road; Dolmuşes leave regularly from Side and Manavgat. Entrance fee*). Their appearance is rather unexceptional (they are only 3m tall!), but the site is ideal for an enjoyable walk along the river's shaded banks arranged like a little park, with drink stands and restaurants. Beware, the site is very popular (especially with Turks) and can be overcrowded in summer.

If you are travelling by car, continue to the village of **Şihlar***, which has pretty stone **houses*** that are several centuries old. On the road, you will pass in front of a beautiful **Ottoman bridge** (*2km from the falls*) crossing the river in five large arches.

Alarahan**

43km from Side, 29km from Manavgat and 39km from Alanya. From Side or Manavgat, take the Alanya road and turn left after Yeşilköy. A small 5km road ends up at the site. Bring a torch, a bottle of water and good shoes if you plan to go up to the citadel. Allow 2hr for the visit.

Lost in the mountains, a castle (*kale*) and a caravanserai (*han*) continue to watch over the Alara, a small river flowing peacefully in between the rocks. Its transparent blue meanders unroll between the tall hills strewn with firs and brushwood. The forgotten and magnificent site bewitches visitors with its wild beauty and Olympian tranquillity.

Near the river (*on the right as you arrive*), next to a ruined bridge, rise the powerful walls of a **Seljuk caravanserai****, a building erected in the 13C by the merchants who travelled the road between Antalya and Alanya. Almost intact, it has retained all of its **vaulted rooms**, illuminated by golden sunlight which pierces through the narrow windows. You stroll inside as you would in a palace, as the architecture is majestically simple and filled with elegant details – niches, rose ornaments, and **torch bearers** with carved lion heads at the base of the walls.

Side

Further down, perched above a steep hill marking the entrance to the gorges, a **citadel**** overlooks the caravanserai and the river. Its stones blend in with the rocks and it is only gradually that your eyes will begin to discern the contours of a **first enclosure***, very well preserved, built half-way up the hill.

The ascent is rather strenuous, but it is really worth the effort for the splendid panorama. Very steep stairs, carved in the rock, lead to the castle. It is time to turn on your torch, since the stairs pass through a **vaulted tunnel,** pitch black and littered with stone blocks, exiting at the level of the first enclosure. This tunnel connected the castle to the caravanserai. Its guests could flee discreetly in case of danger. (Its low entrance is today submerged in the riverbed).

The more athletic will climb up to the **second enclosure**, at the summit, which contains the citadel (in ruins). You will discover the remains of various houses, including the one belonging to the local chieftain, and a **hamam*** still covered by its domes. The site is especially interesting for its magnificent **view***** overlooking the valley and the caravanserai.

Making the most of Side

COMING AND GOING

By bus – *The bus station* is at the entrance to the town, on the left after the tourist information office (C2). Frequent bus services operate to the neighbouring coastal towns.

By shared taxi – Dolmuş stand at the bus station. Services operate to Manavgat.

ADDRESS BOOK

Tourist information – At the entrance to the town, on the left (C2). 8am-7.30pm. The office supplies very little information and a very imprecise street map.

Post office – There are 3 post offices: 2 in the town centre and 1 in the vicinity of the hospital (C1). 8am-8pm.

Bank / change – *Pamukbank*, opposite the main post office (A3), with an automatic cash dispenser. *Yapı Kredi*, in the square with the statue of Atatürk, and another agency at the harbour. Foreign currency can be exchanged at the post office, which also cashes travellers' cheques.

Medical service – *Public hospital*, 200m to the east of the tourist information office (C1), ☎ (252) 412 10 29.

Car rental – *Avis*, Fatih Cad 25, ☎ (242) 753 13 48, Fax (242) 753 28 13.

***Şelale Tours Travel Agency*,** Liman Cad 38 (B3), ☎ (242) 753 39 90 / 753 10 66, Fax (242) 753 29 98.

WHERE TO STAY

The town centre, which is full of hotels and guest houses, is also packed with bars and nightclubs, which makes it an extremely noisy place.

• **Town centre**

US$15

⌂ **Pension Hanımeli**, Turgut Reis Cad 35, ☎ (242) 753 13 19 / 753 17 89 – 12rm. ⌐ ☒ 20m from the beach, this superb little guest house made of stone and wood is a cool haven of peace. With its big garden full of jasmine and lemon trees, and its charming, well-kept rooms, this is the ideal place to seek refuge from all the noise of the town. You will be warmly welcomed by Mehmet Sever, the proprietor. This former archeologist with a passion for history will also be delighted to share his knowledge of the region with you. Open from April to October.

US$30

Hotel Can, Liman Cad 270, ☎ (242) 753 32 40, Fax (242) 753 32 45 – 124rm. ☜ ℰ ⟟ ✕ ❢ [CC] Located next to the beach, 100m from the museum, this hotel is made up entirely of bungalows, and is surrounded by the ancient town walls. Its flower beds make it all the more alluring. The open-air restaurant, surrounded by luxuriant vegetation, is very pleasant. Open from April to November.

Around US$45

Hotel Neptün, on the right at the entrance to the site, ☎ (242) 753 10 86, Fax (242) 753 10 46 – 60rm. ☜ ℰ ✕ [CC] Like the one above, this hotel consists of several bungalows set in a peaceful garden facing the sea. Guarded car park.

• **To the north of the peninsula**

Between US$60 and US$75

Hotel Defne, ☎ (242) 753 18 80, Fax (242) 753 32 33. ☜ ▤ ℰ ✕ ⟟ ✿ [CC] Large, open spaces, luxury, and highly attentive service. A pleasant atmosphere, where you will feel pampered. Excellent value for money.

⊕ **Hotel Sol Muna**, Kumköy Bingeşik Mevkii, ☎ (242) 753 34 46, Fax (242) 753 13 59 – 184rm. ☜ ▤ ℰ ✕ ⟟ ✿ ✾ [CC] A big, modern establishment divided into 8 small units dotted around a large park, offering all sorts of sporting activities. The cuisine is appetising and the service refined.

Hotel Tanyeli, ☎ (242) 753 36 61, Fax (242) 753 28 66 – 36rm. ☜ ℰ ✕ ⟟ ✿ ✾ [CC] Very comfortable, clean and welcoming; a perfect place to relax.

EATING OUT

Most of the restaurants are on the coast all along the peninsula. In general, the fish is excellent but the prices are rather high. **Agora**, Turgutreis Cad 5 (A3-B3). Dinner is served on a very pleasant terrace. The fish is succulent, prepared with the greatest care.

Two other quiet restaurants in Turgut Reis Cad (A3), near the sea, are **Aphrodit** and **Hermès**. Reasonable prices.

HAVING A DRINK

The harbour is teeming with little cafés, each one as friendly as the next. However, the **Apollonik Kafeterya**, the last café when going towards the temple of Apollo, deserves a special mention: its proprietor has had the excellent idea of making a model of ancient Side, which will help to give you a better idea of how the town used to be.

Yes Bar, next to the police station ("Jandarma") (A3). This is where the young techno fans hang out.

Bar Pegasus, Yasemin Sok (B2), set in the ancient town wall. A more laid-back atmosphere, with dimmed lights and cane chairs.

OTHER THINGS TO DO

Excursions – Numerous agencies in the town centre offer rafting trips and walking tours to the Manavgat waterfalls.

Şelale Tours Travel Agency, Liman Cad 38 (B3), ☎ (242) 753 39 90 / 753 10 66, Fax (242) 753 29 98. Offers a multitude of tours to Pamukkale, Cappadocia, Alanya, Antalya and Myra. Also outdoor pursuits, such as rafting in the Taurus Mountains, boat trips and jeep safaris.

ALANYA★★

Antalya Province – Map p 354
131km from Antalya – 82km from Anamur
Pop 110 000 – Mild and sunny weather all year round

Not to be missed
The fortress and the old city.
The sunset over the citadel seen from the sea.

And remember...
Visit the city in the morning, to avoid the heat.
Explore the peninsula by boat at sunset, the colours of the cliffs are spectacular.

Like Side, old Alanya is set on a small peninsula jutting between two bays lined with fine sand. However, Side is flat whereas the Alanya peninsula creates an impressive promontory (200m high), whose steep slopes tumble into the sea. At the summit, a Seljuk citadel wears its crenellated walls like a crown. Its ramparts are wrapped around the red roofs of the old city all the way to the foot of the buttress while it keeps an eye on the port's sleepy fishing boats.

Alanya is a small medieval gem sitting in a jewellery box, made of concrete. At the foot of the promontory the orange and peach trees that used to cast their shadows on the beach have made room for an endless row of impersonal hotels. In only one decade, the site has been ravaged by the tourist industry, drowning the coastline under a layer of breeze block, and asphalt (to the east, the city stretches on for 15km!). Alanya is now an enormous seaside resort highly appreciated by the Germans who colonise it every summer. However, from the top of the battlements, the landscape remains awe-inspiring: on one side the endless blue sea; on the other, the

A crown overlooking the sea: the invincible battlements of ancient Alanya

Y. A. Bertrand/ALTITUDE

The Mediterranean Coast

454

tortuous Taurus ridge. In between the two, the old Alanya hides behind its ramparts, jealously guarding beautiful wooden houses and an atmosphere of bygone days. Spend your time inside the city walls, in the alleys and try to forget about the rest.

The city of pirates

Founded during the Hellenistic period, *Coracesium* earned the reputation of being an uncontrollable city: in 199 BC it was the only town in Cilicia to resist Roman authority and became the most important centre of Cilician pirate activity. As with Side (*see sidebar p 448*), the peninsula represented a very practical base to launch attacks against the coast. In 67 BC, Roman general Pompey the Great decided to raze the corsairs' bastions and his army was able to destroy the entire pirate fleet (nearly 850 ships) gathered at the foot of the promontory. From then on, Alanya was reduced to a modest town, until the Byzantine era. It experienced a rebirth in 1221, by becoming the winter residence of the Seljuk sultan, Alaaddin Keybubat (who lived in the capital Konya, the rest of the time). It was during this period that the city adopted the name of Alanya and the citadel was constructed. The city became a very active port until it was conquered by the Ottomans in 1471.

The Alanya promontory
Allow a half-day to visit.

The heart of the Seljuk city, the tip of the peninsula is the only interesting section of Alanya. The lower enclosure surrounds the promontory for 7km, whereas a second wall, half-way up, protects the old city. Even higher up rise the walls of the citadel's three turrets. Ideally, begin your visit of the city at this point, where you will have a view of the entire site.

From the Tourist Office, take the road which climbs towards the old city, to the summit (3km). For those without private transport, blue shuttle buses leave every hour; the departure point is in front of the Tourist Office. The athletically-inclined can ascend on foot by way of the paths leaving from the Red Tower (in the port). Allow 45min for the climb (steep).

Before leaving the modern quarter, stop by the **museum**, a small building surrounded by a lapidary garden, near the Tourist Office. (A2) (*8am-5pm, all year; closed Mondays. Entrance fee.*) Sarcophagi and **busts** as well as exquisite **jewellery** from Anamurium (*see p 460*) are on display. There is also a rich ethnographic collection, including the reconstruction of a 19C Ottoman house and a local street scene.

The citadel★ (İçkale) (B3)
9am-8pm. Entrance and car park fee. Duration of the visit: 45min.

Not much is left of the buildings which were housed in the İçkale, a fortress built in 1226 on the foundations of the Hellenistic citadel. The only remains are the ruins of a small **Byzantine church** with a dome (6C), dedicated to St George (*to the east as you skirt the rampart*), located next to a large **cistern**. Spend some time along the **ramparts★**, magnificent and well-preserved crenellated walls. The site is especially interesting for its **panorama★★**; from the terrace flanking the northern rampart, your eye is drawn to the roofs of the old city, and follows the contour of the **lower enclosure★★**, a snakelike stone wall adapting itself to every contour of the terrain, punctuated by 143 square towers. Then, it winds off towards the mountains, beyond the sandy Cleopatra beach, where, it is said, the queen would bathe. West of the citadel, facing the sea, a second terrace called **Adam Atacağı** ("the place where men are thrown") overlooks a dizzying precipice from which men condemned to death were tossed.

The old city★★ (Hisariçi and Tophane)

Descending from the citadel, take the path on the left.

Enclosed between the intermediary enclosure and the high walls of the citadel, old Alanya seems to ignore the hectic city of today. It hides among the fruit trees and thick cacti, which, even more so than the walls, form a rampart against the noise and agitation. Underneath the bowers or in the door frame of a home – beautiful white façades with windows encased with dark wood – women weave silk scarves on ageless looms. Stroll about in the streets and flowered terraces overlooking the sea. Along the way, have a look at the **fortified caravanserai** (B3), a warehouse equipped with 26 rooms surrounding a courtyard *(transformed into a hotel)*. It flanks the ruins of a Seljuk **bazaar**. Further north rises the **Süleymaniye mosque** (B3), built in the 17C on the walls of the Seljuk mosque. Lastly, you reach the upper walls of the **Ehmedek bastion** (Ehmedek Kalesi) (B3), a protruding fortress located at the foot of the citadel. It is preceded by a tomb and a small Seljuk era oratory, the **Akçebe Mesçidi**.

The port

Descending towards the east, you will reach the port, which lies at the foot of the walls protecting the city. Facing the pier, in the northeast corner of the enclosure, rises the **Red Tower★** (Kızıl Kule) (C3) *(8am-12noon/1.30pm-5.30pm, closed Mondays. Entrance fee)*, an impressive octagonal-shaped building, 34m high and surrounded by battlements. This observation tower (29m diameter), protecting the port and the arsenal, was erected in 1226 by a Syrian architect. It owes its name to the red brick used in its upper portion. Its five floors house a small **ethnographic museum**, displaying a carpet collection and beautiful Ottoman-period carved doors. From the battlements there is a beautiful **view★** overlooking the old houses hidden behind the ramparts, and the sea.

Around the peninsula★

One-hour boat excursion, departing from the Red Tower.

The cliffs of the promontory hide countless **caves** with exciting names. Trying to make their discovery aboard one of the port's fishing boats makes for a very pleasant excursion and allows an incomparable **view★★** of the fortified city. This is particularly so at the end of the day, when the sun seems to ignite the cliffs. It is also the best way of seeing the **Seljuk arsenal★** (Tersane) *(it can also be reached by a path from the Red Tower)*, a superb boat hangar overlooked by a tower, facing the sea through five large ogee **vaults**. Built in 1227, it was still used at the beginning of the 20C. Beyond the arsenal, the boat skirts the cliffs in search of the **Pirates' Cave** (Korsanlar Mağarası), a small cavern where the corsairs held their prisoners. Then, you reach the **Lovers' Cave** (Aşıklar Mağarası), set at the entrance to **Cilyarda Point**, a long finger of land stretching on the southwest point of the peninsula, edged by Byzantine ruins. The boat circumvents it, before reaching the west coast. Further still, the boat enters the **Phosphorescent Cave** (Fosforlu Mağarası) – the excursion's last stop – which owes its name to the luminous reflections of the water on the walls. You can complete the outing with the **Damlataş Cavern★** (Damlataş Mağarası) (B2), the most interesting, although overly exploited. *(Usually accessed by land, since it is only 100m away from the Tourist Office. 10am-8pm in summer and 10am-5.30pm in winter. Entrance fee.)* It contains a forest of stalactites and stalagmites in a thousand different colours. Its very damp atmosphere is known for its therapeutic qualities, in particular for asthmatics who may enter between 6am and 10am every morning.

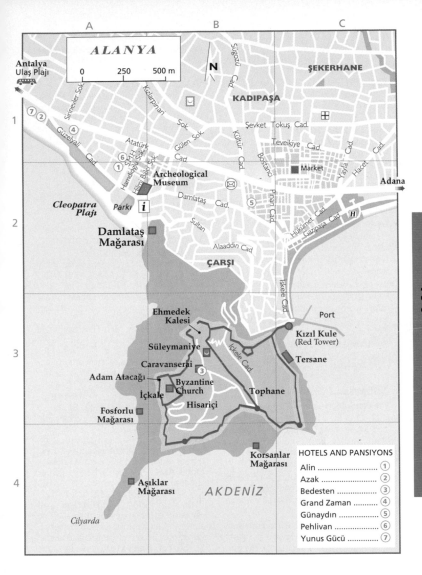

ALANYA

0   250   500 m

N

Antalya
Ulaş Plajı

ŞEKERHANE

KADIPAŞA

Şevket Tokuş Cad.

Tevfikiye Cad.

Market

Adana

Archeological
Museum

Damlataş Cad.

Cleopatra
Plajı

Parkı i

Damlataş
Mağarası

ÇARŞI

Alaaddin Cad.

Sultan

H

Ehmedek
Kalesi

Port

Kızıl Kule
(Red Tower)

Süleymaniye

Caravanserai

Tersane

Adam Atacağı

Byzantine
Church

İçkale

Tophane

Hisariçi

Fosforlu
Mağarası

Korsanlar
Mağarası

Aşıklar
Mağarası

AKDENİZ

Cilyarda

HOTELS AND PANSIYONS	
Alin	①
Azak	②
Bedesten	③
Grand Zaman	④
Günaydın	⑤
Pehlivan	⑥
Yunus Gücü	⑦

Making the most of Alanya

Making the most of Alanya

COMING AND GOING

By bus – *The bus station* is on the road to Antalya, 3km from the centre. Municipal buses (blue) shuttle between the station and town centre approximately every 30min. All the companies are represented there and operate services in the region and to the country's main cities. For Antalya: buses every hour (2hr journey). İstanbul: approximately every 2 hours

(14hr journey). Ankara: roughly every 30min (14hr journey). Variable timetable for İzmir (10hr).

Varan, ☎ (242) 512 00 29 at the bus station, and in town (Damlataş Cad), ☎ (242) 513 33 94.

GETTING AROUND

The local network is simple and traffic flows relatively easily on the main roads. However, it is more difficult to drive around the little streets in the "centre" (area around the tourist information office), particularly in the evening when some of them become pedestrian only.

By bus – Very cheap and relatively fast, the municipal buses (blue) operate in the town centre and on all the town's main roads. Definitely the best way to get around.

By taxi – Convenient, especially in the evening, when the municipal buses stop running. The price (indicated on the meter) is obviously higher than during the day.

By shared taxi – Dolmuşes are white in Alanya. They are slightly cheaper than the taxis and there are more of them.

ADDRESS BOOK

Tourist information – Damlatas Cad 1 (A2), ☎ (242) 513 54 36. Opposite the little square near Cleopatra beach. 8am-6pm from Monday to Friday, 9am-5pm on Saturdays and Sundays. The staff speak English and German.

Main post office – On the corner of Kültür Cad and Atatürk Bul (B2). Post office outlets and phone booths are scattered all over town.

Bank / change – There are numerous banks in the town where you can withdraw money with a Visa card. The currency exchanges are mainly to be found in the shopping district, around Atatürk Cad and Damlataş Cad (B2). 8am-11pm.

Car rental – Sandy, Atatürk Cad 6, ☎ (242) 512 32 51 / 512 11 02. Car and motorcycle hire.

Market – On Fridays (C2). Alanya's bustling, colourful market is definitely worth a visit. It's full of fishmongers.

Airline companies – Turkish Airlines, İskele Cad (C2-3), ☎ (242) 511 11 94.

WHERE TO STAY

Most of the major hotels (outside the old town) – large white concrete boxes devoid of charm – are reserved by regular clients who come back every year. As for the guest houses, they are rather mediocre. Between the two are some hotels, lacking in character but comfortable.

Under US$15

Hotel Günaydın, Kültür Cad 26, ☎ (242) 513 19 43, Fax (242) 512 63 07. ⌁ 𝒫 ✗ Conveniently located right in the town centre. However, it is noisy here (avoid the rooms overlooking the street). Very simple but adequate level of comfort.

Between US$15 and US$30

Hotel Pehlivan, Saray Mah Hacıhamdioğlu Sok 16, ☎ (242) 513 27 81, Fax (242) 513 64 65 – 100rm. ⌁ 𝒫 Very near the tourist information office. Simple level of comfort and quiet, despite its central location. Bar.

Hotel Alin, Saray Mah Hacıhamdioğlu Sok 5, ☎ (242) 513 76 29, Fax (242) 513 76 30 – 40rm. ⌁ 𝒫 ⌱ Next to the one above, with a similar standard of comfort, clean and quiet. Full-board possible.

Between US$30 and US$45

Hotel Yunus Gücü, Atatürk Bul, ☎ (242) 513 30 02, Fax (242) 513 66 13 – 60rm. ⌁ 𝒫 ▤ ✗ ⌱ Bar and car park. Near the sea, this hotel offers a very good level of comfort, is clean and pleasant, and gives good value for money. Lovely terrace restaurant. Half-board possible.

Hotel Azak, Atatürk Cad 161 (right at the end of the avenue), ☎ (242) 513 91 55 or 56, Fax (242) 513 17 59 – 51rm. ⌁ 𝒫 ▤ ✗ ⌱ CC Bar and small car park. More luxurious than the one above, but it gives directly onto the beach. Impersonal decor, but immaculate rooms.

⌂ **Hotel Bedesten**, İskele Cad, ☎ (242) 512 12 34 – 18rm. ⌁ 𝒫 ▤ ✗ ⏣ ⌱ CC Jacuzzi, bar and car park. At the foot of the citadel, up in the old town, the hotel is set in the old restored caravanserai. It is part of a much larger complex which includes the Süleymaniye mosque, the cemetery and the old covered bazaar, whose ruined vaults can still be seen. Ask the proprietor to show you the cistern, a truly magical place. The hotel is slightly out of the way and therefore enjoys more peace and quiet. Good standard of comfort and pleasant decor. Half-board possible.

Over US$60
Hotel Grand Zaman, Saray Mah Atatürk Cad 153, ☎ (242) 512 34 01, Fax (242) 512 48 03 – 136rm. *⌐╕ 🏊 📺* 🍽 ✗ 🏊 CC A luxury hotel with bar, Turkish bath, gym and car park. Excellent standard of comfort.

EATING OUT
If you want to eat Turkish food, give the beach and modern districts a miss. You're more likely to find what you're looking for in the pedestrian streets in the centre of town (Damlataş Cad, for example), where there are some restaurants set in old Ottoman houses opening out onto pleasant terraces, or near the Red Tower. The harbour is, without a doubt, the best place to go.

• **At the harbour**
From the tourist information office, the road which leads up to the citadel is lined with little restaurants, cafeterias and small bars. The liveliest one is the **Türk Ocağı**. You will also find a good number of terrace bars and restaurants at the harbour.
Kaptan Güverte, İskele Cad 62 (B3), ☎ (242) 513 49 00, Fax (242) 513 20 00. Next to the Red Tower. Serves an excellent chocolate soufflé, which you have to order at the beginning of your meal.
İskele, İskele Cad (C2-3), ☎ (242) 513 18 22. At the far end of the harbour, with a sweeping view of the sea. Slightly more expensive than its neighbours, but the service is faultless and the fish specialities delicious.

• **In the town centre**
Old House Eski Ev, Damlataş Cad 44 (B2), ☎ (242) 513 45 54. Attractive garden and traditional dishes.
Ottoman House, Damlataş Cad 31 (B2), ☎ and Fax (242) 511 14 21. A little more expensive than elsewhere, it is also one of the most pleasant restaurants on account of its decor and style. Delicious hummus.
Anfora, Eski PTT Cad Damlataş Cad (B2), ☎ (242) 512 07 19. Retro atmosphere with live synthesiser music. Special menu for those who don't really know what to choose. Reasonable prices. Open until midnight.

HAVING A DRINK
You will find the trendiest bars in İskele Cad (C2) in the harbour area, all with very fashionable decors. The most "in" places are the **Barracuda**, the **James Dean** and the **Bistro Belman**, with its 20m open-air bar.
Internet café – Cybercafé, İskele Cad Kaptan Hotel Yanı (C2), ☎ (242) 511 09 12. Serves non-alcoholic drinks. US$3 per hour.

Nightclubs – Several along the seafront. The **Auditorium Disco**, along the east beach, opposite the Alantur hotel, has a swimming pool.

Casinos – East part of town, in the **Ananas**, **Grand Kaptan** and **Hamdullah** hotels. Open from 2pm to 5am.

OTHER THINGS TO DO
Shopping – Tourism has led to the development of some original local crafts (dried painted gourds, embroidery and lace made by women from the surrounding villages, silk scarves, jewellery etc), but Alanya is an expensive place and, for certain products, it's best to do your shopping in the small neighbouring towns. But do try the ice cream, an ever-welcome speciality of the town, and the "ada çay", a very aromatic sage infusion.

Turkish bath – Büyük Alanya Hamamı, Damlataş Cad Alaattinoğlu Sok (B2), ☎ (242) 511 33 44. With sauna, jacuzzi, hair salon and bar.

Aquatic amusement park – Aquapark, 3km east of the town, on the road to Anamur (left-hand side).

Beaches – Many spaces are reserved by the hotels for their clients. It is much more pleasant to go swimming outside Alanya. **Cleopatra plajı**, on the west side of the peninsula (A2). This beautiful 4km-long stretch of white sand is well-known.
Ulaş plajı, 6km to the west. Frequented more by Turks than foreigners. All kinds of water sports can be practised here.
On the beautiful road to Anamur, bordered with banana groves, you may be tempted to stop at one of the beaches for a swim in the turquoise water. The nearby restaurants serve "gözleme" (savoury Turkish crepes), "ayran" and grilled meats. Make the most of these beautiful places before you reach the less interesting bay of Anamur.

Making the most of Alanya

THE CAPE OF ANAMUR★
THE GATES OF CILICIA
İçel Province
175km from Alanya – 153km from Silifke – Pop 65 000

Not to be missed
The walk along Mamure Kalesi's sentinel round.
An afternoon at the beach in Bozyazı or Anamurium.

And remember...
Bring along a torch for the Mamure Kalesi galleries.
Taste the delicious little bananas sold along the road.

East of Alanya, the landscape becomes rugged, announcing the approach to *Cilicia Tracheia*. Past Gazipaşa, the mountains suddenly advance towards the sea to form sheer cliffs of spectacular beauty. Here and there, the caves and caverns hide narrow inlets where ancient pirates used to lie in wait before slipping onto anchored ships (*see pp 354 and 448*). An impenetrable buttress of the Taurus, the **Taşeli Yarımadası** rises all the way to the gates of Silifke. For more than 200km, a natural land wall rises between the coast and the Anatolian plateau. The road follows the ridge, adapting itself to the curves all the way to the Anamur delta. Then it descends abruptly, offering superb **views**★★ of the sea.

The "muz" of Anamur
Protected by the nearby mountains, the Cilician coast enjoys a mild climate with constant temperatures favouring the growth of olives, figs and **bananas** ("*muz*" in Turkish). Anamur, a small town set at the mouth of the river of the same name, has become its capital. The locals boast that their bananas are the planet's best!

Surrounded by numerous sand or pebble beaches, the town is also a peaceful resort with an old-fashioned charm, attracting numerous Turkish holidaymakers (most of the foreign tourists gather west of Alanya). It has no noteworthy sights, except that it is located close to Anamurium, the ancient Anamur, and Mamure Kalesi, a superb Seljuk and Ottoman fortress overlooking the coast, east of the city. Anamur is also an excellent base for an excursion to the heights of the Taurus where wild scenery and a few unusual treasures of ancient and Byzantine art await the visitor (*see following chapter*).

Anamurium★ (Eski Anamur)

8.5km west of Anamur. Take the road from Alanya for 2km and turn left at the sign indicating the site (2km further). Those without transport will have to take a taxi, since there are neither buses nor dolmuşes. Ask the guardians or guides to point out the most interesting mosaics. 7am-8pm. Entrance fee. Allow 2hr for the visit, 4hr if you climb to the top or if you go to the beach.

Until the Arab invasions which swept the coast in the 7C, Anamurium prospered at the entrance of a small cape marking the gates of the fertile Cilicia **(Anamur Burnu).** Founded by the Phoenicians, the city experienced its golden age under Roman domination when the coast and heights were ridded of the hordes of pirates.

Ravaged by the Barbarians during the first centuries of our era, it was rebuilt by the Byzantines, and was thus given new life.

Although it is ruined, the site is particularly interesting because it clearly illustrates the layout of a Roman and Byzantine city. The city is limited to a small area allowing you to stroll easily about like a Roman going from place to place until you reach the **beach**★, and a superb turquoise bay filled with white pebbles.

A strategic cape

West of Anamurium, the huge radar antennae which cover the cape of Anamur record the smallest air or maritime movement in the eastern Mediterranean. Anamur Burnu is Turkey's closest point to Cyprus, located 40m miles from the coast. On a clear day, Beşparmak Dağları, the "mountain with five fingers" rises on the northern coast of the island. A hand reaching for the sky?

The necropolis★

Beyond the ticket booth, the eye is immediately drawn to the right by the multitude of small "houses" covered with domes clinging to the side of the hill. This is the city's necropolis, a veritable village of 350 souls, overlooked by the remains of a **church** built around 400. Each **tomb** – a real house for the dead – includes two small rooms: one destined for the storage offerings for the deceased in the afterlife, the other enclosing the body. Their walls, composed of cement using a base of plaster and tile pieces, still hide **frescoes** and **mosaics** evoking nature or a mythological event.

On the right, on the side of the road, do not miss the **two tombs** which were restored and can now be seen. One of them displays a few beautiful fragments of decoration. Additional mosaics and paintings remain to be discovered in this maze of mausoleums; take the time to wander or – better yet – have one of the site's guardians guide you.

The city centre★

Higher up on the hill, observe the track of a 3C **aqueduct.** Part of the work is carved in the rock, whereas **monumental arches** make up for the substantial unevenness of the terrain.

Returning to the trail, you reach the wall of the enclosure. Just behind the ramparts, stands the **theatre** *(on the right of the track)*, (2C). You can see the shape of its cavea (in ruins), a 60m-diameter hemicycle facing the sea.

Next to it, the **public baths** (3C) are the most well-preserved buildings on the site and can be reached by a **covered stairway** (still standing). Several rooms have retained their **vaults**, protecting in places beautiful portions of **mosaics**.

Facing it *(on the left side of the track)*, rise the walls of the **bouleuterion**★. They are recognisable by the "battlements" which form windows without lintels. They housed the hemicycle of the municipal assembly and also served as a concert hall (**odeon**). Covered at one time, the steps could accommodate 900 spectators.

From there return to the sea, then walk along the beach until you reach your starting point.

Several **churches** are located on the site (in ruins, unfortunately), built in the 5C in the style of basilicas. The most beautiful among the group is located near the beach, but the apse facing the sea has completely disappeared. However, the walls of the nave are well preserved and numerous ancient pieces and fragments of the **mosaic floors** can be seen. The two other churches, to the northeast, are much more damaged and difficult to distinguish. In one of them, the **baptistery**, recently excavated, has a beautiful floor made of **marble marquetry** protected by a thin film of sand.

The Cape of Anamur

Along the way, you will pass in front of another **bath complex**, a contemporary of the churches, whose heating system, is clearly visible.Here too you will be able to see numerous traces of **mosaic floors**.

On the other side of the ramparts, you will reach a large **sports complex**. It is equipped with **baths** and an **exercise room**, an impressive 1 000sqm rectangle invaded by brush. A colonnaded portico shaded its sides, while geometric mosaics still decorate the floors of the baths. In 660 AD, these baths ceased functioning and a portion of the rooms were converted into **pottery workshops**, judging from the countless oil lamps which were unearthed.

If you are not wearied by mosaics, you can deepen your knowledge by continuing to explore the countless remains which are hidden in the city's houses. It is best to have one of the guardians show you around. Finally, the athletically-inclined can climb up to the **citadel** (built on the foundation of the Hellenistic acropolis), whose walls cap the summit of the hill *(allow one full hour to ascend)*. They will discover a beautiful **view**** of the site and sea. Others may complete their visit by going to the beach.

The Anamur fortress** (Mamure Kalesi)

7km east of Anamur on the raod to Bozyazı.
8am-8pm in summer, 9am-5pm in winter. Entrance fee. Allow one hour for the visit.

Fortress lovers will be delighted: towers (no less than 36), crenellated sentinel paths, loopholes and moats, it is all here and in excellent condition (a large portion was restored). The fortress of Anamur is one of Asia Minor's finest. An impressive land wall facing the sea and continually whipped by its waves, it is also one of the largest, with an outer wall measuring 270m in length and 110m in width.

Built upon the remains of a small Roman fort dating from the 3C AD, the castle was abandoned to the pirates for a while before being included in the numerous strongholds of Leon II, King of Armenia *(see p 357)*. At the beginning of the 13C it fell into the hands of the Lusignan princes of Cyprus, then, in 1221, it came under Seljuk control. Next, the Karamanid Turks razed it to its first level to completely rebuild it and supply it with water through an aqueduct. In 1469, finally, the Ottomans conquered it and renamed it Mamuriye. They installed a mosque and remained there until the final hours of the Empire, in 1923.

Charge!

The building's plan, like a large horn, consists of three parts: two parallel courtyards and an interior citadel. Once you have "conquered" these various sectors, circle the ramparts: the **sentinel's round****, surrounded by **battlements**** in perfect shape, offers great **views****. Skirting the fortifications by the north, you will reach the ancient **main gate** (walled in), topped by an **inscription** signed by the Emir of Karaman: "I brought water – I rebuilt the castle". A 10m-deep **moat** appears at the foot of the walls, which was previously filled with water. Next to the gate, notice the remains of the **aqueduct** which fed the cisterns of the fortress.

Enter the **first courtyard** through a large curved and barrel-vaulted passage, pierced inside one of the large towers of the outer wall. You will notice a small tree filled with countless strips of paper or cloth where childless women leave their requests. In the northeast corner of the courtyard *(on the left as you enter)* rises a tall **turret** *(access by an open staircase)*. Inside, the spiral staircase leads to a terrace where the **view**** of the castle and sea is marvellous.

As you leave the turret, on the right side, a long windowless **gallery** appears *(time to turn on your torch!)*. It is made up of several vaulted rooms which were used for storage or refuge.

Enter the **second courtyard** through a large gap in the wall separating the two areas. On the right rises the small mosque erected by the Ottomans in 1565 (and often remodelled). The courtyard buildings have all disappeared, except for a fountain and the ruins of a hamam.

To the south, the **bastion***, in ruins, is set on the rocky massif at the castle's tip. Its thick walls are partially carved in the rock, covered with battlements. A watchtower and fortress, it protected the building against sea attacks.

Making the most of Anamur

COMING AND GOING

By bus – The bus station and dolmuş stand are in Atatürk Bul in the town centre, at the junction between the highway and the road to Ermenek.

ADDRESS BOOK

Bank / change – Five banks are dotted around the town centre, where you will also find several cash dispensers.

Main post office – In Atatürk Bul. 7am-11pm.

WHERE TO STAY

The best places to stay are in the district of İskele, on the seafront (cheaper), or in **Bozyazı**, a little village just after Anamur on the road to Silifke.

Under US$15

Hotel Meltem, İskele Mah İnönü Cad, ☎ (324) 814 23 16 – 24rm. ⁂⁑ ✗ One of the first hotels you will come across on the seafront. Rudimentary comfort, but it is one of the cheapest.

Between US$15 and US$30

Hotel Anémonia, İskele Mah İnönü Cad, ☎ (324) 814 40 00 – 36rm. ⁂⁑ ℘ Bar. Right at the end of the seafront. Very peaceful and comfortable. Good value for money.

Between US$30 and US$45

Hotel Yan, ☎ (324) 816 48 31 / 814 21 23, Fax (324) 816 48 88. ⁂⁑ ℘ ▤ ✗ No particular charm, but clean and quiet. The music stops at 10pm.

Hotel Hermès, İskele Mevkii, ☎ (324) 814 39 50, Fax (324) 814 39 95 – 70rm. ⁂⁑ ℘ ▤ ✗ ▼ ⚒ CC Sauna and car park. A well-kept hotel, with comfortable rooms and an open-air bar.

• On the road to Bozyazı

Camp site
Pullu camp site, 1km after Mamure Kalesi, near a sandy beach bordered with

pine trees. US$4 per day for a tent and US$6 for a caravan.

• In Bozyazı

US$15
⚐ **Hotel Zeysa**, ☎ (324) 851 20 51 / 851 34 18 – 18rm. ⁂⁑ ✗ Facing the beach. More of a guest house, carefully run by Zeynel, the proprietor, who will give you a most charming welcome. With nothing being too much trouble where his clients are concerned, he prepares the meals himself: delicious fish, cooked green vegetable salads seasoned with olive oil, bulgur with tomatoes, and omelette for breakfast. The Anatolian-style rooms are bright and clean, and the atmosphere very convivial. Half-board possible.

US$40
Hotel Vivanco, 11km after Bozyazı, 17km from Anamur (you will need your own transport), ☎ (324) 85142 00, Fax (324) 851 22 91 – 66rm. ⁂⁑ ▤ ▼ ✗ ⚒ A large luxury hotel facing the beach.

EATING OUT

There is a good selection of fish and pide restaurants on the seafront.

⚐ **Dutaltı**, on the road to Anemurium, just before reaching the site. Although not much to look at, this little eatery is reputed for its fried fish specialities ("lagos") which you can sample in the shade of an enormous mulberry tree. Very cheap and delicious.

BEACHES

You can go for a swim at Anamur (**İskele** beach is 4km east of the town centre), but the pretty pebble beach at **Anemurium** is much better. However, the best one is, without a doubt, **Bozyazı** beach, a long stretch of sand shaded by palm trees, 17km east on the road to Silifke.

CILICIA TRACHEIA ★★

AN EXCURSION IN THE TAURUS REGION

Two-day itinerary – General Map p 354
313km using the Ermenek road – 253km by Gülnar. Lodging in Mut.

Not to be missed
The Alahan Monastery.
And remember...
Rather than drive the steep ascent leading to Alahan by car, go up on foot;
it will give you time to admire the scenery and give your car a rest.

The Mediterranean Coast

Leave the sea to explore another side of Turkey that is unknown to outsiders and deeply Anatolian. After Anamur, instead of continuing along the coast towards Silifke, make a detour to the heights, for a complete change of scenery. Head deep into the Taurus, on the crests of the **Akçalı Dağları★★** and the **Taşeli plateau★★**, in the heart of Cilicia *Tracheia*, and its rough, wild and tortuous countryside. An opportunity to discover superb **karst landscapes★★** – limestone massifs riddled with canyons, gorges, chasms and caverns carved by the impetuous rivers which have altered the appearance of the land.

Not long ago, this labyrinth was the impenetrable refuge of bandits, outlaws, the unruly and all types of social outcasts. Even the roads have difficulty getting through: they snake their way over steep hillsides, between cliffs, revealing **extraordinary views★★★** of the canyons and the summits. Stark steppes, valleys draped with green velvet, forests of pine or wild olive trees, dense brush or rock deserts, the land does not cease to change. Welcome to an infinite palette of colour, fragrance and lights Around the bend of a spur, a village suddenly appears, a cherished sight for the weary traveller. Smiling faces welcome you in the main square where the old moustached men wearing caps drink boiling çay (tea), in between games of okey, a local version of mahjongg. You can lodge modestly in the homes of the inhabitants, who have gone to great lengths to transform their dwellings to make you feel like a king, and eat with them, or at a terrace café. Conversation is based on gestures, improvised Karagöz, which allows everyone to understand each other without a word being spoken. You will feel far away from everything except sheer delight.

Two itineraries

Off the beaten path, this is for those who can do without modern comforts. There is only one choice for lodging, Mut (*pronounced "Moot"*), where you will only find modest accommodation. Two itineraries are suggested. The longest one follows the **Ermenek road** (*117km north of Anamur*) before heading east towards Mut, following the twisted course of the Ermenek Çayı. Allow at least an entire day to reach Mut, where you can make a stop. The following day, visit the Alahan Monastery, 20km north of Mut, on the road to Konya (715). On the way back, all you need to do is follow the Silifke road – marvellous – which reaches the coast (92km).

The second itinerary, slightly shorter, requires leaving Anamur by the coast road (*route 400*) to ascend the mountain only after reaching **Gülnar** (*turn left after Aydıncık, 3hr by road to Mut*). The Gülnar road intersects with the Konya road (715) leading to Mut, where you reach the path of the first itinerary.

Either way, drive slowly. The roads are magnificent; so take the time to admire the scenery. They are winding, so drive cautiously.

The Ermenek Road★★

For those following the first itinerary.

As you leave Anamur, the road first follows the course of a small river, dry in summer, crossing sun-scorched fields. Then, very quickly, it begins to climb, probing into an immense forest of pine and cedar trees clinging to the rocks. At each curve of the river, the scenery becomes lovelier by the minute. Beautiful views appear at each bend overlooking the Anamur plain which fringes the intense blue sea.

The road climbs further, reaching the first summits which already rise at an altitude of nearly 2 000m. It continues in the shade of **Elmakız Dağı** (1 638m), from village to village, allowing you to contemplate the scenery: a mule-drawn cart, women with flowered *şalvars,* a flock of goats marching in formation along the roadside, and ageless houses with sun-bleached façades. The forest thins out as you reach the plateau: barren or green prairies followed by steppes of straw swept by the wind and punctuated by little ochre stones, and finally the desert.

5km before Ermenek, take the road on the right to reach Mut.

Continue along the northern bank of the **Ermenek Çayı**★★, a small river bending among the boulders or along the floor of an arid canyon before drowning in the flow of the Göksu Nehri. The mountains huddle together and grow taller, greyish-green silhouettes, strewn with pine trees which pierce the blue sky. Farther away loom the tallest peaks of the Taurus, blue in the mist.

The Monastery of Alahan★★

99km from Silifke. Take the Konya road (715). Pass by Mut and continue left towards the north until you reach the village of Burunköy (20km). 7km after this village, take the little road on the right which snakes up the mountain amid the pine trees. Further along, turn right again at the Alahan signpost (the 2km-long incline is very steep but in good condition). Bring water. A small pamphlet (not to be removed) can be read at the entrance to the site; useful for finding your way around. Entrance fee.

Perched at an altitude of 1 200m, the Alahan monastery is a forgotten wonder, isolated from the world: a sea of columns and arches suspended high in the mountains, overlooking the Göksu Valley and the powerful massifs of the Taurus. It was a perfect refuge for monks in search of contemplative silence. Today, the site is still magical and imbued with a profound tranquillity. In the shade of the pine trees, shepherds play the flute and the beauty of the ruins is matched by that of the landscape. An enchanting site which you will remember long after your trip.

Founded in the late 5C and early 6C, Alahan is among the first monasteries in Christian history; one of those whose architecture is torn between Antiquity and the new forms of the Byzantine age. Of the Byzantine complex, only two churches remain on the terraces overlooking the entire horizon (a magnificent **view**★★!) Abandoned for centuries, they were rediscovered recently in 1961.

The church of the Evangelists★

Below a large cave – the likely home of an older cult – the church owes its name to the four busts found inside its walls. The latter are razed, but the floor plan is clearly visible: a Paleo-Christian basilica with a narthex leading to three naves with apses, each separated by a Corinthian colonnade. **Six columns**★ facing the spectacle of the mountain are still standing.

Notice the beautiful **portal**★, a heavy stone frame rising in the recess of the narthex, engraved with delicate **reliefs**★. Christ's head appears in the centre of the lintel, flanked by two angels, whereas the sides are occupied by scenes of the Apocalypse and the four creatures seen in Ezekiel's vision *(see sidebar p 577)*. Two archangels appear on the piedroits (heavily damaged). They are St Michael and St Gabriel (standing on a bull), Christian figures raised to fight against pagan myths. In the 5C, Christianity was still in its early stages and its survival a difficult one: the shape of the portal, the handling of the decoration and the interpretation of Christian themes betray the resistance of old ideologies. The mixture is nonetheless stunning!

At the back of the central nave, the **main apse** appears. It is the only portion of the building which has retained a substantial part of its walls (with the apse on the right). Slightly upraised, it has kept its **synthronon**, a series of stone steps where the monks would sit during services. The **altar** rose in the centre (only its foot remains), accompanied by a small **adjoining altar**, decorated with niches with *conch nimbi*, probably reserved for important masses.

Along the ravine toward the east stand the ruins of the **baptistery** *(on your left)*. The small edifice contains two naves and an apse. The baptismal font is still visible; a simple basin shaped like a Greek cross carved in the ground. Beyond, a covered gallery (unfinished) created a portico which gave a beautiful view of the scenery. The building, had it been completed, would probably have been linked to the other church.

The Eastern church**

At the end of the path, on a terrace carved in the rock, rises the monastery's second church. It is located to the east, hence its name. It is more recent (early 6C) and the best preserved. The building copies the basilican plan of its predecessor: three naves (but only one apse) reached through the narthex by an equal number of **doors**, each surrounded by an elegant frieze with carved motifs. Only the narthex, together with its roof, have disappeared. Three large **arched bays***, separated by fine colonnettes, open up to the façade, allowing daylight to illuminate the central nave. As you enter the church, you are struck by the beauty of the lines – gracious arcades against the sky rendered golden by the light. Two superb **Corinthian colonnades**** separate the three bays, whereas a **triumphal arch** marks the entrance to the **apse**, flanked by two **apsidioles** which served as a sacristy (the prothesis and the diaconicon).

Stay here for a while and soak up the peace and tranquillity of this majestic site.

Take the road back to Mut and continue straight on to reach Silifke and the coast.

CILICIA CAMPESTRIS★
FROM SİLİFKE TO KANLIDİVANE
İçel Province – General Map p 354
89km itinerary (1-day trip from Silifke)

Not to be missed
Silifke's yoghurt with cream.
The sunset over Kızkalesi Castle.
The churches and the bas-reliefs of Kanlıdivane.

And remember...
If you have a car, sleep in Narlıkuyu or in Taşucu (in the east);
it will be quieter than in Kızkalesi.
Cennet-Cehennem is a very popular site; go early in the morning
to take advantage of the peace and the fresh air.

Laid out in front of the large Göksu Nehri delta, **Silifke** (the Turkish version of "Cilicia" or "Seleucia"), marks the point of entry into *Cilicia Campestris*, the agrarian Cilicia *(see the region's history, p 357)*: the cliffs to the west have made way for a fertile plain fringed with gently rolling hills. The coast becomes an endless beach guarded by fortresses which continue to watch over the sea, such as Kızkalesi, whose surroundings are today colonised by holiday villages, inexpensive hotels and discotheques belching out noise as soon as the sun sets. The coast has in effect undergone a metamorphosis and become a huge beach resort which gets bigger every year.

■ **Silifke –** For the traveller, Silifke *(pop 85 000)* remains a transit stop of little interest; a compulsory halt to explore the region which includes the heights of the Taurus and the Alahan monastery *(see previous chapter)*, the ancient city of Olba-Diocaesarea, or the coast to the east of the city.

Take advantage of your stay to visit the **Museum of Archeology and Ethnography** located 1km from the city centre on the road to Taşucu *(8am-5pm, except Mondays; entrance fee)*. It contains the Greco-Roman and Byzantine objects found by archeologists in the region *(unfortunately all the display explanations are in Turkish only)*. The numismatic section contains a remarkable collection of **gold and silver coins** representing the kings of Egypt and Syria, together with Alexander the Great. All items originate in the site of Meydancık Kalesi *(75km west of Silifke)* excavated since 1987 by a French team. On the first floor, admire the discoveries made in Gilindire *(Aydıncık, 78km west of Silifke)*: seals, glassware, lachrymatories, fibulae and statuettes. The ethnographic section, although very limited, contains beautiful silver **jewellery** made by the Taurus nomads.

As you leave the city, on the road to Konya, climb to the impressive **Byzantine★ citadel** (Silifke Kalesi) also used by the knights of Rhodes and the Turks. Built in the 7C on the old foundations, it contains two concentric ramparts flanked by 23 towers.

■ Olba-Diocaesarea★ (Uzuncaburç)
Frequent domuş service from Silifke (28km),
facing the Tourist Office (first departure at 11am). 8am-5pm. Entrance fee.

From Olba to Diocaesarea
Surrounded by mountains, the ancient city of Olba spreads its ruins over a small plateau perched at an altitude of 1 184m, among the pine trees. A small city founded by Seleucus, one of Alexander's generals, Olba was governed by priest-kings (the

Teucrids) from the 3C to 2C BC. The latter were devoted to the cult of Zeus, whose sanctuary was located nearby *(the current village of Ura, 4km away)*. In the 1C BC, the Romans took hold of Olba and its sanctuary, developing an entire city around the temple of Zeus. Diocaesarea was born, a flourishing city overshadowing the Hellenistic Olba. The new city prospered during the entire Byzantine period, before declining in its turn, starting in the 11C, with the arrival of the Turks. Diocaesarea was reduced to a modest village (a very picturesque one): **Uzuncaburç**.

The city of Zeus

Park in the city square, in front of the Parade Gate. Begin the visit from the east and cross the site on the main road.

The road linking Korygos (Kızkalesi) to Seleucia (Silifke) crossed the city from east to west from the theatre to the temple of Tyche. A colonnaded **portico** ran on both sides, housing numerous shops. Only the base of this immense colonnade remains and Corinthian capitals are scattered on the ground. Below *(on the right side as you come from the car park)*, the **theatre's** cavea could seat 2500 in a hemicycle (quite damaged) leaning on the hill.

Next, go up the main road to reach the **Parade Gate** (2C AD), a triumphal building marking the heart of the city. A double row of six columns framed a 15.5m-tall arch (five columns on one side have withstood). The magnificent tetrapylon of Aphrodisias *(see p 305)*, today rebuilt, allows a glimpse of the original appearance (actually better!). Further on, to the right, rose the **nymphaeum** whose exedrae – small hemicycle benches – still feature on the basin's perimeter.

On the other side of the road, you soon reach the **Temple of Zeus★** (3C BC), an imposing perimeter of 21x40m still displaying a substantial part of its majestic **colonnade★★**. It is considered to be the oldest Corinthian temple in Asia Minor. An arch and wall fragments appear in various places among the columns, vestiges of its transformation into a church during the Byzantine period. The building was unfortunately damaged by a fire which destroyed its entire roof. Around the temple, the temenos (its sacred area) is covered with frieze fragments, capitals, and a few beautiful **Roman sarcophagi**.

At the end of the main road rise the elegant columns of the façade of the **Temple of Tyche★**. Their grey granite cylinders are topped by immaculate white marble Corinthian capitals.

Further along on the right, you will see the remains of another important way, perpendicular to the first one. It leads to the **northern gate★** (2C AD), a monument consisting of three tall arches facing the sky. It pierced the city's ramparts, which are today in poor sate of repair. The inscriptions appearing on the lintel have revealed the city's Roman name: Diocaesarea.

From there, a path follows the remains of the ramparts all the way to the **city tower**, the only trace we have of the enclosure. Some 22m-tall, it rose like a belfry above the walls and, after its construction during the Hellenistic period, it remained the city's emblem. It even gave the name to the current village, Uzuncaburç, "high tower" in Turkish. At its feet, do not miss the plumbing and the small engineering system which enabled water to flow around the city.

■ **Cennet and Cehennem** (or Narlıkuyu Mağarası) — *17km from Silifke. 8am-8pm. Entrance and car park fees. Bring a torch with you.*

The first stop on this coastal itinerary: Heaven *(cennet)* and Hell *(cehennem)*, no less! They are in fact two large abysses, hidden at the bottom of a valley in a tall thick forest. Since Antiquity, the area has been a pilgrimage site, and it continues to attract crowds – the site is on all the tourist itineraries. The trees surrounding the caves are covered with a multitude of small paper ribbons tied to the branches representing a wish or a prayer.

Cennet★ is a 250m-wide abyss, a deep black pit which descends to a depth of 70m, in the middle of lush vegetation. You descend the 452 steps of the stairs (it is heavy-going the other way!), plunging into a strange atmosphere where the songs of the birds resonate like sirens. At the bottom stands a Paleo–Christian (5C) chapel★, a small building pierced with elegant arched bays. It guards the entrance to a narrow passage leading into the darkness. The obscurity becomes denser and a vague sound can be heard emerging from the depths; a stream, which the Ancients believed was the Styx, that raging river surrounding the domain of Hades, the god of darkness!

In principle, once you met Hades,

The ferryman of souls
To reach the world of the dead, the souls had to cross the Styx. To do so, only one option: hire the services of Charon, a seaman who owned a boat. The souls of the dead would board for a token denarius (coin). It was this obol that the Ancients would place on the deceased's tongue in order for him to reach the other world. Everything has its price, even hell!

you never went back up to the surface. Rest assured, the god of darkness is growing old and you will be able to see the sky again. As you ascend, the heavenly chapel appears in a strange halo of blue mist, like a divine vision. Redemption!

Nearby the second abyss appears. Cehennem is a 120m-deep pit. The Ancients believed it was the den of the monstrous Typhon, a type of winged dragon with several heads who attempted to murder Zeus. The bottom cannot be accessed, therefore it is impossible to verify whether the creature still lurks there.

■ Kızkalesi★

23km east of Silifke, 6km from Cennet–Cehennem.

In a beautiful setting near the shore that real estate agents are quickly disfiguring, the ancient city of Korigos has lost its name in favour of Kızkalesi, a Byzantine fortress emerging from the sea, 200m from the shore. Set on a small promontory, it faces the citadel of Korykos. The two strongholds, once connected by a causeway, defended the city's port, of which nothing remains. Abandoned since the 15C, once the Ottomans arrived, Korykos is now a vast field of ruins dispersed around the surrounding hills and awaiting excavation.

The citadel of Korykos★ (Korykos Kalesi) – *The car park is to the right of the castle, along the shore. 8am–7pm. Entrance and car park fees.*
Witnesses to the prosperity of the port during the Christian period, the two fortresses are the only extant buildings from ancient Korigos. The first – Korykos Kalesi – forms a large quadrilateral composed of two concentric enclosures (the outer enclosure is almost entirely razed).

Erected by the Armenians on the foundations of a small Roman fort, its current walls have existed since the 12C. Past the entrance booth, the path deepens through the scrub until it reaches the foot of the outer walls. They are crossed by a gap leading to the inner enclosure, and on to the Roman gate (2C AD), an arch located in the centre of the western wall. From here, there is a very beautiful view★ of the coast and Kızkalesi.

Continuing to the southwest corner of the wall, you will see the Sea Gate to the south, through which one could enter by boat. It is a beautiful white arch rising from the water and flanked by a large watch tower, now ruined. Continuing along the sea

Cilicia Campestris

A fortress in vain

A prophecy foretold that the daughter of the King of Korigos would die of a snake bite. To protect her, the monarch had a castle built on a deserted island where he locked his daughter away. Unfortunately, a suitor offered her a basket of figs in which a viper lay coiled. When the maiden placed her hand in the basket, she was mortally bitten by the snake. Love, fruit and the snake; a legend which is reminiscent of the lovers of the garden of Eden, Adam and Eve, or the sad end of Queen Cleopatra.

shore, you reach an inner wall and the remains of **two chapels** (one of them has retained its apse). The fortress' **main gate** opened on this side, with a moat defending the entire length (partially filled in).

Kızkalesi castle★ – *Embarkation point on the beach, near the Korykos citadel. 15min crossing. Entrance fee.*

Kızkalesi, the "Maiden's Castle", obtains its name from a legend which says that a king locked up his daughter to protect her from a prophecy warning of her death. History, on the other hand, says that the castle was erected by the Byzantines at the beginning of the 12C, above the walls of a Roman fort. As you approach, you will be impressed by its tall white walls which seem to float on the sea like an enormous stone vessel.

The enclosure rings the entire perimeter of the island, 75m long (190m circumference) defended by eight large **towers★**. Little is left of the buildings which filled the **courtyard**: only a **chapel** and a series of weed–infested **cisterns**. On the other hand, the **ramparts★★** – remodelled by the Ottomans and recently restored – are in a remarkable state of repair. The walk along the watchpath and through the beautiful **vaulted galleries** running along the western wall is especially memorable. The **panorama★★** over the sea and the coastline is of great beauty and the silence which reigns on the island is a welcome contrast to the hubbub of the beach.

■ Kanlıdivane★

33km from Silifke, 10km from Kızkalesi. On the road to İçel, turn left after 7km. 8am-7pm. Entrance fee. Allow 90min for the visit.

Have you ever seen a city rise around an abyss? The Byzantine city of Kanlıdivane (ancient Kanytelis) rose like a rampart on the edges of a large depression with steep walls, the ancient sacred site of a thick forest where numerous birds have found refuge. An unusual site to which the superb ruins add an extraordinary charm: numerous buildings of light-coloured stones, covered by greenery in places.

Founded in the 5C by Emperor Theodosius on the site of a Hellenistic city, Kanlıdivane lived a prosperous and peaceful existence. Away from the coast, it did not fall victim to the successive invaders, which undoubtedly explains the state of conservation of its buildings. In the 8C and 9C, while the Arabs swept along the coast, it even experienced an economic boom until the arrival of the Turks in the 11C. Thereafter it was slowly abandoned.

Around the abyss

Upon arrival, the eye is drawn to the large **square tower**, dating from the Hellenistic period, overlooking the pit. Only half of it is standing now; it formerly housed the city's garrison and controlled the entrance.

Skirting the chasm (*left of the car park*), you will pass in front of the arches of a large church – the **basilica of Papylos★** (*on the left, slightly away from the path*) – whose walls are almost intact. Notice the beautiful **door frames** leading to the naves, as well as the elegant **arched bays** on the first floor.

Backtrack along the path which skirts the cliff and continue to the north.

Further down, on the left, you reach a **monastery** which includes another large **church**, and a vaulted **cistern** in perfect condition pierced by several niches. On the other side, at the edge of the abyss, the terracotta plumbing which supplied the city with water can still be seen. The path descends towards a small terrace overlooking the chasm, where you will be surprised by a number of **wall tombs**★, carved in the rocky wall *(near the square tower)*. All are decorated with **bas-reliefs**★★ representing the deceased – often city notables. Among them, notice the one with six figures in a line.

Continuing towards the north, there is another church, also in excellent condition. Up among the shrubs lies an isolated and imposing **tomb**, a majestic mausoleum in the shape of a temple, also well preserved. Enter through one of the side openings leading to one of the funerary chambers. Each enclosed several sarcophagi, which were affixed to the walls. All around, the vegetation is surrounded by ruins, pieces of friezes and walls weathered by time.

Kanlıdivane, city on an abyss

F. Levillain

Cilicia Campestris

471

The tour of the abyss is completed by the **Governors' Palace****, an impressive building displaying its light-coloured walls across from the city tower, exactly opposite the pit.

Before leaving, you should visit the little village of Çanakçı, near the site *(as you leave, take the track on the right which descends to the village)*. On reaching an isolated sarcophagus, take the path down to the bottom of a green valley, encased between the two red-ochre walls. Note the nine charming **bas-reliefs****, carefully carved in the cliff wall, just above the entrance to the tombs.

Making the most of Silifke

COMING AND GOING

By bus – The bus station is at the very end of İnönü Cad when coming from Kızkalesi.

The **Akdeniz**, **Denizkızı**, **Özkaymak** and **Şimşek** bus companies operate services to İstanbul, Bursa, İzmir, İskenderun, Antakya and Adana. The **Silifke Kooperatifi** runs services to Erdemli, Kızkalesi and Mersin. Several buses depart from Taşucu (the harbour in Silifke) for Konya, Bursa and Mersin.

By shared taxi – Dolmuşes depart for Kızkalesi and Taşucu. In Taşucu, dolmuşes leave for Silifke every 30min, and for Susanoğlu beach (12km from Silifke on the road to Mersin). Others shuttle between here and Uzuncaburç, departing from next to the tourist information office.

By boat – Ferry-boats operate a daily service to Girne (Kyrenia, northern Cyprus): departure at midnight and return at noon. The journey can also be made by hydrofoil, which is much faster (2hr instead of 4hr): departure every day at 11am, return at 7.30pm. All the shipping agencies are at the harbour, along Atatürk Cad.

ADDRESS BOOK

Tourist information – Veli Gürten Bozbey Cad 6, ☎ (324) 714 11 51, Fax (324) 714 53 28. Several foreign languages are spoken and the welcome is very dynamic. Here you will find all the information you need to make the most of the region. From Monday to Friday, 8am-12noon / 1pm-5pm.

Main post office – Cavit Erden Cad, 7am-11pm.

Bank / change – Behind the post office, there are automatic cash dispensers at **İş Bankası**, **Ziraat Bankası** and **Yapı Kredi**, in Menderes Cad.

Market – On Fridays.

WHERE TO STAY

You will find almost everything you need in Kızkalesi.

• **In Silifke**

Under US$15

Pension Arısan, Saray Mah İnönü Cad 89, ☎ (324) 714 39 72. Shared or individual rooms. Communal bathroom. A very clean, new guest house, with simple comforts, built to cater to students. This is the place to come if you want to avoid the big tourist complexes along the coast. It's the only place worth recommending in Silifke.

• In Kızkalesi
Avoid places on the roadside because of the noise. All the establishments below are on the seafront. The most chic hotels are gathered at the end of the beach.

Between US$15 and US$25

Pension Öz Kızkalesi, Mavideniz Mah, ☎ (324) 523 20 97 – 32rm. 🍴 You will find a modest level of comfort, but a warm family atmosphere, in a very pleasant setting (the guest house is surrounded by vegetation and gives directly onto the beach). Watch out for the mosquitoes in the evening!

Etap Motel, Mavideniz Mah 2 Plaj Yolu, ☎ (324) 523 21 32. 🍴✕ A guest house with a simple but adequate level of comfort and no surprises, just like all the surrounding guest houses. Guests have access to a kitchen and washing machine.

Hotel Hantur, near the select clubs, ☎ (324) 523 23 67. 🍴 Minibar. An unpretentious guest house run by a very welcoming proprietor.

Between US$40 and US$55

🌸 ***Hotel Club Barbarossa***, Kızkalesi Mevkii, ☎ (324) 523 23 64 – 103rm. 🍴 🏊 🗒 ✕ 🛥 Bar. Very good value for money. Modern level of comfort and good quality service.

• Taşucu
A little harbour town 11km east of Silifke, Taşucu is quieter than Kızkalesi, but will only be of interest to travellers with their own transport (it is quite far from the sights worth seeing).

Under US$15

Pension Meltem, next to the beach, ☎ (324) 741 43 91 – 18rm. 🍴🗒 A very simple guest house meticulously kept by a young man who has conveniently opened a grocery store on the ground floor.

Between US$15 and US$30

Lades Motel, Atatürk Cad 89, ☎ (324) 741 41 08. 🍴✕🛥 Bar. An ageing establishment with a standard level of comfort, but at more attractive prices than in Kızkalesi.

EATING OUT
There are two restaurants in Silifke (see below), but you will find a greater choice in Kızkalesi, and particularly in Narlıkuyu and Taşucu, where there are some delicious fish specialities.

As a snack, try the fresh pistachio nuts sold by the street vendors in Kızkalesi.

• In Silifke
Kale Restaurant, near the fortress, ☎ (324) 714 15 21. Meze and meats at reasonable prices, served on a terrace which dominates the whole town.

Babaoğlu, Dörtyol Mevkii, near the "otogar", Silifke, ☎ (324) 714 20 41. Convenient for travellers who are just passing through, and very cheap. All the Turkish specialities are served in a simple setting with air conditioning.

• In Taşucu
Denizkızı, in the square with the statue of Atatürk. This place is very popular with the locals, who regularly dine here. Follow their example – the food is delicious.

Tequila, near the Lades Motel, with a terrace looking over the ferry port. On the menu: fish and meze, for around US$10 per person, including drinks.

At the harbour and in the main square of the village, you can also have a drink in one of the many open-air "Çay Bahçesi" (soft drinks, beer, tea and coffee).

• In Kızkalesi
Try the local speciality, "tantuni", a sandwich filled with very finely sliced veal, with lots of parsley, fresh tomatoes and onion, served with half a lemon and very hot little green chillies (optional). You can try them at ***Burg***, just next to the statue of Atatürk.

• In Narlıkuyu
17km from Silifke, on the road to Mersin, this small fishing village abounds with fish restaurants, serving grouper ("horfoz") in particular.

OTHER THINGS TO DO
Silifke hosts an ***International Folk Music Festival*** every year in May.

THE PLAIN OF ÇUKUROVA
TARSUS AND ADANA
Adana Province – Map p 354
Hot and humid climate

Not to be missed
The Church of St Peter of Tarsus.

And remember...
From Tarsus, if you have transport, escape to the heights.
The landscape is beautiful and the silence impressive.
A breath of fresh air before reaching Adana.

The Mediterranean Coast

"The scrub lands of Çukurova begin where the landscaped fields of monochrome clay end. For miles on end, huddled, as if braided, shrubs, bamboo, brambles, wild vines and reeds cover the region with a dark green coat, wilder than a dark forest, darker still."

Yaşar Kemal, *Mehmet the Thin*

When the writer Yaşar Kemal, a native of the region, wrote the first lines of his famous novel, in 1955, the plain of Çukurova was nothing more than a gigantic marsh inhabited by pink flamingos and gazelles. It was virgin territory, barely exploited by landowners with feudal customs, who reigned like lords in the villages of the surrounding hills. Fifteen more years had to go by after Atatürk's death (1938) for the farmers of "the Çukurova" to witness the beginning of dramatic change. The change did occur, the marshes of Adana became immense cotton fields which would eventually transform the region into the country's richest.

Tarsus
31km from İçel (Mersin) and 41km from Adana. Pop 187 600.

After İçel, the agricultural plain of Çukurova – eastern edges of Cilicia – stretches along the foot of the Taurus, a large triangle of land advancing toward the sea, closing off the gulf of İskenderun. A multitude of rivers are lost in meanders, including the Seyhan which feeds Adana, and the Ceyhan, further east. The road flanking the coast heads inland, skirting the foot of the hills and leaving the plain to the south.

Before reaching tumultuous Adana, allow yourself a few hours of rest in Tarsus, a tranquil town located on the banks of the Tarsus Çayı. Except for the large cedars which cast their shade, the city does not have any particular attractions, but the atmosphere is lively, perhaps because the city is filled with numerous students. Tarsus is in fact home to a large American school and the youths will gladly converse in English with you. Take the time to stroll in the old city, which hides a few lovely Ottoman houses and begin your exploration of the (rare) remains of the city of St Paul.

The land of St Paul
Tarsus is a very ancient city: the first traces of life go back to the 14C BC. However, it was during the Hellenistic period that the city began to develop. The Seleucid period (from the 4C to the 2C BC) even turned it into a brilliant intellectual centre, thanks to the presence of the greatest Stoic philosophers. Incorporated into the Roman Empire in 64 BC, the city experienced substantial economic growth as a result of the construction of a canal connecting it to the sea. However, the city is especially known as being the home of Saul, who was to become the apostle Paul and who was born

in the area in 5 or 15 AD. When Christianity was declared the State religion, Tarsus became the seat of an important bishopric. Later, like its neighbours, it fell under the control of the Seljuks, Armenians and finally the Ottomans, in 1515.

Visiting the city

Allow 2hr. All the sights are within walking distance.

As soon as you enter the city *(coming from İçel)*, your eyes are drawn to the **Cleopatra Gate** (Kancık or Kleopatra Kapısı), one of the Roman city's six gates, which Cleopatra supposedly crossed to reach her lover Anthony. The building, a heavily restored simple stone arch is of no exceptional value; but there is the legend.

From the Cleopatra Gate, follow the main road keeping to the right. At the first large intersection, turn right again to enter into the alleys of the old city.

Have a look at the small **Archeological Museum** (Kubad Paşa Medresesi) set up inside a pretty 16C **medrese** *(8am-12noon/1pm-7.30pm in summer, 5pm in winter)*. It contains a few statues and sarcophagi from the Roman era, as well as glass items, jewellery and several objects found in the city surroundings, dating from the Hittite to the Ottoman periods.

Further along *(in the same street, on the left as you leave the museum)*, you reach the large mosque, **Ulu Cami**, a sober 16C Ottoman building built upon the foundations of the Byzantine cathedral dedicated to St Peter. Spend some time in the **covered arcade** (Kırkkaşık Bedesten) located next door, very picturesque with lively cafés, where men sip *çay* as they play cards.

As you leave the arcade, take the small road on the left (Bilal-i Habeşi), then turn left again.

Not far from Ulu Cami rises the **Church of St Paul*** (St Paulus Kilisesi) *(8am-12noon/1pm-5pm; closed Sundays and Mondays)*, converted into a mosque in the 15C. Although neglected, it is undoubtedly the city's finest building, with ochre stone walls and elegant concave vaults. Fragments of **frescoes** appear haphazardly.

Return to the main street and follow Cumhuriyet Alanı, straight on towards the northwest.

Lastly, another interesting site in the city, **St Paul's Well** (Paulus Kuyusu), is located inside the apostle's supposed birthplace *(7.30am-6pm; entrance fee)*. It is in fact a simple water well protected by white walls, but the spot is a pilgrimage site for Christian Turks. Nearby, on Cumhuriyet Alanı, excavations (still in progress, every summer) have brought to light the remains of a **Roman road** and several dwellings.

North of Tarsus

Route 750, which climbs towards the north of Tarsus, crosses beautiful mountainous landscapes unveiling wonderful **views****. Indulge in a little excursion in the heights, for 50km, to the **Cilician Gates*** (Gülek or Camalan Boğazı), an impressive gap barely 20m wide, carved by the Tarsus between two 120m-high walls. Cut in the cliff, a small, very old road probes into the heart of the gorge, towards the summits of the Taurus. This is the passage which was used by the Persians, then by Alexander, to reach the Cilician plain. It is quite an adventure!

Adana

193km from Antakya. Pop 1 034 000.

Facing the plain, at the foot of the first hills of the Taurus, Adana almost monopolises the region's entire economic activity with its cotton mills and its textile and food industries. The country's fourth largest city is as frightening as a giant octopus. However, it is a practical hub from which to explore the region, home to magnificent fortified castles.

The Plain of Çukurova

Crossed by a motorway and served by an international airport, Adana is a busy, dusty city, with large avenues already unable to cope with the ever-growing traffic. Adana's expansion is a recent phenomenon. The intensification and modernisation of the region's agriculture, starting in the 1930s, attracted hundreds of thousands of farmers looking for work. In 50 years its population has exploded, creating severe housing and health problems: numerous *gecekondu* (slums) spring up along the roads and concrete continues to devour the plain.

A quick look at the city
Allow 2hr for the visit

Little remains of the old city which claims the west bank of the Seyhan *(reached by the motorway crossing the heart of the city)*. To the right of the modern road bridge a magnificent **Roman bridge***, the **Taş Köprü**, strides the river. Built in the 2C AD, the work – the city's oldest vestige – is no less than 310m long. Still used but more and more damaged by pollution, it is a marvellous illustration of the talent of Roman architects.

From the bridge, follow the docks *(Ulus Cad)* towards the south to reach the **Ulu Cami** *(Kızılay Cad, at the corner of sokak 74)*, a small mosque (1507) whose **portal*** and minaret are decorated with beautiful bands of black and white marble, as is common in Syrian buildings. The interior is embellished with beautiful İznik and Kütahya tiles. Notice also the **mihrab***, a sober niche of black and white marble.

Close by *(towards the west)* rises another mosque, **Yağ Camii**, built in 1501 inside the walls of a church dedicated to St James. Its name comes from (*yag*: "oil") a legend which claims that when the church was transformed, all of the residents participated financially in the project. An old woman who could not contribute financially offered the olive oil which she sold. Thirty years later the building hosted a **Koranic school** which functions to this day.

Adana, Ulu Cami Mosque

F. Levillain

Arriving from 5 Ocak square, turn at the first street on the left in front of the Kemer Altı mosque. Nearby rises the **Church of St Paul** (Bebek Kilisesi) *(Tepebağ Mah. 10 Sok; 8.30am-12noon/3pm-7pm)*, a reminder of the era when the region was home to a strong Armenian community.

From there, you can reach the **Ethnographical Museum** *(Ziya Paşa Cad; 8am-5pm, closed Mondays, entrance fee)*, located inside a restored church. It harbours a few magnificent examples of carpets and old Korans, musical instruments and a Yörük tent where traditional objects of nomadic life are displayed.

If time allows, have a look at the **Museum of Regional Archeology** *(Fuzuli Cad; 8.30am-12noon/1pm-4.30pm, closed Mondays, entrance fee)*, next to the Merkez mosque *(800m from the city centre)*.

Leaving the city and travelling northwards, you will reach the **Seyhan Dam.** It encloses a large **artificial lake** *(8km from the city centre. Take Gazipaşa Bul, cross the railroad tracks, then Mustafa Kemal Pasa Bul and flank the Seyhan. Those without private transport can take a taxi or dolmuş).* The road leads to the lake, **Adnan Menderes Bulvarı**, a traditional excursion for local families in search of greenery, peace and fresh air. On weekends, the area is lively with local citizens who spend the entire day picnicking and relaxing on the lake's shores.

COMING AND GOING

By air – Şakir Paşa Havaalanı international airport, 4km from the centre. Take the E5 towards İçel (Mersin); the airport is signposted on the left, ☎ (322) 436 92 12.

By bus – The bus station, **Adana Merkez Otogarı**, is quite far from the centre, on the E5 going towards İçel and Ankara. In addition to the major bus companies such as **Varan**, **Metro** and **Has**, numerous local bus companies operate services to all the national destinations: İstanbul, Ankara (an 11hr overnight journey), Bursa, İzmir, Marmaris, Antalya, Sivas, Malatya, Van, Gaziantep and Diyarbakır. There are also connections to Cappadocia, the Black Sea and Bitlis (in Georgia). And, of course, there are several buses per day to Tarsus (2hr) and Antakya (3hr).

By train – The railway station is located to the north of the city, at the end of Atatürk Cad, opposite Ziya Paşa Bul, ☎ (322) 453 31 72. Trains run to the following destinations: Gaziantep (Monday, Wednesday, Friday at 4.50am), Elazığ (every day at 8.40am), Kayseri (every day at 5.50pm), Diyarbakır (every day at 4.20pm), Ankara (every day at 7.30pm), İstanbul (Tuesday, Wednesday, Saturday at 9.45pm). Trains to Mersin depart every 30min from 4.45am to 11pm, and to İskenderun (3 departures per day).

By shared taxi – Main dolmuş stand, Turan Cemal Beriker Bulv, next to the Great Mosque.

ADDRESS BOOK

Tourist information – Atatürk Cad 13, ☎ (322) 363 14 48 / 363 12 87, Fax (322) 363 13 46. Every day, 8am-12noon / 1pm-5pm, except Saturday and Sunday.

Main post office – Kızılay Cad, 8.30am-5.30pm. Telephones and currency exchange. There are two other post offices, one opposite the railway station and one at the bus station.

Bank / change – Automatic cash dispenser at **İş Bankası**, opposite the railway station, and next to the main post office. Banks abound in Özler Cad and Atatürk Cad: **Yapı Kredi**, **Koç Bank**, **Garanti Bankası** and **Akbank**.

Car rental – Avis, Ziyapaşa Bul Hürriyet Apt 5/B, ☎ (322) 453 30 45 / 459 75 58, Fax (322) 453 48 24. At the airport, ☎ (322) 435 59 75 / 435 04 76, Fax (322) 435 04 76.

Budget, Ziyapaşa Bul Hürriyet Apt B Blok 13A, ☎ (322) 459 00 16, Fax (322) 459 11 09.

Europcar, Döşeme Mah Mücahiler Bul Kayalı 2 Apt 87/C, ☎ (322) 453 47 75, Fax (322) 458 15 29. At the airport, ☎ (322) 433 29 57 / 436 25 63.

Decar, Ziyapaşa Bul 10/B, Divan Apt, ☎ (322) 459 04 98/99, Fax (322) 459 04 88.

Hertz, Ziyapaşa Bul Hürriyet Apt 7/A, ☎ (322) 433 21 00 / 458 49 92 / 458 50 62, Fax (322) 453 11 55.

Airline companies – **Türk Hava Yolları** (Turkish Airlines), Atatürk Cad, ☎ (322) 435 91 75 / 435 92 06.

İstanbul Hava Yolları (İstanbul Airlines), Atatürk Cad Büyükşehir Belediyesi Yanı, Uğurlu Pasajı, Asma kat, ☎ (322) 454 41 72, www.istanbulairlines.com.tr. Operates services to İstanbul (4 flights per day) and to some European cities.

Medical service – Hospitals: **Seyhan Hastane**, near the railway station, and **Göğüs Hastanesi**, Mahfaz Sigmaz, in Baraj Yolu, ☎ (322) 227 03 87.
State hospital: **Devlet Hastanesi**, Yamaçli Mah Yüregir ☎ (322) 321 57 52. On the east bank, after the Taş Köprü.

Consulate – **American Consulate**, Atatürk Cad, ☎ (322) 459 15 51, Fax (322) 457 65 91.

WHERE TO STAY

The hotels in Adana are fairly expensive in comparison with the rest of the region. They are mainly frequented by businessmen seeking a modern and standard level of comfort. So don't expect to find any charming little places here. Most of the hotels are in the vicinity of İnönü Cad, on the west bank of the river.

Between US$15 and US$30
Hotel İpek Palas, İnönü Cad, ☎ (322) 351 87 41 – 84rm. ⌐ ℰ With its very rudimentary level of comfort, this hotel is nothing like a palace, despite its name. As a last resort.

Between US$40 and US$55
Hotel Koza, Özler Cad 103, ☎ (322) 353 58 57 / 352 58 52/ 352 59 05, Fax (322) 359 85 71 – 66rm.

⌐ ℰ TV ✕ Car park and discotheque. A comfortable establishment, but the staff only speak Turkish.

Hotel Hosta, Bakımyurdu Cad 3, ☎ (322) 352 37 00 – 36rm. ℰ ⌐ ▤ TV The standard of comfort is not exceptional, but the hotel is clean and you will be welcomed with a smile.

Between US$55 and US$70
Hotel Zaimoğlu, Özler Cad 72, ☎ (322) 351 34 01 – 77rm. ⌐ ℰ TV ✕ Car park, discotheque and bar. Every modern comfort and luxury – you'll feel just like a businessman!

Over US$75
Hotel Seyhan, Turhan Cemal Beriker Bul 30, ☎ (322) 457 58 10 – 100rm. ⌐ ℰ TV ▤ ✕ ᚁ CC Bar. This is one of Adana's most chic establishments and has a casino which is regularly packed with congress attendees.

EATING OUT

The local cuisine is very spicy (Syria is not far away). You will find a wide variety of restaurants near the tourist information office, in Atatürk Bul and Menderes Bul. The local specialities are "piliç şiş", chicken brochettes, fish stuffed with pistachio nuts, and the "Adana Kebab", mutton with cayenne pepper, served on pide. To put out the fire, try the local drink, "şalgam suyu", a turnip, beetroot and carrot based cocktail. A little bitter, but worth a try! Lastly, how about a tasty "bici", a mixture of crushed ice and red-coloured rice flour flavoured with rose water. If you are not tempted by any of this, you can always order an "Adana çorbası", a good vegetable soup with meatballs. You certainly won't go hungry after that.

• **In the city centre**
Yeni Onbaşılar, Atatürk Bul Dörtyolağazı, ☎ (322) 351 41 78. Opposite the tourist information office. Simple service and typical atmosphere.

• **Near the stadium**
🍽 **Agba**, Cemalpaşa Mah 271 Sok 4, ☎ (322) 453 67 30/458 32 31. A very good restaurant with original and tasty Turkish dishes, such as sheep's head, sautéd boiled mutton ("tandır"), cheese

"lahmacun", liver brochettes and "Ali Nazik", a "döner" served with aubergine purée. Around US$5 per meal.

Mesut, Mesatbey Mah 21 Sok. Recently redecorated, this restaurant serves regional specialities at reasonable prices.

Also go to the Kara Soku Mah district, to the **Eski Alışveriş Merkezi** market, which is renowned for its little "Adana Kebab" restaurants.

● **Towards the dam**

The banks of the Seyhan, to the north of town, abound with open-air restaurants where the inhabitants of Adana like to have lunch at weekends.

Okutan Tesisleri, Adnan Menderes Bul Dinazorlu Çocuk Parkı Karşısı 113, ☎ (322) 235 17 36. Opposite the lake, under the trees, a pleasant restaurant with renowned fish specialities.

Hindi, Adnan Menderes Bul 49, ☎ (322) 233 03 05. Restaurant with a bar that plays music on Friday and Saturday evenings. Very pretty lakeside terrace. The "inegöl köfte" are not to be missed.

Menekşe Kardeşler, Beyaz Saray Tesisleri, Adnan Menderes Bul, ☎ (322) 234 35 50, Fax (322) 235 11 05. An attractive restaurant with a view over the lake, in a guarded complex with a swimming pool, dance hall, tennis courts and a wood. Fish, prawn and squid specialities. Around US$15 per person.

HAVING A DRINK

Numerous tea rooms and restaurants line Adnan Menderes boulevard, to the north of the city. Here you will find "bici" served in liquid or solid form. A few addresses: **100 yıl Lünapark**, next to the amusement park. The **Green Bar** and the **Hindi disco**, ☎ (322) 321 34 63, both in Ceyhan Yolu, are more upmarket and more modern.

Internet café – Galaxi Internet Cafe, Gazipaşa Bul Toros Cad 279 Sok (in the stadium area), ☎ (322) 453 47 77. US$3 per hour.

Cake shops – Mavi Köşe Pastanesi, Atatürk Cad and **Samanyolu Pastanesi**, Gazipaşa Bul Toros Cad Alkaya Apt 6, with air conditioning.

OTHER THINGS TO DO

Excursions – Pink Tours, Reşat bey Mah 4 Sok Ümran Apt 16/A, ☎ (322) 459 17 67. Organises tours to Fethiye, Marmaris, Bodrum, the Black Sea and northern Cyprus. Also offers flights to Ankara, İstanbul, İzmir, several European cities, Bakou (in Azerbaijan) and even New York! Depending on demand, the agency can organise trips to Nemrut Dağı.

Parks – Cumhuriyet Parkı, between Atatürk Cad and Ziya Paşa Cad. You can come here to escape the noise of the horns and the urban traffic for a while. With its fountains and palm trees, this shaded park is pleasant indeed in a city where the temperature can reach 35°C in summer. To the north of the city, in Adnan Menderes Bul, there is an **amusement park** (near the Menekşe restaurant) and a **dinosaur park** (opposite the Olutan restaurant) which will keep the children amused.

SHOPPING GUIDE

Try the fresh prickly pears which are sold in the street.

Markets – On Thursdays, near the **stade 5 Ocak**. There is also a market, the **Eski Alışveriş Merkezi**, every day in the district of Kara Soku Mah, where copperware is sold.

There are some large supermarkets in the city centre: **Gima**, in Atatürk Cad, and **Çetinkaya**, in Kuru Köprü Cad.

THE ROAD OF THE FORTRESSES★

NORTHEAST OF ADANA

171km itinerary – One day – General Map p 354
No hotels, only informal accommodation in the villages
A pleasant solution: camping in the Karatepe Natural Park

Not to be missed
Yılanlı Castle and its view.
The scenery and the Hittite ruins in Karatepe National Park.

And remember...
Leave from Adana early in the morning to fully
take advantage of the day and the cool temperature.
Since the region lacks restaurants, pack a picnic before you leave.
Bring good shoes and drinking water.
Avoid Karatepe at weekends, it is filled with people from the city.

East of Adana, the road rushes across huge *pamuk* (cotton) fields. Women emerge with colourful scarves protecting them from the sun and a large bag hanging over their shoulder filled with fluffy white material. After the cotton come the pine trees and the basalt, a tortuous landscape carved by the volcanoes. Here begins a voyage back in time from the Middle Ages to the Hittites, by way of the Byzantines and the Romans. Forget the future: leave the fast roads for the ways of the past, which disappear into the highlands of silence.

Basalt castles

The eastern buttresses of the Taurus are the domain of countless fortified castles, forgotten sentinels of the ephemeral Armenia Minor which covered Cilicia from the beginning of the 12C to the end of the 13C (*see p 357*). Around Yılanlı Kale – the first stop on this itinerary – no less than eight other fortresses rise in a 50km radius, capping the steepest slopes of the surrounding hills. They protected the threshold of the kingdom, watching for the smallest cloud of dust that might arise on the plain, signalling the advance of a cavalry troop. Carved in the rocks, their walls still stand, having withstood attack. Crenellated crests slash the sky and turn to fire as the sun sets. From the watchtowers, the view is dizzying and the spectacle of the plain and the blue tips of the Taurus is unforgettable.

■ Yılanlı Kale★

41km from Adana. Take the Ceyhan road (E400) rather than the motorway, for 39km, then turn right to take the small 3km road which ascends gently. Leave your car in the car park and continue on foot for 500m. The small path from the car park leads to the first enclosure. From there, you will have to climb through fallen rocks to reach the second enclosure. Be very careful, the rocks are slippery and the climb is akin to mountain climbing. If you are subject to vertigo, do not attempt it! Entrance fee. Allow 1hr for the visit.

Cotton fields as far as the eye can see. Suddenly appears a startling vision: rocks point towards the north, preceding a hill covered with a thick rocky plateau. Above it – a stiff silhouette seemingly impossible to reach – Yılanlı Kale (the "snake castle") reveals its battlements above the plain and the meanders of the Ceyhan.

Its history has faded into the past, but its architecture is the work of Leon II, King of Armenia Minor from 1187 to 1219, to whom we can credit nearly all the fortified castles of eastern Cilicia. Probably remodelled by the Seljuks, its battlements, which were originally rectangular, have made way for merlons, pyramidal battlements reminiscent of Syriac citadels.

The fortress hugs the rock closely, drawing an ellipse nearly 200m-long, punctuated by eight large circular towers. Two of them flank the **entrance gate** which opens up at the summit of a large area of fallen rocks *(the climb is quite dangerous)*. It is covered by a relief showing the King's coat of arms: a man armed with a sword (it was long thought to be a snake, hence the castle's name), surrounded by two lions.

As you enter the **courtyard**, on the left, a large **cistern** faces the foot of the wall. The contours of a **chapel** can also be discerned; its walls must have originally been used to lodge the commander of the fortress' troops. The **towers** have a few beautiful **vaulted rooms** and the **watchpath*** affords magnificent **views**** over the plain and the Ceyhan, which forms a sort of long blue snake across the cotton fields. If you do not fear heights, climb to the top of the tower located next to the entrance: to get an impressive **view**** of the castle and the surroundings.

Return to the main road towards Ceyhan-İskenderun. 3km later, turn left in the direction of Kozan and Kadirli (route 817). In Ayşehoca, take the track on the right leading to Anazarbus-Anavarza, 5km further on.

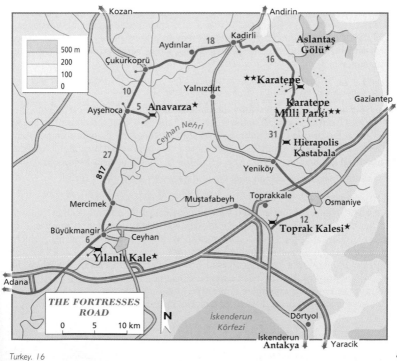

The road of the Fortresses

■ Anazarbus★ (Anavarza)

38km from Yılanlı Kale and 73km northeast of Adana, on the right of the
Kadırlı road. No hotels or restaurants. Allow 90min there and back with the climb.

Continue your trip through time: after the Middle Ages, this is where the Byzantine and Roman era begin. Built on the walls of the ancient Anazarbus, the small village of Anavarza sleeps under the sun, at the foot of a vertiginous cliff surmounted by a citadel. The site has never been excavated and the ruins are dispersed in the greenery, in the fields and in the village. The organisation of this Roman city is therefore not easy to understand, but the young goat herders of the area will gladly abandon their flocks for a moment to guide you across the remains. After that, surrounded by all the caps and moustaches of the entire village, you cannot refuse the traditional glass of çay offered.

Founded by the Romans in the 1C BC, Anazarbus rapidly became a flourishing city. Its role in the economic development of the region made it the capital of eastern Cilicia, in the 5C AD. In spite of the numerous earthquakes which shook it, the city continued its expansion making its neighbours envious. Attacks and pillages succeeded each other inside its walls and the city changed hands: Arabs in the 8C, Armenians in the 11C, then Mamelukes in 1375, only to end up abandoned.

The lower city

At the entrance of the village, the courtyard of a house to the right contains the fragments of two **mosaics** which decorated the basins of two fountains. Next door you will find a map of the site.

Further along, on the left, as you cross the village, a beautiful **triumphal arch**★ (3C AD) opens onto the meadow, a blanket of green grass that goes on for miles. It was one of the city's gates, and it preceded a long avenue lined with **porticoes**. Only a small row of broken grey **columns** remains. A few pieces of wall still stand here and there, vestiges of the Roman **baths,** along with a **church** built by the Byzantines.

Return to the village, then turn left to reach the foot of the cliff where you will find the
stadium (on your right) and the theatre (on your left).

The **stadium** can be recognised by the oblong shape of a few steps carved into the cliff's rock (convict labour!). On the other side of the path, after the ruins of an **oven**, you reach the **theatre**, also quite demolished (its stones are thought to have been used to consolidate the ramparts of the city and citadel). Beyond, the disembowelled **sarcophagi** lost among the greenery, lie on the site of the ancient **necropolis.**

From here, a small stairway carved in the rock allows you to reach the citadel.

The citadel★★

A gigantic natural barrier erected on an infinitely flat plain, Anavarza cliff is striking. At the doorstep of Cilicia, it offered an ideal site for an observation tower and a refuge. Today, still, the fortress continues to withhold many of its secrets, which only experienced mountain climbers can attempt to pierce.

An extraordinary stone crown, the citadel of Anazarbus stretches on for 700m. It follows the edge of the cliff, not missing a single nook or cranny, as if to enhance it further and render it even more impressive. You cannot but ask yourself how these builders managed to heave heavy stone blocks up the steep cliff face.

F. Levillain

Yılanı Kale, the "snake castle"

The only accessible portion, the fortress' **first enclosure** was the refuge of local inhabitants in case of danger. Except for the ramparts, all of the courtyard's buildings – stores, stables and houses – have disappeared. Only the ruins of a **funerary chapel,** which undoubtedly harboured the remains of the kings of Armenia Minor, survive. Its plan is typically Armenian: three naves, each closed off by an apse.

North of the court, a large **tower*** rises in front of the second enclosure, an impressive work with an **inscription** revealing the construction techniques; quite a job, since the base of the tower is carved in the rock and the stones have been sealed with metallic pegs. Go and explore the beautiful **vaults**.

The main reason for coming, however, is to **walk along the watchpath****, a truly memorable experience. From there, the other two **enclosures** of the fortress can be seen. Their beautiful battlements belong only to the vultures and clouds.

Descending on the western side, you will cross a **necropolis**, a forest of thistles strewn with toppled sarcophagi and broken covers. Turn around from time to time: seen from the bottom, the citadel's towers seem to melt into the rock and are really impressive.

Take the Kadirli road (28km). As you leave the village, take the Andirin road and, after 2km, turn right at the "Karatepe" sign, 16km away.

■ Karatepe**

112km from Adana. 8.30am-12.30pm/2pm-5.30pm in summer and 8am-12noon/1pm-3.30pm in winter. Entrance fee. Taking photographs is forbidden. The visit is made with the obligatory "guide" who speaks only Turkish. Allow 1hr. At the site you will see a restaurant, drink stand and a lodge (about $2 per day). Camping is located nearby (tents provided if you do not have one) and you can also take advantage of the beautiful beach on the Aslantaş dam, open for swimming.

After the Romans came the Hittites! Past Kadirli, the road climbs to the heights and penetrates into the heart of a magnificent pine forest filled with the fragrance of resin and thyme. It reaches the shores of the **Aslantaş artificial lake***, created by dams on the Ceyhan. The southern portion of the lake is the domain of the **Natural Park of Karatepe**** (Karatepe Milli Parkı), the magnificent setting of Turkey's most beautiful Hittite site. This open-air museum set in the middle of a pine forest is ideal for delightful walks. Here and there, clearings allow magnificent **views**** of the turquoise waters of the lake and river, and it is difficult to resist the temptation to stretch out or go for a swim as you listen to the crickets.

A Hittite palace

Perched on a pinnacle overlooking the Ceyhan, Karatepe ("the black hill") was the stronghold of King Azitawadda, a vassal of the Hittite sovereign of Adana who reigned at the end of the 8C BC. Controlling the caravan route linking the eastern plains to the Anatolian plateaux, the citadel faced another Hittite fortress – Domuztepe – erected one century earlier on the other side of the river.

The **royal residence,** the only excavated building (the digs continue each year), formed an impressive square (300m on each side), fortified by 4m thick **basalt walls** built in a polygonal form. The entrances were through two gates (still standing), one to the southwest *(upper gate)*, the other to the northeast *(lower gate)*. Each was flanked by two stone **lions*** ("*aslantaş*" in Turkish), with gaping jaws, ready to pounce on any evil presence. From there, you would reach a T-shaped hall leading to the palace's various rooms.

Magnificent bas-reliefs ran the length of the walls, carved on the stones of the first row of rock. All of them have been grouped around two doors which have been set upright. They illustrate, with humour and poetry, the daily life of the court – figures with primitive features, huge eyes, whose subject matter and lines show an Egyptian and Assyrian influence. Take the time to look at them; you will discover numerous details to help you to imagine palace life.

In addition to these bas-reliefs, an **inscription in Hittite** has been discovered. The longest one known to this day: a speech full of grandiloquence by Azitawadda to his people, accompanied by a translation in Phoenician allowing the archeologist Helmut Bossert to decipher the Hittite language.

By taking the path on the right you reach the **Upper Gate**, guarded by a majestic **winged sphinx with a human head**** (notice the severity and the beauty of the face). It is surrounded by superb **reliefs**** displaying here and there the king having a meal, being distracted by musicians (a monkey is hidden under the table) and various hunting and fishing scenes. In addition, there are also several winged divinities and a multitude of animal scenes.

The lower gate* – the best preserved – is still flanked by two **lions***. Among the most beautiful **reliefs**** surrounding it, the most noteworthy are: the ship in the port, wrestling scenes, and a woman breast-feeding her child in the shade of a palm tree. On the stone base of the threshold, notice the door's hinge holes.

As you circle the hill through the woods, the path will take you back to the entrance to the site. From there, continue through the park to descend towards Osmaniye (31km). N.B. Road conditions are poor: very bumpy for a long stretch (between fields of cotton), it gives way to a 8km-long rocky track.

Towards İskenderun
Allow about 30min half a day to visit each fortress.

Now we will return to the Armenian period before heading to İskenderun and the 20C. Slightly before Yenikoy and the Osmaniye junction, the road passes at the foot of the ruins of the Armenian fortress of **Hierapolis-Castabala** (13C) perched on a hill.

20km further on, the dark shadow of **Toprak Kalesi*** appears. Entirely made of greyish-brown basalt, it was one of Cilicia's most important castles, built by Armenians during the same period as the preceding one. The enclosure walls are in good condition, but little is left of the courtyard buildings. Through a gap you enter a large vaulted room leading to a long courtyard with several cisterns on the ground*(watch where you place your feet!)*. The high point of the visit is the **watchpath**, which is supported by a series of vaulted rooms (warehouses, stables, etc.), allowing you to circle the ramparts. From there, there is a very beautiful **view*** of the famous **Issos plain** (towards the east), where Alexander the Great defeated Darius III (in 333 BC), opening up the gates to the Orient.

The road heads south towards the sea *(the motorway which is supposed to go to Hatay is not completed yet, but you may take it all the way to İskenderun)*. It crosses the entire industrial area of İskenderun's outskirts, filled with factory chimneys belching black smoke. After İskenderun, the plain grows green again, right up to the gates of Antakya *(Toprakkale-Antakya: 115km)*.

ANTAKYA
(HATAY)
Capital of Hatay Province – Map p 354
193km from Adana – 56km from the Syrian border (towards the south)
Pop 140 700 – Mild climate all year round

Not to be missed
The Mosaic Museum.
The view from the fortress of Antioch
The tunnel of Seleucia Pieria.

And remember...
Visit old Antakya on foot;
the traffic in the maze of alleys is nightmarish!
Have a picnic at the fortress of Antioch: peace and beauty are guaranteed!
For Seleucia Pieria, bring a torch and wear good shoes.

After the steelworks and oil refineries of Dörtyol and İskenderun (where Iraq's Kirkuk oil pipeline terminates), the road climbs slowly up the flanks of the Nur Dağları, a small mountainous range protecting the green plain of Amik. Here begins Hatay, Turkey's southernmost region, imbued with the soul of its neighbour, Syria.

A cosmopolitan region
Southeast of İskendereun, the road crosses the **Belen pass**, a small gap overlooking the sea (beautiful **view***) which the Romans called the **Syrian Gates**. Beyond lies a cosmopolitan province, squeezed between two cultures: a meeting point between the Orient and the Mediterranean basin, which is extremely fertile. Hatay has always been a coveted piece of land, where man and trade have left their mark. In the streets of Antakya, Arabic is as common as Turkish, the cuisine spicier and the religions more diverse. Muslims, Alawites (Turkish Shiites), Jews, Orthodox Christians mingle in an atmosphere which seems happier and more serene than elsewhere in the country. It is truly enchanting.

Syrian or Turkish?
After the collapse of the Ottoman Empire, at the end of the First World War, the province of Antioch was handed to Syria, which was under French rule at the time. Turkey took it back in 1939. However, the Syrians say it belongs to them and continue to show it on their maps! This does not please Turkey. Whatever the case, the province is Turkish and Ankara plans to keep it that way!

Antioch, the ancient Antakya
On the death of Alexander the Great, his lieutenant Seleucus I Nicator undertook to continue Alexander's work and snatched Syria from Persian control. In 301 BC, he founded the port of Seleucia Pieria and Antioch ad Orontes, which he made capital of the young Seleucid Empire. The city rapidly acquired great prosperity thanks to the richness of the soil, its location on the Silk Road and the intense trading activity of the port of Seleucia, which began to rival Alexandria. An opulent and brilliant city, it attracted the attention of all, including the Romans who took control of it in 81BC. Some 500 000 inhabitants strong – twice as many as in Ephesus – Antioch became the main city of

the Roman province of Syria (64 BC) and one of the ancient world's most important cities. Its intellectual life was as effervescent as that of its Egyptian neighbour, and Antioch could not fail to be interested in the advent of Christianity. It became one of its first centres of activity. It is here that St Paul is said to have founded the first Christian community and that the term "Christian" is to have been born in the 1C.

Splendour and decadence – however, the decline of the Roman Empire also led to the downfall of the city, further weakened by violent earthquakes. Antioch fell prey to invaders. The Arabs took it in 638 before ceding it to the Byzantines in 969, who left it to the Crusaders. In 1268, the Mamelukes of Egypt took control and left it in ashes, putting a permanent halt to its splendour. After their passage, the city long remained a field of ruins; Ottomans conquering the area in 1560 ignored it completely. Antioch owes its renaissance to Atatürk and the agricultural development of the region. Although economic activity is mostly concentrated in İskenderun, Antakya – the new Antioch – is today a busy commercial centre, bustling with activity. German and French visitors have been crossing paths here for quite some time, but the city is still not familiar with tourism and its streets remain deeply Oriental. No one knows what tomorrow will bring, so take advantage of the city's precious Eastern flavour.

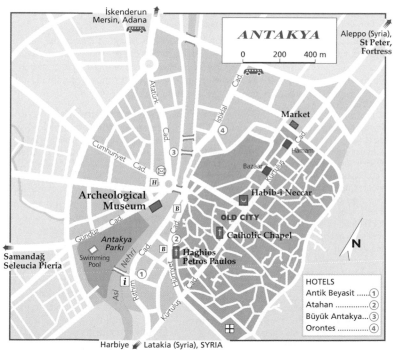

Visiting the city

Allow 3hr. Leave your car in the city centre, near the bridge.

Encased between the steep slopes of the Nur Dağları (to the north) and the Ziyaret Dağı (to the south), facing the green plain of Amik, Antakya stretches along the banks of the ancient Orontes (today's Asi Nehri). The surrounding mountains protect it from the sea winds. The old city is set on the eastern bank, an immense network of small red roofs huddling all the way to the foot of a high cliff, whereas modern Antakya lies on the other bank, facing the fields.

The old city★

A labyrinth of busy alleys, shaded by stately Ottoman or Syrian houses or elegant French buildings, old Antioch overflows with charm. The busy commercial city centre is filled with the aroma of spices, Arabic music, tiny shops inundated with multicoloured materials, and hardware stores submerged with pots and pans, all reminiscent of Oriental souks.

From the bridge, take Hürriyet Cad to Hotel Atahan.

Shortly after the hotel, on the left, a door opens up to a delightful square surrounded by old houses. On the doorsteps, women chat as they peel vegetables, while children play nearby, waiting for the first visitor to come by so that they can scream in unison their best "Hello!". You are immediately charmed by the white **façade★** of the **Haghios Petros Paulos Church★** located on the square. With its large ogee arches, this Syriac Orthodox sanctuary dating from the 19C is reminiscent of a Romanesque villa on an Italian shore. Inside – a delicious harbour of peace – are several beautiful **icons★**.

Return to Hürriyet Cad and turn left to reach Kurtuluş Cad.

On the left, away from the street, stands another sanctuary – Catholic this time – the **Church of the Capuchins** (Katolik Kilise), a pretty chapel with a lovely shaded courtyard *(closed between 12noon and 3pm; daily mass at 5pm in winter, 6pm in summer)*. Further down, you reach the **Habib-i Neccar Camii**, the city's most beautiful mosque (very simple), set inside an ancient 17C **Frankish church**.

Opus tessellatum

Probably invented by the Sumerians and discovered in Mesopotamia, the oldest known mosaics go back to the fourth millennium BC. Consisting of small, coloured clay cones (in red, black and white), set in bitumen or cement, they created all sorts of motifs used to decorate the façades of temples and palaces. The art of mosaics was perfected during the Hellenistic period as a result of the development of pebble floors (Gordion, 8C). Small stone cubes of various colours were made of ceramic or molten glass. However, it was the Romans who gave them their elegant touch, during the Imperial period, when mosaics were used in all buildings, private and public. The art reached its zenith when tiny cubes – as small as 4sqmm! – made it possible to create blended colours as with paint.

The Archeological Museum★★★ (Hatay Müzesi)

Near city hall, 100m from the bridge, on Gündüz Cad. 8.30am-11.30am/ 1.30pm-4.30pm; closed Mondays. Entrance fee.

If you only make one visit in Antalya, go for the museum. It contains the most beautiful objects – jewels, coins, statues, pieces of architecture and, especially, mosaics – brought to light during the excavations in the region in the 1930s.

The first four rooms are dedicated to **mosaics★★★** of impressive dimensions (but don't forget to look at the beautiful statues). They are from neighbouring cities – Tarsus,

G. Degeorge

"Summer", mosaic of the Four Seasons, Antakya Museum

Alexandretta (İskenderun) and Daphne (Harbiye). Created for the most part between the 2C and 4C AD, they illustrate the extraordinary talent of the Roman artists in this field. The majority represent mythological scenes, surrounded by elegant geometric motifs, countless interlaces or figurative friezes.

The first room is mainly occupied by an immense mosaic, with square tableaux representing the **four seasons****. The seasons are portrayed in each corner by small winged figures carrying a different item: a fruit basket (autumn), a bundle of wheat (summer), a flower crown (spring) and lastly a goblet of wine (winter). In between appear several mythological scenes.

In the second room do not miss **Narcissus and Echo***, a bright mosaic with reddish-brown tones. It depicts Narcissus armed with his stick and wearing a shepherd's hat admiring his reflection in the water, encouraged by the rascal Eros.

Room 4, the largest, encloses some of the museum's finest mosaics, **Oceanus and Thetis*** *(on the wall)*, originally part of a huge calendar. Although incomplete, the work is amazingly fine, similar to the art of painting. The two maritime divinities, lifelike and gracious, appear in the middle of shells and fish.

On the ground, the gigantic **Yakto mosaic*** (a site near Daphne) shows a woman (seen in the central medallion) surrounded by a series of hunting scenes.

After the mosaics, admire the beautiful collection of objects dating from the Copper Age to the Persians via the Hittites and the Assyrians. Among the items on display are Hittite basalt **column bases****, decorated with two lions and the very beautiful **Yari-Lim basalt statue*** representing the first known king of the Amorite State of Aleppo. Admire the exquisite Assyrian and Roman **statuettes***, the delicate glass flasks and the Roman heads with realistic features displayed in the last room.

Around Antakya*
Allow at least one day.

Between the great open spaces of the green Amik plain and the steep mountains separating it from the sea, the Antakya region is particularly beautiful. Several astonishing historical sites make for an enjoyable excursion around ancient Antioch.

■ Daphne (Harbiye)

7km south of Antakya. From the city centre, take the road heading for the Syrian border, in the direction of Latakia. The road climbs over the crest of **Ziyaret Dağı***, across some beautiful landscapes. It is in this setting that the ancient **sanctuary of Apollo**, which brought Antioch great fame, once stood. Built on an elevation, among the cypresses, oleanders and the cascades, the temple of Apollo was an important pilgrimage site during the Hellenistic period. Games similar to those of Olympia were often held here. The sanctuary's importance was such that for a while Antioch was known as Epidaphne, the "city close to Daphne."

Daphne's oleander

Apollo, the greatest of seducers, became infatuated with the beautiful Daphne. Unfortunately, she did not respond to the god's charm. To help resist his advances, she asked for her father's help. He had the idea of transforming her into an oleander, Apollo's favourite tree (and one of his symbols, see Didyma, p 326). When the god was about to catch up with Daphne, the nymph transformed herself into a beautiful oleander. The god's honour was unscathed: he wanted a beautiful plant and he got one!

During the Roman era, Daphne became Antioch's garden, its oasis of freshness...and pleasures. The pilgrims made way for the region's wealthy Romans, in search of greenery and frivolity. Palaces sprang up around the temple covered with the most luxurious mosaics (now in the Antakya museum). Tradition has it that Anthony and Cleopatra were married here.

Whatever the case, nothing remains of the great temple of Apollo, and the sumptuous Roman houses which surrounded it have been replaced by many restaurants. Daphne has in fact become the favourite relaxation area for the inhabitants of the region and many Syrians spend their holidays here. The site remains enjoyable but avoid weekends at all costs!

Return to Antakya and take the Altınözü road, towards the northeast.

■ Church of St Peter (Senpiyer Kilisesi) — *about 2km from Antakya. On the road to Altınözü, turn right at the yellow sign. 8.30am-12noon / 1.30pm-4.30pm, closed Mondays. Entrance fee.* After the city of pleasure, make a pious stop at the small Church of St Peter, actually a natural cave. In order to please Pope Pius IX in 1863, the Capuchins decorated it with a pretty oriental-style **façade**. The site is historically renowned because "It was here that the disciples were called Christians first" according to the Scriptures (Acts 11, 26). The cave is believed to have welcomed the first Christian community, founded by Peter, Paul and Barnabas in the year 47. The followers would come to listen clandestinely to the apostles (a tunnel at the end of the cave allowed them to flee in case of danger). Many pilgrims gather here every year and two masses are held every Sunday *(3pm and 4.30pm).* The night of Noah is also celebrated here.

Past the Church of St Peter, continue on the road to Altınözü. Cross the village of Kuruyer, then, after the olive oil factory, turn right and continue for 1km.

■ The Antioch fortress*

Perched at the top of a tall, rocky peak, the ruins of this Byzantine fortress overlook the entire Amik plain and the valley of the Orontes. The **panorama**** is absolutely magnificent. The site is mainly of interest for the view; Nicephorus II Phocas' 10C building is in a sad state of repair. The walk along the ruined ramparts is nevertheless very enjoyable because of the beauty of the site, the fresh air and the relative peace and quiet. If it is time to eat, take out the feta and the tomatoes.

Returning to Antakya, turn off towards the southwest.

Towards the sea

Following the course of the River Asi to its mouth, the road crosses beautiful **scenery***, overlooking the Asi valley encased between the high slopes of the mountain. It passes at the foot of **Samandağ** -"Mount Simeon" – at the top of which the hermit St Simeon Stylites isolated himself before preaching in the entire region. Finally, we reach the village of **Samandağ** *(28km from Antakya)*, drowning among the berry bushes, olive, orange, fig, and lemon trees which blend their aromatic fragrances. A jungle of fruit! Beyond, the sea is fringed by a long beach (unfortunately spoiled by a large group of holiday homes). The area is highly coveted by the local residents, Turks and Syrian alike, who come to spend their weekends or vacations. Unfortunately, the entire coastline is polluted and the beach quite dirty.

Rather than risk bathing, head for Seleucia Pieria, Antioch's ancient port (skirt the beach towards the north, for 6km, until you reach the hamlet of Çevlik).

■ **Seleucia Pieria*** At the mouth of the Orontes, Seleucia Pieria was founded at the same time as Antioch by Seleucus I Nicator *(see history of Antakya above)*. Other than a few meagre vestiges of the ramparts along the beach, almost nothing is left of the warehouses, the dockyard and the markets which made this port so prosperous. The site's interest lies at the foot of the mountain. Climbing towards the cliff overlooking the lower city *(well- indicated concrete stairs)*,

Simeon's mountain

It is in Antioch that St Simeon Stylites was buried, in the 5C, after having spent more than 40 years of his life praying at the top of Mount Simeon – Samandağ – and preaching Christ's word all over the region, perched atop a column (see sidebar, p 331). Towards 520, his most loyal disciple, St Simeon the Younger, in turn ascended Mt Simeon to pray. Two churches, ravaged by successive earthquakes, cap the mountain's summit.

you reach the entrance of a narrow **tunnel**** carved in a pyramidal shape right in the heart of the mountain. Partially enclosed and partially exposed to the sky, it continues for 250m, literally splitting the mountain in two. This stupefying work was conceived during Vespasian's era (79 AD) to supply the city with water and in particular to channel the river whose level could at times be dangerous.

As soon as you enter the first very short tunnel, you feel tiny *(beware of the dripping water making the rocks slippery)*. The outside light barely reaches the depths, and above your head, the two sides of the canal, as smooth as walls, tower towards the sky until they touch. At the end, light and greenery await. The canal, a simple trench in the ground, continues in the open air for an additional 80m, before disappearing once again into the rock, for a length of 140m and a height of 7m. Breathtaking!

Northwest of the tunnel lies the necropolis, also carved out of the mountain. In the middle of the brush and greenery lie two **rock tombs** decorated with bas-reliefs, as well as a church – **Beşikli Kilise***– carved out of a single block in the mass of a cliff. The narthex faces the exterior by way of three arches with columns eroded by time; several tombs have been dug in the ground.

Beyond the second section of the tunnel, you reach the foot of **Musadağı** – Mt Pieria – which can be skirted by following the dry riverbed. It is a wonderful opportunity for a walk among the rocks, the bushes, tall grass and wild olive trees where goats roam. Higher up in the mountain you will find the remains of the **dam** which controlled the flow of the river.

COMING AND GOING

By bus – **The bus station** is 5km from the centre, on the road to Mersin, ☎ (326) 214 91 97. Services depart here for all the main destinations, including Adana (3hr journey), Gaziantep, Ankara, İstanbul, and Aleppo (105km away). There is also a dolmuş shuttle service to Harbiye. **Has Tourizm**, Atatürk Cad, ☎ (326) 216 21 45 / 216 21 46. Connections to Ankara, İstanbul, Mersin, Antalya, İzmir, Marmaris, Taşucu, Çanakkale, Bursa, Konya and Trabzon.

Airline company – **İstanbul Hava Yolları** (İstanbul Airlines), Atatürk Cad 56, ☎ (326) 216 36 01 / 02, Fax (326) 216 36 03.

ADDRESS BOOK

Tourist information office – Vali Ürgen Alanı 47, at the roundabout to the north of Atatürk Cad, ☎ (326) 891 126 36. 8am-5pm, closed at weekends. Note: following the summer 1999 earthquake, this office was requisitioned for the collection of relief supplies for the disaster victims, and the office has been temporarily moved to a building adjoining the Prefecture (Valilik), in Hükümet Cad. It was still there at the date of publication of this guide.

Main post office – In the square in front of the museum, 8.30am-12.30pm / 1.30pm-5.30pm. Telephone and currency exchange.

Bank / change – **Akbank**, in Atatürk Cad. **Ziraat Bankası**, opposite the museum. Cash dispenser at **İş Bankası**, Hürriyet Cad, opposite the Han restaurant. **Döviz** currency exchange in İstiklâl Cad, 20m from the Orontes hotel.

WHERE TO STAY

There is not much choice in Antakya itself. 3 hotels are adequate but a little expensive. You can stay in guest houses for under US$15, but the standard of comfort and cleanliness is far from perfect.

Between US$15 and US$30

Hotel Atahan, Hürriyet Cad 28, ☎ (326) 214 21 40, Fax (326) 215 80 06 – 42rm. ⚞ ♪ 🍽 ✕ In the old town. It's

a pity that it's all rather dusty. It does, however, offer a very acceptable level of comfort, especially considering the town's hotel infrastructure. Avoid the rooms on the top floor, which are like a furnace in summer. The restaurant is simple and good and is one of the most popular places to eat in Antakya.

Hotel Orontes, İstiklâl Cad 58, ☎ (326) 214 59 31 32, Fax (326) 214 59 33 – 35rm. ⚞ 🍽 ✕ CC Car park. The best value for money. English, German and Arabic are spoken here and the welcome is very warm. It is all very clean. Try to book at least 5 days ahead.

Around US$75

Hotel Büyük Antakya, Atatürk Cad 8, ☎ (326) 213 58 60, Fax (326) 213 58 69. ⚞ ♪ TV 🍽 ✕ Car park, bar, discotheque. Very chic but expensive. The hotel belongs to one of the major hotel chains in the country and is very comfortable but lacking in character.

Antik Beyazıt Hotel, Hükümet Cad 4, ☎ (326) 216 29 00, Fax (326) 214 30 89 – 27rm. ⚞ ♪ 🍽 ✕ 🍷 CC Minibar. After being tastefully restored, this early 20C former konak (lavish Ottoman residence), opened in January 1999. Wood, carpets, large armchairs and mirrors make for a refined and warm decor. The ground-floor rooms have a mezzanine.

EATING OUT

The specialities of Antakya have a rather Syrian flavour; such as the "hummus", chickpea purée seasoned with sesame oil, lemon juice and parsley, or the "içli köfte", small elongated pastries stuffed with minced meat, crushed nuts and onions. Even the meze have a more oriental flavour and are, in other words, more spicy. Also, why not try the "çökelek", a salad made with dried yoghurt, tomatoes, cucumber, parsley and chillies. And to cool down, there is nothing quite like a "limonlu dondurma", lime-flavoured sherbet sold in small glasses in the streets, to be eaten on the spot. The best restaurants are in the vicinity of **Hürriyet Caddesi**:

Hotel Atahan, mentioned above. A good, typical restaurant.

Han, opposite the Atahan hotel. Hürriyet Cad 19, ☎ (326) 215 85 38. Its terrace and shaded inner courtyard with fountain are welcome indeed in the hot season. Good meze and traditional "Adana Kebaps" are served here.

• In Harbiye

The site is teeming with restaurants and cafés where the tourists mingle with the inhabitants of Antakya who come here to have a drink in the evening. Good fish and meat dishes are served in flower-covered arbours on the river bank. Among these restaurants is the renowned *Şelâle*, near the waterfall. Many of these establishments also serve as "gazino" in the evening.

Boğaziçi, Defne Mah Ürgen Cad Şelâle Karşısı, ☎ (326) 231 49 33. One of the last restaurants at the end of the village, on the right, with a large terrace on the riverbank. Regional fish specialities and meze. *Hidro*, Çağlayan Mah, ☎ (326) 231 40 06. Although this restaurant is reputedly more chic than the others, you will find the same dishes here as elsewhere. The difference is in the setting.

HAVING A DRINK

The tea rooms which line Atatürk Cad are highly prized by the inhabitants who come here for a drink with their families at the end of the day. The delicious sherbet attracts all the young locals, and the vendor opposite the Büyük Oteli, *Edem*, is a particular favourite.

Internet café – *Prestige*, Hürriyet Cad 1/3, 1/ kat, ☎ (326) 213 58 09. Open until midnight every day. US$2 per hour. Also has several billiard tables.

OTHER THINGS TO DO

Turkish bath – *Saka Hamam*, in the market, at the junction between Saka Sok and Tayfur Sökmen Cad (Akbaba Mah district). A very old traditional Turkish bath, which has been standing for two centuries. For women: 12noon-6pm. For men: 5am-12noon. Very cheap (US$1).

Beaches – You can go to Samandağ, 28km southwest of Antakya, but the beach is not very clean.

SHOPPING GUIDE

Arts and crafts – In the old part of Antakya, you will find everything you could possibly want in the stalls or at the market (on Tuesdays): sponges, spices, oriental pastries etc. The regional speciality is laurel-perfumed soap, but you will also find a selection of colourful wickerwork and lovely cotton and silk fabric. In the villages around *Samandağ*, in particular, the traditional silkworm industry is still very much alive. And don't forget to buy some of the excellent dates (in October) before you leave.

B. Brillion/MICHELIN

Women of Anatolia in traditional colours

CENTRAL ANATOLIA

Between the Taurus and the massifs of the Pontic chain stretches the Anatolian plateau, an immense steppe at an altitude of 1 000m. It is dotted with lakes with turquoise waters and strewn with volcanoes and bare hills. For miles on end, it is an arid ochre-coloured land without boundaries, changing like the sea beneath the clouds and sun. It is here on this austere and almost deserted plateau that the most ancient civilisations of Anatolia blossomed; nine millennia of history, from the first stones of Çatal Höyük – the world's oldest city – to the capital of the young Turkish nation, proud **Ankara**. Hattians, Hittites, Assyrian merchants, Phrygians and Persians succeeded each other; it is here also, in **Gordion**, in the heart of this land, that Alexander the Great cut the legendary Gordian knot which gave him access to the gates of the Orient. Crossed by the great caravan routes, the centre of Anatolia was from then on and for many hundreds of years, the scene of fruitful exchange between Persia and the Aegean.

Today, it is in Ankara that the most beautiful objects of this long history have been assembled, fragments from the life of some of the world's oldest peoples. From here, the traveller can set out to explore the traces of the Hattians and Hittites, from the royal tombs of **Alaca Höyük** to the stone lions of the **Boğazkale** ramparts, by way of the superb rock carvings of **Yazılıkaya**.

Sivas gives an insight into the Seljuk world. Fine tracery, stars and stalactites grace the portals of all of the city's mosques and medrese, evoking the opulence of faraway Persia.

The Orient is found in the west, all the way to **Konya**, capital of the Seljuk sultanate of Rum and a staging-post for many great caravans; Konya the spiritual, the city of the Whirling Dervishes who danced with arms upraised between heaven and earth.

Further west, in the middle of the mountains, relaxation can be found on the peaceful, flowering shores of **Lake Eğirdir** before you explore **Sagalassus**, a brilliant city of ancient Pisidia, high among the peaks.

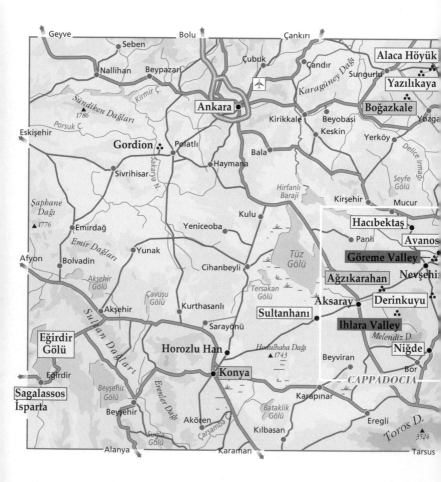

To the east is Cappadocia, an enclave in the heart of the plateau, filled with fabulous landscapes and an extraordinary Byzantine heritage (*the region is described in another section, p 547*).

Towards the banks of the Euphrates, finally, the desert appears, filled with mirages. Like a giant stela laid between Anatolia and ancient Persia, the tumulus of **Nemrut Dağı** flaunts its giant statues above the mountains, one set towards the east, the other towards the west, golden cones placed in the middle of nowhere.

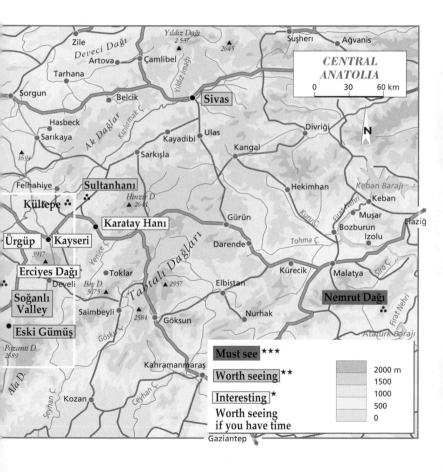

CENTRAL ANATOLIA

0   30   60 km

Must see ★★★
Worth seeing ★★
Interesting ★
Worth seeing if you have time

2000 m
1500
1000
500
0

KONYA★★

Provincial Capital – Map p 496
148km from Aksaray – 250km from Ankara – 215km from Nevşehir
Pop 964 000 – Alt 1 026m

Not to be missed
The Mevlana tekke (Dervish lodge) and the medrese (now museums),
in particular, the ceramics museum.
A stroll in the bazaar, seldom visited by tourists.

And remember...
The city is "conservative". Wear proper attire: trousers or long skirts.

Isolated in the heart of the Anatolian plateau, Konya is a pleasant place, less austere than its reputation as a holy and mystical city might have one believe. Nevertheless, no miniskirts here; the headscarf is the rule, since this cradle of the Whirling Dervishes remains a bastion of conservative-minded people. The area surrounding the city is growing rapidly and is being covered with nondescript buildings; but the old city centre is full of Seljuk monuments.

The Konya region is also Turkey's breadbasket. In the last few decades, the steppes and the goats have made way for farmland, and what was a near-desert, has become a kind of oasis.

Mevlana "our master"
Faced with the Mongol invasion, the Sufi master, Bahaeddin Valad, left his ancestral home on the borders of Persia and Afghanistan, to settle in Konya in the 13C. His son, Celaleddin-i Rumi (1207-1273), became a reputed theologian. At the age of 37, he met a Wandering Dervish, Shams of Tabriz, who initiated him into Sufi mysticism and inspired him to establish a Dervish brotherhood. Celaleddin-i founded the first monastery ("tekke") and his charisma immediately had his disciples calling him "Mevlana" (our master). Recognised as a great poet of mystical ecstasy, he is the author of a considerable body of work written in Farsi (Persian), including the famous "Masnavi", composed of 45 000 verses. After his death, Sultan Veled reorganised the brotherhood and created the order of the "Mevlevi" (Whirling Dervishes) which went to claim followers in all of Anatolia, Syria and even faraway Egypt. The order was dissolved by Atatürk in 1925.

Seljuk capital
Inhabited and invaded since the Bronze Age, Konya became successively Hittite, Phrygian, Lydian, Persian, then Roman (under the name of "Iconium"). In 50 AD, St Paul and St Barnabas passed through it on their way to evangelise Asia Minor. The city reached its apogee at the end of the 11C, when it became the capital of the Seljuk sultanate of **Rum**. It was during this prosperous period that the order of the Whirling Dervishes was founded, to which the city owes much of its fame. Invaded at the end of the 13C by the Mongols, its prosperity declined after it was annexed to the Ottoman Empire in 1466.

The city
Allow one day. If you only have half a day,
visit the Mevlana Museum, the Karatay Medrese and the İnce Minare Medrese.

The Mevlana Museum★★ (D2)
9am-6pm, 10am-6pm on Mondays. Entrance fee.

At the end of Mevlana Caddesi, next to the Selimiye mosque, appears the superb green **dome★★** of the *tekke* of Mevlana, a fluted cone entirely covered with tiles. It houses the tombs of the holy man and his successors, making this monastery one of Turkey's

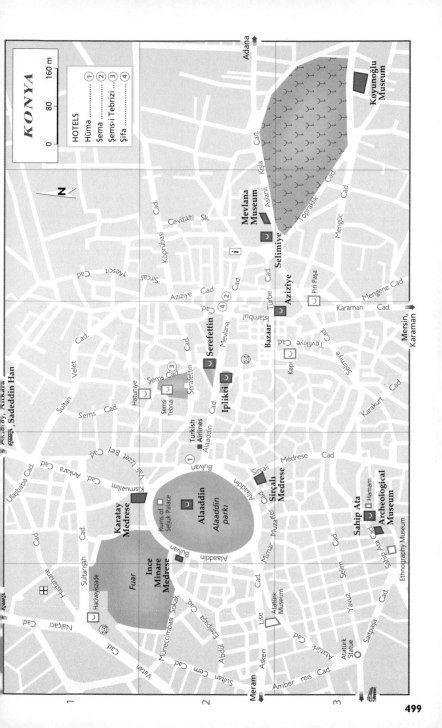

KONYA

	0	80	160 m

HOTELS
Hüma .... ①
Sema .... ②
Şems-i Tebrizi ... ③
Şifa .... ④

N

Adana

Koyunoğlu Museum

Kışla Cad.

Cad.

Aslanli

Mevlana Museum

Toprablik

Menguc Cad.

Selimiye

Cevizalti Sk.

Köprübasi

Mescit Cad.

Sircali Cad.

Aziziye Cad.

i

Türbe Cad.

Aziziye

Piri Paşa

Mengene Cad.

Karaman Cad.

Mersin, Karaman

Serefettin

② ④

Istanbul Cad.

Mevlana Cad.

Bazaar

Kapi

Tevfikiye Cad.

Selimiye Cad.

Karakurt Cad.

Iplikci

Sems Cad.

③

Hatuniye

Semsi Tebrizi

Serafettin Cad.

Cad.

Velet

Sultan

Sems Cad.

Cad.

Akören, Ankara
Sadeddin Han

Ulasbaba Cad.

Ankara Cad.

Vali Izzet Bey Cad.

Kısmullam

Turkish Airlines

Alaaddin Bulvarı

①

Alaaddin

Sircali Cad.

Alaaddin

Sircali Medrese

Médrese Cad

Karatay Medrese

Ruins of Seljuk Palace

Alaaddin parkı

Alaaddin Bulvarı

Minar Muzaffer Cad.

Sultanşah Cad.

Fuar

Ince Minare Medrese

Hacıveyiszade

Ezelpaşa Cad.

Münecimbasi Sokak

Sultan Cem Cad.

Abdül

Atatürk Museum

Lise

Askeri

Atatürk Cad.

Amber reis Cad.

Meram

Hastahane

Nalçacı Cad.

Vatan Cad.

Selim Cad.

Yavuz Cad.

Sahip Ata Cad.

Ethnography Museum

Sahip Ata

Hamam

Archeological Museum

Saltpaşa Cad.

Atatürk Statue

499

Sufi dance and music

In order to become a Dervish, novices had to undergo austere training lasting 1 001 days. Then they could concentrate on praying under the supervision of the master. For their meditation, the Sufi monks would immerse themselves in music. For the Whirling Dervishes this became the obligatory accompaniment for their dance, the "sema", which mimics the movements of the celestial bodies: dressed entirely in white, the monks begin to spin slowly, with the right hand upraised towards the sky, and the left hand towards the ground. This is accompanied by the insistent music of the "ney", an open-tube reed flute with a monotonous sound, or by an orchestra composed of various instruments: the "rebap", a gourd viol, the "küdüm", a double drum, the "kemence", a small violin, the "halile" and the "tef" (cymbals), the "ud" (lute) and the "tambur", a guitar with a long neck.

most venerated pilgrimage sites. Although it was transformed into a museum in 1953, the Mevlana *tekke* has remained a place of worship for the faithful; you must therefore remove your shoes before entering. Also, suitable clothing is required (women must don a headscarf).

The mausoleum is located at the back of an elegant **inner courtyard**, with its **ablutions fountain**. On the right, the monks' cells and kitchens are housed in a series of elegant small buildings with domes and chimneys dating from the Seljuk period. To the left is the *sema* hall (the Dervishes' ritual dance) and the mosque, both built in the 16C by Süleyman the Magnificent.

Once your shoes have been removed and left under the porch, you enter the **mausoleum**** antechamber, with its beautiful walnut doors with silver plaques (16C). The **cenotaphs*** of the master's disciples stand in line, bathed in dim light. At the back, those of the Mevlana and his son, are protected by a beautiful silver grille. Each is covered by a thick gold-

Konya: the Mevlana *tekke*, the sanctuary of the Whirling Dervishes

embroidered **brocade**, on top of which the head-dress has been placed, like a stela. Overhead is an elegant painted wood **dome**. Pilgrims from all walks of life gather with their families in front of the cenotaphs, their palms upraised, moving about in silence in a muffled atmosphere, the sound of footsteps absorbed by thick carpets. Once their respects are paid, they have their picture taken near the ablutions fountain.

Covered by a tall dome, the **sema hall** has several objects belonging to the Dervishes: Sufi musical instruments, clothing, four **mosque lamps** (14C) from Egypt, and beautiful carpets including a 15C *usak*. On the right, **manuscripts** of the *Masnavi* written by the Mevlana can be seen, along with a large **copper tub**, inlaid with gold and silver. This beautiful container was used as a stoop (font): April rain, thought to be miraculous, was gathered and distributed to the faithful.

The **mosque's*** prayer hall *(to reach it, cross the mausoleum antechamber)*, a beautiful area punctuated by tall broken arches, encloses superb **illuminated Korans*** and beautiful **silk prayer rugs**. People meditate in front of a display case containing small wooden **box** with mother-of-pearl. The box contains a few precious hairs from the beard of the Prophet.

On the other side of the courtyard, the kitchens and the monks' cells house a small **ethnography museum** with a beautiful array of Ottoman brocades and carpets. Other rooms show various items used by a Dervish, such as a container for alms. In addition there are reconstructions of a monk's cell and the superior's quarters.

Across the city

On leaving the *tekke*, to the left, is the **Selimiye Camii***, a mosque built in the 16C by Selim II. Its two slim minarets and its vast prayer hall with dome are fine examples of classic Ottoman architecture: great size and a central plan.

At the roundabout, go along Türbe Caddesi.

The **Aziziye Camii** (C3) is a 19C mosque whose Baroque lines evoke the Rococo kiosks of the end of the Ottoman Empire. This building is unusual in a city dominated by Seljuk art. Right behind is the busy **bazaar** (C2-3). In a modern shopping gallery, the *konfeksiyon* shops for women supply local ready-to-wear fashions: long grey, beige or mauve coats which are brightened by printed scarves. Next door is a maze of streets where the local people come to purchase shoes, bags, school uniforms, jewellery etc.

The Konya "look"

Beyond the bazaar, to the right, is the **İplikçi Cami** (C2), a sober brick mosque (13C). Alaaddin Caddesi leads to the park of the same name.

Alaaddin Park (B2)

This vast public garden covers an entire hill in the heart of the city. It is overlooked by the minaret of the **Alaaddin Mosque*** (Alaaddin Camii) (B2) *(8.30am-6pm)*. The mosque is Konya's oldest, completed during the reign of Sultan Alaaddin Keykubat in 1221. An elegant polychrome marble **portal** enhances the austere façade. In the hypostyle prayer hall, the 42 **columns*** are surmounted by reused Roman and Byzantine capitals. A beautiful carved wood **minbar** can be seen as well. Beyond the prayer hall is the inner courtyard with two mausoleums housing cenotaphs of the Seljuk sultans.

Further down, in the park, a concrete structure protects a modest fragment of **wall**, all that remains of the Seljuk sultans' **winter palace**. It was inhabited until the 17C by the Ottoman governors, but an earthquake destroyed it in 1907.

Konya's medreses★

Just to the north of the park is the **Karatay Medrese**★★ (B1-2), one of Konya's most beautiful Seljuk Koranic schools (*9am-12noon/1.30pm-5.30pm; closed Mondays. Entrance fee*). Built in 1251 by the Emir Celaleddin Karatay, it is as interesting for its architecture as it is for the **Ceramics Museum** which it houses. A sober and majestic **portal★** of polychrome marble, decorated with fine twisted colonnettes, *muqarnas* and interlace faces an inner courtyard. At the back is a large room surmounted with a 12m-diameter **cupola★★★**, attached to the walls by four pendentives made up of five triangles. The names of the early prophets and caliphs appear in Kufic-style characters, while a chapter of the Koran runs along the drum of the cupola. The walls of the rooms and the *iwan* are covered with **ceramics★** creating magnificent interlaces in turquoise-blue and black tones.

In the room to the left of the entrance see the very beautiful **ceramic tiles★★** which decorated the walls of the sultan's summer palace, in Kubadabad, on the shores of Lake Beyşehir. Animals, figures with Asian features and hunting scenes, all finely executed, appear in star- or cross-shaped frames. This visualisation of the human being, rare in Muslim art, is a reminder that the Turks came from Asia (*see p 62*). Lastly, in the room next door, the cenotaph of the medrese's founder can be seen.

Going round Alaaddin Park towards the İnce Minare, you skirt the "Fuar", an exhibition hall and amusement fairground which is extremely popular with local people.

The portal of the Karatay medrese, Seljuk Konya

G. Degeorge

Central Anatolia

Another medrese that has been transformed into a museum is the İnce Minare Medrese★ (Slender Minaret) (B2) today housing the **Museum of Wood and Stone Carving** *(9am-12noon/1.30pm-5.30pm; closed Mondays. Entrance fee)*. The medrese owes its name *(ince* means "slim") to the elegant **minaret★** of glazed blue tiles, detached from the building. Before lightning struck it to the ground at the beginning of the 20C, it rose elegantly skyward. The luxuriously decorated and magnificent **portal★★★** is characteristic of Seljuk art in the second half of the 13C, influenced by Iranian art spread by the Mongols. Mixed into the geometric patterns, two large bands of Koran verses run along each side of the door, interlacing and rising up to the cornice, a superb example of calligraphy.

The medrese has the same plan as the Karatay Medrese, the main room being covered by a pretty brick **dome★** decorated with glazed tiles in blue, turquoise and black.

On the walls, the engravings evoke the 13C fortress (only a small portion of the wall remains in Alaaddin Park). The carved **stelae★** with human and animal figures – lions, winged genies, dragons and other chimaeras – came from the main gate of the fortress. The room to the left of the *iwan* has a collection of Seljuk period **wood engravings.**

South of Alaaddin Park hill, the **Sırçalı Medrese★** (B2) is also worth a visit *(8.30am-12noon/1.30pm-5.30pm, closed Sundays. Entrance fee)*. Another 13C Seljuk Koranic school, it is today the **Museum of Funerary Monuments**. Its architecture is more interesting than the Seljuk and Ottoman tombstones it displays. Beyond the **portal★**, richly decorated as usual, is an **iwan** which has retained some of its superb **tiles★★** with geometric turquoise and black patterns.

Nearby, you will be able to see the remains of the **Sahip Ata Camii** (B3), a mosque which was part of a large religious complex built in the 13C. Only the magnificent **portal★★** and one of the two fluted **minarets** are still standing. The cylinder of the minaret is decorated with bricks and glazed in blue and white, creating graceful interlace, and geometric patterns. The original building (with both minarets) must have been the pride of the city.

The Archeology Museum (B3) *(9am-12noon/1.30pm-5.30pm, closed Mondays. Entrance fee. Begin the visit with the room at the back to follow the chronological order. Explanations in Turkish)* is next door, on the left. Among the objects of interest on display are terracotta vases and obsidian objects from the Neolithic site of Çatal Höyük (60km from Konya), a terracotta **bathtub** found in Kara Höyük, going back to the period of the Assyrian colonies (1950 BC) and a white marble **Roman sarcophagus** representing the Twelve Labours of Hercules. The demigod is shown ageing, with his beard growing as the scenes progress.

If there is still time, a tour of Konya can be completed with a visit to **Koyunoğlu Museum** (E3) *(8am-12noon/1.30pm-5pm. Entrance fee. Explanations in Turkish)*, a modern building with several collections that were bequeathed to the city by one of its wealthy inhabitants. It is more a collection of oddities than a museum: minerals, fossils, and Bronze Age objects are flanked by stuffed animals and old pictures of Konya. The ethnographic section includes a beautiful collection of carpets; but the highlight is the **Turkish House** *(next door; the guardian will open the door)*, a superb 19C Ottoman residence, still decorated with woodwork and mural paintings giving a fascinating insight into how an upper class Konya family lived in this period.

Konya

Around Konya

24km to the east, on the Konya-Aksaray road, the **Sadeddin caravanserai*** (Sadeddin Han) appears in the immensity of the steppe (*it is reached from the main road, by a little turning on the left*). This 13C Seljuk *han* has remained isolated and has retained its majestic austerity. The **portal**, an unusual combination of dark basalt with white marble, is the only decorative feature of the exterior, in great contrast with the sobriety of the walls. Inside, the large rectangular courtyard is surrounded by a series of small rooms, while a vast **hall***, on the left, is embellished by four rows of large pillars.

Making the most of Konya

COMING AND GOING

By air – Just one destination from Konya: İstanbul. Three flights per week, on Mondays, Wednesdays and Fridays.

By train – The station is out of town, to the east of Konya. A bus runs to the station from Alaaddin Cad in the town centre. Information and reservations: ☎ (332) 322 36 70. Konya is on the İstanbul-Mardin line (to the east). A night train with couchettes links Konya to İstanbul in 12hr.

By bus – The "otogar" is 3km north of the town centre in the direction of Ankara. You can easily get there by dolmuş from Alaaddin Cad. Several companies operate services all over Turkey, and **Kontur's** double-decker buses to İstanbul, Ankara and İzmir have a no-smoking deck, which is a real godsend. Buses run to the main cities in Turkey every day: Adana (7hr), Ankara (3hr), Antalya (6hr), Bursa (7hr), İstanbul (10hr) and İzmir (7hr).

GETTING AROUND

The main sights are concentrated in a relatively small area, which means that they can easily be visited on foot.

By taxi – Yellow taxis cruise the town. A ride will cost you around US$2 on average.

By shared taxi – Many stops are indicated by a "D" sign in Atatürk Cad and Mevlana Cad.

By rental car – **Avis**, Nalçacı Cad 29 Mayıs Sitesi 39/C, ☎ (332) 236 14 86. 8.30am-7pm.

ADDRESS BOOK

Tourist information – Next to the Mevlana Tekke, Mevlana Cad 21 (D2), ☎ (332) 351 10 74. Open in summer from Monday to Saturday, 8am-5pm. Closed at lunchtimes and on Saturdays in winter. Friendly welcome.

Bank / change – The banks are located in Mevlana Cad (C2, D2). Open Monday to Friday, 8.30am-12.30pm / 1.30pm-5pm. Foreign currency can also be exchanged in the hotels, but the rate is not as good.

Main post office – In Hükümet Meyd (C2). Open every day, 8.30am-7pm. Telephone service available 24 hours a day. Many card-operated phone booths are lined up outside the post office.

Airline company – **Turkish Airlines** (B2) has offices on the 1st floor at Mevlana Cad 7/106, ☎ (332) 351 20 00.

WHERE TO STAY

Between US$25 and US$30
Hotel Sema, Mevlana Cad 15, ☎ (332) 350 46 23, Fax (332) 352 35 21 – 50rm. ⌂ ℘ TV ✕ cc A good, simple and clean hotel in the main avenue. A good, cheap place to stay.

Between US$30 and US$45
⌂ **Hotel Şems-i Tebrizi**, Şems Cad 10, ☎ (332) 350 57 38, Fax (332) 351 17 71 – 32rm. ⌂ ℘ TV Immaculate, bright little rooms, right in the town centre. Good welcome. Best value for money.
Hotel Şifa, Mevlana Cad 55, ☎ (332) 350 42 90, Fax (332) 351 92 51 – 30rm. ⌂ ℘ TV ✕ cc A good hotel, with no particular charm, but in a very good location.

Over US$45

Hotel Hüma, Çifte Merdiven Mah Alaaddin Bul 8, ☎ (332) 350 63 89, Fax (332) 351 02 44 – 30rm. ⁂ ℘ TV ✗ CC Very good welcome in a rather garish oriental decor. The rooms are spacious and bright.

EATING OUT

• **In town**

Between US$5 and US$8

Halil Ibrahim Sofrası (D2), to the left of the Mevlana Tekke: Mevlana Cad Katlı Otopark Bitişiği 9, ☎ (332) 352 72 26. A little restaurant which doesn't look very appealing, but you really should taste its "fırın kebab", mutton, which is rather like a confit, and served by weight. Truly delicious. No alcohol. Open every day; closed in the evening and during Ramadan.

Damla, Hükümet Alanı Şahin Oteli Altı 5, ☎ (332) 351 37 05. Set back from the street, behind the Sahin hotel. Traditional Turkish fare in a smoke-filled masculine atmosphere.

Köşk (D3), Akçeşme Mah Topraklık Cad 66, ☎ (332) 352 85 47. 15min on foot from the Mevlana Tekke, when going towards the Koyunoğlu Museum. Good traditional cuisine served in an old house. Frequented by businessmen. No alcohol.

• **Out of town**

5km to the north, on the road to Ankara, the 13C **Horozlu caravanserai** (Horozlu Han) has been restored and now houses a restaurant.

OTHER THINGS TO DO

Turkish bath – Sultan Hamamı (B3), Uzunharmanlar Cad, on the side of Sahip Ata Camii. A real neighbourhood establishment. Noon-midnight for men; 8am-6pm for women.

Whirling Dervishes Festival – From 10 to 17 December, in commemoration of the death of Mevlana. This event takes place in a covered stadium. In the future, the Dervishes may also perform in summer. Further details can be obtained from the tourist information office.

SHOPPING GUIDE

Market – Very colourful vegetable market behind the bazaar, towards the Archeology Museum.

Antiques and carpets – Galeri Selçuk (D2), Mevlana Cad 53/D, ☎ (332) 351 50 36. Beautiful carpets and silver goods. There are other boutiques on the same side of the street, opposite the carpet bazaar.

Bazaar – It is very pleasant just to stroll around this shopping district, where you will come across the wooden spoons used as musical instruments in the region's folklore.

Making the most of Konya

LAKE EĞIRDIR★
ISPARTA

Eğirdir: 183km from Antalya, 208km from Denizli, 268km from Konya
Map p 496 – Alt: 916m – Mild climate (annual average 13°C)

Not to be missed
The sunset on the lake. The view from the Sagalassus site.
And remember...
The countryside is deeply attached to its traditions:
respect local mores and avoid being skimpily clad in town.
Wear sturdy shoes to visit Sagalassus.

Ancient **Pisidia** is a region of lakes, a multitude of blue patches on the country's map. The lake waters are ever-changing: turquoise, or deep blue, turning suddenly to indigo or cloudy grey, or gold when the sun bursts over the jagged crest of the surrounding mountains. The lakes of Pisidia are mirrors, reflecting the sky and the snow-capped peaks of the 3 000m Taurus Mountains all around.

The lake of roses

There are regions that inspire tranquillity. This is the case of Lake Eğirdir (*Eğirdir Gölü*), undoubtedly one of Turkey's most beautiful. At an altitude of more than 900m, it traces a large S between the mountains, stretching for a length of 48km and barely 10km in width. With a surface area of 517sq km, it is Turkey's fourth largest lake, sitting astride several provinces. It is an important fresh water reservoir irrigating the surrounding fields, feeding the rivers and supplying the region's hydro-electric power stations.

Here, the air is pure, bathed with the fragrance of the famous Isparta roses which carpet the shores of the lake and caress the mountain's slopes. It is possible to swim in the lake's cool waters, take a boat ride, wind-surf, fish for bass or crayfish in the company of a fisherman or relax on the shores surrounded by lovely beaches and villages. A choice site for a relaxing holiday, if simple accommodation is acceptable, since in Eğirdir and Isparta, it is mostly limited to family-run inns and guest houses. This means sharing something of the local, very rural, way of life, getting to know the people and understanding and respecting their customs.

Eğirdir★
Allow half a day.

A small town with 17 000 people, Eğirdir developed at the southern tip of the lake, at the foot of Davas Dağı (2 635m). It stands on a small promontory pointing to a small islet – **Yeşilada** – linked to the mainland by a causeway. There are two things which immediately strike the visitor to Eğirdir: on one side, the lake, a huge limpid stretch of water, on the other, the word *Komando* written in gigantic letters on the mountain. This refers to the elite unit of the Turkish army which has a base here, and which gives the town a distinctly military flavour.

But it is still a quiet sort of place, in the centre, with its lovely reminders of Seljuk customs. Women continue to weave kilims with patterns they inherited from the Yörük, the nomads who still haunt the Taurus. A few old houses have resisted the passage of time among the *pansiyons* which seem to flourish everywhere. **Yeşilada**, especially, has become their stronghold. A little floating garden island in the middle of the lake, it is the ideal place to stay while exploring the region's sights.

Eğirdir rather than Eğridir

Little is left of the rich Roman Prostanna – an important staging post on the royal way between Ephesus and Babylon. The ancient city (yet to be excavated) was on the slopes of Davas Dağı, close to today's *Komando* camp! The site of today's city is due to the Byzantines who migrated to the shores of the lake. Prostanna lost out to Akrotiri ("steep mountain", in Greek), which became an important bishopric. In 1080 it was named capital of a small Seljuk emirate founded by the Hamidoğulları, a wealthy family responsible for most of the city's main buildings.

After the Ottomans conquered it in 1417, Akrotiri became Eğridir, the "dishonest". The name was not appreciated by its inhabitants who fought to have it changed...and were able to do so only 10 years ago: a subtle shift in its spelling, Eğridir became Eğirdir, the name of a small flower. The town's new name is well-earned since it is abloom every spring with roses and apple trees. Along with fishing, they are the region's most important resources.

A Seljuk city

While today's Eğirdir stretches along several kilometres of the lake shore, only the town centre, facing the islet of Yeşilada, has much of interest. Of its prestigious Seljuk past, Eğirdir retains a beautiful mosque, the **Hızır Bey Cami**, built by Emir Hızır Bey in the 14C within the confines of a 13C Seljuk depot. Notice the building's beautiful **wooden doors****, carved with much finesse. The minaret still has its original blue tiles.

Across the way, the Koranic school, **Dündar Bey Medresesi**, was established in 1285 inside the walls of an ancient **caravanserai** (1218), which today has been transformed into a bazaar.

The only remains of ancient Prostanna is the **citadel** (Kale), on the tip of promontory. Built in the 5C, it was enlarged by the Byzantines, then, more ambitiously, by the Seljuks. Not much is left of its massive walls and its once impressive, round towers.

Around the lake**

The minor road that runs along the **western shore**** is of great beauty and gives plenty of magnificent **views**** of the lake and mountains, whose colours change all day long. It crosses the charming village of **Barla**, wedged between the water and the steep wall of Barla Dağı (2 799m). A superb blue-tiled **Seljuk minaret*** rises above the roofs. On the way back, stop at the 1.5km long **Bedre beach** *(11km from Eğirdir)*, undoubtedly the lake's most beautiful *(see "Making the most of Eğirdir", "Other things to do")*.

Isparta

34km south of Eğirdir.
Dolmuşes run regularly between the two towns (30min trip).

The best way of getting to Isparta is not by car or dolmuş, but by steam train. As shiny as a newly-minted coin, the locomotive looks like a prop out of a Buster Keaton movie and runs once in a while between Eğirdir and the city of roses *(the railway station is at the foot of the military camp)*. As a means of transport, the train is as pleasant as it is unusual, allowing its passengers to enjoy the **scenery**** in a perfectly relaxed way. The stops are frequent, since the way is regularly blocked by goats grazing between the tracks.

The rose...

In springtime, the entire region of Isparta is covered with pastel-coloured roses. The women – with the obligatory flowered headscarf and şalvar – tend to the harvest, picking roses by the ton and placing them in wicker baskets. The attar (essential oil) from the petals is then distilled before being exported to international perfume houses. In Turkey, however, the rose is not only appreciated for its fragrance: it is also used to make Turkish delight and delicious preserves.

Surrounded by immense rose gardens, Isparta is a tranquil provincial city (pop 230 000) with beautiful white houses and pink shops filled with bottles, flasks, boxes and even pink plastic canisters. In Isparta everything is related to the rose (attar, in Turkish), including the carpets which use it in the patterns (a carpet auction is held at the end of the year). The Isparta **market** is a very busy place, full of smiling farmers wearing grey caps and well-trimmed moustaches.

Sagalassus★ (Ağlasun)

39km south of Isparta, 75km from Eğirdir and 108km north of Antalya. From Isparta, take the Antalya road. In the village of Ağlasun, turn right onto a narrow road which climbs steeply towards the site, 7km further on. Bring water and avoid the heat. The visit (free) is difficult without your own car. Allow 90min.

The Ağlasun road crosses a magnificent **landscape**★★, a wild and little-known Anatolia. Among the jagged crests of the mountains are bare plateaux and velvet-covered valleys with greyish-green tones. Bunches of tobacco leaves dry upon the rustic trellises, in front of houses with crooked wooden balconies. In a few areas, the sun shines on the red roofs of the forgotten and faraway hamlets. Further south, the Taurus give way to gentler hills and valleys filled with rectangular wheatfields.

High up in the mountains, at an altitude of 1 435m, Sagalassus is a forgotten city, bathed in the silence of its summits, a ghost town whose ruins are scattered among the rocks and the yellow grass swept relentlessly by the wind. Sagalassus is only just beginning to be excavated, and the site's main attraction is the beauty of its **setting**★★ which gives the ruins a spellbinding majesty.

The city rose in terraces on the slopes of Akdağ (2 276m). Each terrace was supported by formidable stone walls. The city is laid out in two districts: the lower city, seat of worship, and the upper city, centre of public life, overlooked by the theatre.

The city of potters

Sagalassus first appears in history with the conquest by Alexander the Great, in 333 BC. It quickly rivalled Antioch of Pisidia *(north of the lake)* and Selge *(to the south, see p 446)*, to finally become Pisidia's most important city under Roman domination. Established along the road linking Pamphylia to the centre of Anatolia, it waxed rich on the flourishing commerce between the two regions. But it owed most of its wealth to the area's agricultural resources and its **clay** soil. It was one of the most important centres of the pottery industry in Asia Minor, especially after the 1C AD when Vespasian attached the region to Lycia and Pamphilya. Pisidia regained its independence in the 4C before falling into the hands of the Byzantines (6C), who transformed Sagalassus into an important religious centre (no fewer than three basilicas have been discovered). Unfortunately, a series of earthquakes and plagues shook the city, making its inhabitants flee to Ağlasun, down in the valley. The new city never recovered the prosperity of the mountain city, and Burdur and Isparta benefited instead.

The site

From the car park, take the path along the ravine. A tour of the site begins with the large **Roman baths** (2C AD), which can be seen below the path *(currently being restored)*. In ruins, only the outline of the massively built walls can be distinguished, but their impressive dimensions – 80x55m – rank them among Asia Minor's largest.

Further along the path over-looking the valley, is the **necropolis**, a romantic chaos of **sarcophagi** lost among the ruins. To the west, are **rock tombs**, with carved façades which look like temples or houses, dug into a rocky spur. There are more sar-chophagi at the foot of the cliff.

Return to the baths and take the little path on the left which climbs to the upper terrace.

The upper city is entered through the ancient **Monumental Gate**, an ele-

Isparta: "la vie en rose"

gant, but very ruined propylaeum with three arches. Further north, next to the mountain, is **Neon's library**, built by a wealthy (and enlightened) citizen in the 2C AD. Inspired by the library of Ephesus, it was undoubtedly one of the city's most opulent buildings. The only remnant of its refined decor is the 120sqm **mosaic**★ floor, showing Achilles' departure for Troy. The central motif (unfortunately badly damaged) is in colour, while the sides are filled with black and white designs.

Just below the library is a **nymphaeum**. Its façade, once decorated with columns, rose above a pool, still paved with marble slabs.

A path leads to the **upper agora** (2C BC), a vast rectangular esplanade strewn with stone blocks. On the northern side, there are some remains of the columns from the stoa, which once ran round the agora.

Return to the library.

On the right, a path climbs gently towards the **theatre**★★, perched at an altitude of 1 574m *(access is blocked by large stone blocks which you will have to climb)*. It is by far the site's most impressive monument, due as much to its seting as to its state of preservation. Leaning against the bare walls of the mountain, the **cavea**★ faces the surrounding summits and offers a magnificent **view**★★. Its terraces could accommodate 9 000 spectators. The earthquakes have made them uneven and the stage wall has mostly collapsed. The frame of a doorway still stands, though its lintel looks

Lake Eğirdir

F. Levillain

ready to drop. On both sides of the cavea, the access galleries still have their beautiful barrel vaults, but the fallen blocks of stone have replaced the comings and goings of the spectators.

The highest part of the city was the **potters' district**, now an immense plateau of low grass, covered with stone blocks and thousands of pieces of terracotta awaiting the archeologists' perusal (do not be tempted to pick up any pieces; all antiquities, whatever they may be, must remain on Turkish soil. Failure to obey this law could create serious problems at customs).

Making the most of Eğirdir

COMING AND GOING

By bus – The bus station is right in the centre of town. A bus shuttle runs between Eğirdir and Isparta every 30min (journey time: 30min) until 6pm in winter and 8pm in summer. Main destinations: Antalya (183km, 2hr journey), Denizli (208km, 3hr), Konya (268km, 4hr), İzmir (418km, 7hr), Ankara (457km, 7hr).

ADDRESS BOOK

Tourist information – İkinci Sahil Yolu 13, ☎ (246) 311 43 88, on the road that borders the lake at the entrance to the town. Open 9am-12noon / 1pm-6pm in summer, and 5.30pm in winter. Closed weekends.

Main post office – Kûrirye Sahil Yolu. Opposite the "otogar", right in the centre. Open until 5.30pm.

WHERE TO STAY

Near the bus station, there is a signpost indicating most of the guest houses in town.

• In Yeşilada

This is the nicest place to stay. The guest houses (with 5 or 6 rooms) are lined up along the lakeside in Yeşilada Mah. They are all simple and homely.

Under US$15

Pension Adac, at *no* 1 in the street, ☎ and Fax (246) 312 30 74. ⁕¶ ✕ The first one you will come across when arriving on the peninsula. Ask for the room with the terrace and view of the lake. The proprietor's sons speak English and they organise walks in Kovada National Park. It's also possible to borrow the small boat belonging to the property at no extra charge to cruise on the lake. Someone will pick you up at the "otogar" if you give advance warning of your arrival.

Between US$15 and US$25

Pension Ali's, at the far end of the island, ☎ (246) 312 25 47 / 312 39 54 – 6rm. ⁕¶ ✕ ⌀ This small quiet hotel has simple but well-kept rooms. Meals are taken on a small terrace overlooking the lake. The owner organises local excursions by minibus.

Pension Göl, ☎ (246) 312 23 70. ⁕¶ ✕ Comfortable and clean. Beautiful room upstairs and roof terrace.

Pension Paris, ☎ (246) 311 55 09. ⁕¶ ✕ This new guest house is a little more "chic" than its neighbours (for the time being). It has the advantage of being isolated on the west bank of the peninsula, so is the quietest one of them all.

• In the town centre

Between US$15 and US$30

Hotel Apostel, Ata Yolu 7, ☎ (246) 311 54 51, Fax (246) 312 35 33 – 27rm. ⁕¶ ✎ Standard level of comfort, simple but pleasant. Good value for money.

EATING OUT

In Yeşilada, 2 restaurants which stand next door to each other are renowned for their freshwater fish specialities. Their terraces provide a perfect spot to watch the sun set over the lake.

🦐 **Adac**, restaurant belonging to the hotel of the same name, ☎ (246) 312 30 74. Here you'll find the best meal on the island served on a small terrace on the lake's edge. You'll love the owner's cooking served by candlelight. Specialties consist of the lake's offerings, meze, meats and desserts – all tasty and inexpensive. The staff is pleasant in this family-like atmosphere. What more could you ask for?

OTHER THINGS TO DO

Beaches – If you like slightly colder water, you'll love it here. The three most beautiful beaches around Eğirdir are: **Belediye**, known as **Halk Plajı**, less than 1km away on the road to Isparta, at Yazla (small rough-sand beach); **Altınkum**, 3km to the north, on the Isparta-Göyceköy road. Its size gives it an advantage over the first beach and there is a camp site right next to it. **Bedre**, 11km to the north on the road to Barla: this is the biggest beach (1.5km long), the most beautiful and the most peaceful. They all have their own little restaurants where you can snack on sandwiches or meze.

Boat trips – In Eğirdir, every guest house has its own boat. Inexpensive and very pleasant.

Apple and Fish Festival – Every year during the first week of September, when the apples are harvested, the Golden Apple and Silver Fish Festival takes place.

Steam locomotive – You can travel to Isparta by a small train pulled by a steam locomotive (normal journey time: 75min at best).

Making the most of Isparta

COMING AND GOING

By bus – The bus station is 2km from the centre, in Süleyman Demirel Bul. Daily bus services to all the main destinations. **Isparta Petrol Turizm**, Mimar Sinan Cad 30, ☎ (246) 218 54 63 / (246) 218 13 00. Open daily 6.30am-1am. Reservations and tickets for Ankara, İstanbul, İzmir, Antalya.

By train – The station is near the city centre, below İstasyon Cad. Trains for Ankara as well as for İstanbul, İzmir, Pamukkale, Afyon, Burdur and Eğirdir depart Tuesdays, Thursdays, and Sundays.

ADDRESS BOOK

Tourist information – 3rd floor of Valilik Binası, the large brown building on Hükümet Meyd. Open 8.30am-12noon / 1.30pm-6pm. Closed weekends.

Bank / change – There are banks everywhere in the town centre, especially in İstasyon Cad and Mimar Sinan Cad, as well as an automatic cash dispenser at **Yapı Kredi bank**, in Hükümet Meyd, that operates 24 hours a day.

Main post office – Opposite the tourist information office. There is another one near the "otogar".

WHERE TO STAY

There are no guest houses in Isparta and the few, very ordinary hotels available are quite expensive.

US$30
🏨 **Hotel Bolat**, Süleyman Demirel Bul 67, ☎ (246) 223 90 01, Fax (246) 218 55 06 – 64rm. ⁴⁷ 🅿 TV ✗ CC This is the best hotel in town, right in the centre. A good standard of comfort for a reasonable rate. Rooms are impeccable, lounges are exquisitely decorated and the fine restaurant on the top floor offers beautiful views of the town.

Hotel Artan, Cengiz Topel Cad 12/B, ☎ (246) 232 57 00, Fax (246) 218 66 29 – 41rm. ⁴⁷ ✗ Here you'll find good value for your money but service is average.

EATING OUT

🍴 **Kebabcılar Arastası**, Hacıbenlioğlu 13, ☎ (246) 218 18 25. A little restaurant, very popular with the locals. Simple and typical atmosphere. Try the delicious and very cheap "Tender kebab".

Alpin, Hükümet Meyd, ☎ (246) 232 22 11. CC In the town centre. A large, quiet restaurant surrounded by vegetation. Serves traditional Turkish cuisine cooked over the fire (kebabs, pide and "köfte") and a few desserts. There's not a lot of choice but the food is good and inexpensive and there's a pleasant atmosphere.

SHOPPING GUIDE

Don't miss the **market** on Wednesdays. A very lively and friendly atmosphere.

Rose products – Turkish delight, jam, soap; and everything is rose-flavoured and sold in rose-coloured boutiques.

ANKARA ★

Capital of the country – Provincial capital – Map p 496
454km from İstanbul – 250km from Konya – 328km from Kayseri – 417km from Samsun
Pop: 2 838 000 – Alt 851m

Not to be missed
The Museum of Anatolian Civilisations.
Atatürk's Mausoleum.
And remember...
Ankara is more than just the Museum of Anatolian Civilisations and a few historical
districts; take the time to explore the modern city.

Ankara lies at the bottom of a secluded valley in the heart of the high and arid plateaux of central Anatolia. It is difficult to imagine that this large bustling city was home to only 30 000 people at the beginning of the 20C. The change, which was brutal, took place in 1923 when **Atatürk** decided to transform it into the capital of the young Turkish nation. Ever since, a huge construction site has developed at the foot of the Byzantine citadel. The new Ankara was born, a modern, dynamic city with all the facilities and institutions of a metropolis: ministries, embassies, administrative offices, universities and large shopping centres.

Angora of Ankara
Ankara, whose ancient name is Angora, gave the famous wool its name. This long-haired wool, which the city continues to produce, is renowned for its silky feel. Angora blankets remain a local speciality and Angora goats still roam the neighbouring steppes and hills.

The sudden development has had its side-effects. To the north, the district of Ulus has kept a narrow maze of colourful streets, while to the south, Atatürk's city is laid out within a rectilinear framework of avenues and boulevards.

Ankara has not stopped growing: new construction bursts forth everywhere, the second underground line is being prepared and *gecekondu* sprout in the outskirts, an unsanitary maze of slums filled with the victims of the rural exodus. Three cities in one, each of them reflecting an aspect of modern Turkey.

The land of the Hittites

Although the first traces of settlement go back to the Hittites (second millennium BC), *Ankyra*, ancient Ankara, first appears in history in the 8C BC, when the Phrygians established their capital in Gordion, 100km away. The region subsequently passed into the hands of the Persians, followed by Alexander the Great (334 BC). Later, a tribe from Gaul, the Galatians, turned it into the capital of Galatia. In 25 BC the Romans annexed the territory, but allowed Ankara to retain its status. The province of Galatia soon became Christian, especially after the sojourn here of St Paul (51 AD), author of the *Epistle of St Paul (the Apostle) to the Galatians*. From the 7C to 12C, the city suffered successive invasions by Persians, Arabs, Byzantines, Seljuks, Mongols (Tamerlane) and Ottomans (1360). It was near Ankara that the troops of Beyazıt I

Capital of modern Turkey
Far from Ottoman İstanbul, in the heart of Hittite Anatolia, Ankara was the ideal site to found the capital of the young Turkish Republic. The choice symbolised Atatürk's will to tap into the most ancient origins of the new nation. Today, Ankara is a large and bustling city, an important commercial centre and a major creator of employment for the region.

Central Anatolia

experienced a heavy defeat at the hands of Tamerlane (1402). However, the Turks quickly recovered and retook the city in 1414. A long period of stagnation ensued only to be broken in the 19C as a result of the trade in angora wool. Even at the beginning of the 20C, it was still a small town, until Mustafa Kemal established his general headquarters here (1919) and proclaimed it capital of Turkey in 1923. It was to be the start of a revolutionary project.

The ancient districts

A half-day is enough to see the main sights (citadel and museum).
Allow more time if you wish to stroll.

From Ulus to Samanpazarı, old Ankara is coiled around the citadel. Ochre-coloured houses cluster on the hillside in a maze of picturesque alleyways lined with poplar trees. Take the time to enjoy a walk after visiting the museum.

The Museum of Antolian Civilisations★★★ (B2)

8.30am-5pm, closed Mondays. Entrance fee. Many guides offer their services (at times too insistently), in English or French. Try to be there at opening time to avoid the crowds. Allow 2hr. To learn more about history, see p 18-19; and individual chapters on the important archeological sites.

If you see only one thing in Ankara, the museum should be it. Its collections are quite exceptional. Displayed inside a beautiful 15C *bedesten* (the offices are in the neighbouring caravanserai), the objects originate from Turkey's most ancient sites. They retrace, in chronological order, the entire history of the peoples of Anatolia, from the Paleolithic era to the arrival of the first Greek settlers.

A tour of the museum begins *(on the right as you enter)*, with **prehistory**, exemplified by flint arrowheads, chiselled stone axes and bone jewellery mostly discovered in the **cave of Karain** (27km from Antalya). It is there that the remains of the oldest Anatolian, 100 000 years old, were brought to light.

The next section *(Displays 2 to 11)* is dedicated to the **Neolithic Age**★ (7000-5000 BC), the age of polished stone which saw the birth of the first villages and pottery techniques. Objects from Çatal Höyük and Hacılar, the oldest Anatolian cities, are assembled here. There is also a reproduction of the **sanctuary of Çatal Höyük★**, a small square room built according to the plan of the period dwellings *(see sidebar p 18)*. Its walls are decorated with bulls heads – symbol of strength and virility – and stunning **paintings**★ with glowing tones, including one representing a volcanic eruption.

Painted pottery, obsidian mirrors (black flint) can be seen in the displays alongside remarkable **terracotta figurines**, fertility divinities with generous bodily attributes. Among them is the statue of an obese **mother goddess**★ *(Display 5)* giving birth between two sacred lions.

Several displays *(12 to 21)* show objects from the **Chalcolithic Age** (Copper Age, 5000-3000 BC), a period in which the cities surrounded themselves with ramparts and a truly urban environment began to develop. All the items on display originate in **Hacılar**: beautiful polychrome pottery, arms and tools in stone and metal which prove the existence of a highly elaborate social organisation. There are also several examples of the **mother-goddess Cybele★** *(Display 15)*.

Another chronological anomaly, (Display 107), is pottery of the **Lydian Kingdom** (700-550 BC) together with a few examples of the first **coins** minted in Sardis – the capital – which made the legendary Croesus enormously wealthy *(see p 264)*.

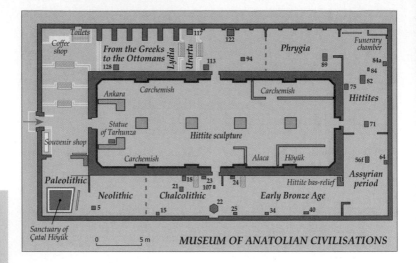

Map labels (from the image):

Toilets
Coffee shop
From the Greeks to the Ottomans
128
Lydia
Urartu
117
122
113
94
Phrygia
89
Funerary chamber
84a
84
82
75
Hittites
Ankara
Carchemish
Carchemish
71
Statue of Tarhunza
Hittite sculpture
Souvenir shop
Carchemish
Alaca   Höyük
56f   64
Assyrian period
Hittite bas-relief
Paleolithic
18   23
21   107
24
Neolithic
Chalcolithic
Early Bronze Age
5
15
22
25   34   40
Sanctuary of Çatal Höyük
0   5 m
MUSEUM OF ANATOLIAN CIVILISATIONS

Central Anatolia

On the left, on either side of the entrance to the central halls, two staircases lead down to the ground floor of the bedesten, where a new room was opened in 1999.

A single room stretches along the entire length of this floor. The right side *(Displays 1 to 14)* contains a great variety of objects, all remarkable: Oriental amulets *(Display 1)*, Phrygian votive stelae (8C BC) *(Display 7)*, red and black Greek vases (4C and 3C BC)*(Displays 11 and 12)*, delicate Ottoman ceramics *(Display 13)*, completed by the works of an "artist of the Republic" *(Display 14, the last one in the section)*.

Dedicated to **ancient Ankara**, the left side of the room is a reminder of the prehistory of Atatürk's city. (It was under Atatürk that Turkish archeologists began work, seen in the historic photographs displayed on the walls.) Beyond the limited number of Bronze Age items *(Display 16)* are the treasures of the Hittite period, exquisitely demonstrated by an astonishing **vase**★ with a wedding scene in relief *(Display 17)*. The Roman period is portrayed by the remains of a theatre discovered on the outskirts of the city and by a **marble satyr**★, a small bearded man with large ears *(Display 19)*. After the reconstructed Roman tomb *(Display 20)*, two showcases show the Ulus district during various periods: Ottoman, Seljuk, Byzantine, with many objects found during the digs.

Further along, among a group of small statues from different periods *(Display 26)* – all from the Ankara region – two heads draw attention. One of them, primitively crafted and with worn contours, represents **Cybele**. The other, next to it, is that of an enigmatic and proud **horseman**★★, with delicate features. Another outstanding work is the bronze bust of the **moon-god**★★, a divinity arising from the combined blending of the Greek pantheon, ancient rituals and oriental influence.

The room leads to the museum's beautiful flower garden. Take a walk around before going upstairs to discover the most interesting part of the collections.

The museum's highlight, the **Early Bronze Age room**★★ (3000-2000 BC) contains the discoveries made in **Alacahöyük**. The **Hatti** civilisation was established in this small fortified city in the centre of Anatolia *(Displays 22 to 41)*. The site's royal tombs (a reconstruction can be seen above Display 25) have yielded a myriad of refined ritual objects in copper, lead, bronze or electrum (a mixture of gold and silver). The **solar standards***** in bronze (*Displays 22-24*) are particularly magnificent. They are decorated with bulls and with stags with giant antlers, and were carried during religious ceremonies (one of them is used as an emblem by the Ministry of Tourism). Notice the **gold jewellery**** – crown, necklace, earrings, as well as little **fertility goddesses***** in silver or electrum (*Displays 34 and 40*), the forms of which seem startlingly modern.

The room's last display cases (*42 to 54*) show a series of statuettes from the Late Bronze Age found near **Alişar** and in **Kültepe** (near Kayseri), figurines of Cybele and other elaborately shaped **idols*** in terracotta.

At the end of the section, is a superb **Hittite bas-relief**** (14C BC). This panel decorated the King's Gate, one of the entrances of the Hittite capital, **Hattuşaş**. It incorporates an armed figure wearing a helmet, identified as the god of war, who kept evil spirits away from the city.

Next, comes the **Middle Bronze Age** (1950-1750 BC). This period saw the first writings and the first exchanges between Asia Minor and Mesopotamia, under the auspices of **Assyrian merchants**. The latter established nine trade companies (*karum*) in Anatolia, with **Kültepe** (near Kayseri) being the most important. Numerous **clay tablets** (*Display 56F*) have been found. Traders used them to write down their calculations using the cuneiform characters.

Here too there are beautiful **rhyta**, libation vases in the shape of animal heads, as well as a smiling ivory **statuette**** of the goddess of fertility (*Display 57*). You can also see minuscule **cylindrical seals*** (*Display 68*) inspired by Mesopotamia, on which hunting, war or cult scenes are engraved with delicate precision.

The section dedicated to the **Hittites** (1750-1200 BC) who established their capital in **Hattutşaş** (Boğazkale) begins at the end of this gallery. The **ritual vases*** with four handles and remarkably decorated with bull heads (*Displays 71 and 75*) originate from there. There are also two superb **rhyta**** shaped like bulls (*Display 82*) with a beautiful red patina and a modern appearance. *Display case 84a* contains a 4cm-tall **figurine** wearing the traditional Hittite pointed hat. A **bronze tablet** – an unusual use of this material – carries the inscription, in cuneiform characters, of a peace treaty established in the 13C between Hattuşaş and a neighbouring kingdom (*Display 84*).

To continue the tour in chronological order, return to the central hall.

The central hall is reserved for **Hittite sculptures****. Here are the magnificent **orthostats** which decorated the base of palace walls, temples and gates of the royal cities. They consist of large stone panels with long bas-relief friezes. Inspired by the Assyrians, this type of architectural decoration persisted for nearly seven centuries, marvellously illustrating the skill of Hittite craftsmen. It is also a fascinating example of the culture and lifestyle of the court.

D. Silberstein/PIX

Solar standard of Alaca Höyük,
Museum of Anatolian Civilisations

The largest area is set aside for the basalt bas-reliefs and sculptures of **Carchemish**** (1000-800 BC), the capital of the most important **neo-Hittite Kingdom** after the collapse of the Empire. A whole series of fictional animals can be seen, along with half-man, half-animal figures accompanying a procession of priests and musicians about to perform a sacrifice. Hunting and banquet scenes depict the king's daily life surrounded by many animals – symbols of the divinities.

On the right of the entrance, sculpted blocks from **Ankara** (800 BC) also represent various mythological creatures.

On the same side, at the back, is the imposing statue of **King Tarhunza** discovered in **Arslantepe** (Malatya, 1100-800 BC). The Assyrian influence is clearly visible: hair-style and clothing (the artist chose the Assyrian sandals and long robe rather than the short tunic and *crakows* (shoes) usually worn by Hittites).

Last but not least, on the other side of the room, are the dark andesite **bas-reliefs**★ of the **Sphynx Gate**★ and the Hittite enclosure of **Alaca Höyük** (1300 BC). The king and queen are represented worshipping a bull, preceded by a procession of animals, acrobats and jugglers.

After the Hittites come the **Phrygians** (8C BC) who established their capital in **Gordion** (100km southwest of Ankara). The items shown (*Displays 89 to 106*) are from the largest tumulus discovered in the region, customarily attributed to King Midas. The most striking among them are a **table**★★ and a **screen**★★ in wood mar-quetry, both exquisitely refined (*Displays 89 and 89a*) as well as a magnificent bronze **cauldron**★★ on a tripod (*Display 94*), with sphinx-shaped handles. The animal-shaped pottery decorated with delicate geometric patterns is particularly fine. On the right side (*Display 122*) is an elegant **statue of Cybele**★, discovered in Boğazkale, accom-panied by two musicians.

The Urartu civilisation (900-600 BC) which blossomed around the shores of Lake Van (eastern Turkey), disappeared in the 7C BC as a result of Assyrian attack. The people were especially gifted in the art of metal craftsmanship: beautiful bronze objects including an enormous **cauldron**★★ on a tripod, are represented (*Display 113*) as well as superb engraved **belts**★★ decorated with human figures. There are also items in ivory, in particular the beautiful **statuette of a lion**★★ (*Display 114*).

The last section of the museum mixes various periods, from the Greeks to the Ottomans (*Displays 123-133*). It contains beautiful **Roman glasswork**, delicate gold jewellery, as well as a substantial collection of **Greek coins** from the 7C BC. A series of bronze griffins (*Display 128*) with wide-open eyes and gaping mouths heralds the end of the tour. The Turks and the Greeks have adopted these fictional apotropaic (to ward off the evil eye) animals of Eastern origin which are very similar to the *garuda* of southeast Asia.

The Citadel★ (B2)
Go round the museum on the right and climb the (very steep) street leading to a small square.

An assortment of stalls huddle at the foot of the citadel's walls. Spice bags and dried apricots fill the air with rich fragrances. Dominating the streets of the lower city, the Byzantine citadel is very well preserved. It harbours a small district of old **wooden Ottoman houses**★, painted blue, mostly restored and transformed into restaurants. The area is charming and it reveals a beautiful **panorama**★ of the city. This is an excellent opportunity for a stroll.

Built between the 7C and 8C to withstand the attacks of the Arabs, two lines of walls defend the citadel, partially built with stone from the old city. The **lower ramparts** – a 1500m belt flanked by 14 bastions – are reached by the **Hisar Gate** (Hisar Kapısı), a massive tower with a clock.

Continuing straight on, the road leads to **Parmak Kapısı**, the only gate of the **upper ramparts⋆** (1 105m). The latter is the oldest and best-preserved wall of the whole complex. Inside, on the right, a tall polygonal tower can be seen. It is the **Sark Kale**, which connects the two walls. On the other side is the **Alaaddin Mosque** *(open during prayer hours)* containing a beautiful 12C **minbar**, and further along Alitaş Sokağı is a small fort of the Seljuk or Ottoman period known as the **Ak Kale**.

Returning to the square, go past the spice market and along the Altaparı Sok, then go down the first street on the right towards the lower city.

Samanpazarı⋆ (B2, C2)

This working-class neighbourhood is reached by way of a maze of steep streets filled with dozens of shops selling spices, basketry and spools of wool. It represents the charming Ankara of olden times in spite of the appearance of souvenir shops.

Built by the Seljuk's in the 13C, the **Arslanhane Mosque⋆** (Ahi Şerafettin Camii) is Ankara's most ancient place of worship *(can be visited outside of prayer hours)*. If it appears plain on the outside, the **prayer hall⋆**, all in wood, deserves a visit. Instead of the traditional dome, it is covered with a simple wooden roof supported by 24 **columns⋆**, also in wood, topped with old stone capitals. The **mihrab⋆** displays its elegant glazed black-and-blue tiles, while the **minbar's⋆**, carved in cedarwood, is equally noteworthy.

Go down Can Sok, until you reach the small square, then continue along Koyunpazarı Sok.

Another example of a wooden interior, the **Ahi Elvan Mosque** (Ahi Elvan Camii) was built at the end of the 14C *(can be visited outside prayer hours)*. Here too, the columns have ancient Roman or Byzantine capitals.

Return to the small square and take the second street on the right: Saraçlar Sok, which will allow you to reach the northern section of Ulus.

The district's streets are all very busy with shops and canopied stalls filled with clothes and linen. At the end of Anafartalar Cad *(on the left)* you reach a very picturesque **vegetable market** (Yeni Haller).

Cross Hisparkı Cad and go along Hükümet Cad, almost opposite.

Ulus⋆ (B1-2)

Above the often very busy esplanade, the ruins of the **temple of Augustus** (B1) are some of the city's rare ancient remains *(closed for restoration)*. Erected in the 1C BC, the building underwent many changes and was converted from a temple to a church (6C), then into a mosque, until it was finally abandoned. Today, the colonnade has disappeared, revealing the walls of the cella, pierced by a very tall **door**. On the walls of the **pronaos**, still partially standing, Augustus had his testament inscribed in Greek and Latin along with a summary of the accomplishments of his reign.

Next to the temple stands the **Hacı Bayram Mosque** (Hacı Bayram Camii) *(cannot be visited during prayer hours)* built during the 15C, before being restored by the great architect, Sinan. A 3m-high section of the **prayer hall's** walls is covered with glazed Kütahya tiles with beautiful blue-and-white motifs.

Most of the city's funerals are held here and it is common to see coffins resting on tables in the esplanade while the families are inside.

Next to the mosque rises the **türbe** of its founder, Hacı Bayram, which is a major pilgrimage site. This explains the large number of shops filled with religious objects and votive offerings in the **arcade**, next to the Roman building.

There are good art books to be found here too *(see "Making the most of Ankara")*.

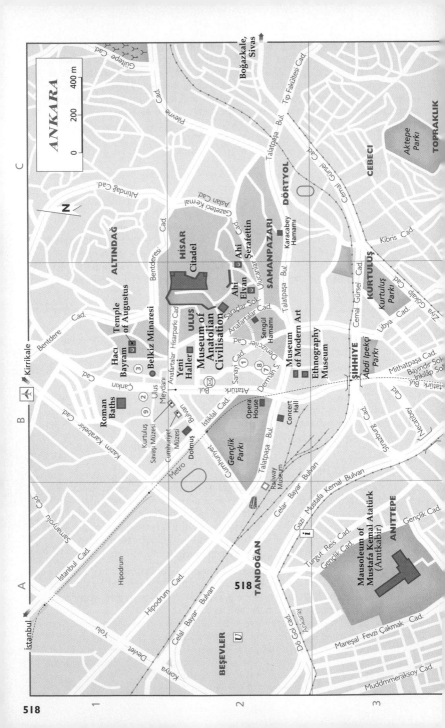

ANKARA

0   200   400 m

N

Kırıkkale

İstanbul

BEŞEVLER

TANDOĞAN

518

ANITTEPE

Mausoleum of
Mustafa Kemal Atatürk
(Anıtkabir)

ALTINDAĞ

HİSAR

ULUS

SAMANPAZARI

DÖRTYOL

CEBECİ

TOPRAKLIK

ŞIHHIYE

KURTULUŞ

Boğazkale, Sivas

Roman Baths

Temple of Augustus

Hacı Bayram

Belkız Minaresi

HİSAR Citadel

Museum of Anatolian Civilisation

Museum of Modern Art

Ethnography Museum

Ahi Elvan

Ahi Şerafettin

Karacabey Hamamı

Sengül Hamamı

Yeni Haller

Opera House

Concert Hall

Gençlik Parkı

Railway Museum

Aktepe Parkı

Kurtuluş Parkı

Abdi İpekçi Parkı

Cumhuriyet Müzesi

Savaş Müzesi

Kurtuluş

Ulus Meydanı

Dolmuş

Metro

Hipodrum

② ③ ①

⑨ ⑦ ⑧

Gültepe Cad.

Altındağ Cad.

Bentdere Cad.

Bentdere Cad.

Bentderesi Cad.

Kazım Karabekir Cad.

Çankırı Cad.

Cad.

Pilevne Cad.

Tıp Fakültesi Cad.

Talatpaşa Bul.

Cemal Gürsel Cad.

Cemal Gürsel Cad.

Gazeteci Kemal Aslan Cad.

Ulucanlar Cad.

Talatpaşa Bul.

Kıbrıs Cad.

Libya Cad.

Ziya Gökalp Cad.

Mithatpaşa Cad.

Bayındır Sok.

İnkılâp Sok.

Necatibey Cad.

Atatürk Bul.

Sezgünü

Saraçlar Sok.

Anafartalar Cad.

Anafartalar Hisarparkı Cad.

Denizciler Cad.

Sanayi Cad.

Dermân S.

İstiklâl Cad.

Atatürk Bul.

Cumhuriyet Bulvarı

Talatpaşa Bul.

Celal Bayar Bulvarı

Gazi Mustafa Kemal Bulvarı

Gençlik Cad.

Gençlik Cad.

Gençlik Cad.

Turgut Reis Cad.

Dö Göl cad. Ankara

Celal Bayar Bulvarı

Hipodrum Cad.

Samsun Yolu

İstanbul Cad.

Devlet Yolu

Konya

Maraşal Fevzi Çakmak Cad.

Muddmmeraksoy Cad.

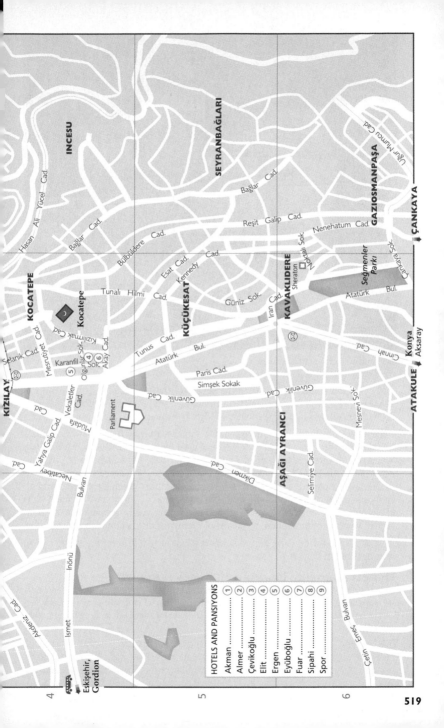

This is a map of central Ankara showing districts including INCESU, KOCATEPE, KIZILAY, SEYRANBAĞLARI, KÜÇÜKESAT, KAVAKLIDERE, AŞAĞI AYRANCI, and GAZİOSMANPAŞA.

HOTELS AND PANSIYONS

Akman	①
Almer	②
Çevikoğlu	③
Elit	④
Ergen	⑤
Eyüboğlu	⑥
Fuar	⑦
Sipahi	⑧
Spor	⑨

Streets and landmarks labelled on the map:

Hasan Ali Yücel Cad., Bağlar Cad., Bülbüldere Cad., Esat Cad., Kennedy Cad., Reşit Galip Cad., Bağlar Cad., Nenehatum Cad., Uğur Mumcu Cad., Tunalı Hilmi Cad., Güniz Sok., Noktalı Sok., Segmenler Parkı, Sheraton, Atatürk Bul., Çankaya Sok., Selanik Cad., Mesrutiyet Cad., Kocatepe Cad., Kızılırmak Cad., Karanfil Sok., Olgunlar Sok., Akay Cad., Iran Cad., Tunus Cad., Atatürk Bul., Paris Cad., Simşek Sokak, Güvenlik Cad., Cinnah Cad., Konya, Aksaray, Vekaletler Cad., Mudafaa, Parliament, Yahya Galip Cad., Necatibey Cad., Güvenlik Cad., Dikmen Cad., Selimiye Cad., Mesnevi Sok., Akdeniz Cad., Inönü Bulvarı, Ismet, Çetin Emeç Bulvarı

ÇANKAYA
ATAKULE

Eskişehir, Gordion

519

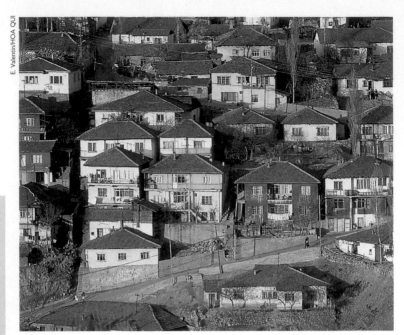

Old Ankara lives on in Ulus

Further on, Hükümet Cad leads to the square of the same name. The **Column of Julian** (Bekiz Minaresi) (B1) was erected in honour of the Emperor during his visit in the 4C. Topped by a Byzantine capital, its 15m shaft is carved with horizontal grooves.

Archeology enthusiasts will want to visit the immense **Roman Baths** (B1) whose ruins extend along the Çankırı Cad *(8.30-12noon/1-5pm; entrance fee; ask the guardian to open the gate)*. Built during the reign of Caracalla (3C), these large baths were linked to the forum of Augustus by an avenue lined with porticos. **Funerary stelae** of various periods are displayed on the left side of the palestra (completely disappeared). Signposts indicate the location of various rooms, some of which have retained signs of plumbing and marble floors. The **hot rooms** are easily recognisable by their impressive array of little **piers**, remnants of the hypocaust heating system *(see p 53)*.

On your way to the city's modern districts is the attractive **Youth Park** (Gençlik parkı) flanking Atatürk Bulvarı.

The Ethnography Museum★ (Etnografya Müzesi) (B2)
Behind the Museum of Modern Art. Facing the Opera, leave Atatürk Bul for Derman Sok. The museum is on the other side of Talatpaşa. Take special care when crossing! 8.30am-12noon/1pm-5pm; closed Mondays. Entrance fee (enter through the back of the building). Allow half an hour.

The building is recognisable by its dome and elegant portico. It was constructed under the auspices of Atatürk, in 1927, to increase knowledge of Turkish culture. As a result, its collections illustrating the way of life of the Turks during the Ottoman period, are remarkably abundant. Traditional Anatolian crafts can also be seen.

On the ground of the main hall, a large white marble plaque marks **Atatürk's first tomb**. It is here, in fact, that his body lay from 1938 to 1953 before its transfer to the Mausoleum.

The rooms on the right of the entrance recreate the atmosphere of **wealthy Ottoman residences***, with mannequins and all sorts of objects of great quality: porcelain, carpets, kilims, clothes and embroideries, including a 17C **wooden cradle inlaid with mother-of-pearl***, originally found in a young man's circumcision chamber.

The room opposite is dedicated to the **Whirling Dervishes**. Beautiful 13C **Seljuk** ceramics, along with arms, Korans and Ottoman-era manuscripts fill the remaining rooms. The museum also houses a collection of wooden architectural items, including a 15C **medrese door***, the doors of the Hacı Bayram mausoleum and a superb 14C **mihrab**** from a mosque in a small Cappadocian village, completely covered in calligraphy.

The **Museum of Modern Art** (Resim ve Eykel Müzesi) is housed inside a beautiful Ottoman-style building. It has a broad range of paintings from the 19C to the present (*9am-12noon/1pm-5pm; closed Mondays. Free*). A few of the works of art (*first floor*) are in the Impressionist style: many Turkish painters studied in France. In the last room, dedicated to architecture, you can see other buildings designed by the museum's architect. On the ground floor, on the right of the entrance, there are interesting portraits of Atatürk, which differ slightly from the ones usually seen across the country.

The modern city
Allow 2hr30, according to traffic conditions.

South of Talatpaşa Bulvarı, another side of Ankara is revealed. An airy city pierced by broad avenues lined by large white buildings. Designed by two European city planners, Atatürk's Ankara needed to be in the same league as European capitals. This area's atmosphere is far removed from that found in the districts surrounding the citadel. Here, moustached old men give way to businessmen, chic women and students. Modern Ankara is also an important commercial centre with the shopping malls of the **Kızılay** and **Atakule** and the adjoining fashionable restaurants. Statues of Atatürk on foot or on a horse can be seen in all the squares.

The Atatürk Mausoleum** (Anıtkabir) (A3)
By taxi or dolmuş. 9am-5pm. Note that the museums within the mausoleum's compound close (usually) between 2pm and 4pm and all day Monday. Allow 1hr.

Perched atop the **Anıttepe** promontory, the immense Atatürk mausoleum recalls the acropolis of Athens, with the addition of a modern Parthenon. The complex covers an area of 75ha and is the work of two architects chosen by an international jury: Emin Onat and Orhan Arda.

Two pavilions marking the entrance to the "sanctuary" are flanked by statues representing the Turkish nation. Inside, an exhibit explains the **chronology of the mausoleum's construction**, with a model and photographs showing the transfer of Atatürk's body in 1953.

Beyond, a **wide promenade*** stretches for 200m and is flanked by **resting lions** directly inspired by the sacred felines of Hittite statuary.

The promenade leads to an **esplanade** surrounded by several buildings (exhibition halls) and corner towers. On the left, monumental stairs lead to the mausoleum flanked by a bas-relief illustrating the history of Turkey.

The mausoleum* – a temple worthy of Jupiter – is surrounded by an impressive peristyle composed of completely unornamented columns. The majestic complex is especially impressive at night when the illuminated portico enhances the simple architectural lines.

The immense inner hall is lined with marble while the ceiling is decorated with red and gold motifs reminiscent of kilims. At the back, almost lost in this austere space, is **Atatürk's cenotaph** (the vault is underneath), a 40-ton monolith. Many visitors pay their respects with quasi-religious fervour.

The **museum** on the left of the esplanade is well worth a visit. Atatürk's personal belongings are displayed here: his famous alpaca suit, his cashmere overcoat and, in particular, a **toiletry case*** given to him by the king of Afghanistan.

Opposite, another pavilion houses the books of **Atatürk's library**, while a third one, at the corner of the lion promenade, contains the photographs relating to Atatürk's efforts to emancipate women. Last but not least, on the other side of the esplanade, on the left, are Atatürk's official and private **cars**. Facing the mausoleum, a portico harbours **the tomb of İsmet İnönü**, the successor (and friend) of Atatürk at the helm of the Republic.

J.-F. Galmiche

Ankara's chic boutiques

Another one of Ankara's monuments, visible from afar, the **Mosque of Kocatepe*** (B4) (*east of Atatürk Bul*) is the city's largest and most recent. It was completed in 1987, after 20 years of construction. Continuing the tradition, it is part of a religious complex containing a library, a conference hall, but also, sign of the times, an immense car park and shopping centre. Built according to the model of the grand Ottoman mosques, it is reminiscent of İstanbul's blue mosque – a style of architecture often revived in current projects.

Making the most of Ankara

COMING AND GOING

By air – Esenboğa airport is 23km north of the city centre (a **Havaş** bus shuttles between the railway station and the airport, another between the "AŞTİ" bus station and the airport). **Turkish Airlines** and **İstanbul Airlines** operate several flights per day to the main European cities via İstanbul. Flights also operate from here to most of the main Turkish cities.

By train – The station is to the west of Ulus, in Talatpaşa Bul (A2). Information: ☎ (312) 311 06 20 / 21. Reservations: ☎ (312) 310 65 15 / (312) 311 49 94. Left-luggage office: 7.30am-11pm. Book your tickets in advance. Services operate mainly to İstanbul (4 trains during the day, 3 at night, 10hr journey) and İzmir (2 couchette trains, 15hr overnight journey). Keep it in mind that, for İstanbul, various categories are available, from an ordinary seat to a couchette. If you are travelling at night, take the Anadolu or Ankara Express, these are the only ones with couchettes.

By bus – The vast "otogar" (also called AŞTİ) is 5km west of the city centre. A dolmuş will get you there in 20min (departing from the dolmuş stand in Cumhuriyet Bul, a 10min walk from the railway station) (B2). You can get to the four corners of Turkey from Ankara. Several services operate every day to the following destinations: Adana (7hr), Alanya (8hr), Antalya (8hr), Bodrum (12hr), Bursa (6hr), Erzurum (13hr), İstanbul (5hr 30min), İzmir (8hr), Kayseri (5hr), Mersin (8hr), Nevşehir (4hr), Sivas (7hr), Trabzon via Amasya, Samsun and the Black Sea coast (12hr).

FINDING YOUR WAY

See the map on p 518-519. Like the "decumanus" of the Roman cities, Ankara is cut in two by a 6km main road – Gazi Mustafa Kemal Bul – which runs from east to west. To the north, the old quarters of Ulus, Hisar and Samanpazarı are huddled around the citadel, while the broad avenues of the modern city stretch out to the south. The main sights are concentrated in the old quarters, which can easily be visited on foot. However, you will need to take a taxi or dolmuş to get around the modern part of the city.

GETTING AROUND

By car – It is difficult to get around by car, because the traffic is always very heavy and the local network rather complex (endless intersections and one-way streets). Also, car parks are few and far between.

By bus – A convenient and inexpensive means of transport (the same fare, whatever the distance), but the buses are packed at rush hour. Their final destination (name of district or terminus) is indicated on the front.

By metro – A new line runs from north to south of the city. One single fare to all destinations.

By taxi or shared taxi – Numerous taxis (yellow, with taximeters) cruise the city. Taxis and dolmuşes are very cheap

and definitely the most convenient way of getting around Ankara.

By rental car – *Avis*, Tunus Cad 68/2, Kavaklıdere (B5), ☎ (312) 467 23 13. *Europcar*, Küçük Esat Cad 25/C, Bakanlıklar, ☎ (312) 398 05 03. *Hertz*, Atatürk Bul 138/B, Kavaklıdere (B6), ☎ (312) 468 10 29. Agencies open every day from 8am-7pm.

ADDRESS BOOK

Tourist information – Gazi Mustafa Kemal Bul 121, Tandoğan (A2), ☎ (312) 231 55 72. Open every day in summer, 9am-5.30pm. It is rather curiously located far away from the tourist area.

Bank / change – There are numerous currency exchanges and banks in Atatürk Bul, Ulus and the modern quarters of Şihhiye (B3) and Kızılay (B4).

Main post office – In Atatürk Bul, just before Ulus Square (B2). Open 24 hours a day. To find the entrance, just look for the big yellow post box. There are two other large post offices in Kızılay (B4) and at the top of Cinnah Cad in Kavaklıdere (B6).

Medical service – *Bayındır Tıp Merkezi* clinic, Kızılırmak Mah 28, Sok 3 (B5), ☎ (312) 287 90 00. *Sevgi Hastanesi* clinic, Tunus Cad 28, Kavaklıdere, ☎ (312) 419 44 44 / 60.

Embassies – *British Embassy*, Şehit Ersan Cad 46/A, Çankaya, ☎ (312) 468 62 30 / 42, Fax (312) 466 29 89. *United States Embassy*, Atatürk Bul 110, Kavaklıdere, ☎ (312) 468 61 10, Fax (312) 467 00 19. *Canadian Embassy*, Nenehatun Cad 75, Gaziosmanpaşa, ☎ (312) 436 12 75 / 76 / 77, Fax (312) 446 44 37. *Australian Embassy*, Nenehatun Cad 83, Gaziosmanpaşa, ☎ (312) 446 11 80 / 87, Fax (312) 446 11 88.

Airline companies – *Air France*, Atatürk Bul 231/7, Kavaklıdere (B5), ☎ (312) 467 44 00.

Austrian Airlines / Swissair, Oscar Turizm ve Ticaret A-S, Tamran Cad 12/10, Kavaklıdere, ☎ (312) 468 11 44, Fax (312) 468 48 45.

Delta Airlines, Atatürk Bul 223/13, Kavaklıdere (B5). Information and reservations: ☎ (212) 231 23 39 / (212) 233 38 20.

İstanbul Airlines, Atatürk Bul 83, Kızılay (B4), ☎ (312) 431 09 20 / 21.

Turkish Airlines, Atatürk Bul 154, Kavaklıdere (B5), ☎ (312) 428 02 00.

Travel agencies – Numerous agencies in the city. One of the good ones is **Angel Tour**, Gölpeli Sok 27/16, Gaziosmanpaşa (C6), ☎ (312) 436 16 17.

WHERE TO STAY

• Ulus (old town)
Since most of the sights are in Ulus, you may as well stay there. This is also where you will find the best value for money. As for the main international hotels (Hilton, Sheraton), they are in Kavaklıdere.

Under US$15
Hotel Sipahi, Kosova Sok 1, ☎ (312) 324 02 35 – 30rm. ⌐ A very busy old hotel with ageless rooms that are basic but clean, as well as a telephone switchboard that is a collectors item and the receptionist's pride and joy.

Hotel Fuar, Kosova Sok 11, ☎ (312) 312 32 88 – 15rm. Communal bathrooms. The rooms are neither particularly clean nor attractive but their rate is unbeatable (around US$5 for a double).

Between US$15 and US$25
Hotel Akman, Opera Meyd Tavus Sok 6, ☎ (312) 324 41 40 – 49rm. ⌐ A simple but comfortable establishment. Check out the kitsch decor in the dining room.

Between US$25 and US$30
Hotel Spor, Rüzgarlı-Plevne Sok 6, ☎ (312) 324 21 65, Fax (312) 312 21 53 – 45rm. ⌐ ✂ ⎡TV⎤ Simple, clean rooms. Good welcome.

Hotel Çevikoğlu, Çankırı Cad Orta Sok 2, near the Column of Julian, ☎ (312) 310 45 35, Fax (312) 311 19 40 – 70rm. ⌐ Clean, with a standard level of comfort.

Between US$30 and US$40
🍴 **Hotel Almer**, Çankırı Cad 17, ☎ (312) 309 04 35, Fax (312) 311 56 77 – 81rm. ⌐ ✂ ⎡TV⎤ ⎡CC⎤ A very well-run establishment, with immaculate and very comfortable rooms (with a small lounge area). Good welcome. Best value for money.

• Kızılay (new town)
Between US$30 and US$40
Hotel Ergen, Karanfil Sok 48, ☎ (312) 417 59 06, Fax (312) 425 78 19 – 48rm. ⌐ ✂ A modern establishment with a standard level of comfort.

Hotel Elit, Olgunlar Sok 10, ☎ (312) 417 46 95, Fax (312) 417 46 97 – 44rm. ⌐ ✂ ⎡TV⎤ ⎡CC⎤ All the usual comforts of a modern hotel, in the heart of this lively district.

Under US$60
🍴 **Hotel Eyüboğlu**, Karanfil Sok 73, ☎ (312) 417 64 00, Fax (312) 417 81 25 – 52rm. ⌐ ✂ ⎡TV⎤ ⎡CC⎤ Spacious, immaculate rooms. A very good place to stay.

EATING OUT
The popular restaurants are grouped together in the districts of Ulus and Kızılay. The ones set in the citadel attract lots of tourists, and are good although a little more expensive than elsewhere. The most chic ones are scattered around the modern part of the city (Kavaklıdere, Gaziosmanpaşa and Çankaya).

• Ulus (old town)
Under US$5
In Atatürk Bul, there are numerous restaurants serving excellent and very cheap "iskender" and "döner kebab". However, they do not serve alcohol.
Gaziantepli Fethibey, Sanayi Cad 35 (B2), ☎ (312) 311 66 54. In a large room with mosaic tiles, authentic dishes, such as smoked "çorba" or fresh pastries, are served at any hour.

Under US$8
In summer, Gençlik Parkı (B2), with its lively restaurants, is a great place to dine. 🍴 **Bulvar**, Çankırı Cad 14/37 (B1), ☎ (312) 311 71 17. It would be nice to eat here every day. This is the ideal cafeteria: you can choose among a number of mouth-watering meals in the kitchen before you sit down in the warm dining area where you can chat with the hip and friendly customers.

Between US$8 and US$15
Zenger Paşa Konağı, in the citadel, Doyran Sok 13 (B2), ☎ (312) 311 70 70. In a superb Ottoman house, with a beautiful view over the city. You can watch the chefs prepare delicious flat bread in large crepe pans. Wide selection of meat and fish.

🍴 **Kınacılar Residence**, in the citadel, Kalekapısı Sok 28, ☎ (312) 312 56 00. Another magnificently restored Ottoman house. Traditional cuisine and excellent welcome.

Central Anatolia

• Kızılay

You will find all sorts of restaurants in Bayındır Sok and İnkilâp Sok, from the most simple to the most chic.

Under US$15

🦞 **Göksu**, Bayındır Sok 22/A **(B3)**, ☎ (312) 431 22 19. Sample the tasty fish on offer in this very pleasant setting (white table cloths and wood panelling). Terrace in summer. Alcohol. A good place to go.

• Kavaklıdere

Over US$8

Hacı Arifbey, Güniz Sok 48 **(B5)**, ☎ (312) 467 00 67. 🎏 Good traditional cuisine (delicious meze, kebabs and "baklavas"). No alcohol.

🦞 **İskender Kebab**, Paris Cad 20/A **(B5)**, ☎ (312) 418 78 88. Excellent "iskender" and a refined setting. No alcohol.

• Gaziosmanpaşa

Over US$8

Pineapple, Uğur Mumcu Cad 64/B **(C6)**, ☎ (312) 446 53 27. Good meat dishes and pizzas on the menu in this very attractive Italian-style restaurant. Very chic. Rather expensive.

Villa Restaurant, Boğaz Sok 13, ☎ (312) 427 08 38. Close to the Sheraton **(B6)**, this is one of the city's trendy restaurants. Pasta and good traditional cuisine in an original, beautifully-lit saloon-style setting (!) with wooden tables.

• Çankaya

Under US$15

Lagos, Farabi Çevre Sok 25/A, to the southeast of the city, ☎ (312) 427 09 73. Closed Sundays. A good fish restaurant, attractively decorated with aquariums and fishing nets on the walls. Alcohol.

HAVING A DRINK

Bars – The fashionable bars are in the south of the city, in the Gaziosmanpaşa **(C6)** and Çankaya districts.

Baron, Köroğlu Cad 54, Gaziosmanpaşa, ☎ (312) 437 45 03. A good place to go for a drink at the end of the day, in a setting reminiscent of a comfortable English club.

🦞 **Salata**, Reşit Galip Cad 57/A, Gaziosmanpaşa, ☎ (312) 446 34 52. An elegant bar with a very cosy atmosphere, where you will receive a warm welcome. Open until 3am. You can snack on a "salata".

Nightclubs – Manhattan Bar, Çevre Sok 7, Çankaya, ☎ (312) 427 28 63. Closed Sundays. Jazz and rock music.

Çengel Café, Noktalı Sok 8/1, Gaziosmanpaşa, ☎ (312) 426 18 51. Opposite the Sheraton. Turkish pop music in a pleasant setting.

Live shows – Opera, Devlet Operave Balesi, Atatürk Bul Opera Meyd **(B2)**, ☎ (312) 324 22 10. For under US$5, you can take in a show at the opera (dance or music). At 8pm, from October to May.

Symphony Orchestra, Cumhurbaşkanlığı Senfoni Orkestrası Salonu, Talatpaşa Bul 38/A, Ulus **(B2)**, ☎ (312) 309 13 43. Concerts at the weekend, from October to May.

OTHER THINGS TO DO

Turkish baths – Karacabey Hamamı, Talatpaşa Bul 101, Ulus **(C2)**, ☎ (312) 311 84 47 or (312) 310 21 55. 6.30am-10.30pm. A "real" Turkish bath with separate sections for men and women, each with its own large relaxation room.

Şengül Hamamı, Acıçeşme Sok 3, Ulus **(B2)**, ☎ (312) 310 22 98. 6am-6pm. Another neighbourhood establishment, clean and pleasant, not mixed.

SHOPPING GUIDE

Market – At the junction of Hisarparkı Cad and Anafartalar Cad, you will find a bustling market selling fruit, vegetables, honey and fish in a riot of colours and aromas.

Arts and crafts – The jewellers and goldsmiths are concentrated in Anafartalar Cad, very near the food market. A little further up, at the entrance to the citadel, stand boutiques selling Anatolian woollen goods and traditional wooden objects (Koyunpazarı Sok). The antique dealers are in Can Sok.

You can see a more western side of Ankara at the beautiful **Karum** shopping centre, next to the Sheraton **(B6)**. 9am-10pm. **Atakule** shopping centre: 9am-9pm.

Book shops – In the Kızılay district. Beautiful art books in English are sold at **Topaloğlu Kitapevi**, Hacıbayram Kitapçılar Çar 2, Kat P 33, Ulus (next to the Temple of Augustus) **(B1)**, ☎ (312) 324 24 77.

GORDİON
Ankara Province – Map p 496
106km west of Ankara, on the road to Eskişehir

Not to be missed
The Royal Tomb.
And remember...
Complete your visit by going to the Museum of Anatolian Civilisations in Ankara.
The items discovered at the site are displayed there.

Coming from Ankara, go through Polatlı, then turn right and head for Yassıhöyük (12km).

The remains of this Phrygian city are quite meagre. It is the Royal Tomb (tumulus), thought to belong to the legendary King Midas, which makes Gordion interesting. No fewer than 90 other tumuli are present in the region (25 have been excavated), creating an unusual landscape of conical hills similar to little volcanoes studding the arid plain with lunar colours.

From Midas to Alexander
An oracle had predicted that "he who untied the knot which fixed the royal cart (in the temple of Zeus) to its yoke would rule all Asia." The knot had been tied by King Gordius, five centuries earlier. In 333 BC, cunning and in a hurry, **Alexander the Great** cut the famous **Gordian knot** with his sword and left once again to conquer all of Mesopotamia.

Other legends are associated with Gordion and its most important king, the Phrygian **Midas**. However, long before him, the Gordion of the Hittites (1900-1100 BC) was already a flourishing city, which profited from its situation on the trade road between Susa and Troy. Legend is then mixed with history, first with the advent of King Gordius, who gave his name to the city, and then with Midas, whose adopted son founded the kingdom of **Phrygia**, by using the name of his homeland, Brygia. It was under his rule that Gordion experienced its golden age (8C BC). A capital, it became one of the most powerful cities of central Anatolia, reputed for its metallurgists – see the magnificent Phrygian cauldrons shown in the Ankara museum – and for the quality of its gold-laced fabric, which was exported east and west of Anatolia.

A king with ass's ears
Legend has it that King Midas took part in a musical contest which pitted Apollo against the old satyr, Marsyas. The god was obviously declared the winner, but Midas boldly challenged his victory, which led him to be humiliated with a set of donkey ears. The only person who was aware of this was his barber. However, the secret was too hard to bear, the barber shared it with the Earth by digging a hole on the riverbank and burying it there. But a reed was listening, and told the secret to its companions. Ever since, whenever the breeze has blown, the reeds can be heard whispering "King Midas has ass's ears."

The city was completely destroyed by the Cimmerians in the 13C BC. Its inhabitants rebuilt it on another hill, until the Persians (6C BC) reconstructed it again on the original site, on the ruins of the first city. Once again destroyed (by an earthquake), then rebuilt in the 4C BC, to be swept away by Alexander the Great, Gordion was no more than a modest village when the Gallic hordes invaded the region and gave it the name **Galatia**. The little city survived until the Roman period, after which it was finally abandoned.

The Royal Tomb (Tumulus)*

Go through the village and continue for 2km. The keys to the site are kept by the museum's warden, across the way. 8.30am-5.30pm. With a diameter of 300m and a height of 53m, the burial mound known as the tumulus of Midas (8C BC) is the most important of all. Access is through a narrow corridor, 70m long, which archeologists have dug to reach the chamber. The chamber itself is closed off, but an opening on the side allows you to view the interior and its construction, as if in section. Some 3m high, the chamber consists of a small and simple rectangular space, 6m long and 5m wide.

All of the region's tumuli follow the same principle: a hill of gravel hiding an underground tomb in a small rectangular room hermetically closed off by a judicious assembly of beams and layers of clay, all reinforced by a thick enclosing wall of building stone. In the interior, in a corner of the room, the body of the deceased was laid out on a bed of cloth, the head pointing to the east, next to a pile of offerings. Having miraculously remained sealed, the royal tomb revealed an extraordinary treasure: when the archeologists penetrated the funerary chamber, everything was in place, including the king's body attired in a tunic held by bronze fibulas and a leather skirt. The **funerary furniture** included 166 bronze objects, including three large cauldrons resting on a tripod, nine three-legged tables, and two screens all of which can be seen in the museum in Ankara (the **local museum** has very little). Surprisingly, perhaps, no gold was ever found…

Gordion's gold

Gordion was reputed for its bronzes, but legend has transformed them into gold. In gratitude for having found his old companion, Silenus, Dionysus offered to grant Midas his greatest wish: to change everything he touched into gold. No sooner said than done. Back at the palace, Midas amused himself by turning all of the furniture into gold. However, at lunch time, the piece of bread and wine that he brought close to his lips also turned to gold! Starving and thirsty, Midas prayed for mercy, and Dionysus agreed, telling him to bathe at the source of the Pactolus river, which Midas did without delay. However, the river's waters remained filled with grains of gold, which, two centuries later, were to make the fortune of famous King Croesus, (for the remainder of the story, see p 264!)

The Phrygian city

On your return from the tumulus, have a look at the ruins of the Phrygian city, 1km from the edge of the village. Opposite the petrol station, turn left on the little path which skirts the hill; the ruins are located behind. The site is closed off by a grille but there is no problem getting in.

Of the ruins of the city of Midas, only the **Phrygian gate** is of interest. Built at the end of the 8C BC, this imposing limestone structure was built at an angle to the city wall, creating a 33m-long corridor with a completely square opening (9x9m).

Beyond the gate are the remains of the city, a chaos of razed walls which are difficult to identify due to the lack of signs. Opposite the gate and slightly to the left, the walls of four **megarons** (*see lexicon p 58*) house a group of buildings which probably belonged to the royal palace and to the temple dedicated to Cybele. It was in this temple, later dedicated to Zeus, that the famous cart with the Gordian knot was located. Beyond are another eight megarons on either side of a path.

Gordion

THE LAND OF THE HITTITES★★
ALACAHÖYÜK – BOĞAZKALE – YAZILIKAYA
50km tour – One day – Map p 496
(250km starting at Ankara; 3.5hr on good roads)
Accommodation in Boğazkale or Sungurlu

Not to be missed
The Sphinx Gate in Alacahöyük.
The postern crossing the southern ramparts of Hattuşaş.
The rock bas-reliefs in Yazılıkaya.

And remember...
Ideally, it is best to visit the three sites chronologically, as outlined below. However, if you stay overnight in Boğazkale, you might prefer to begin with the nearer sites, Hattuşaş and Yazılıkaya. Whatever you decide, be sure to complete your tour by seeing the superb collections in the Ankara Museum.

The territory of one of Anatolia's most ancient people extends two hundred kilometres east of Ankara. Beyond Sungurlu, the Boğazkale road crosses a beautiful **landscape**★ of steppes and arid hills, climbing to an altitude of 1 500m. This is where Hattuşaş, the capital of the Hittite Empire, developed. Nearby, the four-thousand-year-old city of Alacahöyük is among the planet's oldest. The heart of Anatolia was also the centre of the world. *(For more information on the history of the first peoples of Anatolia, see p 18).*

Hittite society
Little is known about the daily life of the Hittites. What we do know comes from the superb bas-reliefs carved on the walls of the palaces, which depict court scenes, processions and acts of homage to the king, and depict a very hierarchical society. However, more precise information is found on the tablets discovered in Hattuşaş, using cuneiform characters, which supplied the names of kings, accounts of battles, summaries of treaties and laws, and numerous historical facts that have taught us about the habits and influences of the period.

A codified society
Inspired by the Assyrian model, Hittite society was headed by a sovereign – simultaneously judge and high priest – who delegated the administration of his provinces to warlords. A code also governed all relations between landowners, artisans, farmers and slaves, not forgetting the conquered peoples, whose customs were often respected and even adopted.

In particular, these tablets have shown that the Hittites were "intelligent" conquerors who knew how to benefit from the culture of the people they encountered. They adopted the cuneiform form of writing of the Assyrians, included numerous Hurrian divinities in their pantheon, and a number of Hittite kings married Mesopotamian princesses.

Gifted metallurgists, the Hittites also proved to be able builders, capable of adapting to uneven terrain and expert in the design of sophisticated defence systems (towers, posterns etc). The base of these constructions – not just fortifications, but also temples and public buildings – were of stone (andesite, basalt, granite or limestone), decorated with bas-reliefs, while the walls, long gone, were in adobe (sun-dried bricks), like those of the dwellings.

Central Anatolia

■ Alacahöyük★

35km from Boğazkale, 39km from Sungurlu, 210km from Ankara
Allow 1hr.

Coming from Ankara, go past Sungurlu, then after 33km, take the minor road on the right in the direction of Höyük (not well signposted). The site, which includes a small museum, is in the middle of the village. 8am-12noon/1.30pm-5.30pm; closed Mondays. Entrance fee. The numbered signs make it easy to find one's way round.

Inhabited by the Hattians from the fourth millennium BC onwards, Alacahöyük reached its apogee around 1900 BC. The 13 tombs brought to light date from this period and contain remarkable objects – arms and jewellery, in bronze, gold or electrum (gold and silver), now in the Ankara museum. The city continued its development during the whole period of Hittite domination (Alacahöyük was probably the site of the first Hittite capital, **Kussar**), before falling into the hands of the Phrygians, in 1100 BC. This period marked the beginning of a slow decline, which continued until the Roman period. Reduced to a modest village, Alacahöyük fell into oblivion.

The Hittite vestiges★

The first sight of the city, the **Sphinx Gate**★, is also the most impressive. These remains are those of the Hittite city of the New Empire, which goes back to the 14C BC. Two stern **sphinxes** flank the passage leading to the ruins, andesite monoliths forming the *piedroits* of the main gate (south). Their presence was supposed to protect the city from evil spirits. On the inner side of the right sphinx, notice the **two-headed eagle** grasping a rabbit in its claws.

A few **stone panels (orthostats)**★ protrude from the wall, on both sides of the gate, forming a magnificent bas-relief frieze *(reproduction, the original is in the Ankara museum)*. On the left the king and queen can be seen worshipping a bull, followed by a line of animals and jugglers, priests and musicians. On the right, the Hurrian solar goddess Arinna-Hepatu, rises in front of a group of worshippers.

The Hattian city

The rest of the site is much less spectacular. Beyond the gate is a vast field of ruins, a chequerboard of the walls and foundations of the pre-Hittite city.

There is a well-preserved underground **drainage system**, and on the right, there are six **Hattian royal tombs**★ *(sign no 8)*. They consist of simple rectangular platforms, 4-6m long, 350m wide. Their walls, barely 1m high, are made of small stones, whereas the roof was made of beams and a layer of soil, hermetically closing off the funerary chamber. Two of these tombs have been rebuilt, and offer a glimpse of the interior: the deceased was laid in a foetal position in a corner of the chamber, near the offerings. In the other tombs, the location of the deceased is indicated by a stone.

Built between 2300 and 1800 BC, these undoubtedly were the burial sites of important people – kings, princes or priests – judging by the wealth of what they contained: standards and solar discs made of bronze, gold jewellery, statuettes of the mother goddess, many treasures which are now in the Ankara museum.

Beyond the royal tombs, the path crosses the ruins of numerous dwellings to reach the city's **western postern**★ *(sign no 9, on the left)*, a narrow underground passage reached by a small set of stairs. Passing underneath the Hittite ramparts, it allowed the inhabitants to flee in case of danger. Part of the **corbel vault**★, made of beautiful stone blocks, has been preserved.

The land of the Hittites

529

The small but interesting **museum** *(by the entrance to the site)* should be visited. It has a few fine objects found on the site: **solar discs**, animal statuettes, and early Bronze Age pottery (royal tomb period), gold jewellery and Hittite hairpins, along with a **bathtub** and weaving weights. There are also examples of of fine Phrygian pottery, decorated with embossed geometric patterns. In the basement is a small ethnographic section.

From Alacahöyük, go to Salman and turn left in the direction of Boğazkale. If you come from Ankara: 8km after Sungurlu, turn right in the direction of Boğazkale; 22km. The site is at the end of the village.

■ Boğazkale★★ (Hattuşaş)

Allow half a day to visit Hattuşaş and Yazılıkaya, the neighbouring site.

38km from Alacahöyük, 30km from Sungurlu and 202km from Ankara. Daily (in season), 8am-5pm. Entrance fee. Small museum in the village, to be visited only if you have the time.

Judiciously set on a small plateau overlooking a river, at an altitude of 1 000m, the city of Hattuşaş was founded in the second millennium BC by the Hattians. However, it only really began to grow during the Hittite period, when it became the capital of King Hattusilis I who gave it its name (1900 BC). Most of the ruins are from the New Empire (14-13C BC), a period marking the apogee of the city. Deserted at the end of the Hittite Empire, it experienced a renewal under the Phrygians, who lived in it from the 9C to the 7C BC. The following centuries saw only sporadic occupation of the site, until it was completely abandoned.

Upon arrival, you will be surprised by the sheer size of the site (2.5km). Hattuşaş was in fact a very extensive city, whose ramparts ran for more than 6km, matching the lines of the uneven terrain. Its ruins seem to spread forever, an impression reinforced by the surrounding **panorama★★**, which takes in an immense steppe, undulating as far as the eye can see. Fortunately, the road crossing the city makes it easier to visit (take advantage of this, if you are travelling by car).

Temple I★ (Büyük Maret)

Beyond the ticket office, on the right is a vast terrace filled up by a gigantic religious complex dedicated to Teshub, the storm god, and to Arinna-Hepatu, the sun goddess. This is the largest known Hittite temple, a quadrilateral measuring 160x 130m and containing all sorts of adjoining buildings, rooms for worship, and shops. More than just a temple, this complex also had an economic purpose, comparable to that of the Roman forum, although more enclosed.

Before you reach the propylaea, you will see a **monolithic basin** which has retained part of its ornamentation: two beautiful **lions with five paws** (only four when seen from the front or from the side).

Once inside the complex, you go from room to room along narrow paved alleyways. The chambers on the right, undoubtedly reserved for the archives, have yielded thousands of **tablets** covered with cuneiform inscriptions. On the other side, a series of large **amphorae** set in the ground, with a capacity of 900-3 000 litres, indicate the location of the storage area. The heart of the complex is formed by the temple, whose rooms surround a large **central courtyard**. On one of the sides, a vestibule once gave access to two **adytons**, inner sanctums, where the statues of the divinities were kept.

Southwest of the temple, the **Workshop House** was a second annex to the complex. It contained shops, housing and workshops related to the functioning and administration of the temple. The tablets brought to light have revealed that more than 200 people concerned with the temple's daily life lived here. The "house" was inside the walls, isolating the complex from the rest of the city, with a single gate linking it to the outside world.

Return to the road which crosses the site. Follow it to the junction and turn right.

The ramparts★

Continuing towards the ramparts of the lower city, the road skirts the foot of the little ruined fortress of **Yenicekale**, built on a rocky peak *(on the left of the road)*. Since the uneven and rocky terrain constituted a natural defence, the city's battlements did not surround it completely. In the south, on the other hand, where the city was open to the valley, a **double fortification** was erected (14C BC) and strengthened by an artificial embankment, whose ruins testify to the Hittites' skill and knowledge of defensive architecture: the inner rampart was reinforced by a lower outer wall, separated by a 6m-wide dry moat. A thick glacis covered the walls, rendering the opponents' manoeuvres even more perilous. Watchtowers protected the access gates, with those on the rear wall staggered in relation to those at the front, giving a clear view and field of fire on all sides. A gallery linked the outer and inner extremities of each gate (vaulted with ogees) which were blocked with heavy wooden doors locked with iron bars. No-one could possibly say that the city wasn't well guarded!

Of the six doors which pierced the walls, three are still visible. The finest is undoubtedly the **Lions' Gate★** (Aslanlıkapı), which owes its names to the two majestic creatures on its outer architraves. The way they have been sculpted (notice how the block of stone is given its curved form by the animal's swelling breast) is reminiscent of their contemporaries, the sphinxes of Alacahöyük. The well-preserved **lion on the right**, is opening its jaw in a silent roar, a deterrent to evil spirits.

Two **monumental stairways** lead to the **Sphinxes' Gate★** (Yerkapı), set on the highest point of the walls (1 245m; very beautiful **view★**). It has lost the large limestone sphinxes which guarded its outer access (to be seen in İstanbul and Berlin); however,

The land of the Hittites

12m below is the opening of a remarkable intact **postern***, a narrow 71m-long underground tunnel crossing the walls from side to side and ending up in the countryside. Its corbel vault is tall enough to allow a horseman to pass. Continuing along the walls to the east, the road skirts the razed walls of four buildings, on the left, prosaically named **Temples 2, 3, 4** and **5**. All have the same layout as Temple 1 (but on a smaller scale): propylaeae precede a central courtyard surrounded by small rooms, while the sacred adyton – reserved for priests – is at the rear.

Further on is the **King's Gate*** (Kralkapı), similar to the Lion's Gate. The inner gate bears, on its left architrave, a magnificent **figure**** thought to be a king *(it is a copy, the original is in the Ankara museum)*. It is in fact the god of war responsible for the protection of the city.

Towards the Büyükkale citadel

Returning towards the city centre, you come to a number of ruins spread up the uneven hillside. On the left are the ruins of the little bastion of **Nişantepe** (14C BC). On a rocky spur just beyond is another small fort, **Sarıkale** (13C BC), while on the right of the road, **Güneykale** ("the castle of the south") occupies a small plateau.

This last bastion rises in front of the impressive **Büyükkale** citadel ("the big fortress"), also built on a plateau. Surrounded by ramparts, it covered an area of 250x140m. Erected by the Hittites (14-13C BC), it was remodelled by the Phrygians (7-6C BC). However, it is the Hittite foundations that have been brought to light by the archeologists. It is thought that the citadel housed the king's residence. A number of buildings surrounding the courtyards made up the complex, including several archive rooms: no less than 3 000 **tablets**, written in cuneiform characters or in Egyptian hieroglyphics, have been discovered. One of them relates the non-aggression pact signed between the Hittites and Pharaoh Ramses II, after the battle of Kadesh. Two superb rhyta (vases) shaped liked bulls and the statue of the mother goddess **Cybele** were also found in the citadel. Both are displayed in the Museum of Anatolian Civilisations in Ankara.

The village **museum** *(8am-5pm, closed Mondays; entrance fee)* houses a few objects from the site (tablets, libation vases, terracotta fragments from the drainage system) as well as a map and photographs of the excavations.

■ Yazılıkaya*

3km from Boğazkale. The road is clearly marked.
Open every day in season, 8am-5pm. Entrance fee, allow 1hr.

Yazılıkaya was the religious sanctuary of Hattuşaş (Boğazkale), founded in the 13C BC by Hattusilis III, and enlarged by his son Tudhaliyas IV (1250-1220). There are several references to Tudhaliyas around the site.

The Hittites' pantheon included a plethora of divinities (almost 1 000), since little by little they assimilated into their own culture the gods belonging to the peoples they encountered or conquered. The gods represented in Yazılıkaya – more than 65 of them – belonged to the Hurrian pantheon.

The various sanctuary buildings have all disappeared; only their foundations, built of stone and not adobe, have withstood the passing of time. On the other hand, the rocky walls separating the sacred rooms have retained extraordinary wall paintings.

Chamber A★

Beyond the entrance, a path lined with hedges flanks the **temple** ruins *(on the left; entrance forbidden)*. This sanctuary followed more or less the same principle as Temple 1 in Boğazkale: beyond the propylaea, a staircase led to a central courtyard and continued on to an **adyton★**, situated here on the left of the courtyard *(to reach it, follow the remains of the temple and make for the deepest opening, on the left)*. The spring feast and the renewal of nature were undoubtedly celebrated here with the king and queen acting as symbolic figures.

However, the adyton of the temple of Yazılıkaya is not really a constructed room: laid out in a sunken area, it is a space open to the sky surrounded by natural rocky walls. The rocks form a background for the beautiful **bas-reliefs★** of the gods in procession, aligned one after the other, in profile, following the artistic canons inherited from Hurrian Mesopotamia. Most of the figures are very worn, but the ensemble remains inspiring. On the left wall appear the gods, wearing Hittite clothing – tunic and pointed hat – whereas the right wall hosts the goddesses wearing traditional long gowns. It is possible to make out the silhouettes of **Teshub** (the storm god) and **Hepatu-Arinna** (the sun goddess) accompanied by a two-headed eagle.

The size of each divinity varies according to its importance in the pantheon, but the tallest figure remains that of King **Tudhaliyas IV★**, simultaneously governor and high priest *(near the goddesses, on the right)*. Thus, Teshub and Hepatu are "only" 2m tall, while, the king, shown crossing a mountain, is 2.6m tall. He wears priest's clothing but holds in his hand the crook of the Hittite shepherd, his sceptre as sovereign. A cartouche in hieroglyphics indicates his name.

Backtrack.

Chamber B★★

On the left, a narrow corridor, guarded by two **winged chimaeras** with lion heads, leads to Chamber B, an impressive corridor open to the sky, cut in the rock, with a length of 20m and a width of 2-4m. It is here that the most beautiful bas-reliefs are located. On the right, **12 gods★★** armed with scimitars are aligned along the wall, like marching soldiers.

Facing them is another depiction of King **Tudhaliyas IV★**, supported by Sharuma, the son of Teshub and Hepatu (the silhouette of the god, smaller and covered with a cape, is difficult to identify). The name of the king is inscribed inside the cartouche next to his head, while the one belonging to the god is represented by a figurine in the king's hand. Beside them is an unusual figure known as the **"sword god★"**. His human head, with a tiara, is shown above the busts of two lions and two lions lying in a vertical position. The whole ensemble forms the handle of a sword, with the blade pointing downwards. It is thought to be a tribute to the king for his victories in Syria.

Making the most of the Hittite sites

COMING AND GOING

By bus – Since the sites are near the Ankara-Samsun road, they are easy to get to by bus. Regular bus services operate to Sungurlu from Ankara on a daily basis. Dolmuşes shuttle between Sungurlu and Boğazkale every hour.

By car – Still the most convenient way to travel around the region.

WHERE TO STAY – EATING OUT

• In Sungurlu

Around US$30

Motel Hitit, on the road to Ankara, in Samsun, on the right when coming from Ankara (near a garage), ☎ (364) 311 80 42, Fax (364) 311 38 73 – 23rm. ⌂ ⊡ ✗ Average level of comfort; the establishment is going downhill. Dining facilities.

• In Boğazkale

The hotel facilities are rather rustic, but Boğazkale is the best place to stay if you want to get an early start in the morning.

Around US$30

Motel Aşıkoğlu, at the entrance to the village, on the opposite side from the site, ☎ (364) 452 20 04, Fax (364) 452 21 71 – 20rm. ⌂ ✗ The rooms are very simple, the atmosphere friendly and the food very good (lunch and evening meals). Closed from December to March.

Motel-Pension Hattuşaş, in the main square in the centre of the village, ☎ (364) 452 20 13, Fax (364) 452 29 57 – 9rm (23 beds). ⌂ ✗ A small, simple, but comfortable hotel with spacious rooms. The friendly owner speaks English well and takes pleasure in providing information on the region. The restaurant is good and nicely decorated with kilims. Open all year round.

ROGER-VIOLLET

Central Anatolia

Yazılıkaya, the procession of the Hittite gods

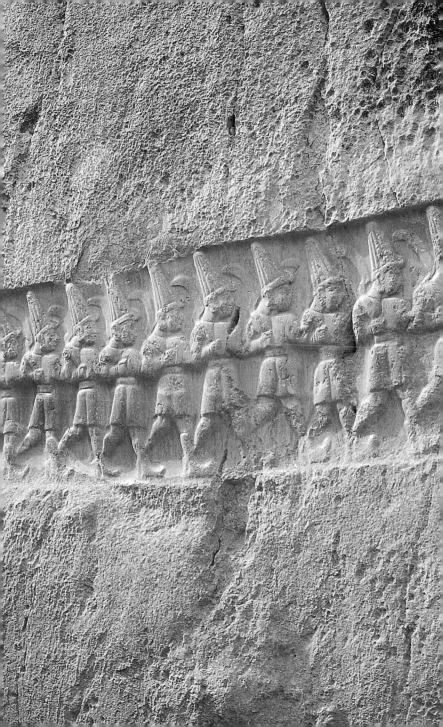

SİVAS★★

Provincial capital – Map p 497
108km from Tokat – 193km from Kayseri – 247km from Malatya
Pop 385 000 – Alt 1 265m

Not to be missed
The Blue Medrese and the Seljuk buildings in Selçuklu Park.
And remember...
Sivas has the reputation of being a highly religious city, and visitors should
dress appropriately (avoid shorts and miniskirts).

Like Konya, whose atmosphere it recalls, Sivas has retained remarkable examples of
Seljuk architecture making it well-worth a visit. Established at the crossroads of some
of the most important caravan routes of the East, the Black Sea and the Aegean, this
little city has always thrived on trade and continues to do so today, with a lively
bazaar, a colourful market and ever noisy streets.

A highly coveted city

Highly coveted throughout its entire history, ancient *Sebastea* was the capital of several
successive states. Converted to Christianity in the 2C, it was the seat of a bishopric
during the Byzantine era, before becoming the capital of a small Armenian state at
the end of the 10C. It was in 1071, when it passed into the hands of Seljuk Turks,
that it acquired its current name. However, at the end of the 11C, a Turcoman dynasty, the Danişmend, created an enclave in the Seljuk Empire, establishing its capital in Sivas. The emirate was short-lived, since the Seljuk Emir of Tokat was able, in

The martyrs of Sebastea
In the 4C, Sebastea experienced a dark
period in its history, often depicted in
Byzantine iconography: refusing to re-
nounce their Christian faith and honour pagan gods, 40 Roman soldiers
from the city's garrison were taken to
the middle of a frozen lake, stripped
and left to die of exposure.

1191, to reclaim Sivas in the name of the Empire. The city later endured the passage of the
Mongols, in the 13C. One of their chiefs,
Eretna, proclaimed himself independent and
made Sivas capital of his little state, which
turned out to be quite prosperous. Most of the
monuments visible today, especially the
medreses, date from this period. However,
the Turco-Mongol Tamerlane, who was attempting to extend his Empire into Anatolia,
took the city and destroyed its ramparts. It was a short-lived conquest, however, since
the Ottomans reclaimed it a few years later and retained it until the 20C. The successive conflicts exhausted Sivas, and although the city is still a busy commercial centre, it has never regained the sparkle of its past.

The city

*The monuments are concentrated in the heart of the city, around the main square, Konak
Meydanı. It is easy to visit the entire city on foot. Allow half a day.*

A tour of the medreses

Selçuklu Park *(near the Konak Meydanı, entrance on İnönü Bul, 8am-8pm)* is the elegant
setting of three superb Seljuk-period Koranic schools. One of them, the Bürüciye
medrese (1271), is closed for restorations, but its main interest lies in its **portal★**,
decorated with a beautiful pediment with *muqarnas* (stalactites).

Behind it is a vestibule leading into a central courtyard surrounded by the facilities typically found in all Koranic schools – rooms for study, student quarters, library etc. A small cell, at the left of the entrance, houses the founder's **türbe**.

The **portal***** is all that remains of the **medrese with Two Minarets***** (Çifte Minare), but it is of outstanding beauty. Like the city's other Seljuk buildings, this medrese was built at the end of the 13C, during the Mongol occupation. The architecture of this period, inherited from Iran and Central Asia is characterised by sumptuous decoration, although mostly concentrated on the portal, which can be defined as Baroque. Flanked by two elegant **minarets****, in glazed blue bricks, the portal of the medrese marvellously illustrates this tendency, a veritable forest of stalactites, geometrical patterns, calligraphy, interlacing and foliage which sparkle like stars.

Across the way is the **Şifaiye medrese**** (8am-8pm, entrance free). It is in fact a hospital that was built at the beginning of the 13C, and later converted into a Koranic school. Its portal is similar to its neighbour's, although slightly less exuberant. It precedes a large vestibule leading to three rooms and giving onto a central courtyard, lined with porticoes. At the back lies the **iwan** (partially destroyed) with its surrounding cells. The medrese houses the founding sultan's **türbe**, its pretty **façade*** covered with glazed bricks and black and blue tiles. The site needs to be restored, however it exudes much charm thanks to the presence of the colourful stalls of carpet sellers and craftsmen. And there is a handy open-air café nearby.

Opposite the park (near the entrance), on the other side of the boulevard is the **Ethnography Museum*** (Atatürk, Kongre & Etnografya Müzesi), housed in an imposing, early 20C administrative building (8am-12noon/1.30pm-5.30pm; closed Mondays; entrance fee). Its collection of Sivas **carpets**, in the central hall, is worth visiting, as are the rooms dedicated to everyday Ottoman life, furnished with fine furniture, opaline lamps etc. Also of interest is the beautiful wooden **minbar*** from the Divrigi mosque. Upstairs, the **Congress hall**, left intact, was the scene of the Congress of Sivas in 1919, at which Atatürk rallied opposition to the Allied moves to dismember Turkey.

Go along İnönü Bul until you reach Cemal Gürsel Cad and turn left.

Further down, on Cemal Gürsel Caddesi is the city's oldest mosque (early 12C), the **Grand Mosque** (Ulu Cami). It is easily recognised because of its large cylindrical **minaret**, added in the 13C. The prayer hall is decorated with 10 rows of broken arches creating a beautiful inner space.

The Blue Medrese*** (Gök Medrese)

Past the Grand Mosque, turn right on Cumhuriyet Cad. You will reach the rear façade of the Blue Medrese, the pride of Sivas (under restoration; 8am-6pm; entrance fee). The building is of great force and majesty, reinforced by the two minarets which soar above the portal. At each corner of the building is a **turret***, with all-over carving, while the **portal***** in the middle of the façade has a pediment with a wonderful cascade of muqarnas. Built in 1271, the Gök Medrese is also very representative of the Baroque wave in Seljuk art. The decor of the two **minarets**** is a fine example of this style: fluted shafts on which bricks alternate with black and blue glazed tiles, creating countless chevrons.

Inside, on the right, is a small **oratory*** which has retained a few beautiful blue tiles. The central courtyard, lined with elegant porticoes, is embellished with three iwans with ogee vaults, while at the back, the **wall*** of marble blocks is decorated with a pretty **frieze*** of calligraphy in bas-relief.

Sivas

Retrace your steps and go along Cumhuriyet Cad all the way to the end. Then, turn right on Hıkıyet Işı.

On the left is the **Güdük Minare**, a large redbrick tower topped with a pointed dome. It is in fact a mausoleum dating from the 14C. It faces the city's merchant quarter where old **caravanserais** house the stalls of spice shops, as scented as they are colourful.

Making the most of Sivas

COMING AND GOING

By bus – Dolmuşes run between the bus station and town centre, 2km away. Daily bus services operate to Trabzon (15hr), Amasya (4hr), Ankara (7hr), Divriği (4hr), Erzurum (7hr), Malatya (for Nemrut Dağı) in 5hr, Kayseri (4hr) and Tokat (2hr).

By train – The town is on the İstanbul Lake Van line. From Sivas you can also get to Samsun, Erzurum, Malatya and Ankara (12hr). You may as well take the bus!

By air – **Turkish Airlines** operates a 1hr flight between Sivas and Ankara on Wednesdays and Fridays. The airport is 23km from the town. Information: **Sivas Tourism**, Seyahat Acentası İstasyon Cad 50 Yıl Sitesi, Vergi Dairesi Altı 78, ☎ (346) 221 11 47. Closed on Sundays.

ADDRESS BOOK

Tourist information – On the 1ˢᵗ floor of the town hall in the main square, ☎ (346) 221 35 35. Open Monday to Friday, 9am-5pm.

Main post office – At the end of Atatürk Bul, on the right, just before the main square. 8.30am-7pm. Telephones available 24 hours a day.

Change – In Atatürk Bul, near the main square. Several banks exchange foreign currency, but only US dollars and deutsche marks.

WHERE TO STAY

Hotels are scarce, but so are the tourists, so you should have no trouble finding somewhere to stay.

Around US$45

🛏 **Hotel Madımak**, Eski Belediye Sok 2. Not far from Atatürk Bul, near the square, ☎ (346) 221 80 27 – 25rm. ⬛ TV ✍ Recently renovated, this little hotel offers simple, clean rooms. Good welcome.

Around US$60

Hotel Büyük Sivas, İstasyon Cad. A 10min walk from the square, ☎ (346) 225 47 62, Fax (346) 225 23 23 – 114rm. ⬛ ✍ TV ✗ CC This immense hotel opened in 1996 and is in perfect condition. Despite its somewhat austere decor, you will find a good standard of comfort.

EATING OUT

In the street behind the post office, you will find several little restaurants serving extremely cheap "döner kebap" and pide. Likewise in the main street.

Under US$5

Büyük Merkez Lokantası, Atatürk Cad 13, ☎ (346) 223 64 34. Join the lunchtime crowd at the market for a good "iskender kebap". Good, copious and very cheap dishes.

SHOPPING GUIDE

Beautiful carpets at **Şifaiye Medrese**, which is now a crafts centre. If you take a stroll around the town, you will also come across spices and wooden goods.

G. Degeorge

Making the most of Sivas

The full exuberance of Seljuk art: the portal of the Bürüciye medrese (Sivas)

NEMRUT DAĞI★★★

70km from Malatya, 49km from Kahta (71 using the Eski Kahta road)
106km from Adıyaman, 414km from Kayseri – Map p 497
Alt 2 935m – Mountain climate, dry and cool

Not to be missed
The sunset seen from the western terrace (the loveliest),
absolutely stunning.
The sunrise (eastern terrace) is not bad either!

And remember...
Because of the political situation, the region is not always very stable, and
it is best to book your tour at the Tourist Office in Kahta or Malatya.
Bring along warm clothing; you are at a high altitude and it can get cold.
The cleanliness of some of the local hotels is dubious; bring along a bed sheet.

At the summit of the mountain, at an altitude of more than 2 000m, a strange pale-coloured and perfectly-formed cone appears against the sky, flanked by two rows of colossi. One row faces the east, the other the west, looking at both sides of the world. This is the monumental tomb of Nemrut Dağı (see photograph; p 42-43).

Whichever road you use – each straddles an extraordinary landscape of mountains – you will not reach Nemrut Dağı by chance. Like an obstacle course, the prize is awarded at the end of the race, and transformed into gold by the sun.

There are two ways of reaching the site: one starting at Malatya, the other from Kahta, depending on whether you are coming from the north or from the south (see "Making the most of Nemrut Dağı). By making a short detour to the west, the second route adds to the interest of a trip to Nemrut Dağı by taking in a number of neglected, but nevertheless fascinating sites.

From Kahta to Nemrut Dağı
*70km tour; allow 2hr with stops for the visits.
Bring along a guide, signposts are rare.*

■ 9km from Kahta, the **Karakuş tumulus** becomes visible from the road. The little hill houses the relics of the mother, daughter and grand-daughter of Mithridates I, the founder of the dynasty of the kings of Commagene (see sidebar p 543).
Three white Doric columns rise at the foot of the royal tumulus, which were respectively crowned by a lion, an eagle (still standing) and a bull.

■ 8km further on, in a splendid **landscape★★**, the road reaches the edge of the Cendere, a small river crossed by the single arch of a pretty **Roman bridge** – the **Cendere Köprüsü** – built in honour of Septimius Severus (late 2C). Two pairs of **columns** stood at each end of the bridge (three are still standing), each representing a member of the Imperial family.

■ Beyond the river is the village of **Eski Kahta** (*5km from the bridge, on the "Gerger-Nemrut Dağı" road*), guarded by the Mameluke fortress of **Yeni Kale★** (14C) high on a rocky peak.
From here, go back 2km, then take the minor road on the left for 3km.

■ **Eski Kale** is the site of the ancient **Arsameia★**, the capital of the Commagene kingdom (*entrance fee*). Founded in the 1C BC, the city was laid out on the plateau stretching along the summit of the hill, while the sanctuary of Mithridates I was built halfway up. The remains are sparse, but they are worth a look, as is the spectacular **panorama★★** overlooking the mountains. The path leads firstly to a large **cistern**, then ends further down at the entrance to a **tunnel** dug in the rock. A majestic **stela★** rises nearby, showing Heracles (recognisable by his club) shaking the hand of Mithridates I. From here, a **monumental staircase** (in ruins) led to the top of the hill to the terrace of the royal palace. The building has disappeared but its beautiful mosaic floors are preserved in the Ankara museum.

The road then passes through several villages before reaching Narince. From here turn left to reach (7km later) the main road leading to Nemrut Daği. The site is 16km further on.

The sanctuary of Antiochus I★★★
20min climb on foot, whether you are coming from Malatya or Kahta. Entrance fee.
At the site, allow 1hr.

What is today an immense desert – a superb **landscape ★★★** of arid mountains – was once a fertile region, covered with forests. The kingdom of Commagene was a wealthy State, strategically located on the borders of the Seleucid Empire and Persia. The magnificent sculptures and bas-reliefs found in the region express this interplay between Hellenistic culture and the Mesopotamian world very well. This synthesis was the pride of the kings of Commagene, in particular, **Antiochus I** (69-23 BC) who claimed to descend from the great Darius I on his father's side, and the no less valorous Alexander the Great on his mother's. True or false? Whatever the truth, he showed his megalomania in the extravagant mausoleum which he had erected at the summit of Nemrut Daği. More than a tomb, it is a major religious complex, destined to honour the gods as well as the king himself, who appears as an equal at their side.

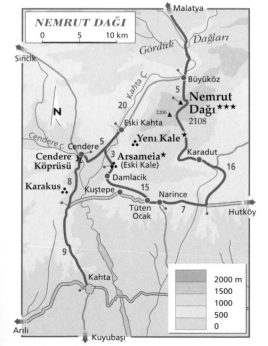

Discovered in 1881 by a Turkish geologist, the sanctuary was not excavated until 1953 by the American Institute of Oriental Research. However, abandoned after five years, the excavations have never resumed and the tomb of Antiochus I, the exact location of which has not yet been determined, lies undisturbed.

The **tumulus★**, consisting entirely of crushed rock, forms a cone with a diameter of 150m and a height of 50m. Three terraces surround it: one to the east, the other to the west – its counterpart – and a third to the north (now destroyed). The latter led to the sacred way where the processions would pass, flanked by a monumental eagle and

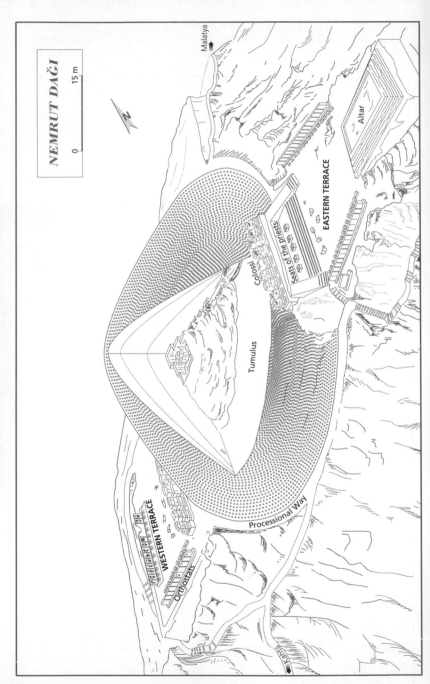

NEMRUT DAĞI

0   15 m

Malatya

Altar

EASTERN TERRACE

Seats of the priests

Colossi

Tumulus

Processional Way

WESTERN TERRACE

Orthostats

lion. The other two, symmetrical, display the same configuration: a row of nine colossi are located in front of a cobblestone esplanade reserved for worship, surrounded by a series of sculpted orthostats (stone panels set vertically).

The colossi, seated, were from left to right: Apollo, Tyche (the goddess of fortune, in the image of Commagene), Zeus, Antiochus (on the left of the "father") and Hercules. The group was flanked on each side by an eagle and a lion.

A kingdom between two worlds

Located north of Syria, between Cilicia and the banks of the Euphrates, the land of the Commagenes was the Seleucid Empire's easternmost province, at the edge of the Iranian plateau. However, in 162 BC Ptolemy, its governor, made it an independent kingdom. At the beginning of the 1C BC, Mithridates I established his capital in Arsameia and founded a dynasty, which his son, Antiochus I, made prosperous. But the glory was short-lived: with the arrival of the Romans, Commagene became a protectorate, before being divided between the Roman provinces of Syria and Cilicia in 72 AD.

Beside these monumental statues (9m high), the orthostats flanked the two terraces showing the king and his illustrious ancestors in the company of gods. While their extremely noble faces are endowed with a realism akin to Hellenistic art, the bodies seem to follow Iranian or Egyptian tradition, and perhaps even the canons of Hittite art.

The **western terrace****** is undoubtedly the most beautiful. Earthquakes have violently shaken the colossi; they have all disintegrated and their **heads****** have toppled. But it is precisely this array of giant heads resting on the ground, their faces peering blindly into infinity, which creates a spectacle of extraordinary majesty. Here, Zeus, recognisable by his beard, there, Tyche with fruit-decorated hair, farther away, Apollo, wearing a hat. It is an amazing sight to the see the sun's rays illuminate one by one at sunrise and sunset. On the left, the **lion** and the **eagle** are still in place, as well as a few **orthostats*** with fine carving.

The colossi of the **eastern terrace**** are in much better condition, but their heads, all toppled, are much more worn. The eastern terrace has one unusual feature compared to its western counterpart: at the end of the esplanade are the remains of an **altar** with an incineration chamber (most likely used to sacrifice animals during religious ceremonies).

Malatya

Provincial capital. 95km from Nemrut Daği, 344km from Kayseri, 247km from Sivas, 410km from Adana. Pop 372 000. Alt 915m

If you are coming from the north, Malatya will be your starting point for Nemrut Daği. Once virtually unknown to visitors from abroad, the city is slowly opening up to tourism. Even so, it is best to avoid wearing shorts and miniskirts. Its population has exploded in the last few years and has completely altered its character and appearance. But Malatya has retained its beautiful orange colour of former years. It is the capital of apricots! They are everywhere, in shops, drying on rooftops, and especially in the stalls of the **apricot market**** *(near the main square)*, undoubtedly the city's most picturesque sight.

Around July 20, there is an **apricot festival**, with numerous festivities. If time allows, have a look at the **ethnography museum** *(at the end of Fuzuli Cad 8am-5pm; closed Mondays. Entrance fee)*. Although dusty, the **Neolithic and Hittite collections** are quite interesting.

Another place to visit is **old Malatya** (Eski Malatýa), 19km from the city *(take a bus, on Sivas Cad., in the direction of Battalgazi)*, an attractive village whose Seljuk **Great Mosque** (Ulu Cami), built in the 13C, has beautiful blue tiles.

Nemrut Daği

Making the most of Nemrut Dağı

COMING AND GOING

Depending on whether you come from the north (from Trabzon or Sivas), from Cappadocia or from the south (from Mersin or Syria), you will pass through either Malatya or Kahta. In both cases, the road leading to the site is of very variable quality and the route complicated. Moreover, the region is relatively unsafe. So, whether you have your own transport or not, we strongly recommend that you do not make the trip unaccompanied: call in at the tourist information office in Malatya or Kahta, both well-practised in the organisation of this "expedition".

Return trip from Malatya – In summer, the Malatya tourist information office runs a tour every day enabling you to see the sun set and rise over the site: departure at noon, sunset at Nemrut Dağı, night at the *Motel Güneş* (the only hotel near the site, 3km away; reservations through the Malatya tourist information office; rustic level of comfort), sunrise and return to Malatya around 10am the following day. The site is a 20min walk or 5min car ride away from the motel.

Return trip from Kahta – The direct route takes 2hr to get to the site (49km).

If you choose to follow the itinerary suggested above, it will take you 4hr 30min (70km). Once you have reached the foot of Nemrut Dağı, it will only take a further 20min to walk up to the tumulus. Kahta suffers from the competition from Malatya, but the tourist office is fighting back, particularly against certain unscrupulous individuals who were still recently selling their services at very high prices. There is now one official rate for the tours and hotel accommodation. You will not, however, find sunset / sunrise tours like those which run from Malatya. But the advantage is that you can choose at what time you go to the site.

Outward trip from Malatya / Return to Kahta – From Nemrut Dağı, take a section of the road which goes down to Malatya, until you reach the village of Büyüköz (the village is not signposted; it is about 30min from the summit). When leaving the village, on the left is a 25km track which skirts the mountain and leads to Eski Kahta, where you can join the road to Kahta. You can make the trip from Nemrut Dağı to Kahta in one morning. The hotel facilities on the way are very modest but can be welcome.

Making the most of Kahta

COMING AND GOING

By bus – The "otogar" is in the centre of the village. Kahta is a long way from the main tourist roads and the local buses are not very comfortable. Several buses make the 30min journey to Adiyaman (large neighbouring town) every day. From there, you can get to Adana (6hr), Ankara (12hr), Kayseri (9hr), İstanbul (19hr), Malatya (3hr) and to eastern Turkey.

ADDRESS BOOK

Tourist information – Mustafa Kemal Cad, near the junction with Nemrut Yölü, ☎ and Fax (416) 725 50 07. Good welcome.

WHERE TO STAY

Between US$20 and US$25
Pension Kommagène, Mustafa Kemal Cad. Next door to the one below, ☎ (416) 715 10 92 – 15rm. Rudimentary

comfort. Some rooms have private bathroom facilities. Breakfast is served in a pleasant little inner courtyard. Closed in winter, but a room can be opened for you. Friendly welcome.

Hotel Nemrut, Mustafa Kemal Cad. On the left at the entrance to the village, ☎ and Fax (416) 725 68 80 – 30rm. ⌗ This establishment could do with a little restoration work but it is still the best

place to stay. Simple level of comfort. Only open in summer.

EATING OUT

Yeni Yudum, Mustafa Kemal Cad 123. On the same side as the two hotels, right at the other end of the village, ☎ (416) 725 52 45. A good place to eat: cheerful welcome, pleasant decor with tablecloths, good food and very attractive prices. What more could you ask for?

Making the most of Malatya

COMING AND GOING

By bus – The bus station is a 5min dolmuş ride from the town centre. Daily bus services operate to Adana (7hr), Ankara (10hr), Antalya (16hr), İstanbul (17hr), İzmir (17hr), Kahta (3hr), Kayseri (5hr), Mersin (7hr) and Sivas (5hr). Book your return ticket as soon as you arrive in Malatya, because the lines are in great demand.

By train – Malatya is on the İstanbul Ankara-Lake Van line. The train also goes to Adana, İzmir and Sivas, but you will get there much faster by bus.

By air – Turkish Airlines operates a daily flight to Ankara. Details from **Arfen Tour**, Atatürk Cad 40/B, ☎ (422) 325 55 88.

ADDRESS BOOK

Tourist information – Hükümet Konağı (on the 1st floor), in the main square, in the little park behind the government building, ☎ (422) 323 30 25. Open Monday to Friday, 9am-5pm.

WHERE TO STAY

It is advisable to book your hotel before you set off on your journey here.

Around US$30

Hotel Sinan, Atatürk Cad 6, ☎ and Fax (422) 321 29 07 – 35rm. ⌗ Small, simple hotel with a basic level of comfort. Good welcome.

Hotel Büyük Malatya, Yeni Cami Karşısı, ☎ (422) 321 14 00, Fax (422) 321 53 67 – 52rm. ⌗ 𝒫 TV CC By far the best hotel in town: both quiet and centrally located, with a friendly welcome and immaculate rooms. Very good value for money.

US$60

Hotel Yeni Kent, PTT Cad 33, ☎ (422) 321 10 53, Fax (422) 324 92 43 – 30rm. ⌗ 𝒫 TV Try this hotel only if the one above is full. Although built not too long ago, the carpets are already stained and the prices are rather high.

EATING OUT

US$8

Mehmet Öztaş (Haci Baba), just behind the town hall, ☎ (422) 321 15 62. The ground floor is deserted: all the clients are enjoying a glass of rakı or beer on the 1st floor terrace. Good traditional cuisine and a lively atmosphere in the evening.

Lokanta Lokanta, PTT Cad 29, ☎ (422) 325 99 88. Another good place to eat, offering an attractive setting (tablecloths) and good food.

SHOPPING GUIDE

Stock up on some delicious apricots from the **bazaar** before setting out on your journey to Nemrut Dağı.

Soğanlı Valley

B. Brillon/MICHELIN

CAPPADOCIA

A fragment of another planet, a mirage of stone in the heart of Anatolia...There are parts of the Earth which do not seem to really belong; Cappadocia is one of them, a strange and spectacular landscape from the pages of science fiction. What could possibly lie behind the creation of such an alien place?

The answer should be sought among the trio of snow-covered volcanic peaks, nearly 4 000m high. It all began in the tertiary era (70 to 25 million years ago), when these giants rose above the plain: Erciyes Dağı to the northeast (near Kayseri), and Hasan Dağı and the Melendiz Dağı chain to the southwest. The three volcanoes covered the entire region with a thick crust of tufa (porous volcanic rock), a conglomeration of ash and small perforated stones. Later, the fire gave way to lava, which extended like a sea, submerging the plateau with tufa over an area of 10 000sq km. A basalt lava which was slowly petrified by the cold and rendered as hard as limestone.

Then the volcanoes were silent. After the fire, wind and rain began their work, hollowing out faults in the basalt to reach the tufa bed. It is here that the real story began; tufa is much more malleable than basalt. As the lava cover cracks and breaks, the tufa slowly erodes. Cones began to appear and with erosion, to separate from one another, carrying a fragment of lava on their head. This is how the **"fairy chimneys"** were born, amazing pointed hats covered with a small basalt plate which would fall eventually. They have sprouted all over: of all sizes (up to 30m high), isolated or in groups, leaning against the cliffs or hidden in the nooks of the valleys.This is Cappadocia: thousands of cones coloured various shades of ochre and pink by the setting sun.

A gem in a jewel case of stone

Erosion continues its work: once the basalt hat falls off, the fairy chimneys are exposed to the forces of nature. Their edges will gently soften, like petrified dunes, then flatten until they become dust. A very fertile dust which the farmers have used to create a productive landscape of vines, orchards and poplars.

But, in a few thousand years, this extraordinary landscape will only be a memory, and the fairy hats will be all be gone. With them, one of humanity's most extraordinary treasures will also disappear. Cappadocia's cones are hollow. However their entrails hide a second Byzantium, dug in the rock, undetectable from the outside. There are few places on earth where man has merged so well with earth, to the point of becoming invisible.

The "land of beautiful horses"

A tortured region with an unruly terrain, Cappadocia remained outside the coveted area and was in particular a land of transit between the Orient and the Mediterranean. It only received its name in the 6C BC when the Persians turned it into one of their satrapies (province). Since the inhabitants paid their tribute with horses, the region was called *Katpatuka*: "the land of beautiful horses", in ancient Persian. Beginning in the 1C AD, Cappadocia came under Roman control. A land where Christians who were persecuted by Romans were welcomed, the region became an important centre of Christianity with the advent of Constantine, the first Christian emperor (313). From then on, it attracted many monks and hermits looking for solitude who built the first churches. Built? No, dug; in the rock, and inside the cones and cliffs.

A rocky Byzantium

So a strange kind of "architecture" was born, monolithic but in the image of already – existing places of worship: from the basilican to the cross or central plan, all existing types of churches, including the Ayasofya of Constantinople were reproduced, in miniature due to the size of the cones. It is all there, narthex, nave, transept, dome or vault, columns, all from a single space, cut inside the tufa. Most of the churches chose a simple plan, a single nave, vaulted or covered with a flat ceiling and closed with a horseshoe-shaped apse.

For the imitation to be complete, the walls were decorated with the most beautiful paintings, an unusual and magnificent illustration of Byzantine art. Yes, Cappadocia is also a land filled with hundreds of images concealed in the rocks, and which on their own would make the trip worthwhile.

The early paintings – With the Arab invasions, starting in the 8C, Cappadocia entered into a long period of troubles. Like the monks, the inhabitants decided to make their homes inside the rock, in the side of the cliffs or beneath their feet. They created underground cities, on several levels, equipped with the traditional paraphernalia of a village. These hiding places, where entire families could live in total autonomy for up to six months, proved to be extremely efficient: they are just beginning to be discovered, often by accident!

Basalt

Tufa

The formation of cones

A few important themes
Cappadocian painting firstly renders homage to Christ. His story is told on the walls of all of the churches and He is often displayed in the apse, in majesty (Pantocrator). When the iconoclasm was in force, a multitude of red crosses signified his presence. Emperor Nicephorus II, who was originally from Cappadocia and defeated the Arabs, often finds himself in the "picture" with St Basil of Caesarea (see page 596). And St Theodore accompanies St George, but only when the latter does not take up the whole space with his dragon.

The 8C and 9C marked the period of **iconoclasm**, "the iconoclastic crisis". Since they were against idolatry, the Byzantine emperors erased faces from the churches, substituting them with all types of symbols and geometric patterns – crosses, vines, fish etc. – simple decoration, often achieved with a simple red line. These iconoclastic decorations are the most ancient ones to be seen in Cappadocia.

The century of monasteries – With the victory of Nicephorus II Phocas against the Arabs (965), Cappadocia found peace once again and monasteries began to increase in number. After the iconoclastic crisis, images began to reappear on the walls (as of 843), depicting all sorts of scenes in colourful tones, like comic book drawings – works by local artists that often appear clumsy (known as "archaic" art). Later in the 11C, the figures began to appear in larger panels filled with red, green or blue. The richer inhabitants even had painters come from Constantinople to give their characters more elegant features and svelte silhouettes. The most beautiful churches date from this period. They are a moving testimony to Byzantine art at its apogee.

The Seljuks and the advent of Islam
In the 11C, the arrival of the Seljuk Turks meant that Cappadocia entered a completely different phase in its historical development. The phase began without confrontation but with peaceful cohabitation between Muslims and Christians (they venerated the same prophets after all).

The opening of a caravan road between Konya and Persia brought incredible economic development to the region. The **Uzun Yol** ("the great road") followed the route of a very ancient commercial road, which already in the second millennium BC connected the Hittite land to Assyria, by passing through **Kültepe** (21km east of Kayseri). The Seljuks therefore linked up again with the Orient and offered Cappadocia its second golden age. From the 11C to 13C, caravanserais sprang up all along the road and the cities of Aksaray, Niğde and Kayseri endowed themselves with prestigious monuments – mosques, medreses and public buildings. More than a simple stop, Cappadocia became a land of exchange. The slow traffic of caravans continued for five centuries, barely troubled by the passage of the Mongols (13C) and the Ottoman Turks (14C). In the 16C, however, the Portuguese opened up a new maritime route which spelt the end of large-scale land trade, and Cappadocia and the entire region began to fall into a deep sleep. The "rediscovery" of its rock churches dates only from the early 20C. It is due to Father de Jerphanion, a French friar who dedicated an important part of his life to studying the area. This was the prelude to a new invasion – tourists this time – from all over the world.

The kingdom of pigeons
In Cappadocia, pigeons are king, since their droppings are an all-powerful fertiliser. All over the valley, you will see hundreds of dovecots dug into the cones and cliffs, small openings surrounded by white chalk, which seem glued against the walls like confetti. The farmers have even set them up in abandoned rock churches!

A fragile world heritage

Cappadocia has retained its rural soul, preserved by agricultural and artistic activities that go back a thousand years. The women, wearing the şalvar, continue to knot **carpets** (the Soğanlı region is one of the country's most important production centres). They also embroider scarves with lace and knit socks and vests. Many of the inhabitants live in the troglodyte dwellings. The **potters** of Avanos continue to spin their wheels, while the farmers enrich their lands with pigeon droppings as they did in former times.

Thanks to tourism, local **craftsmanship** has been experiencing a great renewal, be it traditional or catering for visitors, like the cloth dolls of Soğanlı. However, the influx of tourists threatens to disfigure the region. Concrete has no place in Cappadocia whose beauty resides in the harmony between human settlement and landscape. But, new constructions – usually hotels, of course – are multiplying on the outskirts of the villages and are affecting this marvellous equilibrium.

Yet Cappadocia is a protected area, appearing on the list of UNESCO's World Heritage Sites. Its most beautiful valleys are protected, some churches are closed to conserve them and others are being restored. Many, however, are open and without protection. Worse still, the concentration of tourists in such places as the Göreme Valley leads to the decaying of the frescoes, which are too often subject to the light of torches and the negative effects of human respiration.

Discovering Cappadocia

Although Cappadocia is not an administrative region, it comprises the Aksaray region (to the west), Kayseri (to the east) and Niğde (to the south); a triangular plateau at an altitude of 1 200m corresponding to the "common domain" of the three Cappadocian volcanoes.

The heart of the region, where the most beautiful ensemble of churches and fairy chimneys are concentrated, is limited to the triangle formed by Ürgüp, Üçhisar and Avanos. Our first itinerary leaves from Ürgüp. The distances are short; however, the richness of the sites requires at least two days to do the rounds. Nearly 365 churches have been counted, among which 150 have retained their paintings (and the locals say there are still 600 waiting to be discovered!). This triangle is also the most visited by tourists.

Two other itineraries are also suggested, each lasting one day, which can be undertaken from Ürgüp or any other city in the region. They will take you slightly off the beaten track, one towards the Ihlara Valley, an impressive canyon riddled with churches, the other towards the valley of Soğanlı and the underground cities.

Finally, if there is still some time, follow the caravan road and the traces of the Seljuks. Aksaray, Niğde, Kayseri and the caravanserais which surround the cities are all fascinating.

The land of hikers

The best way to explore Cappadocia is on foot. Everyone is bound to find something to his liking whether it be a one-hour walk, or a day-long trek, on the marked trail or in the chaos of the rocks and churches underground.

The proposed itineraries cover the principal sights; however, Cappadocia is crisscrossed with thousands of paths, at times challenging, which only the local experts know. Have a guide accompany you; it is the safest way to avoid getting lost in the maze and missing important sites. The simplest solution is to contact a local agency. Do not hesitate to ask your hotel staff for advice.

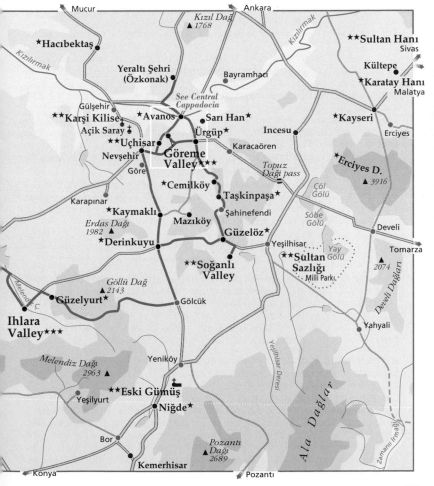

THE HEART OF CAPPADOCIA ★★★
THE ÜRGÜP – ÜÇHISAR – AVANOS TRIANGLE
25km – 2-4 day itinerary
Accommodation in Ürgüp, Göreme or Avanos

Not to be missed
The view from the Üçhisar peak. The Göreme Valley.
A walk in Dovecot Valley or Güllü Valley.
The "fairy chimneys" of Paşabağ.
The sunset overlooking the volcanic rock cones.

And remember...
In summer, plan your excursions in the early morning
or late afternoon to avoid the crowds and take advantage of the
favourable conditions for taking photographs.
Ideally, try to discover the area on foot.
For your walking tours, use the services of a guide: Cappaddocia is a maze of paths.

The villages of Ürgüp (to the east), Üçhisar (to the west) and Avanos (to the north) demarcate the heart of Cappadocia; a "golden triangle" barely 10km on each side, in the middle of which nature and history have carved the most unusual of landscapes, with unparalleled extravagance and originality. In fact, this region constitutes a national park encompassing some of the most beautiful examples of fairy chimneys in Cappadocia. Cones and dunes made of tufa (volcanic rock) are aligned as far as the eye can see, alternating with steppes or valleys strewn with vines, fruit trees and poplars. The concentration of tourists is, unfortunately, almost proportional, but groups pass through rapidly and for the traveller with a little time, the magic of the spot will not fail to cast its spell.

The proposed itinerary begins and ends in Ürgüp – a launching pad – but you can also undertake the same circuit from Göreme or Avanos. Depending on the time at your disposal, you can follow it in its entirety – walks included – or simply opt for the main sites. Ürgüp, Avanos and the Göreme Valley are each described in a separate chapter.

From Ürgüp to Üçhisar
From Ürgüp, take the road to Nevşehir.

On leaving Ürgüp for Nevşehir, the road descends into the heart of a vale surrounded by white cliffs filled with troglodyte dwellings. Beautiful stone houses, a legacy of the Greeks who lived here until 1923, rise in the shade of poplar trees. Some 500m after leaving Ürgüp, in a bend, on the right, souvenir sellers have set up shop in front of a beautiful row of **fairy chimneys★**, perfect cones topped with hats. *3km further on the left, a dirt path leads to the Hallaç monastery (500m further).*

■ **The Hallaç Monastery★** (Hallaç Manastır) – *Entrance fee.* Tucked away in the middle of nowhere, this rock monastery known as "the monastery of the hospital" nonetheless had a short-lived existence. Hollowed out in the 11C, it was abandoned during the Seljuk invasion at the end of the same century. The rooms surround a vast **natural courtyard**, inside the rock and carved with niches. The **main church** is to the right. There follows a large room set on columns (perhaps the refectory), with capitals finely decorated with geometric patterns and animal heads. On the right, there is another smaller church, whose central dome retains an odd carved figure *(on the pendentif on the right in relation to the entrance)*, an enigmatic goblin wearing a pointed hat. Angel or demon?

Return to the Nevşehir road 1km further on, turn right towards the "Panoramic View" (sign).

This narrow road leads to a superb **vantage point**★★ over the Kızıl Çukur and Güllü Dere, two of Cappadocia's most beautiful valleys. They stretch on for 3km, from east to west, one towards Çavuşin, the other towards Avanos. Their narrow green corridor, strewn with vines, poplars and apricot trees, runs between the fairy chimneys, for miles on end. The tufa cones appear in thousands of colours, varying from ochre to purple, which the rays of the setting sun turn to copper and gold.

You enter these valleys at either end. On account of the layout of the main sites (churches), Kızıl Çukur may be visited from the "Panoramic View", and Güllü Dere from Çavuşin (see p 556).

■ **The Kızıl Çukur Valley**★★ – *Entrance fee in season. Allow 2hr30-3hr on foot if you wish to cross the entire valley (with the help of a guide).*

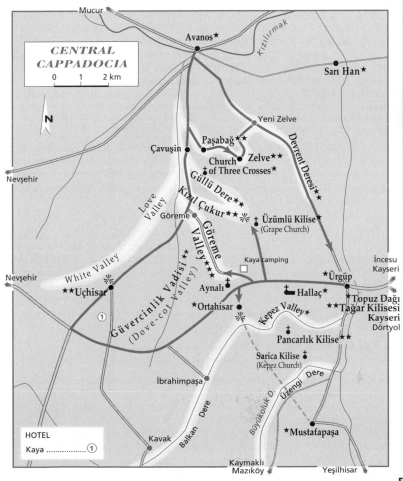

Near the entrance to the site, the little **Grape Church**★ (Üzümlü) is the remains of the hermitage of an 8C stylite. *Access via the path on the left, below the car park (10 min walk).* The church includes a narthex leading to a single narrow nave with a cradle vault. It has retained **frescoes**★ of an incredible brightness, all in yellow, orange and red monochrome. Vine foliage decorates the narthex ceiling, where a large cross stands out. Apostles succeed one another on the walls of the nave, while a majestic *Virgin with Child* – one of the few in Cappadocia – fills the apse, accompanied by two angels.

Return to the Ürgüp-Nevşehir road, continue for 1km, then turn left towards Ortahisar, 4km away.

■ **Ortahisar**★ – *Pop 4 500. Allow 1hr to reach the peak.* Visible from all over, the **rocky peak**★★ of Ortahisar ("The middle citadel", in Turkish) rises above the horizon like a giant belfry. The **village**★ huddles at its feet, traversed by narrow alleyways. In the ochre stones of the walls you will see several doors with ogee arches or covered with a carved pediment. Leaning against the rock, the oldest houses communicate with each other by way of a labyrinth of underground galleries, which the inhabitants have often converted into sheds. Dug underneath the peak and rising up to its tip, like an ant house, these galleries were home to approximately one hundred people. They also served as a refuge in case of invasion as did the citadel **(kale)** sitting atop the peak *(8am–sunset. Entrance fee).* It can be reached by a stairway with 143 steps and a succession of ladders (be brave!). From the summit, there is a very beautiful **view**★★ of the village and the surroundings, a labyrinth of white valleys dotted with poplars. At the beginning of the summer, the rooftops are covered with apricots left to dry in the sun, creating a superb mosaic of orange carpets.

To the southwest of Ortahisar, is the village of İbrahimpaşa, starting point for a hike in the **Balkan Dere ravine** *(allow 2-3hr on foot; good shoes are a must, as is a guide).* Between İbrahimpaşa and Ortahisar, the river has dug a canyon, whose abrupt sides hide a few churches (Cappadocia's oldest). Follow the river for 2km *(4km round trip)*, along a narrow and chaotic path *(be careful, the ground can be slippery)*, which is unfortunately crossed by sewage pipes.

Return to the Ürgüp-Nevşehir road, then take the first road on the right, in the direction of Göreme.

Along the way *(1km, facing the Kaya camp site)*, make a stop at the **Aynalı Monastery** (or Fırkatan). Its façade, carved in the rock, is visible from the road. *(100m from the road; entrance fee. Bring a torch along).* Dug in the 10C, this complex includes several rooms spread out over two floors, as well as a church with three naves which has retained a few **frescoes** from the Iconoclastic period – simple geometric patterns painted in red. From the church, a stairway leads to what might have been the refectory upstairs.

■ **The Göreme Valley**★★★ – *1km beyond Aynalı. See p 564.*
Take the direction of Nevşehir for 4.5km, then turn right towards Üçhisar, 2.5km from there.

■ **Üçhisar**★★ – *Allow 1hr to climb and visit the peak. 8am-sunset; entrance fee, easy stairway with 142 steps (one less than in Ortahisar!).*
Although it is not as high as the one in Ortahisar, the Üçhisar **peak**★★ is no less impressive. An enormous rock set in the middle of nowhere, riddled with holes like a piece of Swiss cheese, it was also used as an observation tower and a refuge for villagers. A tunnel (partially collapsed) allowed the besieged to obtain supplies or escape. From the summit, the **view**★★ over the region is truly superb: dunes of rocks

undulating beneath the sunlight, for miles on end. Inhabited by the Greeks until 1923, the **village** has retained beautiful stone houses with façades decorated with engravings. The many cafés along the way are a good place to stop if you are in need of a rest.

From Üçhisar to Avanos

After Üçhisar *(towards the village of Göreme)*, the road overlooks **Dovecot Valley★★** (Güvercinlik Vadisi), a large canyon with white cliff walls punctuated by fairy chimneys, which continue to the northeast *(the descent into the valley is via the path on the right of the Kaya hotel)*. From the road, the **view★★** is magnificent, especially in springtime when flowering fruit trees fill the valley. Above the vineyards, dovecots have been dug into the rocks in hundreds of small openings, surrounded by nimbi painted white to attract the birds *(see sidebar p 549)*.

From Dovecot Valley, the village of Göreme is a two-hour walk away, via an easy path. At midpoint the path becomes more dangerous. You can avoid it by heading east (to the right), or – better still – by going back 100m to avoid the challenge, turning west (left), before reaching the normal path. Slightly before reaching the village, you will pass in front of the Durmuş Kadir and Yusuf Koç churches (see p 567). Parallel to the valley, the Üçhisar-Avanos road also passes by Göreme, then Çavuşin, 5km further on.

Overlooking the roofs of Üçhisar

J.-F. Galmiche

■ **Çavuşin** – At the foot of a cliff riddled with ancient troglodyte dwellings, Çavuşin is a small and charming village. An important pilgrimage site in the 5C, it retains two rock churches, including the **Nicephorus II Phocas Church**★★ (Çavuşin Kilise), among Cappadocia's finest *(on the outskirts of the village towards Avanos, on the right. 8am–7.30pm. Entrance fee. Allow 30min to visit)*. The church was part of a monastic complex whose annexes are still partially visible. A ladder leads to the narthex whose outer wall has crumbled, bringing to light some very beautiful **frescoes**★★ with red and blue tones. The ones which are in best condition, hidden from the rock, are in the nave, a tall structure leading to an apse with two chapels. The paintings are shown in several successive registers which show the life of Christ and the victories of Nicephorus II Phocas against the Arabs (the Emperor and his family are displayed in the apsidiole on the left). Byzantine soldiers fought in Cappadocia in 964; a fact that enabled a precise date – a rarity in the region – to be given to the building. Also visible is the Ascension framed by medallions depicting the four evangelists. From Çavuşin, you can explore three valleys: Güllü Dere and Kızıl Çukur towards the southeast, and Zelve towards the northeast. It is a perfect opportunity for walking tours amidst some of Cappadocia's most beautiful scenery. *For Kızıl Çukur (which is visited from the Ürgüp-Nevşehir road), see above. For Zelve, see below.*

■ **The Valley of the Roses**★★ (Güllü Dere) – *In Çavuşin, take the road leading to the cemetery. 50m further on, at the end of the village, you reach the valley by way of the second path on the left. Allow a 3hr, slightly difficult walk (uneven ground; wear sturdy shoes). The two main churches of the valley (45min from Çavuşin on foot) are accessible by car.*
The Güllü Dere valley, a magnificent landscape of cones emerging from the vines and the apricot trees, links up with the Kızıl Çukur Valley at the *"Panoramic View"* *(see above)*, 3km to the southeast. Its rocks contain several wall monuments, including the **Church of the Three Crosses**★ *(on the right bank)*, the remains of a 7C monastery. The nave, covered with a flat roof carved with three large crosses, was enlarged at the end of the 9C and decorated with paintings. In the apse is a beautiful **Christ Pantocrator** surrounded by angels and the symbols of the four evangelists.
Nearby, *(5min on foot)*, the **Church of St John the Baptist** (Ayvalı)★ contains beautiful 8C and 9C frescoes, including a representation of the *Apocalypse*. Unfortunately, the church is often closed (it belongs to a farmer who has transformed it into a dovecot!).

Returning to Çavuşin, take the road to Avanos. After 1km, a road on the right leads to the Zelve Valley (4km) via Paşabağ (2km, on the right). The road runs through a very beautiful landscape of fairy chimneys in various phases of formation, a perfect illustration of erosion. Hiking enthusiasts can continue the itinerary on foot, in 1hr (2hr round-trip) starting from the Nicephorus II Phocas Church (in Çavuşin).

■ **Paşabağ**★★ – Paşabağ ("the vines of Paşa") also known as the "valley of the monks" is the epitome of Cappadocia: it is here that the most beautiful fairy chimneys are gathered – cones taller than 10m topped with flat hats, or cylinders crowned with pointed hats. An extraordinary sight which attracts numerous souvenir vendors and as many tourist buses. Despite all this, head down the path through the vineyards and the fruit trees to explore the hidden hermitages dug by stylite monks during the 10C.

■ **Zelve**★★ – *8am–7.30pm. Entrance fee. Allow 1hr to 2hr to visit. Souvenir (and wool pullover) vendors have set up shop at the site entrance, as have small restaurants, good and inexpensive, where you can enjoy a break. There is even a post office and a currency exchange booth. Bring along a torch and sturdy shoes (slippery).*

Surrounded by impressive cliffs, Zelve forms a large horseshoe topped with cones. Here and there, large arches open up in the rock, gaping holes at the back of which can be distinguished stairs climbing up to invisible galleries. A great religious centre from the 9C to the 13C, Zelve in fact housed an important troglodyte city which remained inhabited for more than a thousand years: it was only abandoned in 1950 for safety reasons. Throughout the centuries, its inhabitants dug the rock and created dozens of galleries – churches, living rooms, warehouses – which ended up weakening the entire cliff, threatening its collapse. In addition, there are earthquakes and continuous erosion by the wind. Entire sections of tufa have detached themselves from the cliff and the cones, revealing the hidden houses and littering the bottom of the valley with large boulders.

The site consists of three valleys, inter-linked via a network of tunnels, paths, ladders and stairs. Little can be visited due to the constant threat of collapse. Zelve's interest does not lie herein – most of the churches are in ruins – but rather in its impressive landscape. The curious, and more adventurous, can nevertheless have a look at the ruins of the **monastery** *(in the first valley)*, perched in front of the ancient village mosque (a church to which a minaret was added). *Be careful, climb cautiously; the ground is slippery.*

The second valley is reached through a narrow open tunnel *(time to take out your torch)* above a ladder. The claustrophobic and less athletic can avoid this adventure by walking around the outer wall. Beyond the mosque rises the small **Geyili Church** (also known as "The Deer Church"), so called after the fresco which decorated the vault of the apse, today almost invisible. The church is very damaged and it is best not to enter.

On the left side as you enter the third valley, are a **mill** and a **bread oven**. They precede a **basilica** whose nave is doubled by a sizeable funerary chapel. Two churches in one, which the inhabitants baptised with different names according to the decor of their apses: the **Balıklı Church** ("Fish") corresponds to the main nave, while the **Üzümlü Church** ("Grape") designates the chapel. A few bunches of grapes are still visible, whereas the fish have disappeared. Most of the remaining decoration consists of beautiful red geometric motifs from the pre-Iconoclastic period.

■ **Avanos** – *See p 570. From Avanos, take the road to Ürgüp.*

From Avanos to Ürgüp

The last "side of the triangle", the road from Avanos to Ürgüp crosses an immense plateau sprinkled with cones and rock dunes undulating for miles on end. A strange desert which the sun continually colours with pastel shades. On the right of the road, the **Devrent Valley**★★ is one of the few uninhabited parts of the area, where the rocks have only been carved by erosion. Strange shapes have resulted, like hares, gazelles and camels. When the glorious sun sets, these "animals" change their appearance once again.

ÜRGÜP★

Nevşehir Province
Map p 553
23km from Nevşehir – 13km from Avanos
Pop 11 000 – Alt 1 060m

Not to be missed
The market, every Saturday morning.
Pancarlık Church, near Ürgüp.

And remember...
Base yourself in Ürgüp, it is an excellent centre
for exploring the region.

The only stop on the road from Aksaray to Kayseri, in the heart of Anatolia, Ürgüp has always been a prosperous and lively town. Agricultural products and shelter for travelling merchants have been the bedrock of its livelihood. Today, the travellers it welcomes are tourists who use the city as a base for their Cappadocian itineraries. The old city spreads at the foot of an imposing cliff whose façade includes the homes of troglodytes (cave dwellers), stables and depots, but also wine "cellars". The surrounding hills produce some good wines (all of the hotels and restaurants in the centre stock them; so do not hesitate to try some).

A city of colour and fragrances

The last few years have witnessed great development of the hotel industry's infrastructure, thereby transforming the appearance of Ürgüp: the small streets have been enlivened by restaurants, souvenir and carpet shops giving the old village a completely new atmosphere.

Ürgüp nonetheless retains the charm of former years and its liveliness is very pleasant especially on Saturday mornings, **market★** day, when the square (*east of the bus terminal*) is coloured with the stalls selling regional produce. From dawn onwards, fruit and vegetables, as well as honey and cheese fill the entire neighbourhood with their scents. Women from the country, wearing şalvar and flowered head-scarves also come to sell their embroidered scarves, handkerchiefs and doilies.

Close by, you can take a quick look at the **Archeological Museum** (*8.30am-5.30pm; entrance fee*), where a few fossils are displayed along with traditional clothing and ancient coins.

West of the central square (Cumhuriyet Meydanı), is the maze of the **old city** alleys (*between İstiklal Cad and Ahmet Refik Cad*), which has retained many **Greek houses** built of beautiful ochre stone. Sitting around in a circle, on a doorstep, women chat as they embroider scarves for tourists, while cats stroll by, in search of a sunny stone slab for a nap.

By taking Ahmet Refik Cad (*towards the north*), you reach the **Yahya Efendi Mosque**, a beautiful 15C building. From there, stairs climb up the flank of the cliff towards the **Kaya Kapı** district, a small hill that still exudes the atmosphere of old Ürgüp with its stone houses and rock dwellings. Enjoy the beautiful **view★** of the city.

Around Ürgüp

The valley of Kepez★

See map p 553. The road running south of Ürgüp *(towards Mustafapaşa-Yeşilhisar)* crosses the little valley of Kepez. The **view**★★ of the aligned cones in the valley is magnificent.

6km beyond Ürgüp, a track on the left *("Pancarlık Kilise" sign)* descends towards the two **churches of Kepez** (or Sarıca Kilise). Excavated inside a group of cones, they belong to a large monastery. A few frescoes with red geometric patterns (Iconoclastic period) are still visible in the second church, dug on two levels.

From there, continue 200m along the path on the right and follow the "Pancarlık Kilise" sign.

Below, an isolated cone houses the beautiful **Pancarlık Kilise**★★ (10C), dedicated to St Theodore. Magnificent **frescoes**★ – portraits of saints and scenes of the life of Christ – decorate the flat ceiling of the nave. The figures are enhanced by a green background, a colour rarely used by Cappadocian artists. In the apse, which has retained its altar, there is a Virgin in Majesty.

Towards Kayseri

Two roads lead to Kayseri. However, the scenery along the most direct one, via İncesu, is less interesting. If time allows, opt to travel via **Dörtyol** instead, further to the southeast, whose road climbs up the **Topuz Dağı pass**★ in the middle of a lunar landscape, streaked with valleys and rows of white dunes. Beyond the pass, Mount Erciyes appears with its impressive silhouette against the horizon.

Along the way, do not miss the magnificent **Tağar Kilisesi**★★, another church dedicated to St Theodore *(16km east of Ürgüp; after 8km, turn right towards Karacaören, cross Karain, Karlık and lastly Yeşilöz: there, a signpost points towards the church located next to the village exit; to visit, ask for the keys in the village; entrance fee)*. Founded in the 11C, it was attached to a monastic complex. Its cloverleaf plan (unique in the region) and its very large dimensions make it one of Cappadocia's most original buildings. The transept crossing is covered by a dome resting on a drum, surrounded by a gallery accessible via a flight of stairs.

The **frescoes**★★ are remarkable, in particular those of the main and left apses, both decorated with a beautiful *Deesis* with green and orange tones. Portraits of saints appear in medallions between the arches of the nave.

At the market

B. Brillion/MICHELIN

Ürgüp

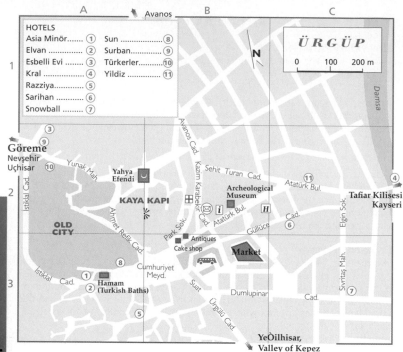

Making the most of Ürgüp

Cappadocia

COMING AND GOING

By bus – *The bus station* (B3) is adjacent to the market place. ***Göreme-Nevtur*** operates daily services to the main cities in western Turkey via Nevşehir (see "Making the most of Nevşehir"). For the eastern regions, you must go to Kayseri (see "Making the most of Kayseri").

GETTING AROUND THE REGION

By bus – A bus service operates through the region with departures every 30min during the week and every hour at the weekend, calling at Avanos, Zelve, Ürgüp, Göreme, Üçhisar and Çavuşin.

By rental car – *Avis*, İstiklal Cad Belediye Pasajı (A3), ☎ (384) 341 21 77. ***Europcar***, İstiklal Cad 10 (A3), ☎ (384) 341 34 88. Agencies open 7 days a week, 8.30am-7pm.

ADDRESS BOOK

Tourist information – Kayseri Cad 37 (B2), next to the museum, access via a small garden, ☎ (384) 341 40 59. 8.30am-8pm in summer, 8.30am-6pm in winter.

Bank / change – Several banks near the main square (B3). 8.30am-12noon / 1.30pm-5pm.

Main post office – Postane Sok, near the tourist information office. 8am-5pm. Foreign currency exchange.

Medical service – *Doctor*: Ahmet Esen (speaks English), ☎ (384) 341 38 99 (surgery), ☎ (384) 341 46 20 (home). ***Pharmacy*** near the main square (B3), open 24 hours a day.

WHERE TO STAY

Ürgüp offers a large selection of hotel facilities from guest houses to international hotels.

Camp sites
Türkerler camp site and hotel, Nevşe-hir Cad, Dereler Mah, ☎ (384) 341 33 54 – 10 pitches. ⌇ You can pitch your tent in a small shaded garden right in the city centre, a few feet from the swimming pool. The charming owner does all that is possible to please his guests. The adjoining hotel is also highly recommended.

Around US$8
Hotel Snowball, Sivritaş Mah Elgin Sok, ☎ (384) 341 23 56 – 12 rm. ⌇ A small, unpretentious establishment with rooms as modest as they are cheap.

☺ **Sun Pension**, Hamam Sok 6, ☎ (384) 341 44 93, Fax (384) 341 47 74 – 9rm. ⌇ A family will welcome you warmly into their old home that has been converted into a hotel and decorated with kilims and plants. Ask for rooms on the terrace which are of unbeatable value.

Pension Sarıhan, Güllüce Cad, ☎ (384) 341 88 13 – 4rm. ⌇ The rooms here are more impersonal but well-kept and overlook a refreshing garden of poplar trees.

Under US$15
Hotel Yıldız, Kayseri Cad, ☎ (384) 341 46 10, Fax (384) 341 46 11 – 18rm. ⌇ A small, very simple guest house offering a very warm welcome. Breakfast is served in a flower garden.

Between US$15 and US$25
☺ **Hotel Asia Minor**, İstiklal Cad 38, ☎ (384) 341 46 45. Near the Turkish bath – 13rm. ⌇ One of the best addresses in town, located in a splendid old home that has recently been renovated. Rooms have a lot of charm and the superb garden is enclosed by Ottoman arches.

☺ **Razziya Guest House**, Yeni Cami Cingilli Bayırı Sok 24, ☎ (384 341 50 89 – 7rm. ⌇ Romi, a delightful Swiss woman, has tastefully redone her superb old house in the old Greek quarter. Her charming rooms are not the only plus – there is also a beautiful garden and individualised walking tours are organised.

☺ **Hotel Surban**, Yunak Mah, ☎ (384) 341 47 61, Fax (384) 341 32 23 – 30rm. ⌇ ℘ ✗ Another charming place where you will get a warm welcome and very good value for money. The hotel is made of locally quarried stone and has some beautiful and very tastefully decorated vaulted rooms. The rooms are immaculate. You get a wonderful view of the village from the open roof-terrace.

Hotel Elvan, İstiklal Cad Barbaros Hayrettin Sok, ☎ (384) 341 41 91, Fax (384) 341 34 55 – 22rm. ⌇ Central location. A very well-run and absolutely spotless hotel. Vaulted ceilings and exposed stone make it all very charming. Breakfast is served on one of the two patios. Good welcome.

Between US$25 and US$30
Hotel Kral, Kayseri Cad, ☎ (384) 341 26 55, Fax (384) 341 26 56 – 30rm. ⌇ ℘ Slightly out of the way, this hotel stands in a pleasant, tranquil setting on the banks of the Damsa. The rooms here are also very charming, with vaulted ceilings, stone walls and refined decoration.

Over US$45
☺ **Hotel Esbelli Evi**, Esbelli Sok 8, ☎ (384) 341 33 95, Fax (384) 341 88 48 – 7rm. ⌇ ℘ A magnificent Ottoman house, very tastefully decorated (carpets, antiques). Large terrace. Excellent welcome. Book ahead because there are not many rooms.

Several high-capacity international hotels have also been built on the road to Kayseri, each with a high level of comfort and a swimming pool.

● **In Mustafapaşa**
Approximately US$15
Old Greek house, ☎ (384) 353 53 06 – 6rm. ⌇ ✗ 300m from the centre. Typical of this tiny village, this old Greek residence has preserved its charm thanks to the careful restoration carried out by its owners. Comfortable rooms and a lively restaurant.

● **In Üçhisar**
Between US$40 and US$45
☺ **Hotel Kaya (Club Med villa)**, 52140 Üçhisar, ☎ (384) 219 20 07, Fax (384) 219 23 63 – 62rm. ⌇ ℘ ✗ ⌇ ᴄᴄ Built to face the Göreme Valley, in a stunning setting. The hotel offers all the amenities found in the Club Med. There is a pleasant welcome and attentive staff. Excellent value for your money.

Deluxe
Hotel Ahbab Konağı, ☎ (384) 219 30 20, Fax (384) 219 30 21, asen@alfa.gen.tr – 19rm (including 2 family suites). ⌇ ℘ ⌇ ᴄᴄ This new establishment was completed in the autumn of 1999. It is well located in front of the citadel and has a lovely panoramic view, particularly at sunset. Some rooms are

equipped with a small private terrace and 6 are in the form of a cave. There are also 2 restaurants, one serving traditional Turkish cuisine. You'll receive a pleasant welcome.

EATING OUT

Under US$5

Restaumicro, Dumlupınar Cad 33, behind the bus station (B3), ☎ (384) 341 20 68. This tiny and intimate restaurant is very good, and cheap. Try the "inegöl köfte" and "ekmek kadayıfı" (dessert).

Between US$5 and US$8

Cappadocia, Dumlupınar Cad, behind the bus station (B3), ☎ (384) 341 40 29. Very good local cuisine. You can eat inside or on the terrace.

Şömine Cafe & Restaurant, in the main square, ☎ (384) 341 84 42. Traditional cuisine served in a pleasant setting (large terrace).

Over US$8

🍴**Ocakbaşı**, Terminal Üstü, next to the bus station (B3), ☎ (384) 341 32 77. You can't go wrong in this upstairs eatery, which draws the locals (always a good sign). The meat is delicious and you will be made to feel welcome.

Han Çırağan, Cumhuriyet Meyd, near the main square, ☎ (384) 341 41 69. Set in a former caravanserai, with a terrace and a patio in the shade of a vine arbour.
Kervan, on the northern side of the main square (B3), on the 1st floor. This place should be avoided – it's a tourist restaurant that has several vegetarian dishes but in general doesn't serve much that is good.

• In Üçhisar

Around US$10

🍴**Hotel Kaya (Club Med villa)**, 52140 Üçhisar, ☎ (384) 219 20 07. At any time of day, and without necessarily being a client of the hotel, you can make the most of its large and copious buffet, which is very convenient.

HAVING A DRINK

Bar – Beautiful vaulted room in the **Han Çırağan** restaurant (see above).

Nightclubs – **Le Harem** (opposite the Han Çırağan restaurant) and **Armağan** (at the top of Suat Ürgülü Cad) (B3).

OTHER THINGS TO DO

Special events – The **International Wine Festival** takes place at the beginning of June. In mid-September, Ürgüp has another wine-related celebration with its **Grape Harvest Festival**.

Excursions – The agencies (in the town centre) all offer tours and trips to the main sights in the region.
Alan Turizm, Yunak Mah (A2), ☎ (384) 341 46 67.
Argeus, İstiklal Cad 13 (A3), ☎ (384) 341 46 88.
Cappadocia is also a good departure point for a safe and easy 2-day trip to **Nemrut Dağı**. Details and reservations at the tourist information office.

Horse riding – Don't miss out on the wonderful treks (1 or more days) led by **Bérangère Şentürk**, Beyaz Yeleçiftlik, Suçuoğlu Sok 12, ☎ (384) 341 51 75.

Turkish bath – In the main square, on the corner of İstiklal Cad, ☎ (384) 341 22 41. In a beautiful early 20C house. 8am-11pm. The Turkish bath is mixed, so mainly frequented by tourists.

SHOPPING GUIDE

Cake shop – Delicious cakes at **Merkez Pastanesi**, in the main square, on the corner of Atatürk Bul.

Wine – Wine tasting in the town's wine co-operatives and at **Turasan**, next to the Surban hotel.

Antiques – A veritable cave at **Antikite Ali Baba**, Kayseri Cad 7 (B2), near the cake shop (not to be mixed up with Aziz Baba, a little further down on the other side of the street), ☎ (384) 341 44 46. Friendly welcome.

Carpets – Numerous shops around Atatürk Bul (B3), near the main square. A good opportunity to watch a carpet demonstration – a real art of seduction! Very wide selection and attractive prices. **Galeri Yunak**, Yunak Mah (A2), ☎ (384) 341 43 25. Run by the proprietor of the Surban hotel.
Goya Tapis, Cumhuriyet Meyd 14 (B3), ☎ (384) 341 43 39. This has an excellent choice and the vendors are experienced at bartering long and hard – and always with a big smile.

Evrasia Press/DIAF

Near Ürgüp: the Uçhisar rock

THE GÖREME VALLEY★★★

Nevşehir Province – Map p 553
12km from Nevşehir – 8km from Avanos and Ürgüp
Pop 5 000

Not to be missed
The Buckle Church (Tokalı) and the Dark Church (Karanlık),
on the outskirts of the "Open-Air Museum."

And remember...
Visit early in the morning or at lunch time
to avoid the crowds.

The Göreme Valley is one Cappadocia's most beautiful jewels. A masterpiece of nature, but also of humanity: the cones and cliffs of this deep-sided circus contain an exceptional collection of churches (30 have been counted), a true "Open-Air Museum" displaying the region's most beautiful frescoes.

Inhabited from the Roman period onwards, the valley of *Korama* and its surroundings welcomed their first recluses in the 4C. Chased out of Caesarea (Kayseri) by the Arabs in the 7C, Christians found refuge by transforming the rocks into houses and monasteries. Under the auspices of Bishop Basil *(see sidebar p 596)*, Göreme became an important home to Christianity reaching its apogee with the victory over the Arabs by Emperor Nicephorus II Phocas (964-965). It was the beginning of a long and peaceful era which lasted until the end of the 11C and saw the construction of many monasteries. The majority have lost their annexes, but time has preserved their churches, unforgettable jewels filled with frescoes.

The Open-Air Museum★★★
(Göreme Açik Hava Müze)

2km from the modern village of Göreme. Parking and entrance fees. The ticket is also valid for the Tokalı church, located outside the site. However, a second ticket (expensive) is required to visit the Karanlık church (purchase it in front of the church). At the entrance to the site, you will find a bank, a post office, restaurants and the inevitable souvenir shops. It is up to you whether you use them or not. However, in order not to encourage their expansion on the site, be aware that the same services are available in Göreme, Avanos and Ürgüp. 8.30am-5.30pm. Allow 2hr for the visit.

Opened to the public in 1950, the Göreme Valley has become the emblem of Cappadocia, its best known site and the most visited. Today, it is being invaded by busloads of tourists. The shops at the site entrance ruin the landscape and the church frescoes are threatened by the large concentration of tourists. As a result, numerous churches are closed for restoration for an unspecified period of time. It is hoped that measures will be taken quickly to protect this fragile heritage so that it may continue to enchant visitors.

After the ticket booths, the visit begins on the right with the small **Church of St Basil** (Basil Kilisesi), excavated in the 11C. The narthex, with a tomb-filled floor, is separated from the nave by a colonnade. The paintings, highly damaged (or unfinished?) are composed mainly of geometric drawings with red lines. In places, however, a few faces with naïve features still appear.

A hundred metres further on, the very beautiful **Apple Church**★★ (Elmalı Kilise), unfortunately restored with abundant use of concrete, is hidden at the end of a narrow tunnel with a low roof. Its vaults display a remarkable decor created with red, ochre, green and blue-grey tones, typical of the 11C. The church probably owes its name to the decor of the dome preceding the apse: the archangel Gabriel holding an apple in his hand (but is it really an apple?), or is the church dedicated to the apple tree outside?

Excavated in the same cone, the **Church of St Barbara** (Barbara Kilisesi) has paintings that are contemporaries of its neighbour, but in a completely different style. In addition to the many geometric drawings and large crosses traced in red, they represent remnants of Iconoclastic themes according to one school of thought, and primitive works by labourers who excavated the church according to another. The symbolic figures portrayed include a strange animal perhaps evoking the devil, flanked by two crosses and a cockerel *(on the wall facing the entrance)*. This simplicity contrasts with the finesse of the lower scene (St Theodore and St George fighting the dragon) or the portrait of St Barbara *(on the left wall of the nave)*. An amusing detail: the architectural components of a church – stone and capitals – are drawn like a trompe l'œil, with a simple red line.

Further down, the **Snake Church** (Yılanlı Kilise) (11C) is entered through a single nave with a bench. The vault is covered with frescoes representing numerous saints. You will recognise *(on the left)* St Theodore and St George with the dragon, the animal being represented by an enormous snake (which gave the church its name). At their side appear St Helena and Emperor Constantine surrounding the Cross. On the right, notice the unusual figure of St Onofrios, half-man, half-woman. According to legend, Onofrios was a reformed prostitute who had asked God to change her into a man. The painter drew a bearded woman whose genitalia are enigmatically concealed behind a plant.

GÖREME
Open-air Museum

0   50   100 m

Göreme Village

Tokalı Kilise (Buckle Church)

P

Cafeteria, toilets

Ticket Office

Ürgüp

Shops, bank

Kızlarin Kalesi (Convent)

Basil Kilisesi (St Basil Church)

Çarıklı Kilise (Sandal Church)

Elmalı Kilise (Apple Church)

Karanlik Kale Kilise (Dark Church)

Barbara Kilisesi (St Barbara Church)

Monastery

Snake Church (Yılanlı Kilise)

N

Nearby, before you reach the other side of the valley, is a large cone filled by the annexes of a **monastery** with several floors. You can see the **refectory** made up of a long table surrounded by benches cut in the rock. No less than 40 monks could sit and drink the wine from the cellar on the right. The walls of the latter are pierced with little niches where oil lamps used to burn. After the banquet it was time for prayer (or a nap!) in the church located above and now ruined.

The Dark Church★★★ (Karan-lık Kale Kilise) – *(Entrance fee, in addition to the museum fee, expensive, but worth it!)* If you are unable to see the Apple Church, you will have an idea of its appearance by visiting the Dark Church – among the "museum's" most beautiful – and its neighbour, *Çarıklı Kilise.* These three 11C churches effectively show numerous architectural and pictorial analogies: they follow the Greek cross plan covered with domes resting on **columns**, and their **frescoes**★★★ were probably painted by the same artists.

Recently restored, those of the Dark Church are the most beautiful. They cover the entire surface of the sanctuary, composing a superb collection of figures – har-

The luminous frescoes of the Dark Church
(Karanlık Kale Kilise)

monies of ochre and reds offset by their navy blue background (a mixture of lapis lazuli powder), which gave the church its name. Take the time to contemplate the realism of the features and the elegance of the silhouettes. Created by a great Constantinople artist, this leads one to believe that the church benefited from a sizeable grant. In fact, four donors appear at Christ's feet: two in the Ascension decorating the narthex (illuminated by a skylight), two others praying *(Deesis)* near Christ rising in the central apse. In the nave, **frescoes**★★★ on the domes and vaults relate the life of Christ, and below them are the four evangelists, the archangels, St Helena and Constantine.

Besides the church, it is still possible to see the annexes of the monastery: the **cellar**, **kitchen** (all blackened by soot) and the **refectory**, with table and benches cut in the rock, as well as the remains of a two-storey basilica.

The neighbouring **Sandal Church** (Çarıklı Kilise), nestled on a hill, hangs in the void since its narthex has collapsed. Enter through a set of metal stairs leading to the side of the nave. There, in the rock at the foot of an **Ascension**, two unusual footprints appear and explain the name given to the church, which tradition has attributed to Christ. The third "column" church, Çarıklı retains beautiful frescoes – unfortunately, heavily damaged – whose figures are reminiscent of those in the Dark Church. Above the church, the monastery's dormitory could once be reached (now a collapsed hollow casing whose stair notches are still visible). The lower floor is home to the **refectory**, with table and stone benches, which accommodated up to 20 monks. The tour of the valley ends with a quick look at the site's only **convent** (Rahibeler Kilisesi, or Kızların Kalesi) *(on the right, towards the exit)*, now a ruin.

The Buckle Church*** (Tokalı Kilise)

On the right of the road coming from the museum. You can enter with the same ticket.
Isolated in the north, outside the Open-Air Museum limits, the Buckle Church is undoubtedly the most beautiful (and largest) in all of Göreme. Its numerous and well-preserved frescoes are of exceptional beauty and illustrate the main trends in Byzantine religious art.

The sanctuary includes in fact two churches, one dug 50 years after the other. The oldest one, **Eski Tokalı**** *(through which you enter the sanctuary)*, goes back to the beginning of the 10C. It consisted of a simple vaulted nave overlooking the apse. During the reign of Nicephorus II Phocas, the latter disappeared in favour of a large transept (10x5m) sustained by two arches and doubled by a narrow gallery leading to three apses.

The original nave has retained all of its paintings in the archaic style, faces in different tones of ochre and pink on a green background, the work of regional artists. The story of Christ is represented in cartoon fashion, in 30 chronological scenes, which are read from top to bottom starting on the right side of the nave.

The frescoes of the **Yeni Tokalı***** *(the "new church")* reproduce the same theme, but using a different approach reflecting the art of Constantinople. The green used as a background for the first paintings gives way to a magnificent navy blue sprinkled with gold, where the silhouettes of the characters stand out like visions, creating a ballet of colours and lines. The artist's sensibility is fully displayed in the **Virgin with Child****, which decorates the left niche of the central apse.

The Village of Göreme

Allow 30min for the visit.

Some 2km west of the Open-Air Museum, the village of Göreme slumbers at the bottom of another valley, inhabited since the time of Roman control. The site today is not of much interest but you can find accommodation and eat there in peace.

Near the village, towards Dovecot Valley, two churches are worth a detour. Dug in the 5C or 6C, the **Basilica of Durmuş Kadir** (Durmuş Kadir Kilise) is one of the most ancient churches in the region *(take the last path on the right before the valley entrance. Free)*. There are no frescoes, yet the interest lies in its size and layout which differ from most of Cappadocia's churches: three vast naves separated by impressive square pillars preceding the choir, isolated behind a colonnade. In the centre of the main apse, you can see a beautiful stone **ambo** (pulpit), perfectly preserved.

The **Yusuf Koç Church** (Yusuf Koç Kilisesi) is hidden 100m from here *(ask to be accompanied, it is difficult to find. Ask for the key at the house located on the other side of the peak. The church is reached by a small ladder)*. Several rooms of the monastery to which the church belonged have remained, including the **refectory**, with bench and table cut in the rock. In the church (11C), it is still possible to see **frescoes** with ochre, yellow and orange tones, all very luminous in spite of their poor condition. An amusing detail: the domes seem to rest on stalactites, since the lower part of the columns supporting them have disappeared.

Making the most of Göreme

COMING AND GOING

By bus – The **Göreme-Nevtur** company operates daily services to the main cities in the west of the country via Nevşehir (see "Making the most of Nevşehir", p 594). Services to eastern Turkey depart from Kayseri (see "Making the most of Kayseri", p 602).

GETTING AROUND THE REGION

By bus – A bus service operates through the region with departures every 30min during the week and every hour at weekends, calling at Avanos, Zelve, Ürgüp, Göreme, Üçhisar and Çavuşin.

By rental car – Next to the "otogar", several agencies hire out mopeds and cars by the day. Pay particular attention to the type of insurance cover offered. In principle, two-wheel vehicles are not insured.

ADDRESS BOOK

Tourist information – In the same square as the "otogar", ☎ (384) 271 25 58. Open every day, 8am-7pm.

Bank / change – There are no banks in the village itself, but there is one at the Open-Air Museum. However, it is possible to exchange foreign currency at the post office.

Main post office – On the road to Avanos, just opposite the fork to the Open-Air Museum. Open every day from April to October, 8.30am-5.30pm. Currency exchange.

Pharmacy – In the centre, near the "otogar".

WHERE TO STAY

Guest houses abound in Göreme, all offering the same minimum level of comfort. Good hotels, however, are more difficult to find, so it is advisable to book ahead.

Camp sites

Kaya camp site, on the road to Ürgüp, 2.5km from Göreme (signposted), ☎ (384) 343 31 00 – 50 pitches. ✗ ♥ ⌇ This camp site has been popular with campers for a number of years. There is plenty of shade, clean facilities, and a small shop for emergencies.

Dilek camp site, on the road to the Open-Air Museum, ☎ (384) 271 23 96 – 80 pitches. ♥ ⌇ This camp site gives the impression of being untidy and although the bathroom facilities are clean, there are very few of them. People stay here for the pleasant atmosphere and the large trees that protect from the sun.

Göreme camp site, on the road to the Open-Air Museum (signposted), ☎ (384) 271 25 23 – 40 pitches. ✗ ⌇ This well-kept camp site is equipped with a large space covered with poplar trees. The setting is superb amidst the fairy chimneys.

Under US$15

Nest Pension, 1st road on the right after the post office when heading towards the centre, ☎ (384) 271 23 82 – 6rm. ⌇ Here you'll stay with local people in their small home adorned with a trellis and a large swimming pool hidden from view.

Starcave, 400m from the "otogar", towards Göreme Valley, ☎ (384) 271 23 57 – 11rm. ⌇ A hotel carved in the tufa of the fairy chimneys that conceal several the original rooms. Don't miss the one with the walls hollowed out with cavities H, converted from a dovecot. There's a very laid-back atmosphere in this long-standing travellers' haunt.

Anatolia Pension, in the same direction as the Open-Air Museum, next to Ufuk Pension, ☎ (384) 271 22 21 – 9rm. ⌇ Rooms are simple when you stay with Isabelle and Bekir (and two of them are in a fairy chimney). Breakfast is a delicious buffet and is served in the flower garden. On certain evenings everyone is served delicious Turkish dishes shared with the family. Moreover, Isabelle knows of walks off the beaten track like the back of her hand.

Pension Tan, on the road to Avanos, after the post office, ☎ (384) 271 24 45 – 14rm. ⌇ A good guest house with immaculate rooms. Breakfast is served in a charming inner courtyard. Cheerful welcome. Good value for money.

Pension Ufuk, in the direction of the Open-Air Museum, ☎ (384) 271 21 57, Fax (384) 271 21 57 – 9rm. Small, simple rooms, 5 of which have their own private bathrooms. Breakfast is served in a little flower garden.

Cappadocia

Between US$15 and US$30
&**Walnut House**, 200m from the "otogar" towards the centre of the village, ☎ (384) 271 25 64 – 8rm. 🛏 This lovely traditional house is a great success. The rooms are cosy and sustained by stone arches. Excellent value for your money.

Hotel Ottoman House, along the canal, towards Dovecot Valley, ☎ (384) 271 26 16, Fax (384) 271 23 51 – 35rm. 🛏 ⟟ 📺 ✖ 🆑 Set in a large, tastefully converted traditional house, this hotel has a good level of comfort. Lunch is served on a vast terrace overlooking the fairy chimneys. Very good value for money.

US$75 (including half-board)
&**Hotel Ataman**, along the canal, at the end of the road leading to Dovecot Valley, ☎ (384) 271 23 10, Fax (384) 271 23 13 – 35rm. 🛏 ⟟ 📺 ✖ An extremely elegant, spacious establishment made out of locally quarried stone. The rooms are very comfortable and decorated with beautiful antique furniture. The atmosphere is equally refined and the food certainly among the best in Göreme. From the terrace, there is a lovely view of the fairy chimneys.

• **In Üçhisar**

Under US$15
Anatolia Pension, on the road where the post office square connects with the road to Göreme, ☎ (384) 219 23 39 – 14rm. 🛏 ⟟ The lovely, elegant and simple rooms look onto a small garden. In the evening the guests can hang out in the bar in an attractive vaulted cave.

Between US$40 and US$45
Hotel Kaya (Club Med villa), 52140 Üçhisar, ☎ (384) 219 20 07, Fax (384) 219 23 63 – 62rm. 🛏 ⟟ ✖ ▭ 🆑 In a magnificent setting facing Dovecot Valley, this hotel enjoys all the amenities of the Club Med. Pleasant welcome and attentive service. Excellent value for money.

Les Maisons de Cappadoce, Belediye Meydan 24, BP 28 Üçhisar, ☎ (384) 219 28 13, Fax (384) 219 27 82 or: 5, rue du Tendat, 81000 Albi, France, Fax (33) 5 63 46 20 09. This is absolute luxury for relatively reasonable rates. In an old part of the village, five houses, each sleeping 4 to 6, and 2 studios have been superbly restored and converted by a French architect who has managed to preserve the traditional character, while at the same time offering modern comfort. Weekly rental approximately

US$300 for a studio, from US$855 for a 6-person house.

EATING OUT

Between US$5 and US$8
Hacının Yeri, on the road to Nevşehir, next to the tomb of Hieron, ☎ (384) 271 23 92. The dining room has been hollowed out of the rock and opens onto a small terrace. Traditional cuisine.

Sedef, in the main square, opposite the bus station. Good traditional cuisine served inside or on the terrace. Good meze.

Orient, on the road to Nevşehir, near the tomb of Hieron, ☎ (384) 271 23 46. The tables are set in a flower garden and a small dining room. Friendly welcome.

Around US$10
&**Hotel Kaya (Club Med villa)**, in Üçhisar, ☎ (384) 219 20 07. Even if you're not a guest, you can enjoy the large, copious buffet at any hour.

Over US$14
Paşa, Belediye, El Sanatları Çarşısı, ☎ (384) 271 23 40. The setting is rather impersonal, but there is a pleasant terrace. Good food (the house speciality is stuffed chicken).

&**Ataman**, along the canal towards Dovecot Valley, ☎ (384) 271 23 10. Very good food in a refined setting with equally refined service.

OTHER THINGS TO DO

Excursions – The travel agencies are all in the centre and offer day-trips to the surrounding areas (Ihlara and Soğanlı) and 2- or 3-day tours to Nemrut Dağı.
Hiro-Tour, at the bus station, ☎ (384) 271 25 42.
Sovalye Tour, at the bus station, ☎ (384) 271 26 22.
Rose Tours, Terminal Karşısı, ☎ (384) 271 20 59.

Walking tours – All the agencies also offer walking tours.

Horse riding – **Rainbow Ranch**, ☎ (384) 271 24 13. Reasonable prices.

Hot-air ballooning – **Kapadokya Lodge**, ☎ (384) 213 99 45, in Nevşehir. You can join this trip from the Ataman hotel, ☎ (384) 271 23 10. Expensive but unforgettable. Departure at dawn to admire the sunrise from on high. The flight lasts 1hr, but you should count 4hr in all, including the preparations.

Making the most of Göreme

AVANOS ★

Nevşehir Province – Map p 553
17km from Nevşehir – 13km from Ürgüp
Pop 11 000 – Alt 950m

Not to be missed
The Sarı Han caravanserai,
especially at sunset.

And remember...
Avanos is a great place for shopping.
Take the time to bargain and, even if you do not make a purchase,
accept the tea which will surely be offered.

A pleasant town set at the foot of İdis Dağı, Avanos stretches along the banks of the **Kızılırmak**, the "red river". The river is Anatolia's longest, undoubtedly named after the colour of the earth which it carries. Founded by the Hittites, the city experienced its first golden age during the Hellenistic period by becoming the centre of an important pilgrimage dedicated to Zeus. Under Roman domination, *Venessa* even rivalled with Caesarea (modern day Kayseri), Cappadocia's most powerful city. Having declined during the Byzantine period, it experienced a second birth in the 13C when the Seljuks opened up new trade routes in Anatolia. Today, Avanos retains the brilliant mark of an Ottoman past with its elegant stone houses decorated with sculpted pediments. From the top of the hill, there is a very beautiful **view★** of the **old city** – small white and ochre cubes descending in steps all the way to the riverbank.

The city of potters

The charm of Avanos also lies in the activities of its craftsmen – **carpet** weaving and the cutting of **onyx** from the nearby quarries. However, the city is especially known for its potters. More than 250 workshops fill its streets *(around the post office and Atatürk Caddesi)*, invading them with pots – pitchers, jars, teapots, vases, plates, bowls, which pile up on the pavements. The craftsmen will invite you to try the potter's wheel or simply watch them as you sip tea at the entrance to the workshop. A tradition that goes back as far as time and whose renown has travelled beyond Cappadocia: Avanos is the twin city of Nuits-St-Georges (France), which explains why so many people in the region speak French.

Around Avanos

Sarı Han★, the yellow caravanserai

6km to the east. Take the road to Ürgüp, then take the first fork on the left (there is a sign). 9am-7pm, closed in winter. Entrance fee.

A spin of the potter's wheel
In Cappadocia, the potter's spinning wheel has been used since the Bronze Age (third millennium BC). Needless to say, it is a technique that gets around! Long before, at the time of the first pots (sixth millennium), the inhabitants of the region had the habit of gathering the red clay from the Kızılırmak. Ever since the earth has not stopped spinning in Avanos.

Hidden away in the middle of an immense steppe, a 13C Seljuk caravanserai proudly displays its mighty walls. Recently restored with stones from the original quarry (the patina of time will eventually blend in the newer stones), it deserves more than ever its name, *sarı*: "yellow", especially at sunset, when the last rays of the sun brighten up the plateau and the limestone gold. A memorable sight.

Cappadocia

You enter the *han* through a beautiful **portal with "muqarnas"*** (a hollow pediment sculpted with stalactites), surmounted by a small mosque. Travellers would settle in for the night in the large room at the back of the courtyard, while the horses and camels found shelter underneath the arches located on the sides.

The underground city of Yeraltı Şehri (Özkonak)

Follow the road from Gülşehir for 12km, then turn right at the junction when you reach the "Özkonak" sign. 8am-6pm. Entrance fee.

Less well-known than Derinkuyu or Kaymaklı, Yeraltı Şehri is less cluttered with tourist buses. Discovered by chance in 1972 by the village muezzin, it held no less than 19 levels of dwellings (for the moment, only four can be visited). All of them follow the same principle of organisation as the other underground cities in Cappadocia: living rooms, cellars, presses, ventilation ducts, water wells and grindstones allowing the entrance to be sealed in case of danger. Were they molehills or anthills? In any event, they are excellent examples of this type of dwelling.

The pottery of Avanos, a millenary craft

N. Thibault/HOA QUI

Making the most of Avanos

COMING AND GOING

By bus – The bus station is on the south bank of the Kızılırmak. The **Göreme-Nevtur** bus company operates daily services (day and night) to the main cities in Turkey. For the west, see "Making the most of Nevşehir". For the Black Sea and the east, see "Making the most of Kayseri". Timetables, which vary according to the day and time of year, are available at the station. It is advisable to buy your ticket in advance.

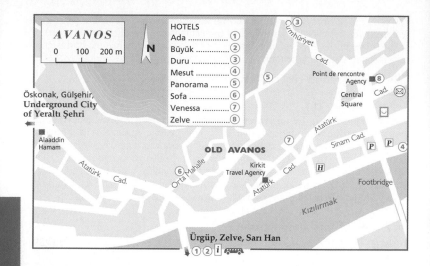

GETTING AROUND THE REGION

By bus – A shuttle operates between Avanos, Çavuşin, Üçhisar and Ürgüp every 30min during the week and every hour at weekends, from 7.30am-6.30pm. Departures from the bus station or from in front of the statue of Atatürk in the main square.

By rental car – Several agencies in the town centre hire out mopeds, scooters and cars by the day or week. Pay particular attention to the type of insurance cover offered: two-wheel vehicle insurance covers material damage, but never personal injury.

ADDRESS BOOK

Tourist information – At the bus station, ☎ (384) 511 43 60. Open every day, 8am-6.30pm.

Bank / change – The banks are gathered around the main square (C1), take Visa cards and are equipped with automatic cash dispensers.

Main post office – In the main street, right next to the square in the town centre (C1). 8am-6pm. You can also exchange foreign currency here.

Pharmacies – 6 dispensaries in the town centre.

WHERE TO STAY

Camp sites

Mesut camp site, on the river banks just after the footbridge, ☎ (384) 511 35 45 – 50 pitches. ✕ ♟ This shaded camp site is ideally located in the heart of Avanos near the river (and its mosquitos). Its restaurant is good and inexpensive and is one of the busiest in the village.

Ada camp site, Yeni Mah Tuzyolu Sok 10, on the road to Nevşehir, 1.2km from Avanos, ☎ (384) 511 24 29 – 100 pitches. ✕ ♟ ⊿ An enormous swimming pool with a bar-restaurant creates a pleasant atmosphere. It's a shame that the camp site is not in the shade.

• **North bank**

Around US$10

Panorama Pension, in old Avanos at the top of the village, signposted from the centre, ☎ (384) 511 46 54 – 18rm. ⌁ Dominating the valley, the simple, clean rooms offer a stunning view. The hotel is well worth the climb it takes to get there!

Between US$15 and US$25

Venessa Pension, Camikebir Mah Hafızağa Sok 20, ☎ (384) 511 38 40 – 8rm. ⌁ An old house in pastel colours, packed full of old things in all the nooks and crannies, with lovely rooms with lots of character. It's a shame the bathrooms are so cramped.

Hotel Sofa, Orta Mahalle 13, ☎ and Fax (384) 511 44 89 – 34rm. ☏ CC This hotel is set in a group of four delightful old houses. The rooms are pleasant and decorated with kilims, but of varying quality. Ask to make your own choice when you arrive, if the hotel isn't full. Book ahead.

Duru Motel, Cumhuriyet Meyd 15, ☎ (384) 511 40 05 – 16rm. ☏ CC High up on the left bank, this hotel has a beautiful terrace where you can dine while enjoying a magnificent view over the village and the surrounding countryside. The rooms are perfectly adequate. Book ahead.

Hotel Zelve, Atatürk Cad, ☎ (384) 511 45 24, Fax (384) 511 46 87 – 30rm. ☏ Rather antiquated, but clean and central.

● **South bank**

Between US$25 and US$40

Hotel Büyük, Kapadokya Cad 46, ☎ (384) 511 35 77, Fax (384) 511 35 77 – 60rm. ☏ ♂ ⌇ CC At the entrance to Avanos. A comfortable, modern hotel with a very large swimming pool which is especially welcome during the hot season.

EATING OUT

Between US$5 and US$8

Damla, slightly out of the way, opposite the Alaaddin Turkish bath (A2). An authentic Turkish restaurant, with formica tables. Very good pide and "köfte".

Çalı Piknik, on the riverside, behind the main square, ☎ (384) 511 43 99. Simple food served in a pleasant setting.

Cihan, in the main square, ☎ (384) 511 40 45. Simple traditional food.

Beyaz Saray, on the waterfront, near the one above. Friendly welcome.

Tafana, in the main square, ☎ (384) 511 48 62. Renowned for its pide.

Over US$8

Tuvanna, next to the one above, ☎ (384) 511 44 97. A good selection of meze, but the place has started to attract groups for which long tables are set aside. Not the place to go for an intimate dinner.

HAVING A DRINK

Sato Bar, on the riverside, ☎ (384) 511 28 84. Live traditional-style music every evening, with guitar, saz and darbouka. Very pleasant atmosphere. You can also have a drink on the terrace. The bar opens at 5pm.

Kervanhan Disco & Bar, near the main square, towards the old town, ☎ (384) 511 35 35. A lively disco where you can dance from 5pm until dawn.

Labirent Dance Club, a little further up than the one above, in the same direction, ☎ (384) 511 22 64. Same opening hours.

OTHER THINGS TO DO

Excursions – The travel agencies, around the main square, offer day-trips in the region around Avanos and to Soğanlı and Ihlara. Tours by minibus for a fixed rate, including lunch. Daily departures in summer. Two good agencies: **Kirkit Voyage**, in Atatürk Cad, ☎ (384) 511 32 59. **Point de Rencontre**, in the main square, ☎ (384) 511 51 71.

Outdoor pursuits – The above same agencies organise exciting treks on horseback or on foot, by the day or the week.

Turkish bath – The **Alaaddin**, on the road to Gülşehir (A2). This establishment is mixed and now frequented only by tourists. But for want of any other…

SHOPPING GUIDE

Local delicacies – You absolutely must try the "pekmez", a sort of grape compote, made with the residue after pressing. It is excellent served with white meat and poultry.

Delicious baklavas at **Aytemur Pasta Salonu**, next to the Tafana restaurant near the main square.

Potteries – The potters' workshops are situated near the town centre, in the vicinity of the post office. There is no shortage of choice, so you are bound to find something to your taste. Here are two addresses, all the same:

– **Galip**, ☎ (384) 511 42 40. In addition to all the usual wares, you will find some beautiful and very original pieces.

– **Amatörler**, on the other side of the square, opposite the Tuvanna restaurant, ☎ (384) 511 41 56. Simple, rough style in a variety of shapes.

THE SOĞANLI VALLEY★★
AND THE UNDERGROUND CITIES
105km circle route from Ürgüp
Map p 551 – Allow one day

Not to be missed
The Keşlik monastery, on the road to Soğanlı.
The rock tombs of Soğanlı Valley.
Visiting an underground city.

And remember...
Have lunch in Soğanlı.
Try to schedule your visits outside peak hours.

Cappadocia

South of Ürgüp, the road crosses a tortuous landscape of cones, sinuous gorges and large vales carpeted with greenery. Further south, from Güzelöz onwards, the terrain rises, creating an immense plateau filled with cracks. This is where the lands of Hasan Dağı (3 258m) begin and the snowy peaks of its big brother, Erciyes Dağı, rise (southwest of Ihlara). Another volcano, another Cappadocia: a harder stone, the lava of the Hasan Dağı has cut basalt ledges at the summit of the hills of Soğanlı. They resemble the crests of the American Grand Canyon often used as a backdrop in western films. Towards the west, completing the loop, you cross an underground land, filled with invisible cities. Like ants' nests excavated in the rock, hidden under your feet, Kaymaklı and its neighbours protected themselves from men and nature. Once this loop is completed, you will have the impression of having crossed several worlds and will realise that Cappadocia is several lands in one.

The Güzelöz road
From Ürgüp, head towards Yeşilhisar-Niğde.
The itinerary is well marked all the way to the Soğanlı Valley.

Some 3km after Ürgüp, the roads splits in two, swinging towards the west *(right)* to Kaymaklı. Follow this direction for 5km, to Mustafa Paşa, a small detour which will enable you to add an excursion to the majestic **Üzengi Valley** (Üzengi Dere), a haven of greenery punctuated by cones. The dovecots have riddled it like a piece of Swiss cheese with dozens of little holes surrounded by white circles. *(Allow a 3hr 30min walk to Mustafa Paşa. Have a guide accompany you, there are numerous paths.)*

■ **Mustafa Paşa★** – Perched at the edge of the valley, this large village, on the cliff, flaunts its beautiful stone houses with carved façades; a heritage from the Greeks who lived in the area until 1923. A witness of its past prosperity, the **Church of St Constantine and Helena** (Aios Constantinos Eleni) sits in the middle of the village, decorated with a **pediment painted** with multicoloured grapes. Near the square, a 14C **medrese** (home to a carpet shop) still shows off its elegantly carved **portal**. Finally, in the village heights, have tea in the **Old Greek House**, a superb 19C Greek house which has been transformed into an inn.
Before leaving, make a last stop at the **St Basil Church★** (Aios Vasilios), near the village *(ask for information at the Mustafa Paşa Tourist Office; a guide will accompany you. Entrance fee)*. It is reached by a small stairway cut in the tufa. Dug in the 8C and restored in the 19C by the Greeks, the church is composed of two vast parallel naves, separated by a colonnade and each bound by an apse with intact iconostasis. The colourful **frescoes** are well preserved.

From Mustafa Paşa, the Yeşilhisar road is reached directly as you head in the direction of Soğanlı. 9km south of Mustafa Paşa, the small village of **Cemilköy** displays its lovely **Greek houses** on the mountainside *(on the right of the road).*

After 2km, a yellow sign indicates "Keşlik Manasteri", on the right.

■ **The Keşlik Monastery** ★ – *At the end of a small path (5min walk). 8am-6pm. Entrance fee. Allow 30min to visit.*
Excavated in the 13C the monastery, known as "the monastery of the archangels" retains two churches and a refectory. **The Black Church** (Kara Kilise) includes two parallel naves, each bound by an apse. Unfortunately, it is difficult to see the frescoes, which have been blackened by smoke. Next to it lies the **refectory**, a large room cut in two by arcades, which could hold 100 people.
Some 50m from the monastery, you reach **St Stephen's Church** ★ (Aios Stephanos), dug in the 9C. This is where the most beautiful **frescoes** appear with bright tones of orange and yellow. The single nave is covered with a flat roof containing a large **cross** lost among grape foliage.

Take the road towards Taşkınpaşa (3km away). On the right of the road, fairy chimneys seem to have lost their way.

■ **Taşkınpaşa** – Last stop before Soğanlı Valley, the village of Taşkınpaşa retains the ruins of a **medrese** *(at the village entrance on the left),* decorated with a remarkable **Seljuk gate** ★★★ with muqarnas (stalactites).
Beyond, after Şahinefendi, the scenery changes radically, giving way to an 11km-long rectilinear plateau as arid as a steppe. At the end, the little village of **Başköy** (or **Güzelöz**) will delight you with tree-shaded squares. As you go by, notice the communal bread oven in the main square.

At the end of the village, turn left towards Soğanlı. After 6km, turn right at the yellow sign. The valley is 5km away.

500m before reaching the site's entrance, signposts indicate two isolated churches, nestled high up on the façade of the cliff above. The small detour will give you an excellent **view** ★ over the valley's entrance. Cut in the white tufa, an abrupt stairway climbs up towards the **Buckle Church** (Tokalı Kilise), the remains of an 11C monastery. The narthex floor contains several tombs brought to light by archeologists, which you have to leap over in order to reach the nave. You will discover several frescoes, geometrical patterns with bright colours (green and red), unfortunately quite damaged.
As you return, have a look at the **Sky Church** (Gök Kilise) *(across the way, 50m below the road, on the right),* a small 10C sanctuary. It is composed of two parallel naves with barrel vaults and painted with beautiful frescoes representing Christ's childhood. The two apses have retained their chancel (barrier).

■ **Soğanlı Valley** ★★
45km from Ürgüp. 8.30am-5.30pm. Entrance fee. The site can be visited by car (two roads cross the valley), but it is much more enjoyable on foot (allow 2hr in this case).

A giant fault, opened by the Titans in the basaltic plateau of the Hasan Dağı, the Soğanlı Valley stretches between two vertiginous slopes. At the summit, abrupt cliffs look more like crowns. On both sides of the Soğanlı, tight rows of tufa cones form a barrier between the arid walls of the valley and the river's green banks. Others are perched half-way up the slopes, in isolated groups. All are riddled with little holes –

The Soğanlı Valley

The valley of tulips

Imagine this valley covered with tulips! In Turkish, "*Soğanlı*" means onion, or tulip bulb in this case. Harvested in Cappadocia for centuries, this flower became very popular at the beginning of the 18C, under the reign of Ahmet III. The latter exported many bulbs to Europe and this is how Holland became the land of the tulip. The Turkish tulip that is!

dovecots surrounded by white limestone to attract the birds. Walk among them to explore the hidden churches or along the river edge in the shade of the poplars. Village women will most likely invite you to ride a donkey, if they have not already shown you their **cloth dolls**, products typical of Soğanlı's craftsmanship.

Visiting the site

Soğanlı's churches were all dug between the 10C and 11C, in the groups of cones set half-way up or in the porous walls of the valley. A peculiarity of the site, some cones have been carved from the exterior in the form of a dome, giving the church a "built" appearance. They are especially reminiscent of the elf houses seen in comic books!

The itinerary skirts the two banks of the Soğanlı. Begin with the right bank and follow the river towards the north, before returning by the other bank towards the village of Soğanlı. The churches are well indicated. You can have lunch at the Kapadokya, located below the car park, in the shade of the apple trees.

First stop of your excursion, the **Black Head Church** (Karabaş Kilise) was part of the monastery set around a natural open courtyard in the rock. The church includes a single barrel-vaulted nave, bound by a large apse which has retained its altar and chancel. On the right you see the paraclesion, which later became a dovecot. The soot-darkened frescoes are barely visible and very damaged. Only the very beautiful **Communion of the Apostles**★ *(in the apse)* remains.

As you continue, notice on the other side of the river, perched on the opposite slope, two **cones** carved in the shape of churches, with small domes, unusual silhouettes which seem right out of Tolkien's fairy tale-like universe.

The second sanctuary of the right bank, the **Snake Church**★ (Yılanlı Kilise) was also part of a monastery which has retained numerous annexes: the refectory, kitchen with the *tandır* (oven carved in the floor) and even several cells. The church itself has experienced much damage and the frescoes, blackened with soot, are almost completely ruined. On the left of the entrance, St George was shown fighting the dragon, represented by a snake, which explains the name of the church. On the vault, on the opposite side, a beautiful scene remains: Abraham, Isaac and Jacob are bearing the heads of 12 children (representing the 12 tribes of Israel) heavenwards.

Cross the river and take the path flanking the other bank from above, in the opposite direction.

This is how the other group of cones is reached. Their tips have been carved in the shape of domes on drums, imitating masonry. One of them houses the **Cupola Church** (Kubbeli Kilise), the upper part of a monastery carved on two levels. Nearby, another cone carved in the shape of a dome contains two churches, one above the other. The lower sanctuary, known as the **Hidden Church** (Saklı Kilise) is a vast basilica with three naves (without frescoes) linked by two tunnels further connecting the upper sanctuary and the neighbouring church.

The path circumvents the village to the east, following the riverbank. It then follows the road climbing towards the right in the direction of the last two large churches on the site.

Deer Church★ (Geyikli Kilise) owes its name to the Vision of St Eustatius, which decorated one of the narthex walls: a deer whose horns locked Christ's head. The hooves are unfortunately no longer visible. Today, the church is interesting because of its unusual **iconostasis**★, carved out of a single piece in the rock. A tunnel links it to

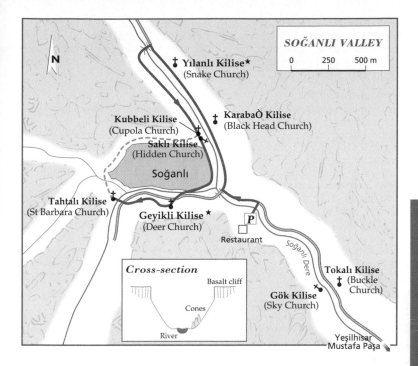

The Soğanlı Valley

The Tetramorphs

In Christian art, the four evangelists are often represented by animals. They are called the Tetramorphs (from the Greek "tetra": four and "morph": form). Tradition assimilates them in effect to the four "living beings" which the prophet Ezekiel describes in his vision, in the first chapter of his Book (1,10): four winged creatures surround God's chariot, each decorated with four faces, one human, another a lion, the third a bull and the fourth an eagle. Following the same order, Matthew – the first evangelist – appears as the man, Mark the lion, Luke the bull and John, the last evangelist, as the eagle.

the neighbouring monastery leading to the **refectory★**, a beautiful room with blind arcades as well as a table and benches carved in the tufa.

On the other side, the **Church of St Barbara★** (Tahtalı Kilise) can be seen through a small narthex covered with a dome and decorated with frescoes. It precedes a single nave with a barrel vault and is closed off by an apse. A paraclesion was carved later, on the side. The **frescoes★**, in good condition (early 11C), display a beautiful harmony of bright tones standing out on a navy blue background. In the apse, Adam and Eve can be seen kneeling at the feet of Christ in Glory, surrounded by the emblems of the four evangelists.

Take the road to Başköy where you will turn left in the direction of Derinkuyu, 25km to the west.

The underground cities

Have you ever dreamed of entering the tunnels of an anthill? Here is a good opportunity! From the 6C to 10C, when Cappadocia was threatened by hordes of invaders, some of the inhabitants decided to protect themselves. They buried themselves completely, reproducing their village directly underneath their feet, like its underground reflection. These cities, invisible from the outside, were an ideal shelter, especially against the rough winters. They developed all over the region (almost 100 have been counted), particularly south of Nevşehir, where the tufa is slightly more malleable. Most of them were discovered haphazardly, in the 1960s. This is proof of the efficacy of these cities!

Monolithic cities

True ant hills (or molehills!) on a human scale, they were organised like autonomous cities, capable of surviving in isolation for several months. Everything was reproduced: stables, warehouses, silos, presses, vats, living quarters, communal rooms, even churches interconnected by galleries which could be obstructed from inside by large millstones. A ventilation system, consisting of several chimneys, allowed the various levels to receive fresh air. These wells could be extended by a water reservoir of equivalent depth. As far as lighting is concerned, oil lamps were ever-present in the rock's niches. Abandoned at the end of the great upheavals, in the 11C, these cities were forgotten until urban construction made them accessible.

Warning to the claustrophobic: the galleries of the underground cities are illuminated by electricity. Occasionally power is cut off and the maze is in total darkness. A torch is therefore quite useful. Try to avoid bus tour peak hours: the corridors are low and narrow, human traffic jams are common. Bring along a sweater: in summer, compared to the outside temperature, the temperature underground is quite cool. These cities are quite similar in appearance; no need to visit all of them.

■ **Derinkuyu*** – *20km south of Nevşehir on the road to Niğde. 8am-6pm. Entrance fee. Follow the red arrows to descend, the blue to climb.* Discovered by chance in 1963 and opened to the public two years later, Derinkuyu ("the deep well" in Turkish) is the deepest and vastest underground city known. It has 18 levels spread over 55m (*only eight can be visited for now*). It has 52 ventilation chimneys averaging a height of 70m and could hold 10 000 people! On the first level, for stables and warehouses – rooms carved with holes where jars were deposited – numerous fragments of Hittite pottery were found. The lower levels house the living quarters, the kitchens and the communal rooms, as well as a very large chapel (*7th sub-level*). An 8km-long tunnel, whose access has not yet been found, linked the city to Kaymaklı.

Take the Nevşehir road to the north (on the right), to Kaymaklı, 10km from here.

■ **Kaymaklı*** – *8am-6pm. Access fee. As in Derinkuyu, follow the red arrows to descend and the blue to ascend.* Although smaller than Derinkuyu, Kaymaklı is the most visited city, simply because it is slightly closer to Nevşehir. It has ten levels, spread out over a depth of 45m. Underneath the stables, always on the first level, several chapels can be seen as well as warehouses, which were permanently used even in times of peace. A ventilation duct with a height of 40m was dug in the centre of the city and extended by a well of equal length (80m in all). Around it, a long corridor descended to the last level like a screw. It was obviously not a good idea to drop the goods being carried!

From Kaymaklı, take the Ürgüp road for 7km, then turn right again towards Mazıköy, located 3km further on.

■ **Mazıköy** – *8.30am-6pm. Access fee.* This is the least visited underground city. It is also by far the smallest and least characteristic: instead of being dug underground and being carved in the rock, it is wedged against the wall of a cliff. A few of its internal walls were actually constructed. Of its five levels, four have been cleared (*you enter through the last but one, from the bottom*). You visit them successively by using the square-shaped vertical chimneys.

Return to the Kaymaklı-Ürgüp road, and turn right to reach Ürgüp, 20km away. If you plan to visit the Ihlara Valley (to the west), you can also reach it without returning to Ürgüp, to sleep there and be ready for the following morning's hike (see "Making the most of Ihlara", p 585).

"Kuş Cenneti", the bird paradise★★
70km from Kayseri, 25km from Soğanlı, 9km from the city of Yeşilhisar.
Organised boat trips at sunrise (US$15). Allow 2hr.

Where do Alsatian storks, pink flamingos from Camargue or small swallows fleeing cold European winters go to? To Kuş Cenneti, of course, in Turkish: the "bird paradise". Such is the name given to the **National Park of Sultan Sazlığı**★★ (Sultan Sazlığı Milli Parkı), a natural range of 17000ha dotted with lakes, at the foot of Erciyes Dağı, where more than 300 types of birds gather every year. Two of these lakes, adjacent to each other, offer a perfect opportunity for an excursion aboard a silent boat. After a never-ending corridor of reeds, the first lake appears with its fresh and crystal clear water. Startled **eagles**, **egrets** and **tufted herons** take flight in unison while **moorhens** dive. After a short break on land, you reach the second lake, much vaster, whose salt water attracts **pink flamingos**★★. During the best season – autumn and spring –, tens of thousands gather, creating an impressionist painting in stunning monochrome. This Eden without tourists awaits discovery.

Making the most of Sultan Sazlığı

COMING AND GOING
By bus – Many buses go to Kayseri stopping in Yeşilhisar. If you call the Sultan Pension, someone will come to pick you up.
By car – From Yeşilhisar, take the road to Konya, then take the first road on the left towards Yahyalı. The entrance to the nature park is signposted on the way, in the village of Ovaçiftliği.

WHERE TO STAY
There is only one guest house, which also offers very good meals and breakfasts.

Under US$15
Sultan Pension, at the end of the road leading to the national park, just before the entrance, Ovaçiftliği, ☎ (352) 658 55 49 / 55 31 – 7rm. ✗ Communal bathroom. A small ochre cube hidden among the reeds, this house is truly a haven of peace. You can admire the birds and the sunset from the rooftop. The rooms have several beds for groups. Basic but cosy. Mesut, the owner, is helpful and efficient.

THE IHLARA VALLEY★★★

Aksaray Province – Map p 551
89km from Ürgüp – 69km from Nevşehir – 48km from Aksaray
Accommodation in Aksaray or Güzelyurt

Not to be missed
The walk from Ihlara to Belisırma
The Selime Monastery
And remember...
Get an early start and take good shoes and a picnic.
Avoid Sundays, the peak day for outings.
Sleep in Ihlara; you will be ready to go the next morning.

The Ihlara Valley (Peristrema in Greek), is in a way Cappadocia's rare jewel. Its exceptional landscape does not include cones, fairy chimneys nor peaks. Ihlara is a canyon, a fault wedged between two cliffs, over 100m high, undulating for over 14km between the villages of Ihlara *(to the southeast)* and Selime *(to the northwest)*. At the far end, the river which created it (the Melendiz) peacefully continues its work in the shade of wild olive trees and poplars, drawing a large green streak at the foot of the ochre-pink cliffs. Nearly invisible from the road, the canyon appears at the last minute, as if the earth suddenly parted at your feet. The view is breathtaking!

An inhabited canyon

As if nature were not beautiful enough, Ihlara hides in its cliffs numerous churches, whose frescoes – although slightly more altered by time than in Göreme – are remarkable gems. More than 100 churches have been counted *(only 10 or so can be visited)* and hundreds of dovecots, granaries and houses are set in the cliffs, proof of a noteworthy human presence. In fact, from the 7C onward, the Ihlara canyon welcomed thousands of Christians expelled from Syria, Palestine and Mesopotamia by the Arabs. The frescoes of their churches display an Eastern and Coptic influence: simple figures and geometric patterns, reminiscent of mosaics, associating the worship of the Cross with that of images, a unique example in Cappadocia.

Ihlara will please hikers: the less athletically-inclined can effortlessly follow the river while adventurers will gladly get lost among the chaotic rocks in search of forgotten churches.

From Nevşehir, two roads lead to the Ihlara valley: the first one – more direct – via Aksaray (in the direction of Aksaray-Konya, towards the west); the other – longer but more beautiful – via Kaymakli and Derinkuyu (in the direction of Niğde, southbound). In Gölcük (17km after Derinkuyu), turn right in the direction of Aksaray.

The Gölcük-Aksaray road crosses the very beautiful village of **Güzelyurt**★ ("the beautiful country"), which is worth a stop. Populated by Greeks until 1924, the village continues to live according to the rhythm of its former inhabitants. Time has stood still in the beautiful 19C stone houses, decorated with elegant carved façades, and numerous villagers still live in the troglodyte houses carved inside the mountain. In the main square, old men chat while they drink *çay* and sit serenely as if they have been there forever. The only change in the village is that

P. Desclos/SCOPE

Ihlara, a canyon hewn from the plateau

the very ancient **Aşaği Church** (4C) has become a mosque. The Greek soul remains: according to the villagers, there is talk of restoring the church and returning it to its original status.

From Güzelyurt, continue for 3km in the direction of Aksaray, then turn left at the signpost "Ihlara-Peristrema" (6km road). Once you have reached Ihlara, a track, on the right as you leave the village, leads to the valley, located 2km away.

Exploring the canyon
The churches of the Ihlara valley are located in two areas: near the Ihlara village, the site's entrance, and in Belisırma, 5km north.

On foot – Ideally, the two groups of churches should be reached on foot, following the river, then according to the time at your disposal, continue to Selime Monastery, at the northern extremity of the canyon *(4km further away)*. It is an easy walk, very enjoyable and in superb surroundings. A whole day is necessary to go from one end of the canyon to the other *(allow approximately 4hr for the walk)*. If you did not bring a picnic, you can have lunch in one of the small restaurants in Belisırma, on the river's edge. In Belisırma and Selime, taxis (or the villagers themselves) bring visitors back to their point of departure.

The Ihlara group is easily visited, but to visit the other churches, you must be accompanied lest you get lost! At the entrance of the site, children will offer to accompany you. Do not hesitate to follow them, they know every nook and cranny of the canyon.

By car – For those in a hurry, a road takes you to the plateau's different sites *(Yaprakhisar road)*. Past Selime, it continues to Aksaray. Those without private transport can come to Ihlara by *dolmuş* or by bus (numerous shuttles from Aksaray; but find out about return schedules. It is best to purchase a tour in an agency in Ürgüp or Aksaray).

The Ihlara group★★★
8am-7pm in summer, 11am-4pm in winter. Entrance fee. Allow 2hr to visit. The main churches (described below) are indicated by a small yellow sign. Many others are hidden in the cliffs; these are for archeology buffs and the more adventurous!

You descend the canyon by way of a large stairway (382 steps!) up against the cliff, which allows a dizzy **view**★★ of the whole site. Shortly before the last step, on the right, you reach the **under-a-Tree Church**★ (Ağaç Altı Kilisesi), the remains of a monastery with three storeys. Enter through the apse of the collapsed chapel. You will see beautiful paintings with bright and clear tones, varying from yellow to green on a white background. The most striking work is undoubtedly the **Ascension**★★ filling the dome: in a mandorla, Christ stands upright, taken to the skies by angels and archangels, while the prophets and apostles assist him, aligned in two friezes in the lower register. On the left wall, notice the **Three Wise Men**★, three little characters wearing pointed hats. The drawing of the composition and the geometric motifs surrounding the scenes show that the work is very ancient, going back to the pre-Iconoclastic period (starting in the 6C).

Backtrack to the stairway and continue all the way down. Take the path on the right for 400m (10min walk) until you reach the "Kokar Kilise" sign, then climb towards the church perched on the cliff above.

The collapsed apse of the **Fragrant Church**★★ (Kokar Kilise) leads into the void. Its single barrel-vaulted nave, extends into two funerary chapels. It also retains numerous paintings (completed at the end of the 9C), unfortunately degraded by Islamic-period graffiti. The technique is closer to folk art than in the previous church, with

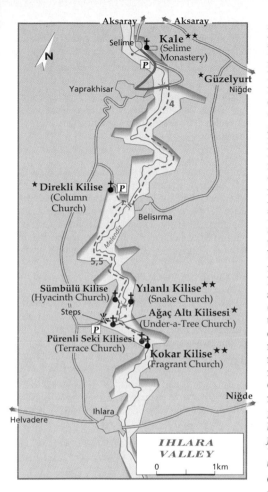

IHLARA
VALLEY

0   1km

a lively palette – red, green, yellow, black and white – large and simple figures, reminiscent of mosaics. A large Greek cross surrounded by white fills the entire vault, decorated with God's hand in the middle, giving a blessing with three fingers, the symbol of the Holy Trinity. On the sides, a few **scenes of the life of Christ**★, the apostles and, remarkably, four of Islam's prophets: Moses, Solomon, Elijah and Jesus (*on the entrance arch*), biblical characters who were also venerated by the first Arabs who arrived in Anatolia.

Below, you can have a look at the **Terrace Church** (Pürenli Seki Kilisesi), a contemporary of the preceding church. In the very dark nave, the frescoes, unfortunately in poor condition, represent scenes of the life of Christ, as shown in several registers.

Backtrack to the stairs and head towards the bridge. Before crossing it, turn left at the "Sümbüllü Kilise" sign. Access to the church is via a stairway.

Cut in the rock, the façade of the **Hyacinth Church** (Sümbüllü Kilise) draws large arches on the cliff wall. The only remains of a two-storey monastery, the very small sanctuary has retained its altar and its chancel as well as frescoes, unfortunately heavily damaged by dripping water. Several isolated paintings can be distinguished – major liturgical feasts – painted in grey, red and ochre tones with great refinement, a characteristic of 11C Byzantine art.

After the bridge, 50m on the left, by means of a stairway, do not miss the **Snake Church**★★ (Yılanlı Kilise), Ihlara's largest sanctuary, excavated at the beginning of the 10C. Here, the frescoes are very clear (in spite of the graffiti), executed in a harmony of vibrant shades of red, yellow and green. Enter through the narthex, barrel-vaulted and flanked by a funerary chapel, then into the nave, topped with a flat roof. The apse, with its original altar, is located all the way at the back. The most beautiful paintings are in the narthex, including the impressive **Last Judgement** (*on the left*): next to the *Weighing of the Souls*, *Hell* is represented by a three-headed monster and a group of four naked women being attacked by snakes punishing them for their sins. In the upper register and overflowing onto the vault, the 40 martyrs of Sebastea align themselves above the 24 old men of the Apocalypse. Two long friezes of highly stylised figures with harsh features betray the eastern origins of the artists.

Cross the bridge once again. Hikers will continue towards Belisırma by following the river (5km, or 1hr 30min on foot).

Between Ihlara and Belisırma, the path follows the river in the shade of willows and olive trees, a very enjoyable and refreshing walk. In places, nevertheless, the path is punctuated by large heaps of rock which have fallen from the cliffs. Rest assured, you need not be an acrobat to cross them.

The Belisırma group*

Numerous churches are hidden around Belisırma, in the niches of the cliffs surrounding the village. Very few of the churches are sign-posted (you should be accompanied). You will also have the opportunity to find the **Church of St George***
(Kırk Dam Altı Kilise) *(before the car park as you arrive from Ihlara)*, a true eagle's nest reached by a climb amid huge boulders. The nave, looking as if it had been sectioned with an axe in the protruding mass of cliff, faces the void. Its flat ceiling, in a magnificent hue of velvety navy blue, displays the delicate works painted at the end of the 13C.

Further on you will see the **Column Church*** (Direkli Kilise), the site's most beautiful *(from the car park in Belisırma, near the restaurants, walk back up the road for approximately 100m)*. On the left of the road *(on the right, if arriving in Belisırma by car)*, notice the façade of the church, a series of niches and arches carved in the cliff side. Excavated at the beginning of the 11C, this sanctuary strikes the visitor by its dimensions. In the centre, a large dome rests on four massive pillars (hence the church's name). Syriac geometric patterns still appear, but most of the extremely fine frescoes are barely visible.

Right before Belisırma's first houses, on the river's right bank, a small terrace restaurant serves excellent grilled fish which you can savour in peace (tour groups usually stop by at the other restaurant, 50m further down towards the bridge).

From Belisırma to Selime**

A 4km excursion, allow 2hr on foot. By car, take the road above the Ihlara car park and turn right towards Yaprakhisar.

Past Belisırma, the cliffs abruptly spread apart and their steep walls become immense cones: from here on you are once again in Cappadocia, with its strange landscape of large pointed hats. The river widens, clearing the way for a valley strewn with rocks where goats gambol under the watchful eye of their young shepherds. In the shade of the poplars huddling alongside the river, the moss-covered banks act as a perfect mattress for sunbathing in-between swims.

The path follows the course of the Melendiz on the eastern bank, until it reaches an intersection. There, take the bridge on the left to reach Yaprakhisar, on the opposite bank. At the village entrance, the road on the right leads to Selime.

The Selime Monastery** (Kale)

Last stop on your excursion, the Selime Monastery hides among a row of volcanic rock cones leaning against the cliff *(in the heights east of the village, on the right. Free)*. The whole building (6C), excavated in several cones, resembles the huddled and slender towers of a fairy-tale castle. Very charming. Since all the annexes are still standing, it is easy to imagine the life of the monks, in particular in the refectory*, a large room with blind arcatures. Many rooms are interconnected with stairs, tunnels and passages, where it is a pleasure to get lost. The very spacious **church** follows the basilican plan: three high naves separated by powerful pillars. The paintings are unfortunately very weathered.

From Selime, a 3km road links up to the Aksaray road. From there, there is a beautiful **view*** of the Hasan Dağı (3 268m) which overlooks the southern horizon.

Making the most of Ihlara

WHERE TO STAY

Ihlara is a convenient place to stay when visiting the major sights of southern Cappadocia (the underground cities and the Soğanlı valley) to avoid having to return to Ürgüp.

Camp sites
Pension Camping Anatolia, 500m before the entrance to the valley, ☎ (382) 453 74 40, Fax (382) 453 74 39 – 10 pitches. ⌐ ✕ Rather than a camp site, this can more accurately be called the guest house garden. It will do at a pinch.

Around US$10
Pension Ihlara, when leaving the village, opposite the road leading to the site, ☎ (382) 453 70 77 – 16rm. ⌐ ✕ Clean rooms, a friendly welcome and a good

dinner (very important, since there are no restaurants in the village). It is advisable to book ahead.

• **Güzelyurt**
Around US$25
Hotel Karballa, at the bottom of the steps when leaving the village square, ☎ (382) 451 21 03, Fax (382) 451 21 07 – 11rm. ⌐ ✕ ☂ ⌐ ⛲ Converted from an old and magnificent stone monastery, this establishment is designed for groups but will also welcome individual travellers. Swimming pool, bar, horseback excursions. It's a closed universe but comfortable. Be aware that meals are very costly. However, there is a restaurant in the square, just a 2min walk away, that serves delicious local cuisine.

Making the most of Ihlara

585

AKSARAY

Provincial capital – Map p 550
226km from Ankara – 148km from Konya – 71km from Nevşehir
Pop 145 000 – Alt 980m

Not to be missed
Ağzıkarahan, the region's most beautiful caravanserai.
And remember...
If comfort is not an absolute must, sleep in the village of Ihlara
perfectly located for your excursion the following morning.

A small town set in the middle of the steppe, Aksaray (the "white palace") is a transit point, a trading stop on the road from the Orient towards İzmir, via Konya. The lorries and trucks filled with goods and tourist buses arriving from Cappadocia have replaced the slow caravans of yesteryear. Aksaray is in particular a stop on the way to the breathtaking Ihlara Valley *(see p 580)*.

A small Seljuk excursion

Before discovering the surroundings, take the time to look at a few of the city's Seljuk marvels *(2hr should suffice)*. Aksaray experienced great prosperity during the rule of the Seljuk sultanate before it was handed over to the Ottomans. When the latter conquered Constantinople, they transferred a portion of the population to render the ancient Byzantine capital more Turkish. Hence the name of the district located west of the Grand Bazaar. On the main street (Bankalar Caddesi), you should visit the **Grand Mosque** (Ulu Cami), erected in the 15C, and recently restored (beautiful Seljuk **minbar***).

At the end of the road, across the river, the old city has an unusual sloping minaret, the **Eğri Minare*** (13C), the local "leaning tower of Pisa", built all in redbrick.

Lastly, behind the city hall, spend some time in the **Zinciriye medrese**, which houses a small **archeological museum** *(8am-5.30pm, closed on weekends; entrance fee)*. The visit is especially interesting because of the building, a beautiful 15C Seljuk construction. Behind the sculpted **portal**, there is a small-domed courtyard. A fountain is located in the middle, whereas the iwan and the students' cells are on the sides.

Around Aksaray

Aksaray is also a good point of departure for visiting the two most beautiful **caravanserais** in central Anatolia, perfect rectangles laid out in the middle of the desert. Like all of the *han* which marked the caravan roads, their impenetrable surrounding wall bears no decoration, other than the portal. The sun alone can transform it into marble or gold.

Ağzıkarahan**

13km away on the road to Nevşehir, heading toward Cappadocia. 8am-7pm. Entrance fee.

Set along the **Uzun Yol**, the caravan road which linked Persia to Konya, the Seljuk capital, Ağzıkarahan is one of the best-preserved caravanserais (13C). Behind its walls, reinforced with turrets, the courtyard houses a small, plain **mosque**, a simple cube of stone on four pillars. All around, warehouses, stables and dormitories are lined up. These vast rooms were heated by braziers. On the left, one of the rooms is lit up by the rays which pass through its collapsed dome. At the end of the courtyard – facing the entrance – a magnificent **portal*** leads to a "large room" preceded by a finely-carved protruding arch.

Sultan Hanı⋆

48km west of Aksaray, in the direction of Konya (Adana exit), in the small village named after it. 9am-7pm. Entrance fee. Another stop on the long way to Konya, Sultan Hanı *(see photograph p 12-13)* is a contemporary of its neighbour (early 13C), but a fire damaged it at the end of the 18C. Recently restored, the caravanserai is once again brand new...too new. Breaking with the austerity of the walls, the **portal⋆⋆** of the Sultan Hanı is a marvel of Seljuk sculpture, an exuberant garden of muqarnas, rosettes and interlaces. It precedes the small **mosque** with four pillars, as well as the warehouse and the lounges. Right at the back, an **iwan** closes off the entrance of the **grand room⋆**, an immense hall divided into five vaulted naves where the animals would rest.

Making the most of Aksaray

COMING AND GOING

By bus – The bus station is a 10min walk from the centre, on the outer boulevard. Daily services to Ankara (4hr), Alanya (10hr), Antalya (8hr), İstanbul (10hr), İzmir (10hr), Konya (2hr), Kayseri (2hr 30min) and the main towns of Cappadocia: Avanos, Göreme, Ürgüp. Journey by day or night, depending on the destination. Timetables available at the station.

By shared taxi – Just behind the "otogar". This is the best way to get to Ihlara, even if the bus drivers are adamant that the dolmuşes don't go there. (Journey time: 1hr). Check the return time.

WHERE TO STAY

Apart from a luxury holiday complex outside the town, Aksaray's hotel infrastructure is rather modest.

Camp sites
Kervan Pension camp site, Sultan Hanı, ☏ (382) 242 23 25 – 15 pitches. ⚐ ✗ Signposted on the road Nevşehir / Konya, 2km from the Sultan Hanı caravanserai. The camp sites are actually in the guest house garden and offer the same conviences.

Under US$15
Çakmak Pension, in the "otogar", ☏ (382) 212 92 90 – 8rm. ⚐ Comfort at a minimum price. Useful if you arrive late or have to leave early in the morning.
Aksaray Pension, Aslan Sok 1, ☏ (382) 212 41 33 – 10rm. ⚐ Take Eski San Cad from the main square and take the 2nd road on the left. Small, inexpensive and decent (English spoken).

Hotel Tezcanlar, Kızılay Cad, ☏ (382) 213 84 82, Fax (382) 215 12 34 – 11rm. ⚐ Located behind the town hall and the main square. Good value for your money with clean and modern rooms.

Between US$15 and US$18
Hotel Yuvam, Kurşunlu Cami Yanı Eski Sanayi Cad Kavşaği, ☏ (382) 212 00 24, Fax (382) 213 28 75 – 16rm. ⚐ ✍ In the main square. A recent establishment with attractively decorated rooms. Best value for money.

US$30
Melendiz Motel, 2km from Aksaray, in the direction of Adana, ☏ (382) 215 24 00, Fax (382) 215 24 10 – 92rm. ⚐ ✍ TV ✗ ♨ CC A lot of groups come here. It does offer a very good level of comfort with a setting to match.

EATING OUT

Between US$4 and US$8
Kar Restaurant, Kılıçaslan Mah Güven Sok 14, ☏ (382) 212 86 04. Good traditional food served in a little courtyard with a refreshing fountain.
Merkez Lokantası, Bankalar Cad Sümerbank Yanı, ☏ (382) 213 10 76. A good little eatery in a central location.
Sultan lahmacun, Kalealtı Sok. Here you'll find delicious Turkish pizza.

OTHER THINGS TO DO

Turkish bath – Paşa hamamı, behind the museum, ☏ (382) 212 04 63. A charming, authentic Turkish bath.

Making the most of Aksaray

NİĞDE★

Provincial capital – Map p 551
104km from Aksaray, 134km from Kayseri, 80km from Nevşehir
Pop 98 000 – Alt 1 217m

Not to be missed
The tomb of Hüdavent Hatun.
The monastery of Eski Gümüş, nearby.
And remember...
The city's mosques are only open at prayer time;
it is an opportunity to participate, but be discreet.

A small agricultural town surrounded by poplars, Niğde flaunts its old fortress standing at the foot of a volcanic massif of the Melendiz Dağları. Neglected by the hordes of tourists travelling across Cappadocia, the city is nevertheless replete with beautiful Seljuk buildings, mosques and mausoleums, which are proof of its brilliant past. You should also take the time to stroll around its small streets, filled with charming old houses with light-coloured façades. Niğde is a good base for visiting the Eski Gümüş monastery, a jewel of Byzantine art.

The flourishing city of the Seljuk sultanate of Rum (late 11C) was devastated after the passage of the Mongols at the beginning of the 13C. However, Niğde experienced a revival with Eretna, the former governor of Sivas, who turned it into his refuge from 1335 onwards. The city's beauty is derived from the buildings dating from this period. Niğde remained in the hands of the Seljuks until 1467, when it became Ottoman.

Visiting the city

*Allow a morning for the visit and the remainder of the day
for the Eski Gümüş monastery.*

From the main square, take Bankalar Cad and turn left at the second street.

In the middle of a small square embellished by an outdoor café, there are two elegant *türbe* with light-coloured limestone walls. This beautiful mausoleum – a real gem! – is the **Hüdavent Hatun Türbesi★★**, a small octagonal building covered with a pyramidal dome, in the purest Seljuk style. Almost all of the decoration is concentrated on the **portal★**, whereas a delicate frieze of geometrical and floral patterns underscores the upper portions of the doors and windows. Built in 1312, this mausoleum harbours the remains of Princess Hüdavent, the sultan's daughter.

Beside it, the **Gündoğolu Türbe** is more modest with a square layout giving it a heavier contour. It is however unique: four of the roof's panels extend halfway over the walls, accentuating the pyramidal shape of the building.

Leave the park on the side opposite the mausoleums. Turn left and follow the large avenue until you reach the third street on the left.

On the right, the **Archeological Museum★** is worth a detour (*8am-12noon/1.30pm-5pm; closed Mondays. Entrance fee*). It houses a beautiful collection of objects going back to the Neolithic and Bronze ages (5000-3000 BC). All are from the region, in particular from the *tell* of **Kosk** (Room 2), a site which can be seen 15km south of Niğde. The Hittites are represented by the excavations from the **Acem Höyük** (1900-1700 BC), a palace of the Assyrian period located 18km north of Aksaray. You should not

Cappadocia

miss the **treasure** consisting of 196 gold coins, minted with the effigy of the last Ottoman sultans, discovered in 1977 in the mosque of Sungur Bey. As you leave the room, notice the imposing **Phrygian funerary vase★** (750-300 BC), before entering Room 3 housing the mummy of a young girl found in the Ilhara Valley (10C). A small ethnographical section displays a few beautiful carpets and kilims, official robes and everyday objects.

Take the street on the right to Bor Cad, then turn right. At the first intersection, cross over to take the street opposite.

On the right you will see the **Ak Medrese** (*closed for restoration, for an undetermined length of time*), a Koranic school founded in 1409. The façade alternates with broken arches surrounding a beautiful Seljuk **portal**. Behind, a central courtyard is encircled by porticoes on three sides and an iwan furnished with a mihrab.

Go down the street until you reach the intersection and the **Sungur Bey Mosque★** (Süngür Bey Camii), constructed in the 14C by the Mongols. The portal, retaining a few ornaments (it should be imagined completely carved) opens up to a lovely **porch★** topped by intersecting ribs. The **northern portal★** is much better preserved, a true lace of stone, creating a multitude of stars and scrolls on a succession of frames, around a beautiful **wooden door**, also heavily crafted. Sitting on both sides, aged Turkish men chat while they await prayer time. Have a look at the **interior★**, a sober space punctuated by columns livened up by red carpets. The only decorative accessory is the **mihrab** which recaptures the portal's structure.

The mosque is flanked by a **türbe** (*on the left of the portal*) and a **bedesten** (*on the right*), a beautiful 16C covered market. Unfortunately it no longer functions.

Leaving the mosque, take the alley in front which climbs up to the **Alaaddin Camii★★** (*on the left*), a beautiful mosque dating from the early 13C. Its massive appearance is due to the buttresses and the limited number of windows. Even the **portal★** is quite subdued with its regular decor consisting of palmettes and arabesques (the two heads with braids are symbols inherited from shamanism). In the corner, the cylindrical **minaret** resembles a lighthouse, solidly anchored on an octagonal base. Tucked away in the half-light, the **prayer room★** is quite lovely with its ogees and its massive pillars. The cold setting is similar to that of a guard room in European medieval castles, except for the small domes sculpted with stalactites, the **mihrab** and the gracious carpets covering the floor.

The citadel (*cannot be visited*), built on the heights overlooking the city rises nearby. Raised in the 11C, by the sultans of Rum, it is Niğde's most ancient remains, although its walls were restored by the Ottomans in the 15C. The latter also erected the ramparts which still enclose part of the knoll. All that remains of the citadel is the impressive **northern tower**, long used as a prison.

Around Niğde

Some 20km south, in the direction of Adana, the **Kemerhisar** road follows an attractive **Roman aqueduct**, whose arches in varying states of repair, run for several kilometres across the countryside, sometimes serving as a fence. Water flowed from a large **marble basin★** filled with the waters of surrounding springs. The acqueduct, in perfect condition, is located 4km from Kemerhisar, in the middle of a wonderful haven of greenery. Built in the 2C, it is still functioning, and it is a treat to drink çay in front of its tranquil waters. The Neolithic site of **Kosk** (*closed to the public*) is located nearby. Its pottery can be seen in the Niğde museum.

Niğde

The monastery of Eski Gümüş**

9km east of Niğde, on the Kayseri road. After 5km, turn right, then left 500m further down. The monastery is 4km from here, in the village of Gümüşler (well indicated). 8am-12noon/1pm-5.30pm. Entrance fee. It is forbidden to take pictures inside the church. However, photos are sold at the counter.

Entirely sculpted in the volcanic rock, the monastery of Eski Gümüş is one of Cappadocia's most beautiful. Vast and remarkably well preserved, it also contains beautiful frescoes. Besides the church, the monastery is adjacent to a small subterranean city, whose first two levels have been uncovered.

From the exterior, its simple volcanic rock wall pierced by a few holes does not appear very impressive. Sculpted in the rock, a corridor leads to an open **inner courtyard***, completely excavated to form a well of light in the centre of the monastery. A few wall-sculpted cells (on the sides) are located underneath the arcades whereas the middle is reserved for tombs, hollowed out in the ground. Through a tunnel, on the left, you enter the **underground city**, a small labyrinth of corridors, cells and shops ventilated by vertical wells. The right side was occupied by the large vaulted room of a **funerary chapel**.

The **church**** is across from the entrance. Access is on the side of the vaulted narthex formerly preceded on the left by an exonarthex (never completed). On the right, the nave, an immense walled area, is as impressive for its dimensions and its verticality as it is for the beauty of its frescoes. A tall central **cupola** rests on four massive circular pillars, decorated with geometrical patterns, and the surrounding façades are covered with countless images with glistening tones, creating a harmonious pattern of colours and lines.

Painted in the 10-11C (and restored in 1962), the **frescoes**** are supposedly the work of three different artists. The characters, whose yellow nimbi look like stars against the navy blue background, create beautiful compositions with red and ochre tones. Take a closer look at the magnificence of each figure's facial expressions and the folds in the clothing.

In the central apse, the Church dignitaries, standing, surround the Virgin, who is in turn surrounded by the apostles and the evangelists. The painting is the work of a different artist to the one who executed the frescoes in the side apses, whose bodies are more elongated. On the left, notice the superb **Virgin with Child**, and on the right St John the Baptist. Lastly, the large composition displayed on the left side is the work of a third artist. The paintings should be observed from the bottom up, illustrating the Annunciation, the Nativity and the Presentation at the Temple. In the middle, the Three Wise Men appear, symbolising the three periods of life.

Making the most of Niğde

COMING AND GOING

By bus – The bus station, Terminal Cad, is a 15min walk from the centre. Several services operate every day to Ankara (4hr 30min), Aksaray (90min), Kayseri (2hr30min), İstanbul (12hr), İzmir (11hr), Konya (3hr 30min) and Nevşehir (90min).

By train – The station is out of the way, on a circular boulevard, at the very end of İstasyon Cad. You can get to Ankara, Adana, Kayseri and Konya from Niğde, but it is faster by bus.

ADDRESS BOOK

Tourist information office, Hükümet Meyd Vakıf İşhanı 1-B, ☎ (388) 232 34 01. 8am-12noon, 1.30pm-6.30pm; closed weekends. Very pleasant welcome. You can find a good street map here.

WHERE TO STAY

Few tourists come here, so there are not many suitable hotels and most of the guest houses are rather grim.

Under US$15
Hotel Murat, Eski Belediye Yanı 5, ☎ (388) 213 39 78 – 16rm. ⁂ In the heart of the old quarter, this decent hotel has clean and colourful rooms – however, they're barely large enough to fit the bed.

Around US$15
Hotel Nahita, Terminal Cad, near the "otogar", ☎ (388) 232 53 66 – 30rm. ⁂ ℘ The hotel must have been nice – once

upon a time. Today, it's decrepit, in need of a facelift and offers only average comfort. It's a bit far from the centre (a 10min walk) but is close to the bus station.

Around US$30
Hotel Evim, Hükümet Meyd, ☎ (388) 232 08 69, Fax (388) 232 35 36 – 48rm. ⁂ ℘ This establishment has recently been renovated and offers comfortable rooms with electric blue carpets. Additional benefits include a hospitable welcome and a central location.

EATING OUT

Some little restaurants along Bor Cad, the shopping street which leads to the main square.
Saruhan Etli Pide Salonu, Bor Cad Çetintürk Sitesi Karşısı, ☎ (388) 232 21 72. Tasty, very cheap pide.
Boğaziçi, Bor Cad 29, ☎ (388) 213 60 90. Across from a small park you can sample pide and kebabs in a calm and cool setting.

SHOPPING GUIDE

Delicacies – A sweet tooth's paradise: Niğde has numerous cake shops and outlets selling dried fruits and seeds. They are mainly to be found along Bor Cad and İstasyon Cad, in the vicinity of the main square.

Carpet market – On Wednesdays and Thursdays, near the Sungur Bey mosque. A wide selection at very interesting prices. A good opportunity to drink tea and try your hand at haggling.

NEVŞEHİR

Provincial capital – Map p 551
75km from Aksaray – 110km from Kayseri – 217km from Konya
Pop 113 000 – Alt 1 160m

Not to be missed
The Church of St John, nearby.

And remember...
If you have limited time to visit the region,
pass rapidly through Nevşehir and head straight
for the heart of Cappadocia (see p 552).

Nevşehir is the province's most populated city, a stone's throw from the heart of Cappadocia. However, it seems oblivious to the crowds of tourists streaming by without ever stopping. Facing the steppe, the city clings to the traditions of ancient Anatolia: in the streets, the women wear large headscarves and at times even face veils.

Nevşehir experienced its golden age in the 18C, when Damat İbrahim Paşa, one of the city's distinguished citizens, had the honour of becoming the son-in-law of Sultan Ahmet III. Almost nothing remains of this prestigious period. However, if you have the time, head north of the city to visit the legendary *tekke* (monastery) of Hacı Bektaş, the "Precious Pilgrim".

A short tour of the city

Overlooked by the ruins of a Seljuk fortress, the old quarter of Nevşehir stretches between the two main streets of the city, Atatürk Bulvarı and Lâle Caddesi. In the heart of its tortuous alleys rises the **İbrahim Paşa Mosque** (Nevşehirli İbrahim Paşa Külliyesi), the only large Ottoman mosque in the region. Built in the 18C by İbrahim Paşa, it was part of a large complex including a medrese (still operating), a library, an *imaret* (hospice) and a hamam. The latter is still functioning but it has become mixed, causing the Turks to flee (to the tourists' advantage) *(see "Making the most of Nevşehir")*.

Although it is slightly out of the way, the **Archeological Museum** is worth a detour *(Kayseri Cad, the extension of Atatürk Cad. 8am-12noon/1pm-5pm, closed Mondays. Entrance fee)*. It houses an interesting collection of Bronze Age pottery (third millennium), a statue of a **Hittite lion**, an exquisite **Urartian metal belt**, Roman glassware and delicate **mother-of-pearl medallions** from the Byzantine era. A small ethnographic section also displays elegant regional costumes, manuscripts and jewellery. On the first floor, pretty miniatures and engravings representing prosperous 18C Nevşehir can be seen.

...and beyond

A 90km (round-trip) excursion north of Nevşehir. Allow 3hr.

"Through Syria and Anatolia, wandering from country to country, I have searched for and never found, a foreigner like me."

Yunus Emre, Sufi poet.

Penetrate into the deep Anatolia of hermits, monks and Sufi masters. The straight road crosses the steppe, a large ochre space caressed by the clouds. From time to time you will encounter a painted cart drawn by a donkey.

■ The Church of St John✶✶ (Karşı Kilise)

21km from Nevşehir, on the left, before Gülşehir.

On the way to Hacıbektaş, take the time to visit this church, one of the rare ones to have had its **façade carved** into the rock. In the chapel surmounting the nave, you will discover remarkable, recently-restored 10C or 11C **frescoes✶✶**, illustrating the life of Jesus. The images, in varying red and ochre tones, stand out against their magnificent navy blue background. The elegance of the *folds*, the svelte silhouettes and the finesse and realism of the features reveal the work of a great Constantinople artist.

■ The Hacıbektaş Monastery✶

45km from Nevşehir. 8am-12noon/1.30-5.30pm; closed Tuesdays. Entrance fee.

The small town of Hacıbektaş owes its renown to the tekke founded by Hacı Bektaş Veli (1248-1270), a mystic originally from Iran. Converted into a museum in 1964, it has remained a sacred site and thousands of pilgrims travel from all over Turkey (especially on August 16) to pay homage to the tomb of the Sufi master. Once their respects are paid, they jostle in the nearby shops to purchase posters, plates, medallions, rings or clocks with the effigy of Bektaşı Dervishes.

B. Brillon/MICHELIN

Souvenir from Hacıbektaş...
an around-the-clock reminder!

With its low buildings, covered with zinc roofs, the tekke is simple and functional, a reminder of the life of the sages *(pir)* who came here to meditate.

At the back of the courtyard, near the small **mosque** *(Tekke Camii)*, you may visit the **kitchen** cluttered with its large **cauldrons**, as well as a small room *(on the left)* which includes various objects from the Dervishes' daily life. In the **Meydan Evi**, a large central room where judgements were pronounced and ceremonies held, various musical instruments and the monks' felt headgear are displayed. Continuing, you come to a **garden** flowering with various types of convolvulus. Facing the *türbe* of Bakim Sultan, a hundred-year-old mulberry tree disappears under a multitude of cloth strips which the pilgrims tie to branches in order to have their wishes granted. At the back rise the sober **türbe of Hacı Bektaş** and his disciple, Güvenç Abdal. Underneath a beautiful wooden ceiling, the master's tomb is truly venerated: the faithful lay a cotton scarf on the floor, and then circle around the tomb on their knees with their foreheads touching the ground.

Hacı Bektaş Veli

Little is known concerning the origins of Hacı Bektaş Veli (1248-1270). A few claim he is descendent of the prophet Ali and one legend has it that he arrived in Anatolia in the form of a crane, the totemic animal of the shamans. This explains the crane dance which the Bektaşı dervishes perform during their prayers. The ideology of Hacı Bektaş Veli mixed various principles of the cults of the Orient and the Byzantine world, both Muslim and Christian. Its teachings were based on love, charity, great tolerance and especially a deep understanding of the self through bodily awareness. Very influential among the military (the Bektaşı were the army "chaplains" of the Janissaries), they played a major political role during Ottoman rule, and the brotherhood had many followers in the Empire, including the Balkans. The order was banned in 1936, by Atatürk.

Making the most of Nevşehir

COMING AND GOING

By bus – *The bus station* is 1km from the town centre, on the road to Gülşehir. To travel east, you have to take a bus to Kayseri where you can buy a ticket for your destination. For the main cities in the west of Turkey, the **Göreme-Nevtur** bus company operates daily services to: Adana (11hr), Ankara (5hr), Antalya (11hr), Bodrum (14hr), Bursa (11hr), Denizli (10hr), Eskişehir (8hr), Fethiye (13hr), İstanbul (11hr), İzmir (13hr), Kayseri (1hr), Konya (4hr), Marmaris (14hr) and Mersin (6hr). It is advisable to purchase tickets in advance.

ADDRESS BOOK

Tourist information – In Atatürk Bul, at the junction of Lale Cad, next to the hospital, ☎ (384) 213 36 59. 8.30am-5.30pm. There is a second office at the "otogar". Open 7am-9pm, May to September.

Car rental – At the *Dedeman hotel*, Ürgüp Yolu, on the way into town, ☎ (384) 213 99 00.

WHERE TO STAY

Apart from the big hotels on the outskirts, accessible only to those with their own transport, the town's hotel infrastructure is limited. You can, however, easily make do with the small establishments in the town centre.

Under US$15

Hotel Şems, Atatürk Bul 29, ☎ (384) 213 35 97 – 32rm. ☝ The rooms are a bit dated but are still relatively decent and the price is right.

Between US$15 and US$25

Hotel Seven Brothers, Kayseri Cad Tusan Sok 25, ☎ and Fax (384) 213 49 79 – 30rm. ☝ ♪ Slightly out of the centre, towards the museum. Simple but adequate.

Between US$30 and US$40

Hotel Orsan, Kayseri Cad 15, ☎ (384) 213 21 15, Fax (384) 213 42 23 – 95rm. ☝ ♪ ♨ Very beautiful lobby decorated with carpets. The rooms are more impersonal, but very comfortable.

EATING OUT

Sölen Restaurant, Atatürk Bul 15, ☎ (384) 231 07 41. A traditional "salonu" in a long room with formica tables. All the dishes are appetizing and are displayed in the window.

Aspava Restaurant, Atatürk Bul 29, ☎ (384) 212 10 51. A popular restaurant with good pide and kebabs at cheap prices.

Bostan Restaurant, Atatürk Bul 32, ☎ (384) 213 44 87. Right in the town centre. Tables inside and in a pleasant garden. It's a pity that the food is mediocre and rather expensive.

OTHER THINGS TO DO

Market – All day Monday, at the junction between Atatürk Bul and the road to Ankara.

Turkish bath – On the side of Lale Cad, ☎ (384) 213 26 58. 8am-9pm. Since the establishment is mixed (the ladies are massaged by a man), it is frequented only by tourists. But the steam is still deliciously relaxing.

Helicopter ride – Expensive but unforgettable! Departure at dawn to admire the sunrise from on high. 4hr trip (1hr flight time) organised by **Kapadokya Lodge**, ☎ (384) 213 99 45.

B. Brillion/MICHELIN

On the road to Hacıbektaş

KAYSERI★

Provincial capital
Map p 551
328km from Ankara – 336km from Konya – 193km from Sivas – 90km from Ürgüp
Pop 605 000 – Alt 1 050m

Not to be missed
The citadel tower.
One of the two beautiful caravanserais close to Kayseri:
Sultan Hanı or Karatay Hanı.

And remember...
Taste some of the city's culinary specialities,
including the tasty "pastırma" (see "Making the most of Kayseri").

Is it the seething atmosphere permeating the air, the construction work which overwhelms the city centre or the dark stones of its walls? First impressions do not suggest a joyous town. Around its dark basalt citadel, frenetic activity prevails in the streets, and entire neighbourhoods are undergoing construction work disturbing the past. Kayseri is a modern city bustling with activity. An important food industry centre, it is known for its culinary specialities – including the famous *pastırma* (*see "Making the most of Kayseri"*) – but also for its textile industry and its silk carpets which rival those of Hereke. Nevertheless, the "city of 24 mausoleums" has not forgotten its precious heritage – a last glimpse of a great central Anatolian city. At the eastern border of Cappadocia, Kayseri is an Eastern city which can be seen in its countless Seljuk buildings. The interlaces and stars of its portals evoke distant Persia, hidden behind the tall silhouette of Erciyes Dağı which rules over the steppe, as its white summit disappears among the clouds.

Caesar's city
Although it was in Kültepe that the first traces of Hittite occupation in Anatolia (1700 BC) were found, Kayseri does not seem to have developed before the Hellenistic period. The city lived through a prosperous era under Roman domination, the period in which it received the name *Caesarea*, in honour of Emperor Tiberius (14-37 AD). With the advent of Christianity, it became an important bishopric, represented by the brilliant figure of its bishop, Basil. Weakened by Arab invasions which shook Cappadocia in the 7C and 8C, it was not able to fend off the Seljuks who occupied its walls for more than two centuries from the 11C to the 13C. One of them, the Daniş mend Prince Tursan, even made it the capital of his emirate, a powerful entity encompassing all of Cappadocia and the provinces of Sivas and Amasya. At the end of the 12C, Kayseri fell again to the Seljuks of Rum, but they in turn were expelled permanently in 1243 by the Mongols, who remained masters of the city for more than a century. In 1515, the city became part of the Ottoman Empire.

Saint Basil of Caesarea
Born in Caesarea in the middle of the 4C, Basil became its bishop in 370 AD. Being very productive, he prompted the Christians of Cappadocia to organise themselves into small farming communities, according to the monastic model. He wrote two important collections for his followers: *Longer Rules* and *Shorter Rules*, as well as a liturgy which is still in use today. Seen as a kind of father figure, Basil became a popular character in Cappadocia. Local artists have often represented him in churches with a wrinkled but firm face and a long black beard. In his hands, he carries an elegant book and around his neck, his bishop's stole covered with gold crosses.

Visiting the city

Allow half a day to see the main monuments, which are grouped around Cumhuriyet Meydanı, the main square. If you add a few hours, you can pursue your exploration with the Çifte Medrese and the Archeological Museum.

The citadel★ (Kale) (B2)

There are two entrances. From the main square, a vaulted passage leads to the interior. Free.

An imposing basalt wall, the citadel raises its sombre silhouette in the heart of the city, which is slowly being invaded by the shops which overflow from the bazaar. It constitutes one of the rare examples of defensive medieval architecture in Anatolia, and one of the best preserved. Erected in 1224 by the Seljuk sultan, Alaaddin Keykubat I, it rises on the walls of a Byzantine fortress going back to the reign of Justinian (6C). In the 13C, the city itself was surrounded by a similar **basalt land wall**. A few remaining ruins are visible near Kıçıkapı Meydanı and on Talaş Caddesi. Remodelled in the 15C, the citadel boasts no less than 19 towers, linked by a watch-path. The double main entrance consists of an ingenious defence system: from the **outer gate**, guarded by **two lion heads**, you penetrate the interior through an impressive **barbican**, an open air corridor, 30m-long, running at the foot of a large watchtower. This "sieve" rendered entry extremely difficult to the assailants. In the inner courtyard, in the middle of carpet merchants and *pastırma* vendors, rises the **bedesten**, a handsome covered market built in the 15C and recently restored, which used to welcome silk merchants in former times. Close by, its contemporary, the **Fatih Mosque** (Fatih Camii) stands against the stone walls.

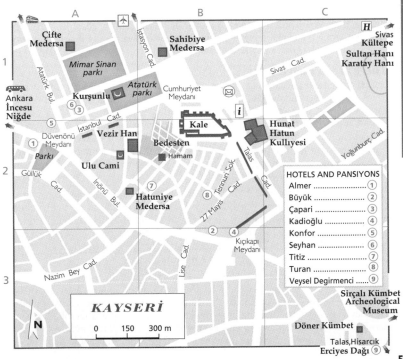

Kayseri

The Hunat Hatun Complex★ (Hunat Hatun Külliyesi) (B2)

Completed between 1228 and 1238, Hunat Hatun Külliyesi is the first complex which the Seljuks founded in Anatolia. It owes its name to the wife of Sultan Alaaddin Keykubat I, who financed the project. The complex includes a mosque, mausoleum, medrese and a hamam, precious examples of this period's architecture.

The mosque★ (Hunat Hatun Camii) opens up through a narrow portal with a carved façade, flanked on the right by a fine cylindrical minaret. The prayer hall★, a vast forest of columns, is divided into eight naves. A small dome on pendentives covers the mihrab, carved in the black lava. The grand central dome is not part of the original layout: it was added in the 19C to cover the traditional central courtyard, which was not adapted to withstand the rigours of the Anatolian winter.

Between the mosque and the medrese is the mausoleum of the founder (Hunat Hatun Türbe). It is a small octagonal structure covered with a pyramidal cone (access through the medrese). Armenian by birth, Hunat Hatun converted to Islam when her son acceded to the throne. Her granddaughter lies next to her.

The medrese (Hunat Hatun Medresesi) houses an interesting Ethnography Museum (8.30am-5.30pm; entrance fee). Its traditional plan includes a central courtyard embellished with a fountain and surrounded on three of its sides by elegant porticoes (it is a pity that the windows hide the arcades). Two iwans face each other (inside one of them there is a nomad tent), and eight cells are aligned on each side. Various objects from the Seljuk and Ottoman periods are displayed; in particular, beautiful star-shaped turquoise tiles, representing stylised characters, which are from the neighbouring hamam. At the back, on the right, you enter the Hunat Hatun türbe, described above.

Nearby, the hamam still functions. Although it has been stripped of its sparkling tiles, the setting is still charming and you should take advantage of it while you are in town (see "Making the most of Kayseri").

The bazaar district (B2)

Behind the citadel stretches the bazaar, bustling with life. The pastırma and suçuk stores are interspersed amongst the jewellers, shoe-makers, the pots and pans of the hardware shops, the clothes, linen and carpet shops.

At the far end of the bazaar, furthest from the citadel, you reach the Vezir Han, a caravanserai built in the 18C by Damat İbrahim Paşa. This large, grey lava building rises on two storeys. In former times, this is where the city's commercial activities were concentrated. Today, unfortunately, its rooms house only a few wool wholesalers and the remainder seem abandoned.

Facing it, the Grand Mosque (Ulu Cami) has a beautiful redbrick minaret★, a fine cylindrically-shaped building which is surrounded at the top by an elegant band of blue tiles. Built in the 12C, the mosque was restored in the 13C. Its unique feature: the arcades of the prayer hall are covered by a flat ceiling★ composed of beams. Do not miss the minbar, in multicoloured wood, which has carved inscriptions in Kufic characters, nor the beautiful white marble mihrab.

Returning towards Cumhuriyet Meydanı, you will reach the Kurşunlu Mosque (Kurşunlu Camii) (A1), recognisable by its five lead domes. Built in the 16C, it is thought to be the work of Sinan, the famous architect, or one of his pupils. Whichever is the case, the building retains all the characteristics of Ottoman mosques: the hypostyle prayer room, dear to the Seljuks, is replaced here by a bright space with white walls, illuminated by the stained glass of a tall central dome.

Across the city

If you still have a bit of time, head towards **Mimar Sinan Park** to visit the **Çifte Medrese** (A1), a 12C Seljuk medical complex which has been transformed into the **Museum of Medicine** *(closed Mondays and Tuesdays, 8am-12noon/1pm-5pm; entrance fee)*. It includes two large buildings; on one side there is the hospital, on the other the school of medicine (Anatolia's first) which was added a bit later. You enter through two beautiful **portals**, the only outside decoration. In the centre, the traditional open courtyard is surrounded by four iwans. The hospital and the school are linked by a large vaulted corridor.

Enter through the **School of Medicine** (Giyasiye Medresesi). On the right is the tomb of Princess Nesibe, the sultan's sister and initiator of the project. The classrooms are located around the central fountain where drawings of medicinal plants are displayed *(the explanations are only in Turkish, unfortunately)*. Next, follow the corridor to reach the **hospital** (Şifaiye), where the operating room can still be seen. At the back, dark **cells** are aligned along a corridor, almost as sinister as a dungeon. They are in fact rooms which held mental patients.

Continuing to the east, you will come to the **Sahibiye medrese** (B1), an early 13C Koranic school. Four **turrets** mark the corners of the building, and lion-shaped **gargoyles**, protruding from the dark walls, surround a lovely **portal★** with stalactite decoration.

The inner courtyard with its fountain is surrounded by porticoes on three sides; the fourth side is occupied by an iwan (closed off by windows). Its cells are now home to a handicrafts centre and pleasant book market.

South of the city, the **Döner Kümbet★** (C3), one of the most beautiful mausoleums in Kayseri, rises in the centre of a small square surrounded by watermelon vendors. Its cylindrical shape gave it its nickname "the revolving mausoleum" *(döner, in Turkish)*. Topped with a conical roof, it rests on a square base with cut angles. An inscription above the door indicates that it was constructed in 1275 to house the tomb of a princess. The exterior decor is remarkably fine with its blind arcades, enhanced with long bands of geometrical and animal patterns – winged leopards, griffins and double-headed eagles (the Seljuk emblem of royalty). On both sides of the door there are two fan-shaped palm trees.

On the side of the square, towards the Archeological Museum, another mausoleum can be seen, the **Sırçalı Kümbet** (14C) which has unfortunately lost all of its tile decor.

Arriving from the citadel, take the road on the left from Döner Kümbet, near the train station, then the first road on the right (Kışla Cad).

Enclosed in a small modern building, the **Archeological Museum★** houses the discoveries made in the nearby Hittite site of **Kanesh** (Kültepe), as well as various objects from the Hellenistic, Roman and Byzantine periods *(8.30am-5.30pm; closed Mondays. Entrance fee. Signs in English. Arrows guide you from room to room)*.

In the first room, dedicated to the Bronze Age, there are alabaster **idols★** with two or three heads, representations of the **mother goddess** and cuneiform **clay tablets★**. The latter are proof of the trading activity of *Karum*, the district of Kanesh where Assyrian traders would gather. Also notice the terracotta **bathtub** of the Hittite period (1900-1200 BC) and the elegant neo-Hittite sculpted stelae.

East of Kayseri

Kültepe, the ancient Kanesh

22km northeast of Kayseri, in the direction of Sivas. After 19km, turn left towards Karahöyük for 3km. 8am-5pm (officially). Entrance fee (the guardian appears as you arrive).

Kanesh will essentially interest those who have a passion for Hittite archeology, since its remains are quite modest. Founded in the fourth millennium BC, Kanesh gained in importance in the second millenium BC with the arrival of the Hittites who had fruitful trade relations with the Assyrians. However, the city was ravaged by two fires, one in 1850, the other 50 years later, which made it lose much of its prosperity. It was further weakened during the invasion of the Peoples of the Sea, who pillaged it and caused the downfall of the Hittite Empire. The site remained occupied until the Roman period, but Kanesh had by then become a modest village.

The site extends on both sides of the road. On the left, the razed walls of the **palace** and several temples can be seen on the top of a knoll, indicating the site of the **citadel**. At its foot stretched the **karûm** district, the home of Assyrian traders and their families. A few remnants of their houses are still visible on the flanks of the hill on the right of the road. This district provided a great quantity of clay **tablets** (preserved in the museums of Kayseri and Ankara) on which the Assyrians and Hittites recorded all the stages of their trading transactions, in cuneiform writing.

Sultan Hanı★★

45km north east of Kayseri, in the direction of Sivas; at the junction, turn left towards Tuzhisar. Cross the village. The caravanserai is located in the next village, on the right. 9am-5pm (officially). Entrance fee. The guardian arrives with the key as soon as he hears a car. NB, there is another caravanserai with the same name, near Aksaray (see p 587).

Built during the reign of Sultan Alaaddin Keykubat at the beginning of the 13C, this superb han was a refuge for the caravans on the **Uzun Yolu**, a great trade road linking the Orient to Konya, the capital of the Seljuk kingdom of Rum *(see p 498)*.

On both sides of the portal, its walls are reinforced by fine **turrets**, like juxtaposed columns, which also serve to underline every corner of the building. After the portal you enter into a vast courtyard in the middle of which rises a **mosque★**, superbly restrained with its large arches opening up to a single room. At the back lies the vast high-ceilinged **communal room**, punctuated by colonnades; porticoes run the length of the sides (overly restored). At the right of the entrance, a small set of stairs leads to the roof, surrounded by a series of lion-headed gargoyles.

Karatay Hanı★

From Sultan Hanı, return to the Sivas road. Turn right, then take the direction of Bünyan, for 10km. In Bünyan, take the large road on the left towards Malatya, then, after 20km, turn right towards Elbaşı, 6km from there. Pass the village and continue towards Karatay for 5km. The caravanserai is at the end of the village, on the right. Since the building is always closed, you must obtain the keys from the villagers. Free; a small tip ("bahşis") will be welcomed.

Built in 1240 by the vizier Emir Celaleddin Karatay, this forgotten caravanserai exudes charm with the weeds that have invaded its courtyard and the large iron grille that grates beneath the portal. Although it was entirely restored in the 1960s, the building is seldom visited, yet it radiates a sort of tranquillity conducive to

Erciyes Dağı, at the dawn of time...

daydreaming. Like the Sultan Hanı, superb **turrets**** which are in harmony with the stalactite decor of the pediment girdle the remarkably crafted **portal**. Unlike most caravanserai, the mosque is not located in the central courtyard, but rather on the right of the iwan preceding the entrance. On the same side, several small rooms are aligned – for sleeping and storage – whereas a portico shades the building's left wing. At the rear, a portal marks the entrance of a large hypostyle room. Before leaving, have a look at the village: time seems to have stood still.

Erciyes Dağı* (Mt Aergius) *24km south of Kayseri, via the Hisarcık road (well indicated)*. An unrealistic silhouette with ever-changing pastel tones, the ancient Mt Aergius rises above the steppe, poking its tip above the clouds, at an altitude of 3 916m. Erciyes Dağı is one of the three volcanoes to which Cappadocia owes its origins and extraordinary landscape *(see p 547)*. In summer, its flanks are assaulted by hikers who circle it (100km), discovering grandiose **landscapes**** each step of the way. In winter (from December to April), **Kayak Evi** resort is filled with skiers. A good road goes up to the village, where a ski-lift takes you to the summit.

İncesu

31km west of Kayseri, on the road to Niğde.

Perched at an altitude of 1 075m, this little-known village hides a beautiful **külliye***, a small 17C Ottoman complex, made of red stone. It included a bedesten, mosque, medrese and a hamam, as well as a **caravanserai**, in good condition, and which can still be visited. The road entrance is closed, but you can enter through one of the **bedesten's** boutiques. Many of the shops are now closed, but a few artisans continue to make its old walls live on by making small horse-hair seats that look like saddles. On the square, the noble grandfathers who spend the day in the shade of the trees will not fail to invite you to share a *çay* with them. Let yourself be tempted, the ambience is so congenial.

Making the most of Kayseri

COMING AND GOING

By air – The military airport of Erkilet is 3km north of Kayseri. One single destination: İstanbul. 2 flights per day in summer, one flight per day in winter (flight time 90min).

By train – The station is located north of İstasyon Cad, on Çevre Yolu, ☎ (352) 231 13 13. Kayseri is quite a large station, at the junction of several railway lines: from İstanbul to Lake Van, from Ankara to Adana and the one from Sivas to Ankara. However, the bus remains the most convenient way of getting to Ankara (west) or Malatya (east), since the train journeys are always long.

By bus – The "otogar" is located to the west of Kayseri and can be easily reached by dolmuşes which leave from the town centre, near the citadel. You can travel to every part of Turkey from here. Several companies operate daily services, travelling by day and/or night, to the following destinations: Adana (5hr), Ankara (5hr), Antalya (11hr), Bursa (11hr), Avanos, Göreme and Ürgüp in 90min, Edirne (13hr), Kahta (8hr), İstanbul (11hr), Malatya (6hr), Mersin (5hr), Niğde (2hr 30min), Samsun (9hr), Sivas (3hr). For Nemrut Dağı, book your seat for Malatya (via the north) or Kahta (via the south) as soon as possible.

GETTING AROUND

On foot – Since the main monuments are near the citadel, it's easiest just to get around on foot.

By car – It is easy to get around Kayseri by car, since the local network is not complicated. It is therefore a good way of getting to the Archeological Museum, which is rather out-of-the-way, and also handy for a trip to Mount Erciyes.

By rental car – *Europcar*, Osman Kavuncu Cad, on the Ankara-Niğde road, ☎ (352) 336 42 22.
Avis, Atatürk Bul, ☎ (352) 222 61 96. Agencies open 7 days a week, 8.30am-7pm.

By taxi – Numerous yellow taxis, fitted with taximeters, cruise the town. A taxi ride will cost you around US$3 on average.

ADDRESS BOOK

Tourist information – Kağnı Pazarı Hunat Camii Yanı 61, to the side of the citadel (B1). 8.30am-5.30pm. Information mainly in English. Very cordial welcome.

Bank / change – Numerous banks in Park Cad and in the shopping streets (27 Mayıs and Talaş Cad) south of the citadel (B2).

Main post office – In the main square, opposite the citadel, on the corner of Sivas Cad (B1). Open 7 days a week, 8.30am-7pm.

Airline companies – *Turkish Airlines (THY)*, Sahabiye Mah Yıldırım Cad 1, ☎ (352) 222 38 58.

WHERE TO STAY

Under US$15

Hotel Seyhan, Gevher Nesibe Mah Seyhan Sok 6/D, Düvenönü, ☎ (352) 222 43 66 – 30rm. ☝ A large hotel is hidden behind this modest façade. Excellent value for your money. Rooms are simple but clean and you'll receive a hospitable reception.

Between US$15 and US$25

Hotel Büyük, İnönü Bul 55, ☎ (352) 232 53 40 – 28rm. ☝ An unpretentious and well-kept hotel, offering unoriginal but bright rooms.

☝ **Hotel Titiz**, Camikebir Mah Maarif Cad 7, ☎ (352) 222 50 40, Fax (352) 222 55 42 – 32rm. ☝ ✗ You'll appreciate this hotel for its kitsch decoration – midnight blue façade, the interior covered with mirrors, the crimson rooms; its bar and restaurant on the top floor that offer panoramic views; its reception, and finally, its very reasonable prices.

Hotel Kadıoğlu, Kıçıkapı Serdar Cad 45, ☎ (352) 231 63 20, Fax (352) 222 82 96 – 26rm. A good little hotel with a simple level of comfort.

Between US$25 and US$30

Hotel Konfor, Atatürk Bul 5, ☎ (352) 320 01 84, Fax (352) 336 51 00 – 45rm. ☐ ☐ ☐ ☐ Bright rooms with beautiful bathrooms. Very good welcome. Excellent value for money.

Hotel Turan, Turan Cad 8, ☎ (352) 222 55 37, Fax (352) 231 11 53 – 70rm. ☐ ☐ ☐ An old hotel with faded charm. Ask for one of the rooms which have been redecorated, because some of the others are in a pitiful state.

Between US$30 and US$45

Hotel Almer, Çankırı Kavuncu Cad 15, ☎ (352) 320 79 70, Fax (352) 320 79 74 – 77rm. ☐ ☐ ☐ ☐ ☐ An upmarket international hotel which caters to Turkish businessmen. Immaculate rooms and excellent buffet dinner.

Hotel Çapari, Gevher Nesibe Mah Donanma Cad 12, ☎ (352) 222 52 78, Fax (352) 222 52 82 – 44rm. ☐ ☐ ☐ ☐ ☐ Same good quality amenities as the one above, although the welcome is more impersonal.

• **On the road to Erciyes Dağı**
US$55

Veysel Değirmenci, ☎ (352) 342 20 31 – 53rm. ☐ Establishment offering an average level of comfort, open all year round. It is advisable to book ahead.

EATING OUT

You absolutely must try the town's local delicacies, such as "mantı", tiny ravioli stuffed with minced meat, "sucuk" (large beef sausage, dried and spicy) and "pastırma" (dried, spicy beef, cut into fine slices). They are served in all the little restaurants in town.

Between US$4 and US$8

Avcılar İskender, Düvenönü Park Cad Park İşmerkezi 10/A (A2), ☎ (352) 222 70 45. Towards the Almer hotel. Very good beef or chicken "iskender" served in a railway-station-style setting.

Gözde lokantası, Tennuri Sok 33/A (B2), ☎ (352) 222 81 77. Authentic and delicious Turkish cuisine. Families gather here to get away from the noise of the boulevards.

İskender Salonu, 27 Mayıs Cad 27 (B2), ☎ (352) 231 27 69. On the corner of the main square, opposite the citadel. Upstairs. All the "iskender" enthusiasts of Kayseri come here. The "iskender" tastes the same as anywhere else, but the lively atmosphere makes this place worth a visit.

Between US$8 and US$15

Restaurant of the Almer hotel, Osman Kavuncu Cad 15 (A2), ☎ (352) 320 79 70. Open to non-clients. Excellent buffet dinner at a reasonable price. Good for a change.

OTHER THINGS TO DO

Turkish bath – Right in the town centre, next to Hunat Hatun Camii (B2). A pleasant establishment with old-fashioned charm. It is frequented by Turks and has separate sections for men and women. 8.30am-6pm.

Excursions – Erciyes Dağı is 25km south of Kayseri. You can get there by renting a car or taxi for the day. The town is also a good point of departure for going to **Nemrut Dağı**: the tourist information office organises a safe 2-day trip at a reasonable price.

SHOPPING GUIDE

In the authentic atmosphere of a tourist-free bazaar you will find goldsmiths and merchants selling wool, material and carpets, and, of course, the local culinary delicacies.

Carpets – Kayseri is renowned for its silk carpets; you will find numerous shops all over town, especially at the bazaar.

THE BLACK SEA

A Turkish Switzerland! The ochre steppes of central Anatolia disappear, hidden behind the crest of the Pontic range which accumulate all the rain on their northern flank. The escarpments of the mountains are covered with thick forests of beeches and firs whose dark green, velvet needles drown in the mist. Large roofs with four slopes and wooden walls make the houses look like chalets. This is the face of another country, a cool, green Turkey more reminiscent of Europe than the Orient. You might think you were in the Alps. if it were not for the beautiful Seljuk medreses and the fine minarets of Ottoman mosques which suddenly transport the visitor to Persia. The depths of the valleys hide a few unknown treasures: **Safranbolu**, **Amasya**, and **Tokat**, small forgotten cities whose superb wooden *konak* recall the beauty of the villages of former times.

At the foot of the mountain, facing the sea, a long green ribbon unfolds: an immense orchard of cherry trees, tea bushes, tobacco and hazelnuts (the Black Sea plantations make Turkey the world's top hazelnut producer!). Along the coast, tall cliffs alternate with beaches and an infinity of small fishing ports dot the landscape from east to west, all the way to frenetic **Trabzon**. The ancient Trebizond is undoubtedly the Black Sea's finest city, and the busiest, ever since trade with Russia, the Caucusus and Eastern Europe resumed.

Colonised from the 7C BC onwards by Greeks who arrived from the Aegean coast, the shores of the Black Sea were to see in succession Persians and Alexander the Great before Mithridates, a local potentate, proclaimed himself King of Pontus in the 3C BC. The dynasty he founded was so powerful that he was able to weaken the Roman grip in Asia Minor. However, after a long period of instability, the province was finally annexed by the Empire (74 BC), before being recovered by Byzantium in the 6C. Trebizond was the last bastion of the Byzantine Empire, surviving for an additional eight years after its fall. However, İstanbul took the whole of its commercial activity, and the Black Sea coast became isolated from the modern world. Since the collapse of the USSR, another era heralding an economic revival has begun.

Neglected by tourists, especially Westerners (Turkish and Russian vacationers are more numerous), the Black Sea coast still retains the appearance of an authentic Turkey which is profoundly Anatolian and where traditions still live on. Travelling to this region takes you back in time and allows a glimpse of daily life in the Turkey of the past. Avoid waiting too long; go before "progress" alters it.

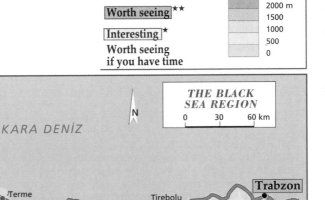

SAFRANBOLU ★★

Zonguldak province – Map p 604
225km from Ankara, 77km from Amasra, 372km from Amasya
Pop 40 000 – Alt 350m

Not to be missed
An early morning walk in the city's sleepy streets.
And remember...
Look for a hotel room as soon as you arrive, or better yet, reserve in advance.
Visit the Bağlar district, in the city heights.

Safranbolu is the jewel of the Black Sea region. As if spellbound, time has stood still since the 18C and its Ottoman houses are still terraced on the flank of the hills, nestled along the cobblestone streets. If you would like to see what an Ottoman city looked like, go to Safranbolu: nowhere else in Turkey will you find such a large concentration of ancient houses which are, in addition, very refined and well preserved. Listed in 1994 on the UNESCO World Heritage Site list, the most beautiful have been converted into hotels or museums. Take your time, explore the shops, bazaar, small stone bridges on the river and the ubiquitous street corner fountains, living and charming illustrations of what life was like during the time of the Ottomans.

The city of saffron

Linking the centre of Anatolia to the shores of the Black Sea, Safranbolu was in a choice location. Successively in the hands of the Persians, the Romans and the Byzantines, it became Ottoman in 1392 and entered into an era of great prosperity. It reached its apogee in the 18C thanks to the trade of saffron – used in pharmaceuticals and dyeing, which gave its name to the city. After World War I, a quarter of its population, Greeks, left Turkish soil to head for Greece. Today, Safranbolu suffers from the expansion of Karabük, the neighbouring industrial city. Far from tourist itineraries, it is trying to attract visitors by slowly reviving its precious heritage.

The houses of Safranbolu

All of the houses, or **konak,** are based on the traditional Ottoman plan, adapted to the rigours of the regional winter. The richer families own summer homes in **Bağlar,** on the upper green hills of the city. Covered by a large roof of tiles with four sides, *konak* includes two floors with the upper one protruding in relation to the bottom one; the first two floors follow the contours of the street exactly. The numerous floor windows are aligned on the four sides and surrounded by wooden lintels which time has rendered almost black. They illuminate several small rooms (8-10), each heated by a fireplace. The walls of the ground floor are of stone and almost windowless, in accordance with Muslim tradition which prefers that private life not be shown to the outside world. The big metal lock closing the entrance door hides an ingenious lever system allowing the residents to enter without key. It opens up to an interior courtyard **(hayat)** refreshed by a small fountain used by the stables and the vegetable garden.

The layout of the interior space follows the rules of communal life inherited from a nomadic lifestyle, leaving only a few private enclaves. The kitchen is located on the first floor, a level reserved for daily household chores. It is the women's quarters **(haremlik)**, whereas the men's quarters **(selâmlik)** occupy the floor above. It is

The Black Sea

composed of the **sofa**, a vast central vestibule leading to the four corner rooms. Well isolated from each other, these rooms each house a family unit, the *sofa* being the meeting point for the whole family. Sparsely decorated, these spaces are used as dining rooms and bedrooms. A bench runs the length of the three sides, facing the fireplace and the two large cupboards which are encased in the wall. Besides the mattress, they also house the lavatory, and the water is heated by the fireplace. A simple copper tray resting on a trivet stands in the middle of the room during meals.

Çarşı, the old city★★

Çarşı, Safranbolu's old district (also known as "Eski Safranbolu") is easily visited on foot. To reach it as you come from Karabük, the modern city needs to be crossed, then the upper city of Bağlar, where you descend 2km to the central square of the old city (Çarşı Meydanı), overlooked by the small Kasdağlı mosque and the old Cinci hamam. Allow 2-3hr.

By taking the street which heads southwest (Arasta Sokak), you reach **Yemeniciler Arastası**, a vast market surrounded by walls and closed off by two large heavy doors. Two small narrow alleys, filled with a multitude of shops (48 in all!) cross the area. It was once the leather bazaar, uniting shoe-makers and leather clothing merchants. Restored in 1990, it now houses crafts shops as well as a very pleasant Oriental tea house, the **Boncuk Café**, where sipping a *çay* is a delight. Next door, the shop of one of the last shoe-makers has been transformed into a small **leather museum**.

Behind the bazaar, on Kunduracılar Sokak, the small **Köprülü Mosque** (17C) boasts a **sundial** in the middle of its interior courtyard. Proceeding to the end of the street, we land in front of the **Cinci caravanserai★** (Cinci Hanı), an imposing 17C building, currently being restored. Its walls, true ramparts, house a large rectangular courtyard surrounded by two floors of **arcades**.

Safranbolu, an Ottoman house

G. Degeorge

Walk around the han and take the road climbing right behind. Further away, a small plaque shows the way to the museum, located in a street on the right.

Now a museum, the **Kaymakamlar Evi★** is one of Safranbolu's most beautiful Ottoman houses (*9am-12noon/1.30pm-5pm, closed Mondays; entrance fee*). Next to the door, notice a cool-to-the-touch hollow stone which the inhabitants used to stock their perishables. In the inner courtyard, the plans of several of the city's Ottoman houses are laid out, whereas the upper floors reconstruct daily life in former times (*you will have to walk on felt pads, to preserve the floors*).

Assisted by her English dictionary, your "guide" will take you from room to room, removing blankets from closets, and showing you the china and beauty accessories. Notice the refined decor of the wooden **ceiling★**.

Leaving the house, take the street on the right to reach the summit of **Hıdırlık Tepesi**, a small hill overlooking the city to the southeast, strewn with a few stelae belonging to 19C Ottoman tombs. The spot is especially beautiful for its **view★★** of the city and its brown roofs.

Go down towards the city by turning left.

The path descends steeply incline towards the river. Below, in the alley on the right, you should not miss the **Mektepçiler Evi**, another delightful 18C house, whose **façade★** is decorated with stucco. Nearby, a beautiful **fountain** flows.

After the house, turn left to reach Manifaturacılar Sokak and the bazaar, where the fine **minaret** of the **İzzet Mehmet Paşa Mosque★** pierces the sky. Built at the end of the 18C, it was restored in 1903. Preceded by a portico, the square prayer hall is surmounted by a tall dome.

Go back and continue down the street towards the south.

On the right-hand side, located near the river's edge, you will see the ruined remains of the **grain market** (Zahire Pazarı) and **livestock market** (Hayvan Pazarı). From there take the bridge crossing the Akçasu, after the mosque. You will have a stunning **view★** of the city, wedged between two steep hills. On the other side of the bridge lies the picturesque **metal bazaar** (Demirciler Çarşısı), where artisans still work iron and copper.

Lastly, all the way on the far north side, via one of the cobblestone alleys leading up to Bağlar, you reach the **Asmalar Havuzlu Konağı★**. This magnificent *konak* has been transformed into a luxurious hotel *(1km from the central square; see "Making the most of Safranbolu")* which is like a museum. Even if you do not stay overnight, do not hesitate to have lunch or have a drink in the **salon**, an exquisite atrium embellished by a pond.

Do not leave Safranbolu without visiting the **Gümüş** and **Bağlar** districts, north of Çarşı. You will see many other beautiful houses terraced on the hills among the vineyards.

Nearby

Yörük Köyü★

14km from Safranbolu, in the direction of Kastamonu. After 13km, take the little road on the left. A signpost shows the way to Yörük.

If Safranbolu pleased you, don't miss Yörük Köyü: this little-known village has no less than **124 Ottoman houses★** dating from the 16C, seemingly oblivious to the passing of time. In other words, it is a small Safranbolu, but more authentic: here, there are no hotels or museums. Not one of the houses has been restored, their inhabitants continue to live as they did in the past and in the quaint cobblestone streets there are no tourists. The **Yörük Merkez mosque**, which burned down a few years ago, is being renovated. A replica of its superb **wooden ceiling** is going to be produced.

Making the most of Safranbolu

COMING AND GOING

By bus – Daily departures for Ankara (4hr 30min) and the Black Sea (Bartın). A bus to İstanbul departs from Karabük, 10km away.

ADDRESS BOOK

Tourist information – Arasta Çarşısı 5, in the covered market (Yemeniciler Arastaşı), ☎ (370) 712 38 63. 8am-5pm. You will be given a warm welcome and a street map. Open 7 days a week.

Bank / change – *Türkiye Bankası*, Kapucuoğlu Sok, in Çarşı. 9am-12noon / 1.30pm-5.30pm.

WHERE TO STAY

The relatively few hotels here are rather expensive. Stay in Çarşı if you can, it is definitely the most pleasant quarter.

• Çarşı

Around US$30

Pension Arasna, Çeşme Mah Arasta Arkası Sok 4, ☎ (370) 712 41 70, Fax (370) 712 38 80 – 8rm. ⚐ Adequate rooms, but make sure to ask if you are the only occupant(s)! The ground-floor bar plays music late into the night, so ask for a room on the 2nd floor and take some earplugs if you want to have an early night. If not, it's a good opportunity to party and the guest house is in a great location.

Around US$45

Hotel Tahsinbey Konağı, Hükümet Sok 50, ☎ (370) 712 60 62, Fax (370) 712 55 96 – 11rm. ⚐ ℰ TV In the heart of the old part of Safranbolu. Charming little rooms in a very attractively restored house.

TTOK Asmazlar Havuzlu Konak, Çelik Gülersoy Cad 18. On a corner to the right on the road leading down to the old part

of Safranbolu from the new town, ☎ (370) 725 28 83, Fax (370) 712 38 24 – 11rm. ⚐ ℰ CC In a superb house set in a walled garden, with rooms furnished in an old-fashioned style. Very refined setting and delightfully haughty staff. Make sure you book long in advance.

• Kıranöy (new town)

Around US$45

Hotel Uz, Arap Hacı Sok 3, ☎ (370) 712 10 86, Fax (370) 712 22 15 – 30rm. ⚐ ℰ TV ✗ The rooms were recently redecorated and offer a good level of comfort. Pleasant welcome. This is a good place to stay if you have your own form of transport for getting to the old quarter.

EATING OUT

Under US$5

Çelik Palas, İnönü Mah Arap Hacı Sok 1, in the new town, next to the Uz hotel, ☎ (370) 712 12 63. Simple food at very good prices.

Under US$8

Kadioğlu, Çeşme Mah Arasta Sok 8, in the old quarter, ☎ (370) 712 50 91. Good traditional fare, served in a pleasant setting. Very good pide.

OTHER THINGS TO DO

Turkish bath – Cinci Hamamı, an authentic Turkish bath from the Ottoman era, in Çarşı Meydanı, the main square in the old town. 9.30am-6.30pm.

SHOPPING GUIDE

Souvenir and crafts shops have been set up in the restored and very picturesque **market** quarter, with its paved alleyways and old doors which are closed in the evening.

AMASYA★★
Provincial Capital – Map p 605
129km from Samsun – 112km from Tokat – 220km from Sivas
Pop 163 000 – Alt 392m

Not to be missed
The Torumtay Mausoleum and the Blue Medrese.
A stroll in the old districts, along the Yeşilırmak.

And remember...
An "authentic" Turkey does exist. Allow yourself 3 days to discover it, via the small
Seljuk and Ottoman towns of Amasya, Tokat (see p 614) and Sivas (p 536).

Amasya is one of Anatolia's most beautiful cities, perhaps even more so than
Safranbolu. Wedged between the façades of two rocky hills, it stretches along the
green banks of the Yeşilırmak, creating a magnificent mosaic of red roofs which can
be observed in a leisurely manner from the top of its citadel. The city has retained
a few lovely Seljuk and Ottoman buildings (including numerous mausoleums), proof
of its fruitful past. Today, however, there are two Amasyas. Separated by the river,
two periods face each other: on the right bank, the modern city pulsates around the
old monuments. The left bank is a string of Ottoman houses, more than 200 years
old, set on the river's edge under the watchful eye of the amazing rock tombs
hollowed out of the cliff for the Pontic kings.

Capital of Pontus
Amasya became an important city long ago (it is here that the eminent geographer,
Strabo was born, before leaving to go to study in Nyssa; *see p 293*). It was even
named capital twice: the first time, under the kings of Pontus (4-3C BC) powerful
rivals of the Romans; the second time, in the 11C, when the king of eastern Armenia
traded his kingdom of the east with the Byzantines, in exchange for this region. At
the end of the same century, the Seljuk Turks seized it and turned it into a powerful emirate. Fought over by the Turks and the Mongols, the city was later linked
to the Ottoman Empire (1392) after which it slowly began to decline.

*The main monuments are located in the modern city, on the right bank (south) of the river.
We suggest that you visit it on foot. On the left bank (north), a car will come in handy to
climb up to the citadel, before strolling in the older districts.*

The right bank★
*Leave from the end of the main road (Atatürk Cad), heading towards Tokat.
Allow 2hr for the visit.*

The Blue Medrese★ (Gök Medrese)
Near the mausoleum. Open during prayer hours.

Built in 1266, the old Koranic school is used as a mosque today. Its walls, high and
massive, are reinforced at each angle by buttresses giving it the appearance of a
fortress. The portal, a simple broken arch, is very sober with its traditional *muqarnas*
located on the two small surrounding windows.

A **türbe** flanks the medrese and is covered by a superb, octagonal brick **dome★**
which is underscored by a blue tile band (unfortunately in poor shape).

The **Torumtay Türbesi★** *(9am-5pm)*, another mausoleum, is located nearby. It houses
the tomb of the medrese's founder, who died in 1276. These simple yet elegant
buildings create a charming ensemble.

On the same side of the road as the medrese, returning towards the centre, stop at the **Museum**★ (Amasya Müzezi), which has a few interesting exhibits, from the Hittites to the Romans *(8.15-11.45am/1.15-4.45pm; closed Mondays. Entrance fee. Limited explanations in English)*. On the ground floor, admire the heavy carved **wooden doors**★ which closed off the Blue Mederse, transferred here to better protect them. Two majestic **Hittite lions** stand guard at the foot of the stairs leading to the first floor, where the archeological section is located. Pottery, Bronze Age jars, cult objects, Hittite and Phrygian jewellery share the space with items from the Byzantine and Ottoman epochs. Observe the **bronze statuette**★ from Teshup (1200 BC), the Hittite storm god, wearing the traditional pointed hat. The ethnological section (2nd floor) displays several objects of daily Ottoman life, including a **trunk**★ embedded with mother-of-pearl. An unusual sight, at the back of the garden, the **mausoleum of Sultan Mesut** houses six perfectly preserved mummies of the Mongol period (14C).

The Mosque of Sultan Beyazıt II★ (Sultan Beyazıt Camii)
100m from the museum, on the other side of the road (it is the rear of the mosque which you see).

Erected in the 15C by Sultan Beyazıt II, this small mosque was part of a complex including a medrese (on the side), library, mausoleum and several annexes. It rises today in the middle of a pleasant public garden where children play, groups of women chatter and which men cross on their way to prayer. Two fine **minarets** soar above the domes, brilliantly coloured with red brick chevrons. Behind a large **portico** sustained by antique columns, you will find the prayer hall hiding an elegant marble minber and **glazed tiles** (on the tympanum above the windows).

The adjoining **medrese** consists of three groups of buildings also flanked by porticoes housing cells and study halls.

Across the city★
On the other side of the street, you reach a pavement café. From there, take the small, crowded merchant alley which climbs to the right.

On the left, the **Taş Han** is a ruined caravanserais used as a warehouse, adjoining the **Burmali Minare Camii** (1241), recognisable by its superb **minaret**★ with large roped flutes (*burmali*, in Turkish). With the mountains as a backdrop, the mosque and its little octagonal mausoleum in blond stone create a delightful setting. All around, white umbrellas shade vegetable stalls.

Descend towards the main street, until you reach the square where Atatürk's statue stands. Then take the boulevard (Mustafa Kemal Bul) running the length of the river.

Facing the modest kiosk of the Tourist Office, you can see the impressive **portal**★ of the **Bimarhane medrese**, erected during the Mongol period (14C). It flanks the **Mehmet Paşa Mosque** which today harbours a Koranic school reserved for girls. Continuing on the same side, after the bridge, you get to the **Beyazıt Paşa Mosque**★, a beautiful 15C Ottoman building built according to the plan of the Bursa mosques. Enter through an elegant **portico**★ offset by arcades with red and white voussoirs.

The left bank★★
Cross the river in the direction of Samsun. Allow 2hr.

Immediately after the bridge, do not miss the attractive **Büyük Ağa medrese** (15C), with its original octagonal plan. It is now a Koranic school for boys. Surrounded by beautiful broken arcades, the central courtyard is home to the playground. With a bit of daring (and discretion), have a look.

Amasya

Climbing up to the heights, you reach the **citadel** (Kale), set at the summit of a rocky buttress. Below, other walls can be seen, remains of various bastions which looked over the gorge. The path leading to it is very steep *(by car, take the direction of Samsun, then Kultur Sok, on the left, which climbs to the top of the fortress)*. Erected during ancient times, the citadel has retained numerous portions of its original walls. The attractive façades can easily be distinguished from the older walls, added on through the centuries and during invasions all the way to the Ottoman period. From above, the **view★★** of Amasya is magnificent.

As you descend, take Elmasye Cad to follow the river.

Huddled one against the other along the river, like a set of yellow, ochre or brown cubes, the **Ottoman houses★★** align their sober façades, overlooked by the impressive walls of the mountains. A beautiful picture! The upper floors jut out over the water, overhanging the stone walls of the ground floors, creating an authentic rampart along the river. Behind, other houses are terraced along the flanks of the hill, a picturesque district where time seems to stand still. An old set of stairs climbs up between the roofs towards the cliff where several **rock tombs★**, last homes of the **Pontic kings** *(free)*, stand out. As if suspended above the river, they can be seen from any point in the city, their small temple-shaped façades guarding the city for the last two millennia.

As you descend, do not miss the **Hazeranlar Konağı** *(near the stairs)*, a superb 17C Ottoman house exquisitely restored and transformed into a museum *(8am-5pm; entrance fee)*. As in Safranbolu, the daily life of its inhabitants has been reconstructed. The back rooms have a view of the Yeşilırmak and the sight of the river incites the spectator to daydream.

As you exit, take the time to stroll around the surrounding alleys, to discover the **old homes★** of the district, still beautiful in spite of their decaying state. A programme of renovation is in progress and a few homes, housing charming inns *(see "Making the most of Amasya")* have been renovated. Hopefully all of them will be saved.

Pontic tombs overlooking the Ottoman houses of old Amasya

P. Bordas/DIAF

COMING AND GOING

By bus – Dolmuşes run between the town centre and the bus station which stands outside town in the direction of Erzincan. Daily bus services depart for the Black Sea up to Trabzon (11hr), Samsun (2hr 30min), Ankara (5hr), İstanbul (12hr), Kayseri (8hr), Sivas (4hr) and Tokat (2hr).

By train – The town is on the Samsun-Sivas line. Trains run to these 2 destinations every day, but the journey takes much longer than by bus.

By air – The nearest airport is at Samsun, a 2hr 30min bus ride from Amasya. One flight per day to İstanbul and 2 per week to Ankara, on Mondays and Thursdays.

ADDRESS BOOK

Tourist information – Mustafa Kemal Bul 27. A small kiosk which is, in principle, open from Monday to Friday (9.30am-12noon/1pm-5pm). Meagre documentation.

Bank / change – Emek Kuyumculuk, Amasya Lisesi Altı Belediye Dükkanları 37, ☎ (358) 218 04 05. Open Monday to Saturday, 8am-6pm.

WHERE TO STAY

Hotels are few and far between, rather expensive and badly run. Instead, go for the simple but homely guest houses set in traditional and often attractively restored houses.

US$30

Pension Emin Efendi, left bank, Hatuniye Mah Hazeranlar Sok 73, ☎ (358) 212 08 52, Fax (358) 212 18 95 – 5rm. Very pretty rooms in an old, recently restored house. You will feel more like you're staying with friends than in a hotel.

Hotel Maden, right bank, Mustafa Kemal Paşa Cad 5, ☎ (358) 218 60 50, Fax (358) 218 60 17 – 40rm. Very mediocre level of comfort. This place could certainly do with some restoration work to live up to the description in the old brochures.

Between US$26 and US$45

Pension Ilk, right bank, Gümüşlü Mah Hitit Sok 1, ☎ (358) 218 16 89, Fax (358) 218 62 77 – 6rm. In an old house with bags of charm (cloth pads to be worn to preserve the parquet floors). The rooms are tastefully decorated, each in a different style (and at a different price).

EATING OUT

Under US$3

Güney, Atatürk Cad Sato Ap Altı 1. Next to the Pension Ilk. If you want to lunch Turkish-style, this little pub serves good "Adana kebap" for next to nothing.

Under US$8

Bahçeli Bahar, Yüzevler Cad 96/3, ☎ (358) 211 13 16. Lively atmosphere (crowded in the evening). In addition to the traditional food, beer is served behind the curtains, away from prying eyes.

TOKAT★★
Provincial capital – Map p 605
112km from Amasya, 108km from Sivas
Pop 309 000 – Alt 625m

Not to be missed
The Gök Medrese museum.
The old Ottoman houses.

And remember...
Take the time to stroll in the steep alleyways on the hills.
Enjoy the authentic Ali Paşa hamam.

Overlooked by two tall and rocky hills, Tokat spreads peacefully along the shores of the Yeşilırmak. Neglected by tourists, its Seljuk monuments and old Ottoman houses continue to weather the wrath of time and its treasures of the past are quite run down. However, this patina, which has been erased in Safranbolu by the restoration work, adds to the city's charm. Tokat offers an authentic look into deepest Turkey. It ignores the commotion of the modern era and is unconcerned about its appearance.

Founded around 3000 BC, Tokat was among the most powerful cities of the kingdom of Pontus during the period of Roman domination (3C BC). In hibernation under the Byzantines, annexed by the Seljuks (11C), conquered by Tamerlane's Mongols, it was handed over in the 13C to Eretna, the Mongol governor of Sivas (*see p 536*). In 1392, the city was linked to the Ottoman empire and became a very active agricultural and economic centre, thanks to the mining of copper in the nearby hills. Since then, its prosperity has sharply declined, but the glow of the main street's shops and the liveliness of its old *bedesten* prove that the city is very busy and industrious.

Visiting the city

The main monuments are located on the main artery, Gültekin Topçam Cad, which crosses the city from north to south. Tokat is not widespread and the visit is easily made on foot (allow 2-3hr).

At the entrance to the city, arriving from Sivas, you will see the **Latifoğlu Konağı★** (Müze Evi), a beautiful 19C wooden building which has been entirely renovated and converted into a museum (*8am-4pm, closed Mondays; entrance fee*). Furnished in a traditional manner, the interior reconstructs the daily life of a rich Ottoman family, in a highly refined decor (notice the sumptuous wooden **ceilings★**). Upstairs, the **Paşa's room** (Paşa odası) is lit up by pretty stained-glass windows with stellar motifs. Behind the museum, a small road follows the course of the **Behsai Deresi**, flowing parallel to the main avenue.

Moving on to another period, old **Ottoman houses** filled with cracks line both sides of the river. They seem to overflow onto the crowd which fills the street, their pale façades contrasting with the colourful stalls protruding from the innumerable shops.

G. Degeorge

The Orient in Anatolia: The Seljuk tiles of the Gök Medrese (Tokat)

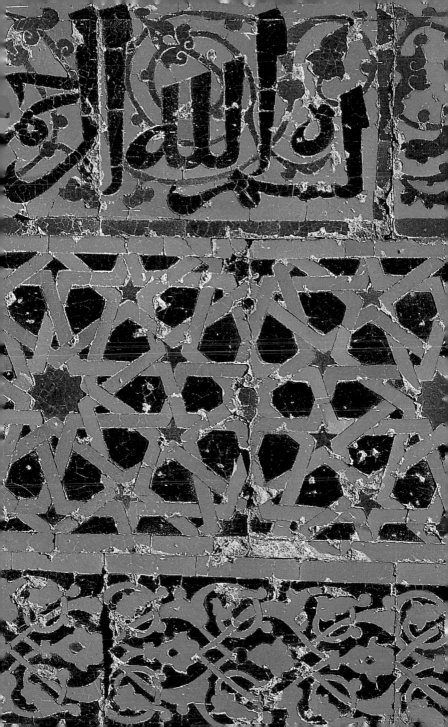

Your walk will lead you to the **bedesten**, the covered market filled with fruits and vegetables. In the heart of the bustle rises the **Hatuniye Mosque** (Meydan Camii) erected in 1485 by Sultan Beyazıt II in honour of his mother. An elegant portico precedes the prayer hall, a simple square surmounted by a dome.

Returning to the main street, head towards the river *(to the north)* until you reach the **mausoleum of Sümbul Baba**, a small 13C Seljuk tomb easily recognisable by its conical roof. A Mongol mausoleum (14C), rises slightly farther away on the same side of the street (in ruins).

From here, the energetic may take the small road climbing up to the **Ottoman citadel**, perched on a small, rocky buttress. Not much is left and the ascent is steep. However, the site allows a delightful **view**★ of the city.

The Gök Medrese★★ (Gök Medersa Muzezi)
Near the mausoleum. 8am-12noon/1pm-5pm; closed Mondays. Entrance fee.

Converted into a museum, the "blue medrese" is especially interesting for its beautiful architecture, typical of Seljuk art (13C). Its **façade**★, an elegant alternation of pink and white stones, is pierced by an exquisite **portal**★★ decorated with stalactites. The vestibule leads to an open-air central courtyard with an iwan. The magnificent but unfortunately damaged remains of the turquoise, black and blue **glazed tiles and bricks**★★ appear everywhere. The motifs of the bricks consist of geometrical patterns, calligraphy, foliage, and stars which reveal their Persian origins.

Surmounted by a passage, a portico runs along the three sides, opening onto the former study lounges and student dormitories. This area is off-limits, only the ground floor rooms, reserved for the **museum**★, can be visited. They house several objects found in the region's archeological sites: Bronze Age statuettes, Hittite pottery, as well as beautiful Byzantine icons and a pulpit from an Armenian church. The ethnographic section displays the kilims of the region, several objects of the 19C, as well as the **stamps** used to print patterns on tablecloths, a crafts typical of Tokat. In the garden, at the back of the museum, you may admire beautiful **funerary stelae**.

Next door, the **Taş Hanı** (17C), an ancient caravanserai, has become a centre for second-hand dealers and crafts shops. Farther to the south near the main square, you will reach the **Ali Paşa Camii**, a 17C Ottoman mosque. The neighbouring garden hides the **Bibi Hatun Mausoleum**, a small hexagonal building surmounted by a dome. Across the street, the **Ali Paşa Hamam** aligns its breast-like domes. It is still operating, so do not hesitate to go in and relax.

But first have a walk around the neighbouring alleys, behind the Taş Han and the Ali Paşa mosque, and discover the old wooden homes which exude the city's antiquated charm. They flank the remains of a few **caravanserais** which testify to Tokat's flourishing period (the city had 14!). Most are in ruins, but a few are still active, such as the **Gazioğlu Han** where cotton is dyed.

Making the most of Tokat

COMING AND GOING

By bus – The "otogar" is 2km northeast of the centre. Daily services to Trabzon (13hr), Samsun (4hr 30min), Amasya (2hr), Ankara (7hr), İstanbul (14hr), Kayseri (6hr) and Sivas (2hr).

ADDRESS BOOK

Tourist information – In the main square, in the building occupied by the prefecture ("Vilayet"). 8am-1pm. You will be given a warm welcome and a street map.

Bank / change – *Safir*, Kuyumcular Çarşısı 25, ☎ (356) 212 83 83. Open Monday to Saturday, 8am-6pm.

WHERE TO STAY

Since Tokat is not a great tourist destination, it has not developed a good hotel infrastructure. You will find mainly guest houses with a rather rustic degree of comfort. However, here are two addresses:

US$26

Hotel Burcu, Gazi Osman Paşa Bul 48, ☎ (356) 212 84 94, Fax (356) 212 23 27 – 24rm. ⁎] ℰ The most comfortable establishment in the town centre. Plain, very clean rooms, and a pleasant welcome.

Around US$60

Hotel Büyük Tokat, in the northwest, on the other side of the Yeşilırmak, 3km from the centre, ☎ (356) 228 16 61, Fax (356) 228 16 60 – 59rm. ⁎] 📧 ℰ 📺 ✕ 🍴 cc An upmarket establishment with very comfortable rooms. A good place to stay if you have your own transport.

EATING OUT

The local speciality is "Tokat kebap", a sort of stew made of mutton, potatoes, aubergines and tomatoes and cooked in the oven. It is good, but a little more expensive than the usual dishes and it requires a certain amount of preparation. Don't order it if you're in a hurry.

Under US$5

Saray Lokanta, Buzluk Sok 7. In the main square, ☎ (356) 214 45 01. This popular little restaurant is constantly packed with people clamouring for its excellent "doner kebap". Very cheap.

Between US$5 and US$8

Cim Cim, Gazi Osman Paşa Bul, ☎ (356) 214 10 49. Behind the curtains, out of sight, you can enjoy a good beer with your "Tokat kebap". Unfortunately you have to put up with the blaring TV.

OTHER THINGS TO DO

Turkish bath – *Ali Paşa Hamamı*. A very old establishment whose beautiful cupolas can be seen from the museum, on the other side of Gazi Osman Paşa Bul. The entrance is 50m away in the street which runs at right angles. Open every day, 9am-5pm.

SHOPPING GUIDE

The *Taş Han* is teeming with antique shops. It's worth taking a good look around – you may well stumble across a rare find.

In the alleyways in the area behind the Taş Han, you will find beautiful block-printed *cotton tablecloths*. Nearby, there are craftsmen making little wooden objects: spoons, tablemats etc.

TRABZON★★
Provincial capital – Map p 605
346km from Samsun, 244km from Erzincan, 300km from Erzurum
Pop 312 000 – Cold and rainy winters, mild summers

Not to be missed
The church of Hagia Sophia (Church of the Divine Wisdom)
The busy streets west of Park Meydanı.
The view from the bridges above the two ravines overlooking the old district.

And remember...
Take the time to stroll around the city.
Since it is quite spread out, wear comfortable shoes!

Facing the Black Sea and an endless stream of ships coming from Russia, Trabzon is a busy commercial city. Its sinuous streets, filled with people, climb up to the surrounding hills. Its old ramparts rise between the two ravines which split the city in two like a double-axe mark. The uneven terrain of this metropolis only serves to highlight the appeal of ancient Trebizond, whose churches remind us that it was an important centre of Byzantine culture.

After the city, escape to the superb outback. The low mountains preceding the Pontic chain (Kalıkandı Dağları) create one of Turkey's most beautiful landscapes, enveloped by the dark green of the immense fir forests. This is where Sumela Monastery is hidden, a fairy-like icon of rocks clinging to the wall of a cliff in the middle of nowhere.

Trebizond, the Byzantine
Founded in the 7C BC by Greek colonists arriving from Arcadia, the ancient Trapezus rapidly developed into a large trading port. Established at the Silk Road's point of departure, linking the Black Sea to Persia, the city prospered throughout Antiquity.

However, it was under Byzantine rule that it lived its days of glory. Firstly, thanks to Justinian, who completely transformed it and equipped the city with ramparts (6C); then especially with the arrival of the **Comneni Dynasty** who gave the city an overwhelming vigour. In 1204, in fact, Constantinople had just been taken by the crusaders, and the sons of the emperors found refuge in Trebizond. They founded the brilliant dynasty, "The Empire of Trebizond", whose sparkle lasted until the 15C. After the fall of Constantinople (1453), the city became the last bastion of Byzantine civilisation before falling, in turn, eight years later.

A trading centre
Under Ottoman rule, the city nevertheless continued to prosper, thanks to its intense economic activity. At the end of the Greco-Turkish war (1920-1923), the departure of the Greek community, in addition to the construction of the Ankara-Erzurum railway, spelled the decline of the city.

But the activity of its port never stopped, and since the 1970s Trabzon has been showing steady growth, benefiting from its privileged location between Iran and the countries of eastern Europe which are in full boom.

The Black Sea

Visiting the city

Allow one day. Begin with Hagia Sophia, which is out of the way, then backtrack to Park Meydanı to discover the city.

The church of Hagia Sophia★★ (Aya Sofia)

3km west of the city centre, in the direction of Samsun. From Park Meydanı, take the "kuruçeşme" (large local dolmuş) "Hat C", or a taxi. 8.30am-5pm. Entrance fee.

Perched on the summit of a hill overlooking the sea, the Byzantine church raises its beautiful fair walls in the middle of greenery, near a 15C **clock tower**. The original building, a basilica with three naves, was transformed in the 13C to reproduce a Greek cross plan, topped by a central dome and flanked by three porches. During the Ottoman period, the church was converted into a mosque, before becoming a museum in 1964. Besides its beautiful architecture, Hagia (Saint) Sophia hides remarkable **Byzantine paintings★**, most likely from the 13C. The majority are quite run down, but the coloured images imbued with so much elegance are quite moving. Before entering, have a look at the very stately **southern porch**, with its three arcades. A **carved frieze** ran along its pediment which can still be seen in parts, representing Adam and Eve (damaged).

In the **nave**, four marble columns sustain a tall and narrow **dome**, decorated with a Christ in Majesty. On the drum, underscored by a frieze with angels, are the **apostles** and the prophets, whereas the pendentives feature the saints. There is a **Virgin with Child** in the central apse, accompanied by an *Ascension* (on the vault). On the opposite side, topping the access to the narthex, notice the beautiful scene of the **Last Supper**.

The paintings of the **narthex** are completely unlike the other paintings: on the central vault, the geometrical motifs encircle all types of scenes with warm reddish tones. The symbols of the **Four Evangelists★** *(see sidebar p 577)* appear in a setting surrounded by angels, whereas the door facing the nave is flanked by two large scenes, one illustrating the **Miracle of the loaves and fishes** and the other, the *Anointing of the Sick*.

Across the city

Returning to Park Meydanı, follow **Uzun Caddesi**, one of the city's busiest shopping streets, invaded by people and fish stalls.

Go beyond the Zeytinlik Sok junction, and continue to Hüsamoğlu Sok, on the left. As it climbs (steeply!) the street becomes Bilaloğlu Sok, then Cumhuriyet Sok.

The small soulless buildings begin to make way for the older houses, a reminder of Greek Trebizond. The street enters the heart of the city, a hive of activity. As the road climbs, the homes become sparser. A maze of small cobblestone streets flanked by grey houses, all crooked, with heavy red tile roofs awaits you. Former gardens now serve as warehouses, and logs for winter fires overflow on the pavement.

After this effort, you reach **Yeni Cuma Mosque** (Yeni Cuma Camii) (B3), formerly known as the **Church of St Eugenius** (12C). Dedicated to the patron saint of Trebizond, the primitive building was a basilica. Imitating Hagia Sophia and most of the city's churches, it was topped with a dome on a drum in 1340 (following a fire). In the 15C, the Ottomans converted the church into a mosque by adding a small porch roof *(to the north)*, a minaret and an elegant stone **mihrab**.

Leaving the mosque, and behind the houses flanking it to the west, you will discover a beautiful **panorama**★ overlooking the ramparts and the impressive uneven terrain of the city. The oldest section of this **enclosure**★ goes back to the 6C, but the current walls, particularly well preserved towards Reşadiye Caddesi, date from the Ottoman period. The **citadel** (kale), is on the contrary very damaged *(accessible via Refik Cesur Cad, facing the Ortahisar Fatih)*.

Backtrack along the same path until the end of Uzun Cad and cross the first ravine.

From here, there is a stunning and almost vertiginous **view**★★ of the houses lining the river below. Once the bridge is crossed, on the left, an ancient Russian dwelling of the early 20C houses the **Cultural Centre** (Kültür Merkesi), exhibiting handicrafts.

Across the way, the **Ortahisar Fatih Mosque** (Ortahisar Fatih Camii) (B2) was laid out in the 15C in one of Trebizond's oldest churches, known as the **Gold-topped Church of the Virgin** (Panaghia Chrysokephalos). Here too, the basilican plan with three naves gave way in the 13C to a layout centred on a dome. Gold-plated copper plaques coated the dome which explains its "gold-topped" nickname. Its **raised narthex** is probably from the same period, whereas the **porch with three arcades** of the north entrance is from the Ottoman period.

Walk around the mosque from the back by taking Zağnos Cad and cross the second ravine.

On the way, enjoy the **panorama**★ overlooking the city whose contours hug every nook and cranny. Past the bridge, do not miss the pretty **Abdullah Paşa fountain** (19C), an elegant plaque of carved marble standing against the wall.

On the other side of the rampart you reach a small square where old Turkish men with white beards chat away in the shade of the **Gülbahar Hatun Mosque** (Gülbahar Hatun Camii) (A2). Built in the 16C by Sultan Selim in honour of his mother Gülbahar (whose *türbe* is located alongside), the building was part of a small complex which included a medrese, an *imaret* and a hamam, today no longer existing.

Follow Resadiye Cad, along the rampart, until you reach the large intersection. There, take Kahramanmaraş Cad, on the right, via the gateway.

Just beyond the bridge crossing the river, the street runs alongside a picturesque covered market (on the left) selling fruit and vegetables. A short stroll away stands the **Armenian Church of St Anne** (Küçük Ayvasil Kilisesi) (C1), one of the city's oldest (9C). The building is closed. Nevertheless it is the exterior which is particularly interesting. Above the door there is a marble **bas-relief**, undoubtedly taken from a Roman frieze.

On the other side of the street, enter the old merchants' quarter, a true open-air bazaar overflowing with small shops. In the middle of this liveliness rises the **Çarşı Camii**, the city's largest mosque (19C). In the glowing interior, six *trompe-l'œil* columns enhance the pillars sustaining the turquoise dome. North of the mosque, you can see the ruins of the ancient **bedesten.**

Return to Park Meydanı via Semerciler Cad and Kunduracilar Cad.

Conclude your visit by going to **Boztepe**, one of the hills above the city, 3km to the south. Romantic couples will keep you company as you sip *çay* in an outdoor café and enjoy a beautiful **view**★ overlooking Trabzon and the roofs descending towards the sea.

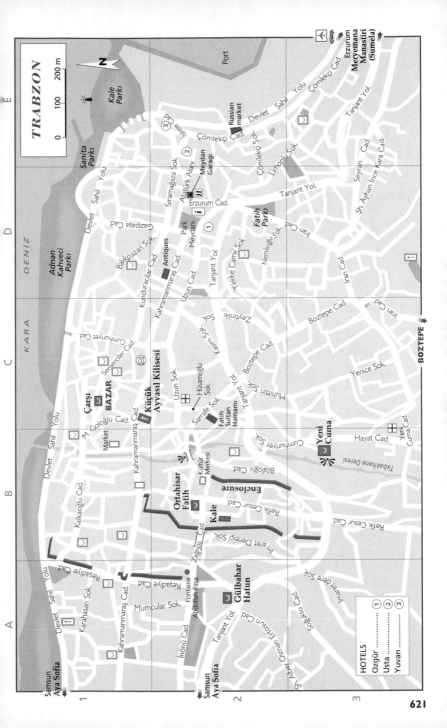

TRABZON

0 100 200 m

621

The Sumela Monastery★★
(Meryemana Manastiri)

45km from Trabzon. Take the road to Erzurum for 30km, until Maçka, then turn left as you leave the city. It can also be reached by dolmuş (departure from Meydan Garagı; 9am-5pm). Enclosed in a natural park (Altındere Vadisi Milli Parkı). Entrance fee. Beyond the ticket counter, at the park entrance, follow the small road to the foot of the cliff, where a car park and an open-air restaurant are located. From there, a very steep but easy path leads to the monastery (30min walk). Do not forget your ticket at the bottom! Allow a half-day, trip included.

The excursion is worth more for the landscape – absolutely splendid – than for the monastery. The road leading to it crosses the heart of a tortuous **landscape★★★** reminiscent of the precipitous Carpathian Mountains: deep gorges, vertiginous cliffs, peaks strewn with firs, emerging with difficulty through the mist and forests. However, this is not the land of Nosferatu! At the end of the road following the sinuous flow of a stream, the cliffs part to make way for the monastery which appears like a miraculous vision (*see photograph, p 625*): as if suspended above the tips of the tallest firs, the building's light-coloured walls seem glued to the abrupt flank of a steep rocky buttress. Dexterity – and devotion – were needed for the workers to build a monastery in such a place.

Splendour and ruin

Dedicated to Mary, Sumela is thought to have been founded in the 4C by two Orthodox monks from Athens, Barnabas and Sophron, to whom the Virgin had appeared. Very quickly, the monastery became a pilgrimage site and many enlargements were undertaken across the centuries to house all the faithful.

Even Islam did not manage to shatter its importance. Better still, the Ottoman sultans placed it under their protection and the monastery remained in operation until 1923, when the Greeks had to leave Turkish soil following the Greco-Turkish war. It was the end of 15 centuries of splendour. Since then, numerous acts of vandalism have damaged the site. What was once a jewel of Byzantine architecture, still intact almost 50 years ago, has become a virtual ruin. Today, construction worker helmets are distributed to visitors and a sign tells you to "beware of falling rocks". The entire construction is supported by beams!

Shortly before going into the monastery's enclosure, the path passes in front of a modern **aqueduct** (1860), literally attached to the cliff.

Among the monastery's oldest rooms, some have been carved directly in the rock. It is partially the case of the astonishing **Church of the Assumption★**, whose nave and apse stand out against the rocky wall, protected by an impressive natural vault. A small **chapel** was added in the 18C. The church's walls are completely covered with **frescoes**, inside as well as outside. Those outer ones, still very visible at the beginning of the 20C, were hammered away and their images have been largely erased. Inside, the paintings are fortunately better preserved. Painted in the 18C, they contain older motifs going back to the 15C. To the right of the entrance, you can admire a majestic *Madonna with Child*. The buildings of the **convent★★**, which make up the essence of the current monastery – the immense façade which is seen as you arrive on the site – were built in the 14C. They span **five floors** and hold 72 cells, a vast refectory and warehouse.

Unfortunately, the convent is now an empty shell. Looking through one of the windows overlooking the fantastic scenery of the Pontic chain, it is easy to understand why the site was conducive to prayer and contemplation.

COMING AND GOING

By air – The airport is 8km east of Trabzon, beyond the "otogar". **Turkish Airlines and İstanbul Airlines** operate daily services to İstanbul (4 or 5 flights, depending on the time of year) and Ankara (3 or 4 flights). Turkish Airlines runs a fare-paying bus shuttle between the airport and the city centre 90min before the departure of each flight. Dolmuşes also make the same trip, of course.

By bus – The "otogar" is 3km east of the city centre, on the way to the airport. Like everywhere else in Turkey, the bus is the most convenient form of transport. Several companies run daily services to the following destinations: Adana (16hr), Amasya (10hr), Ankara (14hr), Hopa (3hr), İstanbul (20hr), Kayseri (14hr), Malatya (15hr), Mersin (16hr), Rize (1hr), Samsun (8hr), Sivas (14hr) and Tokat (12hr).

GETTING AROUND

By taxi – The numerous yellow taxis cruising the city are all equipped with a taximeter. They are very convenient and inexpensive.

By shared taxi – Dolmuşes and "kuruçesme", a local kind of shared taxi, leave from Meydan Garagı, on the corner of the main square, next to the city hall, and will take you anywhere in the city and the surrounding area. They will even take you to Hagia Sophia for a modest fee.

On foot – This is still the best way to visit the city, even though it stretches out over a fairly large area.

By rental car – In a street at right angles to the main square: **Avis**, Gazipaşa Cad 20/B, ☎ (462) 322 37 40. **Europcar**, Gazipaşa Cad Rıza Aksu İşhanı, ☎ (462) 322 41 64. Agencies open 7 days a week, from 8.30am-7pm.

ADDRESS BOOK

Tourist information – In the main square (Park Meydanı) (D2), ☎ and Fax (462) 223 49 29 / 321 46 59. 8am-5pm, 7 days a week in summer, Monday to Friday in winter. A mine of useful information.

Bank / change – In the main square: **Ayka döviz**, Maraş Cad 6/C, ☎ (462) 321 36 81. Open Monday to Friday, 8.30am-7pm. You will also find banks in Atatürk Alanı and Kahramanmaraş Cad.

Main post office – In Kahramanmaraş Cad, before the bazaar (C1). Open 7 days a week, 8.30am-7pm.

Airline companies – Concentrated in the main square (Park Meydanı) (D2). **Turkish Airlines**, Kemerkaya Mah Park Meydanı 37/A, ☎ (462) 321 16 80. **İstanbul Airlines**, Kaazazoğlu Sok 9, Sanat İş Hanı (on the 1st floor), ☎ (462) 322 38 06.

Travel agency – **Afacan Tur Seyahat Acentası**, İskele Cad 40 (E2), ☎ (462) 321 58 04. Open 7 days a week in summer, 9am-7pm. Very friendly welcome. They organise trips to Sumela, in particular.

WHERE TO STAY

As in most Turkish towns where there is little tourist activity, the hotel infrastructure in Trabzon is inadequate and a little more expensive than elsewhere.

Under US$15

Hotel Yuvan, Güzelhisar Cad, ☎ (462) 326 68 23. ♨ ♪ This recent hotel, built in 1996, has small, very clean rooms. A good alternative if you can't stay at the Usta hotel (below), but breakfast is not served here.

Between US$30 and US$40

Hotel Ozgür, Atatürk Alanı 29, ☎ (462) 326 47 03, Fax (462) 321 39 52. If only the rooms were kept in better condition... If all else fails.

Between US$45 and US$55

Hotel Usta, Telegrafhane Sok 3, ☎ (462) 326 57 00, Fax (462) 322 37 93 – 86rm. ♨ ♪ TV CC The only upmarket establishment in the city centre. It is a little expensive, but so much better than all the others.

EATING OUT

Around Park Meydanı, especially in Atatürk Alanı (D2).

Under US$5

🦆 **Çardak**, Uzun Cad 4 **(C2)**, ☎ (462) 321 76 76. You can sample the delicious pide served in an arbour. No alcohol.

Polat, Kunduracılar Cad 111 **(C1, D2)**, ☎ (462) 322 19 03. A popular restaurant serving good "döner" (sold by weight) and pizzas. Handy for a short break from sightseeing.

US$8

Kıbrıs, Atatürk Alanı 17, ☎ (462) 321 76 79. Mainly frequented by men. If you can stand the smoky atmosphere, you will appreciate the traditional cuisine (served upstairs). Alcohol is served here. Open 7 days a week.

Güloğlu, Atatürk Alanı 4/E, ☎ (462) 321 53 32. A very lively place. Excellent "doner" and "iskander kebap". No alcohol. Open 7 days a week.

HAVING A DRINK

Bar – In the city centre: **Meydan Fıçı Bira**, Atatürk Alanı **(D2)**, ☎ (462) 322 45 35. A clientele made up exclusively of male smokers. You can drink a beer and watch television here.

Nightclub – Towards the sea, **Vivalas**, Gazipaşa Cad, after the Avis agency **(D2)**. A lively atmosphere, particularly at the end of the week.

OTHER THINGS TO DO

Excursions – The tourist information office and local travel agencies organise daytrips to **Sumela**, with a departure at 9am

and return at 4pm, which gives you time to visit the monastery and take a walk in the surrounding forest. You can also get there by dolmuş (from Meydan Garagı) or take the Ulosoy bus (on the corner of Taksim square, towards the tourist information office).

Turkish bath – Fatih Sultan Hamamı, Bilaloğlu Sok **(B2)**, ☎ (462) 322 54 09. Open to women on Wednesdays, and to men the rest of the time. It is a little down-at-heel.

SHOPPING GUIDE

Antiques – Abdullah Tabak and Hasan Tabak, Kahramanmaraş Cad Bahar Sok 14 (in the area of the bazaar) **(C1)**, ☎ (462) 321 25 70. Beautiful Ottoman-style silver objects just waiting to be discovered.

Russian market – To the east, along Sahil Yolul **(E2)**. The easiest way is to take İskele Cad and go down the steps to Çömlekçi Cad. To tell the truth, the Russian market no longer lives up to its name; it is mainly an amazing bric-a-brac of Turkish objects. But it is definitely worth a visit, if only to soak up the atmosphere.

Textiles – A lot of clothes and household linen are sold in Kunduracilar Cad **(C1)**, the shopping street which leads to the bazaar. Parallel to this street runs the bustling Uzun Cad (just before Ortahisar Fatih Camii), which is jam-packed with all kinds of stalls selling jewellery and topstitched bedspreads.

G. Sioen/RAPHO

Sumela, the suspended monastery

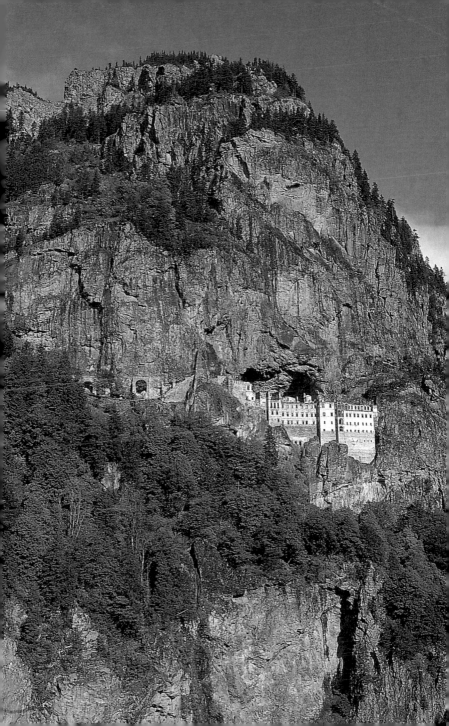

NOTES

NOTES

NOTES

NOTES

NOTES

NOTES

INDEX

Alanya: site description or place name
Constantine I: historical figure
Mosaics: general term with an explanation (historical, for example)

A

Abdülvahap (tomb)	202
Achaemenids	20
Adana	475
Ağlasun (see Sagalassus)	508
Agriculture	38
Ağzıkarahan	586
Akçalı Dağları	464
Akkadians	19
Aksaray	586
Alacahöyük	18, 514, 529
Alahan (monastery)	465
Alanya	454
Alarahan	451
Alawites	66
Alcetas	437
Alexander the Great	20, 356, 526
Altınkum	328
Amasya	610
Amos	367
Anadolu Hisarı	185, 186
Anadolu Kavağı	185, 187
Anamur (fortress)	462
Anamurium	460
Anatolian homes	83
Anavarza (Anazarbus)	482
Andriake	399
Ankara	512
Atatürk Mausoleum	521
Citadel	516
Ethnography Museum	520
Museum of Anatolian Civilisations	513
Samanpazarı	517
Ulus	517
Antakya (Hatay)	486
Antalya	424
Antioch	486
Antioch (fortress)	490
Antiochus I	541
Antiques	124
Aphrodisias	302
Aphrodite	362
Apollo	326
Arabesk (music)	87
Arabs	22

Ararat (mount)	15
Argonauts	187
Armenia Minor	357
Armenians	63, 68
Arsameia	540
Artemis	284, 440
Arycanda	413
Aşık	88
Aslantaş (lake)	484
Aspendos	444
Assos	230
Assyrians	19
Atatürk	29
Attalids	238
Attila	140
Avanos	570
Aynalı (monastery)	554
Ayvalık	234

B

Başer (Tevfik)	72
Bafa (lake) (Bafa Gölü)	330
Balkan Dere (ravine)	554
Balkan War	29
Bananas	460
Barbarossa	27
Barla	507
Basil of Caesarea	596
Battle of Kadesh	19
Bazaar	77
Beçin Kalesi	339
Bedre (beach)	507
Bektaşis	67
Belisırma	584
Bellorophon	418
Bey Dağları	420, 429
Bias	314
Boğazkale	19, 530
Bodrum	342
Halicarnassus Mausoleum	344
St Peter's castle	344
Books (second-hand)	158
Bosphorus	184

Bosphorus (bridge) 184
Bozburun (peninsula) 367
Budget 107
Bursa 204
   Green Mausoleum 206
   Green Mosque 205
   Murat II complex 210
   Yeşil Cami 205
   Yeşil Türbe 206

C

Calligraphy 51
Camels (fights) 90
Çandarlı Halil Hayrettin Paşa
   (mausoleum) 202
Çanakkale 216
Cappadocia 547
Caravanserais 48
Caria 228-229, 373
Çatal Höyük 18
Çavuşin 556
Cedars (islands) 368
Cemilköy 575
Cendere Köprüsü 540
Cennet-Cehennem 468
Çeşme 266
Çetibeli 370
Cherkessians 63
Chimaera 418
Çiftlik 367
Cilicia 357
Circumcision 78
Claros 289
Coffee (Tukish) 96
Colophon 291
Colophony 291
Comneni (dynasty) 618
Constantine I 21, 140
Constantinople (capture of) 26, 141
Copperware 121
Credit cards 107
Crimean War 28
Croesus 264
Crusaders 25
Çukurova (plain) 474
Curetes 282
Currency 106
Customs 106
Cybele 285, 513
Cyprus 32

D

Dalyan 372
Daphne 490
Dardanelles (battle) 218
Dardanelles (straits) 216
Dardanus 217
Datça 360
Demre (see Myra) 408
Derinkuyu 578
Devrent (valley) 557
Didyma 326
Dilek (national park) 308
Diving 118
Dolmuş 114
Dovecot (valley) 555
Düden (falls) 429

E

Eğirdir 506
Eğirdir (lake) 506
Eceabat 217
Edirne 190
   Kırkpınar Festival 190
   Selimiye Camii 192
Elbeyli 202
Emergencies 124
Emirğan (park) 185, 187
Emre (Yunus) 70
Endymion 333
Eolia 228
Ephesus 276
   Artemision 285
   Grotto of the Seven Sleepers 285
Erciyes Dağı 601
Eretna 536
Erim (Kenan Tevfik) 306
Erksan (Metin) 72
Ermenek (road) 464
Eski Anamur 460
Eski Datça 361
Eski Gümüş (monastery) 590
Eskihisar 339
Euphrates 16
Euromos (temple) 336
Evil eye (göz) 84, 387

F-G

Fairy chimneys 547
Fatih Mehmet (bridge) 186
Fethiye 378
Finike 412
Foça 248
Frescoes 163

Friendly (Arthur)	451	Hippodamian plan	316
Funerals	79	*Hippodamus of Miletus*	316
Galatas	21, 140	Hisarönü (bay)	367
Galen	241	Hittites	18, 484, 528
Gallipoli	218	*Hoca (Nasreddin)*	93
Gecekondu	81		
Gelemiş	394	**I**	
Gelibolu	218		
Gelibolu (historical park)	217	Iasos	337
Gemili Adasi	380	İçmeler	370
Glazed tiles (earthenware)	50, 199	Iconoclasm	23, 44, 549
Golden fleece	187	Icons	46
Gordian knot	526	Ihlara (valley)	580
Gordion	526	İncesu	601
Göreme (valley)	564	Insurance	107
Göreme Buckle Church	567	Ionians	228
Gören (Şerif)	73	*Isidorus of Miletus*	322
Göz	84, 387	Isparta	507
Greeks	63	İstanbul	138
Gülek Boğazı	475	Archeological Museums Complex	156
Güllü Dere (valley)	556	Askeri Müze	169
Güllük	340	Ayasofya	145
Gümbet	347	Beyazıt Square	158
Gündogan (bay)	346	Beylerbeyi Palace	174
Güney (Yilmaz)	72	Blue Mosque	150
Güver (gorge) (Güver Uçurumu)	437	Bozdoğan Kemeri	162
Güvercinlik Vadisi	555	Burned Column	158
Güzelçamlı	309, 312	Caravanserais	160
Güzelöz	574	Çemberlitaş	158
Güzelyurt	580	Church of St Saviour-in-Chora	162
Gypsies	63	Church of St Sergius and St Bacchus	151
		Church of Theotokos	
H		Pammakaristos	164
		Çiçek Pasaj	169
Hacı Bektaş Veli	593	Complex of Eyup	172
Hacıbektaş	593	Complex of Fatih Mehmet	164
Hacılar	18	Divan Yolu	157
Halicarnassus	342	Dolmabahçe Palace	170
Hallaç (monastery)	552	Dolmabahçe Sarayı	170
Hamam (Turkish bath)	77, 119	Egyptian bazaar	160
Harbiye	490	Eyüp cemetery	172
Harem	154	Fethiye Camii	164
Harpies	390	Flower Passage	169
Hatay (Antakya)	486	Galata hill	166
Hatay (region)	358	Galata Tower	166
Hattis	18, 529	Grand Bazaar	158
Hattuşaş	19, 530	Hippodrome	150
Hegira	64	İstiklal Caddesi	168
Helle	216	Kapalı Çarşı	158
Hellespont	216	Kariye Camii	162
Heracleitus	276	Küçük Aya Sofya Camii	151
Herakleia	332	Misir Çarşısı	160
Herodotus	342	Making the most of İstanbul	174
Hierapolis-Kastabala	485	Military Museum	169
		Museum of Calligraphy	158
		Museum of Turkish and Islamic Arts	151
		New Galata Bridge	165
		Ortaköy Mosque	171

Palace of Constantine	
Porphyrogenitus	162
Pera Palas Hotel	168
Rüstem Paşa Mosque	160
Sokollu Mosque	152
Süleyman Mosque	161
Sultan Ahmet Camii	150
Sunken Palace	147
Tekfur Sarayı	162
Tekke of the Whirling Dervishes	166
Topkapı Palace	152
Türk ve İslam Eserleri Müzesi	151
Valens aqueduct	162
Wall of Constantinople	162
Yıldız Park	171
Yeni Galata Köprüsü	165
Yerebatan Sarayı	147
İzmir	**252**
Agora	254
Alsancak (district)	257
Bazaar	254
Kadifekale	254
Konak (district)	256
İznik	**198**
İznik (glazed tiles)	199
İztuzu (beach)	**374**

J-K

Janissaries	25
Jason	187
Jews	63, 68, 253
Justinian	22, 141
Kıral (Erden)	73
Kaş	398
Kadırga (bay)	231
Kahta	540
Kale (see Myra)	408
Kaleköy (Simena)	401
Kalkan	393
Kanesh	600
Kanlıca	186
Kanlıdivane	470
Karşı Kilise	593
Karagöz	92, 215
Karain (cave)	18
Karakus (tumulus)	540
Karatay Hanı	600
Karatepe	19, 484
Kaunos	373
Kaya Köy	379
Kaymaklı	578
Kayseri	596
Kekova (bay)	399
Kemal (Mustafa) (see Atatürk)	29
Kemal (Namik)	71
Kemal (Yasar)	71

Kepez (valley)	559
Keslik (monastery)	575
Kilyos	188
Kızıl Adalar	188
Kızıl Çukur (valley)	553
Kızılırmak	16
Kızkalesi	469
Knidos	360
Konak	606
Konya	498
Alaaddin Park	501
İnce Minare Medrese	498
Karatay Medrese	502
Tekke of Mevlana	503
Köprülü Kanyon (canyon)	447
Koran (the)	64
Korykos (citadel)	469
Köşk	589
Köyceğiz (gulf)	372
Kuş Cenneti (Bird Paradise)	579
Kuşadası	308
Kültepe	600
Kurds	30, 63

L

Lascaris, Theodore	198
Latmos	333
Lazes	63
Leatherware	84, 121
Leto	391
Letoön	391
Levantines	253
Limyra	412
Loryma	367
Lycia	357
Lydians	20
Lysimachus	20, 276

M

Magnesia ad Meandra	288
Malatya	543
Mamure Kalesi	462
Manavgat (falls)	451
Manisa	263
Manto	290
Marmaris	366
Marriage	78
Mausolus	20, 330, 373
Maziköy	579
Measuring units	125
Median Wars	20
Medrese	64
Meerschaum	84, 121
Mehmet II	26

Meryemana	286
Meryemana Manastiri	622
Mevlana Celaleddin-i Rumi	67, 70, 498
Meze	94
Michael VIII Paleologus	25
Midas	526
Milas	339
Miletus	320
Miniatures	46
Monk seal	249
Mosaics	46, 163, 488
Muhammad (prophet)	64
Murat II	190
Music (instruments)	88
Mustafa Paşa	574
Myra	408

N

Narlıkuyu Mağarası	468
Neanderthal man	356
Nemrut Dağı	540
Nevşehir	592
Nicaea	198
Niğde	588
Nika (riots)	140
Nomads	63
Notium	290
Nyssa	292

O

Olba-Diocaesarea	467
Olgaç (Bilge)	73
Olive (cultivation)	229
Ölüdeniz (bay)	380
Olympos	416
Onyx	121
Ortahisar	554
Ortakent	347
Osmanlı	25
Ottomans	25, 62
Özkonak	571

P

Pınara	386
Paşabağ	556
Pactolus	264
Paleologus	46
Pamphylia	357
Pamuk (Orhan)	71
Pamukkale-Hierapolis	294
Pancarlık Kilise	559
Parchment	239
Patara	392
Perga	438

Pergamum	238
Acropolis	242
Asclepion	241
Phaselis	420
Phocaeans	249
Photography	125
Phrygians	20
Pigeons	549
Pirates	416, 448, 455
Pompeus	356
Pontic (mountains)	15
Pontus (kingdom)	610, 612
Post	111
Pottery	570
Prayer	65
Press	36
Priene	314
Princes' ısles	188
Burgaz Ada	188
Büyük Ada	188
Heybeli Ada	188

R

Rakı	96
Refiğ (Halit)	72
Roses (of Isparta)	506
Rumeli Hisarı	185, 186
Russians	160

S

Sadeddin (caravanserai)	504
Safranbolu	606
Sagalassus	508
Sailing	118
Saint John	270
Saint Nicholas	380, 408
Saint Paul	228, 277, 474
Saint Simeon Stylites	331, 491
Samandağ	491
Sarı Han	570
Sarıyer	187
Sardis	262
Sarıalan	212
Schliemann (Heinrich)	220
Seal (monk)	249
Sebast	536
Sebast (martyrs)	536
Selçuk	270
Basilica of St John	271
Seleucia ad Pieria	491
Seleucids	20
Seleucus Nicator	20
Selge	446
Selime (monastery)	584
Seljuks	62

Senpiyer Kilisesi	490	Theodore Metochites	164
Seven Wise Men	314	Tigris	16
Seven Wonders of the World	228	Tipping	125
Şeytan Sofrası	234	Tire	287
Shariah (Islamic law)	67	Tlos	381
Shiites	66	Toilets (Turkish)	98
Shop hours	110	Tokalı Kilise	567
Side	448	Tokat	614
Şile	188	Trabzon	618
Şihlar	451	Travel agency	109
Silifke	467, 472	Trebizond	618
Silk	204	Troy (Truva)	220
Simena (Kaleköy)	401	Tulips	576
Sinan (Mimar)	49, 90, 141	Türkbükü	346
Şirince	287	Turkomans	62
Sivas	536	Turgut Reis	347
Smyrna	252	Turko-Mongols	62
Soğanlı (valley)	575	Turtles (caretta)	374
Soccer (football)	75		
Sonku (Cahide)	73	**U-V**	
Sponge fishing	346		
St John (church)	593	Üçhisar	554
St Nicholas (church)	408	Uludağ	558
St Nicholas (island)	380	Underground cities	577
St Peter (church)	490	Urartu (kingdom)	20
St Theodore (church)	559	Ürgüp	558
Strabo	293, 610	Üzengi (valley)	574
Stratonicia	339	Uzun Yolu	549
Sufi	500	Uzuncaburç	467
Süleyman the Magnificent	27, 141	Veil (Islamic)	80
Sultan Hanı (near Aksaray)	587	Virgin Mary	277
Sultan Hanı (near Kayseri)	600	Walks (nature)	117, 551
Sultan Sazlığı (national park)	579	Water (drinking)	217
Sumela (monastery)	622	Whirling Dervishes	67, 500
Sunna	64	Whirling Dervishes (festival)	505
Sunnite	66	Wrestling	90
Syriacs	68		

T		**X-Y-Z**	
Tağar (church)	559	Xanthos	388
Taşeli (plateau)	464	Yakabağ	388
Taşkinpaşa	575	Yanartaş	418
Tamerlane	25	Yalakuzdere	429
Tanzimat	70	Yazılıkaya	532
Tarabaya	187	Yeni Kale	540
Tarsus	474	Yeraltı Şehri	571
Taurus (mountains)	15	Yılanlı Kale	480
Teimiussa	403	Yılmaz (Atıf)	72
Tekirova	422	Yörük (nomads)	83, 428
Telephone	111	Yörük Köyü	608
Termessus	434	Young Turks	29
Tetramorphs	577	Zelve (circus)	556

Maps and Plans

Aegean Coast	226-227	Map II (historical district)	148-149
Alanya	457	Map III (Beyoğlu)	167
Ankara	518-519	Topkapı Palace	153
Museum of Anatolian Civilisations	514	İzmir	255
Antakya (Hatay)	487	Kaş	402
Antalya	427	Kayseri	597
Aphrodisias	305	Konya	499
Avanos	572	Kuşadası	309
Bay of Kekova	399	Lake Bafa (Herakleia)	332
Black Sea region	604-605	Marmara region	136-137
Boğazkale (Hattuşaş)	531	Mediterranean Coast	354-355
Bodrum	345	Miletus	323
Bosphorus (the)	185	Nemrut Dağı (road to)	541
Bursa	208-209	Pamukkale-Hierapolis	296
Byzantine Empire (rise and fall)	22	Perga	439
Cappadocia (main map)	550-551	Pergamum	240
Central Anatolia	496-497	Priene	317
Central Cappadocia	553	Selçuk	
Decline of the Ottoman Empire	28	Basilica of St John	271
Edirne	195	Side	449
Ephesus	278-279	Soğanlı valley	577
Fortresses road	481	Termessus	435
Göreme valley	565	Trabzon	621
Ihlara valley	583	Troy	223
Ionia	354	Turkey	
İstanbul		(country map) inside front cover	
Map I (general map)	142-143	Ürgüp	560
		Xanthos	389

Manufacture Française des Pneumatiques Michelin
Société en commandite par actions au capital de 2 000 000 000 de francs
Place des Carmes-Déchaux – 63000 Clermont-Ferrand (France)
R.C.S. Clermont-Fd B 855 200 507

© Michelin et Cie, Propriétaires-éditeurs, 2000
Dépôt légal avril 2000 – ISBN 2-06-855601-4 – ISSN 0763-1383
No part of this publication may be reproduced in any form without
the prior permission of the publisher.

Printed in the EU 04-2000/1
Compograveur : Nord Compo – Villeneuve d'Ascq
Imprimeur : IME – Baume-les-Dames

Cover photography :
Paşabağ, Cappadocian scenery R. Mattes/EXPLORER
Sesame seed bread vendor E. Valentin/HOA QUI
The Medusa of Didyma B. Morandi/DIAF

Your opinion matters!

In order to make sure that this collection satisfies the needs of our readers, please help us by completing the following questionnaire with your comments and suggestions and return to:

Michelin Travel Publications   or
The Edward Hyde Building
38 Clarendon Road
Watford, UK

Michelin Travel Publications
P.O. Box 19008
Greenville, SC 29602-9008
USA

■ YOUR HOLIDAYS/VACATIONS:

1. In general, when you go on holiday or vacation, do you tend to travel... (Choose one)

☐ Independently, on your own
☐ Independently, as a couple
☐ With 1 or 2 friends

☐ With your family
☐ With a group of friends
☐ On organised trips

2. How many international holidays or vacations of 1 week or more have you taken in the last 3 years? _____

Last 3 destinations: Month/Year:

_____   _____

_____   _____

_____   _____

3. What do you look for most when planning a holiday or vacation?

	Not at all	Sometimes	Essential
Somewhere new and exotic	☐	☐	☐
Real experience/meeting people	☐	☐	☐
Experiencing the wildlife/scenery	☐	☐	☐
Cultural insight	☐	☐	☐
Rest & relaxation	☐	☐	☐
Comfort & well-being	☐	☐	☐
Adventure & the unexpected	☐	☐	☐

4. When travelling, do you take a travel guide with you?

☐ Always   ☐ Usually   ☐ Sometimes   ☐ Never

■ You and the Michelin NEOS guides

5. About your purchase of a NEOS Guide

How long was your holiday where you used the NEOS guide?
How many days? _____
For which country or countries? _____
How long before your departure did you buy it? How many days? _____

6. What made you choose a NEOS Guide?

Highlight everything that applies.

☐ Something new and interesting
☐ The layout
☐ Easy to read format
☐ Cultural details

☐ Quality of the text
☐ Quality of the mapping
☐ Practical Information
☐ Michelin quality

7. Which sections did you use most during your holiday or vacation?

Score 1-4   (1 = least used)   (4 = most used)

	1	2	3	4
"Setting the Scene"	☐ 1	☐ 2	☐ 3	☐ 4
"Meeting the People"	☐ 1	☐ 2	☐ 3	☐ 4
"Practical Information"	☐ 1	☐ 2	☐ 3	☐ 4
"Exploring ..."	☐ 1	☐ 2	☐ 3	☐ 4

8. How would you rate the following aspects of your NEOS guide?

Score 1-4   (1 = Poor)   (4 = Excellent)

	1	2	3	4
Cover design	☐ 1	☐ 2	☐ 3	☐ 4
Chapter Order	☐ 1	☐ 2	☐ 3	☐ 4
Layout (photos, diagrams)	☐ 1	☐ 2	☐ 3	☐ 4
Ease of reading (typeface)	☐ 1	☐ 2	☐ 3	☐ 4
Style of writing	☐ 1	☐ 2	☐ 3	☐ 4
Text boxes and stories	☐ 1	☐ 2	☐ 3	☐ 4
Plans & Maps	☐ 1	☐ 2	☐ 3	☐ 4
Star ratings system	☐ 1	☐ 2	☐ 3	☐ 4
Format	☐ 1	☐ 2	☐ 3	☐ 4
Weight	☐ 1	☐ 2	☐ 3	☐ 4
Durability	☐ 1	☐ 2	☐ 3	☐ 4
Price	☐ 1	☐ 2	☐ 3	☐ 4

9. Did you use other travel guides during your trip? ☐ Yes ☐ No
If yes, which ones? _____

10. Please give your NEOS guide a rating out of 20: ___/20 (with 20 as top rating)
Would you use a NEOS guide for your next trip? ☐ Yes ☐ No
If no, why not? _____
Which other destinations would you like NEOS to cover? _____

11. Any other comments or suggestions: _____

_____

_____

_____

_____

_____

_____

Surname/Last Name: _____ First Name: _____

Address: _____

Age: _____ Sex: ☐ M ☐ F

Profession: _____

Where did you purchase your NEOS Guide: What type of store?
                                         Which country?

Data collected may be used by Michelin Travel Publications for internal purposes only and not for resale.